BLACKSTONE'S GUIDE TO
The Disability Discrimination Legislation

BLACKSTONE'S GUIDE TO

The Disability Discrimination Legislation

Karon Monaghan

OXFORD
UNIVERSITY PRESS

OXFORD
UNIVERSITY PRESS

Great Clarendon Street, Oxford OX2 6DP

Oxford University Press is a department of the University of Oxford.
It furthers the University's objective of excellence in research, scholarship,
and education by publishing worldwide in

Oxford New York

Auckland Bangkok Buenos Aires Cape Town Chennai
Dar es Salaam Delhi Hong Kong Istanbul Karachi Kolkata
Kuala Lumpur Madrid Melbourne Mexico City Mumbai Nairobi
São Paulo Shanghai Singapore Taipei Tokyo Toronto

Oxford is a registered trade mark of Oxford University Press
in the UK and in certain other countries

Published in the United States
by Oxford University Press Inc., New York

© Karon Monaghan, 2005

The moral rights of the author have been asserted
Database right Oxford University Press (maker)

First published 2005

British Library Cataloguing in Publication Data

Data available

Library of Congress Cataloging in Publication Data
Monaghan, Karon.
Blackstone's guide to the disability discrimination legislation / Karon Monaghan.
    p. cm
Includes index.
ISBN 0–19–927919–5
1.   People with disabilities—Legal status, laws, etc.—Great Britain. 2.
Discrimination against people with disabilities—Law and legislation—Great Britain.
3.   Great Britain. Disability Discrimination Act 1995.   I. Title: Guide to the
disability discrimination legislation. II. Title.
    KD737.M66 2005
    343.4108'7—dc22
                                        2005001538

ISBN 0–19–927919–5
EAN 978–0–19–927919–7

1 3 5 7 9 10 8 6 4 2

Typeset by Hope Services (Abingdon) Ltd.
Printed in Great Britain
on acid-free paper by
Biddles Ltd., King's Lynn

To Thea

Foreword

Legislation is frequently more complex than it initially appears and this is certainly true of the Disability Discrimination Act 1995. Further layers of complexity are added when subsequent Acts of Parliament amend the original Act. In an attempt to bring clarity, decisions by the Employment Appeal Tribunals, the Court of Appeal, Court of Session and the House of Lords can alter the interpretation of the principal Act. Yet this is more than an intellectual game of semantics. For disabled people, their life style, freedom from discrimination and sometimes life itself depend on others, and especially the legal profession, understanding not only the wording of the legislation but the purpose for which it was enacted and what it is meant to achieve.

This book is not a mere snapshot of the current position but rather a short video recording of a rapidly changing scene and one to which the proposed Disability Bill, expected to be approved by Parliament in 2005, will bring further change. It is important that all those involved in helping disabled people to exercise their rights, or defending those accused of violating those rights, have available at their elbow an authoritative guide to the DDA and how it has been interpreted by the judicial system. This book is such a guide and, on behalf of the Disability Rights Commission, I warmly welcome it. It should not remain pristine but should become grubby with extensive use and play its role in creating a society in which all disabled people can participate as equal citizens.

Bert Massie CBE, Chairman,
Disability Rights Commission
November 2004

Preface

This Labour Government has, at best, a mixed record on social policy issues and fundamental rights. Disability legislation is one of the few areas where the news has not always been bad. Although the Disability Discrimination Act 1995 was an important piece of social policy legislation it was seriously flawed. It was itself only enacted thirty years after the first significant piece of anti-discrimination legislation (the 1965 Race Relations Act) and after sixteen failed private members' bills on the subject. It omitted the important areas of education and transport from its coverage and allowed for the justification of all the forms of discrimination against which it offered protection.

The 1997 Labour manifesto contained a commitment to comprehensive and enforceable civil rights for disabled people, and to assist it in delivering this promise a Disability Task Force was appointed. This was shortly followed by the Disability Rights Commission Act 1999, which established the Disability Rights Commission. In 2001 the Special Educational Needs and Disability Act filled an important lacuna left by the 1995 Act. If, as expected, the Disability Discrimination Bill is enacted in 2005, it will remedy other defects in the Act. It will give legislative recognition to the fact that institutionalized discrimination cannot be addressed by the conferring of individual equality rights alone. It will do so by the introduction of a series of statutory duties on public authorities to have due regard to the need to eliminate discrimination against disabled persons and to promote equality of opportunity between disabled persons, amongst other things.

Even with the changes described, the legislation remains imperfect and the government has been characteristically slow and cautious in addressing its flaws. The small employer exception provides a very good illustration of this point. Although the Labour party resisted this provision when in opposition, the Government only removed it when forced so to do by the hand of European Community law. One of the greatest weaknesses of the Disability Discrimination Act is that it is largely predicated on the assumption that 'impairments' are personal; that disability is not a social construct and discrimination can be addressed accordingly. Many campaigners have highlighted the flaw in this approach. In addition, it is strongly arguable that the balance between the rights of disabled people and other societal needs remains in the wrong place. In the main, disability discrimination can still be justified (direct discrimination and harassment in limited fields being the exception) and the Disability Discrimination Act is not prioritized over other legislation and so must give way to the compulsion of other enactments (section 59).

The legislation is over-complicated, even by the standards of anti-discrimination law. Disability discrimination law is now found in the Disability Discrimination Act 1995, in European Community law, and in the developing case-law under the Human Rights Act 1998. I hope this book makes it all a little easier to navigate.

There are many good quality web sites that provide information in this area and on which the latest developments can be followed:

- The Disability Rights Commission's web site provides details of latest developments in the law, copies of the Codes of Practice, and recent case-law (http://www.drc-gb.org/)

- Case-law and legislation from the UK and elsewhere can be found on BAILII's web site (http://www.bailii.org/)

- Copies of the judgments of the Employment Appeal Tribunal are on the Employment Appeal Tribunal web site (http://www.employmentappeals.gov.uk/index.html);

- Campaigning web sites include those of the Disability Alliance (http://www.disabilityalliance.org/about.htm); Disability Awareness (http:// www.daa.org.uk/); and the British Council of Disabled People (http://www. bcodp.org.uk/). All contain information about disabled people, legal and policy developments, and links to other sites

- Government policy, draft legislation, and pre-legislative materials can be found on the Government's web site (http://www.disability.gov.uk/).

I have been assisted by many people over the years in my work in discrimination law. I would like to make particular mention of my clients to whom I owe a special debt of gratitude: discrimination and inequality are usually most keenly understood by those who experience them. I would like to thank the following for specific support and assistance with this book: Ulele Burnham; Barbara Cohen; Catherine Casserley; Nicola Dandridge; Thomas Kibling; Aileen McColgan; Mary Stacey; Hugh Tomlinson; Lesford Williams; and David Wolfe. Thanks also to the following members of the Matrix research panel for all their help: Gillian Ferguson, Urfan Khaliq, Kavita Modi, and Richard Moules. Finally, thanks to the very patient Katie Allan of OUP. Any mistakes are obviously mine. I hope there are not too many but I would be pleased to have them pointed out to me. The book is up to date to 1 October 2004 (although I have been able to include a few references after that date).

Karon Monaghan
Matrix Chambers
Gray's Inn
London WC1R 5LN
3 October 2004

Contents—Summary

Contents

Table of Cases

Table of UK Statutes

Table of UK Secondary Legislation

Table of International Legislation

Disability Discrimination Act 1995 (as amended)

Table of Commencement

Provision	Date in force	Amending provisions	Date in force of amendment
1	EWS: 17 May 1996 (SI 1996/1336) NI: 30 May 1996 (SR 1996/219)		
2	EWS: 17 May 1996 (SI 1996/1336) NI: 30 May 1996 (SR 1996/219)		
	(1), (4)	Special Educational Needs and Disability Act 2001	1 Sep 2002 (SI 2002/2217)
3	EWS: 17 May 1996 (SI 1996/1336) NI: 30 May 1996 (SR 1996/219)		
	(3), (3A)	Special Educational Needs and Disability Act 2001	1 Sep 2002 (SI 2002/2217)
3A, 3B		SI 2003/1673	3 July 2003 (for certain purposes) (SI 2003/1673) 1 Oct 2004 (for remaining purposes) (SI 2003/1673)

Provision	Date in force	Amending provisions	Date in force of amendment
4 (as originally enacted)	2 Dec 1996 (SI 1996/1474; SR 1996/280)		
4 (new), 4A–4F		SI 2003/1673	3 July 2003 (for certain purposes) (SI 2003/1673) 1 Oct 2004 (for remaining purposes) (SI 2003/1673)
4G–4K		SI 2003/2770	Partly as from 1 Dec 2003 wholly as from 1 Oct 2004 (SI 2003/2770)
5		SI 2003/1673	3 July 2003 (for certain purposes) (SI 2003/1673) 1 Oct 2004 (for remaining purposes) (SI 2003/1673)
(1)–(5)	2 Dec 1996 (SI 1996/1474; SR 1996/280)		
(6), (7)	6 June 1996 (E, W, S) (SI 1996/1474) 11 July 1996 (NI) (SR 1996/280)		
6		SI 2003/1673	3 July 2003 (for certain purposes) (SI 2003/1673) 1 Oct 2004 (for remaining purposes) (SI 2003/1673)

Provision	Commencement		
(1)–(7), (11), (12)	2 Dec 1996 (SI 1996/1474; SR 1996/280)		
(8)–(10)	6 June 1996 (E, W, S) (SI 1996/1474) 11 July 1996 (NI) (SR 1996/280)		
6A–6C		SI 2003/1673	3 July 2003 (for certain purposes) (SI 2003/1673) 1 Oct 2004 (for remaining purposes) (SI 2003/1673)
7	2 Dec 1996 (SI 1996/1474; SR 1996/280)	SI 2003/1673	3 July 2003 (for certain purposes) (SI 2003/1673) 1 Oct 2004 (for remaining purposes) (SI 2003/1673)
7A–7D		SI 2003/1673	3 July 2003 (for certain purposes) (SI 2003/1673) 1 Oct 2004 (for remaining purposes) (SI 2003/1673)
8 (renumbered (1) as s 17A by SI 2003/1673)	2 Dec 1996 (SI 1996/1474; SR 1996/280)	Employment Rights (Dispute Resolution) Act 1998	1 Aug 1998 (SI 1998/1658)
		SI 2003/1673	3 July 2003 (for certain purposes) (SI 2003/1673) 1 Oct 2004 (for remaining purposes) (SI 2003/1673)

Provision	Date in force	Amending provisions	Date in force of amendment
(1A)–(1C)		SI 2003/1673	3 July 2003 (for certain purposes) (SI 2003/1673) 1 Oct 2004 (for remaining purposes) (SI 2003/1673)
(2), (5)	2 Dec 1996 (SI 1996/1474; SR 1996/280)	Employment Rights (Dispute Resolution) Act 1998	1 Aug 1998 (SI 1998/1658)
(3), (4)	2 Dec 1996 (SI 1996/1474; SR 1996/280)		
(6)	6 June 1996 (E, W, S) (SI 1996/1474) 11 July 1996 (NI) (SR 1996/280)		
(7)	6 June 1996 (E, W, S) (SI 1996/1474) 11 July 1996 (NI) (SR 1996/280)	Employment Tribunals Act 1996	22 Aug 1998 (s 46)
(8)	2 Dec 1996 (SI 1996/1474; SR 1996/280)	Employment Rights (Dispute Resolution) Act 1998	1 Aug 1998 (SI 1998/1658)
9	2 Dec 1996 (SI 1996/1474; SR 1996/280)	SI 2003/1673	3 July 2003 (for certain purposes) (SI 2003/1673) 1 Oct 2004 (for remaining purposes) (SI 2003/1673)

Section	Subsection			
10 (renumbered as s 18C by SI 2003/1673)		2 Dec 1996 (SI 1996/1474; SR 1996/280)		
11		2 Dec 1996 (SI 1996/1474; SR 1996/280)	SI 2003/1673	3 July 2003 (for certain purposes) (SI 2003/1673) 1 Oct 2004 (for remaining purposes) (SI 2003/1673)
12			SI 2003/1673	3 July 2003 (for certain purposes) (SI 2003/1673) 1 Oct 2004 (for remaining purposes) (SI 2003/1673)
	(1), (2)	2 Dec 1996 (SI 1996/1474; SR 1996/280)		
	(3), (6)	6 June 1996 (E, W, S) (SI 1996/1474) 11 July 1996 (NI) (SR 1996/280)		
	(4), (5)	2 Dec 1996 (SI 1996/1474; SR 1996/280)		
13 (as originally enacted)		2 Dec 1996 (SI 1996/1474; SR 1996/280)		
13 (new)			SI 2003/1673	3 July 2003 (for certain purposes) (SI 2003/1673) 1 Oct 2004 (for remaining purposes) (SI 2003/1673)

Provision		Date in force	Amending provisions	Date in force of amendment
14 (as originally enacted)	(1)	2 Dec 1996 (SI 1996/1474; SR 1996/280)		
	(2)	1 Oct 1999 (SI 1999/1190; SR 1999/196)		
	(3)	2 Dec 1996 (SI 1996/1474; SR 1996/280)		
	(4), (5)	1 Oct 1999 (SI 1999/1190; SR 1999/196)		
	(6)	6 June 1996 (E, W, S) (SI 1996/1474) 11 July 1996 (NI) (SR 1996/280)		
14 (new), 14A–14D			SI 2003/1673	3 July 2003 (for certain purposes) (SI 2003/1673) 1 Oct 2004 (for remaining purposes) (SI 2003/1673)
15			SI 2003/1673	3 July 2003 (for certain purposes) (SI 2003/1673) 1 Oct 2004 (for remaining purposes) (SI 2003/1673)
	(1)(a), (2)–(10)	1 Oct 1999 (SI 1999/1190; SR 1999/196)		
	(1)(b)	Never in force		

16 (renumbered as s 18A by SI 2003/1673)	(1)		SI 2003/1673	3 July 2003 (for certain purposes) (SI 2003/1673) 1 Oct 2004 (for remaining purposes) (SI 2003/1673)
	(2), (4)	2 Dec 1996 (SI 1996/1474; SR 1996/280)		
	(3)	17 May 1996 (E, W, S) (so far as it relates to the definitions 'sub-lease' and 'sub-tenancy') (SI 1996/1336) 30 May 1996 (NI) (so far as it relates to the definitions 'sub-lease' and 'sub-tenancy') (SR 1996/219) 2 Dec 1996 (otherwise) (SI 1996/3003; SR 1996/560)		
	(5)	See Sch 4, Pt I (paras 1–4) below		
16A–16C			SI 2003/1673	3 July 2003 (for certain purposes) (SI 2003/1673) 1 Oct 2004 (for remaining purposes) (SI 2003/1673)
17			SI 2003/2770	Partly as from 1 Dec 2003 and wholly as from 1 Oct 2004 (SI 2003/2770)

Provision		Date in force	Amending provisions	Date in force of amendment
	(1), (2), (4)	2 Dec 1996 (SI 1996/1474; SR 1996/280)		
	(3)	6 June 1996 (E, W, S) (SI 1996/1474) 11 July 1996 (NI) (SR 1996/280)		
17A		See the entry for s 8 as originally enacted above	SI 2003/1673	3 July 2003 (for certain purposes) (SI 2003/1673) 1 Oct 2004 (for remaining purposes) (SI 2003/1673)
17B, 17C			SI 2003/1673	3 July 2003 (for certain purposes) (SI 2003/1673) 1 Oct 2004 (for remaining purposes) (SI 2003/1673)
18	(1), (2)	2 Dec 1996 (SI 1996/1474; SR 1996/280)		
	(3), (4)	6 June 1996 (E, W, S) (SI 1996/1474) 11 July 1996 (NI) (SR 1996/280)		
18A		See the entry for s 16 as originally enacted above	SI 2003/1673	3 July 2003 (for certain purposes) (SI 2003/1673) 1 Oct 2004 (for remaining purposes) (SI 2003/1673)

18B		SI 2003/1673	3 July 2003 (for certain purposes) (SI 2003/1673) 1 Oct 2004 (for remaining purposes) (SI 2003/1673)
18C	See the entry for s 10 as originally enacted above	SI 2003/1673	3 July 2003 (for certain purposes) (SI 2003/1673) 1 Oct 2004 (for remaining purposes) (SI 2003/1673)
18D		SI 2003/1673	3 July 2003 (for certain purposes) (SI 2003/1673) 1 Oct 2004 (for remaining purposes) (SI 2003/1673)
	(2)	SI 2003/2770	Partly as from 1 Dec 2003 and wholly as from 1 Oct 2004 (SI 2003/2770)
19	(1)(a), (c), (d), (2)–(4), (5)(a), (b), (6)	2 Dec 1996 (SI 1996/1474; SR 1996/280)	
	(1)(b)	1 Oct 1999 (SI 1999/1190; SR 1999/196)	
Special Educational Needs and Disability Act 2001	(5)(a), (aa), (ab)	1 Sep 2002 (SI 2002/2217)	
Learning and Skills Act 2000	(5)(aa), (ab)	1 Apr 2001 (SI 2001/654)	

Provision	Date in force	Amending provisions	Date in force of amendment
5(c)	6 June 1996 (E, W, S) (SI 1996/1474) 11 July 1996 (NI) (SI 1996/280)		
(5A), (6)		Special Educational Needs and Disability Act 2001	1 Sep 2002 (SI 2002/2217)
20	2 Dec 1996 (SI 1996/1474; SR 1996/280)		
(1), (3), (4)			
(2), (5), (9)	1 Oct 1999 (SI 1999/1190; SR 1999/196)		
(6)–(8)	6 June 1996 (E, W, S) (SI 1996/1474) 11 July 1996 (NI) (SR 1996/280)		
21	1 Oct 1999 (SI 1999/1190; SR 1999/196)		
(1), (2)(d), (4), (6), (10)			
(2)(a)–(c)	1 Oct 2004 (SI 2001/2030; SR 2001/439)		
(3), (5)	26 Apr 1999 (SI 1999/1190; SR 1999/196)		
(7)–(9)	NOT YET IN FORCE		
21A		SI 2003/1673	3 July 2003 (for certain purposes) (SI 2003/1673) 1 Oct 2004 (for remaining purposes) (SI 2003/1673)

22, 23				
24	(1)–(4)	2 Dec 1996 (SI 1996/1474; SR 1996/280)		
	(5)	6 June 1996 (E, W, S) (SI 1996/1474) 11 July 1996 (NI) (SR 1996/280)		
25	(7)–(9)	2 Dec 1996 (SI 1996/1474; SR 1996/280)	SI 2003/1673	3 July 2003 (for certain purposes) (SI 2003/1673) 1 Oct 2004 (for remaining purposes) (SI 2003/1673)
26	(1A)	2 Dec 1996 (SI 1996/1474; SR 1996/280)	SI 2003/1673	3 July 2003 (for certain purposes) (SI 2003/1673) 1 Oct 2004 (for remaining purposes) (SI 2003/1673)
27	(1), (2), (4)	1 Oct 2004 (SI 2001/2030; SR 2001/439)		
	(3)	9 May 2001 (E, W, S) (SI 2001/2030) 31 Dec 2001 (NI) (SR 2001/439)		

Provision	Date in force	Amending provisions	Date in force of amendment
28 (as originally enacted)	(5) See Sch 4, Pt II (paras 5–9) below 17 May 1996 (E, W, S) (SI 1996/1336) 30 May 1996 (NI) (SR 1996/219)		
28 (new)		Disability Rights Commission Act 1999	25 Apr 2000
28A–28C		Special Educational Needs and Disability Act 2001	1 Sep 2002 (SI 2002/2217)
28D		Special Educational Needs and Disability Act 2001	1 July 2002 (E) (for the purpose of making regulations) (SI 2002/1721) 1 Sep 2002 (E) (otherwise) (SI 2002/2217) 8 Oct 2003 (W) (SI 2003/2532)
	(14)	Education Act 2002	1 Sep 2003 (E) (SI 2003/1667) NOT YET IN FORCE (W)
28E		Special Educational Needs and Disability Act 2001	1 July 2002 (E) (for the purpose of enabling the Secretary of State to issue guidance) (SI 2002/1721) 1 Sep 2002 (E) (otherwise) (SI 2002/2217) 8 Oct 2003 (W) (SI 2003/2532)

28F, 28G	(5), (6), (8)	Education Act 2002	26 July 2002 (SI 2002/2002)
		Special Educational Needs and Disability Act 2001	1 Sep 2002 (SI 2002/2217)
28H		Special Educational Needs and Disability Act 2001	1 Sep 2002 (SI 2002/2217)
	(2)	Education Act 2002	31 Mar 2003 (SI 2002/3185)
	(3)	Education Act 2002	1 Sep 2003 (SI 2002/3185)
28I		Special Educational Needs and Disability Act 2001	1 Sep 2002 (SI 2002/2217)
	(1), (3), (5)	Education Act 2002	1 Sep 2003 (SI 2003/3185)
28J		Special Educational Needs and Disability Act 2001	1 July 2002 (for the purpose of making regulations) (SI 2002/1721) 1 Sep 2002 (otherwise) (SI 2002/2217)
	(2A), (3)—(8)	Education Act 2002	1 Sep 2003 (SI 2003/3185)
28K		Special Educational Needs and Disability Act 2001	1 Sep 2002 (SI 2002/2217)
	(2), (5)	Education Act 2002	26 July 2002 (SI 2002/2002)
28L		Special Educational Needs and Disability Act 2001	1 Sep 2002 (SI 2002/2217)
	(2)(a), (5)(a)	Education Act 2002	20 Jan 2003 (E) (SI 2002/2952) 9 Jan 2004 (W) (SI 2003/2961)
	(2)(b), (5)(b)	Education Act 2002	26 July 2002 (SI 2002/2002)

Provision	Date in force	Amending provisions	Date in force of amendment
28M (6)		Education Act 2002	1 Sep 2003 (E) (SI 2003/1667) NOT YET IN FORCE (W)
28M		Special Educational Needs and Disability Act 2001	1 Sep 2002 (except insofar as it gives the National Assembly for Wales power to give directions under sub-ss (1), (3) above, or makes provision in relation to such a direction) (SI 2002/2217) 8 Oct 2003 (SI 2003/2532) (otherwise)
28N, 28P (5)		Education Act 2002	1 Sep 2003 (SI 2002/3185)
28N, 28P		Special Educational Needs and Disability Act 2001	1 Sep 2002 (SI 2002/2217)
28Q		Special Educational Needs and Disability Act 2001	1 Sep 2002 (SI 2002/2217)
28Q (7)		Education Act 2002	1 Sep 2003 (E) (SI 2003/1667) NOT YET IN FORCE (W)
28R (12)		Education Act 2002	26 July 2002 (SI 2002/2002)
28R		Special Educational Needs and Disability Act 2001	30 May 2002 (for the purpose of allowing the designation of educational institutions under sub-ss (6)(c), (7)(e)) (SI 2002/1647) 1 Sep 2002 (for remaining purposes) (SI 2002/2217)

Section	Subsection		Act	Commencement
28S–28V			Special Educational Needs and Disability Act 2001	1 Sep 2002 (SI 2002/2217)
28W			Special Educational Needs and Disability Act 2001	30 May 2002 (SI 2002/1647)
28X			Special Educational Needs and Disability Act 2001	1 Sep 2002 (SI 2002/2217)
29			Special Educational Needs and Disability Act 2001	1 Sep 2002 (SI 2002/2217)
30	(1), (2)	Never in force		
	(3)	31 July 1996 (SI 1996/1474)		
	(1)	31 July 1996 (SI 1996/1474)	Learning and Skills Act 2000	1 Apr 2001 (E) (SI 2001/654) / 1 Apr 2001 (W) (SI 2001/1274)
	(2)–(4)	31 July 1996 (SI 1996/1474)		
	(5)	31 July 1996 (SI 1996/1474)		
	(6)	31 July 1996 (SI 1996/1474)	Special Educational Needs and Disability Act 2001	1 Sep 2002 (SI 2002/2217)
31	(7)–(9)	Never in force	Education Act 1996	1 Nov 1996 (s 583(2))
	(3)	31 July 1996 (SI 1996/1474)	Special Educational Needs and Disability Act 2001	1 Sep 2002 (SI 2002/2217)
31A–31C			Special Educational Needs and Disability Act 2001	1 Sep 2002 (SI 2002/2217)
32–6		NOT YET IN FORCE		

Provision	Date in force	Amending provisions	Date in force of amendment
37	1 Dec 2000 (E, W) (for the purposes of the issue of certificates pursuant to s 37(5)–(7) and the prescription of the notices pursuant to s 37(8)(b)) (SI 2000/2989) 31 Mar 2001 (E, W) (otherwise) (SI 2000/2989) 1 June 2001 (NI) (for the purposes of the issue of certificates pursuant to s 37(5)–(7) and the prescription of the notices pursuant to s 37(8)(b)) (SR 2001/163) 1 Aug 2001 (NI) (otherwise) (SR 2001/163) NOT YET IN FORCE (S)		
37A		Private Hire Vehicles (Carriage of Guide Dogs etc) Act 2002	31 Dec 2003 (for certain purposes) (SI 2003/3123) 31 Mar 2004 (otherwise) (SI 2003/3123)
38	1 Dec 2000 (E, W) (SI 2000/2989) 1 June 2001 (NI) (SR 2001/163) NOT YET IN FORCE (S)		

Provision	Date in force	Amending provisions	Date in force of amendment
(3), (5), (6)	1 Jan 1996 (E, W, S) (SI 1995/3330) 2 Jan 1996 (NI) (SR 1996/1)		
(4)	1 Jan 1996 (E, W, S) (SI 1995/3330) 2 Jan 1996 (NI) (SR 1996/1)	Employment Rights (Dispute Resolution) Act 1998	1 Aug 1998 (SI 1998/1658)
52	1 Jan 1996 (E, W, S) (SI 1995/3330) 2 Jan 1996 (NI) (SR 1996/1)		
(1)–(10), (12)		Disability Rights Commission Act 1999	25 Apr 2000 (SI 2000/880)
53A		Disability Rights Commission Act 1999	25 Apr 2000 (SI 2000/880)
(1)–(1B)		Special Educational Needs and Disability Act 2001	1 July 2002 (SI 2002/1721)
(1), (9)		SI 2003/1673	3 July 2003 (for certain purposes) (SI 2003/1673) 1 Oct 2004 (for remaining purposes) (SI 2003/1673)
(8), (8A)		Special Educational Needs and Disability Act 2001	1 Sep 2002 (SI 2002/2217)
53	6 June 1996 (E, W, S) (SI 1996/1474) 11 July 1996 (NI) (SR 1996/280)		

54	(1)–(3), (8), (9)	6 June 1996 (E, W, S) (SI 1996/1474) 11 July 1996 (NI) (SR 1996/280)	Disability Rights Commission Act 1999	25 Apr 2000
	(5)	2 Dec 1996 (SI 1996/1474; SR 1996/280)	Employment Rights (Dispute Resolution) Act 1998	1 Aug 1998 (SI 1998/1658)
55	(1)–(7), (9)		Disability Rights Commission Act 1999	25 Apr 2000 (SI 2000/880)
56	(1), (3A)		Special Educational Needs and Disability Act 2001	1 Sep 2002 (SI 2002/2217)
	(5), (6)		SI 2003/1673	3 July 2003 (for certain purposes) (SI 2003/1673) 1 Oct 2004 (for remaining purposes) (SI 2003/1673)
	(5)	6 June 1996 (E, W, S) (SI 1996/1474) 11 July 1996 (NI) (SR 1996/280)	SI 2003/2770	Partly as from 1 Dec 2003 and wholly as from 1 Oct 2004 (SI 2003/2770)

Provision	Date in force	Amending provisions	Date in force of amendment
(1), (3)		SI 2003/1673	3 July 2003 (for certain purposes) (SI 2003/1673) 1 Oct 2004 (for remaining purposes) (SI 2003/1673)
(5)		Employment Rights (Dispute Resolution) Act 1998	1 Aug 1998 (SI 1998/1658)
57	2 Dec 1996 (SI 1996/1474; SR 1996/280)		
(1), (6)		Special Educational Needs and Disability Act 2001	1 Sep 2002 (SI 2002/2217)
58	2 Dec 1996 (SI 1996/1474; SR 1996/280)		
59	17 May 1996 (E, W, S) (SI 1996/1336) 30 May 1996 (NI) (SR 1996/219)		
(2A), (3)		SI 2003/1673	3 July 2003 (for certain purposes) (SI 2003/1673) 1 Oct 2004 (for remaining purposes) (SI 2003/1673)
60	2 Dec 1996 (SI 1996/1474; SR 1996/280)		
61	2 Dec 1996 (SI 1996/1474; SR 1996/280)		

62	(1), (2), (7)	17 May 1996 (E, W, S) (SI 1996/1336) 30 May 1996 (NI) (SR 1996/219)	Employment Tribunals Act 1996	22 Aug 1996 (s 46)
	(3)–(6)	Never in force		
63	(1), (2), (4)–(6)	17 May 1996 (E, W, S) (SI 1996/1336) 30 May 1996 (NI) (SR 1996/219)	Employment Tribunals Act 1996	22 Aug 1996 (s 46)
	(3)	Never in force		
64	(2), (2A), (5)–(8)	2 Dec 1996 (SI 1996/1474; SR 1996/280)		
64A			SI 2003/1673	3 July 2003 (for certain purposes) (SI 2003/1673) 1 Oct 2004 (for remaining purposes) (SI 2003/1673)
65		2 Dec 1996 (SI 1996/1474)	SI 2003/1673	3 July 2003 (for certain purposes) (SI 2003/1673) 1 Oct 2004 (for remaining purposes) (SI 2003/1673)

Provision	Date in force	Amending provisions	Date in force of amendment
(2)		Employment Rights Act 1996	22 Aug 1996 (s 243)
(5)		Employment Rights (Dispute Resolution) Act 1998	1 Aug 1998 (SI 1998/1658)
66	2 Dec 1996 (SI 1996/1474)	SI 2003/1673	3 July 2003 (for certain purposes) (SI 2003/1673) 1 Oct 2004 (for remaining purposes) (SI 2003/1673)
67	17 May 1996 (E, W, S) (SI 1996/1336) 30 May 1996 (NI) (SR 1996/219)		
(5)		Disability Rights Commission Act 1999	25 Apr 2000 (SI 2000/880)
68	17 May 1996 (E, W, S) (SI 1996/1336) 30 May 1996 (NI) (SR 1996/219)	SI 2003/1673	3 July 2003 (for certain purposes) (SI 2003/1673) 1 Oct 2004 (for remaining purposes) (SI 2003/1673)
(1)		SI 2000/2040	27 July 2000 (SI 2000/2040)
		Private Hire Vehicles (Carriage of Guide Dogs etc) Act 2002	31 Dec 2003 (SI 2003/3123)
(2)–(5)	2 Dec 1996 (E, W, S) (SI 1996/1474); (NI) (SR 1996/280)		

	Provision		Commencement
69	(2), (2A)–(2D), (4A), (5)	SI 2003/1673	3 July 2003 (for certain purposes) (SI 2003/1673) 1 Oct 2004 (for remaining purposes) (SI 2003/1673)
	(1)–(3), (6), (8)		17 May 1996 (E, W, S) (SI 1996/1336) 30 May 1996 (NI) (SR 1996/219)
70	(4)		8 Nov 1995 (s 70(2))
	(5)		2 Dec 1996 (SI 1996/1474; SR 1996/280)
	(5A), (5B), (6)		See entry for Sch 7 below
	(7)	SI 2003/1673	3 July 2003 (for certain purposes) (SI 2003/1673) 1 Oct 2004 (for remaining purposes) (SI 2003/1673)
		Disability Rights Commission Act 1999	25 Apr 2000 (SI 2000/880)
Schedule	**paragraph**		
1	1–6		17 May 1996 (E, W, S) (SI 1996/1336) 30 May 1996 (NI) (SR 1996/219)

Provision	Date in force	Amending provisions	Date in force of amendment
7	2 Dec 1996 (SI 1996/1474; SR 1996/280)		
8	17 May 1996 (E, W, S) (SI 1996/1336) 30 May 1996 (NI) (SR 1996/219)		
2	17 May 1996 (E, W, S) (SI 1996/1336) 30 May 1996 (NI) (SR 1996/219)		
2, 2A, 2B, 4A–4E		Special Educational Needs and Disability Act 2001	1 Sep 2002 (SI 2002/2217)
2C, 3, 4		SI 2003/1673	3 July 2003 (for certain purposes) (SI 2003/1673) 1 Oct 2004 (for remaining purposes) (SI 2003/1673)
3, 4		SI 2003/2770	Partly as from 1 Dec 2003 and wholly as from 1 Oct 2004 (SI 2003/2770)
3	2 Dec 1996 (SI 1996/1474; SR 1996/280)		
1		Employment Tribunals Act 1996	22 Aug 1996 (s 46)
2–4		SI 2003/1673	3 July 2003 (for certain purposes) (SI 2003/1673) 1 Oct 2004 (for remaining purposes) (SI 2003/1673)

Provision	Act / SI	Commencement
2	SI 2003/2770	Partly as from 1 Dec 2003 and wholly as from 1 Oct 2004 (SI 2003/2770)
3	Employment Rights (Dispute Resolution) Act 1998	1 Aug 1998 (SI 1998/1658)
4	Employment Relations Act 1999	16 July 2001 (SI 2001/1187)
6	Disability Rights Commission Act 1999	25 Apr 2000 (SI 2000/880)
9–15	Special Educational Needs and Disability Act 2001	1 Sep 2002 (SI 2002/2217)
10	Education Act 2002	1 Sep 2003 (SI 2002/3185)
3A	SI 2003/1673	3 July 2003 (for certain purposes) (SI 2003/1673); 1 Oct 2004 (for remaining purposes) (SI 2003/1673)
1, 2	SI 2003/1673	2 Dec 1996 (SI 1996/1474; SR 1996/280); 3 July 2003 (for certain purposes) (SI 2003/1673); 1 Oct 2004 (for remaining purposes) (SI 2003/1673)
4	SI 2003/1673	3 July 2003 (for certain purposes) (SI 2003/1673); 1 Oct 2004 (for remaining purposes) (SI 2003/1673)
3	6 June 1996 (E, W, S) (SI 1996/1474); 11 July 1996 (NI) (SR 1996/280)	3 July 2003 (for certain purposes) (SI 2003/1673); 1 Oct 2004 (for remaining purposes) (SI 2003/1673)

Provision	Date in force	Amending provisions	Date in force of amendment
4	17 May 1996 (E, W, S) (SI 1996/1336); 30 May 1996 (NI) (SR 1996/219)	SI 2003/1673	3 July 2003 (for certain purposes) (SI 2003/1673); 1 Oct 2004 (for remaining purposes) (SI 2003/1673)
5–7	1 Oct 2004 (SI 2001/2030; SR 2001/439)		
8, 9	9 May 2001 (E, W, S) (SI 2001/2030); 31 Dec 2001 (NI) (SR 2001/439)		
10–14		Special Educational Needs and Disability Act 2001	30 May 2002 (SI 2002/1647)
4A		Special Educational Needs and Disability Act 2001	1 Sep 2002 (SI 2002/2217)
1		Education Act 2002	1 Sep 2003 (E) (SI 2003/1667) NOT YET IN FORCE (W)
4B, 4C		Special Educational Needs and Disability Act 2001	1 Sep 2002 (SI 2002/2217)
5	1 Jan 1996 (E, W, S) (SI 1995/3330); 2 Jan 1996 (NI) (SR 1996/1)	Disability Rights Commission Act 1999	25 Apr 2000 (SI 2000/880)
6	2 Dec 1996 (SI 1996/1474; SR 1996/280)		

7		
5, 42, 50	2 Dec 1996 (repeals of or in Disabled Persons (Employment) Act 1944, ss 1, 6–14, 19, 21, subject to a saving and transitional provisions; Disabled Persons (Employment) Act 1958) (E, W, S) (SI 1996/1474)	
33, 35, 52	2 Dec 1996 (repeals of Disabled Persons (Employment) Act (Northern Ireland) 1945, ss 1, 6–14, 19, 21 subject to saving and transitional provisions; Disabled Persons (Employment) Act (Northern Ireland) 1960) (NI) (SR 1996/280)	
33	NOT YET IN FORCE (otherwise)	
47	8 Nov 1995 (s 70(2))	

8		
SI 1996/1921	24 Sep 1996 (art 1)	
Northern Ireland Act 1998	1 Oct 1999 (SI 1999/2204)	
SI 1996/1919	24 Sep 1996 (SI 1996/1919)	
SR 2000/8	9 Mar 2000 (SR 2000/8)	

1

INTRODUCTION TO THE DDA

1.1. INTRODUCTION

The Disability Discrimination Act 1995 (DDA) was the third of the trio of main anti-discrimination statutes. It was enacted only after sixteen failed private members' Bills introduced by disability rights campaigners and significant lobbying by disability rights organizations.[1] It followed some twenty years after the Sex Discrimination Act 1975 (SDA) and the Race Relations Act 1976 (RRA) and to a large extent followed the model adopted by those Acts. Like the SDA and the RRA, the DDA defines 'discrimination' for the purposes of its provisions and creates a series of statutory torts wherein discrimination as defined is made unlawful. There are, however, significant differences between the Acts and these are addressed in Chapter 2 below. To this trio of Acts has now been added the Employment Equality (Religion or Belief) Regulations 2003 SI 2003/1660 and the Employment Equality (Sexual Orientation) Regulations SI 2003/1661, which expressly regulate, for the first time in UK domestic law,[2] religious and sexual orientation discrimination in a limited number of fields.[3]

---

[1] Fredman, *Discrimination Law* (OUP, 2002) 58–9; and see, ed McColgan, 'Achieving Equality at Work' (2003) IER 69–70.

[2] That is, outside the protection afforded by the Human Rights Act 1998; by the RRA, in the case of members of religious groups that also constitute 'ethnic groups' within the meaning of the RRA, eg Jews and Sikhs (*Seide v Gillette Industries* [1980] IRLR 427; *Mandla v Dowell Lee and O'rs* [1983] 2 AC 548); by some provision in the Education Acts regarding the employment of teachers, eg Section 30 Education Act 1944; and by the Fair Employment and Treatment (Northern Ireland) Order 1998 SI 1998/3162 (NI 21) as now amended by the Fair Employment and Treatment Order (Amendment) Regulations (Northern Ireland) 2003 SR 2003/520.

[3] Namely, in employment and related fields. Both giving effect to the obligations upon Member States in the Framework Directive 2000/78/EC to outlaw such discrimination. See, De Marco, *Blackstone's Guide to the Employment Equality Regulations 2003* (OUP, 2004).

Prior to the enactment of the DDA no enforceable rights against disability discrimination were conferred upon disabled people. The Disabled Persons (Employment) Act 1944, introduced to address the concerns about returning wounded servicemen, provided a quota system for the employment of disabled people. The Act was not enforceable by individuals but only by criminal sanction; it allowed employer-wide exemptions and was honoured more in breach than in observance. Indeed, despite widespread non-compliance there was not a single criminal prosecution under it.[4]

Disability discrimination was nevertheless widespread and remains so. It is likely that at least 8.5 million people are 'disabled' people within the meaning of the DDA definition. A further 1.5 million have had a disability that also qualifies them for protection under the DDA.[5] There is now widespread recognition of the disadvantages faced by disabled people but still significant prejudice and misunderstanding about the nature of 'disability' and its impact on the potential of disabled people to engage fully in society. It is now understood that a significant cause of disadvantage is that civil society constructs its arrangements for engagement on the basis of a 'non-disabled' norm. Thus there are physical barriers to buildings making access for disabled people difficult or impossible; communication modes have been adopted that are inaccessible to certain parts of the community; and attitudinal barriers are created that obstruct the proper and fair engagement of disabled people in social life.[6] As has been observed, individual assumptions can become part of an organization's policies and practices, resulting in institutional discrimination.[7] The impact of these barriers is seen in the statistical evidence that indicates that disabled people are twice as likely as non-disabled people to be unemployed and to have no formal qualifications.[8] Disabled people are disproportionately concentrated in low paid and vulnerable atypical work. Thus for example, 15 per cent of home workers are disabled, whereas disabled people make up 12.7 per cent of the employed population.[9] The barriers to employment faced by disabled people are compounded when they have additional responsibilities as parents. Thus disabled parents are significantly more likely to be unemployed than non-disabled parents, and less than one-third of disabled lone parents are in work.[10] Research

---

[4] Palmer, Gill, Monaghan, Moon, and Stacey, ed McColgan, *Discrimination Law Handbook* LAG, (2002) 133.

[5] 'From Exclusion to Inclusion, Final report of the Disability Rights Task Force', November 1999, Chapter 1, paragraph 7. See Chapter 4 below for the meaning of 'disability'.

[6] See Chapter 2 below for further discussion on this.

[7] 'From Exclusion to Inclusion', *supra* note 5.

[8] *Ibid.*, *supra* note 5, paragraph 8.

[9] Disability Rights Commission submission to the Department for Trade and Industry's review of the Employment Relations Act 1999, section 23, cited in 'Achieving Equality at Work', *supra* note 1.

[10] Ballard 'Disabled Parents and Employment', (2004) EOR 126, 20.

also demonstrates that around 42 per cent of disabled people still have problems accessing goods and services.[11]

1.2. OVERVIEW OF THE DDA

In short summary, the DDA was enacted in 1995[12] and in its original enactment regulated disability discrimination in the following areas:

- employment and related fields (sections 4–18);
- access to and provision of goods, facilities, and services[13] (sections 19–21); and
- the management, buying, or renting of land or property (sections 22–24).

In addition, in its original enactment the DDA made provision in the fields of education and transport but importantly did not outlaw discrimination or provide any individually enforceable rights in these fields.[14]

Much of the DDA was brought into force in 1996.[15] Other provisions were introduced on various dates thereafter.

As to employment and related fields:[16]

- since December 1996 it has been unlawful to treat disabled people less favourably than other people for a reason relating to their disability, unless such treatment is justified;[17]

- since December 1996 it has been unlawful to fail to comply with a duty to make reasonable adjustments for a disabled person who is placed at a substantial disadvantage in comparison with people who are not disabled by reason of any arrangements made or any physical feature of premises occupied, unless such failure is justified;[18]

- since December 1996 it has been unlawful to treat any person less favourably by reason that that person has brought proceedings under the DDA; given evidence or information in connection with proceedings under the DDA;

---

[11] Government's final response to Task Force recommendations, March 2001, paragraph 1.2. See also the Analytical Report 'Improving the Life Chances of Disabled People' published by the Prime Minister's Strategy Unit: http://www.strategy.gov.uk/output/Page5046.asp.

[12] The DDA extends to Northern Ireland, section 70(6).

[13] Excluding education and transport, sections 19(5) and (6).

[14] Sections 29–31, 32–49.

[15] See (for the main commencement provisions), Disability Discrimination Act 1995 (Commencement No 1) Order SI 1995/3330; Disability Discrimination Act 1995 (Commencement No 2) Order SI 1996/1336; Disability Discrimination Act 1995 (Commencement No 3 and Saving and Transitional Provisions) Order SI 1996/1474.

[16] Below is set out a short summary. Details of each set of provisions and relevant exceptions are set out below.

[17] Part II DDA. See Chapters 5 and 6 below.

[18] *Ibid.*

otherwise done anything under the DDA; alleged that any person has contravened the DDA; or because it is believed or suspected that s/he has done or intends to do such things.[19]

As for service providers:

- since December 1996 it has been unlawful for service providers to treat disabled people less favourably than other people for a reason relating to their disability, unless such treatment is justified;[20]
- since October 1999 it has been unlawful for service providers to fail to comply with the duty to make reasonable adjustments for disabled people where the existence of a practice, policy, or procedure makes it impossible or unreasonably difficult for disabled people to make use of a service provided, unless such failure is justified;[21]
- since October 1999 it has been unlawful for service providers to fail to comply with the duty to make reasonable adjustments so as to provide a reasonable alternative method of making the service in question available to disabled people where the existence of a physical feature makes it impossible or unreasonably difficult for disabled people to make use of a service provided, unless such failure is justified;[22]
- since October 1999 it has been unlawful for service providers to fail to comply with the duty to take reasonable steps to provide auxiliary aids or services to enable or facilitate the use by disabled people of services that the service provider provides, unless that would necessitate a permanent alteration to the physical fabric of a building or unless such failure is justified;[23]
- since December 1996 it has been unlawful for service providers to treat any person less favourably in the context of access to or provision of services by reason that that person has brought proceedings under the DDA; given evidence or information in connection with proceedings under the DDA; otherwise done anything under the DDA; alleged that any person has contravened the DDA; or because it is believed or suspected that s/he has done or intends to do such things.[24]

---

[19] Section 55 and Part II DDA. See Chapters 5 and 6 below.

[20] Sections 19 and 20(1) DDA. See Chapters 5 and 7 below.

[21] Sections 19, 20(2), and 21(1) brought into force by Disability Discrimination Act 1995 (Commencement Order No 6) Order SI 1999/1190. See Chapters 5 and 7 below.

[22] Sections 19, 20(2), and 21(2)(d) DDA.

[23] Sections 19, 20(2), and 21(4) DDA; Disability Discrimination (Services and Premises) Regulations 1999 SI 1999/1191, Regulation 4.

[24] Sections 19 and 55. See Chapters 5 and 7 below.

As for landlords and sellers of premises:

- since December 1996 it has been unlawful for a person with power to dispose of any premises to treat disabled people less favourably than other people for a reason relating to their disability, unless such treatment is justified;[25]
- since December 1996 it has been unlawful for a person managing premises to treat a disabled person occupying those premises less favourably than other people for a reason relating to their disability, unless such treatment is justified;[26]
- since December 1996 it has been unlawful for a person whose licence or consent is required for the disposal of any leased or sub-let premises to discriminate against a disabled person by withholding that licence or consent, unless such treatment is justified;[27]
- since December 1996 it has been unlawful for a person concerned with disposing of premises or managing premises or with the granting of licences or consent to treat any person less favourably by reason that that person has brought proceedings under the DDA; given evidence or information in connection with proceedings under the DDA; otherwise done anything under the DDA; alleged that any person has contravened the DDA; or because it is believed or suspected that s/he has done or intends to do such things.[28]

There were a number of exemptions and lacunae in the DDA, some of which have been removed or filled. For example, discrimination in the field of 'education' was subject to a specific exemption.[29] However, new duties came into effect in September 2002 under Part IV of the DDA as amended by the Special Educational Needs and Disability Act (SENDA). These provisions require schools, colleges, universities, and providers of adult education and youth services to ensure that they do not discriminate against disabled people.[30] In addition a duty to provide auxiliary aids in certain circumstances, pursuant to the reasonable adjustment duty under Part IV of the DDA, as amended by the SENDA, came into force in September 2003. The enforcement mechanisms are distinct from those applicable to the other unlawful acts created by the DDA (which are enforced in the Employment Tribunals and County Courts or Sheriff Courts[31] in the usual way[32]).

---

[25] Sections 22(1) and 24(1) DDA. See Chapters 5 and 7 below.
[26] Section 22(3) and 24(1) DDA. See Chapters 5 and 7 below.
[27] Sections 22(4) and 24(1) DDA. See Chapters 5 and 7 below.
[28] Sections 24(1) and 55. See Chapters 5 and 7 below.
[29] Section 19(5) and (6).
[30] See Chapter 8 below.
[31] In Scotland.
[32] Sections 17A and 25 and see Chapter 11 below.

Transport, however, remains separately regulated. The DDA allows the government to set minimum standards to help disabled people to use public transport easily but does not create any individually enforceable rights.[33]

The DDA defines 'disability' and 'discrimination' for the purposes of its provisions. Both sets of definitions are cumbersome and problematic. They are addressed below in Chapters 4 and 5 respectively.

The DDA did not create an enforcement body with powers analogous to those of the Equal Opportunities Commission (EOC) or the Commission for Racial Equality (CRE). It created the now defunct National Disability Council[34] that had no powers to support individual litigants in claims under the DDA and had no enforcement powers of its own.[35] This defect was remedied by the enactment of the Disability Rights Commission Act 1999 (the DRCA), by which the Disability Rights Commission Act (DRC) was established. There remain important distinctions between the powers of the EOC, the CRE, and the DRC and these are discussed in Chapter 12 below.

1.3. OVERVIEW OF CHANGES TO THE DDA IN FORCE FROM OCTOBER 2004

The DDA, though having many faults, represented a considerable and radical shift in the nature of the rights afforded to disabled people. Such was the potential impact of those rights that not all provisions were brought into force at the same time. In particular, the provisions requiring service providers to make physical adjustments to their premises[36] were given a nine-year lead in time. Accordingly, these provisions came into force on 1 October 2004,[37] from which date:

• where a physical feature (for example, one arising from the design or construction of a building or the approach or access to premises) makes it impossible or unreasonably difficult for disabled persons to make use of a service, the service provider will be under a duty to take reasonable steps to remove the feature; alter it so that it no longer has that effect; or provide a reasonable means of avoiding the feature;[38]

---

[33] See Chapter 9 below. This will change when the Disability Discrimination Bill, discussed in Chapter 13 below, is enacted.

[34] Section 50.

[35] Its constitution, powers, and duties were prescribed by section 50 and schedule 5 of the unamended DDA (now repealed by the Disability Rights Commission Act 1999).

[36] Section 21(2) DDA.

[37] Disability Discrimination Act 1995 (Commencement No 9) Order 2001/2030.

[38] Sections 19, 20(2), and 21(2) DDA. The duty to provide a reasonable alternative method of making the service in question available to disabled persons in such circumstances was brought into force in 1999, see above.

- the duty upon service providers to comply with the duty to take reasonable steps to provide auxiliary aids or services to enable or facilitate the use by disabled people of services that the service provider provides applies even to such steps as would necessitate a permanent alteration to the physical fabric of a building.[39]

This important change is fully explained and considered in Chapter 5 below.

In addition, the European Community has recently, and pursuant to new powers contained in the EC Treaty,[40] enacted legislation in the field of disability law. Thus the Council Directive of 27 November 2000 'Establishing a General Framework for Equal Treatment in Employment and Occupation' (2000/78/EC) ('the Framework Directive') requires Member States to take measures to combat disability discrimination in the employment and related fields. Member States are required to give effect to these new laws by no later than 2 December 2006.[41] The UK Government has given effect to the disability provisions of the Framework Directive by the making of the Disability Discrimination Act 1995 (Amendment) Regulations 2003[42] (the 2003 Regulations). The 2003 Regulations amend the DDA by introducing new concepts of disability discrimination, widening the scope of the employment-related provisions, and removing certain exemptions from the DDA. They also came into force on 1 October 2004.[43] In summary, the 2003 Regulations:

- introduce new concepts of discrimination, namely 'less favourable treatment on the ground of a disabled person's disability' and 'harassment' (neither of which can be justified);[44]
- widen the scope of the obligation upon employers, and related bodies, to make adjustments to cover any 'provision, criterion, or practice';[45]
- extend the scope of the DDA to cover all employers, save for the armed forces, so repealing the small employer exception;
- extend the scope of the DDA to cover new occupations, such as office holders, barristers, the police, and partners in firms;
- extend the scope of the DDA to cover practical work experience, whether paid or unpaid;

---

[39] Sections 19, 20(2), and 21(4) DDA; Disability Discrimination (Services and Premises) Regulations 1999 SI 1999/1191, Regulation 4. See Chapters 5 and 7 below

[40] As amended by the Amsterdam Treaty.

[41] Article 18 of Council Directive 2000/78/EC, which extends the end date for implementation of the provisions on disability discrimination from the primary three-year period, when the provisions on sexual orientation and religion and belief must have been implemented, to six years, if necessary.

[42] SI 2003/1673.

[43] Though the burden of proof provisions will have an impact on cases brought before that date but not yet determined as well as cases brought after that date: see Regulation 2(1). See further, Chapter 11 below.

[44] See Chapter 5 below.

[45] See Chapters 5 and 6 below.

- extend the scope of the DDA to cover qualifications bodies;
- create new prohibitions on discriminatory advertisements;
- introduce new provision in relation to employment services;
- remove the justification defence for a failure to make reasonable adjustments so that a failure to make an adjustment that is reasonable for a person to have to make is unlawful; and
- make important changes to the burden of proof.

The 2003 Regulations cover discrimination only in the employment and related fields.

In addition, the Disability Discrimination Act 1995 (Pensions) Regulations 2003[46] (the Pensions Regulations) make provision in relation to pensions. They give effect to the provisions of the Framework Directive that address 'pay'.[47] The Pensions Regulations make unlawful a number of acts in relation to the provision of pension benefits.[48] They came into force on 1 October 2004.[49] In short summary, the Pensions Regulations:

- insert a new non-discrimination rule into every occupational pension scheme (requiring trustees or managers to refrain from discriminating against a relevant disabled person in carrying out their functions in relation to the scheme and refrain from harassing such a person in relation to the scheme);
- make unlawful any act of discrimination or harassment by a trustee or manager contrary to the non-discrimination rule;
- impose a duty to make reasonable adjustments on trustees or managers of schemes in relation to provisions, criteria, or practices (including scheme rules) applied by them and physical features of premises occupied by them, where these place a relevant disabled person at a substantial disadvantage in comparison with persons who are not disabled;
- ensure that where a relevant disabled person presents a complaint to an Employment Tribunal that trustees or managers of a scheme have acted in a way that is unlawful, the employer in relation to the scheme is to be treated as a party to the complaint;
- make provision in relation to remedies for a person discriminated against in the context of an occupational pension scheme; and
- identify the classes of persons who are protected by various provisions of the Pension Regulations.[50]

---

[46] SI 2003/2770.   [47] Article 3(c).

[48] For a full analysis see Chapter 6 below.

[49] Though they will have an impact in relation to benefits accrued before that date insofar as the servicing of them is concerned, see Chapter 6.

[50] A 'relevant disabled person in relation to an occupational pension scheme' means a disabled person who is a member or prospective member of the scheme: section 4K(2) DDA, as inserted by

1.4. CODES OF PRACTICE

The DRC has issued a re-revised Code of Practice on 'Rights of Access, Goods, Facilities, Services and Premises'.[51] This Code replaces the first revised Code. This new Code takes account of the further duties on service providers to make adjustments when the physical features of their premises make it impossible or unreasonably difficult for disabled people to use their services. Although these remaining duties did not come into force until 1 October 2004, this Code was issued in May 2002 in order to encourage service providers to be proactive and to assist them in preparing for these significant extended obligations.[52]

In addition, following extensive consultation, the DRC has issued two new Codes of Practice. These incorporate guidance on the new provisions that came into force in October 2004 in the employment and related fields. These are the Code of Practice on Employment and Occupation[53] and the Code of Practice on Trade Organisations and Qualifications Bodies.[54] These were laid before Parliament for approval pursuant to the negative resolution procedure, as required, and came into force on 1 October 2004.[55] These are considered in detail in Chapters 5 and 6 below.

Other relevant guidance is contained in the 'Guidance on matters to be taken into account in determining Questions relating to the Definition of Disability';[56] the Code of Practice for Schools;[57] and the Code of Practice for Providers of Post-16 Education and Related Services.[58]

---

the Pensions Regulations. However, certain protection extends to a disabled person who is entitled to present payment of dependants' or survivors' benefits under an occupational pension scheme or is a pension credit member of such a scheme: section 4K(1) DDA, as amended by the Pensions Regulations.

[51] ISBN No 0 11 702860 6.

[52] Commencement date 27 May 2002, Disability Discrimination Code of Practice (Goods, Facilities, Services and Premises) (Appointed Day) Order 2002 SI 2002/720.

[53] (2004) DRC ISBN 0 11 703419 3; Disability Discrimination Codes of Practice (Employment and Occupation, and Trade Organisations and Qualifications Bodies) Appointed Day Order 2004, SI 2004/2302.

[54] (2004) DRC ISBN 0 11 703418 5; Disability Discrimination Codes of Practice (Employment and Occupation, and Trade Organisations and Qualifications Bodies) Appointed Day Order 2004, SI 2004/2302.

[55] *Ibid.* See also DDA, section 53A.

[56] This guidance came into force on 31 July 1996 (SI 1996/1996) and is discussed in Chapter 4 below.

[57] Disability Rights Commission reference COPSH July 2002. This Code came into force on 1 September 2002, Disability Discrimination Codes of Practice (Education) (Appointed Day) Order 2002, SI 2002/2216. This is addressed in Chapters 5 and 8 below.

[58] Disability Rights Commission reference COPP16 July 2002. This Code came into force on 1 September 2002, Disability Discrimination Codes of Practice (Education) (Appointed Day) Order 2002, SI 2002/2216. This is addressed in Chapters 5 and 8 below.

1.5. DRAFT DISABILITY BILL

The Government has committed itself to introducing primary legislation to implement the outstanding recommendations of the Disability Task Force. In December 2003 the Government published the draft Disability Discrimination Bill[59] for pre-legislative scrutiny.

The draft Disability Discrimination Bill if enacted (as is expected in 2005) will amend the Disability Discrimination Act 1995 (DDA) in a number of very significant ways. In summary:

- the scope of the prohibition on discriminatory advertisements will be extended so as to make publishers liable for publishing discriminatory advertisements;
- the coverage by the DDA of group insurance will be simplified;
- the coverage in relation to transport will be extended and improved;
- the scope of the DDA will be extended so as to cover the 'functions' of public authorities not already covered (subject to some exceptions);
- clubs and associations with twenty-five or more members will be brought within the scope of the DDA;
- the DDA's duties on landlords and managers of premises will be extended to include a duty to make reasonable adjustments to policies, practices, and procedures and to provide auxiliary aids and services, where reasonable, to enable a disabled person to rent a property and facilitate a disabled tenant's enjoyment of the premises;
- a new duty will be placed upon public authorities to have due regard to the need to eliminate discrimination of and harassment against disabled people, and to promote equality of opportunity and the DRC will be given power to enforce specific duties imposed by Order and to issue Codes of Practice in relation to such duties;
- the definition of disability will be extended so as to deem people with HIV infection, cancer or multiple sclerosis 'disabled' from the point of diagnosis;
- the questionnaire procedure[60] will be extended to cover non-employment claims; and
- additional clauses will prohibit local authorities discriminating against disabled councillors.[61]

The draft Bill is fully considered in Chapter 13 below.

---

[59] CM 6058-1. Easy to read version at http://www.parliament.uk/documents/upload/Draft DisabilityBillEasyread.pdf. This is addressed in Chapter 13 below.

[60] See Chapter 11 below.

[61] Introduced in February 2004, after the draft Bill was published; see Joint Committee on the Draft Disability Discrimination Bill (May 2004), paragraph 18.

The Joint Committee on the Draft Disability Discrimination Bill, established for the purpose, has considered the Bill and it has published its first Report (May 2004). The Report makes significant recommendations and these are considered in Chapter 13 below. The Government has indicated that it will accept many, though by no means all, of the recommendations.[62]

---

[62] http://www.dss.gov.uk/mediacentre/pressreleases/2004/july/cfd1507-dfres.asp. See Chapter 13 below for a fuller discussion.

2

THE DDA: ITS PROGRESS, STRENGTHS, AND WEAKNESSES

2.1. THE DDA: INTRODUCTION

The Disability Discrimination Act 1995 is without doubt an unusually complex piece of legislation which poses novel questions of interpretation. This . . . should not . . . be taken as a criticism of the Act or its drafting . . . The whole subject presents unique challenges to legislators and to tribunals and courts, as well as those responsible for the day to day operation of the Act in the workplace. Anyone who thinks there is an easy way of achieving a sensible, workable and fair balance between the different interests of disabled persons, of employers and of able bodied workers, in harmony with wider public interests . . . has probably not given much serious thought to the problem. (*Clark v TDG Ltd t/a Novacold*, *per* Mummery LJ).[1]

The DDA protects 'disabled' people[2] against defined forms of discrimination in prescribed areas of social and public life (employment; the provision of goods, facilities, and services; the disposal and management of premises; and education). The scheme it adopts is particularly complex. The importance of the DDA cannot, however, be overstated. Though societal prejudice cannot be addressed by legislation alone, it is an essential tool in tackling in particular entrenched disadvantage. As has been observed:

a comparison can be drawn between age discrimination, where the Government has promulgated a non-statutory code of practice, and disability discrimination, where there are statutory codes of practice which can be used in proceedings under the DDA, as well as being benchmarks for action plans imposed with non-discrimination notices by the DRC.

---

[1] [1999] ICR 951, [1999] IRLR 318.

[2] Save in the case of victimization where the status of the complainant is immaterial: see Chapter 5 below.

All the employers in . . . case studies . . . said that the voluntary code would be ineffective, and none of them had taken measures to combat age discrimination, although they conceded that it was widespread. On the other hand, they praised the codes on disability because of their practical recommendations, which were backed by the force of law.[3]

2.2. THE DDA'S PROGRESS

At an early stage in its life, it was recognized that the DDA would have to be carefully reviewed to monitor its impact. In December 1997 the Government established the Disability Rights Task Force. Their role was to consider the full range of issues that affect disabled people's lives and to advise the Government on how best to deliver the Government's manifesto commitment to secure comprehensive and enforceable civil rights for disabled people.[4] Its formal terms of reference were:

To consider how best to secure comprehensive, enforceable civil rights for disabled people within the context of our wider society, and to make recommendations on the role and functions of a Disability Rights Commission. To provide the latter by March 1998 and to provide a full report of its recommendations on wider issues no later than July 1999. The Task Force will take full account of the costs as well as the benefits of any proposals, so far as is quantifiable and practicable, and in particular ensure that its recommendations for a Disability Rights Commission achieve value for money for the taxpayer.[5]

In April 1998 the Task Force produced an interim report on the role and functions of a Disability Rights Commission. This highlighted one of the main difficulties with the DDA as originally enacted. As mentioned in Chapter 1 above, it contained no enforcement body with powers analogous to the Equal Opportunities Commission (EOC) or the Commission for Racial Equality (CRE). It created the National Disability Council with very limited powers: none to assist litigants in claims under the DDA and none to take enforcement action in their own name. The National Disability Council (created by section 50 of the unamended DDA) had as its primary function the advising of the Secretary of State on, amongst other things, matters relevant to the elimination of discrimination against disabled persons and persons who have had a disability.[6] It also had responsibility for preparing proposals for codes of practice.[7]

---

[3] Hepple, Coussey, and Choudhury, *Equality: A New Framework, Report of the Independent Review of the Enforcement of the UK Anti-discrimination Legislation* (Hart, 2000) paragraph 3.3.

[4] http://www.disability.gov.uk/drtf/.   [5] *Ibid.*

[6] DDA section 50(2).

[7] Which would be subject to approval by the Secretary of State and then by each House of Parliament pursuant to the negative resolution procedure (DDA sections 51 and 52).

In response to the Task Force's first report, made to Government in March 1998, the Government issued a White Paper consultation in July of the same year: 'Promoting disabled people's rights—creating a Disability Rights Commission fit for the 21st Century'.[8] This in turn led to the Disability Rights Commission Bill, which received Royal Assent in July 1999 and became the Disability Rights Commission Act 1999. This established the Disability Rights Commission (DRC) from April 2000 and abolished the National Disability Council.[9] The Disability Rights Commission, its establishment, powers, and obligations are considered fully in Chapter 12 below.

The Task Force made a number of further recommendations for change in its final report, *'From Exclusion to Inclusion, Final Report of the Disability Rights Task Force'* (November 1999). Many of these have been implemented (see Chapter 8 below for the changes in education, for example). Many more (though not all) will be implemented when the Disability Discrimination Bill is enacted (see Chapter 13 below).

The Task Force, in particular, recommended that there be major extensions to the coverage of the DDA. The DDA as enacted in 1995 excluded education from the scope of the unlawful acts it created.[10] This was a significant flaw which the Task Force recommended should be remedied by the creation of new rights for disabled people not to be discriminated against by schools, local education authorities, or by further, higher, and adult education institutes.[11] The Task Force recommended that the partial exclusion of transport from the DDA[12] should be removed.[13] Importantly too, the Task Force recommended that 'the public sector should have a duty to promote the equalisation of opportunities for disabled people'.[14] The Task Force recommended that the definition of disability should be extended to cover people with HIV from diagnosis and people with cancer from when it has significant consequences on people's lives.[15] As to the impact of the Draft Disability Discrimination Bill (2003) on these areas see Chapter 13 below.

In November 1999, the Government acknowledged the inadequacies of the DDA in its published Equality Statement in which it explained its approach and its recognition of the problems inherent in the DDA. It stated that:

eliminating unjustified discrimination where it exists and making equality of opportunity a reality is at the heart of the Government's agenda . . . It is not only inherently right, it

---

[8] ISBN 0 10 139772 0.

[9] Section 1, Disability Rights Commission Act 1999. See SI 2000/880, Article 2, Schedule 2 for the bringing into force of the relevant provisions of the Disability Rights Commission Act 1999.

[10] DDA section 19(5)(a) and (6).

[11] 'From Exclusion to Inclusion, Final Report of the Disability Rights Task Force', November 1999, Chapter 2, paragraph 4.

[12] DDA section 19(5)(b).

[13] 'From Exclusion to Inclusion, Final Report of the Disability Rights Task Force', November 1999, Chapter 2, paragraphs 15–16 and Chapter 7, paragraph 7.2.

[14] *Ibid.* Chapter 2, paragraph 7.   [15] *Ibid.* Chapter 2, paragraph 11.

is also essential for Britain's future economic and social success . . . We will ensure that the right legislative framework and institutional arrangements are in place . . . to challenge discrimination and deliver fair treatment to allow everyone to develop and contribute to their full potential.

In addition it acknowledged that '[t]he Disability Discrimination Act lags behind sex and race legislation in the protection it provides for disabled people. The establishment of a Disability Rights Commission . . . will address one of the Act's major weaknesses but there are other gaps in coverage . . . we are committed to improving the rights of disabled people'.[16]

The Government provided an interim response to the Task Force's recommendations in March 2000.[17] In that response the Government confirmed its commitment to introducing legislation to address the recommendations on rights for disabled children and adults in education. It also addressed those aspects of the Task Force's recommendations that required non-legislative action, for example its recommendation that Government should do more to raise awareness amongst owners of premises of the benefits of physical adaptations that increase accessibility for disabled people,[18] amongst other things.

In its final response to the Task Force's final report, 'Towards Inclusion' (March 2001), the Government invited views from disabled people, their representative bodies, employers, service providers, and public bodies on the recommendations made by the Task Force that required legislation.[19] In addition the Government itself made proposals regarding those legislative changes that it intended to make. Thereafter the Special Educational Needs and Disability Bill was put before Parliament on 7 December 2000 and enacted to become the Special Educational Needs and Disability Act 2001 (SENDA), on which see Chapter 8 below. In addition, and in the meantime, the Council of Ministers agreed the terms of the Council Directive 'Establishing a General Framework for Equal Treatment in Employment and Occupation' (2000/78/EC) ('the Framework Directive') then enacted on 27 November 2000 pursuant to new powers under the Article 13 of the EC Treaty (on which see Chapter 3 below).

There were then significant developments in the field of disability law, many of which recognized the inadequacies in the original scheme provided for by the DDA.

In January 2003 the Government announced its intention to introduce a draft Disability Bill later in the year[20] to implement those recommendations of the Disability Rights Task Force accepted by the Government in its response, 'Towards Inclusion' (March 2001).

---

[16] Equality Statement, November 1999, cited in Government's final response to the Task Force recommendations, March 2001 at paragraphs 1.1 to 1.3.

[17] 'Interim Government Response to the report of the Disability Rights Task Force' (2000).

[18] Recommendations 6.28 and 6.29.

[19] Government final response to Task Force recommendations, 'Towards Inclusion', March 2001, Foreword by Margaret Hodge, MP, Minister for Disabled People.

[20] 'Disability Equality: Making it Happen' April 2003, DRC, page 8.

In April 2003, the Disability Rights Commission published its first review of the DDA, 'Disability Equality: Making it Happen'.[21] In that review it called upon Government to include in the draft Disability Bill those proposals made in its review in addition to those made by the Disability Rights Task Force. It observed that, 'Civil rights legislation for disabled people needs to be comprehensive. This is necessary both to establish a clear public principle of equality, and to ensure that all the barriers to disabled people's full participation are removed'.[22]

The DRC also recommended 'consistency' across the different parts of the DDA and where possible between disability and other anti-discrimination legislation.[23] Criticism is regularly made about the existing legislative scheme on the basis that there are significant inconsistencies. This makes understanding anti-discrimination law problematic and creates a hierarchy of grounds promoting race, ethnicity, and national origins discrimination to a position where protection is most comprehensive with, now, religion, belief, and sexual orientation discrimination being the least well protected.[24] In addition and importantly the DRC acknowledged that proposals were needed that 'promote[d] systemic change'; that the legislative scheme needs to 'move from relying on individual enforcement towards a proactive approach to disability equality'.[25]

The review addressed those areas that had been the subject of recommendation by the Task Force, but not carried forward by the Government, and some additional matters. By the time of the review, draft Regulations amending the DDA to, amongst other things, give effect to the Framework Directive had been published.[26] In addition a Private Member's Bill had been introduced (though it was eventually unsuccessful) by Bridget Prentice, which included a statutory duty upon public authorities to promote equality of opportunity for disabled people.[27] A further Private Member's Bill, sponsored by Neil Gerrard, was

---

[21] April 2003, DRC.   [22] *Ibid.* page 10.   [23] *Ibid.* page 10.

[24] See Race Relations Act 1976 as amended by the Race Relations (Amendment) Act 2000 and the Race Relations Act 1976 (Amendment) Regulations 2003, SI 2003/1626, which together provide protection against race discrimination, with discrimination being given a wide meaning, across a whole range of activities and introduce statutory duties upon public authorities to, amongst other things, 'have due regard to the need [in carrying out their functions] (a) to eliminate unlawful racial discrimination; and (b) to promote equality of opportunity and good relations between persons of different racial groups', see sections 71 and 71D and E for enforcement. This might be contrasted with the position in relation to sexual orientation and religion and belief where protection extends across a much narrower range of activities (employment and related fields only) and where there are no comparable statutory duties: Employment Equality (Religion or Belief) Regulations 2003, SI 2003, 1660 and Employment Equality (Sexual Orientation) Regulations, SI 2003/1661. See, Hepple, Coussey, and Choudhury, *Equality: A New Framework*, *supra* note 3, for a review and discussion of the inconsistencies which then existed and which with new regulation now have increased in number.

[25] 'Disability Equality: Making it Happen' April 2003, DRC, page 10.

[26] *Ibid.* reference to the same pages 13–14.

[27] *Ibid.* reference to the same page 14.

passed in November 2002: the Private Hire Vehicles (Carriage of Guide Dogs etc) Act 2002, which had the effect of implementing the Task Force's recommendations that private hire vehicles should not be allowed to refuse to carry assistance animals.[28]

In its review, the DRC made a number of recommendations for change. Many of these have been given effect by the new Regulations or will be given effect when the draft Disability Discrimination Bill is finally enacted. The full impact of such changes is considered and explained in Chapters 6 and 13 below. Not all recommendations have been carried forward, however, and readers should be alive to the possibility of continuing change in disability discrimination law. In particular, the Draft Disability Discrimination Bill has now been considered by a joint Parliamentary scrutiny committee established for the purpose: The Joint Committee on the Draft Disability Discrimination Bill. They have published their first report[29] in which they endorse many aspects of the Bill but make further recommendations for change. The government has responded and indicated that it will accept some of their recommendations but not others.[30] This is discussed further in Chapter 13 below.

2.3. THE DDA'S STRENGTHS AND WEAKNESSES

2.3.1. 'Disability'

One of the main criticisms from disability campaigners about the model adopted by the DDA is that it, principally,[31] adopts a medical rather than a social concept of disability. A social model acknowledges that there is a 'close connection between the limitations experienced by individuals with disabilities, the design and structure of the environments and the attitudes of the general population' (United Nations Standard Rules on the Equalisation of Opportunities for Persons with Disabilities, paragraph 5).[32] The medical model, on the other hand, addresses disability by regarding it as that of the individual person and their particular impairment. As it was put by Ann Begg MP, expressing her view in the House of Commons second reading debate on the Disability Rights Commission Act: 'It is not my disability that stops me playing an equal part in society, it's the fact that some people put steps in buildings that I can't get into. I have no limi-

---

[28] See recommendations 7.3 and 7.4. See further Chapter 9 below.

[29] 'Joint Committee on the draft Disability Discrimination Bill: First report' (2004), available at http://www.parliament.uk/parliamentary_committees/ddb.cfm.

[30] 'The Government's Response to the Report of the Joint Committee on the draft Disability Discrimination Bill' (15 July 2004), available at http://www.disability.gov.uk/legislation/ddb/response.asp.

[31] Important exceptions are the coverage to past disabilities and severe disfigurements, see Chapter 4 below.

[32] Cited by B Doyle, 'Disabled Workers' Rights, the Disability Discrimination Act and the UN Standard Rules' (1996) 25 ILJ 1, 11.

tations in what I can do in a fully accessible building . . . It is society that has built the physical barriers and it is people in society who have the attitudes that cause the problem—not the disability.'[33]

The DRC has described the social model of disability as follows:

Here the notion of discrimination is the key, in other words, disabled people do not face disadvantage because of their impairments but experience discrimination in the way we organise society. This includes failing to make education, work, leisure and public services accessible, failing to remove barriers of assumption, stereotype and prejudice and failing to outlaw unfair treatment in our daily lives.

'Disability . . . the disadvantage or restriction of activity caused by contemporary social organisation which takes little or no account of people who have physical impairments and thus excludes them from the mainstream of social activities' (UPIAS1976).[34]

As can be seen, the idea of disability as a social construct places the focus on 'how society (consciously or otherwise) compounds a person's impairment by constructing social and economic processes that fail adequately to take account of the disability in question. In other words, the focus is . . . on how society disables by failing to provide equal opportunities for participation'.[35]

The 'Union of the Physically Impaired against Segregation' (UPIAS), a group of disabled people formed as long ago as 1975, regarded disability in these terms and aimed to have all segregated facilities for physically impaired people replaced by arrangements allowing disabled people to participate fully in society.[36]

The duties to make reasonable adjustments (discussed in Chapter 5 below) do at least go some way to satisfying these aims and to some extent acknowledge the social model of disability. However, the emphasis in the definition of 'disability' upon a medical diagnosis undermines any aspiration that the DDA will successfully address disability discrimination as a social phenomenon.

2.3.2. 'Discrimination'

The DDA as originally enacted proscribed three forms of discrimination:

- a failure to comply with a duty to make reasonable adjustments;
- less favourable treatment for a reason relating to disability ('disability-related discrimination'); and
- victimization.

---

[33] Cited in McColgan *Discrimination Law, Text, Cases and Materials* (Hart, 2000) 454.

[34] http://www.drc-gb.org/citizenship/howtouse/socialmodel/index.asp, in its citizenship and disability pages.

[35] Gerrard Quinn, 'Human Rights for People with Disabilities', in ed. Alston, *The EU and Human Rights* (OUP, 2000) page 287.

[36] See 'Policy Statement' adopted 3 December 1974 and amended 9 August 1976 at http://www.leeds.ac.uk/disability-studies/archiveuk/upias/upias.pds.

Such discrimination is still outlawed in the areas covered by the unlawful acts created by the DDA. In addition, two new forms of discrimination are outlawed from 1 October 2004:

- 'direct' discrimination. This is direct discrimination as it is usually understood (and in contrast to the 'old' form of direct disability discrimination, namely 'disability-related discrimination') and it is now also proscribed in consequence of the amendments made to the DDA by the Disability Discrimination Act 1995 (Amendment) Regulations 2003.[37] This form of direct discrimination ('on the ground of the disabled person's disability, he treats the disabled person less favourably than he treats or would treat a person not having that particular disability whose relevant circumstances, including his abilities, are the same as, or nor materially different from, those of the disabled person'[38]) more closely matches the meaning of direct discrimination in the SDA and the RRA.[39] Importantly it cannot be justified; and

- 'harassment'. This is a new concept introduced into the anti-discrimination legislation in consequence of EC law.[40]

In the employment and related fields, it is sometimes that disability-related discrimination has become less important as the new direct discrimination provisions provide more rigorous protection against less favourable treatment[41] and given that the duties to make reasonable adjustments require proactive action to secure substantive equal treatment for disabled persons. However, the disability-related provisions will continue to prove important in addressing some forms of indirect disability discrimination. As is discussed in Chapter 5 below, the comparison exercise required for disability-related discrimination is quite different to that required for the new form of direct discrimination. In cases of disability-related discrimination the disability-related characteristics (including relevant abilities) upon which the treatment is based are ignored for the purpose of carrying out the comparison exercise. This provides in some respects wider protection against disability discrimination than the new direct discrimination provision, albeit that disability-related discrimination can be justified (unlike the new direct discrimination). This is fully discussed in Chapter 5 below. Discrimination based on perceived disability and discrimination based on a person's association with a disabled person remain unprotected.

---

[37] SI 2003/1673. [38] Section 3A(5) DDA.

[39] Section 1(1)(a) SDA and RRA.

[40] See Chapters 3 and 5 below.

[41] See 'Code of Practice on Employment and Occupation' (2004) DRC ISBN 0 11 703419 3 (Disability Discrimination Codes of Practice (Employment and Occupation, and Trade Organisations and Qualifications Bodies) Appointed Day Order 2004, SI 2004/2302), paragraph 4.1 and the order in which the forms of discrimination are addressed.

As mentioned above the duties to make reasonable adjustments are particularly significant. As has been observed in commenting upon the important case of *Archibald v Fife Council*:[42]

As Baroness Hale puts it: 'The 1995 Act . . . does not regard the differences between disabled people and others as irrelevant. It does not expect each to be treated in the same way. It expects reasonable adjustments to be made to cater for the special needs of disabled people. It necessarily entails an element of more favourable treatment.' This, Lord Hope characterises as 'positive discrimination' in favour of a disabled person. That is one way of putting it. Another way is to regard providing reasonable adjustments as what equality means for disabled people, helping them to overcome disadvantage and placing them on an equal footing.[43]

In the employment and related fields the duty is only triggered where a provision, criterion, practice, or a physical feature of premises disadvantages a particular disabled person;[44] it is therefore a *reactive* duty. In certain areas outside the employment and related fields the duties are even more significant because they are *anticipatory*, that is, they do not require a particular disabled person to be disadvantaged for the duties to be triggered. In the provision of goods, facilities, and services, for example, it is enough that the existence of a practice, policy, or procedure makes it impossible or unreasonably difficult for disabled persons to make use of the service provided for the duty to be activated.[45] This requires service providers to plan for and take proactive action to address possible disadvantage to disabled persons arising out of physical or organizational obstacles. Such duties are very important indeed. They have become even more important with the coming into force on 1 October 2004 of the duty to make adjustments to the physical features of premises in such circumstances. The extensive advertising of the coming into force of this duty highlights its importance.[46] A failure to comply with the reasonable adjustment duties, outside the employment and related fields, is nevertheless capable of being 'justified' and this represents a weakness. It is now not possible to justify a breach of the duties to make reasonable adjustments in the employment and related fields.[47] These concepts are fully explained in Chapter 5.

2.4. THE DDA, THE SDA, AND THE RRA

As mentioned in Chapter 1 above, in many respects the DDA follows the model adopted in the Sex Discrimination Act 1975 (SDA) and the Race Relations Act

---

[42] [2004] UKHL 32, [2004] IRLR 651.

[43] 'IRLR *Highlights*' (August 2004) IRLR 589.   [44] See Chapter 5 below.

[45] A cause of action will arise when an unlawful act is thereby committed; see sections 19 and 20 DDA and Chapter 5, paragraph 5.7 below.

[46] See 'Open 4 All' campaign (2004) DRC, http://www.drc.org.uk/open4all/about/orderO4 Acampaignp.asp.

[47] See Chapter 5 below.

1976 (RRA). It creates a number of statutory torts[48] enforceable through the courts and tribunals in the normal way.[49] It makes employers and principals liable for the acts of their agents.[50] It creates self-contained definitions of discrimination applicable for the purposes of the DDA alone.[51] In all these respects it mirrors the approach adopted by the SDA and the RRA.[52] It will often be appropriate to interpret the SDA, the RRA, and the DDA consistently: 'Since the [RRA] is one of a trio of Acts (with the Sex Discrimination Act 1975 and the Disability Discrimination Act 1995) which contain similar statutory provisions although directed to different forms of discrimination, it is legitimate if necessary to consider those Acts in resolving any issue of interpretation which may arise on this Act.'[53] In addition, it will always be appropriate to interpret the DDA purposively:

The legislation now represented by the race and sex discrimination Acts currently in force broke new ground in seeking to work upon the minds of men and women and thus affect their attitude to the social consequences of difference between the sexes or distinction of skin colour. Its general thrust was educative, persuasive, and where necessary coercive. The relief accorded to the victims, or potential victims, of discrimination went beyond the ordinary remedies of damages and an injunction introducing, through declaratory powers in the court or tribunal and recommendatory powers in the relevant Commission, provisions with a pro-active function, designed as much to eliminate the occasions for discrimination as to compensate its victims or punish its perpetrators. These were linked to a code of practice of which courts and tribunals were to take cognizance. Consistently with the broad front on which it operates, the legislation has traditionally been given a wide interpretation: see eg *Savjani v. Inland Revenue Commissioners* [1981] Q.B. 458, 466–467, where Templeman L.J. said of the Race Relations Act 1976:
    'the Act was brought in to remedy a very great evil. It is expressed in very wide terms, and I should be slow to find that the effect of something which is humiliatingly discriminatory in racial matters falls outside the ambit of the Act'.[54]

These observations apply equally to the DDA.[55]

The DDA also reflects many of the limitations of the SDA and the RRA. It does not provide comprehensive coverage.[56] Like the SDA and the RRA, its provisions are complex. As to the concept of 'discrimination', those complexities

---

[48] See eg sections 4, 13, 19, and 22.

[49] Sections 17A and 25.

[50] Section 58(1) and (2).

[51] Eg sections 3A and 3B; 14(1) and (2); 20(1) and (2); and Section 55.

[52] See Parts I and II of the SDA and RRA; sections 63 and 66 of the SDA; sections 54 and 57 of the RRA; sections 41(1) and (2) of the SDA; and sections 32(1) and (2) of the RRA.

[53] *Anyanwu v South Bank Students' Union & Others* [2001] UKHL 14, [2001] ICR 391; [2001] IRLR 305, paragraph 2.

[54] *Jones v Tower Boot Ltd* [1997] ICR 254 at 262, [1997] IRLR 168 at paragraph 31, *per* Waite LJ.

[55] *Anyanwu v South Bank Students' Union & Others* [2001] UKHL 14, [2001] ICR 391; [2001] IRLR 305, paragraph 2.

[56] *Rhys-Harper v The Relaxion Group plc and Others* [2003] ICR 867, 901, [2003] IRLR 484, paragraph 133, per Lord Hobhouse.

are even more pronounced in the DDA.[57] Apart from the meaning of discrimination, the DDA creates a difficult threshold test for 'disability'.[58]

As stated, the scope of the DDA is not comprehensive and so there are activities which fall outside the scope, as with the SDA and the RRA. As compared to the RRA, very many significant activities fall outside the DDA (including the functions of public authorities, save where they fall within the ambit of one of the other narrow provisions of the Act,[59] though this will change with the enactment of the Draft Disability Discrimination Bill).

However, notwithstanding its complexity and other weaknesses, the DDA has and continues to have advantages over the SDA and the RRA. In particular, it does introduce positive obligations on employers, service providers, and others covered by the DDA to make 'reasonable adjustments'. This is a form of 'positive action' which acknowledges that mere formal equal treatment would do little to address the disadvantages faced by disabled people in a society that organizes itself around a non-disabled norm. These duties are addressed below, in Chapter 5. According to Lady Hale:

According to its long title, the purpose of the 1995 Act is 'to make it unlawful to discriminate against disabled persons in connection with employment, the provision of goods, facilities and services or the disposal or management of premises . . .' But this legislation is different from the Sex Discrimination Act 1975 and the Race Relations Act 1976. In the latter two, men and women or black and white, as the case may be, are opposite sides of the same coin. Each is to be treated in the same way. Treating men more favourably than women discriminates against women. Treating women more favourably than men discriminates against men. Pregnancy apart, the differences between the genders are generally regarded as irrelevant. The 1995 Act, however, does not regard the differences between disabled people and others as irrelevant. It does not expect each to be treated in the same way. It expects reasonable adjustments to be made to cater for the special needs of disabled people. It necessarily entails an element of more favourable treatment. The question for us is when that obligation arises and how far it goes.[60]

As can be seen, however, the DDA does not protect non-disabled persons (except by protection against victimization).[61] This is so even where adverse treatment is based on disability or is on the 'ground' of disability and as such does not protect against discrimination based on *perceived* disability or discrimination by *association* (this might be contrasted with the RRA[62]). As to the impact of EC law in this respect, see Chapter 3 below (it is likely that this omission is incompatible with EC law).

In addition, the DDA does not include a definition of 'indirect discrimination' or provide express protection against it. Whilst the wider form of 'direct'

---

[57] See Chapter 5 below. [58] See Chapter 4 below.

[59] See by comparison section 19B of the RRA.

[60] *Archibald v Fife Council* [2004] UKHL 32, [2004] IRLR 651, at paragraph 47.

[61] Eg a non-disabled person who supports a disabled person's complaint of discrimination, see Chapter 5 below.

[62] Section 1(1)(a) RRA.

disability discrimination (disability-related discrimination) provided for in the DDA is such as to catch some incidences of indirect discrimination, other incidences of institutional disability discrimination will fall outside. As to the impact of EC law in this respect, see Chapter 3 below (again it is likely that this omission is incompatible with EC law).

It should not therefore be assumed that the SDA and the RRA will always assist in the construction of the DDA, in particular insofar as those concepts of discrimination unique to the DDA are concerned (disability-related discrimination and the duties to make reasonable adjustments).

The concepts of discrimination provided for in the DDA and the unlawful acts created by the DDA are fully described in the following chapters.

3

EUROPEAN COMMUNITY AND HUMAN RIGHTS LAW

3.1. EC LAW: INTRODUCTION

The regulation of discrimination across a wide range of grounds in European Community law is a relatively recent phenomenon. Whilst protection against gender discrimination (and the requirement for equal pay in particular) and nationality discrimination was provided for in the original Treaty[1] there was no provision permitting legislative action against discrimination more widely.

'Soft law' measures addressing disability discrimination have been in place for some time but these have no binding force. For example Council Recommendation (EEC) 86/379 of 27 July 1986 on the employment of disabled people in the Community[2] recommended to Member States that they (amongst other things):

1. . . . [T]ake all appropriate measures to promote fair opportunities for disabled people in the field of employment and vocational training, including initial training and employment as well as rehabilitation and resettlement.

---

[1] Articles 119 (renumbered Article 141) and 48 (renumbered Article 39) of the Treaty establishing the European Economic Community (EEC), usually referred to as the Treaty of Rome. Note Article 48 (renumbered Article 39) concerns only discrimination against nationals of Member States and does not protect third-country nationals.

[2] [1986] OJ L225/43. Recommendations are non-binding, Article 249 EC Treaty.

The principle of fair opportunity for disabled people should be applied in respect of:
(a) access to employment and vocational training, whether normal or special, including guidance, placement and follow-up services;
(b) retention in that employment or vocational training and protection from unfair dismissal;
(c) opportunities for promotion and in-service training.
2. ... [C]ontinue and, if necessary, intensify and re-examine their policies to help disabled people, where appropriate after consulting disabled people's organizations and both sides of industry; such policies should take account of measures and specific activities implemented in the other Member States which have proved effective and worthwhile.
These policies should provide in particular for:
(a) Elimination of negative discrimination . . .
(b) Positive action for disabled people . . .
3. [R]eport to the Commission on the measures they have taken to implement this Recommendation . . .

Annexed to the Recommendation is guidance on a number of possible measures that Member States are required to consider in implementing the Recommendation, including:

• promoting and supporting projects that train and prepare disabled people to create their own business or that identify new employment opportunities in the media or in services on behalf of other disabled people;

• implementing schemes for creating new jobs for disabled people in these fields. Drawing up special national policies for the re-employment of mentally handicapped [sic] workers who lose their jobs because of changes in the character of the employment market;

• creating more opportunities for part-time employment for disabled workers;

• giving a high priority to improving the availability and quality of vocational preparation and training for disabled people, with particular regard to the following (amongst other) aims:

—giving equal consideration to the needs of workers who incur disability through accident or disease and to the needs of young people whose disability is congenital or was incurred in childhood or adolescence;

—adapting the content of the training courses available to match more realistically the needs of the labour market;

—encouraging disabled trainees to take, as far as possible, a more active part in planning their own training programmes;

• encouraging trade unions to give any necessary support to disabled workers and to ensure that their interests are properly catered for in representative structures;

• ensuring that disabled workers who lose their jobs or who cannot find employment after vocational rehabilitation do not find themselves thereafter, purely because of their disability, financially worse off than other workers in similar circumstances;

- ensuring that benefit systems do not act as disincentives to part-time employment, to trial periods of employment or to the gradual take-up of a job or
return to it, whenever any of these patterns is desirable from the disabled
worker's and employer's point of view;

- ensuring that disabled people live in an environment that makes it possible for
them to benefit from further education and training and to make their full contribution to the economy;

- encouraging and coordinating social research, for which national databases
should be established, both in order to analyse needs and possibilities and to
evaluate the effectiveness of measures undertaken;

- giving particular priority to the active involvement of disabled people, whether
in a representative or personal capacity, in the taking and implementation of
decisions concerning them.

In addition, the Community Charter of the Fundamental Social Rights of
Workers (1989)[3] makes specific reference to disabled workers. It provides that
'all disabled persons' should be entitled to concrete measures aimed at improving their social and professional integration. Such measures are to include
vocational training, ergonomics, accessibility, mobility, means of transport, and
housing.[4]

On 7 December 2000 the Council, Parliament, and Commission solemnly
proclaimed the Charter of Fundamental Rights of the European Union.[5] The
Charter contains important provisions in the context of disability discrimination.[6] It provides that:[7]

- 'Human dignity is inviolable. It must be respected and protected.'[8]

- 'Everyone has the right to respect for his or her physical and mental integrity.'[9]

- 'No one shall be subjected to torture or to inhuman or degrading treatment or
punishment.'[10]

- 'Everyone has the right to respect for his or her private and family life, home
and communications.'[11]

---

[3] Adopted on 10 December 1989. OJ COM 89/248, 9.12.89.
[4] Articles 24 and 25.   [5] [2000] OJ C364, 18.12.2000 page 1.
[6] Including under Chapter III, headed 'Equality'.
[7] Provision is made permitting the limitation of these rights in certain narrow circumstances:
Article 52(1) provides: 'Any limitation on the exercise of the rights and freedoms recognised by this
Charter must be provided for by law and respect the essence of those rights and freedoms. Subject
to the principle of proportionality, limitations may be made only if they are necessary and genuinely
meet objectives of general interest recognised by the Union or the need to protect the rights and freedoms of others.'
[8] *Ibid.* Article 1.   [9] *Ibid.* Article 3(1).
[10] *Ibid.* Article 4.   [11] *Ibid.* Article 7.

- 'Every worker has the right to working conditions which respect his or her health, safety and dignity.'[12]
- 'Everyone is equal before the law.'[13]
- 'Any discrimination based on any ground such as sex, race, colour, ethnic or social origin, genetic features, language, religion or belief, political or any other opinion, membership of a national minority, property, birth, disability, age or sexual orientation shall be prohibited.'[14]
- 'The Union recognises and respects the right of persons with disabilities to benefit from measures designed to ensure their independence, social and occupational integration and participation in the life of the community.'[15]

The impact of the Charter is as yet unclear. Article 51 of the Charter provides that: 'The provisions of this Charter are addressed to the institutions and bodies of the Union with due regard for the principle of subsidiarity and to the Member States only when they are implementing Union law. They shall therefore respect the rights, observe the principles and promote the application thereof in accordance with their respective powers.'[16] It appears then that the Charter's provisions are likely to be taken into account in interpreting any European legislation.[17] However, until 2000 there was no legislation addressing disability discrimination and, until shortly before then, no basis in the Treaty allowing for such legislation.

Article 13 of the EC Treaty now provides the Community with the competence to legislate in the field of disability discrimination. Article 13 was inserted by Article 6A of the Amsterdam Treaty[18] into the Consolidated Treaty Establishing The European Community. Article 13 provides that:

Without prejudice to the other provisions of this Treaty and within the limits of the powers conferred by it upon the Community, the Council, acting unanimously on a proposal from the Commission and after consulting the European Parliament, may take appropriate action to combat discrimination based on sex, racial or ethnic origin, religion or belief, disability, age or sexual orientation.

Pursuant to this power the Council has indeed enacted legislation requiring Member States to regulate discrimination on a wide number of grounds, including disability. This is addressed below.

---

[12] *Ibid.* Article 31(1).
[13] *Ibid.* Article 20.
[14] *Ibid.* Article 21.
[15] *Ibid.* Article 26.
[16] *Ibid.* Article 51.

[17] See, Advocate General Tizzano in his Opinion in Case C-173/99, *R (Broadcasting, Entertainment, Cinematographic and Theatre Union) v Secretary of State for Trade and Industry* [2001] 1 WLR 2313, paragraphs 27–8. See too discussion in Bell, *Anti-Discrimination Law and the European Union* (2002) OUP 13 and 23–7. Indeed it is likely that all the instruments described above will be relevant to the interpretation of any material Community legislation.

[18] OJ C340 10.11.1997, page 1.

In addition, and importantly, the Constitution for the European Union adopted in June 2004[19] contains provisions addressing disability. Article I-2 describes the Union's values as including 'the values of respect for human dignity, . . . equality, . . . and respect for human rights. These values are common to the Member States in a society of pluralism, tolerance, justice, solidarity and non-discrimination.' The Union's objectives are stated as (amongst others) combating 'social exclusion and discrimination, and . . . promot[ing] social justice and protection'.[20] There is a duty placed on the Union to 'observe the principle of the equality of citizens'.[21] The Charter of Fundamental Rights is incorporated in Part II of the Constitution and the 'Equality' chapter of the Charter is included in full.[22] The Constitution's list of competencies reproduces, with modifications, Article 13, described above.[23]

3.2. DIRECTIVE 2000/78/EC

Council Directive 2000/78/EC of 27 November 2000 'establishing a general framework for equal treatment in employment and occupation'[24] (the Directive) was adopted by the Council pursuant to the powers conferred upon it under Article 13 (see above).

In short summary, the Directive enacts a framework for the regulation of discrimination on the ground of, amongst others, disability.[25] The Directive is addressed to Member States[26] and Member States are required by its terms to 'adopt the laws, regulations and administrative provisions necessary to comply with [the] Directive'[27] by 2 December 2003. However, special provision is made for disability, so that:

In order to take account of particular conditions, Member States may, if necessary, have an additional period of 3 years from 2 December 2003, that is to say a total of 6 years, to implement the provisions of this Directive on . . . disability discrimination. In that event they shall inform the Commission forthwith. Any Member State which chooses to use this additional period shall report annually to the Commission on the steps it is taking to tackle . . . disability discrimination and on the progress it is making towards implementation.[28]

---

[19] Draft Treaty Establishing a Constitution for Europe [2003] OJ C169/1. At the time of writing the consolidated final text of the Constitution was unavailable.

[20] *Ibid.* Article I-3(3).   [21] *Ibid.* Article I-44.

[22] See above.

[23] For a discussion, see Bell, 'Equality and the European Constitution' (2004) ILJ 33, 242.

[24] OJ L303, 02.12.2000 pages 16–22.

[25] For its impact on sexual orientation discrimination and discrimination on the ground of religion and belief see De Marco, *Blackstone's Guide to the Employment Equality Regulations 2003*, (OUP, 2004).

[26] Directive 2000/78/EC Article 21.   [27] *Ibid.* Article 18.

[28] *Ibid.* The UK has availed itself of the benefit of this provision. The Regulations, discussed below, which give effect to the Directive, came into force only on 1 October 2004.

As will be seen in the following chapters, the Directive has required the UK to introduce changes to the DDA so as to extend the concept of disability discrimination and the scope of the DDA. This has been effected by the making of regulations under section 2 of the European Communities Act 1972. The Regulations, as summarized in Chapter 1 above, are the Disability Discrimination Act 1995 (Amendment) Regulations 2003[29] and the Disability Discrimination Act 1995 (Pensions) Regulations 2003.[30] The means by which the UK has determined to give effect to the provisions of the Directive are very important indeed. This is discussed further below (see 3.4). In summary, however, if any provision of the Regulations goes beyond that provided for by the Directive it will be *ultra vires* the European Communities Act 1972 and invalid.

3.2.1. Recitals

The Directive contains a number of Recitals (as is usual) that might be used to assist in the construction of its substantive terms. The material Recitals are as follows:

(1) In accordance with Article 6 of the Treaty on European Union, the European Union is founded on the principles of liberty, democracy, respect for human rights and fundamental freedoms, and the rule of law, principles which are common to all Member States and it respects fundamental rights, as guaranteed by the European Convention for the Protection of Human Rights and Fundamental Freedoms and as they result from the constitutional traditions common to the Member States, as general principles of Community law.

[. . .]

(6) The Community Charter of the Fundamental Social Rights of Workers recognises the importance of combating every form of discrimination, including the need to take appropriate action for the social and economic integration of elderly and disabled people.

[. . .]

(8) The Employment Guidelines for 2000 agreed by the European Council at Helsinki on 10 and 11 December 1999 stress the need to foster a labour market favourable to social integration by formulating a coherent set of policies aimed at combating discrimination against groups such as persons with disability. They also emphasise the need to pay particular attention to supporting older workers, in order to increase their participation in the labour force.

(9) Employment and occupation are key elements in guaranteeing equal opportunities for all and contribute strongly to the full participation of citizens in economic, cultural and social life and to realising their potential.

[. . .]

(11) Discrimination based on religion or belief, disability, age or sexual orientation may undermine the achievement of the objectives of the EC Treaty, in particular the

---

[29] SI 2003/1673.   [30] SI 2003/2770.

attainment of a high level of employment and social protection, raising the standard of living and the quality of life, economic and social cohesion and solidarity, and the free movement of persons.

(12) To this end, any direct or indirect discrimination based on religion or belief, disability, age or sexual orientation as regards the areas covered by this Directive should be prohibited throughout the Community. This prohibition of discrimination should also apply to nationals of third countries but does not cover differences of treatment based on nationality and is without prejudice to provisions governing the entry and residence of third-country nationals and their access to employment and occupation.

[. . .]

(16) The provision of measures to accommodate the needs of disabled people at the workplace plays an important role in combating discrimination on grounds of disability.

(17) This Directive does not require the recruitment, promotion, maintenance in employment or training of an individual who is not competent, capable and available to perform the essential functions of the post concerned or to undergo the relevant training, without prejudice to the obligation to provide reasonable accommodation for people with disabilities.

(18) This Directive does not require, in particular, the armed forces and the police, prison or emergency services to recruit or maintain in employment persons who do not have the required capacity to carry out the range of functions that they may be called upon to perform with regard to the legitimate objective of preserving the operational capacity of those services.

(19) Moreover, in order that the Member States may continue to safeguard the combat effectiveness of their armed forces, they may choose not to apply the provisions of this Directive concerning disability and age to all or part of their armed forces. The Member States which make that choice must define the scope of that derogation.

(20) Appropriate measures should be provided, ie effective and practical measures to adapt the workplace to the disability, for example adapting premises and equipment, patterns of working time, the distribution of tasks or the provision of training or integration resources.

(21) To determine whether the measures in question give rise to a disproportionate burden, account should be taken in particular of the financial and other costs entailed, the scale and financial resources of the organisation or undertaking and the possibility of obtaining public funding or any other assistance.

[. . .]

(23) In very limited circumstances, a difference of treatment may be justified where a characteristic related to religion or belief, disability, age or sexual orientation constitutes a genuine and determining occupational requirement, when the objective is legitimate and the requirement is proportionate. Such circumstances should be included in the information provided by the Member States to the Commission.

[. . .]

(26) The prohibition of discrimination should be without prejudice to the maintenance or adoption of measures intended to prevent or compensate for disadvantages suffered by a group of persons of a particular religion or belief, disability, age or sexual orientation, and such measures may permit organisations of persons of a particular religion or belief, disability, age or sexual orientation where their main object is the promotion of the special needs of those persons.

(27) In its Recommendation 86/379/EEC of 24 July 1986[31] on the employment of disabled people in the Community, the Council established a guideline framework setting out examples of positive action to promote the employment and training of disabled people, and in its Resolution of 17 June 1999 on equal employment opportunities for people with disabilities, affirmed the importance of giving specific attention *inter alia* to recruitment, retention, training and lifelong learning with regard to disabled persons.

Recitals are important. Whilst they are not legally binding they can be used to assist in interpreting the substantive provisions of the Directive (the Articles), which are the only legally obligatory provisions.[32] The Recitals set out above provide a significant context for the interpretation of the substantive provisions of the Directive. In particular, they make it clear that the elimination of discrimination should now be regarded as a key Community aim given that its existence undermines the achievement of the objectives of the Community. It is also clear that the substantive provisions must be construed consistently with the European Convention on Human Rights (see 3.5 below). In addition, they provide a context for understanding the exemptions in relation to, for example, the armed forces. They are therefore instructive and will usually operate as an important aid to interpretation.

3.2.2. Principle of Equal Treatment

As to its substantive terms, Article 1 describes the purpose of the Directive in the following terms: 'The purpose of this Directive is to lay down a general framework for combating discrimination on the grounds of religion or belief, disability, age or sexual orientation as regards employment and occupation, with a view to putting into effect in the Member States the principle of equal treatment'.

The 'principle of equal treatment' is defined by Article 2(1) as follows: 'the "principle of equal treatment" shall mean that there shall be no direct or indirect discrimination whatsoever on any of the grounds referred to in Article 1'.

The Directive defines direct and indirect discrimination and makes provision for addressing 'harassment' and 'victimization'. These concepts are defined by Articles 2, 3, and 11.

---

[31] Referred to above at 3.1.

[32] The Recitals serve to discharge the obligation under Article 235 EC that: 'Regulations, directives and decisions adopted jointly by the European Parliament and the Council, and such acts adopted by the Council or the Commission, shall state the reasons on which they are based and shall refer to any proposals or opinions which were required to be obtained pursuant to this Treaty'. Accordingly, the Recitals explain the *reasoning* for a particular act but they create no *obligation* on a Member State to take particular measures (see for discussion, Schermers and Waelbroeck, *Judicial Protection in the European Union* (6th edn, Kluwer, 1992) paragraphs 773–7 and Brent, *Directives: Rights and Remedies in English and Community Law* (LLP, 2001) paragraphs 6.06–6.08) and as such cannot be relied upon for the purposes of the exercising of the law-making powers under section 2 European Communities Act 1972, on which see 3.4 below.

Article 2 provides that:

For the purposes of paragraph 1—
(a) direct discrimination shall be taken to occur where one person is treated less favourably than another is, has been or would be treated in a comparable situation, on any of the grounds referred to in Article 1;
(b) Indirect discrimination shall be taken to occur where an apparently neutral provision, criterion or practice would put persons having a particular religion or belief, a particular disability, a particular age, or a particular sexual orientation at a particular disadvantage compared with other persons unless—
  (i) that provision, criterion or practice is objectively justified by a legitimate aim and the means of achieving that aim are appropriate and necessary; or
  (ii) as regards persons with a particular disability, the employer or any person or organisation to whom this Directive applies, is obliged, under national legislation, to take appropriate measures in line with the principles contained in Article 5 in order to eliminate disadvantages entailed by such provision, criterion or practice.

By Article 3:

Harassment shall be deemed to be a form of discrimination within the meaning of paragraph 1, when unwanted conduct related to any of the grounds referred to in Article 1 takes place with the purpose or effect of violating the dignity of a person and of creating an intimidating, hostile, degrading, humiliating or offensive environment. In this context, the concept of harassment may be defined in accordance with the national laws and practice of the Member States.

In addition the Directive provides at Article 2(4) that '[a]n instruction to discriminate against persons on any of the grounds referred to in Article 1 shall be deemed to be discrimination within the meaning of paragraph 1'.

In the context of disability discrimination law the Directive has had an immediate and significant effect. In the first place, as described in Chapter 2 above, the meaning of 'direct' disability discrimination was quite different to the meaning of direct discrimination provided for in the SDA and the RRA, in the latter case matching that provided for under the Directive in all material respects.[33] In addition no provision was made for 'indirect' discrimination, though again, as observed above, the wider meaning of 'direct' discrimination provided for in the DDA (disability-related discrimination) catches some incidents of indirect discrimination. 'Harassment' was not expressly defined or prohibited under the DDA. As will be seen in Chapter 5 below, the 'detriment' provisions of the DDA have been construed (in line with the same provisions in the SDA and the RRA) as wide enough to protect against harassment. Indeed harassment as defined under the 'detriment' provisions of the Acts is in some respects wider in scope than apparently provided for under the Directive, and this has had an impact on the way in which the harassment provisions have been transposed into

---

[33] Section 1(1)(a) RRA.

domestic UK law.[34] Further, there was no prohibition in the DDA on instructions to discriminate.[35]

In some areas the reach of the Directive is entirely unclear because of a lack of Community law learning on the point. Thus, for example, the Directive does not define 'disability'. It is by no means certain that the very medically based meaning given to 'disability' in the DDA would satisfy the requirements of the Directive. It might be noted in this regard that the UN Standard Rules[36] recognize a social model of disability.[37] In particular, the Rules adopt a concept that indicates 'the close connection between the limitation experienced by individuals with disabilities, the design and structure of their environments and the attitude of the general population' (UNSR Introduction paragraph 5). This is to be distinguished from the model adopted by the DDA.

3.2.3. Scope

Article 3 of the Directive (headed 'Scope') provides that:

(1) Within the limits of the areas of competence conferred on the Community this Directive shall apply to all persons, as regards both the public and private sectors, including public bodies, in relation to—
  (a) Conditions for access to employment, to self employment or to occupation, including selection criteria and recruitment conditions, whatever the branch of activity and at all levels of the professional hierarchy, including promotion;
  (b) Access to all types and to all levels of vocational guidance, vocational training, advanced vocational training and re-training, including practical work experience;
  (c) Employment and working conditions, including dismissals and pay;
  (d) Membership of, and involvement in, an organisation of workers or employers, or any organisation whose members carry on a particular profession, including the benefits provided for by such organisations.'

Accordingly the Directive's scope extends only to employment, occupation, and related fields.[38] Nevertheless, it extends beyond those areas covered by the DDA

---

[34] See section 3B DDA. However, section 3B only protects a 'disabled person' against such discrimination. The Directive appears to protect all persons subject to harassment 'related to any of the grounds referred to in Article 1', including disability, affording wider protection (eg against harassment on the ground that a person's partner is disabled or on the ground that they are, wrongly, perceived to be disabled). See Chapter 5 below.

[35] See now section 16C DDA and see Chapter 6.

[36] UN Standard Rules on the Equalization of Opportunities for Persons with Disabilities (UNSR) adopted at the end of 1993, General Assembly Resolution 48/96 of 20 December 1993.

[37] See Doyle, 'Disabled Workers Rights, the Disability Discrimination Act and the UN Standard Rules' (1996) ILJ vol 25, 1 for an overview and insight into the Rules.

[38] This might be contrasted with the 'Race Directive' (Council Directive of 29 June 2000 'implementing the principle of equal treatment between persons irrespective of racial or ethnic origin' 2000/43/EC), which covers discrimination on the grounds of racial or ethnic origin in the fields of employment and occupation and in addition in relation to social protection, including social security and healthcare; social advantages; education; and access to and supply of goods and services that are available to the public, including housing, see Article 3.

as originally enacted. The Regulations that give effect to the Directive therefore increase the DDA's coverage to include all employers except the armed forces.[39]

The Directive makes specific provision in relation to disability. In so doing it recognizes the special position of disabled persons having regard to the social barriers that disadvantage disabled people. Accordingly, the Directive provides at Article 5 (under the heading 'Reasonable Accommodation for Disabled Persons') that:

In order to guarantee compliance with the principle of equal treatment in relation to persons with disabilities, reasonable accommodation shall be provided. This means that employers shall take appropriate measures, where needed in a particular case, to enable a person with a disability to have access to, participate in, or advance in employment, or to undergo training, unless such measures would impose a disproportionate burden on the employer. This burden shall not be disproportionate when it is sufficiently remedied by measures existing within the framework of the disability policy of the Member State concerned.

The 'reasonable adjustment' duty in the DDA obviously goes some way to meeting the requirements of Article 5. However, it was recognized early on that the 'justification' defence which existed for a failure to make reasonable adjustments[40]—so that a failure to make an adjustment that is reasonable for a person to have to make could still be lawful even if unreasonable—was not consistent with the Directive.[41]

The Directive also makes provision for 'positive action'. Article 7 provides that:

(1) With a view to ensuring full equality in practice, the principle of equal treatment shall not prevent any Member State from maintaining or adopting specific measures to prevent or compensate for disadvantages linked to any of the grounds referred to in Article 1.
(2) With regard to disabled persons, the principle of equal treatment shall be without prejudice to the right of Member States to maintain or adopt provisions on the protection of health and safety at work or to measures aimed at creating or maintaining provisions or facilities for safeguarding or promoting their integration into the working environment.

The 'reasonable adjustment' duty, of course, is a form of positive action. Indeed the DDA itself, notwithstanding its defects, might be described as a form of positive action, providing as it does asymmetrical protection[42] by the

---

[39] See Part II DDA.   [40] See Chapter 5 below.

[41] See for example section 5(2) and now see section 3A of the amended DDA. See also the domestic case-law that preceded the Directive by only a short time and that limited the scope of the defence in this context so that it did not permit justification of a breach of section 6 to be established by reference to factors properly relevant to the establishment of a duty under section 6: *Collins v Royal National Theatre Board Ltd* [2004] EWCA Civ 144; [2004] IRLR 395.

[42] As described in Chapter 2 above, though this is not without its problems, as also discussed in Chapter 2.

prohibitions on discrimination against disabled persons but not non-disabled persons (except in the case of discrimination by victimization: see Chapter 5 below).

The Directive also makes important provision in relation to remedies and enforcement under its Chapter 2. By Article 9, Member States are required to ensure that 'judicial and/or administrative procedures, including where they deem it appropriate, conciliation procedures, for the enforcement of obligations under this Directive are available to all persons who consider themselves wronged by failure to apply the principle of equal treatment to them, even after the relationship in which the discrimination is alleged to have occurred has ended'. In addition, Article 17 provides that 'Member States shall lay down the rules on sanctions applicable to infringements of the national provisions adopted pursuant to this Directive and shall take all measures necessary to ensure that they are applied. The sanctions, which may comprise the payment of compensation to the victim, must be effective, proportionate and dissuasive.' The comparable provision in the Equal Treatment Directive[43] has proved very significant in its impact on UK law. Thus in *Marshall v Southampton and South West Hampshire Health Authority (Teaching) (No 2)*[44] the European Court of Justice (ECJ) considered the impact of Article 6 of the Equal Treatment Directive.[45] This provides that 'Member States shall introduce into their national legal systems such measures as are necessary to enable all persons who consider themselves wronged by failure to apply to them the principle of equal treatment . . . to pursue their claims by judicial process after possible recourse to other competent authorities'. The ECJ held that where a Member State chose compensation in order to achieve the objective of 'real and effective equality of treatment', then to comply with Article 6 the compensation had to be adequate in that it had to enable the loss and damage actually sustained as a result of the discrimination to be made good in full. Accordingly, a statutory upper limit on compensation and the exclusion of an award of interest were not permissible. This is an important guarantee and it may raise the question whether the absence of any power to order reinstatement of a dismissed disabled employee under the DDA[46] is sufficient to give effect to the requirement under Article 9 of the Directive.

The requirement in Article 9 of the Directive that disabled persons must be able to enforce the principle of equal treatment even after the relationship in which the discrimination is alleged to have occurred has ended (although not very elegantly worded) addresses the issue that arose in a line of domestic cases

---

[43] 76/207/EEC, see Article 6, which does not provide in clear terms that a remedy must be available for a breach of the principle of equal treatment after the relationship in which the discrimination is alleged to have occurred has ended but the case-law makes it clear that this is implicit: Case C-185/97 *Coote v Granada Hospitality Ltd* [1998] ECR I-5199; [1998] IRLR 656; see further below.

[44] Case C271/91 [1994] QB 126.   [45] 76/207/EEC.

[46] See Chapter 11.

and indeed before the ECJ. It had been unclear whether discrimination that occurred after the relevant relationship had ended (for example, by failing to provide a reference to an employee on grounds of race, sex, or disability after the employment relationship had terminated) fell within the scope of the SDA, RRA, and the DDA. Following a reference from the Employment Appeal Tribunal the ECJ ruled that Article 6 of the Equal Treatment Directive[47] prohibited discrimination in the employment field after the employment relationship had ended, where it 'was as a reaction to legal proceedings brought to enforce compliance with the principle of equal treatment'.[48] Domestic law followed so that the SDA, the RRA, and the DDA were all interpreted as covering discrimination in the employment field,[49] after the termination of the employment relationship so long as the discrimination was sufficiently connected to the employment relationship.[50] The Regulations, which give effect to the Directive, amend the DDA so as to protect expressly against discrimination occurring after the employment relationship has ended.[51]

Article 9(2) of the Directive provides that Member States must 'ensure that associations, organisations or other legal entities which have, in accordance with the criteria laid down by their national law, a legitimate interest in ensuring that the provisions of this Directive are complied with, may engage, either on behalf or in support of the complainant, with his or her approval, in any judicial and/or administrative procedure provided for the enforcement of obligations under this Directive'. The Disability Rights Commission is not permitted to act as substitute complainant in proceedings[52] so cannot act 'on behalf' of a litigant but does have power to support individual litigants. This appears to comply with the obligations under Article 9(2).

The Directive provides for the shifting of the burden of proof in claims of disability discrimination. By Article 10:

(1) Member States shall take such measures as are necessary, in accordance with their national judicial systems, to ensure that, when persons who consider themselves wronged because the principle of equal treatment has not been applied to them establish, before a court or other competent authority, facts from which it may be presumed that there has been direct or indirect discrimination, it shall be for the respondent to prove that there has been no breach of the principle of equal treatment.

(2) Paragraph 1 shall not prevent Member States from introducing rules of evidence which are more favourable to plaintiffs.

---

[47] 76/207/EEC.

[48] *Coote v Granada Hospitality Ltd, supra* note 43.

[49] At least. The scope of the other unlawful acts was not considered.

[50] *Rhys-Harper v Relaxion Group plc and others* [2003] UKHL 33, [2003] ICR 867; [2003] IRLR 484.

[51] See section 16A DDA.

[52] Section 7, Disability Rights Commission Act 1999. They have limited power to act in their own name and intervene in litigation: see Chapter 12.

This shift does not apply to criminal proceedings.[53] This shift has been given effect by regulations in the employment and related fields.[54]

The Directive requires Member States to protect employees against victimization. Victimization is dealt with below in Chapter 5.

In addition, the Directive requires Member States:

- to take care that the provisions adopted pursuant to the Directive, together with the relevant provisions already in force, are brought to the attention of the persons concerned by all appropriate means, for example at the workplace, throughout their territory;[55]

- to take, in accordance with their national traditions and practice, adequate measures to promote dialogue between the social partners with a view to fostering equal treatment, including through the monitoring of workplace practices, collective agreements, codes of conduct, and through research or exchange of experiences and good practices;[56]

- to encourage the social partners, without prejudice to their autonomy and where consistent with their national traditions and practice, to conclude at the appropriate level agreements laying down anti-discrimination rules in the fields referred to in Article 3 which fall within the scope of collective bargaining;[57]

- to encourage dialogue with appropriate non-governmental organizations which have, in accordance with their national law and practice, a legitimate interest in contributing to the fight against discrimination on any of the grounds referred to in Article 1 with a view to promoting the principle of equal treatment;[58]

- to take the necessary measures to ensure that:
  (a) any laws, regulations, and administrative provisions contrary to the principle of equal treatment are abolished;
  (b) any provisions contrary to the principle of equal treatment which are included in contracts or collective agreements, internal rules of undertakings, or rules governing the independent occupations and professions and workers' and employers' organisations are, or may be, declared null and void or are amended.[59]

- to communicate to the Commission, by 2 December 2005 at the latest and every five years thereafter, all the information necessary for the Commission to draw up a report to the European Parliament and the Council on the application of the Directive.[60]

---

[53] By Article 10(3) 'Paragraph 1 shall not apply to criminal procedures'. The other provisions of Article 10 are as follows: by Article 10(2) 'Paragraph 1 shall not prevent Member States from introducing rules of evidence which are more favourable to plaintiffs.' By Article 10(4) 'Paragraphs 1, 2 and 3 shall also apply to any legal proceedings commenced in accordance with Article 9(2)', eg by the DRC. By Article 10(5) 'Member States need not apply paragraph 1 to proceedings in which it is for the court or competent body to investigate the facts of the case', ie inquisitorial proceedings.

[54] Section 17A(1C) DDA. See Chapter 11 below.

[55] The Directive, Article 12.   [56] *Ibid.* Article 13(1).   [57] *Ibid.* Article 13(2).

[58] *Ibid.* Article 14.   [59] *Ibid.* Article 16.

[60] *Ibid.* Article 19(1). See Green Paper, 'Equality and non-discrimination in an enlarged European Union' Com (2004) 379 Final, 28 May 2004, for the European Commission's analysis on the progress in tackling discrimination so far.

3.3. PRINCIPLES OF COMMUNITY LAW

European law and the principles of Community law interpretation have become increasingly important in the context of disability discrimination. This is because, as discussed above, there is now specific legislation at Community level addressing disability discrimination. There are a variety of possible remedies for any apparent failure by the UK to implement the Directive properly. These are discussed below.

3.3.1. Interpretation

In interpreting the Directive and the Regulations the following Community law principles are relevant:

- domestic legislation that gives effect to Community law must be construed purposively, so as to give it a meaning consistent with Community law insofar as is possible.[61] This is so whether that legislation was passed before or after the coming in to force of the relevant Community law. This means that the DDA and the Regulations must be interpreted consistently with the Directive, insofar as it is possible to do so;

- this interpretative obligation is a very compelling one and may require an interpretation that is inconsistent with the natural and ordinary meaning of the words being interpreted and may require the reading-in of words;

- it is presumed that no provision of Community law is intended to infringe human rights and Community law is therefore to be interpreted and applied accordingly.[62] The importance of fundamental rights to the observance of Community law obligations cannot be overstated. The ECJ has repeatedly held that fundamental rights form part of the traditions of the European Community and will be taken into account in interpreting its laws. In addition, Article 6 of the EU Treaty now provides in terms that the European Union is founded on the principles of liberty, democracy, respect for human rights and fundamental freedoms, and the rule of law. These are principles which, as Article 6 observes, are common to the Member States. The Community is also now, as a matter of Treaty obligation, to respect fundamental rights as guaranteed by the European Convention for the Protection of Human Rights and Fundamental Freedoms and as they result from the constitutional traditions common to the Member States, as general principles of Community Law.[63]

---

[61] *Litster v Forth Dry Dock and Engineering Co Ltd* [1990] 1 AC 546; *Marleasing SA v LA Comercial Internacional de Alimentacion* [1990] ECR I-4135.

[62] Bennion, *Statutory Interpretation* (4th edn, Butterworths, 2002) section 400 and cases cited thereunder.

[63] *Ibid.* Article 6.

This means that the Directive and the Regulations must be interpreted in a way which is compatible with fundamental rights including those contained in the European Convention on Human Rights;[64]

- it is presumed that Community law is intended to be effective to achieve its ends, and any court applying that law is required to act accordingly.[65] This means that the Directive should be interpreted purposively so as to afford it proper effectiveness.

These principles are self-evidently important in interpreting the Directive, the DDA, and the Regulations.

3.3.2. Direct Effect

In addition, and very importantly, much Community law has direct effect. This means that it has binding force in Member States whether or not action has been taken by a Member State to implement it. As section 2(1) of the European Communities Act 1972 provides:

All such rights, powers, liabilities, obligations and restrictions from time to time created or arising by or under the Treaties, and all such remedies and procedures from time to time provided for by or under the Treaties, as in accordance with the Treaties are without further enactment to be given legal effect or used in the United Kingdom shall be recognised and available in law, and be enforced, allowed and followed accordingly.

EC Treaty provisions may have direct effect and have been held so to do even where this is not explicit.[66] Where it is not possible to interpret national legislation consistently with a directly effective Treaty provision, the incompatible domestic provisions must be disapplied in any proceedings.[67]

In addition, and as to Directives, Article 249[68] of the EC Treaty provides that: 'A Directive shall be binding, as to the result to be achieved, upon each Member State to which it is addressed, but shall leave to the national authorities the choice of form and methods'.

Provisions of Directives which are 'sufficiently clear, precise and unconditional' may have direct effect and in such circumstances they may be relied upon against the State or an emanation of it (though not as against private bodies).[69]

---

[64] See further below.   [65] Bennion, *supra* note 62, section 402 and cases cited thereunder.

[66] *Bennion, supra* note 62, section 411 and cases cited thereunder. For examples in the discrimination law sphere, see *Defrenne (No 2) Case 43/75* [1976] ECR 455 and *Bilka-Kaufhaus GmbH v Weber von Hartz* Case 170/84 [1986] ECR 1607 on the direct effect of Article 141 (ex Article 119); *Van Duyn v Home Office* Case 41/74 [1974] ECR 1337 on the direct effect of Article 39 (ex Article 48).

[67] See, for example, *Bossa v Nordstress Ltd* [1998] ICR 694; [1998] IRLR 284.

[68] Ex Article 189.

[69] The State being the party to whom the Directive is addressed. This is known as 'vertical direct effect'. See, *Marshall, supra* note 44; *Foster v British Gas plc* Case 188/89 [1990] ECR I-3313; [1990] IRLR 353.

Where it is not possible to interpret legislation consistently with a directly effective provision of a Directive, the incompatible domestic provisions must be disapplied in any proceedings involving the State or an emanation of it.

3.3.3. Remedies against the State for Non-Implementation

Where the State fails to give effect to Community law, a person suffering damage in consequence may have a remedy in compensation against the State if the breach is sufficiently serious: *Brasserie Du Pecheur SA v Federal Republic of Germany; R v Secretary of State for Transport, ex parte Factortame Ltd and others (No 4).*[70]

In addition, a person may complain to the European Commission, which may take action under Article 226[71] of the EC Treaty, which provides that: 'Where the Commission considers that a Member State has failed to fulfil an obligation under this Treaty, it shall deliver a reasoned opinion on the matter after giving the State concerned the opportunity to submit its observations. If the State concerned does not comply with the opinion within the period laid down by the Commission, the latter may bring the matter before the Court of Justice.'

Accordingly, the Commission may itself take action against a Member State if it considers that it has not fulfilled any obligations arising under the Treaty or other law (including a Directive) directed at the Member State.[72]

3.3.4. References to the European Court of Justice

Article 234[73] of the EC Treaty permits the European Court of Justice to give preliminary rulings on the proper interpretation of Community law, following 'a reference' from a national court. This procedure is extremely important. Any national court may make such a reference where 'it considers it necessary to enable it to give judgment'. However, except where the legal provision concerned is *acte clair* (that is, sufficiently clear) the highest court (in the UK, the House of Lords) *must* ask for such a preliminary ruling.[74]

---

[70] (Joined Cases C-46/93 and C-48/93) [1996] QB 404 '. . . [w]here, in a field governed by Community law in which national legislatures had a wide discretion, as in the present cases, there was a breach of Community law attributable to the national legislature, individuals suffering loss or injury thereby had a right flowing directly from Community law to reparation where (i) the rule of Community law breached was intended to confer rights on individuals, (ii) the breach of Community law was sufficiently serious, in that the member state had manifestly and gravely disregarded the limits on its discretion, and (iii) there was a direct causal link between the breach and the damage sustained', held. And see, *R v Secretary of State, ex parte Factortame Ltd (No 5)* [2000] 1 AC 524.

[71] Ex Article 169.

[72] An example of such action in the discrimination law field can be seen in *Commission v UK* Case 61/81 [1982] ECR 2601; [1982] ICR 578.

[73] Ex Article 177.

[74] For a full discussion, see Schermers and Waelbroeck, *Judicial Protection in the European Union*, *supra* note 32, paragraphs 572–81.

3.4. THE EUROPEAN COMMUNITIES ACT 1972 AND THE DISABILITY DISCRIMINATION ACT 1995 (AMENDMENT) REGULATIONS 2003

Section 2 of the European Communities Act 1972 provides that:

(1) All such rights, powers, liabilities, obligations and restrictions from time to time created or arising by or under the Treaties, and all such remedies and procedures from time to time provided for by or under the Treaties as in accordance with the Treaties, are without further enactment to be given legal effect or used in the United Kingdom shall be recognised and available in law, and be enforced, allowed and followed accordingly; . . .

(2) Subject to Schedule 2 to this Act, at any time after its passing Her Majesty may by Order in Council, and any designated Minister or department may by regulations, make provision—

    (a) for the purpose of implementing any Community obligation[75] of the United Kingdom, or enabling any such obligation to be implemented, or of enabling any rights enjoyed or to be enjoyed by the United Kingdom under or by virtue of the Treaties to be exercised; or

    (b) for the purpose of dealing with matters arising out of or related to any such obligation or rights or the coming into force, or the operation from time to time, of subsection (1) above

and in the exercise of any statutory power or duty, including any power to give directions or to legislate by means of orders, rules, regulations or other subordinate instrument, the person entrusted with the power or duty may have regard to the objects of the Communities and to any such obligation or rights as aforesaid.

The Community obligation for the implementation of which the Regulations were enacted is the obligation under Article 18 of the Directive to adopt the laws, regulations, and administrative provisions necessary to comply with it by 2 December 2006.

As stated above, regulations made to implement Community obligations will where possible be construed so as to be compatible with those Community law obligations (and the obligation to interpret domestic law compatibly with the Community law to which it gives effect is a very compelling one, see 3.3.1 above). However, the interpretation of national legislation is a matter of judgement to be determined by national courts and to be derived from the language of the legislation considered in the light of the circumstances prevailing at the time of the enactment.[76] Where the language of the regulations cannot be reconciled with that of the Community obligation, the regulations must be held to be invalid and disapplied to the extent that they exceed the Community obligation or fail

---

[75] Defined by Schedule 7 to the Act as 'any obligation created or arising by or under the Treaties, whether an enforceable Community obligation or not'.

[76] *Per* Lord Templeman in *Duke v Reliance Systems* [1988] 1 AC 618 at 638G.

to fulfil it.[77] That is so because the exercise of the power under section 2(2) of the European Communities Act is conditional upon the existence of a Community obligation.[78] Accordingly if any provision of the Regulations goes beyond that provided for by the Directive it will be *ultra vires* the European Communities Act 1972 and invalid.

This has important implications for the interpretation and application of the Disability Discrimination Act 1995 (Amendment) Regulations 2003[79] (the 2003 Regulations) and the Disability Discrimination Act 1995 (Pensions) Regulations 2003 (the Pensions Regulations).[80] There are a number of areas of possible challenge:

- the meaning of 'disability'. The 2003 Regulations do not amend the DDA meaning of disability, which, as mentioned above and below,[81] is very medically based. The Directive does not define 'disability' but it is possible that some of the exceptions to and requirements of the DDA definition could be held by the ECJ to be too limiting (eg the requirement that a mental impairment be 'clinically well recognized', the requirement that the effects of any impairment be 'long term' and that the impairment be symptomatic). In this regard, it can be noted that the UN adopts a more social model;[82]

- the meaning of 'direct' discrimination. The 2003 Regulations amend the DDA to include a new form of direct discrimination (in the employment and related fields) such that 'a person directly discriminates against a *disabled person* if, on the ground of the *disabled person's*[83] disability, he treats the disabled person less favourably than he treats or would treat a person not having that particular disability whose relevant circumstances, including his abilities, are the same as, or not materially different from, those of the disabled person'.[84] The Directive, however, defines direct discrimination as occurring where 'one person is treated less favourably than another is, has been or would be treated in a comparable situation, on . . . [the] grounds' of disability.[85] The Directive's meaning would therefore protect a person who is not disabled but who is perceived to be so; or is treated less favourably because of their association with a disabled person. The 2003 Regulations introduce into the DDA a much narrower meaning and therefore apparently do not give proper effect to the Directive;

---

[77] *Addison v Denholm Ship Management* [1997] ICR 770 at 785 (EAT) (Lord Johnston). See also *R v Secretary of State for Trade and Industry ex parte Unison* [1996] ICR 1003, 1013 (QBD) (Otton LJ).

[78] *R v Secretary of State for Health ex parte Imperial Tobacco and others* [2001] 1 WLR 127 at 134–5, *per* Lord Hoffmann. See further Lord Nicholls in *R v Secretary of State for the Environment, Transport and the Regions ex parte Spath Holme Ltd* [2001] 2 AC 349 at 396.

[79] SI 2003/1673.   [80] SI 2003/2770.

[81] See Chapters 2 above and 4 below.

[82] United Nations Standard Rules on the Equalization of Opportunities for Persons with Disabilities, see Chapter 2 above, at 2.3.1.

[83] Emphasis added.   [84] Section 3A(5) DDA.   [85] Article 2(2).

- the absence of provision on 'indirect discrimination'. The DDA contains no provision on indirect discrimination. The Directive requires Member States to regulate indirect discrimination and such discrimination 'shall be taken to occur where an apparently neutral provision, criterion or practice would put persons having a particular religion or belief, a particular disability, a particular age, or a particular sexual orientation at a particular disadvantage compared with other persons' unless justified.[86] An exception is provided for where 'as regards persons with a particular disability, the employer or any person or organisation to whom this Directive applies, is obliged, under national legislation, to take appropriate measures in line with the principles contained in Article 5 in order to eliminate disadvantages entailed by *such* provision, criterion or practice'.[87] However, it is doubtful whether the 'reasonable adjustment' duties in the DDA in the employment and related fields are sufficient.[88] It is not anticipatory in nature as is required (*would put persons having a particular disability*);

- the meaning of 'harassment'. The 2003 Regulations and the Pensions Regulations amend the DDA to include 'harassment' (in the employment and related fields). However, 'harassment' as defined under the amended DDA again covers only 'a disabled person'[89] whereas 'harassment' under the Directive is defined as 'unwanted conduct related to any of the grounds referred to' including disability.[90] As with direct discrimination, this would protect non-disabled people harassed because of a mis-perception that they were disabled or, for example, because of their association with a disabled person or disabled people;

- the remedies available. There is no provision in the DDA permitting an Employment Tribunal to order reinstatement as a remedy for a discriminatory dismissal. The power to make recommendations which does exist is a power to make non-binding recommendations and the courts have construed this power narrowly.[91] The remedy of compensation may be inadequate in circumstances where what is valued is the opportunity to work and the power to order reinstatement does exist for unfair dismissals (where an employee has the requisite length of service). Arguably the absence of a power in the DDA to order reinstatement puts the UK in breach of Article 17 of the Directive, though this point has not been tested.[92]

---

[86] Article 2(2)(b). [87] Article 2(2)(b)(ii). Emphasis added.
[88] Section 4A DDA. [89] Section 3B DDA.
[90] Article 2(3).
[91] *Noone v NW Thames Regional Health Authority [1998] IRLR 195; Noone v NW Thames Regional Health Authority (No 2)* [1988] IRLR 530; *British Gas v Sharma* [1991] IRLR 101.
[92] See *Marshall, supra* note 44.

3.5. HUMAN RIGHTS

3.5.1. The European Convention for the Protection of Fundamental Rights and Freedoms [1950]

The European Convention for the Protection of Fundamental Rights and Freedoms [1950][93] contains important provisions that may form a significant backdrop to the development of disability discrimination law. The UK has signed and ratified the Convention and as a State is therefore bound by its terms. The UK's system of law, however, is such that international treaties do not become part of domestic law without further action.[94] The UK has given significant domestic effect to the Convention by the enactment of the Human Rights Act 1998 (HRA) and this is addressed below (see 3.6).

In addition, as stated above (see 3.2), the Directive refers in its Preamble to the European Convention on Human Rights ('the Convention') and is for that reason to be construed consistently with it. In addition, it is well established that Community legislation has to be construed in the light of the general principles of Community law, which include the principle of respect for human rights, in particular as reflected in the Convention.[95]

The most relevant provisions of the Convention are Articles 2, 3, 8, and 14.

3.5.1.1. *Article 2*
Article 2 provides that: 'Everyone's right to life shall be protected by law. No one shall be deprived of his life intentionally save in the execution of a sentence of a court following his conviction of a crime for which this penalty is provided by law.'

There are exceptions provided for in Article 2(2) but they are not relevant to this work.[96] For the purposes of the issues likely to be raised in the context of disability discrimination, the right conferred by Article 2 is therefore absolute.

Article 2 imposes on Member States substantive obligations not to take life without justification and also to establish a framework of laws, precautions, procedures, and means of enforcement that will, to the greatest extent reasonably practicable, protect life. In addition, Article 2 imposes on Member States a procedural obligation to initiate an effective public investigation by an independent

---

[93] CETS No: 005.

[94] For discussion on this 'dualist' system and the impact of the Convention pre-statutory incorporation, see Clayton and Tomlinson, *The Law of Human Rights* (OUP, 2000) paragraphs 2.09 *et seq.*

[95] See 3.2 and 3.3.1 above.

[96] Deprivation of life shall not be regarded as inflicted in contravention of Article 2(1) when it results: from the use of force which is no more than absolutely necessary; in defence of any person from unlawful violence; in order to effect a lawful arrest or to prevent the escape of a person lawfully detained; or in action lawfully taken for the purpose of quelling a riot or insurrection.

official body into any death occurring in circumstances in which it appears that one or other of the foregoing substantive obligations has been, or may have been, violated and it appears that agents of the State are, or may be, in some way implicated.[97] As Lord Bingham remarked: 'Compliance with the substantive obligations referred to above must rank among the highest priorities of a modern democratic state governed by the rule of law. Any violation or potential violation must be treated with great seriousness.'[98]

Unsurprisingly, Article 2 issues have arisen in the context of disability. In *Regina (Pretty) v Director of Public Prosecutions (Secretary of State for the Home Department intervening)*[99] Mrs Pretty suffered from a progressive and degenerative terminal illness and faced the imminent prospect of a distressing and humiliating death. She was mentally alert and wished to control the time and manner of her dying but her physical disabilities prevented her from taking her life unaided. She wished her husband to help her and he was willing to do so provided that in the event of his giving such assistance he would not be prosecuted under section 2(1) of the Suicide Act 1961. Mrs Pretty therefore sought an undertaking from the Director of Public Prosecutions ('DPP') that he would not consent to such a prosecution; he refused and Mrs Pretty applied for a judicial review of that decision. In particular she claimed that Article 2 protected a right to self-determination, entitling her to commit suicide with assistance. In addition, she argued that the failure to alleviate her suffering by refusal of the undertaking amounted to inhuman and degrading treatment within the meaning of Article 3 (see below) and that in breach of Article 14 (see below) she suffered discrimination because a person without her disabilities might exercise the right to suicide whereas her disabilities prevented her from doing so without assistance. The House of Lords concluded that the terms of Article 2 reflected the sanctity of life and expressed protection of the right to life and prevention of the intentional taking of life, except in closely defined circumstances, and that, so framed, it could not be interpreted as conferring a right to self-determination in relation to life and death and assistance in choosing death. Article 3 was complementary to Article 2, and required the state to respect the physical and human integrity of individuals within its jurisdiction, but did not engage a right to live or to choose not to live. The 'treatment' it prohibited did not bear an unrestricted or extravagant meaning and could not apply to the claimant's suffering, which derived from her illness and not from any action or inaction by the DPP or indeed anyone else. Accordingly, there was no infringement of Mrs Pretty's rights under Articles 2 and 3.[100] Further, according to the House of Lords, even if Article 14 was engaged, the 1961 Act, in decriminalizing suicide, did not confer a right to commit that act and the policy of the law remained adverse to it;

---

[97] *Regina (Middleton) v West Somerset Coroner and another* [2004] UKHL 10; [2004] 2 AC 182, paragraphs 2–3, *per* Lord Bingham, and cases cited therein.

[98] *Ibid.* at paragraph 5.

[99] [2001] UKHL 61; [2002] 1 AC 800.   [100] *Ibid.* at paragraphs 5–15.

that, since the criminal law applied to all, giving weight to personal circumstances when prosecution or penalty was under consideration, section 2(1) could
not be said to be discriminatory.[101]

The European Court of Human Rights also found no violation of Mrs
Pretty's Convention rights.[102]

The ethical issues that arise from such a case are obviously important and
complex. The DRC has adopted the following policy statement:

The Disability Rights Commission is addressing a range of ethical issues impacting on
disability, including genetics, rights to medical treatment and resuscitation, voluntary
euthanasia and assisted suicide. Throughout its programme of work on ethical issues, the
DRC will be guided by two principles: equality between disabled people and non-disabled
people, and the right of individuals to make informed, autonomous choices.

The Commission is not making a general moral judgement on whether voluntary
euthanasia or assisted suicide should be legalised, but is basing its view on the effect that
such legalisation would have on the lives of disabled people. The DRC takes very seriously the principle of autonomy expressed in the phrase 'a right to die'. However, we
believe that the right to live is equally important. Alongside the wishes of people like
Reginald Crew and Dianne Pretty, we hear the voices of disabled people who express a
real fear that their lives will be put at risk if voluntary euthanasia or assisted suicide were
legalised.

Moreover, choice occurs in a context. If someone believes they will be a 'burden', has
no access to services to enable them to live independently, or does not have the equipment
that would enable them to communicate, then any 'choice' they may make to die is not a
true choice. When non-disabled people state that they want to die, the usual response
from society is to offer support, to try to enable them to see that life may be worth living.
To this end the Government has set targets to reduce suicide. The position should be no
different in the case of disabled people. If a disabled person expresses the wish to die the
first task must be to try to enable them to make the choice to live. Until disabled people
are treated equally—their lives accorded the same value as the lives of non-disabled
people, their access to necessary services guaranteed, their social and economic opportunities equal to those of non-disabled people—then the 'right to die' may jeopardise
people's right to live.

The DRC is not aware of any country that has managed to frame a law that allows
assisted suicide or voluntary euthanasia, for people with terminal illness, as in the case
. . . of Mrs Pretty, whilst ensuring that disabled people are protected from coercion, pressure, and involuntary euthanasia. We have therefore commissioned independent
research, to seek out and weigh up the evidence, and the arguments, for and against the
legalisation of assisted suicide and voluntary euthanasia, as it affects disabled people. The
Commission will review its position in early summer, following completion of this
research.

However, such are the implications of this most profound of legal proposals, that until
we are convinced that sufficient regulation and safeguards can, and will be, put in place

---

[101] *Ibid.* at paragraphs 35–6.   [102] *Pretty v UK* (2002) 34 EHRR 1.

to ensure the right to life of disabled people, we will not support the legalisation of assisted suicide and voluntary euthanasia.[103]

That policy so far has the support of the law.

Article 2 has also been held not to apply to decisions to withdraw artificial nutrition and hydration in respect of people in a permanent vegetative state where that is intentionally to, and inevitably would, bring about the patient's death. For these purposes, the phrase 'deprivation of life' in Article 2 means a deliberate act as opposed to an omission, by someone acting on behalf of the State, which resulted in death; that a responsible decision by a medical team based on clinical judgment to discontinue providing such treatment on the basis that it was no longer in the patient's best interest was an omission to act and could not amount to an intentional deprivation of life by the State within the meaning of Article 2.[104] Where the patient's death would be the result of the illness or injury from which he suffered, an omission could only violate Article 2 where the circumstances were such as to impose a positive obligation on the State to take steps to prolong or protect the patient's life.[105]

A decision by a competent patient to *refuse* treatment must be respected even though death will follow.[106] To this extent, the principle of the sanctity of human life must yield to the principle of self-determination:[107]

This situation gives rise to a conflict between two interests, that of the patient and that of the society in which he lives. The patient's interest consists of his right to self-determination—his right to live his own life how he wishes, even if it will damage his health or lead to his premature death. Society's interest is in upholding the concept that all human life is sacred and that it should be preserved if at all possible. It is well established that in the ultimate the right of the individual is paramount.[108]

However, where a disabled person sought to insist upon life-saving treatment that was considered clinically non-beneficial, different considerations appeared to apply. Indeed, guidance issued by the General Medical Council (GMC), 'Withholding and Withdrawing Life-Prolonging Treatments: Good Practice in Decision-Making', made little allowance for such a situation. A recent legal challenge to this guidance argued that it was incompatible with Articles 2, 3, 6,[109] 8, and 14: *R (on the application of Burke) v (1) The GMC (2) The DRC (as*

---

[103] http://www.drc-gb.org/publicationsandreports/campaigndetails.asp?section=he&id=307.

[104] *NHS Trust A v M; NHS Trust B v H* [2001] Fam 348. See also, *Airedale NHS Trust v Bland* [1993] AC 789.

[105] *Ibid.*

[106] *Re B (Adult: Refusal of Medical Treatment)* [2002] EWHC 42a (Fam); [2002] 2 All ER 449 and cases cited therein.

[107] *Airedale NHS Trust v Bland* [1993] AC 789, 864 *per* Lord Goff.

[108] *Re T (Adult: Refusal of Treatment)* [1993] Fam 95, 112, *per* Lord Donaldson of Lymington MR.

[109] 'In the determination of his civil rights and obligations . . . everyone is entitled to a fair and public hearing within a reasonable time by an independent and impartial tribunal established by law.'

interested parties) and (3) The Official Solicitor.[110] The guidance provided that it was the responsibility of the consultant or general practitioner in charge of a patient's care to make the decision about whether to withhold or withdraw a life-prolonging treatment, taking account of the views of the patient or those close to the patient. In cases where a patient lacked capacity to decide for themselves and their wishes could not be determined, regard was to be had to the fact that 'where there is a reasonable degree of uncertainty about the likely benefits or burdens for the patient of providing either artificial nutrition or hydration, it may be appropriate to provide these for a trial period with a pre-arranged review to allow a clearer assessment to be made'; 'where death is imminent, in judging the benefits, burdens or risks, it usually would not be appropriate to start either artificial hydration or nutrition'; 'where death is imminent and artificial hydration and/or nutrition are already in use, it may be appropriate to withdraw them if it is considered that the burdens outweigh the possible benefits to the patient'; and 'where death is not imminent, it usually will be appropriate to provide artificial nutrition or hydration'. However, the guidance provided also that 'circumstances may arise where . . . a patient's condition is so severe, and the prognosis so poor that providing artificial nutrition or hydration may cause suffering, or be too burdensome in relation to the possible benefits' when, subject to certain steps being taken, the same could be withdrawn. Whilst the GMC guidance included advice on circumstances where a patient was competent and resisted treatment, none was provided for the converse: that treatment which a patient wished to have commenced or continued was regarded as inappropriate by the clinicians and refused.

The court set out certain guiding principles including, importantly, that:

- the right to personal autonomy embraced such matters as how one chose to pass the closing days and moments of one's life and how one managed one's death, and Articles 3 and 8[111] embraced the right to die with dignity and the right to be protected from treatment, or from a lack of treatment, which would result in one dying in avoidably distressing circumstances. Accordingly, in principle it was for the competent patient, and not his doctor, to decide what treatment should or should not be given in order to achieve what the patient believed safeguarded his dignity most and in order to avoid what the patient would find distressing;

- under the Convention, as at common law, if the patient is competent, or, although incompetent, has made an advance directive which is both valid and relevant to the treatment in question, his refusal to accept artificial nutrition and hydration is determinative;

- if the patient is competent, or, although incompetent, has made an advance directive which was both valid and relevant to the treatment in question, his

---

[110] [2004] EWHC 1879 (Admin).   [111] See below.

decision to require the provision of artificial nutrition and hydration, which he believes is necessary to protect him from what he sees as acute mental and physical suffering, is likewise in principle determinative;

- to withdraw artificial nutrition and hydration at any stage before the claimant finally lapsed into a coma would in principle involve clear breaches of both Article 3 and Article 8, for it was clear that if artificial nutrition and hydration were to be withdrawn he would be exposed to acute mental and physical suffering;

- the position of an incompetent patient was likely in practical terms to be the same. If artificial nutrition and hydration was providing some benefit it should be provided unless the patient's life, if thus prolonged, would from the patient's point of view be intolerable;

- it was hard to envisage any circumstances (other, perhaps, than where the provision of artificial nutrition and hydration to a patient with severe and deteriorating dementia could be very distressing) in which a withdrawal of artificial nutrition and hydration from a sentient patient, whether competent or incompetent, could be compatible with the Convention;

- assuming that the patient was otherwise being treated with dignity, and in a manner which was in all other respects compatible with his rights under Article 3 and Article 8, there would be no breach of either Article 3 or Article 8 nor of Article 2 if artificial nutrition and hydration was withdrawn in circumstances where it was serving absolutely no purpose other than the very short prolongation of the life of a dying patient who had slipped into his final coma and lacked all awareness of what was happening;[112]

- where it was proposed to withhold or withdraw artificial nutrition and hydration the prior authorization of the court was required as a matter of law where there was doubt or disagreement or a lack of unanimity amongst the doctors.[113]

In the light of those principles, the content of the guidance was properly vulnerable to criticism in four respects:

- the emphasis throughout the guidance was on the right of the competent patient to refuse treatment rather than on his right to require treatment;

- the guidance failed sufficiently to acknowledge that it was the duty of a doctor who was unable or unwilling to carry out the wishes of his patient to go on providing the treatment until he could find another doctor who would do so;

- the guidance failed sufficiently to acknowledge the heavy presumption in favour of life-prolonging treatment and to recognize that the touchstone of best interests was intolerability;

---

[112] At paragraphs 178–9.　　　　[113] At paragraph 202.

- the guidance failed to spell out the legal requirement to obtain prior judicial sanction for the withdrawal of artificial nutrition and hydration in the circumstances set out above.[114]

The DRC intervened in *Burke* and, in addition, issued its own statement of views. In particular, the DRC called for 'quality of life' factors to be removed from GMC guidelines. The DRC contended that such factors are subjective and may reflect a doctor's personal opinion about the quality of life of a disabled person. In place, the DRC argued, should be the much higher 'intolerability test' so that such threshold should be used when a decision is made whether to withdraw treatment from a person. Importantly too, 'intolerability' must be measured from the perspective of the particular disabled person. Their submissions were influential as can be seen from the decision.[115]

Article 2 might appear to be relevant to 'Do Not Resuscitate' (DNR) orders and notices. However, the courts have held that where a State 'has made adequate provision for securing high professional standards among health professionals and the protection of the lives of patients, . . . matters such as error of judgement on the part of a health professional or negligent co-ordination among health professionals in the treatment of a particular patient are not sufficient of themselves' to breach the positive obligations in Article 2.[116] Thus 'Article 2 does not entitle anyone to force life-prolonging treatment on a competent patient who refuses to accept it. Article 2 does not entitle anyone to continue with life-prolonging treatment where to do so would expose the patient to 'inhuman or degrading treatment' breaching Article 3. On the other hand, a withdrawal of life-prolonging treatment which satisfies the exacting requirements of the common law, including a proper application of the intolerability test, and in a manner which is in all other respects compatible with the patient's rights under Article 3 and Article 8 will not, . . . give rise to any breach of Article 2.'[117]

Article 2 does not apply pre-natally.[118] It cannot be used, therefore, in support of an anti-abortion argument. There are concerns about the *discriminatory* nature of the Abortion Act 1967. Section 1(1) Abortion Act 1967 provides that the legal abortion limit is twenty-four weeks save where the woman's life is put in danger by a continuation of the pregnancy, or she would be caused grave permanent injury, or, at any time, where 'there is a substantial risk that if the child were born it would suffer from such physical or mental abnormalities as to be seriously handicapped'. Where the baby is likely to be disabled there may therefore be no legal limit to the time at which an abortion may take place. The

---

[114] At paragraphs 219–22.

[115] See also [2004] EWHC 1879, at paragraph 34.

[116] *Powell v UK* (unreported) 4 May 2000 ECtHR at 18; *Glass v UK* [2004] Lloyd's Med Rep 76; [2004] 1 FLR 101a; see too, *Burke, supra* note 110, at paragraphs 152–62.

[117] *Burke, supra* note 110, at paragraph 162.

[118] *Paton v United Kingdom* (1980) 19DR 244; *Vo v France (2004)* Application No 53924/00, 8 July 2004, ECtHR.

discriminatory nature of this measure (as opposed to abortion *per se* which raises different issues) is controversial. It gives rise to real concern that the life of a disabled person is legally viewed as less valuable or complete than that of a non-disabled person and that legislation and decisions are made with that unconscious prejudice in mind. So far the cases under the Convention and the HRA have prioritized the rights of human beings who have been born to personal autonomy even where they conflict with the views of others including medical practitioners. This approach is supported by the DRC. Nevertheless they, like others, wish to see the discriminatory measure in the Abortion Act 1967 repealed because of its obvious offensive connotations: 'In common with a wide range of disability and other organisations, the DRC believes the context in which parents choose whether to have a child should be one in which disability and non-disability are valued equally. In a positive manner the medical professions and others should ensure that parents receive comprehensive balanced information and guidance on disability, the rights of disabled people and on the support available.'[119]

3.5.1.2. *Article 3*
Article 3 provides that 'No one shall be subjected to torture or to inhuman or degrading treatment'.

Article 3 is unqualified: it absolutely prohibits inhuman and degrading treatment. It is possible to contemplate very serious incidents of disability discrimination that might meet that threshold of 'inhuman' or 'degrading' treatment (for example, seriously inadequate care in prisons and other state institutions).[120] Importantly too, Article 3 imposes positive obligations on the State. 'Vulnerable individuals, in particular, are entitled to State protection, in the form of effective deterrence, against . . . serious breaches of personal integrity.'[121]

Dignity interests are 'at the core of the rights protected by Article 3'.[122] Whether a particular set of circumstances constitutes 'inhuman or degrading treatment' is a matter of fact and degree, but to meet Article 3 standards the treatment complained of must reach a fairly high threshold. As the Court said in *Price v United Kingdom*

The Court recalls that ill-treatment must attain a minimum level of severity if it is to fall within the scope of Article 3. The assessment of this minimum level of severity is relative;

---

[119] http://www.drc-gb.org/publicationsandreports/campaigndetails.asp?section=he&id=325.

[120] *Price v United Kingdom* (2002) 34 EHRR 1285. For a discussion on Article 3 see Clayton and Tomlinson, *The Law of Human Rights*, *supra* note 94, paragraphs 8.13 *et seq*. See also *Chartier v Italy* (1982) 33DR 41, Ecomm HR: though no breach was found the Commission did suggest that the Italian authorities might take steps to mitigate the effects of or terminate the detention in circumstances where the applicant suffered from an heredity illness causing obesity.

[121] *Lopes-Ostra v Spain* (1994) 20 EHRR 277 at 295, paragraph 51.

[122] *R (on the application of (1) A (2) B (by their litigation friend the Official Solicitor) (3) X (4) Y) v East Sussex County Council and the Disability Rights Commission* [2003] EWHC 167 (Admin) at paragraph 87.

it depends on all the circumstances of the case, such as the duration of the treatment, its physical and mental effects and, in some cases, the sex, age and state of health of the victim. In considering whether treatment is 'degrading' within the meaning of Article 3, one of the factors which the Court will take into account is the question whether its object was to humiliate and debase the person concerned, although the absence of any such purpose cannot conclusively rule out a finding of violation of Article 3.[123]

Price concerned a four-limb-deficient thalidomide victim with numerous health problems including defective kidneys who had been committed to prison for contempt of court in the course of civil proceedings. A breach of Article 3 was established in consequence of the conditions in which she was detained. The Court observed that:

There is no evidence in this case of any positive intention to humiliate or debase the applicant. However, the Court considers that to detain a severely disabled person in conditions where she is dangerously cold, risks developing sores because her bed is too hard or unreachable, and is unable to go to the toilet or keep clean without the greatest of difficulty, constitutes degrading treatment contrary to Article 3.[124]

And as was observed by Judge Greve (agreeing that there had been a violation of Article 3):

It is obvious that restraining any non-disabled person to the applicant's level of ability to move and assist herself, for even a limited period of time, would amount to inhuman and degrading treatment—possibly torture. In a civilised country like the United Kingdom, society considers it not only appropriate but a basic humane concern to try to ameliorate and compensate for the disabilities faced by a person in the applicant's situation. In my opinion, these compensatory measures come to form part of the disabled person's bodily integrity. It follows that, for example, to prevent the applicant, who lacks both ordinary legs and arms, from bringing with her the battery charger to her wheelchair when she is sent to prison for one week, or to leave her in unsuitable sleeping conditions so that she has to endure pain and cold—the latter to the extent that eventually a doctor had to be called—is in my opinion a violation of the applicant's right to bodily integrity. Other episodes in the prison amount to the same.

The applicant's disabilities are not hidden or easily overlooked. It requires no special qualification, only a minimum of ordinary human empathy, to appreciate her situation and to understand that to avoid unnecessary hardship—that is, hardship not implicit in the imprisonment of an able-bodied person—she has to be treated differently from other people because her situation is significantly different.

As can be seen, Article 3 is important in protecting disabled people and may require the different treatment of disabled people in certain situations to avoid a violation of Article 3.

In addition, Article 3 will often be engaged in cases where decisions are to be made by disabled people and clinicians about appropriate treatment, particularly that which might prolong or end life.[125] It is important to observe that this

---

[123] *Price, supra* note 120 at 1292, paragraph 24.
[124] *Ibid.* at 1294, paragraph 30.   [125] 3.5.1.1 above.

is so not just where the disabled person concerned is sentient and self-conscious. All of us have 'dignity interests protected by the law and which assert that a patient's best interests embrace a dignified death'.[126]

3.5.1.3. *Article 8*

Article 8 provides that,

(1) Everyone has the right to respect for his private and family life, his home and his correspondence.
(2) There shall be no interference by a public authority with the exercise of this right except such as is in the interests of national security, public safety, or the economic well-being of the country, for the prevention of disorder or crime, for the protection of health or morals, or for the rights and protections of others.

Article 8 (which secures the right to respect for 'home') will have obvious relevance in complaints of discrimination falling under the 'premises' provisions, which protect disabled people against discrimination in the disposal and management of premises (see *Council of the City of Manchester v (1) Romano (2) Samari* [2004] EWCA Civ 834 and Chapter 7 below).

In addition, the concept of 'private life' in Article 8 has been held to encompass personal identity and integrity. Respect for private life comprises 'to a certain degree the right to establish and develop relationships with other human beings'[127] and protects personal autonomy while an individual is alive.[128]

In *Botta v Italy* the EctHR said: 'Private life, in the Court's view, includes a person's physical and psychological integrity; the guarantee afforded by Article 8 of the Convention is primarily intended to ensure the development, without outside interference, of the personality of each individual in his relations with other human beings'.[129]

In order to comply with its obligations under Article 8, the State may be obliged to take positive action to secure respect for private life:

While the essential object of Article 8 is to protect the individual against arbitrary interference by the public authorities, it does not merely compel the State to abstain from such interference: in addition to this negative undertaking, there may be positive obligations inherent in effective respect for private or family life. These obligations may involve the adoption of measures designed to secure respect for private life even in the sphere of the relations of individuals between themselves . . . In order to determine whether such obligations exist, regard must be had to the fair balance that has to be struck between the general interest and the interests of the individual.[130]

---

[126] *R (on the application of Burke) v (1) the GMC (2) the DRC (as interested parties) and (3) the Official Solicitor*, *supra* note 110, at paragraph 147.

[127] *Neimetz v Germany* (1992) 16 EHRR 97 paragraph 29.

[128] *Regina (Pretty) v Director of Public Prosecutions (Secretary of State for the Home Department intervening)*, *supra* note 99, at paragraph 23 (although it does not confer a right to decide when or how to die: *ibid.*); *Pretty v UK* [2002] 35 EHRR 1.

[129] (1998) 26 EHRR 241 at 257, paragraph 32.   [130] *Ibid.* at 257, paragraph 33.

As can be seen, Article 8 is significant in the context of disability discrimination. However, whilst there have been cases challenging barriers to equal access to public spaces, the ECtHR has not been particularly sympathetic. In *Botta* the complainant, a disabled person, complained that his Article 8 rights were violated when he was unable to visit a particular private beach because it was inaccessible. The Court rejected his complaint holding that:

the right asserted by Mr Botta, namely the right to gain access to the beach and the sea at a place distant from his normal place of residence during his holidays, concerns interpersonal relations of such broad and indeterminate scope that there can be no conceivable direct link between the measures the State was urged to take in order to make good the omissions of the private bathing establishments and the applicant's private life.[131]

However, in *Botta* the Court was concerned with the tenuousness of the link between the failure of the State and the complainant's private life. The complaint was that the State was in breach of its positive obligations under Article 8 and having regard to the particular facts of the case, the omissions of a private actor (the beach owners) were not sufficiently serious to engage the State's positive obligations. However, this leaves open the question whether failures which more directly affect a person's ability to engage in social life will breach Article 8. The judgment in *Botta* clearly indicates that not all access issues fall outside Article 8.

Importantly, too, the Convention is not a static instrument:

[H]aving regard to the fact that the Convention is a 'living instrument which must be interpreted in the light of present-day conditions', the Court considers that certain acts which were classified in the past as 'inhuman and degrading treatment' as opposed to 'torture' could be classified differently in future. It takes the view that the increasingly high standard being required in the area of the protection of human rights and fundamental liberties correspondingly and inevitably requires greater firmness in assessing breaches of the fundamental values of democratic societies.[132]

Thus increasingly high standards are required.

As can be seen above, Article 8 is qualified (Article 8(2)). Not all intrusions into the rights protected by Article 8 will also violate it. However, interferences with private life are permitted only where they are 'in accordance with the law' and 'necessary in a democratic society' in the interests of one of the values listed in Article 8(2) of the Convention. For an interference to be 'necessary in a democratic society' to achieve one of the legitimate aims, case-law indicates that the following four elements must be satisfied:

(a) that there is a pressing social need for some restriction;

(b) that the restriction corresponds to (ie has a rational connection with) that need;

---

[131] *Ibid.* paragraph 35. See too *Zehnalova v Czech Republic* (2002) (Application No 38621/97, ECtHR).

[132] *Selmouni v France* (2000) 29 EHRR 403 at 442, paragraph 101.

(c) that the restriction is a proportionate response to that need; and

(d) that the reasons advanced by the authorities are 'relevant and sufficient'.[133]

In addition, regard must be had to the hallmarks of a democratic society, namely 'pluralism, tolerance and broadmindedness'.[134]

3.5.1.4. *Article 14*

Article 14 of the ECHR provides that: 'The enjoyment of the rights and free-doms set forth in this Convention shall be secured without discrimination on any ground such as sex, race, colour, language, religion, political or other opinion, national or social origin, association with a national minority, property birth or other status'.

By Article 14 a person has an entitlement to enjoy the Convention rights free from discrimination. Relevant Convention rights include Articles 2, 3, 6, and 8, and Articles 1 (protection of property), 2 (right to education), and Article 3 (right to free elections) of the First Protocol.

Though disability is not explicitly mentioned in Article 14 the grounds are *inclusively* described and there can be no doubt that disability falls within its scope.[135]

Article 14 complements the other substantive provisions of the Convention. It has no independent existence since it has effect solely in relation to 'the enjoy-ment of the rights and freedoms' safeguarded elsewhere in the Convention. However, in order for Article 14 to be engaged, a complainant does not need to show that there has been a breach of a substantive provision, but merely that the facts of his case fall within the ambit of one of the substantive provisions.[136]

Five questions arise in an Article 14 inquiry,[137] though 'a rigidly formulaic approach is to be avoided.'[138]

(i)   Do the facts fall within the ambit of one or more of the Convention rights?

(ii) Was there a difference in treatment in respect of that right between the com-plainant and others put forward for comparison?

---

[133] *Handyside v United Kingdom* (1976) 1 EHRR 737; *Barthold v Germany* (1985) 7 EHRR 383.

[134] *Handyside, supra* note 133, paragraph 49.

[135] It was not suggested otherwise in *Botta* though no breach was found because the complaint was found not to fall within the scope of one of the other Convention rights (Article 8).

[136] *Abdulaziz Cabales and Balkandali v UK* (1985) 7 EHRR 471; *Ghaidan v Godin-Mendoza* [2004] UKHL 30, [2004] 3 WLR 113, *per* Lady Hale, paragraph 133. See also Karon Monaghan, 'Limitations and Opportunities: A Review of the Likely Domestic Impact of Article 14 ECHR' (2001) EHRLR 167; Robert Wintermute, 'Within the Ambit: How Big is the "Gap" in Article 14 ECHR?' [2004] EHRLR 366

[137] *Ghaidan v Godin-Mendoza, supra* note 136, *per* Lady Hale, paragraph 133, based on the approach of Brooke LJ in *Wandsworth London Borough Council v Michalak* [2003] 1 WLR 617, 625, paragraph 20, as amplified in *R (Carson) v Secretary of State for Work and Pensions* [2002] EWHC 978 (Admin), paragraph 52, [2003] EWCA Civ 797, [2003] 3 All ER 577.

[138] *Ibid.* at paragraph 134.

(iii) Were those others in an analogous situation?

(iv) Was the difference in treatment objectively justifiable? Ie did it have a legitimate aim and bear a reasonable relationship of proportionality to that aim?

(v) Is the difference in treatment based on one or more of the grounds proscribed, whether expressly or by inference, in Article 14.

The concept of discrimination under Article 14 is broad enough to incorporate some forms of indirect discrimination and a requirement to make adjustments: 'the right not to be discriminated against in the enjoyment of the rights guaranteed under the Convention is also violated when States without an objective and reasonable justification fail to treat differently persons whose situations are significantly different'.[139]

Discrimination under Article 14 may be justified by an objective and reasonable justification. Any reliance upon such justification must be carefully scrutinized and the burden of establishing the same rests with the Respondent in any case.[140]

3.6. THE HUMAN RIGHTS ACT 1998

The Human Rights Act 1998 (HRA) to a large extent incorporates the Convention rights (including those described above[141]) into domestic UK law.

Section 3 HRA provides that: 'So far as it is possible to do so, primary legislation and subordinate legislation must be read and given effect in a way which is compatible with the Convention Rights'.

Section 3 provides the primary remedy[142] for addressing incompatibility. It is Parliament's intention that legislation must be read *and* given effect to in a way which is compatible with the Convention rights and the courts must give effect to that intention.[143] Section 3:

• does not depend on any existing ambiguity, indeed the legislation may admit of *no* doubt but section 3 may still require a different meaning;[144]

• is apt to require a court to read in words that change the meaning of the enacted legislation so as to make it Convention-compliant. The intention of Parliament in enacting section 3 was to an extent bound only by what is 'possible' and may require the court to depart from the intention of the enacting Parliament;[145] and

---

[139] *Thlimmenos v Greece* (2000) 31 EHRR 411 at paragraph 44.
[140] *Thlimmenos, supra* note 139.   [141] Section 1 Human Rights Act 1998.
[142] See *Ghaidan, supra* note 137, paragraph 46, *per* Lord Steyn.
[143] *Ibid.* paragraph 26, *per* Lord Nicholls.
[144] *Ibid.* paragraph 29, *per* Lord Nicholls.   [145] *Ibid.* paragraph 30, *per* Lord Nicholls.

- creates a very compelling and mandatory obligation and may require reading in words or reading them out. However, there is no necessity for over-emphasis on linguistic features.[146]

This means that, if the natural reading of a statute gives a meaning that is incompatible with a Convention right, then the court must strive to give it a compatible meaning. This is so whatever the actual words of the statute, so long as a completely opposite meaning to the purpose intended is not given to the statutory scheme, that is, as long as it is not 'as drastic as changing black into white' or 'remov[ing] the very core and essence, the "pith and substance" of the measure that Parliament had enacted'.[147]

A recent example of the operation of section 3 can be seen in *X v Y*[148] in which the Court of Appeal held that section 98(4) of the Employment Rights Act 1996 (unfair dismissal) must be read and given effect in a way which is compatible with an employee's Convention rights so that a dismissal in breach of a Convention right would normally be unfair unless justified. On the facts of that particular case no breach was found but the principle is of general application.

Where a statute cannot be read compatibly with Convention rights (and this will be a rare event, having regard to the guidance above) a court may make a 'declaration of incompatibility' under section 4. A court for these purposes does not include a tribunal, which has no power to make a declaration of incompatibility. Such a declaration may only be made by the High Court and above.[149] A declaration of incompatibility does not affect the validity of any legislation and may be ignored by Parliament.[150] However, a Minister who 'considers that there are compelling reasons for [so] proceeding, . . . may by order make such amendments to the legislation as he considers necessary to remove the incompatibility'.[151]

In addition, section 6 of the HRA creates a new duty and cause of action. It provides that: '(1) It is unlawful for a public authority to act in a way which is incompatible with a Convention right.'

Section 6(3) defines a 'public authority' as including:

(a) a court or tribunal,
(b) any person certain of whose functions are functions of a public nature, but does not include either House of Parliament or a person exercising functions in connection with proceedings in Parliament.

Section 6(5) provides: 'In relation to a particular act, a person is not a public authority by virtue only of subsection (3)(b) if the nature of the act is private'. Importantly, Courts are therefore required themselves to act compatibly

---

[146] *Ghaidan, supra* note 137, paragraphs 38–52, *per* Lord Steyn; paragraphs 111 and 121, *per* Lord Rodger.

[147] *Ibid.* paragraph 111, *per* Lord Rodger.   [148] [2004] EWCA Civ 662.

[149] Section 4(5).   [150] Section 4(6).   [151] Section 10(2).

with Convention rights, bolstering their interpretative obligations under section 3.[152]

A breach of section 6 is actionable under section 7, which provides that:

(1) A person who claims that a public authority has acted (or proposes to act) in a way which is made unlawful by section 6(1) may—
  (a) bring proceedings against the authority under this Act in the appropriate court or tribunal, or
  (b) rely on the Convention right or rights concerned in any legal proceedings,
but only if he is (or would be) a victim of the unlawful act.[153]

Proceedings in respect of such a claim must be brought before the end of the period of one year beginning with the date on which the act complained of took place or such longer period as the court or tribunal considers equitable having regard to all the circumstances,[154] subject to such stricter time limits as apply to the particular proceedings (eg judicial review).[155]

Proceedings must be brought in an 'appropriate court or tribunal' meaning such court or tribunal as may be determined in accordance with rules; and proceedings against an authority include a counterclaim or similar proceeding.[156] An Employment Tribunal is not such a court or tribunal: it has no jurisdiction to hear claims under section 6.[157]

On a finding of a breach of section 6 a court 'may grant such relief or remedy, or make such order, within its powers as it considers just and appropriate'.[158]

In conclusion, all courts and tribunals must read and give effect to legislation in way which is compatible with the Convention rights. In addition, proceedings will lie against a public authority in respect of any breach of a Convention right.

3.7. PROTOCOL NO 12

As seen above, Article 14 does not provide 'freestanding' protection against discrimination. A new Protocol No 12 to the ECHR[159] has been drawn up within the Council of Europe by the Steering Committee for Human Rights. It was opened for signature by the Member States of the Council of Europe on 4 November 2000. It provides that:

---

[152] For a discussion on the distinction between private and public bodies, see Wadham, Mountfield, and Edmundson, *Blackstone's Guide to the Human Rights Act 1998* (3rd edn, OUP, 2004) 76–80.

[153] See section 7(3) and (4) for the meaning of 'victim' in judicial review proceedings. See for example in the disability sphere: *R (on the application of (1) A (2) B (by their litigation friend the Official Solicitor) (3) X (4) Y) v East Sussex County Council and The Disability Rights Commission*, *supra* note 122.

[154] Section 7(5).   [155] Section 7(5).   [156] Section 7(2).

[157] Employment Tribunals Act 1996, sections 2 and 3.

[158] Section 8(1). See also Section 8(2) to (4).   [159] CETS No: 177.

Article 1—General prohibition of discrimination

1. The enjoyment of any right set forth by law shall be secured without discrimination on any ground such as sex, race, colour, language, religion, political or other opinion, national or social origin, association with a national minority, property, birth or other status.

2. No one shall be discriminated against by any public authority on any ground such as those mentioned in paragraph 1.

The Protocol therefore provides protection against discrimination in the enjoyment of rights already set down by law and in addition creates a prohibition against discrimination by public authorities. When in force it will plainly provide greater protection against discrimination than the weaker Article 14.

The Protocol will enter into force three months after the date on which ten Member States of the Council of Europe have ratified it. There have so far been seven ratifications.[160] The UK Government has not signed or ratified Protocol No 12 and they have indicated that they do not presently intend to ratify it.[161] If it is eventually ratified by the UK it is important to note that, though the UK will be bound by it as a matter of international law and individuals will be permitted to petition the ECtHR in reliance on it, it will not have any domestic force unless it is expressly incorporated, as many of the other Convention rights have been through the HRA.

3.8. UNITED NATIONS' STANDARDS

As mentioned above in Chapter 2, the United Nations have developed and adopted[162] 'Standard Rules on the Equalization of Opportunities for Persons with Disabilities' (1993). Although not a legally binding instrument, the Standard Rules represent a strong moral and political commitment by Governments to take action to attain equalization of opportunities for persons with disabilities. The rules serve as an instrument for policy-making and as a basis for technical and economic cooperation.[163] They include, for example, the requirements that:

• States should take action to raise awareness in society about persons with disabilities, their rights, their needs, their potential, and their contribution;

---

[160] As of 26 July 2004 see: http://conventions.coe.int/Treaty/Commun/ChercheSig.asp?NT=177&CM=8&DF=7/26/04&CL=ENG.

[161] Written Answer 37, Parliamentary Under Secretary of State Home Office, Lord Bassam of Brighton (11 October 2000: Column WA37). For a critique of the reasons given by Government for not ratifying Protocol No 12, see Equal Opportunities Review (2002) 105, 21–4.

[162] Adopted by the United Nations General Assembly, 48th Session, Resolution 48/96, Annex, of 20 December 1993.

[163] http://www.un.org/esa/socdev/enable/dissre00.htm.

- states should ensure that responsible authorities distribute up-to-date information on available programmes and services to persons with disabilities, their families, professionals in the field, and the general public. Information to persons with disabilities should be presented in accessible form;
- states should initiate and support information campaigns concerning persons with disabilities and disability policies, conveying the message that persons with disabilities are citizens with the same rights and obligations as others, thus justifying measures to remove all obstacles to full participation;
- states should encourage the portrayal of persons with disabilities by the mass media in a positive way; organizations of persons with disabilities should be consulted on this matter;
- states should ensure that public education programmes reflect in all their aspects the principle of full participation and equality; and
- states should invite persons with disabilities and their families and organizations to participate in public education programmes concerning disability matters.'[164]

In addition, and importantly, the United Nations has resolved[165] to establish an Ad-Hoc Committee to consider proposals for a 'comprehensive and integral international convention to promote and protect the rights and dignity of persons with disabilities, based on the holistic approach in the work done in the fields of social development, human rights and non-discrimination'. This Ad-Hoc Committee has met to consider proposals and formed a working group to draft a proposed text. At the third Session of the Ad-Hoc Committee (24 May–4 June 2004) that text was considered. Work continues on the text.

---

[164] Rule 1.
[165] 56/168. Resolution adopted by the General Assembly [on the report of the Third Committee (A/56/583/Add. 2)].

4

THE MEANING OF 'DISABILITY'

4.1. INTRODUCTION

As observed above, the DDA affords protection against discrimination to 'disabled persons' only (except in the case of victimization[1]). The DDA defines a 'disabled person' for the purposes of its provisions. It is important to note that the concept of disability does not have an autonomous meaning. The meaning given to 'disability' and 'disabled person' under the DDA applies only for the

---

[1] See Chapter 2 above. See Chapter 5 below for explanation of the terms 'discrimination' and 'victimization'.

purposes of the DDA and is quite distinct from the meaning afforded to these concepts in other contexts. The fact therefore, that a person might be 'disabled' for the purposes of some other set of provisions will not afford them the protection of the DDA unless they can also demonstrate that they are disabled within the meaning of the DDA itself. This is important to bear in mind because a person might be 'disabled' for the purposes of a social security benefit (for example, Disability Living Allowance) but not 'disabled' for the purposes of the DDA (though see 4.4 below for persons who have been registered disabled).

The meaning given to the expression 'disability' as provided for by the DDA, as explained below, is very medical and functional based (with limited exceptions, for example the provision in respect of severe disfigurements and past disabilities; see 4.4 and 4.20 below). It is concerned with diagnosis and the functional ability of persons who wish to be classified as 'disabled' under its terms. As observed in Chapter 2 above, the DDA does not adopt a social model of disability, and this is one of its weaknesses. It does not protect against discrimination on the basis of perceived disability. Nor does it protect persons who are treated less favourably by reason of their association with a disabled person (for example, because they have a parent with a disability arising out of a genetic predisposition or because they have a disabled child).[2]

4.2. THE MEANING OF 'DISABILITY'

The meanings of 'disability' and 'disabled person' are addressed in the first place by section 1 DDA, which provides that:

(1) Subject to the provisions of Schedule 1, a person has a disability for the purposes of this Act if he has a physical or mental impairment which has a substantial and long-term adverse effect on his ability to carry out normal day-to-day activities.
(2) In this Act 'disabled person' means a person who has a disability.

A 'disability' therefore, for the purposes of the DDA must comprise:

• a physical or mental impairment, which
• has a substantial and long-term adverse effect
• on the person's ability to carry out normal day-to-day activities.

Each of these elements is further defined by Schedule 1.

---

[2] This may be inconsistent with European Community law in the context of employment and related fields: see section 3A(5) of the DDA, which protects disabled persons only against less favourable treatment on the ground of that disabled person's disability. This is apparently inconsistent with the wider concept of direct discrimination under Directive 2000/78/EC, which defines direct discrimination as occurring 'where one person is treated less favourably than another is, has been or would be treated in a comparable situation, on any of the grounds referred to', including disability. It does not require that the complainant is a disabled person, merely that the less favourable treatment is on the ground of disability. This difference is discussed further in Chapter 5 below.

Provision is made for persons who have had a disability in the past. Section 2 provides that: '(1) The provisions of this Part and Parts II [to 4] [*sic*] apply in relation to a person who has had a disability as they apply in relation to a person who has that disability'.

Section 2 applies whether or not, at the time the person concerned had a disability, the DDA was in force, but the question of disability is to be determined as if the DDA was in force at the material time.[3] Further provision is made for the purposes of determining whether a person has had a 'disability' for the purposes of the DDA in Schedule 2 of the DDA. This is addressed below. In addition regulations have been made addressing particular impairments.[4] These are addressed in 4.4 and 4.6 below.

Schedule 1 contains further detail about the meaning of 'disability' for the purposes of the DDA. It provides that:

- 'mental impairment' includes an impairment resulting from or consisting of a mental illness only if the illness is a clinically well-recognized illness;[5]
- the effect of an impairment is a long-term effect if
  (a) it has lasted at least 12 months;
  (b) the period for which it lasts is likely to be at least 12 months; or
  (c) it is likely to last for the rest of the life of the person affected;[6]
- where an impairment ceases to have a substantial adverse effect on a person's ability to carry out normal day-to-day activities, it is to be treated as continuing to have that effect if that effect is likely to recur.[7]

In addition, an impairment is to be taken to affect the ability of the person concerned to carry out normal day-to-day activities only if it affects one of the following:

(a) mobility;
(b) manual dexterity;
(c) physical coordination;
(d) continence;
(e) ability to lift, carry, or otherwise move everyday objects;
(f) speech, hearing, or eyesight;
(g) memory or ability to concentrate, learn, or understand; or
(h) perception of the risk of physical danger.[8]

It is important to note that each element of the definition of 'disability' must be satisfied. The existence of an impairment alone will be insufficient to establish disability.

---

[3] Section 2(4) and (5) DDA.

[4] Pursuant to the powers to do so under Schedule 1 of the DDA. These Regulations are the Disability Discrimination (Meaning of Disability) Regulations 1996, SI 1996/1455.

[5] Schedule 1, paragraph 1(1) DDA. [6] *Ibid.* paragraph 2(1).

[7] *Ibid.* paragraph 2(2). [8] *Ibid.* paragraph 4(1).

4.3. GUIDANCE

The DDA gives the Secretary of State power to issue guidance about the matters to be taken into account in determining certain questions arising out of the statutory meaning of 'disability'.[9] The Secretary of State has issued such guidance: 'Guidance on Matters to be taken into Account in Determining Questions Relating to the Definition of Disability'[10] ('the Guidance').

Section 3(3) DDA requires 'an adjudicating body' (being a court, a tribunal, or any other person who, or body which, may decide a claim under Part 4)[11] to 'take into account any guidance which appears to it to be relevant' when it is determining 'whether an impairment has a substantial and long-term adverse effect on a person's ability to carry out normal day-to-day activities'.[12]

The Guidance has no legally binding force in the sense that an adjudicating body is not legally bound to follow it. However, the Guidance was formulated only after consultation[13] and was subject to parliamentary approval (under the negative resolution procedure)[14] and is therefore, regarded as important and authoritative.[15] In addition, in addressing whether an impairment has a substantial and long-term adverse effect on a person's ability to carry out normal day-to-day activities, an adjudicating body *shall* take into account any guidance which to it appears relevant.[16]

Explicit reference should always be made to any relevant provision of the Guidance that has been taken into account.[17] However, as has been observed, in most cases the question whether a person has a disability for the purposes of the DDA will be clear, and in such cases 'it would be wrong to search the guide and use what it says as some kind of extra hurdle over which the complainant must jump'.[18]

As the Guidance itself makes clear: 'In the vast majority of cases there is unlikely to be any doubt whether or not a person has or has had a disability, but this guidance should prove helpful in cases where it is not clear'.[19]

In *Goodwin v Patent Office*[20] Morrison J (then President of the Employment Appeal Tribunal) gave the following guidance on determining 'disability' for the purposes of the DDA:

---

[9] Section 3 DDA.

[10] This guidance came into force on 31 July 1996 (SI 1996/1996).

[11] Part 4 contains the education provisions. See section 3(3A) DDA for the meaning of an 'adjudicating body'.

[12] Section 3(3) DDA. For the relevance of 'substantial and long-term adverse effect' etc.

[13] Section 3(4) and (5) DDA. [14] Section 3(6) to (8) and (12) DDA.

[15] *Ibid.* [16] Section 3(3) DDA, emphasis added.

[17] *Goodwin v The Patent Office* [1999] ICR 302 at 307, *per* Morrison J.

[18] *Ibid.* [19] Paragraph 1.

[20] *Goodwin v The Patent Office, supra* note 17.

- When faced with a disability issue, the tribunal should look carefully at what the parties have said in their originating application and response (the ET1 and ET3). Generally speaking it will be unsatisfactory for the disability issue to remain unclear and unspecific until the hearing itself. In many, if not most, disability discrimination cases it will be good practice either to make standard directions designed to clarify issues or to arrange a directions hearing. It may well be that parties will wish to present expert evidence to assist the tribunal and it would be quite undesirable for any such evidence to be given without proper advance notice to the other party and the early provision of a copy of any expert report to be referred to.

- The role of the Employment Tribunal contains an inquisitorial element as Rule 14(2) and (3)[21] of their Rules of Procedure indicates. There is a risk of a genuine 'Catch-22' situation. Some disabled persons may be unable or unwilling to accept that they suffer from any disability; indeed, it may be symptomatic of their condition that they deny it. Without the direct assistance of the tribunal at the hearing, there may be some cases where the claim has been drafted with outside assistance but which the complainant, for some reason related to his disability, is unwilling to support.

- The tribunal should bear in mind that with social legislation of this kind a purposive approach to construction should be adopted. The language should be construed in a way which gives effect to the stated or presumed intention of Parliament, but with due regard to the ordinary and natural meaning of the words in question.

- With the DDA, tribunals are given explicit assistance in two forms, which should detract from the need to adopt a loose construction of the language:

  —Guidance issued on 25 July 1996 under section 3 of the DDA by the Secretary of State (SI 1996/1996) with statutory effect from 31 July 1996 [as described above]; and

  —Code of Practice issued on 25 July 1996 but with statutory effect from 2 December 1996 [now SI 2004/2302, see Chapter 6].

- At least during the early period of the DDA's operation, reference should *always* be made, explicitly, to any relevant provision of the Guidance or Code that has been taken into account in arriving at its decision.

- In addressing the question whether the adverse effect of a physical or mental impairment is 'substantial' and 'long-term' an Employment Tribunal 'shall' take such Guidance into account. However, as the Guidance makes clear, in

---

[21] Previously Rule 9 of the Employment Tribunals (Constitution and Rules of Procedure) Regulations 1993, SI 1993/2687, Schedule 1. Subsequently Rule 11(1) of the Employment Tribunals (Constitution and Rules of Procedure) Regulations 2001, SI 2001/1171, Schedule 1. Now Rule 14(2) and (3) Employment Tribunals Rules of Procedure, Employment Tribunals (Constitution and Rules of Procedure) Regulations 2004, SI 2004/1861.

many cases the question whether a person is disabled within the meaning of the DDA can admit of only one answer. In such clear cases it would be wrong to search the Guidance and use what it says as some kind of extra hurdle over which the complainant must jump.[22]

This Guidance was given in the context of a claim falling within the employment field, but is equally applicable to cases falling within the scope of the other activities caught by the DDA.

4.4. DEEMED EFFECT AND DEEMED DISABILITY

The DDA and regulations made thereunder deem certain impairments and conditions in certain circumstances to have a substantial adverse effect even where that is not the present experience of the disabled person. In addition, certain people are deemed disabled whatever the nature or experience of their impairment.

Thus an impairment which would be likely to have a substantial adverse effect on the ability of the person concerned to carry out normal day-to-day activities, but for the fact that measures are being taken to treat or correct it, is to be treated as having that effect.[23] In other words the effect of treatment is to be ignored. 'Measures' include, in particular, medical treatment and the use of a prosthesis or other aid.[24] Although medical treatment is not defined in the DDA, the Court of Appeal has confirmed that counselling with a consultant clinical psychologist falls within the meaning of medical treatment.[25] It appears, however, that such 'measures' may involve non-medical treatment or aids ('measures' being non-exhaustively defined). This provision may, for example, therefore apply to regulating sleep (where irregular sleep may result in, for example, epileptic seizures) or diet. This provision applies even where the measures result in the effects being completely under control or not at all apparent.[26]

However, this deeming provision does not apply in relation to the impairment of a person's sight to the extent that the impairment is correctable by spectacles or contact lenses.[27] In relation to sight corrections, the only effects that are to be

---

[22] See also *Vicary v British Telecommunications plc* [1999] IRLR 680, paragraph 11, in which the Employment Appeal Tribunal held that, in determining whether the effect of an individual's impairment is 'substantial', the Guidance is of assistance in marginal cases only.

[23] Schedule 1, paragraph 6(1) DDA.

[24] Schedule 1, paragraph 6(2) DDA. In *Vicary v British Telecommunications, supra* note 22, at paragraph 19, the Employment Appeal Tribunal indicated that it thought the use of an automatic can opener was probably not an 'aid' but that 'aid' referred, for example, to Zimmer frames, sticks, and wheelchairs and not to household objects, though the point was not necessary for decision and was not decided.

[25] *Kapadia v Lambeth LBC* [2000] IRLR 699 paragraphs 9, 18, and 23.

[26] Guidance, paragraph A12.　　　　　　　　[27] Schedule 1, paragraph 6(3) DDA.

considered are those which remain when the spectacles or contact lenses are used.[28]

In addition where a person has a progressive condition (such as cancer, multiple sclerosis, muscular dystrophy, or infection by the Human Immunodeficiency Virus ('HIV')) and as a result of that condition he has an impairment which has (or had) an effect on his ability to carry out normal day-to-day activities but the effect is not (or was not) a substantial adverse effect, he nevertheless is to be taken to have an impairment that has a substantial adverse effect if the condition is likely to result in his having such an impairment.[29] This does not protect a person by reason only of a diagnosis of a progressive condition where the condition has always been asymptomatic,[30] though the effect need be neither continuous nor substantial.

A wide meaning should be given to the expression 'as a result of that condition he has an impairment', so that impairments resulting directly from the progressive condition, as well as impairments resulting from standard and common operative procedures for the progressive condition are covered. In *Kirton v Tetrosyl Ltd*[31] Mr Kirton had some urinary incontinence that was caused by an operation comprising a radical prostatectomy and pelvic node clearance undertaken in consequence of a diagnosis of cancer of the prostate. He claimed that he was a 'disabled' person arguing, amongst other things, that he had a progressive condition (cancer) and an impairment as a result of that condition (incontinence) and accordingly the 'progressive conditions' provisions of the DDA applied. The Employment Tribunal (in a decision upheld by the Employment Appeal Tribunal) concluded that the words 'as a result of that condition' must mean as a direct result of the condition, rather than as an indirect result of the condition, so that although the operation would not have been carried out if Mr Kirton had not had cancer, the side effects or consequences of the operation could not properly be said to result from his condition, and accordingly the 'progressive conditions' provisions of the DDA did not apply.

The Court of Appeal allowed an appeal holding that the particular impairment (urinary incontinence) did result from the cancer, within the meaning of paragraph 8(1), schedule 1 of the DDA (the 'progressive conditions' provisions). In so concluding the Court of Appeal had regard to the fact that the surgery conducted was a standard response to the form of cancer diagnosed, and that whenever such surgery is conducted there is a significant possibility that urinary

---

[28] *Ibid.*   [29] Schedule 1, paragraph 8(1) DDA.

[30] Guidance, paragraph A15. See too *Mowat-Brown v University of Surrey* [2002] IRLR 235: it is not enough simply for an applicant to establish that he has a progressive condition and that it has or has had an effect on his ability to carry out normal day-to-day activities. The claimant must also show that it is more likely than not that at some stage in the future he will have an impairment, which will have a substantial adverse effect on his ability to carry out normal day-to-day activities. See Chapter 13 below, at 13.2, for the changes proposed by the Draft Disability Discrimination Bill.

[31] [2003] ICR 1237, [2003] IRLR 353.

incontinence will result, and in those circumstances the impairment was as a result of the cancer, notwithstanding the intervening act of the surgical treatment for the cancer. Accordingly, a wide meaning is to be given in this context to the word 'result' so as to include an impairment that results from a standard and common form of operative procedure. Though the Court of Appeal indicated that in cases 'with other medical scenarios, the result could well be different' (at paragraph 18), their judgment suggests that impairments resulting from standard and common forms of treatment are covered and there seems no reason to distinguish operations from drug therapy or other treatments in this regard.

An impairment that consists of a severe disfigurement is to be treated as having a substantial adverse effect on the ability of the person concerned to carry out normal day-to-day activities, whatever its actual effect.[32] Examples of disfigurements are scars, birthmarks, limb or postural deformation, and diseases of the skin. Assessing severity will be mainly a matter of the degree of the disfigurement. It may be necessary to take account of where the feature in question is: for example on the back as opposed to on the face.[33]

A disfigurement that consists of a tattoo (which has not been removed) is not to be treated as a severe disfigurement. Also excluded is a piercing of the body for decorative purposes including anything attached through the piercing.[34]

Certain people are deemed to be disabled whether or not the nature of their impairment is such that it would constitute a 'disability' within the meaning of the DDA. In particular, persons who were registered as disabled persons under section 6 of the Disabled Persons (Employment) Act 1944 on both 12 January 1995 *and* 2 December 1996[35] are deemed to have a disability for a period of three years beginning on 2 December 1996 and thereafter to have had a disability and hence to have been a disabled person during that period,[36] and are therefore deemed to have had a disability in the past if such disability does not remain present. (See further 4.20 below.)

A person is also deemed to have a disability,[37] and hence to be a disabled person, where he is certified as blind or partially sighted by a consultant ophthalmologist in accordance with the relevant guidance *or* he is registered as blind or partially sighted in the relevant registers.[38] The 'relevant guidance' is:

---

[32] Schedule 1, paragraph 3(1) DDA.   [33] Guidance, paragraphs A16 and 17.

[34] Disability Discrimination (Meaning of Disability) Regulations 1996, SI 1996/1455, Regulation 6 and Guidance, paragraph A16.

[35] When this provision came into force: SI 1996/1474, Article 2(3), Part III of the Schedule.

[36] Schedule 1, paragraph 7(1), (2), and (7) DDA.

[37] Disability Discrimination (Blind and Partially Sighted Persons) Regulations 2003, SI 2003/712.

[38] In England and Wales, in the register maintained by or on behalf of the local authority under section 29 of the National Assistance Act 1948, or in Scotland, in a register maintained by or on behalf of a local authority.

- in relation to a consultant ophthalmologist in England and Wales, the Department of Health Circular LASSL(90)1 entitled 'Certification of Blind and Partially Sighted People: Revised form BD8 and the Procedures' and

- in relation to a consultant ophthalmologist in Scotland, the Social Work Services Group Circular SWSG8/86, NHS 1998 (PCS) entitled 'Registration of Blind and Partially Sighted People'.[39]

4.5. IMPAIRMENT

As observed above, the definition of 'disability' provided for by the DDA requires that the person concerned has a 'physical or mental impairment'. The DDA does not define 'physical impairment' or 'mental impairment' (apart from providing that in the latter case it must be 'clinically well recognized'[40]). The Guidance provides only that:

The definition requires that the effects which a person may experience arise from a physical or mental impairment. In many cases there will be no dispute whether a person has an impairment. Any disagreement is more likely to be about whether the effects of the impairment are sufficient to fall within the definition. Even so, it may sometimes be necessary to decide whether a person has an impairment so as to be able to deal with the issues about its effects. [. . .][41] *Physical or mental impairment* includes sensory impairments, such as those affecting sight or hearing.[42]

The Guidance does not otherwise provide any explanation as to the meaning of 'impairment'. It has been held that 'impairment' for the purposes of the DDA may 'include medical "conditions" of various kinds; . . . the expression may include some damage or defect not itself a clinically treatable medical condition such as a disfigurement'.[43] 'Impairment' therefore, has been taken to mean 'some damage, defect, disorder or disease compared with a person having a full set of physical or mental equipment in normal condition. The phrase "physical or mental impairment" refers to a person having (in everyday language) something wrong with them physically, or something wrong with them mentally.'[44] 'Impairment' in the DDA 'bears its ordinary and natural meaning . . . [it] may result from illness or it may consist of an illness'.[45]

---

[39] Disability Discrimination (Blind and Partially Sighted Persons) Regulations 2003, SI 2003/712. Provision is made for the provision of 'conclusive evidence' of the matters identified by the Regulations under Regulation 4 thereof.

[40] See 4.2 above.

[41] Guidance, paragraph 10. As to excluded conditions, see 4.6 below.

[42] Guidance, paragraph 12.

[43] *Rugamer v Sony Music Entertainment UK Ltd*; *McNicol v Balfour Beatty Rail Maintenance Ltd* [2002] ICR 381; [2001] IRLR 644 at paragraph 29.

[44] *Ibid.* paragraph 34.

[45] *McNicol v Balfour Beatty Rail Maintenance Limited* [2002] EWCA Civ 1074, [2002] ICR 1498, [2002] IRLR 711, paragraph 17, *per* Lord Mummery.

It seems clear that it is not necessary to consider how an impairment was caused. Even if the cause is a consequence of a condition which is excluded (for example an illness caused by alcohol dependency) it will still count as an impairment for the purposes of the DDA:[46] 'That the *identification* of an "impairment" for the purposes of the Act is a different thing from the *causes* that give rise to its being present, and also from its *effects* in terms of the limitations it places on a person's functions and ability to carry out activities, is apparent . . . from the structure of the legislation'.[47]

Accordingly:

[Nothing] in the Act or the Guidance expressly require[s] that the primary task of the ascertainment of the presence or absence of physical impairment has to, or is likely to, involve any distinctions, scrupulously to be observed, between an underlying fault, short-coming or defect of or in the body on the one hand and evidence of the manifestations or effects thereof on the other. The Act contemplates (certainly in relation to mental impair-ment) that an impairment can be something that results from an illness as opposed to itself being the illness—Schedule 1 paragraph 1(1). It can thus be cause or effect. No rigid distinction seems to be insisted on and the blurring which occurs in ordinary usage would seem to be something the Act is prepared to tolerate.[48]

The concept of 'impairment' then has a wide meaning. The World Health Organization's 'International Classification of Impairment, Disability and Handicap' (ICD-10) provides that 'impairment' might be any 'loss or abnor-mality of psychological, physiological or anatomical structure or function'.[49]

4.6. EXCLUDED CONDITIONS

A number of 'impairments' are excluded from the scope of the DDA. The Disability Discrimination (Meaning of Disability) Regulations 1996[50] expressly exclude the following conditions:

• addiction to alcohol,
• addiction to nicotine, and
• addiction to any other substance.[51]

'Addiction' for these purposes includes 'a dependency'.[52]

---

[46] Guidance, paragraph 11. See also *Power v Panasonic UK Ltd* [2003] IRLR 151, see 4.6 below.
[47] *Rugamer v Sony Music Entertainment, supra* note 43, at paragraph 32, original emphases.
[48] *College of Ripon and York St John v Hobbs* [2002] IRLR 185 at paragraph 32, approved by Lord Mummery in *McNicol, supra* note 45 at paragraph 18.
[49] See http://www.who.int/whosis/lcd10/.   [50] SI 1996/1455.
[51] Disability Discrimination (Meaning of Disability) Regulations 1996, Regulation 3(1).
[52] *Ibid.* Regulation 2.

This exemption does not apply to addiction that was originally the result of the administration of medically prescribed drugs or other medical treatment.[53]

In addition, the following conditions are to be treated as *not* amounting to impairments:

- a tendency to set fires;
- a tendency to steal;
- a tendency to physical or sexual abuse of other persons;
- exhibitionism;
- voyeurism;[54] and
- seasonal allergic rhinitis (commonly known as hayfever).[55]

However, these exceptions are more limited than at first glance might appear. In particular, a condition, such as a tendency to violence, falls within the exception only where it is a freestanding condition, and not where it is a condition that is the direct consequence of a physical or mental impairment within the meaning of section 1(1) DDA. Where the consequence of a recognized illness is a tendency to commit acts of violence, the disabled person retains the protection of the DDA.[56]

In addition, as observed at 4.5 above, an impairment *caused* by an excluded condition is not itself excluded. In *Power v Panasonic UK Ltd*,[57] the complainant was absent from work and was both depressed and drinking heavily. Expert evidence was called by both sides and both experts tried to identify which came first, the depression or the alcohol abuse. The Employment Tribunal ruled that the complainant failed to show that she was a disabled person for the purposes of the DDA relying upon the exemption above.[58] The Employment Appeal Tribunal concluded that it was not material to a decision whether a person has a disability within the meaning of the DDA to consider how the particular impairment was caused. It was material only to ascertain whether the impairment was a disability within the meaning of the DDA or whether, where relevant, it was an impairment which was excluded by reason of the Regulations from being treated as such. This, the Employment Appeal Tribunal concluded, was consistent with the Guidance, which provides that: 'It is not necessary to consider how an impairment was caused, even if the cause is a consequence of a condition which is excluded. For example, liver disease as a result of alcohol dependency would count as an impairment.'[59]

---

[53] *Ibid.* Regulation 3(2).   [54] *Ibid.* Regulation 4(1).

[55] But this shall not prevent that condition (only) from being taken into account for the purposes of the DDA where it aggravates the effect of another condition (*ibid.* Regulation 4(2) and (3); this might be relevant, for example, to conditions such as asthma).

[56] *Murray v Newham Citizens' Advice Bureau Ltd* [2003] ICR 643, [2003] IRLR 340 EAT (violent behaviour resulting from paranoid schizophrenia).

[57] [2003] IRLR 151.

[58] Disability Discrimination (Meaning of Disability) Regulations 1996; see *supra* notes 50 and 51.

[59] Guidance, paragraph 11.

In this case the complainant suffered from depression and it was therefore for the Tribunal to judge whether this had a substantial long-term adverse effect on her ability to carry out normal day-to-day activities, regardless of its cause.

4.7. PHYSICAL IMPAIRMENTS

As mentioned above, the DDA does not define 'physical impairment'. 'Sensory impairments' are, however, included.[60] It is impossible to provide a comprehensive list of all the physical impairments that might be covered by the DDA. They will include common conditions, such as epilepsy, asthma, damage to limbs or bones, muscle damage, cancer, diabetes, and physical injury. As stated, sensory impairments are caught, and thus deafness, other hearing impairments, blindness, and sight impairments are also covered.[61]

There is no requirement that the physical impairment be 'clinically well recognized' as in the case of a mental impairment.[62] Accordingly, the meaning is apparently wide enough to cover any physical impairment even if it has not been conclusively diagnosed.[63] In cases where there is any doubt, it will be necessary to make a finding on the question whether or not the impairment is a physical or a mental impairment, having regard to the distinct approach taken by the DDA.[64]

The following have been held to constitute physical impairments:

- ME (myalgic encephalomyelitis);[65]
- soft tissue injury to the back;[66]
- epilepsy;[67]
- photosensitive epilepsy;[68]
- cerebral palsy;[69]

---

[60] See 4.5 and note 42 above.

[61] See 4.5 above.

[62] See 4.2 above and 4.8 below.

[63] See *Howden v Capital Copiers (Edinburgh) Ltd* ET Case No S/400005/97, cited in 'Disability Discrimination' (2002) IDS, 35 in which the complainant experienced sharp, gripping pains that forced him to lie down as well as having other adverse effects on his well-being. Though no satisfactory cause was found for his pain, the tribunal accepted that his condition amounted to a physical impairment even in the absence of an exact diagnosis.

[64] Though this is likely to change. The Government has announced that it proposes to accept the recommendation of the Joint Scrutiny Committee that the requirement that the condition be clinically well recognized be removed from the DDA (Joint Committee on the Draft Disability Bill (May 2004) and see the DWP's announcement at http://www.dss.gov.uk/mediacentre/pressreleases/2004/july/cfd1507-dfres.asp). See also Chapter 13 below, at 13.2.

[65] *O'Neill v Symm & Co Ltd* [1998] ICR 481.

[66] *Clark v TDG Ltd, t/a Novacold* [1999] ICR 951, [1999] IRLR 318.

[67] *British Gas Services Ltd v McCaull* [2001] IRLR 60.

[68] *Ridout v TC Group* [1998] IRLR 628.

[69] *Kenny v Hampshire Constabulary* [1999] ICR 27, [1999] IRLR 76.

- multiple sclerosis;[70] and
- migraine (migrainous neuralgia).[71]

Difficulties have arisen in relation to 'functional overlay' cases. These are cases where the complainant has physical symptoms and these are unexplained by any organic or physical cause but are the manifestation of the complainant's psychological state. This phenomenon is described as 'functional or physical overlay'. Such a condition does *not* amount to a physical impairment for the purposes of the DDA. In *McNicol v Balfour Beatty Rail Maintenance Limited*[72] the Court of Appeal was required to consider the question of disability in circumstances where the complainant contended that he had a physical impairment resulting from a compression injury to his spine but about which there was no evidence before the Employment Tribunal of any organic physical pathology. The medical evidence before the Employment Tribunal suggested that the explanation for the complainant's symptoms lay in some psychological or psychiatric impairment or that they were fabricated. The Employment Tribunal concluded that the complainant was not disabled. The Court of Appeal rejected an appeal by the complainant principally on the basis that there was no error of law disclosed by the decision of the Employment Tribunal. In so doing the Court of Appeal observed that the claim had been advanced as one of physical impairment and that the case highlighted the importance of (a) complainants making clear the nature of the impairment on which the claim of discrimination is advanced and (b) both parties obtaining relevant medical evidence on the issue of impairment.[73] It was made clear by the Court of Appeal that it was for the Tribunal to make a decision in each case on whether the available evidence established that the complainant had a physical or mental impairment with the stated effects.[74]

This approach creates real complexities and does not appear to reflect the approach of the Guidance, nor indeed earlier authority expressly endorsed by Mummery LJ in *McNicol*.[75] In *College of Ripon and York St John v Hobbs*[76] Lindsay J gave the guidance set out above (see 4.5). Mummery LJ endorsed this guidance. As is apparent from the above discussion, the focus of the DDA and the Guidance suggests that no fine distinctions are made between the origins of the *effects* founding the basis of the claim in disability[77] but that the focus is on the impact of that upon the person's ordinary life. Nevertheless, consistent with the guidance of Mummery LJ in *McNicol*, where disability is in issue a complainant must expect to establish an impairment and to establish whether it is a physical or mental impairment.

---

[70] *Buxton v Equinox Design Ltd* [1999] ICR 269, [1999] IRLR 158.
[71] *London Clubs Management Ltd v Hood* [2001] IRLR 719.   [72] *Supra* note 45.
[73] *Ibid.* paragraph 16, *per* Lord Mummery.
[74] *Ibid.* paragraph 19, *per* Lord Mummery.
[75] *Ibid.* paragraph 18, *per* Lord Mummery .   [76] *Supra* note 48 at paragraph 32.
[77] Save in the case of a mental impairment where it must be at least clinically well recognized.

The facts of *College of Ripon and York St John v Hobbs* are also somewhat difficult to reconcile with the judgment of Mummery LJ in *McNicol*. In *College of Ripon and York St John v Hobbs* a joint medical expert found that the complainant had symptoms of muscle fasciculation consisting of twitching, and muscle weakness that created difficulty in mobility. He also found that the complainant had muscle cramps leading to muscle spasms. He reported that the complainant required help in undertaking shopping, cooking, and cleaning and that she used taxis for most journeys because of her difficulty in mobility; her gait was slow and she walked with the aid of a stick. However, he concluded that there was 'no evidence to indicate presence of a disease affecting the central or . . . nervous system to account for [the complainant's] described disability'. He concluded that there was 'no organic disease process causing the symptoms described by [the complainant] and that her disability [was] not therefore organic'. He felt unable to provide an opinion as to whether there was a significant psychological disability present. Notwithstanding this report, the Employment Tribunal concluded that the complainant was a disabled person within the meaning of the DDA. They concluded that she had a 'physical impairment' on the basis that in the DDA the same meant that 'there is something wrong with the body as opposed to the mind'. They noted the extent of the complainant's muscle twitching, which they said suggested that 'this symptom or manifestation is a product of a physical impairment'. It had regard to the fact that the complainant needed a stick to support herself and that she suffered pain and discomfort caused by attacks of muscle cramps and characterized these as 'physical manifestations'. The Tribunal therefore concluded that the complainant had a 'physical impairment' and that it was not necessary for them to know what underlying disease or trauma had caused the physical impairment. This decision was upheld by the Employment Appeal Tribunal. The Employment Appeal Tribunal contrasted the case with *Rugamer*,[78] noting that the complainant had not 'nailed . . . her colours to one of only . . . two possible masts', namely a physical or alternatively a mental impairment.[79] The Employment Appeal Tribunal concluded that the Tribunal were concerned with whether or not the complainant had a disability rather than some question differentiating between physical and mental impairment. The Employment Appeal Tribunal concluded that it was correct for the Tribunal to ask itself whether there was evidence before it on which it could hold directly or by ordinary reasonable inference that there was something wrong with 'the complainant' physically, something wrong with her body,[80] and that the catalogue of symptoms and effects of symptoms described were sufficient to allow the Tribunal to conclude that there existed a physical impairment within the meaning of the DDA.[81] The medical evidence by itself indicated that there was nothing 'organic' to explain the symptoms but, the Employment Appeal

---

[78] See *supra* note 43.   [79] See *supra* note 48 at paragraph 10.   [80] *Ibid.*, paragraph 33.
[81] *Ibid.* at paragraph 34.

Tribunal concluded, that was not necessarily sufficient to point to a conclusion that there was no 'physical impairment'.[82] Accordingly the Tribunal's decision was permissible. This case sits uncomfortably with *McNicol*.

4.8. MENTAL IMPAIRMENTS

As observed above (see 4.2) some further elaboration on the meaning of 'mental impairment' is provided for by Schedule 1.

In addition, section 68 of the DDA[83] provides that: ' "Mental impairment" does not have the same meaning as in the Mental Health Act 1983 or the Mental Health (Scotland) Act 1984 but the fact that an impairment would be a mental impairment for the purposes of either of those Acts does not prevent it from being a mental impairment for the purposes of this Act.'

The Mental Health Act 1983 defines 'mental impairment' as 'a state of arrested or incomplete development of mind (not amounting to severe mental impairment[84]) which includes significant impairment of intelligence and social functioning and is associated with abnormally aggressive or seriously irresponsible conduct on the part of the person concerned and "mentally impaired" should be construed accordingly'.[85] It is quite clear that the meaning of 'mental impairment' provided for by the DDA embraces a much wider range of conditions than those provided by the Mental Health Act 1983.

To constitute a mental impairment for the purposes of the DDA, such impairment must be 'clinically well recognized' (though this will change with the enactment of the Disability Discrimination Bill).[86] The Guidance indicates that such an impairment will be one which is recognized by a respected body of medical opinion:[87] 'This would include those specifically mentioned in publications such as the World Health Organization's International Classification of Diseases'.[88] Chapter V (F) of WHO ICD-10 classifies a whole series of conditions that might be described as mental impairments, including Alzheimer's disease; schizophrenia; mood (affective) disorders, including bipolar affective disorder (manic depression); and phobic anxiety disorders.[89] Similarly, the Diagnosis and Statistical Manual of Mental Disorders (DSM-1V)[90] classifies Alzheimer's; schizophrenia; manic depression; major depressive disorder; psychotic disorder; Aspberger's disorder; and many others.

---

[82] *Ibid.* at paragraph 35.　　[83] The interpretation section.　　[84] Which is also defined.

[85] Section 1(2), Mental Health Act 1983.

[86] Schedule 1(1). See Chapter 13 below, at 13.2 for the impact of the Disability Discrimination Bill.

[87] Guidance Part 1, paragraph 14.

[88] World Health Organization International Classification of Diseases and Related Health Problems, 10th Revision, vol 1, 1993. Also see World Health Organization's ICD-10 Classification of Mental and Behavioural Disorders, 1998.

[89] *Ibid.* Also see *Morgan v Staffordshire University* [2002] ICR 475, [2002] IRLR 190 at paragraph 9.

[90] Published by the American Psychiatric Association, this provides another classification system for the identification of mental impairments.

An impairment that falls within either of these classification systems will be regarded as 'clinically well recognized'.[91] It follows that if an impairment is recognized within one classification system, but not another, it may nevertheless be 'clinically well recognized' for the purposes of the DDA: the DDA does not require that it be universally well recognized. The WHO ICD-10 and DSM-IV manuals, for example, are not identical and they may contain different diagnostic criteria for the same condition. This means that the application of certain criteria can produce different outcomes according to which classification system is relied upon. In *Blackledge v London General Transport Services Ltd*[92] the complainant claimed that he suffered from post-traumatic stress disorder arising out of experiences whilst serving in the Coldstream Guards when he saw a friend being killed and witnessed shootings and deaths. In consequence he suffered flashbacks and intrusive memories of the violence he had witnessed. He was seen by a clinician and diagnosed with post-traumatic stress disorder with a co-morbid alcohol- and drug-dependent syndrome. The diagnosis was made in accordance with the diagnostic criteria set out in WHO ICD-10. Thereafter he was seen by a consultant psychiatrist instructed on behalf of the respondents who concluded that whilst the complainant had experienced post-traumatic stress symptoms his condition did not warrant a diagnosis of post-traumatic stress disorder according to the diagnostic criteria set out in DSM-IV. Both classifications require the witnessing of or exposure to an exceptionally threatening or catastrophic event or situation and both classifications require recurrent, repetitive, and intrusive recollections. However, the DSM-IV requires the disturbance to cause clinically significant distress or impairment in social, occupational, or other important areas of functioning which WHO ICD-10 does not not. WHO ICD-10 states that the disorder should generally arise within six months of the traumatic event, whereas DSM-IV has no time limit but expects the medical reviewer to specify if the onset of symptoms occurred six months or more after the stress or event. In the particular case the complainant's evidence was that his symptoms were not such as to prevent him from getting on with his job or his day-to-day life. Accordingly the Tribunal found that they did not warrant a diagnosis of post-traumatic stress disorder having regard to DSM-IV. The Employment Appeal Tribunal allowed an appeal on the basis that the Tribunal at first instance had applied different aspects of the two classification systems. The Appeal Tribunal noted that WHO ICD-10 was the classification recognized by the NHS and it was therefore difficult to see why that classification was not used by the Tribunal. In addition, the extra requirement in DSM-IV for impairment in functioning seemed more relevant to deciding the effect on function of a mental impairment than to deciding whether a mental impairment exists.[93]

It appears then that reliance should be placed on one or other classification system and the conflation of more than one may impose a threshold upon the

---

[91] Guidance Part 1, paragraph 14. Also *Morgan v Staffordshire University, supra* note 89.
[92] [2001] UKEAT 1073/00/0308, [2003] WL 21491959.   [93] *Ibid.* at paragraphs 18–20.

complainant which is unfair. There seems to be some indication that WHO ICD-10 should be used in preference, at least where it does not disadvantage a complainant.

Four possible routes to establishing the existence of a mental impairment within the meaning of the DDA have been identified. In *Morgan v Staffordshire University* Lindsay J observed as follows:

[T]here will be three or possibly four routes to establishing the existence of 'mental impairment' within the terms of the DDA, namely:

(i)   proof of a mental illness specifically mentioned as such in the World Health Organization's International Classification of Diseases ('WHOICD');

(ii) proof of a mental illness specifically mentioned as such in a publication 'such as' that classification, presumably therefore referring to some other classification of very wide professional acceptance;

(iii) proof by other means of a medical illness recognised by a respected body of medical opinion.

A fourth route, which exists as a matter of construction but may not exist in medical terms, derives from the use of the word 'includes' in paragraph 1(1), Schedule 1 to the Act. If, as a matter of medical opinion and possibility, there may exist a state recognisable as mental impairment yet which neither results from nor consists of a mental illness, then such state *could* be accepted as a mental impairment within the Act because the statutory definition is inclusive only, rather than purporting to exclude anything not expressly described by it. This fourth category is likely to be rarely if ever invoked and could be expected to require substantial and very specific medical evidence to support its existence.[94]

Thus, there may be cases where a person has a 'mental impairment' which does not arise from a mental illness; this presumably might include mental impairments arising from congenital conditions as with some forms of learning disabilities. Though Lindsay J assumes such an impairment will be 'rare' there is no reason to suppose this is so. As the Guidance makes clear, 'mental impairment' includes a wide range of impairments, including what are often known as learning disabilities, relating to mental functioning. Such impairments apparently do not need to be 'clinically well recognized' in the same way as impairments arising from mental illness (Schedule 1, 1(1)) but they would require proof by specific medical evidence.

Many mental impairments have been found to constitute 'mental impairments' for the purpose of the DDA. Below is a sample:

- *Goodwin v The Patent Office*[95]—schizophrenia;
- *Kapadia v The London Borough of Lambeth*[96]—depression;
- *Holmes v Bolton Metropolitan Borough Council*[97]—dyslexia; and
- *Hewett v Motorola Ltd*[98]—Asperger's syndrome.

---

[94] *Supra* note 89 at paragraph 9.   [95] *Supra* note 17.   [96] *Supra* note 25.

[97] ET Case No. 2403516/98, cited in 'Disability Discrimination' (2002) IDS 49.

[98] [2004] IRLR 545.

As to establishing the existence of a mental impairment, whatever its origin, guidance can be found in *Morgan v Staffordshire University*:

(1) Advisers to parties claiming mental impairment must bear in mind that the onus on a claimant under the DDA is on him to prove that impairment on the conventional balance of probabilities.

(2) There is no good ground for expecting the Tribunal members (or Employment Appeal Tribunal members[99]) to have anything more than a layman's rudimentary familiarity with psychiatric classification. Things therefore need to be spelled out. What it is that needs to be spelled out depends upon which of the three or four routes . . . described . . . is attempted. It is unwise for claimants not clearly to identify in good time before the hearing exactly what is the impairment they say is relevant and for respondents to indicate whether impairment is an issue and why it is. It is equally unwise for Tribunals not to insist that both sides should do so. Only if that is done can the parties be clear as to what has to be proved or rebutted, in medical terms, at the hearing.

(3) As the WHOICD does not use such terms without qualification and there is no general acceptance of such loose terms, it is not the case that some loose description such as 'anxiety', 'stress' or 'depression' of itself will suffice unless there is credible and informed evidence that in the particular circumstances so loose a description nonetheless identifies a clinically well recognised illness. In any case where a dispute as to such impairment is likely, the well advised claimant will thus equip himself, if he can, with a writing from a suitably qualified medical practitioner that indicates the grounds upon which the practitioner has become able to speak as to the claimant's condition and which in terms clearly diagnoses either an illness specified in the WHOICD (saying which) or, alternatively, diagnoses some other clinically well recognised mental illness or the result thereof, identifying it specifically and (in this alternative case) giving his grounds for asserting that, despite its absence from the WHOICD (if such is the case), it is nonetheless to be accepted as a clinically well recognised illness or as the result of one.

(4) Where the WHOICD classification is relied on, then, in any case where dispute is likely, the medical deponent should depose to the presence or absence of the symptoms identified in its diagnostic guidelines. When a dispute is likely, a bare statement that does no more than identifying the illness is unlikely to dispel doubt nor focus expert evidence on what will prove to be the area in dispute.

(5) This summary we give is not to be taken to require a full consultant psychiatrist's report in every case. There will be many cases where the illness is sufficiently marked for the claimant's GP by letter to prove it in terms which satisfy the DDA. Whilst the question of what are or are not 'day to day activities' within the DDA is not a matter for medical evidence . . . the existence or not of a mental impairment is very much a matter for qualified and informed medical opinion. Whoever deposes, it will be prudent for the specific requirements of the Act to be drawn to the deponent's attention.

(6) If it becomes clear, despite a GP's letter or other initially available indication, that impairment is to be disputed on technical medical grounds then thought will need to be given to further expert evidence . . .

---

[99] And the same must apply to judicial members of other courts and tribunals.

(7) There will be many cases, particularly if the failure to make adjustments is in issue, where medical evidence will need to cover not merely a description of the mental illness but when, over what periods and how it can be expected to have manifested itself, either generally or to the employer in the course of the claimant's employment. Thus claimants' advisers, before seeking medical evidence, must consider also whether it will be enough to prove a present impairment and whether, instead or in addition, they will need to prove it at some earlier time or times and to prove how it could, earlier or at present, have been expected to have manifested itself.

(8) The dangers of the tribunal forming a view on 'mental impairment' from the way the claimant gives evidence on the day cannot be overstated. Aside from the risk of undetected, or suspected but non-existent, play acting by the claimant and that the date of the hearing itself will seldom be a date as to which the presence of the impairment will need to be proved or disproved, tribunal members will need to remind themselves that few mental illnesses are such that their symptoms are obvious all the time and that they have no training or, as is likely, expertise, in the detection of real or simulated psychiatric disorders.

(9) The tribunals are not inquisitorial bodies charged with a duty to see to the procurement of adequate medical evidence . . . But that is not to say that the tribunal does not have its normal discretion to consider adjournment in an appropriate case, which may be more than usually likely to be found where a claimant is not only in person but (whether to the extent of disability or not) suffers some mental weakness.[100]

4.9. 'NORMAL DAY-TO-DAY ACTIVITIES'

As has been seen above, the definition of 'disability' requires that the impairment has an adverse effect on the disabled persons 'ability to carry out normal day-to-day activities'. As such the DDA adopts a 'functional' model, that is it focuses on how a person's functions are actually affected, as opposed to the social model described above in Chapter 2.[101]

As set out above, Schedule 1, paragraph 4(1) DDA[102] provides that an impairment is to be taken to affect the ability of the person concerned to carry out normal day-to-day activities only if it affects one of the 'abilities, capacities or capabilities'[103] listed. This is an exhaustive list.[104] It excludes certain functions that might be regarded as constituting 'normal day-to-day activities', for example:

- the ability to care for oneself;
- the ability to communicate and interact with others; and

---

[100] *Supra* note 89 at paragraph 20.   [101] See 2.3.   [102] See 4.2 above.
[103] *Ekpe v The Commissioner of Police of the Metropolis* [2001] ICR 1084, [2001] IRLR 605 at paragraph 30.
[104] See 4.2 above.

- the perception of reality (though the concept of 'understanding' may include understanding normal social interaction among people, and/or the subtleties of human non-factual communication[105]).

Such capacities are not to be regarded as relevant to determining whether a person has a disability unless they also fall within one of the enumerated capacities in Schedule 1, paragraph 4(1) DDA as set out in 4.2 above.[106]

In determining whether or not an activity is a 'normal day-to-day activity', regard should be had to the fact that this expression is not intended to include activities that are normal only for a particular person or group of people. In this respect, in deciding whether an activity is a 'normal day-to-day activity' account should be taken of how far it is normal for most people and carried out by most people on a daily or frequent basis.[107] Thus the expression does not, for example, include work of any particular form because no particular form of work is 'normal' for most people:[108] 'The same is true of playing a particular game, taking part in a particular hobby, playing a musical instrument, playing sport or performing a highly skilled task. Impairments which affect only such an activity and have no effect on "normal day to day activities" are not covered.'[109]

Though, as indicated, work of any particular form is not to be regarded as 'normal' for most people, there is case-law indicating that the boundary between particular work and 'normal day-to-day activity' cannot be regarded as precisely drawn. So, for example, where a person's work includes normal day-to-day activities, evidence of that work and the way that person performs it can be relevant.[110] For example, the making of beds, housework and minor DIY tasks, sewing, travelling by underground or aeroplane, putting in hair rollers, or applying make-up have all been held to have been illustrations of 'normal day-to-day activities'[111] and each of these might be material to both work and otherwise depending on the nature of one's work. Further, evidence of a person's ability to carry out normal day-to-day activities at work could have a bearing upon their credibility and the extent to which they were able to carry out normally day-to-day activities outside of work.

In addition, in *Cruickshank v Vaw Motorcast Ltd*[112] the complainant's asthma was triggered by his work environment and it was held (by the Employment

---

[105] *Hewett v Motorola Ltd, supra* note 98. See also Joint Committee on the Draft Disability Discrimination Bill, First Report, (May 2004), paragraph 88. See further Chapter 13, at 13.2 below.
[106] *Ibid.*   [107] Guidance, paragraph C2.
[108] *Ibid.* paragraph C3.   [109] *Ibid.* paragraph C3.
[110] *Law Hospital NHS Trust v Rush* [2001] IRLR 611: the complainant was a nurse and the Employment Tribunal erred insofar as it intended to imply that the extent to which the complainant was able to perform her nursing duties was not a relevant factor for deciding whether or not she was disabled.
[111] *Vicary v British Telecommunications, supra* note 22; *Abadeh v British Telecommunications plc* [2001] ICR 156, [2001] IRLR 23; *Ekpe v Metropolitan Police Commissioner* [2001] ICR 1084, [2001] IRLR 605.
[112] [2002] ICR 729, [2002] IRLR 24.

Appeal Tribunal) that in a case where the effect of an impairment on the ability to carry out normal day-to-day activities fluctuates and may be exacerbated by conditions at work, the Tribunal should consider whether the impairment has a substantial and long-term adverse effect on the employee's ability to perform normal day-to-day activities both while at work and while not at work. 'Normal day-to-day activities' are only a 'yardstick' for deciding whether an impairment is serious enough to qualify for protection under the Act. In assessing whether a disability has a substantial and long-term effect on the ability to do everyday tasks, it is not appropriate to confine the evaluation to the extent to which the complainant is disabled only in a normal day-to-day environment. If, while at work, a complainant's symptoms are such as to have an effect on his ability to perform day-to-day tasks, such symptoms are not to be ignored simply because the work itself may be specialized and unusual, so long as the disability and its consequences can be measured in terms of the ability of a complainant to undertake day-to-day tasks.[113] *Cruickshank v Vaw Motorcast Ltd* indicates that a person might be disabled for some jobs but not others. The Appeal Tribunal were obviously concerned that to conclude otherwise in that case 'would risk turning the Act on its head'.[114] If an employer were able to avoid liability to make reasonable adjustments at work by dismissing the employee, even though this would result in an improvement in the condition and especially where the working environment contributed to the illness, this would be inconsistent with the purpose of the DDA.

This appears difficult to reconcile with the Guidance and the concept of 'normal' day-to-day activities. However, it does suggest that a person who is adversely affected by the conditions in which they are placed by reason of a relevant relationship[115] is entitled to have those effects taken into account.

In determining whether an activity is a *normal* day-to-day activity, no regard should be had to the question whether it is normal for the particular complainant. Thus where travelling by underground might be regarded as a normal day-to-day activity, the fact that the particular complainant does not live or work in London is immaterial (save that it may mean that the effect of the impairment is not substantial).[116] Transport should be viewed overall. Travelling by car or public transport can be regarded as normal day-to-day activities for most people and an inability to use such forms of transport marks an adverse affect on day-to-day activities.[117] However, what is to be regarded as 'normal' 'can not sensibly depend on asking the question whether the majority of people do it. The antithesis for the purposes of the Act is between that which is "normal" and that which is "abnormal" or "unusual" as a regular activity, judged by an objective population standard.'[118]

---

[113] *Ibid.* paragraph 28. [114] *Ibid.* paragraph 21.
[115] Employment; tenant/landlord; recipient of goods and services; student etc.
[116] *Abadeh, supra* note 111 at paragraphs 35–7 and 42. [117] *Ibid.*
[118] *Ekpe, supra* note 111 at paragraph 32.

4.10. ADVERSE EFFECTS

It is important to bear in mind that in determining whether or not an impairment has an adverse effect on a person's ability to carry out normal day-to-day activities, the focus of the DDA is on what a person *cannot* do or can only do with difficulty.[119] Thus concentrating on what a person *can do* will be an error:[120]

The determination of whether there is a substantial adverse impact must depend upon what a person cannot do, rather than what he can still do. It is not a question of balancing individual losses of function directly against retained abilities . . . [I]f . . . the focus should be upon whether or not the *ability referred to in paragraph 4(1) of the Schedule* has been affected, there is little room for drawing up such a balance sheet to answer the question whether there has been any adverse impact; the question 'Has manual dexterity been affected?' in circumstances where a person manipulates buttons only with difficulty cannot sensibly be answered by the riposte: 'Well she can still write a letter without difficulty . . . '.[121]

In *Ekpe v The Commissioner of Police of the Metropolis*[122] the complainant was required to move to a job that involved keyboard duties and felt that she could not do the job because she had a physical impairment which consisted of a wasting of the intrinsic muscles of her right hand. She complained of disability discrimination and her employers disputed that she fell within the definition of a disabled person. The Employment Tribunal concluded that Mrs Ekpe could not carry heavy shopping, scrub pans, peel, grate, sew, or put rollers in her hair. However, they concluded that the complainant's impairment did not have a 'substantial . . . adverse effect' on her ability to carry out normal day-to-day activities because she could, for example, cook normally and although she could not scrub pans normally she could scrub them by adjusting her grip. The Employment Tribunal also held that putting in rollers and applying make-up were not normal day-to-day activities because they were almost exclusively undertaken by women. The Employment Appeal Tribunal concluded that the Employment Tribunal erred because they had addressed item by item the specific aspects of the effects of the complainant's impairment. In so doing '[I]t was in danger of failing to see the wood for the trees, and to recognise that the functions that were debated before it were no more than illustrative aspects of the alleged loss of ability it had to consider'.[123] It ought to have asked 'whether or not taking the evidence as a whole, the admitted impairment has an adverse effect upon either or both manual dexterity and the ability to lift, carry or move

---

[119] *Vicary v British Telecommunications, supra* note 22 at paragraph 5

[120] *Goodwin v The Patent Office, supra* note 17 at paragraph 34; *Leonard v Southern Derbyshire Chamber of Commerce* [2001] IRLR 19.

[121] *Ekpe v The Commissioner of Police of the Metropolis, supra* note 111 at paragraph 28, original emphasis.

[122] *Ibid.*   [123] *Ibid.* paragraph 36.

everyday objects'.[124] In addition, the tribunal ought to have considered what the complainant could not do rather than what she could still do.[125]

This is consistent with the Guidance, which provides that:

In many cases an impairment will adversely affect the person's ability to carry out a range of normal day-to-day activities and it will be obvious that the overall adverse effect is substantial or the effect on at least one normal day-to-day activity is substantial. In such a case it is unnecessary to consider precisely how the person is affected in each of the respects listed in paragraph C4. For example, a person with a clinically well-recognised mental illness may experience an adverse effect on concentration which prevents the person from remembering why he or she is going somewhere; the person would not also have to demonstrate that there was an effect on, say, speech. A person with an impairment which has an adverse effect on sight might be unable to go shopping unassisted; he or she would not also have to demonstrate that there was an effect on, say, mobility.[126]

Furthermore, regard must be had to the fact that disabled people may 'play down' the effect that their disabilities have on their daily lives. The fact that a disabled person can manage their day-to-day activities does not mean that there is no adverse effect upon them or that their 'ability to carry them out has not been impaired'.[127]

Regard must also be had to the fact that disabled people may change the way in which they perform normal day-to-day activities, or indeed refrain from certain of them entirely, consistent with medical advice or otherwise. That must be taken to evidence an indirect effect rather than the absence of an effect.[128] In addition, the fact that a person is able to perform certain activities but that they cause pain or fatigue is to be regarded as a relevant effect.[129] In addition, as mentioned above, disabled people may develop coping strategies or play down the effects of an impairment: this will not obviate the existence of the effect.

4.11. BABIES AND YOUNG CHILDREN

The Guidance observes that the effect of an impairment on babies and young children may not be apparent or so apparent because they are too young to have developed the ability to act in the respects contemplated by Schedule 1, paragraph 4(1). The Disability Discrimination (Meaning of Disability) Regulations 1996[130] makes provision in respect of the same. Regulation 6 provides:

For the purposes of the Act where a child under six years of age has an impairment which does not have an effect falling within paragraph 4(1) of Schedule 1 to the Act that impairment is to be taken to have a substantial and long-term adverse effect on the ability of that child to carry out normal day-to-day activities where it would normally have a

---

[124] *Ibid.*   [125] *Ibid.* paragraph 37.

[126] Guidance, paragraph C5.

[127] *Goodwin v The Patent Office, supra* note 17 at paragraphs 34–5.

[128] *Ibid.* paragraph C6.   [129] *Ibid.*

[130] SI 1996/1455.

substantial and long-term adverse effect on the ability of a person aged six years or over to carry out normal day-to-day activities.

Accordingly, the impairment upon which the disability is founded will have to be hypothetically transposed onto an adult to determine the likely effect.

4.12. WHEN THE EFFECT OF AN IMPAIRMENT IS TO BE MEASURED

The effect of an impairment is to be determined at the time of the alleged discrimination.[131]

4.13. 'SUBSTANTIAL' ADVERSE EFFECTS

Section 1 of the DDA requires that the effects of an impairment on a person's normal day-to-day activities must be *adverse* and *substantial*.[132]

'Substantial' is not defined by the DDA. The Guidance provides that 'a substantial' effect is one which is more than 'minor' or 'trivial'.[133]

The Guidance explains that: 'The requirement that an adverse effect be substantial reflects the general understanding of "disability" as a limitation going beyond the normal differences in ability which may exist among people. A "substantial" effect is more than would be produced by the sort of physical or mental conditions experienced by many people which have only minor effects.'[134]

The time taken by a person to carry out a normal day-to-day activity should be considered when assessing whether the effect of that impairment is substantial.[135] The time should be compared with the time that might be expected to be taken if the person did not have the impairment.[136] In addition, the way in which a person carries out a normal day-to-day activity should be considered when assessing whether the effect of an impairment is substantial.[137] The comparison should be with the way the person would be expected to carry out the activity if he or she did not have the impairment.[138]

The Guidance gives a series of examples of what it would, and what it would not, be reasonable to regard as substantial adverse effects. However, these are indicators and not tests. They do not mean that if a person can do an activity listed then he or she does not experience any substantial adverse effects; the

---

[131] *Cruickshank, supra* note 112 at paragraph 28.　　[132] Section 1(1) DDA.

[133] Paragraph A1.

[134] *Ibid.* Also see *Ekpe, supra* note 111 at paragraph 32, where the Employment Appeal Tribunal concluded that anything which is more than 'insubstantial' is to be regarded as 'substantial'.

[135] Guidance, paragraph A2.　　[136] *Ibid.*

[137] *Ibid.* paragraph A3.　　[138] *Ibid.*

person may be inhibited in other activities, and this instead may indicate a substantial effect.[139] The examples include, by way of illustration, effects on 'mobility', as follows:

It would be reasonable to regard as having a substantial adverse effect:
• inability to travel a short journey as a passenger in a vehicle;
• inability to walk other than at a slow pace or with unsteady or jerky movements;
• difficulty in going up or down steps, stairs or gradients;
• inability to use one or more forms of public transport;
• inability to go out of doors unaccompanied.
It would not be reasonable to regard as having a substantial adverse effect:
• difficulty walking unaided a distance of about 1.5 kilometres or a mile
• inability to travel in a car for a journey lasting more than two hours without discomfort.[140]

Similar lists of examples are provided in respect of each of the capacities identified in Schedule 1, paragraph 4.[141]

The question whether or not the effect of an impairment is substantial is not a medical one. It is a question of fact to be determined on the evidence of the complainant and his or her witnesses who can give evidence on the question of the severity of the effect of any impairment.[142]

4.14. EFFECTS OF BEHAVIOUR: COPING

As has been observed, disabled people may be inclined to 'play down' the effects of an impairment. On the other hand, in determining whether the effects of an impairment are 'substantial' for the purposes of the DDA the Guidance provides that 'account should be taken of how far a person can reasonably be expected to modify behaviour to prevent or reduce the effects of an impairment on normal day-to-day activities'.[143] If a person can behave in such a way that an impairment ceases to have a substantial adverse effect on his or her ability to carry out normal day-to-day activities, the person no longer satisfies the definition of disability.[144]

Where a person has 'coping' strategies which cease to work in certain circumstances (for example, when under stress) regard should be had to the possibility that their ability to manage the effects of an impairment will break down so that effects will still sometimes occur and this should be taken into account when assessing the effects of an impairment.[145] In addition, this must be contrasted with a situation where a person is receiving advice by a medical practitioner to behave in a certain way in order to reduce the impact of a disability when such

---

[139] *Ibid.* paragraph C9 and 10.   [140] *Ibid.* paragraph C14.

[141] See also Guidance, paragraph C5.

[142] *Vicary v British Telecommunications, supra* note 22 at paragraph 16; and *Abadeh v British Telecommunications, supra* note 111 at paragraph 9.

[143] *Ibid.* paragraph A7.   [144] *Ibid.*

[145] *Ibid.* paragraph A8.

behaviour might count as 'treatment', and therefore, be disregarded.[146] The question where the line is drawn as between mere coping strategies and treatment, particularly given that such treatment need not be medical, is unclear.

In addition a court or tribunal should be cautious about relying on stereotypical assumptions. As has been pointed out:

a relatively small proportion of the disabled community are what one might describe as visibly disabled, that is people in wheelchairs or carrying white sticks or other aids. It is important therefore, that when [courts and tribunals] are approaching the question as to whether someone suffers from a disability, they should not have in their minds a stereotypical image of a person in a wheelchair or moving around with considerable difficulty. Such persons may well have a physical impairment within the meaning of the Act and are thus to be treated as disabled, but it of course does not follow that other persons who are not in such a condition are inherently less likely to have a physical or mental impairment of a sort which satisfies the terms of the legislation.[147]

4.15. CUMULATIVE EFFECTS

In determining whether an impairment has a substantial adverse effect, regard should be had to the cumulative impact of such impairment. So when an impairment has an adverse effect on more than one of the eight capacities, abilities, or capabilities set out in Schedule 1 of the DDA its cumulative impact should be considered: 'An impairment might not have a substantial adverse effect on a person in any one of the . . . respects [listed], but its effects in more than one of these respects taken together could result in a substantial adverse effect on the person's ability to carry out normal day-to-day activities'.[148]

Accordingly, a person with mild cerebral palsy may experience minor effects in a number of the respects listed in Schedule 1 which together could create substantial adverse effects on a range of normal day-to-day activities: fatigue may hinder walking, visual perception may be poor, coordination and balance may cause some difficulties.[149] In addition, a person may have more than one *impairment*, any one of which alone would not have a substantial effect. Again, account should be taken of whether the impairments together have a substantial effect overall on a person's ability to carry out normal day-to-day activities.

4.16. EFFECTS OF ENVIRONMENT

The question whether adverse effects are substantial may depend on environmental conditions which might vary, for example temperature, humidity, time of

---

[146] *Ibid.* paragraph A9; see also 4.4.
[147] *Vicary v British Telecommunications, supra* note 22 at paragraph 20.
[148] Guidance, paragraph A4.   [149] *Ibid.* paragraph A5.

day or night, how tired the person is, or how much stress he or she is under.[150] In determining whether adverse effects are substantial, the extent to which such environmental factors are likely to have an impact should also be considered.[151]

4.17. RECURRENT EFFECTS

If an impairment has had a substantial adverse effect on a person's ability to carry out normal day-to-day activities but that effect ceases, the substantial effect is treated as continuing if it is likely to recur; that is, if it is more likely than not that the effect will recur.[152]

In the case of a past disability, the question is whether a substantial adverse effect has in fact recurred.[153]

Conditions which recur only sporadically or for short periods (for example, epilepsy)[154] can still qualify.

According to the Guidance:

Likelihood of recurrence should be considered taking all the circumstances of the case into account. This should include what the person could reasonably be expected to do to prevent the recurrence; for example, the person might reasonably be expected to take action which prevents the impairment from having such effects (eg avoiding substances to which he or she is allergic). This may be unreasonably difficult with some substances. In addition, it is possible that the way in which a person can control or cope with the effects of a condition may not always be successful because, for example, a routine is not followed or the person is in an unfamiliar environment. If there is an increased likelihood that the control will break down, it will be more likely that there will be a recurrence. That possibility should be taken into account when assessing the likelihood of a recurrence.[155]

What is critical is whether the substantial effect of the illness on normal day-to-day activities is likely to occur, and not whether the illness itself is likely to occur. Thus the court or tribunal should ask itself: (1) was there at some stage an impairment that had a substantial effect on the complainant's ability to carry out normal day-to-day activities? (2) Did the impairment cease to have a substantial adverse effect on the complainant's ability to carry out normal day-to-day activities and, if so, when? (3) What was the substantial adverse effect? (4) Is that substantial adverse effect likely to occur? The Tribunal must be satisfied that the same effect is likely to occur and will again amount to a substantial adverse effect on the complainant's ability to carry out normal day-to-day activities.[156]

---

[150] *Ibid.* paragraph A10.
[151] *Ibid.*
[152] Schedule 1, paragraph 2(2).
[153] Schedule 2, paragraph 5.
[154] Guidance, paragraph B3.
[155] *Ibid.* paragraph B5.
[156] *Swift v Chief Constable of Wiltshire Constabulary* [2004] ICR 909, [2004] IRLR 540, at paragraphs 20–7.

4.18. 'LONG-TERM' IMPAIRMENT

The substantial and adverse effects of a person's impairment must be 'long-term' for the protection of the DDA to apply. An effect of an impairment is long-term if:

• it has lasted for at least twelve months; or
• it is likely to last for at least twelve months; or
• it is likely to last for the rest of the affected person's life.[157]

In the case of a past disability, the effect of an impairment is long-term if it has lasted for at least twelve months.[158]

As the Guidance makes clear, it is not necessary for the effect to be the same throughout the relevant period. An effect may change, as where activities which are initially very difficult become possible to a much greater extent. Indeed the main adverse effect might even disappear temporarily or permanently whilst another effect continues or develops. So long as the impairment continues to have, or be likely to have such an effect throughout the period, there is a long-term effect.[159]

'Likely' for the purposes of determining whether the effect of an impairment is likely to last for at least twelve months or for the rest of the person's life, simply means 'more probable than not that it will happen'.[160]

4.19. WHEN 'LONG-TERM' IS TO BE MEASURED

As to when the likelihood of an effect lasting for any period should be tested, the Guidance confirms that the total period over which the effect exists should be taken into account.[161] This therefore includes any time before the point when the discriminatory behaviour occurred as well as any time afterwards.[162] As has been made clear, this means that the effects of the complainant's impairments right up to the hearing of any claim might be taken into account.[163]

4.20. PAST DISABILITIES

As mentioned above (see 4.2), the DDA applies in relation to a person who has had a disability in the past as they apply in relation to a person who currently has that disability.[164]

---

[157] Schedule 1, paragraph 2(1). See also recurrent effects, at 4.17 above.
[158] Schedule 2, paragraph 5.   [159] Guidance, paragraph B2.
[160] *Ibid.* paragraph B7.   [161] *Ibid.* paragraph B8.
[162] This may be contrasted with the question of substantial and adverse effect, which is to be tested at the time of the alleged discrimination. See, for example, *Cruickshank, supra* note 112.
[163] *Greenwood v British Airways plc* [1999] ICR 969, [1999] IRLR 600.   [164] Section 2.

Further guidance is provided by Schedule 2 of the DDA. By Schedule 2, paragraph 2, 'References in Part II [to 4] to a disabled person are to be read as references to a person who has had a disability'. By paragraph 2A, references in the education provisions to a disabled pupil are similarly to be read as references to a pupil who has had a disability. By paragraph 2B, references to a disabled student are to be read as references to a student who has had a disability and similar and consequential changes are made.

In determining whether the effect of an impairment is long-term where the disability is a past disability and where an impairment ceases to have a substantial adverse effect on a person's ability to carry out normal day-to-day activities, the impairment is to be treated as continuing to have that effect if that effect recurs.[165] In *Greenwood v British Airways plc*[166] the complainant was off work between October 1993 and March 1994 due to 'nervous tension'. He was thereafter absent on three occasions on dates between December 1996 and February 1997 which, along with his earlier absence, triggered the sickness absence procedure. He was refused a promotion shortly afterwards on the ground, among others, that he was viewed as unreliable due to his previous sickness record. He went sick with depression in August 1997 and when he was refused promotion brought a complaint under the DDA on the basis that he had been discriminated against for a reason relating to his disability. Overturning the decision of the Employment Tribunal, the Employment Appeal Tribunal concluded that the complainant had had a disability in the past which was covered by section 2 of the DDA; the Tribunal had failed to have regard to the fact that the adverse effect of the complainant's depression recurred and he was therefore to be regarded as having had a past disability by virtue of paragraph 5(2) of Schedule 2.

4.21. FUTURE DISABILITIES

The DDA does not protect persons who have a disposition to become disabled in the future, by reason of some genetic condition or otherwise. This is by reason of the functional nature of the test for disability and the fact that a person who is and remains symptom-free will not be caught by the test provided for in the DDA. It can be noted that paragraph 16 of Annex 1 to the first Code of Practice 'for the elimination of discrimination in the field of employment against disabled persons or persons who have had a disability' and Annex B of the new Code[167]

---

[165] Schedule 2, paragraph 5(2) DDA. See also 4.18 above.

[166] *Supra* note 163.

[167] Commencement 2 December 1996, SI 1996/1996; and now see Code of Practice on Employment and Occupation (2004) DRC ISBN 0 11 703419 3; Disability Discrimination Codes of Practice (Employment and Occupation, and Trade Organisations and Qualifications Bodies) Appointed Day Order 2004, SI 2004/2302. As to progressive conditions, see 4.4 above.

provide that: 'If a genetic condition has no effect on ability to carry out normal day-to-day activities, the person is not covered. Diagnosis does not in itself bring someone within the definition. If the condition is progressive, then the rule about progressive conditions applies.'

As observed in 1.5 above (see also Chapter 13 below, at 13.2) it is likely that there will be legislative change so that certain conditions, even while they remain symptom-free, will be caught by the definition of disability. These will not, however, include genetic conditions where they remain latent and this is an area of some concern.

4.22. PROVING 'DISABILITY'

Except in cases where disability is conceded, a medical report will be required to establish, at least, the fact of an impairment, save in the most obvious cases. This is so especially in the case of a mental impairment because of the additional requirement that it be clinically well recognized. However, a report will often be required to establish the length of time over which the effects of an impairment have lasted or will last; whether the effects will recur; the effects of treatments; and so on.

In addition, whilst the question whether an impairment has a substantial adverse effect is a matter of fact and not expert evidence where there is doubt about the credibility of the complainant, medical evidence may bolster the complainant's account of the effect of any impairment.[168] Furthermore, evidence will often be required where a progressive condition is relied upon to establish that the condition is indeed progressive. In cases where knowledge of the disability is material[169] medical evidence may be required to establish that the impairment manifests itself and indeed how it manifests itself.

Guidance on expert evidence has been provided in the context of the Employment Tribunals in *De Keyser Ltd v Wilson*[170] and more generally in Rule 35 of the Civil Procedure Rules.

4.23. LEGISLATIVE CHANGE

As observed in Chapter 1 above, the Disability Discrimination Bill when enacted will extend the definition of disability so as to deem people with HIV infection, cancer, or multiple sclerosis 'disabled' from the time of diagnosis.

---

[168] See *Vicary v British Telecommunications plc supra* note 22 at paragraph 16; *Morgan v Staffordshire University supra* note 89 at paragraph 20; see also 4.13 above.

[169] In some cases where a failure to make reasonable adjustments is relied upon: see Chapter 5 below, or where the new form of direct discrimination is relied upon: see Chapter 5 below.

[170] [2001] IRLR 324.

The Joint Committee on the Draft Disability Discrimination Bill[171] has reported, and whilst it has endorsed many of the proposals for change it has also made many other recommendations for strengthening the Bill and its impact. The Committee noted that the definition of disability is extremely significant. The DRC has criticized the current definition as being too narrow and has quoted research indicating that 16 per cent (one in six) of decided cases involve complainants who lost because tribunals ruled that they had not met the statutory definition of disability.[172] Indeed this was the most common reason for a claim to fail. The Committee noted that a social model of disability identifies 'disabling barriers' rather than any 'impairment' as the cause of disadvantage and uses the term 'disability' to refer to disabling barriers rather than to any impairment. As the Committee observed: 'A disabled person might say, therefore, "my impairment is the fact that I can't walk; my disability is the fact that the bus company only provides inaccessible buses". By contrast the medical model, on which the DDA is based, focuses on impairment as being the cause of limited opportunities and life chances.'[173]

The Committee concluded that '[t]he focus of anti-discrimination legislation should be on the extent and nature of discrimination, not on the extent and nature of the impairment'.[174] They therefore preferred a social model approach.[175] As a consequence they recommended that the DRC consider and consult on whether the law should be amended to provide protection against discrimination on grounds of impairment, regardless of the level or type of impairment, and provide entitlements to the removal of disabling barriers.[176]

The Committee recommended that all progressive conditions which are currently covered under the DDA when they begin to have an effect should be included from the point of diagnosis.[177]

They further recommended that the requirement that a mental illness be 'clinically well recognized' be removed. Instead they recommend that the medical evidence should be required only to establish the effect of the condition on the person. The requirement that an illness be 'clinically well recognised' apparently originated in a belief that absent such a requirement there would be 'the possibility of claims based on obscure conditions unrecognised by reputable clinicians, which courts and tribunals would find extremely difficult to assess . . . [and the] need to make it clear that the [DDA] does not cover . . . mild or

---

[171] The Committee was established by motions of the House of Commons on 15 January 2004 and the House of Lords on 21 January 2004, see Joint Committee on the Draft Disability Discrimination Bill, First Report available at: http://www.publications.parliament.uk/pa/jt200304/jtselect/jtdisab/82/ 8204.htm. 27 May 2004. The Government's response is available at http://www.disability.gov.uk/ legislation/ddb/response.asp.

[172] Joint Committee on the Draft Disability Discrimination Bill, *First Report* (My 2004) paragraph 34. See also Chapter 13 below

[173] *Ibid.* paragraph 35. See also Chapter 2 above, at 2.3.

[174] *Ibid.* paragraph 47.

[175] *Ibid.*   [176] *Ibid.* paragraph 50.   [177] *Ibid.* paragraph 63.

tendentious conditions'.[178] According to the DRC there is no evidence that this restriction has fulfilled this role.[179] The fact that this requirement applies only to mental impairments is, according to the DRC, discriminatory in itself.[180] The Government in their Response to the Report of the Joint Committee on the Draft Disability Discrimination Bill have accepted the Committee's recommendation that the 'clinically well recognised' requirement be removed and have indicated that they will use the Disabilty Discrimination Bill to remove the requirement.[181] People with mental illnesses, like those with other mental and physical impairments, will continue to need to demonstrate that their impairment has a substantial and long-term adverse effect on their ability to carry out normal day-to-day activities.

The Committee also recommended that the following activities be added to the list of 'normal day-to-day activities' in Schedule 1 DDA:

• the ability to care for oneself;
• the ability to communicated and interact with others; and
• the perception of reality.[182]

The Government has indicated that they consider that the current approach is 'comprehensive and effective'. However, they have indicated that they will revise the Statutory Guidance on the definition of disability to ensure that developments in case-law and legislative changes are covered.[183] For a full discussion of the Draft Disability Discrimination Bill, including its provisions and the Government's response to the same, see Chapter 13 below.

---

[178] William Hague MP during the passage into law of the DDA in 1995 whilst Minister for Disabled People, House of Commons Standing Committee Debates (E), 7 February 1995, Column 104. See the *First Report* of the Joint Committee of the Draft Disability Discrimination Bill, *supra* note 172.

[179] Joint Committee on the Draft Disability Discrimination Bill, *First Report* (May 2004) paragraph 74.

[180] *Ibid.* paragraph 75.

[181] http://www.disability.gov.uk/legislation/ddb/response.asp.

[182] Joint Committee on the Draft Disability Discrimination Bill, *First Report*, paragraph 88.

[183] The Government's response is at http://www.disability.gov.uk/legislation/ddb/response.asp.

5

THE MEANING OF 'DISCRIMINATION'

5.1. INTRODUCTION

The DDA defines 'discrimination' in four ways. In short summary, 'discrimination' for the purposes of the DDA occurs where there is:

- less favourable treatment of a disabled person on the ground of that disabled person's disability ('direct discrimination'). Such discrimination cannot be justified;

- less favourable treatment of a disabled person for a reason which relates to that disabled person's disability ('disability-related discrimination'). Such discrimination can be justified;

- a failure to comply with the duty to make reasonable adjustments. Such discrimination can be justified in limited fields;

- less favourable treatment of a person (whose disability status is immaterial) by reason that that person has done a 'protected act' or the discriminator believes or suspects that he has done or intends to do 'a protected act' ('victimization'). Such discrimination cannot be justified.

'Harassment' is also a form of discrimination, though not so described, which is outlawed in certain circumstances. 'Harassment' cannot be justified.

The statutory concepts of direct discrimination and harassment have been introduced into the DDA's employment and related provisions in consequence of the Directive.[1]

'Discrimination' is outlawed by the DDA (in very short summary) in the following fields:

• employment and occupation;
• the provision of goods, facilities, and services;
• housing and premises; and
• education.[2]

Not all forms of discrimination apply to all the activities covered by the DDA:

• direct discrimination applies only in the employment and related fields;
• harassment applies only in the employment and related fields;
• the duty to make adjustments is differently defined depending on the activity concerned.

Accordingly, discrimination for the purposes of the DDA will occur differently depending upon the context. For this reason the meaning of discrimination is dealt with under the different heads of activity as set out below.

It is important to observe that although these concepts define 'discrimination' for the purposes of the DDA, they do not create any unlawful acts by themselves. Harassment, therefore, in a context outside one of the relevant unlawful acts, will not be made unlawful by the DDA, even if related to disability. Similarly, treating a person less favourably because they have brought proceedings under the DDA, though meeting the definition of 'victimization',[3] is not unlawful of itself.[4]

As mentioned above and as will be seen below, the DDA imposes a series of duties upon persons concerned with activities caught by the unlawful acts created by the DDA. These duties are collectively described as the duties 'to make reasonable adjustments'. The precise scope of these duties varies according to the activity concerned. However, in each case the duties operate, at least to some extent, so as to place disabled people on an equal footing with non-disabled people. They represent a form of 'positive' action, in that they require certain specified persons and bodies to take positive measures to secure that equality. However, they also reflect more closely a social model of disability, acknowledging that 'disability' may be much less about individual impairment and

---

[1] 2000/78/EC, Article 2. See Chapter 3 above, at 3.2. See also Disability Discrimination Act 1995 (Amendment) Regulations 2003, SI 2003/1673.

[2] These are all addressed in detail in Chapters 6–8 below.

[3] Section 55 DDA, see below.

[4] *Bruce v Addleshaw Booth & Co* UKEAT 00555/04/1309 [2004] EOR 131, 17; *Nagarajan v Agnew* [1995] ICR 520, [1994] IRLR 61.

much more about environmental and societal obstacles to equal participation.[5] As mentioned, because the duties are differently described, according to the activity concerned, the duties are dealt with under discrete heads below. However, there is one important distinction that it is convenient to identify at the outset. The activation of some of the duties depends upon disadvantage actually being established by a disabled person in consequence of any arrangements made or by a physical barrier, for example. Certain of the duties, however, are *anticipatory* in nature and therefore it is not necessary to show that a disabled person is in fact disadvantaged by any arrangements or physical feature of premises, for example; the duty applies in any event.[6] In the latter class of case, these duties are concerned with ensuring that service providers, for example, take steps in advance to ensure that their premises and services are accessible to disabled people without waiting for disadvantage to be experienced. As stated, in the former case the duty will not be triggered until such disadvantage is demonstrated.

Importantly, there are relevant Codes of Practice issued by the DRC.[7] These Codes give clear and helpful guidance on the means by which discrimination can be avoided and are referred to further below. There are, however, limits to the assistance the Codes can provide. In particular, where discrimination occurs in a context regulated by other legal measures, the impact of those measures may have to be taken into account and they will not necessarily be addressed by the Codes. Such measures include the HRA,[8] amongst others.[9]

5.2. EMPLOYMENT

Discrimination in employment is outlawed by section 4 DDA. In short summary, discrimination against prospective employees, existing employees, and ex-employees is outlawed:[10] see Chapter 6 below.

'Discrimination' for the purposes of the employment provisions of the DDA[11] is defined by sections 3A, 3B, and 55. It comprises:

---

[5] This is discussed in Chapter 2 above, at 2.3.

[6] Though an individual cause of action will not arise unless the particular claimant has been impeded in some way in consequence of the breach of duty, see eg s 19(1)(b) DDA and see *Roads v Central Trains Ltd* [2004] EWCA Civ 1541 at paragraph 12.

[7] And afforded Parliamentary approval consequent upon the negative resolution procedure applicable to the Codes: see Chapter 1 above, at 1.4.

[8] See Chapter 3 above and *Council of the City of Manchester v (1) Romano (2) Samari* [2004] EWCA Civ 834, paragraph 75.

[9] See, for example, *Council of the City of Manchester v (1) Romano (2) Samari, supra* note 8 paragraphs 18–19, 55, 115, 123. See the suggestion by Brooke LJ that the example given by the relevant Code on a discriminatory eviction may be 'inept . . . in the eyes of anyone who knows anything about the law relating to residential tenancies': *ibid.* at paragraph 55.

[10] Sections 4 and 16A DDA.   [11] Section 4 DDA.

- direct discrimination;
- a failure to comply with a duty to make reasonable adjustments;
- disability-related discrimination; and
- vitimization.

In addition, harassment is outlawed in those areas falling within the scope of the unlawful acts created in the employment and related fields.

Part II DDA also outlaws discrimination in the context of various occupations and occupational related circumstances: see Chapter 6 below. The meaning of 'discrimination' for these other occupational related unlawful acts is addressed below at 5.3–5.5.

The DRC has issued a new 'Code of Practice on Employment and Occupation' ('the Employment Code of Practice').[12] This provides guidance on the impact of the meaning of discrimination and harassment.[13]

5.2.1. 'Direct Discrimination'

Section 3A(5) of the DDA provides that:

A person directly discriminates against a disabled person if, on the ground of the disabled person's disability, he treats the disabled person less favourably than he treats or would treat a person not having that particular disability whose relevant circumstances, including his abilities, are the same as, or not materially different from, those of the disabled person.

Section 3A(5) was inserted by the Disability Discrimination Act 1995 (Amendment) Regulations 2003 ('the 2003 Regulations')[14] and came into effect on 1 October 2004. It purports to give effect to the requirement in the Directive[15] that Member States outlaw direct discrimination in the employment and related fields.[16]

However, as observed in Chapter 3 above, at 3.4, the DDA meaning is somewhat narrower than that provided for in the Directive. It protects disabled people only, and then only where the discrimination is based on their disability. It does not cover discrimination by association (eg less favourable treatment on the ground that the complainant has a disabled partner/friend/parent/child); or discrimination based on a misperception that a person is

---

[12] (2004) DRC ISBN 0 11 703419 3; Disability Discrimination Codes of Practice (Employment and Occupation, and Trade Organizations, and Qualifications Bodies) Appointed Day Order 2004, SI 2004/2302.

[13] The Code of Practice is issued under section 53A DDA. A failure to observe any provision of the Code of Practice does not of itself make a person liable to any proceedings but where a provision of the Code of Practice appears to a court or tribunal to be relevant, it must take that provision into account: section 53A(8) and (8A) DDA.

[14] SI 2003/1673. It applies only to the unlawful acts created by Part II of the DDA (employment and related activities): see Chapter 6 below.

[15] 2000/78/EC.   [16] Article 2(2)(a).

disabled; or discrimination based on a refusal to comply with discriminatory instructions.[17] To this extent it would appear not to give proper effect to the Directive.[18]

5.2.1.1. *'Less favourable treatment'*

'Less favourable treatment' is a concept wide enough to cover any disadvantage. It is not necessary for the complainant to suffer tangible loss or other damaging consequences.[19] Indeed a favourable financial outcome might conceal unlawful discrimination: one cannot buy a right to discriminate.[20] A mere deprivation of choice will be sufficient to found a claim of less favourable treatment.[21] Words or acts of discouragement can amount to less favourable treatment of the person discouraged.[22]

The test of 'less favourable treatment' is now largely subjective[23] and sets a low threshold.

5.2.1.2. *The proper comparator and the relevant circumstances*

Direct discrimination requires that a comparison be undertaken between the treatment afforded the disabled person and the treatment which was or would have been afforded a person not having that particular disability. As the wording indicates it is not necessary for there to be an actual comparator: a hypothetical comparator will suffice. However, in either case the chosen comparator's 'relevant circumstances, including . . . abilities' must 'be the same as, or not materially different from, those of the disabled person'.[24]

---

[17] See by analogy the cases arising under section 1(1)(a) of the RRA which provides that 'A person discriminates against another in any circumstances relevant for the purposes of any provision of this Act if—on *racial grounds* he treats that other less favourably than he treats or would treat other persons' (emphasis added); *Weathersfield Ltd t/a Van & Truck Rentals v Sargent* [1999] ICR 425, [1999] IRLR 94; *Showboat Entertainment Centre Ltd v Owens* [1984] ICR 65, [1984] IRLR 7 (instructions to white employees that they refuse services to black customers held to be unlawful direct discrimination against white employees).

[18] For the remedies for this defect, see Chapter 3 above.

[19] *Chief Constable of West Yorkshire v Khan* [2001] UKHL 48, [2001] 1WLR 1947, [2001] ILR 1065; [2001] IRLR 830, paragraphs 52–3; *Gill v El Vinos Co Ltd* [1983] QB 425. Much of the case-law treats the test of less favourable treatment as equivalent to the meaning of 'detriment' (see eg section 4(2)(d)).

[20] *Ministry of Defence v Jeremiah* [1980] QB 87.

[21] *Gill, supra* note 19, and *R v Birmingham City Council* ex parte *Equal Opportunities Commission* [1989] AC 1155, [1989] IRLR 173.

[22] *Simon v Brimham Associates* [1987] ICR 596, [1987] IRLR 307, though the result in this case is somewhat unfathomable; see, 'Highlights' [1987] IRLR 305–6.

[23] *Chief Constable of West Yorkshire v Kahn, supra* note 19; *Shamoon v Chief Constable of the Royal Ulster Constabulary* [2003] UKHL 11, [2003] ICR 337; [2003] IRLR 285. Though some objective assessment is required, *ibid.* And see eg *Smith v Vodafone UK Ltd* (EAT No: 0054/01) EOR DCLD Number 49D, 7, in which a purely subjectively felt but unjustified sense of grievance was inadequate to make out an unlawful act.

[24] Section 3A(5).

The comparator must be a person without the complainant's disability, that is a non-disabled person or a person with a different disability.[25]

As stated, the *relevant* circumstances of the complainant and the comparator must be the same or not materially different. This does not mean that all the circumstances must be identical as between them. It is only necessary that the relevant circumstances are not materially different. For example, if an employer is recruiting for qualified social workers without regard to where that qualification was obtained then the fact that a complainant studied in a different institution to the comparator will be immaterial. The Employment Code of Practice gives the following examples:[26]

A disabled person with arthritis who can type at 30 words per minute (wpm) applies for an administrative job which includes typing, but is rejected on the ground that her typing speed is too slow. The correct comparator in a claim for direct discrimination would be a person not having arthritis who also has a typing speed of 30 wpm (with the same accuracy rate).

A disabled person with a severe visual impairment applies for a job as a bus driver and is refused the job because he fails to meet the minimum level of visual acuity which is essential to the safe performance of the job. The correct comparator is a person not having that particular disability (for example, a person who merely has poorer than average eyesight) also failing to meet that minimum standard.

A disabled person with schizophrenia applies for a job as an administrative assistant with his local authority, and declares his history of mental illness. The local authority refuses him employment, relying on a negative medical report from the authority's occupational health adviser which is based on assumptions about the effects of schizophrenia, without adequate consideration of the individual's abilities and the impact of the impairment in his particular case. This is likely to amount to direct discrimination and to be unlawful. The comparator here is a person who does not have schizophrenia, but who has the same abilities to do the job (including relevant qualifications and experience) as the disabled applicant: such a person would not have been rejected without adequate consideration of his individual abilities.

The case-law on direct discrimination under the SDA and the RRA[27] is relevant for undertaking the proper comparison exercise. In particular, it is clear that the characteristics of a *reasonable* person in the position of the discriminator (*a hypothetical discriminator*) are immaterial. The only question is how the particular discriminator would have treated other non-disabled persons.[28] If a person treats all people, irrespective of disability status, equally poorly then direct discrimination is not made out.[29]

---

[25] *Ibid.* [26] Paragraphs 4.13 and 4.20.

[27] Though some caution must be demonstrated because, as mentioned above, see note 17, the tests are somewhat different under the RRA.

[28] Or persons not having the complainant's disability.

[29] *Shamoon v Chief Constable of the Royal Ulster Constabulary, supra* note 23. *Zafar v Glasgow CC* [1998] ICR 120; [1998] IRLR 36. Though unreasonable treatment may be relevant in proving discrimination: see below, at 5.2.14.

In addition, the only relevant *circumstances* are the actual circumstances of the particular case. An Employment Tribunal should not have regard to hypothetical circumstances or alternate possible circumstances for determining whether or not there has been comparatively less favourable treatment. In *Smyth v Croft Inns Ltd*[30] a Catholic barman employed in a pub with Protestant customers in a Loyalist area of Belfast learned of a message having been sent to the chargehand barman stating that he should be advised not to be in the bar the following week. Instead of providing support, the bar manager telephoned the Catholic barman and told him he could stay or go. The barman resigned and claimed constructive dismissal on the ground of his religion. The Northern Ireland Court of Appeal (NICA) ruled that the proper comparison for determining whether or not direct discrimination had been made out was between the Catholic barman and the hypothetical Protestant barman working in the same bar who would not have been subject to the same treatment on the ground of his religious belief. In so holding the NICA rejected the argument that the proper comparator was a hypothetical Protestant barman working in a Catholic bar in a Nationalist area (who it was presumed would have been treated in the same way). As the NICA observed:

[i]f an employer owned a bar in a Protestant neighbourhood, patronised by Protestants, in which he employed a Roman Catholic barman, and a second bar in a Roman Catholic neighbourhood, patronised by Roman Catholics, in which he employed a Protestant barman, and the employer dismissed both barmen on the grounds that the customers in the respective bars did not like being served by a barman of a religious belief which differed from their own, then on the Appellant's argument the employer would not be guilty of religious discrimination because he did not treat either barman less favourably than the other. I consider that this argument is fallacious. In my opinion the employer would be guilty of religious discrimination against both barmen.[31]

The 'relevant circumstances' cannot by themselves be tainted with discrimination.[32] It would be no answer to a claim brought by a disabled person that they had been treated less favourably on the ground of their disability that the employer would treat all disabled persons in the same way. Otherwise the direct discrimination provisions would be largely deprived of their teeth.

As observed above, an actual comparator is not required for the purposes of establishing direct discrimination. A hypothetical comparator is sufficient. However, constructing a hypothetical comparator and undertaking the relevant

---

[30] [1996] IRLR 84.

[31] Paragraph 28. And see *R v Commission for Racial Equality ex parte Westminster City Council* [1985] ICR 827, [1984] IRLR 230 at 233 and 234. See also *Grieg v Community Industry and Ahern* [1979] ICR 356, [1979] IRLR 158.

[32] By analogy, though bearing in mind the slightly different wording in the SDA and the RRA, see *James v Eastleigh BC* [1990] 2 AC 751, [1990] IRLR 288. See also *Carter* (sued on his own behalf and on behalf of the other members of the Labour Party) *v Ashan* [2004] UKEAT 0907/03. This approach might be contrasted with *Dhatt v McDonald Hamburgers Ltd* [1991] ICR 226, [1991] IRLR 130, though *James* is a House of Lords decision, whilst *Dhatt* is a Court of Appeal decision, and the former should therefore be regarded as binding.

comparison exercise has not always proved easy in practice. Where the treatment is explicitly based on a protected ground (here disability) then it will be fairly easy to convince an Employment Tribunal that a person of a different status would not have been afforded the same treatment. But however overt the treatment, a comparison must always be undertaken and discrimination is not to be presumed.[33] It will always be necessary to undertake a comparison with a real comparator where one exists. If there is no real comparator an Employment Tribunal is bound to consider whether a hypothetical comparator of a different status would have been treated in the same way.[34] This is important because in some cases there will be no actual comparator, or as the evidence emerges the chosen comparator might prove to be in materially different circumstances. It is necessary then to consider the position of the hypothetical comparator.

Constructing a hypothetical comparator is conceptually difficult. However, it is permissible to rely on persons who do not prove to be actual comparators but whose circumstances are, though non-identical, not wholly dissimilar. In *Chief Constable of West Yorkshire v Vento*[35] Lindsay J[36] gave the following guidance:

We would readily accept that the treatment of an actual male comparator whose position was wholly akin to Mrs Vento's in relation to the . . . incident was not in evidence. It followed that the tribunal had to construct a picture of how a hypothetical male comparator would have been treated in comparable surrounding circumstances. One permissible way of judging a question such as that is to see how unidentical but not wholly dissimilar cases had been treated in relation to other individual cases. That is one approach. Another permissible approach is to ask witnesses how the hypothetical case that requires to be considered would have been dealt with, although great care has to be exercised in assessing the answer to questions such as that, because the witness will be aware that it will be next to impossible to disprove any answer to a hypothetical question and also witnesses will know, by the time of the tribunal hearing, what sort of answer is convenient or helpful to the side that they might wish to support . . . As for constructing the hypothetical case from actual but dissimilar cases, the tribunal refer in some detail to four actual comparators . . . but the tribunal did not treat any of the four cases . . . as being a relevant actual comparator. That is why the tribunal turned, as it had to, to a *hypothetical* male officer in the same circumstances. The tribunal used the four actual cases as building blocks in the construction of the neighbourhood in which the hypothetical male officer

---

[33] Joined cases *MacDonald v Advocate General for Scotland* [2003] UKHL 34, [2003] ICR 937; *Pearce v Governing Body of Mayfield Secondary School* [2003] UKHL 34, [2003] ICR 937, [2003] IRLR 512 in which the House of Lords overruled a line of cases that indicated that where treatment was race- or gender-specific (and by analogy disability-specific) no comparison exercise was required but that of itself constituted less favourable treatment on the protected ground. It is now necessary to undertake a comparison exercise and conclude that the treatment was on one of the protected grounds.

[34] *Balamoody v UK Central Council for Nursing, Midwifery and Health Visiting* [2001] EWCA Civ 2097, [2002] ICR 646, [2002] IRLR 288.

[35] [2001] IRLR 124 at paragraphs 7 and 15.

[36] When President of the Employment Appeal Tribunal.

was to be found. For the tribunal to have relied on the four actual comparator cases in that way was not only not an error of law, it was, as it seems to us, the only proper way in which to proceed on the evidence put before it.

As to the position of the complainant, just as the alleged discriminator must be taken as he is, with no hypothetical characteristics imputed, so the disabled person with their actual abilities must be considered as they are in fact. In some cases, there will be particular reasonable adjustments which an employer is required by the DDA to make,[37] but in fact has failed to make. It may be that those adjustments would have had an effect on the disabled person's abilities to do the job. However, in making the comparison for direct discrimination purposes, the disabled person's abilities should be considered as they in fact were, and not as they would or might have been had adjustments been made. By the same token, however, if adjustments have in fact been made which have had the effect of enhancing the disabled person's abilities, then it is those enhanced abilities that should be considered. In all cases the disabled person's abilities must be considered as they in fact were at the material time (and not as they might have been if the adjustments had been made in the former case or had they not been made in the latter case).[38] The Code of Practice gives the following examples:

A disabled person who applies for an administrative job which includes typing is not allowed to use her own adapted keyboard (even though it would have been reasonable for the employer to allow this) and types a test document at 30 wpm. Her speed with the adapted keyboard would have been 50 wpm. A non-disabled candidate is given the job because her typing speed on the test was 45 wpm with the same accuracy rate. This is not direct discrimination, as the comparator is a non-disabled person typing at 30 wpm.[39]

A disabled person with arthritis who applies for a similar job is allowed to use an adapted keyboard and types a test document at 50 wpm. A non-disabled candidate types at 30 wpm with the same accuracy rate. However, the disabled candidate is rejected because of prejudice and the other candidate is offered the job instead. This is direct discrimination, as the comparator would be a person not having arthritis who could type at 50 wpm.[40]

The question whether any treatment was less favourable as compared to that afforded an appropriate comparator and the question whether or not the treatment was on the ground of a disabled person's disability are often closely related. In such circumstances a single enquiry might be more appropriate: 'did the claimant, on the proscribed ground, receive less favourable treatment than others?'[41] This can be most simply analysed by asking the question 'Why' a person was treated as they were: if it was on the ground of their disability then

---

[37] See below, at 5.2.2.   [38] Code of Practice, paragraph 4.22.

[39] But the disabled person would be likely to have good claims in respect of two other forms of discrimination: a failure to make reasonable adjustments and disability-related discrimination; see 5.2.2 and 5.2.3 below. Code of Practice, paragraph 4.22.

[40] Code of Practice, paragraph 4.22.

[41] *Shamoon, supra* note 23, *per* Lord Nicholls at paragraph 8.

they were plainly treated less favourably than a person not possessing those characteristics. If not, then they were not:[42]

Thus, on this footing also, the less favourable treatment issue is incapable of being decided without deciding the reason-why issue. And the decision on the reason-why issue will also provide the answer to the less-favourable-treatment issue. This analysis seems . . . to point to the conclusion that . . . tribunals may sometimes be able to avoid arid and confusing disputes about the identification of the appropriate comparator by concentrating primarily on why the claimant was treated as she was. Was it on the proscribed ground which is the foundation of the application? . . . If [so] . . . there will be usually no difficulty in deciding whether the treatment afforded to the claimant on the proscribed ground, was less favourable than was or would have been afforded to others.[43]

The 'reason why' question must, however, be distinguished from any question of intent or motivation, which are not required. See 5.2.1.3 below.

5.2.1.3. *On the ground of the disabled person's disability*
In determining whether treatment was on the ground of a disabled person's disability, a simple causation test is to be applied: 'But for' the complainant's disability status would he or she have been treated as he or she was?[44] Disability status need not be the sole ground for the treatment complained of so long as it has a significant influence on[45] or was an important factor[46] in the outcome.

It is important to bear in mind that motive and intention are not material. A person may have a very benign motive for treating a person less favourably on the ground of their disability or on some other objectionable ground (perhaps to protect them from hostility from others[47]) but this is immaterial:[48]

[I]n every case it is necessary to enquire why the complainant received less favourable treatment. This is the crucial question. Was it on [proscribed] grounds . . . ? Or was it for some other reason, for instance, because the complainant was not so well qualified for the job? Save in obvious cases, answering the crucial question will call for some consideration of the mental processes of the alleged discriminator. Treatment, favourable or unfavourable is a consequence which follows from a decision. Direct evidence of a deci-

---

[42] *Shamoon, supra* note 22, at paragraph 10.   [43] *Ibid.* at paragraphs 10 and 11.

[44] *James v Eastleigh Borough Council* [1990] 2 AC 751, [1990] IRLR 288; *R v Birmingham City Council ex parte EOC, supra* note 21.

[45] *Nagarajan v London Regional Transport* [2000] 1 AC 501, [1999] ICR 877, [1999] IRLR 572 at paragraph 14, *per* Lord Nicholls.

[46] *Owen and Briggs v James* [1982] ICR 618, [1982] IRLR 502, in a claim of direct race discrimination but on an issue that would not appear to be materially affected by the difference in the definition of direct discrimination. See also *(1) Chamberlain Solicitors (2) Mr T Emezie v Ms I Emokpae* [2004] IRLR 592.

[47] See *Smyth, supra* note 30.

[48] *Nagarajan v London Regional Transport, supra* note 45; see also *R v Commission for Racial Equality ex parte Westminster City Council, supra* note 31, concerning the withdrawal of an offer of employment to a black road sweeper by a manager who feared industrial action in consequence, which was held to be racially discriminatory.

sion to discriminate on racial grounds will seldom be forthcoming. Usually the grounds of the decision will have to be deduced, or inferred, from the surrounding circumstances.

The crucial question just mentioned is to be distinguished sharply from a second and different question: if the discriminator treated the complainant less favourably on [proscribed] grounds, why did he do so? The latter question is strictly beside the point when deciding whether an act of . . . discrimination occurred.[49]

The reason why an alleged discriminator acts as they do is therefore irrelevant.

Unintentional, accidental, and benign acts of less favourable treatment are covered by the direct discrimination provisions where they are done on the grounds of a disabled person's disability. This might occur particularly where there is a reliance on, for example, stereotyping.[50]

[If] the less favourable treatment occurs because of the employer's generalised, or stereotypical, assumptions about the disability or its effects, it is likely to be direct discrimination. This is because an employer would not normally make such assumptions about a non-disabled person, but would instead consider his individual abilities.[51]

A blind woman is not short-listed for a job involving computers because the employer wrongly assumes that blind people cannot use them. The employer makes no attempt to look at the individual circumstances. The employer has treated the woman less favourably than other people by not short-listing her for the job. The treatment was on the ground of the woman's disability (because assumptions would not have been made about a non-disabled person).[52]

In addition, less favourable treatment that is disability-specific, or which arises out of prejudice about disability (or about a particular type of disability) is also likely to amount to direct discrimination.

An employer seeking a shop assistant turns down a disabled applicant with a severe facial disfigurement solely on the ground that other employees would be uncomfortable working alongside him. This would amount to direct discrimination and would be unlawful.[53]

Discrimination may be unconscious as well as conscious. People hold prejudices that they do not admit even to themselves and disabled people are entitled to be and are, as a matter of law, protected against unintentional discrimination as well as intentional discrimination.[54]

5.2.1.4. *Proving direct discrimination*
There is specific provision regarding the burden of proof and the shifting of it in certain circumstances. This is described in Chapter 11 below.

---

[49] *Nagarajan, supra* note 45, *per* Lord Nicholls at paragraphs 13–14.
[50] *Coleman v Sky Rail Oceanic Ltd* [1981] ICR 864, [1981] IRLR 398; *Horsey v Dyfed County Council* [1982] ICR 755, [1982] IRLR 395.
[51] Employment Code of Practice, paragraph 4.8.   [52] *Ibid.*
[53] Employment Code of Practice, paragraph 4.9.
[54] *Nagarajan v London Regional Transport, supra* note 45; *King v Great Britain China Centre* [1992] ICR 516, [1991] IRLR 513; Employment Code of Practice, paragraph 4.11.

However, in the context of direct discrimination there has been much relevant guidance from the courts on proving direct discrimination, particularly in cases where the ground for the treatment is not overt (as, for example, in the case of abuse). That guidance was summarized most recently by Lord Justice Sedley in *Anya v University of Oxford and another*:[55]

Deciding such questions is not easy. The problem was classically addressed in this court by Neill LJ in *King v Great Britain China Centre* [1992] ICR 516. In a well known passage, at pp 528–529, which the industrial tribunal clearly had in mind, he summarised the relevant principles in this way:

> 'From [the] several authorities it is possible, I think, to extract the following principles and guidance. (1) It is for the applicant who complains of . . . discrimination to make out his or her case. Thus if the applicant does not prove the case on the balance of probabilities he or she will fail. [*This is now to be treated as qualified by the burden of proof changes.*[56]] (2) It is important to bear in mind that it is unusual to find direct evidence of . . . discrimination [on a proscribed ground]. Few employers will be prepared to admit such discrimination even to themselves. In some cases the discrimination will not be ill-intentioned but merely based on an assumption that "he or she would not have fitted in". (3) The outcome of the case will therefore usually depend on what inferences it is proper to draw from the primary facts found by the tribunal. These inferences can include, in appropriate cases, any inferences that it is just and equitable to draw . . . from an evasive or equivocal reply to a questionnaire.[57] (4) Though there will be some cases where, for example, the non-selection of the applicant for a post or for promotion is clearly not on [proscribed] . . . grounds, a finding of discrimination and a finding of a difference in [status[58]] will often point to the possibility of . . . discrimination. In such circumstances the tribunal will look to the employer for an explanation. If no explanation is then put forward or if the tribunal considers the explanation to be inadequate or unsatisfactory it will be legitimate for the tribunal to infer that the discrimination was on [proscribed] . . . grounds. This is not a matter of law but, as May LJ put it in *North West Thames Regional Health Authority v Noone* [1988] ICR 813, 822, "almost common sense". (5) . . . At the conclusion of all the evidence the tribunal should make findings as to the primary facts and draw such inferences as they consider proper from those facts. They should then reach a conclusion on the balance of probabilities, bearing in mind both the difficulties which face a person who complains of unlawful discrimination and the fact that it is for the complainant to prove his or her case.'

It should be made clear that, when Neill LJ refers under head (4) to discrimination, he means it in its literal, not its objectionable, sense: that is to say, he is referring simply to a choice or a process of selection such as occurred here. It is not unduly onerous, as has sometimes been suggested, to proceed from the simple fact of such a choice, if it is accompanied by difference in [status], to a request for an explanation. In the allocation of jobs

---

[55] [2001] EWCA Civ 405, [2001] ICR 847, paragraphs 7–8, *per* Lord Justice Sedley. See also *Qureshi v Victoria University of Manchester* now reported at [2001] ICR 863 for the very helpful guidance of Lord Justice Mummery.

[56] Author's notes in square brackets. See further Chapter 11 below.

[57] For the questionnaire procedure, see Chapter 11 below.

[58] Eg race, sex, or disability status.

by any sensibly-run institution, the explanation will be straightforward: the candidates were interviewed by an unbiased panel on an equal footing, using common criteria which contained no obvious or latent elements capable of favouring one . . . group over another; and the best one was chosen. By parity of reasoning, evidence that one or more members of the panel were not unbiased, or that equal opportunities procedures were not used when they should have been, may point to the possibility of conscious or unconscious . . . bias having entered into the process.

It is important in all cases to have regard to the circumstantial evidence where such evidence might indicate one way or another whether objectionable discrimination has occurred. Such evidence might include evidence relating to an alleged discriminator's compliance with good equal opportunities practice (see the observations of Lord Justice Sedley above) and compliance with the relevant provisions of the Codes of Practice. Statistical evidence may be relevant where it suggests a discernible pattern of treatment by the alleged discriminator towards a particular group.[59] In addition, the questionnaire procedure is a very important tool for the drawing of inferences. The questionnaire procedure is explained in Chapter 11 below. An Employment Tribunal is entitled to infer direct discrimination from all such evidence (and since the burden of proof changes may be *required* so to do[60]).

In considering the surrounding circumstances, an Employment Tribunal is not required to determine that they themselves are tainted with disability discrimination (though if they are—eg in the case of disabilist abuse—that will be very relevant indeed). Instead a tribunal is required to make primary findings of fact on all the circumstantial evidence relied upon and then decide, having regard to those primary findings, whether or not the proper inference to draw from all those facts is an inference of unlawful discrimination in respect of the particular complaint of disability discrimination made.

As observed above (see paragraph 5.2.1.2) unreasonable treatment without more is not objectionable discrimination. However, 'hostility *may* justify an inference' of discrimination 'if there is nothing else to explain it: whether there is such an explanation . . . will depend not on a theoretical possibility that the employer behaves equally badly to [all] employees . . . but on evidence that he does'.[61] Such an inference may also be rebutted by the employer leading evidence of a genuine non-discriminatory reason for the hostility.[62]

---

[59] *West Midlands PTE v Singh* [1988] ICR 614, [1998] IRLR 186.

[60] See Chapter 11 below.

[61] *Anya, supra* note 55, at paragraph 14, *per* Lord Justice Sedley.

[62] *Bahl v (1) Law Society (2) Robert Sayer (3) Jane Betts* [2004] EWCA Civ 1070, [2004] IRLR 799.

5.2.1.5. *Absence of a justification defence*

It is important to bear in mind that direct discrimination *cannot* be justified. However benign, well intentioned, or non-deliberate it may appear to be, no defence of justification is available in a claim of direct discrimination.[63]

5.2.2. The Duties to Make Reasonable Adjustments

By section 3A(2) DDA, 'a person . . . discriminates against a disabled person if he fails to comply with a duty to make reasonable adjustments imposed on him in relation to the disabled person'.

The duty to make reasonable adjustments in the context of employment and related activities is described in the first place by section 4A(1) of the DDA which provides that:

(1) Where—
    (a) a provision, criterion or practice applied by or on behalf of an employer, or
    (b) any physical feature of premises occupied by the employer,
places the disabled person concerned at a substantial disadvantage in comparison with persons who are not disabled, it is the duty of the employer to take such steps as it is reasonable, in all the circumstances of the case, for him to have to take in order to prevent the provision, criterion or practice, or feature, having that effect.

By section 4A(2) 'the disabled person concerned' means—

    (a) In the case of a provision, criterion or practice for determining to whom employment should be offered, any disabled person who is, or has notified the employer that he may be, an applicant for that employment;
    (b) in any other case a disabled person who is—
        (i) an applicant for the employment concerned, or
        (ii) an employee of the employer concerned.

The duty has changed in consequence of the 2003 Regulations.[64] The introduction of a requirement that reasonable adjustments be made in respect of 'a provision, criterion or practice' follows from the Directive.[65] It is intended to address the requirement that Member States outlaw indirect disability discrimination in the employment and related fields.[66] Indirect discrimination in the Directive is defined so as to address indirectly discriminatory provisions, criteria, and practices.[67] Though the duty to make reasonable adjustments goes some

---

[63] Section 3A(4) DDA. This is consistent with the position under sections 1(1)(a) of the SDA and the RRA (direct sex and race discrimination) but is not uncontroversial: see Bowers and Moran, 'Justification in Direct Sex Discrimination Law: Breaking the Taboo' (2003) 31 ILJ 307; Gill and Monaghan, 'Justification in Direct Discrimination: Taboo Upheld' (2003) 32 ILJ 115.

[64] SI 2003/1673.   [65] 2000/78/EC.

[66] 'Towards Equality and Diversity, Implementing the Employment and Race Directives' (2001), The Cabinet Office, 46.

[67] See Chapter 3 above, at 3.2.2.

way to addressing indirect discrimination, there is considerable concern about the limits of the duty. It is not anticipatory in nature (this might be contrasted with the meaning given to indirect discrimination in the Directive[68]) and it requires an employer to know of a disabled person's disability (or at least reasonably be expected to know).[69] It is therefore by no means entirely clear that the duties as described in section 4A give proper effect to the Directive.[70]

The duty arises in respect of all employment-related activities, namely recruitment, employment, dismissal, and other activities arising out of and closely connected with the employment relationship.[71] The scope of the duty is wider than before the 2003 Regulations came into force. Unlike the previous position, the duty applies unequivocally to 'dismissals' and 'detriments'. It also applies to all employers, however few their employees,[72] so that it applies now even to private households. Section 6 of the DDA (in force prior to the 2003 Regulations) set out a number of factors which, in particular, were required to be taken into account in determining whether it was reasonable for an adjustment to have to be made by an employer (see below). The 2003 Regulations add two new factors:

• the nature of the employer's activities and the size of his undertaking; and

• where the step would be taken in relation to a private household the extent to which taking it would
  —disrupt the household; or
  —disrupt any person residing there.[73]

The DDA also sets out some specific examples of steps that an employer might have to take (under section 18B DDA). These reflect the examples previously provided under section 6 DDA prior to 1 October 2004. To the existing examples have been added express reference to training (see further 5.2.2.5 below).

In addition the defence of justification, which was available in a case where there had been a failure to make reasonable adjustments, has now been repealed.[74]

Though the duty is owed at the recruitment stage as well as in respect of existing and ex-employees, it is likely that the extent of the duty will vary depending on the position of the disabled person concerned. Thus, for example, it is likely

---

[68] *Ibid.* and 3.4. It can be noted that the DRC has recommended that the duty should be anticipatory to ensure institutional barriers are properly addressed: 'Disability Equality: Making it Happen, First Review of the Disability Discrimination Act 1995' (2003) DRC, 27.

[69] Section 4A(3) DDA.

[70] For remedies in respect of the same see Chapter 3 above.

[71] See section 4 and section 16A DDA. See also Chapter 6 below.

[72] The small employer exemption has been repealed: ex-section 7 DDA.

[73] Section 18B DDA. In the latter case this reflects the fact that the small employer exemption has been repealed (ex-section 7 DDA).

[74] Section 5(4) DDA is repealed.

that more extensive duties will be owed to employees than to people who are merely thinking about applying for a job. More extensive duties are likely to be owed to current employees than to former employees.[75] But each case will always turn on its own facts.

Importantly a breach of the duty gives rise to a discrete complaint of discrimination (so long as the treatment or activity concerned falls within the scope of one of the unlawful acts). It is not dependent on a finding of direct discrimination or less favourable treatment.[76]

5.2.2.1. *Knowledge of the disabled person's disability*

As has been seen above, and as will be seen below, it is not necessary for an employer to know that a disabled person has a disability within the meaning of the DDA for the purposes of the direct discrimination provisions[77] or for the purposes of disability-related discrimination.[78]

However, in relation to the duty to make adjustments, no duty is imposed upon an employer in relation to a disabled person if the employer does not know and could not reasonably be expected to know—

• in the case of an applicant or potential applicant, that the disabled person concerned is, or may be, an applicant for the employment; or

• in any case, that that person has a disability and is likely to be put to a substantial disadvantage by reason of a provision, criterion, or practice applied by or physical feature of premises, or occupied by, the employer.[79]

If an employer's agent or employee, such as an occupational health adviser or personnel officer, knows in their capacity as such that the disabled person concerned has a disability, an employer will not usually be able to claim that it did not know of that disability, for the purposes of the reasonable adjustment duties.[80] Importantly, therefore, knowledge by an employer's agent or employee will be imputed to the employer, save in the most exceptional of circumstances. The Employment Code of Practice recommends that employers ensure that where information about disabled people comes through different channels there is a means in place (with appropriate respect for confidentiality) for bringing that information together so as to make it easier for the employer to fulfil its duties under the DDA.[81]

---

[75] Employment Code of Practice, paragraph 5.6.

[76] Section 3A(2) DDA. *Clark v TDG Ltd t/a Novacold* [1999] ICR 951, [1999] IRLR 318.

[77] Though of course knowledge may be highly material to the question whether any less favourable treatment was on the ground of the disabled person's disability.

[78] To establish less favourable treatment for a reason relating to disability, knowledge of the disabled person's disability is not required: *HJ Heinz Co Ltd v Kenrick* [2000] ICR 491, [2000] IRLR 144. In this respect the less favourable treatment for a reason relating to disability test is an objective one.

[79] Section 4A(3).   [80] Employment Code of Practice, paragraph 5.15.

[81] *Ibid.*

However, where an employer arranges for the provision of services to employees independently of the employer, information received by the providers of those services will not necessarily be imputed to the employer. Thus where an employer contracts with an agency to provide independent counselling services to its employees under contracts which provide that counsellors are not acting on the employer's behalf while acting in that role, any information about a person's disability obtained during such counselling will not ordinarily be imputed to the employer and accordingly will not ordinarily trigger a duty to make adjustments.[82]

A transferee of an undertaking will be deemed to have relevant knowledge obtained by the transferor.[83]

The burden of establishing absence of the requisite knowledge rests with an employer, who must show that he did not know and could not reasonably be expected to have known of the disability in question.

In *Ridout v TC Group*[84] an applicant for employment stated in her medical questionnaire that she had photosensitive epilepsy, controlled by medication. She was not contacted about interview arrangements and, in the event, the interview room had bright fluorescent lighting. When she entered the room, wearing sunglasses around her neck, she did make some comments as to the effects of the lighting and that she might be disadvantaged by it. However, the employers assumed that this was an explanation relating to her sunglasses. In the event Ms Ridout never used the sunglasses and did not tell the employers that she was in any way unwell or felt disadvantaged. The Employment Tribunal dismissed her complaint that the employers had failed to make a reasonable adjustment to the physical features of the premises (that is, by the lighting) on the basis that the applicant could have been 'much more forthcoming about what she regarded as being required'. The Employment Appeal Tribunal dismissed Ms Ridout's appeal on the grounds that she had a very rare form of epilepsy and the tribunal was entitled to conclude that no reasonable employer could be expected to know, without being told explicitly by her, that the arrangements which were made for the interview might disadvantage her. This was so notwithstanding that Ms Ridout had informed the employers that she had a disability and that she had 'photosensitive' epilepsy indicating plainly that this related to 'light'. Given that the Directive requires, in the case of disability discrimination, that indirect discrimination will only be excusable where it is objectively justified or where the

---

[82] *Ibid.* paragraph 5.16.

[83] *Jolley v (1) Namdarkham (2) Greene King Retail Services Ltd* (ET Case No 2602411/03) [2004] EOR 132, 21. This is consistent with the purpose of the Transfer of Undertakings (Protection of Employment) Regulations 1981, SI 1981/1794. If a transferee were to evade the reach of the DDA by arguing that they did not have relevant knowledge, when such knowledge was available to the transferor, arguably Regulation 5(2) (all transferor's duties and liabilities shall be transferred to the transferee) would not be given full effect.

[84] [1998] IRLR 628.

employer is obliged to and has provided reasonable accommodations[85] such an interpretation, if it were to be followed now, would not give proper effect to the Directive. As far as the Directive is concerned, knowledge of the disability does not appear to be requisite and, in any event, does not appear to impose a burden on an employee any greater than that described by the circumstances in *Ridout*. The *Ridout* case can therefore be regarded as unduly restrictive.

However, on any analysis, once the duty arises, the issue of knowledge becomes immaterial. The question whether the employer has discharged the duty upon him is to be determined by an objective test regardless of knowledge (actual or imputed) as to the extent and effects of that disability.[86]

5.2.2.2. *Provisions, criteria, and practices*

The words 'provision', 'criterion', and 'practice' are not exclusively defined by the DDA. However, they are words capable of attaching to a wide range of arrangements. Section 18D DDA provides explicitly that 'provision, criterion or practice includes any arrangements'.

These words are clearly wider in scope than 'condition' and 'requirement' (though wide enough to embrace them) found in the indirect discrimination provisions of the SDA and the RRA as originally enacted. Both the SDA and the RRA have been amended since the enactment of Community legislation requiring that the concept of indirect discrimination provided for in domestic law be wide enough to protect against indirectly discriminatory provisions, criteria, and practices.[87] It can properly be assumed therefore that Parliament considered that the concepts of 'condition' and 'requirement' which had before then formed the basis of the only indirect discrimination provisions in the SDA and the RRA were too narrow to meet the requirements of Community law. Certainly, the words 'condition' and 'requirement' in the SDA and RRA have been narrowly interpreted so as to attach only to mandatory rules.[88] This has meant that challenges could not be mounted to criteria which were 'desirable' or non-mandatory. Plainly, the expressions found in the DDA reasonable adjustment duty are wider than this.

---

[85] Namely the taking of appropriate measures, where needed in a particular case, to enable a person with a disability to have access to, participate in, or advance in employment, or to undergo training (unless such measures would impose a disproportionate burden on the employer): Article 2(2)(b) and Article 5. See further Chapter 3 above.

[86] *Wright v (1) The Governors of Bilton High School (2) Warwickshire County Council Respondents* [2002] ICR 1463. And see *British Gas Services Ltd v McCaull* [2001] IRLR 60.

[87] Section 1(2)(b) SDA and section 1(1A) RRA both inserted in consequence of, in the first case, the 'Burden of Proof' Directive 97/80/EC and, in the second case, the 'Race Directive' 2000/43/EC. It should be noted that these new definitions of indirect discrimination in the SDA and RRA apply only to certain of the unlawful acts created therein. A full discussion is outside the scope of this work.

[88] *Meer v London Borough of Tower Hamlets* [1988] IRLR 399. Though there was a liberalizing of this very strict approach in later years, exemplified by, for example, the case of *Falkirk Council v Whyte* [1997] IRLR 560, this was because of the impact of European Community law in the field of gender discrimination in particular.

The duty will apply to procedures, for example, for determining whom to select for employment, contractual arrangements, working conditions, arrangements for determining whom to dismiss, and dismissal procedures, even where the rules are non-mandatory (as in the case, for example, of 'desirable' or 'preferred' qualifications).[89]

5.2.2.3. *Physical features*

Section 18D(2) DDA defines a 'physical feature', in relation to any premises, as including:

any of the following (whether permanent or temporary)—
(a) any feature arising from the design or construction of a building of the premises,
(b) any feature on the premises of any approach to, exit from or access to such a building,
(c) any fixtures, fittings, furnishings, furniture, equipment or material in or on the premises,
(d) any other physical element or quality of any land comprised in the premises.

Thus the duty to make reasonable adjustments in respect of physical features is very wide. Physical features include steps, stairways, kerbs, exterior surfaces and paving, parking areas, building entrances and exits (including emergency escape routes), internal and external doors, gates, toilets and washing facilities, lighting and ventilation, lifts and escalators, floor coverings, signs, furniture, and temporary or movable items, amongst other things.[90]

There may be legal impediments or consequences to making an adjustment to a physical feature of premises. Various measures address those circumstances and these are discussed in 5.6 below.

5.2.2.4. *When does the duty arise?*

As can be seen the duty to make reasonable adjustments arises only where a provision, criterion, or practice applied by or on behalf of an employer, or any physical feature of premises occupied by the employer, in fact places the disabled person concerned[91] at a substantial disadvantage compared with people who are not disabled. The duty is not 'anticipatory' (as discussed in 5.2.2 above) and thus substantial disadvantage must be shown in the particular case.

'Substantial' for the purposes of measuring the disadvantage simply means more than 'minor' or 'trivial'.[92]

It is not necessary for a disabled person to point to an actual non-disabled person who is not placed at a substantial disadvantage by reason of the particular

---

[89] Employment Code of Practice, paragraphs 5.8, 7.1 *et seq*, 8.1 *et seq*, and 8.24 *et seq.*

[90] Employment Code of Practice, paragraph 5.10.

[91] As to which, see 5.2.2 above.

[92] Employment Code, paragraph 5.11. See also *Cave v Goodwin* [2001] EWCA Civ 391. See further *HJ Heinz Co Ltd v Kenrick, supra* note 78 (in the context of justifications, on which see 5.2.3.5 below).

provision, criterion, or practice or physical feature of the premises occupied by an employer. In addition, the fact that the same would not substantially disadvantage another disabled person is irrelevant. The duty is owed specifically to the individual disabled person:[93] it is not a duty owed to disabled people at large.[94]

5.2.2.5. *How is the duty discharged?*
In determining what adjustments an employer must make for the purposes of discharging the duty upon him, regard must be had to section 18B DDA. This provides guidance on whether it might be reasonable for a person to have to take a particular step in order to comply with a duty to make reasonable adjustments (in the employment and related fields) and provides examples of steps which a person might need to take in order to comply with such a duty.

As to the sorts of steps an employer might have to take in order to comply with the duty to make reasonable adjustments once it arises, the following examples are provided (and they are examples only):

• making adjustments to premises;
• allocating some of the disabled person's duties to another person;
• transferring him to fill an existing vacancy;
• altering his hours of working or training;
• assigning him to a different place of work or training;
• allowing him to be absent during working or training hours for rehabilitation, assessment, or treatment;
• giving, or arranging for, training or mentoring (whether for the disabled person or any other person) [which might include eg disability awareness training];
• acquiring or modifying equipment;
• modifying instructions or reference manuals;
• modifying procedures for testing or assessment;
• providing a reader or interpreter;
• providing supervision or other support.[95]

The Employment Code of Practice gives many practical examples of the steps an employer might have to take under each of these heads, including the following:[96]

---

[93] Employment Code of Practice, paragraph 5.4.

[94] And this might be contrasted with the duties under Part III in respect of service providers and certain duties under Part IV in respect of education providers; see 5.7 and 5.9 below.

[95] Section 18B(2)(a) to (l).

[96] Employment Code of Practice, paragraphs 5.18 *et seq.*

An employer makes structural or other physical changes such as widening a doorway, providing a ramp or moving furniture for a wheelchair user; relocates light switches, door handles or shelves for someone who has difficulty in reaching; or provides appropriate contrast in decor to help the safe mobility of a visually impaired person.

A disabled man returns to work after a six-month period of absence due to a stroke. His employer pays for him to see a work mentor, and allows time off to see the mentor, to help with his loss of confidence following the onset of his disability.

The format of instructions and manuals might need to be modified for some disabled people (eg produced in Braille or on audio tape) and instructions for people with learning disabilities might need to be conveyed orally with individual demonstration.

In some cases a reasonable adjustment will not work without the cooperation of other employees and (subject to considerations of confidentiality) employers must ensure that such cooperation is provided.[97] An employer who argues that his staff are obstructive and unhelpful is unlikely to be able to avail himself of any defence under the DDA.[98]

In determining whether it is reasonable for a person to have to take a particular step in order to comply with the duty to make reasonable adjustments, the following factors must be had regard to:

- the extent to which taking the step would prevent the effect in relation to which the duty is imposed;
- the extent to which it is practicable for him to take the step;
- the financial and other costs which would be incurred by him in taking the step and the extent to which taking it would disrupt any of his activities;
- the extent of his financial and other resources;
- the availability to him of financial or other assistance with respect to taking the step;
- the nature of his activities and the size of his undertaking;
- where the step would be taken in relation to a private household the extent to which it would
  —disrupt that household; or
  —disturb any person residing there.[99]

Examples from the Employment Code of Practice include the following:[100]

A disabled employee cannot physically access the stationery cupboard at work. It is unlikely to be reasonable for the employer to have to make the cupboard accessible, unless distribution of stationery was a significant part of the employee's job.

---

[97] Employment Code of Practice, paragraph 5.22.

[98] An employer is, of course, liable for the acts of his employees: section 58(1) DDA. See Chapter 10 below.

[99] Section 18B(1)(a) to (g) DDA.   [100] Paragraphs 5.28–5.31.

It might be impracticable for an employer who needs to appoint an employee urgently to have to wait for an adjustment to be made to an entrance. How long it might be reasonable for the employer to have to wait would depend on the circumstances. However, it might be possible to make a temporary adjustment in the meantime, such as using another, less convenient entrance.

It would be reasonable for an employer to have to spend at least as much on an adjustment to enable the retention of a disabled person—including any retraining—as might be spent on recruiting and training a replacement.

Many adjustments, of course, involve little or no cost or disruption to an employer and in such circumstances it is very likely to be reasonable for an employer to have to make them.[101] Even where there is an increased cost, regard must be had to the overall cost effectiveness of taking a particular step (having regard to the difficulties that might arise otherwise, the length of an employee's likely employment, and so on). In addition to those factors described above, to which the DDA expressly requires regard must be had, other factors may be relevant to determining whether or not the taking of a particular step is reasonable. The Employment Code of Practice gives the following examples:

• effect on other employees;
• adjustments made for other disabled employees;
• the extent to which the disabled person is willing to co-operate.[102]

Particular illustrations of the application of the duty in the employment sphere are provided in Chapter 6 below.

There is now a body of case-law indicating that the duty to make reasonable adjustments imposes a real and significant burden on an employer to identify and take such steps as it is reasonable for him to take in order to prevent the substantial disadvantage which triggers the imposition of the duty. Thus, in *Cosgrove v Caesar and Howie*[103] the Employment Appeal Tribunal held that an Employment Tribunal had erred in regarding the employee's views and that of a doctor as decisive on the question of reasonable adjustments. The employer has a duty to consider whether reasonable adjustments could be made even though there is no guarantee that they will work. In addition it is incumbent upon the employer to consider the extent to which *all* the adjustments requested by an employee might alleviate any of his or her symptoms and, as the case may be, assist a return to work.[104]

The duty is therefore compelling. It has been held to embrace the possibility of adjusting sick pay entitlement so as to secure sick pay for a disabled employee in circumstances where it would not otherwise be payable,[105] and an adjustment

---

[101] Employment Code of Practice, paragraph 5.25.
[102] Employment Code of Practice, paragraph 5.42.   [103] [2001] IRLR 653.
[104] *Fu v London Borough of Camden* [2001] IRLR 186. See also *Nottinghamshire County Council v Meikle* [2004] EWCA Civ 859, [2004] IRLR 703.
[105] *London Clubs Management v Hood* [2001] IRLR 719; *Nottinghamshire CC v Meikle, supra* note 104.

to permit an employee to work from home on a temporary basis so as to ensure that his skills were maintained in circumstances where the job was one which could not be done permanently from home.[106] In addition a failure to make adjustments to a grievance/harassment procedure may breach the duty.[107] In *Beart v HM Prison Service*[108] the Court of Appeal upheld an Employment Tribunal's decision that there had been a breach of the duty to make reasonable adjustments in circumstances where the complainant was not offered a transfer to work at another prison when the medical evidence was such that she would not be able to return to work at the prison in which she was presently employed due to depression which had resulted from conflict with another member of staff. In *Beart* the Employment Appeal Tribunal gave the following guidance:

[The duty to make adjustments] does not require of a particular step that it should prevent the effect in question but that the employer, in considering whether he was under a duty to take the step, is entitled to have regard to the extent to which the step would prevent the effect in question. There will be many steps . . . which, ahead of their being taken, could not be guaranteed to 'work' in the sense of totally removing the disadvantage which the disabled person is encountering but that, of itself, is no reason to absolve the employer from the duty to take it or is such, without more, to deny the step the appellation 'reasonable'. The Tribunal's view that there was substantial possibility that relocation would have 'worked' was, in effect, a finding that even if the Prison Service had considered the merits and demerits of a relocation (which seems not to have been proved), the case for not taking the step on the grounds that it would or might not totally succeed had not been demonstrated and would not in any event have availed the Service.[109]

In addition, the duty to make adjustments may encompass the assessment by the employer of what adjustments may be necessary. Thus, in *Mid Staffordshire General Hospitals NHS Trust v Cambridge*[110] the Employment Appeal Tribunal held that the Employment Tribunal did not fall into error when it found that the employers had failed to comply with the duty to make reasonable adjustments when they did not carry out an assessment to enable them to decide what steps would be reasonable to prevent the complainant from being at a disadvantage:

A proper assessment of what is required to eliminate the disabled person's disadvantage is a necessary part of the duty imposed . . . since that duty cannot be complied with unless the employer makes a proper assessment of what needs to be done. The submission that the Tribunal had imposed on the employer an antecedent duty which was a gloss [on the statutory provisions] could not be accepted. The making of that assessment cannot be separated from the duty imposed . . . because it is a necessary precondition to the fulfilment of that duty and therefore part of it. There must be many cases in which a disabled person has been placed at a substantial disadvantage in the workplace, but in which the

---

[106] *Royal College of Nursing v Ehdaie* [2002] EAT 0789/00.   [107] *Ibid.*

[108] [2003] EWCA Civ 119, [2003] ICR 1068, [2003] IRLR 238.

[109] EAT 650/01 paragraph 29, *per* Lindsay J (President). This was not interfered with by the Court of Appeal.

[110] [2003] IRLR 566.

employer does not know what it ought to do to ameliorate the disadvantage without making enquiries. To say that a failure to make those enquiries would not amount to a breach of the duty imposed on employers . . . would render [the statutory provision] practically unworkable in many cases. That could not have been Parliament's intention.

It is now plain that the duty to make adjustments in the employment field extends to transferring an employee to another post at a higher grade or level of pay without a competitive interview if that would remove the disadvantage the disabled person would otherwise face.[111] This is consistent with the wording of section 18B(2)(c), which envisages that a transfer to an existing vacancy may be a reasonable adjustment without qualifying that by any words indicating that the same must be at the same or a lower grade. As Baroness Hale has said, the DDA 'does not regard the differences between disabled people and others as irrelevant. It does not expect each to be treated in the same way. It expects reasonable adjustments to be made to cater for the special needs of disabled people. It necessarily entails an element of more favourable treatment.'[112]

The duty to make adjustments may not extend to matters unrelated to the job, so that employers may not be under a statutory duty to provide carers to attend to their employees' personal needs such as assistance in going to the toilet.[113] However, an employer might still be obliged to make adjustments to accommodate the presence of a personal carer provided by the disabled employee himself.[114]

In all cases it must be remembered that the duty to make adjustments is on the employer, and it is no answer that the disabled person has not shown what adjustments would have been reasonable.[115]

5.2.2.6. *Applying the reasonable adjustment duty*
In *Morse v Wiltshire County Council*[116] the Employment Appeal Tribunal gave guidance on the proper approach to applying the reasonable adjustment duty, as follows:

Firstly, the tribunal must decide whether the provisions of [section 4A DDA][117] impose a . . . duty on the employer in the circumstances of the particular case. If such a duty is imposed, the tribunal must next decide whether the employer has taken such steps as it is reasonable, in all the circumstances of the case, for him to have to take in order to pre-

---

[111] *Archibald v Fife Council* [2004] UKHL 32, [2004] ICR 954, [2004] IRLR 651, overruling the rather bizarre decision (apparently counter to the purpose of the legislation) of the Scottish Court of Session. For an illustration of the duty in operation, see *Moreland v Northern Ireland Railways Company Ltd* [2000] DCLD 45, 12.

[112] *Archibald, supra* note 111, paragraph 47.

[113] *Kenny v Hampshire Constabulary* [1999] ICR 27, [1999] IRLR 76.

[114] *Ibid.*   [115] *Cosgrove, supra* note 103.

[116] [1998] ICR 1023, [1998] IRLR 352.

[117] This case, of course, referred to the previous provision imposing a duty to make adjustments, namely section 6 DDA. The changes occurring from October 2004 are minimal in respect of the duty to make adjustments: see 5.2.2 above.

vent the [provision, criterion, or practice][118] or feature having the effect of placing the disabled person concerned at a substantial disadvantage in comparison with persons who are not disabled. This in turn involves the tribunal enquiring whether the employer could reasonably have taken any steps including any of the steps set out in [section 18B(2)]. The purpose of [section 18B(2)] is to focus the mind of the employer on possible steps which it might take in compliance with its . . . duty, and to focus the mind of the tribunal when considering whether an employer has failed to comply with a [section 4A] duty. At the same time, the tribunal must have regard to the factors set out in [section 18B(1)].[119]

It may not be necessary for the tribunal to set out in its decision its findings on each of the matters specified in section 18B (ex section 6(4)) DDA: the extent to which a Tribunal must spell out such findings depends on how controversial the issues are. If the Tribunal clearly had the provisions of section 18B in mind that will suffice.[120]

5.2.2.7. *Justification*
No defence of justification is now available where there has been a failure to comply with the duty to make reasonable adjustments.[121]

5.2.3. Disability-Related Discrimination

Section 3A(1) DDA defines disability-related discrimination as follows:

a person discriminates against a disabled person if—
(a) for a reason which relates to the disabled person's disability, he treats him less favourably than he treats or would treat others to whom that reason does not or would not apply, and
(b) he cannot show that the treatment in question is justified.

Such discrimination has always been outlawed in the employment and related fields by the DDA.[122] Notwithstanding the amendments made to the DDA by the 2003 Regulations (and in particular the introduction of protection against

---

[118] *Ibid.*

[119] *Per* Bell J at paragraphs 41–4. It can be noted that the holding in this case that the duty to make adjustments extended to dismissals was overturned by the Court of Appeal in *Clark v Novacold, supra* note 76, in which the Court of Appeal drew a distinction between pre-dismissal breaches of the DDA and the dismissal itself, but the guidance remains good. It can also be noted that the new provisions of the DDA in relation to the duty to make adjustments do cover dismissals so that line of cases remains of historical interest only. See also *Beart v HM Prison Service, supra* note 108.

[120] *Travis v Electronic Data Systems Ltd* [2004] EWCA Civ 880.

[121] Section 5(4) DDA was abolished by the 2003 Regulations. The defence was in any event rendered largely ineffectual by the decision in *Collins v Royal National Theatre Board Ltd* [2004] EWCA Civ 144, [2004] IRLR 395 in which it was held that the only workable construction of section 5(4), in the context of the DDA and its manifest objects, was that it did not permit justification of a breach of section 6 to be established by reference to factors properly relevant to the establishment of a duty under section 6, thus foreshadowing its demise (see also: *Law v Pace Micro Technology plc* [2004] EWCA Civ 923).

[122] Ex-section 5(1) DDA.

'direct' discrimination: see above) it remains an important form of discrimination[123] perhaps overlooks its importance for less overt incidences of discrimination). The same treatment might constitute both direct discrimination and disability-related discrimination,[124] but importantly 'direct' discrimination cannot be 'justified'. Accordingly, 'disability-related discrimination' will only be relevant where the complaint is incapable of amounting to direct discrimination. However, such complaints are likely to remain prominent and, as will be seen below, protection against disability-related discrimination remains very important.[125]

5.2.3.1. *Less favourable treatment*
'Less favourable treatment' has the same meaning as have the same words in 'direct discrimination' (see 5.2.1.1 above).

5.2.3.2. *Reason related to disability*
For disability-related discrimination, it is necessary to determine whether the less favourable treatment of a disabled person was 'for a reason which relates to the disabled person's disability'.

This is a wider concept of discrimination than that afforded by 'direct discrimination'.[126] It does not depend upon the treatment being on the 'ground' of disability but has a much wider reach. It is a concept wide enough to embrace some acts of 'indirect discrimination'.[127] There must, however, be a relationship between the disabled person's disability and the reason for the treatment.[128]

The following are examples of 'disability related' discrimination:

- the dismissal of an employee in consequence of a period of sickness absence caused by disability;[129]

- the refusal to offer an applicant employment because of a history of violent behaviour connected with schizophrenia;[130]

---

[123] The observation that it can be regarded as a 'residual' form of discrimination. See first draft Employment Code of Practice, DRC (changed significantly before issue) paragraph 4.22.

[124] For example, a dismissal in consequence of prolonged sick absence caused by disability, in circumstances where a non-disabled person would not have been dismissed, would constitute both 'direct' discrimination and 'disability-related' discrimination.

[125] Note that this form of discrimination is outlawed in the employment and related fields (section 3A covering the whole of Part 2); in relation to the provision of goods, facilities, and services (section 20(1) DDA); in relation to the disposal and management of premises (section 24(1) DDA); and in relation to the provision of education (sections 28B and 28S DDA); see further below.

[126] See 5.2.1 above.

[127] *Clark v TDG Ltd T/A Novacold, supra* note 76.

[128] *Council of the City of Manchester v (1) Romano (2) Samari, supra* note 8, especially at paragraph 93.

[129] *Clark v TDG Ltd T/A Novacold, supra* note 76; *HJ Heinz Co Ltd v Kenrick, supra* note 78.

[130] *Murray v Newham Citizens' Advice Bureau Ltd* [2003] ICR 643, [2003] IRLR 340.

- The dismissal of an employee with dyslexia for failing to take the minutes of a meeting;[131] and
- the failure to pay full pay when absent on sick leave caused by disability.[132]

The Employment Code of Practice gives the following example.[133]

A woman takes three periods of sickness absence in a two-month period because of her disability, which is multiple sclerosis (MS). Her employer is unaware that she has MS and dismisses her, in the same way that it would dismiss any employee for a similar attendance record. Nevertheless, this is less favourable treatment for a disability-related reason (namely, the woman's record of sickness absence) and would be unlawful unless it can be justified.

5.2.3.3. *Proper comparator*

In determining a claim of disability-related discrimination, the proper comparator will be quite different to that required for direct discrimination. Unlike direct discrimination, in identifying the proper comparator the disability-related characteristics upon which the treatment is based are *ignored*. Accordingly, the proper comparator is a person to whom the reason for the treatment complained of does not or would not apply. This is so because the statutory test requires a comparison between the treatment afforded the disabled employee and the treatment that was or would have been afforded 'others to whom that reason does not or would not apply'. This is not a like-for-like comparison of the sort required by the direct discrimination provisions. The statutory focus is narrower, being the reason for the treatment, and it is that which informs the identity of the proper comparator: a person to whom that reason does not or would not apply. The effect is that, whilst acts of 'direct' discrimination which are explicitly based on a person's disability (abuse, decisions based on stereo-typing prejudice, etc) are covered, so too are incidents of treatment which are disability-neutral (eg no dogs allowed, dismissal after six months' absence, etc).[134]

This is best illustrated by the case of *Clark v TDG Ltd T/A Novacold*.[135] Mr Clark suffered a back injury at work and was diagnosed as having soft tissue injuries around the spine. He was absent for a prolonged period and his employers obtained medical reports which indicated that it was extremely difficult to anticipate his return to work in the near future. Eventually and on that basis his employers dismissed him and he in turn commenced proceedings in disability discrimination. Novacold, his employers, submitted that the reason for dismissing Mr Clark was that he was no longer capable of performing the main func-

---

[131] *Chadwick v Eurodis HB-Electronics Ltd* [2001] EOR DCLD 50, 7.

[132] *Nottinghamshire County Council v Meikle, supra* note 104.

[133] Paragraph 4.31.

[134] Which would be addressed by the indirect discrimination provisions in the context of the SDA and the RRA.

[135] *Supra* note 76.

tions of his job and there were no available or suitable vacancies in alternative work. The Employment Tribunal concluded that there was no discrimination within the meaning of section 3(A)[136] because the proper comparator was another employee who was off work for the same length of time but for a non-disablement reason. The Employment Tribunal concluded that such an employee would have been treated no differently from Mr Clark. This analysis was problematic: indeed it had the potential to seriously undermine the protection afforded by the DDA. The case reached the Court of Appeal, and Lord Justice Mummery analysed this concept of discrimination as follows:

The two questions posed by the statutory provisions are—
(1) Was Mr Clark dismissed for a reason which relates to his disability?
(2) If so, did Novacold treat him less favourably than they would treat others to whom that reason would not apply?
Question (1) is one of fact.
. . .
In order to answer Question (2) it is necessary to compare Novacold's treatment of Mr Clark with the treatment of others to whom 'that reason' would not apply.
What is meant by '*that* reason'?
On the one hand, it is argued on behalf of Novacold that it refers to the whole of the first clause of the paragraph. That imports two requirements: first, the existence of 'a reason' for the treatment (in this case, the dismissal); secondly, the causal link between the reason and the disabled person's disability. It must be a reason 'which relates to the disabled person's disability'. Thus '*that* reason' embraces the significant causal link to the disability. On this approach the person to whom '*that* reason' would not apply would be one who, like the disabled person, is incapable of performing the main functions of his job, but for a reason which does *not* relate to disability . . . On the factual findings of the tribunal this interpretation leads to the conclusion that Mr Clark was not treated less favourably than others incapable of performing the main functions of their job for a non-disability reason.
A contrary interpretation is submitted on behalf of Mr Clark. His argument is that '*that* reason' refers only to the first three words of the paragraph—'for a reason'. The causal link between the reason for the treatment and the disability is not the reason for the treatment. It is not included in the reason for the treatment. The expression 'which relates to the disability' are words added not to identify or amplify the reason, but to specify a link between the reason for the treatment and his disability which enables the disabled person (as opposed to an able-bodied person) to complain of his treatment. That link is irrelevant to the question whether the treatment of the disabled person is for a reason which does not or would not apply to others. On this interpretation, the others to whom '*that* reason' would not apply are persons who would be capable of carrying out the main functions of their job. Those are the 'others' proposed as the proper comparators. This comparison leads to the conclusion that Mr Clark has been treated less favourably; he was dismissed for the reason that he could not perform the main functions of his job, whereas a person capable of performing the main functions of his job would not be dismissed.

---

[136] Ex-section 5(1)(a) of the unamended DDA.

Linguistically section 5(1)(a) is ambiguous. The expression 'that reason' is, as a matter of ordinary language, capable of bearing either of the suggested meanings. The ambiguity must be resolved by recourse to the context of the ambiguous language and to the aim of the legislation.

. . .

In the historical context of discrimination legislation, it is natural to do what the industrial and the appeal tribunal (though 'without great confidence') did, namely to interpret the expression 'that reason' so as to achieve a situation in which a comparison is made of the case of the disabled person with that of an able-bodied person and the comparison is such that the relevant circumstances in the one case are the same, or not materially different, in the other case. This might be reasonably considered to be the obvious way of determining whether a disabled person has been treated less favourably than a person who is not disabled.

But, as already indicated, the 1995 Act adopts a significantly different approach to the protection of disabled persons against less favourable treatment in employment . . .

The result of this approach is that the reason would not apply to others even if their circumstances are different from those of the disabled person. The persons who are performing the main functions of their jobs are 'others' to whom the reason for dismissal of the disabled person (ie inability to perform those functions) would not apply.

In the context of the special sense in which 'discrimination' is defined in section [3A] of the 1995 Act it is more probable that Parliament meant 'that reason' to refer only to the facts constituting the reason for the treatment, and not to include within that reason the added requirement of a causal link with disability: that is more properly regarded as the cause of the reason for the treatment than as in itself a reason for the treatment. This interpretation avoids the difficulties which would be encountered in many cases in seeking to identify what the appeal tribunal referred to as 'the characteristics of the hypothetical comparator' . . .

This interpretation is also consistent with the emphasis on whether the less favourable treatment of the disabled person is shown to be justified. That defence is not available in cases of direct discrimination under the other discrimination Acts.

It is also more consistent with the scheme of the 1995 Act as a whole.[137]

In adopting this analysis and in reaching the conclusion he did, Lord Justice Mummery[138] drew on certain of the observations made by the Minister promoting the Bill during its progression in the Commons. This is discussed further below (see 5.7.2). In summary, Lord Justice Mummery noted that the employer's argument, if accepted, would mean that a restaurant owner could lawfully refuse access to a sight-impaired customer accompanied by an assistance dog so long as he refused access to all customers seeking entry with a dog.[139] Such an approach would obviously undermine the aims of the DDA and would not reflect the intention of Parliament.

The Employment Code of Practice gives the following example.[140]

A disabled woman is refused an administrative job because she cannot type. She cannot type because she has arthritis. A non-disabled person who was unable to type would also

---

[137] Paragraphs 52–63.
[138] With whom the other Lordships agreed.
[139] Paragraphs 68–71.
[140] Paragraph 4.30.

have been turned down. The disability-related reason for the less favourable treatment is the woman's inability to type, and the correct comparator is a person to whom that reason does not apply—that is, someone who can type. Such a person would not have been refused the job. Nevertheless, the disabled woman has been treated less favourably for a disability-related reason and this will be unlawful unless it can be justified. There is no direct discrimination, however, because the comparator for direct discrimination is a person who does not have arthritis, but who is also unable to type.

5.2.3.4. *The relevance of knowledge*

As illustrated by the extract from the Employment Code of Practice above (see 5.2.3.3), knowledge of the person's disability is not required for disability-related discrimination to be made out.

As observed above, nothing in the statutory language requires that the relationship between the disability and the treatment should be judged subjectively through the eyes of the employer. The correct test is an objective one: whether the relationship between less favourable treatment and disability exists, not whether the employer knew of it.[141] If the test were not objective, difficulties would arise 'with credible and honest yet ignorant or obtuse employers who fail to recognise or acknowledge the obvious'.[142]

5.2.3.5. *Justification*

Unlike 'direct' discrimination, 'disability-related discrimination' can be justified.

Section 3A(3) DDA provides that: 'Treatment is justified for the purposes of subsection (1)(b)[143] if, but only if, the reason for it is both material to the circumstances of the particular case and substantial'. The justification defence sets a 'very low' threshold for an employer.[144]

Controversially,[145] in *Jones v Post Office*[146] the Court of Appeal ruled that the function of Employment Tribunals in determining whether justification is made out is 'not very different from the task which they have to perform in cases of unfair dismissal'. In cases of unfair dismissal, a tribunal's role is to determine whether the dismissal was within 'a range of reasonable responses'; in 'justification', it is to consider the materiality and substantiality of the employer's reason: 'In both cases, the members of the tribunal might themselves have come to a different conclusion on the evidence, but they must respect the opinion of the employer, in the one case if it is within the range of reasonable responses and in the other if the reason given is material and substantial'.[147]

---

[141] *HJ Heinz Co Ltd v Kenrick, supra* note 78. And see *London Borough of Hammersmith and Fulham v Farnsworth* [2000] IRLR 691.

[142] *Ibid.* at paragraph 26.   [143] See 5.2.3 above.

[144] *Heinz v Kenrick, supra* note 78.

[145] *DLA*, 'Briefings' vol 13, 212; 'Highlights' IRLR [2001] June 321.

[146] [2001] EWCA Civ 558, [2001] ICR 805, [2001] IRLR 384.

[147] *Per* Lord Justice Pill, at paragraph 28.

This means that the justification test under the DDA requires a much less rigorous scrutiny of an employer's actions than that required in indirect race and sex discrimination.[148] In *Jones* itself, therefore, the Court of Appeal allowed an appeal against an Employment Tribunal's decision that Mr Jones, who was employed as a mail delivery driver, was unlawfully discriminated against when he was removed from driving duties. Mr Jones had non-insulin dependent diabetes but was eventually diagnosed with insulin dependent diabetes and was then removed from his driving duties in accordance with the Post Office's medical fitness standards. It was conceded by the employers that, by removing Mr Jones from all driving duties, they had discriminated against Mr Jones. An Employment Tribunal concluded the 'decision in this case as to what is justified must be ours'. It concluded that a correct appraisal of Mr Jones' medical condition would have led to the conclusion that he should have been allowed to drive throughout his shift. The Tribunal heard expert evidence for Mr Jones that the deterioration in his condition signalled by his reliance on insulin made no material difference to the existing risk that he would experience a hypoglycaemic episode while driving a Post Office van. Since it considered that the employers' conclusion was wrong, the Tribunal held that the justification could not be either 'material' or 'substantial' and was therefore not justified. The Court of Appeal concluded that the Tribunal's approach was wrong and remitted the case back for a fresh hearing.

Given that many cases of disability-related discrimination will be instances of indirect discrimination it is difficult to see how *Jones* can survive the Directive. As has been seen, the Directive requires Member States to outlaw indirect discrimination save where such discrimination is:

• justified by a legitimate aim and the means of achieving that aim are appropriate and necessary; or

• as regards persons with a particular disability, the employer is obliged, under national legislation, to make reasonable accommodations (or adjustments) to eliminate disadvantages entailed by such provision, criterion, or practice and that obligation has been discharged.[149]

As will be seen below, consistent with the Directive, disability-related discrimination cannot be justified where the employer is under a duty to make reasonable adjustments in relation to a disabled person but fails to comply with that duty, unless it would have been justified even if he had complied with that duty.[150]

---

[148] Sections 1(1)(b) SDA and RRA and see: *Bilka-Kaufhaus GmbH v Weber von Hartz* Case 170/84 [1986] ECR 1607, [1986] IRLR 317; *Hampson v DES* [1991] 1 AC 171, [1990] IRLR 302; *Webb v EMO Air Cargo (No 2)* [1995] ICR 1021, [1995] IRLR 645 HL; *Allonby v Accrington & Rossendale College* [2001] EWCA Civ 529, [2001] ICR 1189, [2001] IRLR 364.

[149] Directive, Articles 2(2)(b) and 5, 2000/78/EC; see Chapter 3 above.

[150] Section 3A(6) DDA. This is an important limitation on the defence of justification for disability-related discrimination: *Nottinghamshire County Council v Meikle*, *supra* note 104 at paragraphs 63–6.

However, the justification defence provided for in *Jones* is a long way from that required by the Directive and EC law.[151] It is likely that the defence of justification will now have to give way to an EC compatible meaning.

The Employment Code of Practice gives some guidance as to the meaning of justification:

Where less favourable treatment of a disabled person is capable of being justified (that is, where it is not direct discrimination), the Act says that it will, in fact, be justified if, but only if, the reason for the treatment is both material to the circumstances of the particular case and substantial. This is an objective test. 'Material' means that there must be a reasonably strong connection between the reason given for the treatment and the circumstances of the particular case. 'Substantial' means, in the context of justification, that the reason must carry real weight and be of substance.[152]

Health and safety considerations and medical evidence may justify disability-related discrimination. However, in each case, the reason for the treatment must be both material to the circumstances of the particular case and substantial. This means that treatment based on generalized assumptions is unlikely to be justified. The fact that a person has a disability does not necessarily mean that he represents an additional risk to health and safety, for example.[153] In addition, it is important to note that health and safety law does not require employers to remove all conceivable risk, but to ensure that risk is properly appreciated, understood, and managed.[154]

5.2.3.6. *Relationship between justification and reasonable adjustments*
Disability-related discrimination cannot be justified where the employer is under a duty to make reasonable adjustments in relation to a disabled person but fails to comply with that duty, unless it would have been justified even if he had complied with that duty.[155] Accordingly, it is necessary to consider not only whether there is a material and substantial reason for the less favourable treatment, but also whether the treatment would still have been justified even if the employer had complied with its duty to make reasonable adjustments:

In relation to disability-related discrimination, the fact that an employer has failed to comply with a duty to make a reasonable adjustment means that the sequence of events for justifying disability-related less favourable treatment is as follows:
• The disabled person proves facts from which it could be inferred in the absence of an adequate explanation that:

---

[151] See cases cited under note 148 and see Chapter 3 above for remedies for the impact of EC law on domestic law and remedies for a breach of EC law.

[152] Paragraph 6.3.   [153] See Employment Code, paragraph 6.7.

[154] Employment Code, paragraph 6.8. See also *(1) Lane Group plc (2) North Somerset Council v Farmiloe* [2004] EAT UKEAT 0352/03/DA & UKEAT 0357/03/DA on the relationship between health and safety law and the DDA: at the time of writing this case is on appeal to the Court of Appeal. See also *Fytche v Wincanton Logistics plc* [2004] UKHL 31 on employers' duties.

[155] Section 3A(6) DDA.

a. for a reason related to his disability, he has been treated less favourably than a person to whom that reason does not apply has been, or would be, treated, and

b. a duty to make a reasonable adjustment has arisen in respect of him and the employer has failed to comply with it.

• The employer will be found to have discriminated unless it proves that:

a. the reason for the treatment is both material to the circumstances of the particular case and substantial, and

b. the reason would still have applied if the reasonable adjustment had been made.[156]

This operates as an extremely important limitation on the defence of justification available in claims of disability-related discrimination, and mitigates the adverse effect of the judgment in *Jones*.[157]

The Employment Code of Practice gives the following example.

An applicant for an administrative job appears not to be the best person for the job, but only because her typing speed is too slow as a result of arthritis in her hands. If a reasonable adjustment—perhaps an adapted keyboard—would overcome this, her typing speed would not in itself be a substantial reason for not employing her. Therefore the employer would be unlawfully discriminating if, on account of her typing speed, he did not employ her or provide that adjustment.[158]

5.2.3.7. *Proving disability-related discrimination*

As with direct discrimination, disability-related discrimination may be inferred from all the circumstances.[159]

5.2.4. Harassment

Harassment remains common both inside and outside the workplace; twelve million workers in Europe consider themselves to be victims of harassment.[160]

Harassment can and often does have a very debilitating effect on its victims. The Employment and Social Affairs Committee of the European Commission recently reported that:

The effects of harassment on the health are devastating. The victim suffers stress, nervous tension, headaches/migraines and depression, and develops psychosomatic illnesses such as stomach ulcers, colitis, thyroid problems, insomnia, high blood pressure and skin diseases. In most cases victims of harassment take long-term sick leave or even resign from their jobs. In addition, harassment has significant effects on the productivity and economic performance of the firm or public-service department concerned because of the

---

[156] Employment Code of Practice, paragraph 6.6.

[157] See *Nottinghamshire County Council v Meikle*, *supra* note 104.

[158] Employment Code, paragraph 6.5.

[159] Revised Code of Practice of Practice, Rights of Access, Goods, Facilities, Services and Premises (2002) DRC, paragraph 3.5.

[160] 'Second European Survey on Working Conditions in the European Union', European Foundation for the Improvement of Living and Working Conditions [1997], Office for Official Publications of the European Communities.

absenteeism it generates and the costs and benefits that have to be paid as a result of sickness or redundancy. The cost of harassment to businesses and society is therefore very high.[161]

A recent study by a European Health and Safety Agency identifies bullying in the work place as one of the new occupational 'risk' factors with a psychological dimension.[162] When proved it is usually treated very seriously indeed by courts and tribunals. Most of the very high awards of compensation in discrimination cases are in those cases arising out of complaints of harassment. For example, in *Yeboah v London Borough of Hackney*[163] an award of £380,000[164] was made to a senior black African employee of Hackney after he complained of a prolonged campaign of harassment. In *HM Prison Service v Salmon*[165] an award of £76,344.88 was made to a woman prison officer subject to sexual harassment which eventually resulted in a diagnosis of a depressive illness.[166]

The DDA now contains specific provision addressing harassment and this is addressed below. Importantly, however, for many years 'harassment' has been deemed a form of 'detriment' for the purposes of the anti-discrimination statutes. The SDA, RRA, and DDA outlaw direct, and in the case of the DDA, disability-related, discrimination across a range of activities where such discrimination causes 'detriment'.[167]

A very subjective concept of harassment has developed under the domestic anti-discrimination statutes and the concept of 'detriment'.[168] The European Commission's Code of Practice on Sexual Harassment[169] has been adopted in a series of cases[170] as affording a workable definition (with appropriate modifications depending on the ground for the treatment). It defines sexual harassment as follows:

'Unwanted conduct of a sexual nature, or other conduct based on sex affecting the dignity of women and men at work'. This can include unwelcome physical, verbal or non-verbal conduct.

---

[161] 'Harassment at the Workplace', July 2001 doc ref 2001/2339(INI).

[162] 'The State of Occupational Safety and Health in the European Union' [2000], the European Agency for Health and Safety at Work cited in the Report of the Employment and Social Affairs Committee of the European Commission, on 'Harassment at the Workplace', July 2001 doc ref 2001/2339(INI).

[163] [1998] ET case no 56617/94.

[164] The sum was ordered to be paid by consent.   [165] [2001] IRLR 425.

[166] See too guidance in *Vento v Chief Constable of West Yorkshire Police (No 2)* [2002] EWCA Civ 1871, [2003] ICR 318, [2003] IRLR 102; and see Chapter 11 below for remedies generally.

[167] For example, section 6(2)(b) SDA, section 4(2)(c) RRA, and section 4(2)(d) DDA.

[168] *Driskel v Peninsula Business Services Ltd and others* [2000] IRLR 151, paragraph 12.

[169] Annexed to the European Commission's Recommendation on the Protection of Dignity of Women and Men at Work: 91/131/EEC.

[170] Which indicate a largely, though of course not wholly, subjective approach: 'It is for the Tribunal hearing the case to determine upon "an objective assessment . . . of all the facts" ', *Driskel v Peninsula Business Services Ltd and Others*, *supra* note 168. See too, *Smith v Vodafone UK Ltd*, *supra* note 23.

Thus, a range of behaviour may be considered to constitute sexual harassment. It is unacceptable if such conduct is unwanted, unreasonable and offensive to the recipient; a person's rejection of or submission to such conduct on the part of employers or workers (including superiors or colleagues) is used explicitly or implicitly as a basis for a decision which affects that person's access to vocational training or to employment, continued employment, promotion, salary or any other employment decisions; and/or such conduct creates an intimidating, hostile or humiliating working environment for the recipient.

The essential characteristic of sexual harassment is that it is unwanted by the recipient, that it is for each individual to determine what behaviour is acceptable to them and what they regard as offensive. Sexual attention becomes sexual harassment if it is persisted in once it has been made clear that it is regarded by the recipient as offensive, although one incident of harassment may constitute sexual harassment if sufficient serious. It is the unwanted nature of the conduct which distinguishes sexual harassment from friendly behaviour which is welcome and mutual.[171]

Neither motive nor intention is necessary.[172]

This definition of harassment, whether covering sexual harassment, or adapted to cover disability harassment, is plainly wide enough to cover: abuse, disability-related 'jokes', and other offensive conduct which is explicitly disability-based (gesticulating; depicting offensive disability-related materials and slogans; distributing disability-offensive publications; and so on).

It is also wide enough to cover much more petty acts of harassment, which taken together cause indignity to workers in the workplace, for example:

- not passing on messages;
- hiding or moving work;
- ostracizing;
- allocating menial tasks; or
- allocating too much work.[173]

As stated, the DDA now expressly prohibits harassment in the employment and related fields. Such provision is made in consequence of the amendments made by the 2003 Regulations and these in turn have been made in consequence of the Directive.

The Directive defines 'harassment' as follows:

Harassment shall be deemed to be a form of discrimination . . . when unwanted conduct related to any of the grounds referred to in Article 1 takes place with the purpose or effect of violating the dignity of a person and of creating an intimidating, hostile, degrading, humiliating or offensive environment. In this context, the concept of harassment may be defined in accordance with the national laws and practice of the Member States.[174]

The grounds referred to in Article 1 include disability.

---

[171] Eg *Wadman v Carpenter Ferrer Partnership* [1993] IRLR 374; *Insitu Cleaning Co Ltd v Heads* [1995] IRLR 4; *Driskel v Peninsula Business Services Ltd, supra* note 168.

[172] *Ibid.*

[173] See eg Report of the Employment and Social Affairs Committee of the European Commission, on 'Harassment at the Workplace', July 2001 doc ref 2001/2339(INI).

[174] Article 2(3).

The Directive addresses discrimination in the employment and related fields only and the explicit definition of harassment accordingly only applies to those fields (Part II, DDA).

As can be seen, the Directive concept of 'harassment' appears somewhat narrower than that provided for under the 'detriment' provisions as described above, in particular, by requiring both that the conduct was intended to violate the dignity of the victim or that it actually had that effect *and* that the conduct was intended to create an intimidating, hostile, degrading, humiliating, or offensive environment for the victim or that it actually did have that effect. The Directive contains a 'non regression' clause[175] and accordingly 'under no circumstances' could the Government use the Directives to *reduce* the protection currently available. The 2003 Regulations therefore enact a wider meaning of harassment than that provided for by the Directive.

5.2.4.1. *DDA meaning of 'harassment'*

Section 3B DDA now provides that:

(1) For the purposes of this Part, a person subjects a disabled person to harassment where, for a reason which relates to the disabled person's disability, he engages in unwanted conduct which has the purpose or effect of—

    (a) violating the disabled person's dignity, or

    (b) creating an intimidating, hostile, degrading, humiliating, or offensive environment for him.

This means that conduct which is intended to violate a disabled person's dignity or create an intimidating etc environment for him will constitute harassment, whatever the actual effect. To this extent, the meaning is wider than under previous case-law which focused on the effect on the victim. The Employment Code of Practice gives the following example:[176]

A man with a learning disability is often called 'stupid' and 'slow' by a colleague at work. This is harassment, whether or not the disabled man was present when these comments were made, because they were said with the intention of humiliating him.

In other cases, the test for determining whether treatment constitutes harassment is a mixed objective/subjective test. Section 3A(2) provides that 'Conduct shall be regarded as having the effect specified in paragraph (a) or (b) of subsection (1) only if, having regard to all the circumstances, including in particular the perception of that other person, it should reasonably be considered as having that effect.'

Some concern has been expressed that the new meaning given to harassment is regressive[177] because of the introduction of the concept of 'reasonableness' by section 3A(2).[178] It is also a dangerous and unwelcome development. The ques-

---

[175] Article 8(2).   [176] Employment Code, paragraph 4.39.

[177] 'New Discrimination Regulations: An EOR Guide' EOR 119, 21.

[178] And an indication under the same definition in the amended RRA that Government's intention was that regard should be had to the intention of the perpetrator, *ibid.*

tion whether treatment amounts to 'harassment' should be principally determined from the perspective of the victim, as section 3A(2) appears to acknowledge.[179] Any other construction would be regressive and would breach the terms of the Directive.

Unlike direct discrimination and harassment falling with the scope of the 'detriment' provisions, no comparator is required.[180]

5.2.4.2. *Relationship with 'detriment'*
Section 18D DDA provides that, except in relation to section 16C(2)(b) (pressure to discriminate[181]) 'detriment' does not include 'conduct of the nature referred to in section 3B (harassment)'.

Thus all conduct falling within the definition of harassment will now fall outside the scope of 'detriment' notwithstanding the old case-law.

The old case-law remains instructive however. Given the non-regression obligation imposed by the Directive,[182] the pre-2003 Regulations case-law sets the minimum threshold for protection against harassment.[183] It is also possible that some acts of harassment will fall outside the definition contained in section 3B and will therefore fall to be considered under the detriment provisions. It is difficult to conceive of such a case. However, to the extent that it might ever be argued that a harasser's motive or intention is relevant under section 3B, such that conduct which would otherwise be regarded as harassment is found not to be so, section 3A(1) and (5) (disability-related and direct discrimination) and the 'detriment' provisions might still prove relevant.

5.2.4.3. *One-off acts*
It can be seen from the above that the concept of harassment suggests a course of conduct or a number of incidents which together undermine the victim's dignity. However, a one-off act can constitute harassment, if sufficiently serious.

In *Insitu Cleaning Co Ltd and Another v Heads*[184] the Employment Appeal Tribunal upheld the finding by an Employment Tribunal that Mrs Heads had been unlawfully discriminated against when a manager, the son of one of the directors of the company for whom she worked, said to her in a meeting 'Hiya, big tits'. The Employment Appeal Tribunal concluded that the Employment Tribunal was entitled to conclude that the one incident was sufficiently serious to amount to sexual harassment and accordingly a detriment under the SDA. The Employment Appeal Tribunal held that the question whether any act

---

[179] Domestic case-law had become largely subjective, eg *Reed v Stedman* [1999] IRLR 299; *Driskel v Peninsula Services, supra* note 168; and see the very subjective meaning given to 'detriment' (under which term harassment cases are litigated) in *Chief Constable of West Yorkshire v Khan, supra* note 19.

[180] See above and see *Pearce v Governing Body of Mayfield Secondary School, supra* note 33.

[181] See Chapter 6 below.   [182] See Article 8(2).

[183] For example, *Cox v Rentokil Initial Services Ltd* (ET Case No 2405154/00) [2002] EOR 103, 20.

[184] *Supra* note 171.

amounted to a detriment was largely a matter of fact for the Employment Tribunal and that whether a single act of verbal sexual harassment was sufficient to found a complaint is also a question of fact and degree:

It seems to be the argument that because the Code of Practice refers to 'unwanted conduct' it cannot be said that a single act can ever amount to harassment because until done and rejected it cannot be said that the conduct is 'unwanted'. We regard this argument as specious. If it were correct it would mean that a man was always entitled to argue that every act of harassment was different from the first and that he was testing to see if it was unwanted: in other words it would amount to a licence for harassment . . . The word 'unwanted' is essentially the same as 'unwelcome' or 'uninvited'. No one, other than a person used to indulging in loutish behaviour, could think that the remark made in this case was other than obviously unwanted.[185]

Thus even a single act of harassment that affects the dignity of the victim may amount to unlawful treatment.

5.2.4.4. *Proving harassment*
As mentioned above, there is specific provision regarding the burden of proof and the shifting of it in certain circumstances. This is described at Chapter 11 below.

In approaching claims of harassment regard can be had to the following guidance:

• When looking at acts, particularly which by themselves appear petty, it is important to look at the whole picture because the overall picture is often more serious than first appears from a look at its component parts.[186] An Employment Tribunal should be invited to make findings in respect of each of the incidents relied upon but should be urged to consider all the acts *together* in determining whether or not they might properly be regarded as harassment. In *Driskel v Peninsular Business Services Ltd and Others*,[187] Mrs Driskel complained of sexual harassment when the head of her department subjected her to sexual banter and comments over a period of three months or so. On the day before she was due to have an interview with him for promotion, he recommended to her that she should 'wear a short skirt and see-through blouse showing plenty of cleavage if she wanted to be successful'. She complained of sexual harassment. The Employment Tribunal accepted Mrs Driskel's account of the earlier incidents in which comments had been made with a sexual connotation, but concluded that she had not objected at the time and that her head of department could not have known that she found them offensive. The Employment Tribunal also found that as to the comments

---

[185] Paragraphs 8–11.

[186] The same approach is taken to determining complaints of direct discrimination: *Anya v Oxford University, supra* note 55, see 5.2.1.4 above.

[187] *Supra* note 168.

made before the promotion interview, whilst they accepted the comments were made, the remarks were intended as flippant and could not reasonably have been taken seriously and were not taken seriously by Mrs Driskel. The Employment Tribunal therefore rejected Mrs Driskel's complaints. At the Employment Appeal Tribunal Mrs Driskel's appeal was allowed and the following guidance given:

[T]he tribunal's approach should be as follows:
(a) The tribunal hears the evidence and finds the facts. As has already been pointed out, it is desirable not to include in this exercise judgments as to the discriminatory significance, if any, of individual incidents—judgment thus far should be limited to the finding of all facts that are *prima facie* relevant. If *ad hoc* assessments 'discrimination or no' are made the result is a fragmented and discursive judgment; more importantly, there is the potential . . . for ignoring the impact of totality of successive incidents, individually trivial.
(b) The tribunal then makes a judgment as to whether the facts as found disclose apparent treatment of the female applicant by the respondents as employers in one or more of the respects identified in Section 6(2)(a) and (b)[188] that was less favourable than their treatment, actual or potential, of the male employee.
(c) The tribunal further considers any explanation put forward on behalf of the respondent employers. In the light of any such explanation is the discrimination so far potentially identified real or illusory?[189]

The Employment Appeal Tribunal concluded that had the Employment Tribunal found all the facts before making a judgment as to whether or not the acts complained of amounted to unlawful discrimination it would have, amongst other things, put each of the incidents in context and would 'readily have found that that which was complained of amounted *prima facie* to discrimination of a high order'.[190] Accordingly, observations, remarks, or other treatment which may appear trivial when looked at alone may evidence disability-related harassment when they are seen in their overall context.

• The absence of a contemporaneous complaint regarding any incidents of *prima facie* harassment does not necessarily negate a finding that the incident complained of was 'unwanted'.[191] In considering the relevance of any failure to complain, an Employment Tribunal must consider the circumstances. In Mrs Driskel's case, for example, any 'instinct to complain must perforce be inhibited by the fact that she wanted the promotion that would come from the approval of [the harasser]'.[192]

• Intention is largely irrelevant. In *Driskel*, the Employment Appeal Tribunal commented that the Employment Tribunal's finding that the remark regarding Mrs Driskel attending the interview in sexually provocative dress 'was flippant and was not meant to be taken seriously' missed the point.[193] The

---

[188] Of the SDA, the relevant unlawful acts in that case, including 'detriment'.
[189] *Driskel v Peninsular Business Services Ltd, supra* note 168, paragraph 12.
[190] *Ibid.*, paragraph 14.   [191] *Ibid.*   [192] *Ibid.*   [193] *Ibid.*

Employment Appeal Tribunal concluded that it was irrelevant that the harasser did not actually expect Mrs Driskel to attend the interview in sexually provocative dress 'what is relevant is that by this remark (flippant or not) he was undermining her dignity as a woman'.[194]

This guidance, as with much of the case-law in the harassment field, arises in the context of sexual harassment but it is equally applicable to disability harassment.

5.2.5. Victimization

Victimization is a quite different form of discrimination from those forms described above. It is not concerned with protecting against adverse treatment based on the personal characteristics of a complainant, nor is it concerned with a complainant's disability status. The victimization provisions protect persons, whether disabled or not, seeking to enforce the DDA, either as complainants or witnesses, and those assisting them.

Section 55 DDA provides, as follows:

(1) For the purposes of Part II[195] [Part 3[196] or Part 4[197]] a person ('A') discriminates against another person ('B') if—
  (a) he treats B less favourably than he treats or would treat other persons whose circumstances are the same as B's; and
  (b) he does so for a reason mentioned in subsection (2).
(2) The reasons are that—
  (a) B has—
    (i)   brought proceedings against A or any other person under this Act; or
    (ii) given evidence or information in connection with such proceedings brought by any person; or
    (iii) otherwise done anything under this Act in relation to A or any other person;[198] or
    (iv) alleged that A or any other person has (whether or not the allegation so states) contravened this Act; or
  (b) A believes or suspects that B has done or intends to do any of those things.

Subsection (1) 'does not apply to treatment of a person because of an allegation made by him if the allegation was false and not made in good faith.'[199]

The acts set out under (2) are usually described in short hand as the 'protected acts'.

---

[194] Paragraph 14.   [195] Discrimination in the employment field, see Chapter 6 below.
[196] Discrimination in the provision of goods and services and housing, see Chapter 7 below.
[197] Discrimination in the field of education, see Chapter 8 below.
[198] With modifications for certain purposes in the employment and related fields, see section 55(6) DDA and see 5.2.5.5.3 below.
[199] Section 55(4) DDA.

Importantly, the victimization provisions do not themselves make any act unlawful. The victimization provisions merely *define* one form of discrimination for the purposes of the other parts of the DDA.[200] In order to breach the DDA there must also be a 'prohibited act' such as a failure to recruit or promote.[201] This is plain from the terms of the legislation itself, and has been confirmed by case-law.[202]

5.2.5.1. *Who is protected*
The victimization provisions, unlike all the other provisions of the DDA that define discrimination, protect persons who have done a protected act whether or not they are disabled.[203]

5.2.5.2. *'Less favourable treatment'*
'Less favourable treatment' has the same meaning as in direct discrimination.[204] Any 'disadvantage'[205] or deprivation of choice[206] might constitute less favourable treatment (see 5.2.1.1 above).

5.2.5.3. *The proper comparator*
In order to show that a person has been less favourably treated, a comparison must be made between the person who has done one of the protected acts set out in section 55(2)(a) to (b) DDA and another real or hypothetical comparator.

As mentioned above, the disability status of the person victimized is irrelevant to any comparison which must be undertaken and must be disregarded.[207]

The proper comparison is between a person who has done one of the protected acts and a person who has not done one of the protected acts. The circumstances must otherwise be the same.

There has been considerable controversy about the relevant circumstances for the purposes of the comparison required in a victimization case, but the issue has now been settled by the decision of the House of Lords in *Chief Constable of West Yorkshire v Khan*.[208] Sergeant Khan complained of race discrimination when he was refused promotion over a number of years because of assessments made by his managers. The promotion assessments identified weaknesses in

---

[200] Section 55(1) DDA.

[201] Under, for example section 4 DDA.

[202] *Bruce v Addleshaw Booth & Co, supra* note 4; *Nagarajan v Agnew & others, supra* note 4.

[203] Section 55(5); section 19(4); section 22(7); section 28A(6); section 28R(4) DDA. See modification in the context of education, addressed at 5.9.1.5 below (in respect of the provisions affecting schools and education, references to 'B' in (2) above, include references to B's parent and a sibling of B. This means that a child's parents and siblings are equally protected but only in respect of protected acts done in the context of the educations provisions, section 55(3A) DDA).

[204] See 5.2.1.1 above.

[205] *MOD v Jeremiah, supra* note 20, paragraph 27, in which the question of *less* favourable treatment and detriment were subsumed into one question by Lord Brandon.

[206] *Gill v El Vinos, supra* note 19.   [207] Section 55(3) DDA.

[208] *Supra* note 19.

Sergeant Khan which made him unsuitable for promotion to a more senior post.

While Sergeant Khan was awaiting a Tribunal hearing of his race discrimination complaint, he applied to a different police force for a promoted post. The second police force requested a reference from the Chief Constable of West Yorkshire, Sergeant Khan's employer. Any reference would have been based on the promotion assessments about which Sergeant Khan complained in his race discrimination case. The Chief Constable took advice and refused to provide a reference because of the outstanding proceedings. He responded to the reference request to the effect that there was an outstanding claim in respect of his failure to support Sergeant Khan's application for promotion and that he would make no further comment for fear of prejudicing his own case.

Sergeant Khan commenced proceedings for victimization arising out of the refusal to provide him with a reference. The question was then whether he should be compared with a person who had brought proceedings against the Chief Constable other than under the RRA, or whether he should be compared to a person who had not brought proceedings at all. The evidence before the Employment Tribunal was that the Chief Constable would have refused a reference to any person who had brought proceedings against him where the accuracy of the reference was going to be the subject matter of dispute in the proceedings, whether or not the proceedings were brought under the RRA. Identifying the proper comparator was therefore very important.

The House of Lords held that the proper comparator was a person who had not brought proceedings against the Chief Constable at all:

> The statute is to be regarded as calling for a simple comparison between the treatment afforded to the complainant who has done a protected act and the treatment which was or would be afforded to other employees who have not done the protected act. Applying this approach, Sergeant Khan was treated less favourably than other employees. Ordinarily West Yorkshire provides references for members of the force who are seeking new employment.[209]

Thus the proper comparator in a victimization complaint is a person who has not done the act which is said to give rise to the less favourable treatment. It is not someone who has done the same act, but in circumstances unconnected with the DDA.[210]

The treatment of the complainant must have been less favourable than that which the discriminator afforded a real comparator, or would have afforded a hypothetical comparator, in the 'same' circumstances. Where a complainant is relying on a real comparator a complainant should therefore ensure their circumstances are the same. If a complainant is relying on a real comparator it is usually wise to rely on a hypothetical comparator in the alternative.

---

[209] At paragraphs 27–28, *per* Lord Nicholls.

[210] Indeed, any other construction is likely to be inconsistent with the Directive 2000/78/EC. See Chapter 3 above.

As with direct discrimination,[211] in constructing a 'picture of how a hypothetical comparator would have been treated' an Employment Tribunal is entitled to take account of how the employer has treated other persons, who have not done protected acts, in different but not dissimilar circumstances.[212]

5.2.5.4. *'For a reason mentioned in subsection (2)'*
Section 55 DDA provides that the less favourable treatment must be 'by reason' that the person victimized has done a protected act.[213]

In *Nagarajan v London Regional Transport*[214] the House of Lords held that in determining whether or not a person has been less favourably treated 'by reason'[215] that he or she has done one of the protected acts, an Employment Tribunal is not required to determine whether the discriminator was *consciously* motivated or influenced by the fact that the person victimized had done the protected act. Further, the fact that the complainant had done a protected act need not be the *sole* cause of the less favourable treatment: it need only have had a 'significant influence'[216] or be the 'principal' or 'important' cause.[217]

According to the House of Lords in *Nagarajan*: 'although victimisation has a ring of conscious targeting, this is an insufficient basis for excluding cases of unrecognised prejudice'[218] from the victimization provisions. The relevant question is: 'why did the alleged discriminator act as he did? What, consciously or unconsciously, was his reason?'[219]

The test for victimization is not a simple 'but for' test. A subjective analysis of why the discriminator treated the complainant less favourably is required. Where the protected act has caused the less favourable treatment it will usually mean that the less favourable treatment was 'by reason' of it. But this will not always be the case, particularly where proceedings are pending. This is an important distinction, because the fact that a complainant has done a protected act will frequently cause another person to act in a particular way, although the latter may have a reason unconnected with the DDA for so acting.

In *Khan* the House of Lords held that, although the fact that Sergeant Khan had brought proceedings caused the Chief Constable to refuse a reference, this did not establish that the refusal was 'by reason' of the fact that he had brought proceedings:

---

[211] See 5.2.1.2 above.

[212] *Chief Constable of West Yorkshire v Vento, supra* note 35.

[213] Or A believes or suspects that B has done or intends to do a protected act: Section 55(2)(b) DDA.

[214] *Supra* note 45.

[215] The words used in the RRA, though there is no material difference between this and the wording adopted by the DDA (for [such] a reason' (section 55(1)(b)).

[216] *Per* Lord Nicholls, paragraph 19.   [217] *Per* Lord Steyn, paragraph 34.

[218] *Per* Lord Nicholls, paragraph 18.

[219] *Khan, supra* note 19 *per* Lord Nicholls, paragraph 29.

Employers, acting honestly and reasonably, ought to be able to take steps to preserve their position in pending discrimination proceedings without laying themselves open to a charge of victimisation. This accords with the spirit and purpose of the Act. Moreover, the statute accommodates this approach without any straining of the language. An employer who conducts himself in this way is not doing so because of the fact that the complainant has brought discrimination proceedings. He is doing so because, currently and temporarily, he needs to take steps to preserve his position in the outstanding proceedings. Protected act (a) ('by reason that the person victimised has—(a) brought proceedings against the discriminator . . . under this Act'[220]) cannot have been intended to prejudice an employer's proper conduct of his defence, so long as he acts honestly and reasonably. Acting within this limit, he cannot be regarded as discriminating by way of victimisation against the employee who brought the proceedings.[221]

Importantly, the House of Lords in *Khan* was influenced by the fact that Sergeant Khan's complaint of race discrimination was outstanding. Their Lordships held that the pending proceedings had the effect of changing the relationship between Sergeant Khan and the Chief Constable. Once proceedings had been commenced they were not just employer and employee, but also adversaries in litigation. The Chief Constable was entitled to protect himself in respect of that litigation. He could have been roundly criticized and ordered to pay more compensation if he provided a reference based on the promotion assessments when Sergeant Khan was complaining that they were racially discriminatory, and that issue had not been decided. Lord Hoffmann gave the following guidance:

A test which is likely in most cases to give the right answer is to ask whether the employer would have refused the request if the litigation had been concluded, whatever the outcome. If the answer is no, it will usually follow that the reason for refusal was the existence of the proceedings and not the fact that the employee had commenced them. On the other hand, if the fact that the employee had commenced proceedings under the Act was a real reason why he received less favourable treatment, it is no answer that the employer would have behaved in the same way to an employee who had done some non-protected act, such as commencing proceedings otherwise than under the Act.[222]

On the facts of *Khan* the House of Lord's decision is understandable. It may be that in many cases where proceedings are outstanding employers have to take steps in connection with those proceedings that are 'less favourable' to the person who brought the proceedings (by, for example, collecting evidence against an employee; making statements that are adverse to an employee, etc). But an employer will need to show, as in *Khan*, that there was a reason apart from the fact that proceedings were commenced that caused the less favourable treatment. An Employment Tribunal is likely to be satisfied that any less favourable treatment was caused by the bringing of the proceedings where the conduct of the employer is unreasonable, unconnected with the proceedings, or

---

[220] Section 55(2)(a)(i) DDA.
[221] *Per* Lord Nicholls, paragraph 31.
[222] Paragraph 60.

dishonest. In *IRC v Morgan*,[223] for example, the Employment Appeal Tribunal upheld a finding of victimization made by an Employment Tribunal arising out of a memo sent by a manager to staff addressing a race discrimination claim brought by one of their colleagues. The memo gave 'a general warning' that because of the complainant's complaints of race discrimination details of personnel records might possibly become public knowledge. The Employment Appeal Tribunal concluded that the Employment Tribunal was entitled to find that that the circulation of the memo constituted less favourable treatment of the complainant and victimization.

5.2.5.5. *What acts are protected*

The victimization provisions protect persons who have taken steps to enforce rights under the DDA.

The protected acts are those set out under section 55(2) and a complainant will need to identify the subsection under which their complaint is brought. If there is any doubt they can be relied upon in the alternative.

These acts are 'protected' whether or not the employer knew they were done in connection with the DDA.[224] However, there are limitations, largely imposed by the case-law, on the reach of the protection afforded by these provisions. These are discussed below.

5.2.5.5.1. *'Brought proceedings against A or any other person under this Act'* As can be seen from *Khan* and the discussion above, where the 'protected act' is the bringing of proceedings, a complainant will need to show that the reason for the less favourable treatment was something other than an honest and reasonable step in the proceedings.

5.2.5.5.2. *'Given evidence or information in connection with such proceedings brought by any person'* This protected act is self-explanatory. The proceedings in respect of which evidence or information are given must be proceedings under the DDA, as the reference to 'such proceedings' in section 55(2)(a)(ii) makes clear. This is a reference back to section 55(2)(a)(i) which refers to 'this Act' (that is, the DDA). There is some case-law indicating that this subsection cannot be relied upon where proceedings have not yet been brought at the time of the less favourable treatment (even if they are brought thereafter).[225]

---

[223] *Commissioners of Inland Revenue and another v Morgan* [2002] IRLR 776. See also *St Helens MBC v J E Derbyshire & 38 Ors* (2004) UKEAT/0952/03.

[224] *Nagarajan v London Regional Transport, supra* note 45.

[225] *Kirby v Manpower Services Commission* [1980] ICR 420, [1980] 1 WLR 725, [1980] 3 All ER 334, [1980] IRLR 229, paragraph 15. Note: the approach to the comparison exercise undertaken in this case was departed from by the House of Lords in *Khan, supra* note 19; see, for example, Lord Nicholls, paragraph 27.

5.2.5.5.3. *'Otherwise done anything under this Act in relation to A or any other Person'* This protected act protects a person who does anything under the DDA, for example serving a questionnaire under the DDA.[226]

This protected act is modified for the purposes of Part II and to the extent that it relates to the provision of employment services under Part III.[227] In such cases, section 55(2)(a)(iii) is to be read as, 'otherwise done anything under *or by reference*[228] to this Act in relation to A or any other person'.

This widens the scope of this protected act, in relation to employment and related fields and in relation to employment services, and brings the DDA into line with the SDA[229] and the RRA.[230] Where a complainant relies on something done *under* the DDA, case-law indicates that a specific provision of the DDA (under which the act is done) must be capable of identification and be identified.[231] The words 'by reference to' import a wider reach. Thus, for example, a report made to the Community Relations Council by an employee of a Job Centre about racially discriminatory client employers was something done *by reference to* the RRA.[232] Similarly, it would be unlawful to subject an employee to any detriment where he attends an Employment Tribunal not to give evidence but purely to offer support to the complainant in proceedings under the DDA because this would be something which is done by reference to the Act.[233]

5.2.5.5.4. *Alleged that A or any other person has (whether or not the allegation so states) contravened this Act* Where the protected act relied upon is the making of an allegation of a contravention of the DDA[234] the allegation must be one which is capable of constituting a contravention of the DDA. By analogy, in *Waters v Commissioner of Police for the Metropolis*[235] brought under materially the same provisions of the SDA[236] the Court of Appeal held that an Employment Tribunal correctly dismissed WPC Waters' complaints of victimization by her employer, when the 'protected act' she relied on was a complaint made to her employer of sexual harassment by a male colleague. This was because the Employment Tribunal found that the sexual harassment complained of took place outside the course of her male colleague's employment and accordingly was not unlawful under the SDA.[237]

The Court of Appeal held that the allegation relied on, though it did not need to include an explicit statement that an act of discrimination contrary to the SDA had occurred (as is plain from section 55(2)(a)(iv) DDA) must be such that the asserted facts relied upon are capable of amounting in law to an unlawful act of discrimination.

---

[226] Section 56 DDA. See Chapter 11 below.   [227] See Chapter 6.

[228] Emphasis added.   [229] Section 4 SDA.   [230] Section 2 RRA.

[231] *Kirby v Manpower Services Commission, supra* note 225.   [232] *Ibid.*

[233] Employment Code of Practice of Practice, paragraph 4.33.

[234] Section 55(2)(a)(iv) DDA.   [235] [1997] ICR 1073, [1997] IRLR 589.

[236] Section 4(1)(d) DDA.

[237] See section 41 SDA and Chapter 10 for the provisions addressing liability.

The effect of the decision in *Waters* is that the SDA, and by necessary implication the DDA, requires the person victimized to show that s/he has made an allegation that a person has committed an act which, if proved, would amount to a contravention of the DDA. This is a very narrow interpretation. An allegation of unlawful discrimination by a person will amount to a contravention of the DDA only if all the necessary ingredients of unlawful discrimination are made out. A person victimized may very well not know whether all the ingredients of the legal wrong can be proved. However, similarly, a generalized complaint of some unspecified discrimination may be insufficient.[238]

It is wise therefore, as indicated above, to plead any complaint of victmization in the alternative where there is any doubt about which of the subsections the act relied upon falls within. If an allegation proves not to be capable of constituting an unlawful act under the DDA, it may nevertheless be something done 'by reference' to the DDA.[239]

5.2.5.6. *Bad faith*

There is a statutory defence available in respect of a complaint of victimization. Under section 55(4) DDA, the victimization provisions do not apply to treatment of a person because of an 'an allegation made by him if the allegation was false and not made in good faith'.

These requirements are conjunctive and accordingly both elements must be satisfied. A person who makes an allegation in good faith that turns out to be false will be protected, as will a person who makes an allegation of discrimination that is true, but which is made for some improper motive. In practice this defence is very rarely relied upon.

5.2.5.7. *Proving victimization*

As mentioned above, there is specific provision regarding the burden of proof and the shifting of it in certain circumstances. This is described at Chapter 11 below.

An Employment Tribunal is entitled to infer that the less favourable treatment of a person who has done one of the protected acts was by reason of his or her having done the protected act, without proof of intent, motive, or otherwise, where there is an otherwise inadequate explanation by the discriminator for such treatment.[240]

---

[238] In *Benn v London Borough of Hackney* (ET Case No 22956/91) EOR DCLD Number 19, 1994, the ET held that allegations of a racist or sexist 'culture' did not amount to an allegation that the Acts had been contravened.

[239] Section 55(2)(a)(iii). The Employment Appeal Tribunal in *Kirby, supra* note 225, observed that there is some overlap between the equivalent provisions in the RRA, see paragraph 18.

[240] *Nagarajan, supra* note 45, *per* Lord Nicholls at paragraphs 17–19.

5.3. CONTRACT WORKERS, OFFICE HOLDERS, ETC

The provisions addressing 'discrimination' (direct discrimination, reasonable adjustments, disability-related discrimination, and victimization) and 'harassment'[241] as defined above[242] apply equally to those provisions addressing contract workers, office holders, partnerships, barristers, and advocates under Part II DDA. The persons caught by these unlawful acts are identified below. There are some differences in relation to the duty to make reasonable adjustments, reflecting the particular circumstances of the occupations concerned, and these are addressed below. Otherwise, the guidance above applies equally.

The unlawful acts are considered fully in Chapter 6 below.

5.3.1. Contract Workers

The DDA makes it unlawful for 'principals' to discriminate against disabled contract workers or to subject disabled contract workers to harassment.[243] In addition, the duty to make reasonable adjustments applies to contract workers.[244] The duty to make adjustments is defined in the same way as under the employment provisions.[245] A duty is imposed upon both principal and employer.[246]

In the case of employers, the duty arises where, 'by virtue of a provision, criterion or practice applied by or on behalf of all or most of the principals' to whom a disabled contract worker 'is or might be supplied, or a physical feature of premises occupied by such persons, he is likely, on each occasion when he is supplied to a principal to do contract work, to be placed at a substantial disadvantage in comparison with persons who are not disabled which is the same or similar in each case'.[247] In such circumstances, the employer must take such steps as he would have to take under section 4A (employers' duty to make reasonable adjustments) if the provision, criterion, or practice were applied by him or on his behalf or (as the case may be) if the premises were occupied by him.[248]

In the case of principals, the duty arises in precisely the same circumstances as in the context of employment and as if the principal and contract worker were employer and employee (or prospective employer and employee) respectively.[249] However, exceptionally, a principal is not required to take a step in relation to a disabled contract worker if the disabled contract worker's employer is required to take the step in relation to him.[250] Additionally, of course, where the contract work is for a very short period or at short notice this may be relevant to the

---

[241] Sections 3A, 3B, and 55 DDA.
[242] Under 'Employment'. See 5.2 above.
[243] Section 4B(1) and (2) DDA.
[244] Section 4B(4)–(7) DDA.
[245] Section 4A DDA.
[246] Section 4B(4)–(7) DDA.
[247] Section 4B(4) DDA.
[248] Section 4B(5) DDA.
[249] Section 4B(6) DDA.
[250] Section 4B(7) DDA.

extent of the steps required by the duty. It might be, subject to the particular facts, unreasonable for a principal to have to make certain adjustments if the contract worker was to be engaged for a very short time only.[251] Conversely, the Employment Code of Practice gives the following example:[252]

A travel agency hires a clerical worker from an employment business to fulfil a three month contract to file travel invoices during the busy summer holiday period. The contract worker is a wheelchair user, and is quite capable of doing the job if a few minor, temporary changes are made to the arrangement of furniture in the office. It is likely to be reasonable for the travel agency to make these adjustments.

5.3.2. Officer Holders

The DDA makes it unlawful for 'relevant persons' to discriminate against disabled office holders (or prospective disabled office holders)[253] or to subject disabled office holders (or prospective disabled office holders) to harassment.[254] In addition, the duty to make reasonable adjustments applies to office holders.[255]

In relation to office holders,[256] again the duty to make adjustments is defined in materially the same way as under the employment provisions.[257] A disabled person is only protected by the duty where:

- in the case of a provision, criterion or practice for determining who should be appointed to, or recommended or approved in relation to, an office or post to which this section applies, he is a disabled person who
  —is, or has notified the relevant person that he may be, seeking appointment to, or seeking a recommendation or approval in relation to, that office or post; or
  —is being considered for appointment to, or for a recommendation or approval in relation to, that office or post.
- In any other case, he is:
  —a disabled person who is seeking or being considered for appointment to, or a recommendation or approval in relation to, the office or post concerned: or
  —a disabled person who has been appointed to the office or post concerned.[258]

A 'relevant person' means:[259]

- in a case relating to an appointment, the person with power to make the appointment;

---

[251] See, for example, Employment Code of Practice, paragraph 9.8.
[252] *Ibid.* paragraph 9.9. [253] Section 4D(1)–(3) DDA.
[254] Section 4D(4) DDA. [255] Section 4E DDA.
[256] *Ibid.* [257] *Ibid.*
[258] Section 4E(2), DDA. [259] Section 4F(2) DDA.

- in a case relating to the making of a recommendation or approval a Minister of the Crown, a Government department, the National Assembly for Wales or any part of the Scottish Administration, with power to make that recommendation or give that approval;

- in a case relating to a term of an appointment, the person with power to determine that term; and

- in a case relating to a working condition, the person with power to determine that working condition or, where there is no such person, the person with power to make the appointment;

- in a case relating to the termination of an appointment, the person with power to terminate the appointment.[260]

A duty arises in respect of any physical feature of premises only where they are under the control of the relevant person and the functions of an office or post are performed from those premises.[261]

As with the duty to make adjustments in the employment context, no duty arises in relation to office holders where the relevant person does not know and could not reasonably be expected to know that the disabled person concerned is or may be seeking appointment to, or a recommendation for office or is being considered for appointment to or for a recommendation in relation to that office or in any case that the person has a disability and is likely to be affected in a way which gives rise, or would otherwise give rise, to the duty to make adjustments.[262]

5.3.3. Partners

The DDA makes it unlawful for a firm to discriminate against a disabled partner (or a prospective disabled partner)[263] or to subject a disabled partner (or prospective disabled partner) to harassment.[264] In addition, the duty to make reasonable adjustments applies to partners.[265]

In relation to partners, again the duty to make adjustments is defined in materially the same way as under the employment provisions.[266] The duty is owed:

- in the case of a provision, criterion, or practice for determining to whom the position of partner should be offered, to any disabled person who is, or has notified the firm that he may be, a candidate for that position; and

---

[260] It should be noted that where the complaints relate to other forms of discrimination, particularly in a case of complaints about detriment or harassment, the relevant person is any of the previous persons, depending on the particular context: section 4F(2)(f) DDA.

[261] Section 4E(1)(b) DDA. [262] Section 4(E)(3) DDA, see 5.2.2.1 above.

[263] Section 6A(1) DDA. [264] Section 6A(2) DDA.

[265] Section 6B DDA. [266] Section 4E DDA.

- in any other case, to a disabled person who is a partner or a candidate for the position of partner.[267]

The duty is owed by the firm concerned.[268]

As with the duty in other cases, no duty arises where the firm does not know and cannot reasonably be expected to know that the disabled person concerned is a candidate or potential candidate for the position of partner or in any other case that that person has a disability and is likely to be affected in a way which would otherwise give rise to the duty.[269]

As to the expenses incurred by a firm in making any adjustments, the cost of taking those steps is to be treated as an expense of the firm.[270] Where the disabled person concerned is or becomes a partner, his contribution to that cost is not to exceed an amount that is reasonable having regard in particular to the proportion in which he is entitled to share in the firm's profits.[271] This ensures that the entire costs attributable to making adjustments are not borne by the disabled person to whom the duty is owed. The Employment Code of Practice gives the following example:[272]

A disabled person who uses a wheelchair as a result of a mobility impairment joins a firm of architects as a partner, receiving 20% of the firm's profits. He is asked to pay 20% towards the cost of a lift which must be installed so that he can work on the premises. This is likely to be reasonable.

The greater any disparity between the percentage profit share and contribution to costs (where they exceed the percentage profit share), the less likely that the contribution requirement will be 'reasonable'.

5.3.4. Barristers, pupils, etc

The DDA makes it unlawful for barristers and barristers' clerks to discriminate against disabled barristers who are tenants, pupils, or squatters[273] (or prospective tenants, pupils, or squatters)[274] or to subject a disabled tenant, pupil, or squatter (or prospective tenant, pupil, or squatter) to harassment.[275] In addition, the DDA makes it unlawful for any person to discriminate against a barrister[276] or an advocate in Scotland[277] in relation to the giving or withholding of instructions or to subject a disabled advocate to harassment.[278] The duty to make reasonable adjustments applies to barristers, barristers clerks, and advocates (in Scotland).[279]

---

[267] Section 6B(2) DDA.
[268] Section 6B(1) DDA.
[269] Section 6B(3) DDA, see 5.2.2.1 above.
[270] Section 6B(4) DDA.
[271] Section 6B(4) DDA.
[272] Paragraph 9.31.
[273] The meaning of these terms is described in Chapter 6 below, at 6.6.
[274] Section 7A(1) and (2) DDA.
[275] Section 7A(3) DDA.
[276] In England and Wales: section 70(5A) DDA.
[277] Section 70(5B) DDA.
[278] Sections 7A(4) and 7C(4) DDA.
[279] Sections 7B and 7D DDA.

In relation to barristers,[280] again the duty to make adjustments is defined in materially the same way as under the employment provisions.[281] The duty is owed:

- in the case of a provision, criterion, or practice for determining to whom a pupillage or tenancy should be offered, to any disabled person who has notified a barrister or barrister's clerk that he may be an applicant for a pupillage or tenancy; and

- in any other case, to a tenant, a pupil, or an applicant for a pupillage or tenancy.[282]

The duty is owed by any barrister or barrister's clerk and, where the duty applies in relation to two or more barristers in a set of chambers, the duty is owed by each of them.[283]

The same principles apply to pupils in Scotland[284] though no duty to make adjustments is owed to advocates (reflecting the differences in the way they organize practice, as compared to barristers in England Wales).[285]

In the case of both barristers and advocates, as with others in the employment field, no duty arises where there is no relevant knowledge (that is, that the disabled person is an applicant or potential applicant for a pupillage or tenancy or that the disabled person has a disability and is likely to be affected in such a way as would otherwise give rise to the duty).[286]

5.3.5. Practical Work Experience

The DDA makes it unlawful for a placement provider to discriminate against a disabled person seeking or undertaking a work placement[287] or to subject such a disabled person to harassment.[288] In addition, the duty to make reasonable adjustments applies to disabled persons seeking or undertaking a work placement.[289]

Again the duty to make adjustments is defined in materially the same way as under the employment provisions.[290] The duty is owed:

- in the case of a provision, criterion, or practice for determining to whom a work placement should be offered, to any disabled person who has notified the placement provider that he may be an applicant for that work experience; and

- in any other case a disabled person who is an applicant for the work placement concerned or undertaking a work placement with the placement provider.[291]

---

[280] Section 7B(1) DDA.   [281] Section 4A DDA.   [282] Section 7B(3) DDA.
[283] Section 7B(2) DDA.   [284] Section 7D DDA.
[285] See further Chapter 6 below, at 6.6.
[286] Sections 7B(4) and 7D(3) DDA, see 5.2.2.1 above.
[287] Section 14C(1) DDA, see Chapter 6 above, at 6.7.
[288] Section 14C(2) DDA.   [289] Section 14D DDA.   [290] *Ibid.*
[291] Section 14D(2) DDA.

The duty is owed by the placement provider[292] who is the person providing the work placement.[293]

As with the employment and related provisions, no such duty arises if the placement provider does not know that the disabled person is an applicant for the work placement or that the disabled person has a disability and is likely to be affected in a way that would otherwise give rise to the duty.[294]

The length of any placement is likely to be relevant in determining the extent of any adjustment required.[295] It should also be borne in mind, however, that some disabled students undertaking work placements may be able to fund their own adjustments out of the Disabled Student's Allowance.[296] In addition, some disabled people may have their own equipment that they are prepared to use in the workplace and in such a case the placement provider may have to make reasonable adjustments in order to facilitate the use of that equipment (for example, by ensuring that it is transported and stored safely and adequately insured whilst in the workplace).[297]

5.4. TRADE ORGANIZATIONS AND QUALIFICATIONS BODIES

The DDA regulates discrimination and harassment by trade organizations and (since 1 October 2004) qualifications bodies. The provisions addressing 'discrimination' (direct discrimination, reasonable adjustments, disability-related discrimination, and victimization) and 'harassment' as defined above[298] apply equally to the provisions addressing trade organizations and qualifications bodies.[299] The persons caught by these unlawful acts are identified below. There are some differences in relation to the duty to make reasonable adjustments as between employment, trade organizations, and qualifications bodies, reflecting the particular circumstances concerned, and these are addressed below. Otherwise, the guidance above applies equally.

The unlawful acts are considered fully in Chapter 6 below.

The DRC has prepared and issued a Code of Practice in respect of trade organizations and qualifications bodies: 'The Code of Practice on Trade Organisations and Qualifications Bodies' ('Trade Organisations and Qualifications Bodies Code').[300] This provides guidance on the impact of the meaning of discrimination and the reasonable adjustment duty.[301]

---

[292] Section 14D(1) DDA. [293] Section 14C(4) DDA.

[294] Section 14D(3) DDA, see 5.2.2.1 above.

[295] See Employment Code, paragraph 9.48, and see generally section 18B DDA.

[296] Employment Code, paragraph 9.48. [297] *Ibid.*

[298] Under 'Employment'. See 5.2 above. [299] Sections 3A, 3B, and 55 DDA.

[300] (2004) DRC ISBN 0 11 703418 5; Disability Discrimination Codes of Practice (Employment and Occupation, and Trade Organizations and Qualifications Bodies) Appointed Day Order 2004, SI 2004/2302.

[301] The Code of Practice is issued under section 53A DDA. As with the Employment Code, a failure to observe any provision of the Code of Practice does not of itself make a person liable to any

5.4.1. Trade Organizations

The DDA makes it unlawful for a trade organization to discriminate against a disabled member (or prospective member)[302] or to subject such a disabled person to harassment.[303] In addition, the duty to make reasonable adjustments applies to disabled members (and prospective members).[304]

The duty to make adjustments is expressed in the same way as it is under the employment provisions.[305] Whilst the duty to make reasonable adjustments arose in relation to trade organizations before the amendments made by the Regulations, the duty as it applied to 'physical features' was only brought into force on 1 October 2004 with the making of the 2003 Regulations.[306]

The duty is now owed in the case of a provision, criterion, or practice for determining to whom membership should be offered, to any disabled person who is, or has notified the organization that he may be, an applicant for membership[307] and in any other case a disabled person who is a member of the organization or an applicant for membership of the organization.[308]

The duty is owed by the trade organization.[309]

As with duties in other contexts, no duty is imposed where the organization does not know, and could not reasonably be expected to know:

• in the case of an applicant or potential applicant, that the disabled person concerned is, or may be, an applicant for membership of the organization; or

• in any case that that person has a disability and is likely to be affected in a way that would otherwise trigger the duty.[310]

5.4.2. Qualifications Bodies

The DDA now makes it unlawful for a qualifications body to discriminate against a disabled person[311] or to subject such a disabled person to harassment.[312] In addition, a duty to make reasonable adjustments applies.[313] The test

---

proceedings but where a provision of the Code of Practice appears to a court or tribunal to be relevant, it must take that provision into account: section 53A(8) and (8A) DDA.

[302] Section 13(1) and (2) DDA.   [303] Section 13(3) DDA.

[304] Section 14(2) DDA.

[305] Section 14(1) DDA. See 5.2.2 above. See also Disability Discrimination Act 1995 (Commencement Order No 6) Order 1999, SI 1999/1190.

[306] Section 14 substituted by the Regulations SI 2003/1673.

[307] Section 14(2)(a) DDA.   [308] Section 14(2)(b) DDA.

[309] Section 14(1) DDA.

[310] Section 14(3) DDA. See paragraph 5.2.2.1 above.

[311] Section 14A(1) DDA, introduced by the 2003 Regulations, SI 2003/1673 in consequence of the requirements imposed by Directive 2000/78/EC.

[312] Section 14A(2) DDA.   [313] Section 14B DDA.

of justification in relation to disability-related discrimination is modified in certain instances described below ('competence standards').

The duty to make reasonable adjustments is expressed in the same way as it is under the employment provisions[314] with an important qualification that is discussed below. The duty is owed:

- in the case of a provision, criterion, or practice for determining on whom a professional or trade qualification is to be conferred, any disabled person who is, or has notified the qualifications body that he may be, an applicant for the conferment of that qualification; and

- in any other case, a disabled person who holds a professional or trade qualification conferred by the qualifications body or applies for a professional or trade qualification which it confers.[315]

The Trade Organisations and Qualifications Bodies Code of Practice gives the following examples:[316]

A woman with a mental health problem is informed that an oral examination for a diploma in interpreting and translation has been arranged for 8:30 am. The timing of the examination would substantially disadvantage the woman, because a side effect of her medication is extreme drowsiness for several hours after taking her morning dose—which prevents her from concentrating well. The qualifications body agrees to her request to take the examination later in the day.

A man who lip-reads because of his hearing impairment is due to have a practical test as part of his beauty therapy course. The qualifications body instructs an assessor working on its behalf to face the man when she issues instructions during the assessment and to talk clearly.

The duty to make adjustments does not, however, apply to a 'competence standard'.[317] This is addressed below.

As with the duty arising in the employment field, no duty is imposed where the qualifications body concerned does not know and could not reasonably be expected to know, in the case of an applicant or potential applicant, that the disabled person concerned is, or may be, an applicant for the conferment of a professional or trade qualification or in any case, that that person has a disability and is likely to be affected in a way which would otherwise trigger the duty.[318]

Where it applies, the duty to make reasonable adjustments is likely to affect arrangements in relation to taking tests and examinations, renewing qualifications, and the like, as can be seen from the examples above.

As the Code of Practice advises,[319] qualifications bodies should set up systems for working with educational institutions and other bodies with whom they work to ensure that qualifications bodies obtain the information they need to

---

[314] Section 14B(1) DDA.
[316] Paragraph 8.20.
[318] Section 14B(3) DDA. See 5.2.2.1 above.

[315] Section 14B(2) DDA.
[317] Section 14B(1)(a) DDA.
[319] Paragraph 8.23.

make adjustments for disabled students. Whilst no duty arises where a qualifications body does not know of a disabled person or of their disability, they are deemed to know what they could reasonably be expected to know.[320] It would therefore be prudent to have systems in place to ensure that such information as would provide them with such knowledge is actually made available.

5.4.2.1. *'Competence standards'*

The duty to make reasonable adjustments does not apply to a 'competence standard'.[321] Further, the defence of 'justification' available in a case of disability-related discrimination is modified where the application of a competence standard constitutes the discrimination complained of.[322]

A 'competence standard' means an academic, medical, or other standard applied by or on behalf of a qualifications body for the purpose of determining whether or not a person has a particular level of competence or ability.[323] It is extremely important to identify whether a particular measure constitutes a 'competence standard' because it will determine whether a duty to make adjustments applies and will affect the test for any defence of justification that may be available.

The Trade Organisations and Qualifications Bodies Code of Practice gives certain examples that illustrate those standards which might properly be described as 'competence' standards and those which might not. Thus, for example, having a certain standard eyesight is a competence standard required for a pilot's qualification.[324] On the other hand, a condition that a person has, for example, a certain length of experience of doing something will not be a competence standard if it does not determine a particular level of competence or ability.[325] In general terms there will be a difference between a competence standard and the process by which attainment of the standard is determined. Thus the passing of an examination may not involve a competence standard or impose one, whilst the knowledge necessary to pass it will be a competence standard.[326] There will be occasions where the process of assessing whether a competence standard has been achieved is inextricably linked to the standard itself so that the

---

[320] Section 14B(3)DDA. See 5.2.2.1 above.

[321] Section 14A(5) and (4) DDA. One as yet untested issue relates to a possible situation where membership of a trade organization is itself a qualification (within the meaning of Section 14(A)(5) (see Chapter 6 below, at 6.12.2) in which case the trade organization would be subject to the duties to make reasonable adjustments under section 14(1) DDA whilst apparently also falling under section 14A (as in such case they would also constitute a qualifications body) and thereby subject to the exemption in relation to such duties under section 14(A)(3) and (4) DDA. Given that no 'competence standard' exemption applies to trade organizations, it appears that the duties to make adjustments may continue to apply (see, 8.4 and 8.7 below and Code of Practice on Trade Organisations and Qualifications Bodies; see also Chapter 6 below, at 6.11 and 6.12, for further discussion).

[322] Section 14A(3) DDA. [323] Section 14A(5) DDA.

[324] Trade and Qualifications Code of Practice, paragraph 8.72. [325] *Ibid.* paragraph 8.29.

[326] *Ibid.* paragraph 8.30.

ability to take the test may itself amount to a competence standard.[327] The Trade Organisations and Qualifications Bodies Code of Practice gives the following examples:[328]

An oral examination for a person training to be a Russian interpreter cannot be done in an alternative way, eg as a written examination, because the examination is to ascertain whether someone can speak Russian.

A driving test for a heavy goods vehicle licence cannot be done solely as a written test because the purpose of the test is to ascertain whether someone can actually drive a heavy goods vehicle.

A practical test in tree surgery cannot be taken on the ground because the test is to ascertain whether someone can actually cut the branches of trees, including the high branches.

As to disability-related discrimination, less favourable treatment of a disabled person for a reason relating to his disability may be justified where the same relates to the application of a competence standard, but only where the qualifications body can show[329] that:

- the standard is, or would be, applied equally to persons who do not have his particular disability; and

- its application is a proportionate means of achieving a legitimate aim.[330]

The Trade Organisations and Qualifications Bodies Code of Practice gives the following example:[331]

A qualifications body refuses to grant a qualification to a man who fails a fitness test. This does not amount to direct discrimination because anyone, disabled or non-disabled, failing the fitness test would be treated in the same way. But it is less favourable treatment for a reason related to the man's disability. The treatment could be justified if the fitness test was applied equally to all candidates **and** the fitness test was a proportionate way of showing that the person was fit enough to carry out the essential requirements of the job to which the qualification relates.

In the above situation the qualifications body had not reviewed the fitness standards to see if they were proportionate to the requirements of the job. If it had done so, it would have found that the fitness standard demanded was much higher than many people actually working in that job could now achieve (even though these people achieved that standard at the time of qualification). The qualifications body would therefore be unlikely to be able to justify this competence standard.

It is important to note that the test of justification in relation to competence standards is *objective*. It therefore sets a higher threshold than that set by the

---

[327] *Ibid.* paragraph 8.31.   [328] *Ibid.*   [329] The burden is on them.
[330] Section 14A(3) DDA. This reflects in substance the test of 'indirect discrimination' in Directive 2000/78/EC, Article 2. See also the exemption for 'occupational requirements' provided for in Article 4 of the Directive, which incorporates materially the same test.
[331] Paragraph 8.36.

Court of Appeal in *Jones v Post Office*.[332] This test reflects the test of justification in European Community law.[333] Justification, therefore, does not depend on an individual assessment of the disabled person's circumstances, but depends instead on an assessment of the purpose and effect of the competence standard.[334] Importantly too, the modified test of justification only applies to the actual application of a competence standard. If a qualifications body applies a competence standard incorrectly, then it is not, in fact, applying the standard and these rules do not operate. In such circumstances the ordinary test of justification[335] applies (unless the application of the standard is directly discriminatory).

Direct discrimination cannot be justified whatever the circumstances and whether or not it concerns the actual application of a competence standard. Therefore if a standard is applied differentially according to whether the person concerned is disabled or not, or according to whether the person concerned has a particular disability, such will be unlawful and not capable of justification.[336]

5.5. EMPLOYMENT SERVICES

Part III DDA addresses discrimination in relation to employment services.[337] However, the meaning given to discrimination in the context of employment services more closely mirrors that in the employment field (rather than that provided for under Part III[338]).

The DDA makes it unlawful for a provider of employment services to discriminate against a disabled person[339] or to subject a disabled person to whom he is providing such services (or who has requested him to provide such services) to harassment.[340] In addition, a duty to make reasonable adjustments applies.[341] These provisions were inserted by the 2003 Regulations[342] to give effect to the Directive.[343]

'Discrimination' is defined in a hybrid way. It reflects in some respects the employment related provisions and in some respects those under the goods, facilities, and services provisions. Thus, it is unlawful to discriminate directly in

---

[332] *Supra* note 146.

[333] See, for example, *Bilka Kaufhaus GmbH v Weber von Hartz* (170/84) *supra* note 148, 317; *O'Flynn v Adjudication Officer* [1996] ECR I-2617.

[334] Trade and Qualifications Bodies Code, paragraph 8.37.

[335] Section 3A(1)(b) DDA.   [336] Sections 3A(4) and 14A(3)–(4) DDA.

[337] Section 21A DDA.   [338] As to which see 5.7 below.

[339] Section 19(1) read with section 21A DDA.

[340] Section 19(1) read with section 21A(2) DDA.

[341] Section 19(1) read with section 21A(4), (5) and (6) DDA.

[342] SI 2003/1673, prior to which employment services were not separately regulated but fell to be considered under section 19 DDA.

[343] 2000/78/EC, Article 3. See Chapter 3 above.

the provision of employment services (and direct discrimination does not usually apply outside the employment field).[344]

In addition, the concept of reasonable adjustments is defined so as to reflect the wording under the employment provisions. It covers practices, policies, and procedures[345] and is triggered where such a practice, policy, or procedure places disabled persons at a substantial disadvantage in comparison with persons who are not disabled.[346] A 'practice, policy, or procedure' includes a 'provision or criterion', so bringing the breadth of the duty expressly in line with the employment provisions.[347] Where a provider of such services fails to comply with the duty to make reasonable adjustments to a practice, policy, or procedure, such a failure cannot be justified.[348]

In addition, in the context of employment services, it is unlawful to subject a disabled person to whom he is providing such services or who has requested him to provide such services to harassment within the meaning of section 3B DDA, although harassment is not outlawed explicitly by the other provisions of Part III DDA.

Otherwise, the unlawful acts created by section 21A are to be addressed in the same way as the unlawful acts falling within Part III DDA. Importantly, in this context, the duties to make reasonable adjustments under Part III DDA[349] are anticipatory in nature. They are owed not simply to an individual disabled person but to disabled people at large. Providers of employment services therefore (unlike other relevant persons operating within the employment field) are duty-bound to consider the need for reasonable adjustments in advance of any adverse impact upon a disabled person. This is discussed in 5.1 above. In addition, the provisions governing leases and other binding obligations, applicable in relation to the duty upon providers of employment services to make adjustments to physical features, are those which apply to Part III, not Part II. This is addressed in 5.7 below.

5.6. MAKING REASONABLE ADJUSTMENTS TO PREMISES: LEGAL RAMIFICATIONS IN THE EMPLOYMENT AND RELATED FIELDS

There are obvious legal ramifications for occupiers of premises in complying with the duty to make adjustments to premises where obligations under leases and other statutory obligations are engaged. Whether a person occupies

---

[344] Section 21A(5)(c) DDA.   [345] Section 21A(6) DDA.

[346] Section 21A(4), inserting section 19(1)(aa) DDA where the complaint relates to employment services, and section 21A(6) DDA.

[347] Section 21A(6) DDA. See 5.2.2 above on the meaning of these words.

[348] Section 21A(5) read with section 20(1) and (2) and section 21 DDA. The same does not apply to physical features or auxiliary aids: section 21A(5) DDA.

[349] Which is discussed in 5.7 below.

premises under a lease, or as a freeholder, or pursuant to any other arrangements, is immaterial to the question whether a duty to make adjustments arises. However, the status of the employer or other relevant occupier (falling within Part II DDA) in relation to the premises may be relevant.

In addition, where adjustments are made to premises, building and planning regulations may be relevant. These are not overridden by the provisions of the DDA.[350]

5.6.1. Building Regulations etc and the Duty to Make Adjustments to Physical Features

Any requirement to obtain statutory consent such as planning permission, Building Regulations approval, listed building consent, schedule monument consent, and fire regulations approval, for example, is not overridden by the DDA.[351]

However, it should be borne in mind that where a physical adjustment is pending approval, a person falling within Part II may be required to make an interim or other adjustment pursuant to its obligation to make reasonable adjustments.

The design and construction of new buildings, or a material alteration to an existing one, must comply with the Building Regulations.[352] In respect of buildings in England and Wales, Part M (Access to and Use of Buildings) of the Building Regulations is designed to ensure that reasonable provision is made for disabled people to gain access to and use a building.[353] Similar provision is made in relation to Scotland under the Technical Standards for Compliance with the Building Standards (Scotland) Regulations 1990[354] and associated technical handbooks. These standards are considered further under 5.7 below. However, the fact that the design and construction of a building, or the physical feature of a building, which an employer occupies meets the requirements of the Building Regulations does not in any way limit the employer's duty to make reasonable adjustments in respect of the building's physical features.[355] The Building Regulations are concerned with providing a minimum standard of accessibility and do not, of course, address the specific needs of individuals.

The Employment Code of Practice recommends that in assessing the access requirements of disabled people, it is likely to be helpful to refer to British Standard 8300:2001, 'Design of Buildings and their Approaches to meet the

---

[350] Section 59 DDA. For a full discussion on section 59, see Chapter 10 below.

[351] Section 59 DDA.

[352] Building Regulations 2000, SI 2000/2531, and Building (Amendment) Regulations 2003, SI 2003/2692. See 5.7.1.7.1 below.

[353] Schedule 1, M.

[354] And from May 2005 under the Building (Scotland) Regulations 2004.

[355] It should be noted that whilst there is a partial exemption from the duty to make adjustments to physical features in relation to service providers (on which see below) this does not apply in relation to employers or other bodies falling within the scope of Part II DDA.

needs of Disabled People: Code of Practice'. This Code of Practice followed a research study commissioned by the former Department of the Environment, Transport, and the Regions. It is 167 pages long and covers a wide range of different design standards to improve access to the built environment, including many considerations for sensory impairments that had been lacking in previous guidance. The design recommendations in BS8300:2001 were based on user trials and validated desk studies that formed part of the research project commissioned in 1997 and 2001 by the then Department of the Environment, Transport and the Regions.[356]

The Employment Code of Practice advises that: 'It is unlikely to be reasonable for an employer to have to make an adjustment to a physical feature of a building which it occupies if the design and construction of the physical features of the building is in accordance with BS8300'.[357] Whilst this guidance is important it ought not to be taken as a statement of the law. The duty to make adjustments arises in individual cases and the obligations are therefore idiosyncratic. A generalization of this kind is therefore informative but not conclusive.

The Employment Code of Practice also advises that: 'In addition, although less comprehensive than BS8300, guidance accompanying the Building Regulations (known as 'Approved Document M') sets out a number of "provisions" as suggested ways in which the requirements of the Regulations might be met. It is unlikely to be reasonable for an employer to have to make an adjustment to a physical feature of a building which is occupied if that feature accords with the relevant provisions of the most up to date version of Approved Document M'.[358] For the same reason, this guidance should be treated with appropriate circumspection. This is particularly so given that the requirements of BS8300:2001 and Approved Document M are not identical. It is therefore conceivable that a building would comply with one standard and not the other but in a particular case the duty to make adjustments is such that the other should be complied with. As has been noted:

The 2004 edition Approved Document M when implemented in May 2004 has adopted many of the BS8300 standards and in some cases the standards contained in Approved Document M are higher than those contained within the British Standard. It would seem that for those standards that are higher, these are additional standards that should be applied to physical adaptions to work towards meeting design requirements under the DDA.[359]

In addition regard should be had to the fact that financial assistance may be available from Access to Work to help meet the cost of making reasonable

---

[356] See Forward to BS8300:2001.   [357] Employment Code of Practice, paragraph 12.9.
[358] Employment Code of Practice, paragraph 12.10.
[359] 'Access to the Built Environment: Disability Discrimination Act 1995: British Standard 8300:2001, Design of Buildings and their Approaches to meet the needs of Disabled People—Code of Practice of Practice; etc', presentation by Paul Day, 12 March 2004, Centre for Disability Studies, School of Sociology and Social Policy, University of Leeds.

adjustments to the physical features of a building which an employer occupies. Where this is available, it will always be relevant to the question whether a failure to make an adjustment is reasonable.[360]

5.6.2. Leases and Other Binding Obligations

Where a person is bound by the terms of an agreement or other legally binding obligation (for example, a mortgage, charge, or restrictive covenant or, in Scotland, a feu disposition) under which it cannot alter the premises without another's consent, the DDA provides that:

- it is always reasonable for such person to have to request that consent before making the alteration in question;[361]
- it is never reasonable for such a person to have to make the alteration in question before having obtained that consent.[362]

In this way, any binding agreement or obligation is given precedence over the duty to make adjustments.[363] However, where a person occupies premises under a lease and the terms of the lease *prevent* him from making an alteration to the premises, then the DDA does take precedence over the terms of the lease. By section 18A(2) DDA, the lease is deemed to have effect as if it provided:

- for the occupier to be entitled to make the alteration to premises with the written consent of the lessor, where the alteration is one which the occupier proposes to make in order to comply with his duty to make adjustments;
- for the occupier to have to make a written application to the lessor for consent if he wishes to make such alteration;
- for the lessor not to withhold consent to such an alteration unreasonably;
- for the lessor to be entitled to make his consent subject to reasonable conditions.[364]

Where a lessee fails to apply to the lessor in writing for consent to the making of the alteration, he cannot rely on any constraints attributable to the fact that he occupies the premises under a lease (on a provision prohibiting him making the alteration, for example) in defending any claim that he has failed to comply with his duty to make reasonable adjustments.[365] Accordingly, anything in the lease that prevents the alteration being made is to be ignored in deciding whether it was reasonable for that person to have made the alteration. As stated, in this

---

[360] Employment Code of Practice, paragraphs 8.19 *et seq.*

[361] Section 18B(3) DDA. [362] *Ibid.*

[363] It should be noted that whilst it is always reasonable for a person to have to seek consent, that does not include taking steps to apply to a court or tribunal: section 18B(4) DDA. The obligation is therefore not onerous.

[364] Section 18A(2) DDA. [365] Schedule 4, Part 1, paragraph 1 DDA.

way the DDA prioritizes the duty to make adjustments over any provisions in a lease.

Where the lessor has a superior lessor, such that he is prevented from consenting to the alteration without the consent of his landlord, the superior lease is deemed modified so as to require the lessee of that lease to apply in writing to its lessor where it wishes to consent to the alteration. Again, such consent may not be withheld unreasonably but reasonable conditions may be attached to it.[366]

Regulations make provision for the obtaining of consent and the effect of a refusal to grant this consent. The Disability Discrimination (Employment Field) (Leasehold Premises) Regulations 2004[367] provides that a lessor has twenty-one days from receipt of an application for consent to reply in writing to the person occupying the premises and if he does not he is to be taken to have unreasonably withheld his consent to the alteration (subject to any longer period which is reasonable in the circumstances).[368] In addition, where a lessor replies consenting to the application subject to obtaining another's consent (the superior lessor, for example) but fails to seek the consent of that other person within twenty-one days of receiving the application (or such longer period as may be reasonable) he will be taken to have withheld his consent. These Regulations[369] also make provision deeming certain refusals to provide consent unreasonable and others reasonable. Regulation 5 provides that where the lease provides that consent shall or will be given to an alteration of the kind in question, any refusal to provide consent will be deemed unreasonable. Regulation 6 provides that any refusal to give consent where there is a binding obligation requiring the consent of another person to the alteration and steps have been taken to seek that consent and such consent has not been given or has been given subject to a condition making it reasonable for him to withhold his consent, then the withholding of that consent is deemed reasonable. In addition, Regulation 6 provides that a lessor will be taken to have acted reasonably in withholding consent where he is bound by an agreement which allows him to consent to the alteration concerned subject to a condition that he makes a payment and the condition does not permit him to make his own consent subject to a condition that the occupier reimburse him in respect of that payment.

Outside of these circumstances, the issue of reasonableness will depend on the particular facts. Relevant considerations will include, for example, any substantial reduction in the value of the lessor's interest in the premises, the extent of any disruption that might be caused by an adjustment to other tenants, and inconvenience.[370]

As to the conditions which it might be reasonable for a lessor to impose when giving consent, the Disability Discrimination (Employment Field) (Leasehold

---

[366] Regulation 9 Disability Discrimination (Employment Field) (Leasehold Premises) Regulations 2004, SI 2004/153.

[367] *Ibid.*   [368] *Ibid.* Regulation 4.   [369] *Ibid.*

[370] Employment Code of Practice, paragraph 12.22.

Premises) Regulations 2004[371] provide some guidance in Regulation 7. In particular, it will be reasonable for a lessor to impose conditions that the occupier obtain necessary planning permission and any other consent or permission required by law; that the occupier submit plans or specifications for the alteration to the lessor for approval and that the work is carried out in accordance with them; that the lessor be permitted to a reasonable opportunity to inspect the work when completed; and that the occupier repay to the lessor the costs reasonably incurred in connection with the giving of consent.[372] In addition, it will be reasonable for a lessor to impose a condition that upon expiry of the lease the occupier[373] reinstate any relevant part of the premises which is to be altered to its state before the alteration was made.[374] However, such a condition will only be reasonable where it would have been reasonable for the lessor to have withheld consent completely. Where it would be unreasonable for a lessor to withhold consent, it will not necessarily be reasonable (each case will turn on its facts) for the lessor to impose a condition requiring such reinstatement.

In proceedings brought by a disabled person where a failure to make adjustments to premises is relied upon and that failure is attributable to a failure by a lessor to grant consent, the lessor may be joined as a party in those proceedings.[375] Where a lessor is joined, the Employment Tribunal may determine whether he unreasonably refused consent to the alteration, or consented subject to unreasonable conditions, and in either case make an appropriate declaration, make an order authorizing the employer to make a specified alteration, and order the lessor to pay compensation to the disabled person.[376]

5.7. GOODS, FACILITIES, AND SERVICES

Discrimination in the provision of goods, facilities, and services is outlawed by Section 19, in Part III, DDA. In short summary, discrimination by a failure or refusal to provide a disabled member of the public with services which are otherwise provided to members of the public: discrimination by a failure to comply with a duty to make reasonable adjustments where the effect of that failure is to make it impossible or unreasonably difficult for the disabled person to make use of any such service, and discrimination in the standard, manner or terms of service provided to disabled persons are outlawed. See Chapter 7 below.

'Discrimination' for these purposes is defined by section 20 and section 55 DDA.[377] It comprises:

• a failure to comply with a duty to make reasonable adjustments;

---

[371] *Supra* note 366.　　　　[372] Regulation 7(1).　　　　[373] Or any assignee or successor.
[374] Regulation 7(2).　　　　[375] Schedule 4, Part 1, paragraph 2 DDA.
[376] *Ibid.* Where compensation is ordered against the lessor, it may not be ordered against the employer as well: Schedule 4, Part 1, paragraph 2(9).
[377] Victimization: see 5.7.4 below.

- disability-related discrimination; and
- victimization.

Both a failure to comply with a duty to make reasonable adjustments and disability-related may be justified.[378]

Direct discrimination and harassment are not outlawed explicitly. However, as discussed below, some instances of direct discrimination and harassment will constitute disability-related discrimination (see 5.7.2 below).

Part III DDA also outlaws discrimination in relation to the disposal and management of premises[379] and in relation to employment services.[380] The 'premises' provisions are dealt with under a separate heading at 5.8 below because the meaning given to 'discrimination' is narrower than that provided for under the goods, facilities, and services provisions. In addition, the 'employment services' provisions are dealt with following employment and related fields above, at 5.5. This is because the meaning given to 'discrimination' in the context of 'employment services' more closely mirrors the meaning provided for under the 'employment' provisions and so is more conveniently dealt with there.

The DRC has prepared and issued a re-revised Code of Practice on 'Rights of Access, Goods, Facilities, Services and Premises'[381] ('Goods, Facilities, Services and Premises Code of Practice'). This Code of Practice replaces the first revised Code. As mentioned in Chapter 1 above, this new Code of Practice takes account of the further duties on service providers to make adjustments when the physical features of their premises make it impossible or unreasonably difficult for disabled people to use their services. Although these remaining duties did not come into force until 1 October 2004, this Code of Practice was issued in May 2002 in order to encourage service providers to be proactive and to assist them in preparing for these significant extended obligations.[382]

5.7.1. The Duty to Make Reasonable Adjustments

The duty to make reasonable adjustments in the context of goods, facilities, and services has become more extensive since 1 October 2004. As originally enacted, the DDA:

- made it unlawful for service providers to fail to comply with the duty to make reasonable adjustments for disabled people where the existence of a practice, policy, or procedure made it impossible or unreasonably difficult for disabled

---

[378] Though see 5.7.3 below for the limits of this defence in its application to a failure to make reasonable adjustments.

[379] Section 22 DDA.   [380] Section 21A DDA.   [381] ISBN 0 11 702860 6.

[382] Commencement date 27 May 2002, Disability Discrimination Code of Practice (Goods, Facilities, Services and Premises) (Appointed Day) Order 2002, SI 2002/720.

persons to make use of a service provided, unless such failure was justified.[383] However, these provisions were not brought into force until October 1999;[384]

• made it unlawful for service providers to fail to comply with the duty to take reasonable steps to provide auxiliary aids or services to enable or facilitate the use by disabled people of services provided, unless such failure was justified.[385] However, these provisions were not brought into force until October 1999, and then only in part.[386] The duty was restricted so that devices, structures, or equipment the installation, operation, or maintenance of which would necessitate making a permanent alteration to or which would have a permanent effect on the physical fabric of premises, fixtures, fittings, furnishings, furniture, equipment, or materials were not to be treated as auxiliary aids or services.[387] This limitation was only removed upon the coming into force of the duty to make adjustments to the physical features of premises on 1 October 2004;[388]

• made it unlawful for service providers to fail to comply with the duty to make reasonable adjustments to physical features (for example, one arising from the design or construction of a building or the approach or access to premises) where such a feature made it impossible or unreasonably difficult for disabled persons to make use of a service, unless such failure was justified.[389] However, these provisions were not brought into force until 1 October 2004. Until then, the duty to make adjustments to physical features extended only to providing a reasonable alternative method of making the service in question available to disabled persons.[390]

Thus there have been significant and recent changes to the meaning of 'discrimination' for the purposes of the goods, facilities, and services provisions of the DDA. The significance of these changes cannot be overstated and is recognized by the very long lead-in time given to their implementation.[391]

---

[383] Sections 19(1)(b), 20(2) and sections 21(1), 21(2)(d), 21(4), 21(6), and 21(10) brought into force by Disability Discrimination Act 1995 (Commencement Order No 6) Order, SI 1999/1190.

[384] *Ibid.*

[385] Sections 19(1)(b), 20(2), and 21(4) brought into force, in part, by Disability Discrimination Act 1995 (Commencement Order No 6) Order, SI 1999/1190.

[386] *Ibid.* See also Disability Discrimination (Services and Premises) Regulations 1999, SI 1999/1191, which restricted the scope of the duty so as to exclude any requirement to make permanent adjustments to physical features: Regulation 4(1) and (2).

[387] *Ibid.*

[388] *Ibid.* Regulation 4(2) and see Disability Discrimination Act 1995 (Commencement No 9) Order, SI 2001/2030.

[389] Sections 19(1)(b), 20(2), and 21(2) DDA brought into force by the Disability Discrimination Act 1995 (Commencement No 9) Order, SI 2001/2030.

[390] Section 21(2)(d) DDA, which came into force on 1 October 1999: Disability Discrimination Act 1995 (Commencement Order No 6) Order, SI 1999/1190.

[391] 4 years and 9 years in the case of practices, policies and procedures, and 9 years in the case of physical features, respectively.

Section 21 DDA, as it is now in force[392] (and so far as is material) provides that:

(1) Where a provider of services has a practice, policy or procedure which makes it impossible or unreasonably difficult for disabled persons to make use of a service which he provides, or is prepared to provide, to other members of the public, it is his duty to take such steps as it is reasonable, in all the circumstances of the case, for him to have to take in order to change that practice, policy or procedure so that it no longer has that effect.

(2) Where a physical feature (for example, one arising from the design or construction of a building or the approach or access to premises) makes it impossible or unreasonably difficult for disabled persons to make use of such a service, it is the duty of the provider of that service to take such steps as it is reasonable, in all the circumstances of the case, for him to have to take in order to—

(a) remove the feature;

(b) alter it so that it no longer has that effect;

(c) provide a reasonable means of avoiding the feature; or

(d) provide a reasonable alternative method of making the service in question available to disabled persons.

. . .

(4) Where an auxiliary aid or service (for example, the provision of information on audio tape or of a sign language interpreter) would—

(a) enable disabled persons to make use of a service which a provider of services provides, or is prepared to provide, to members of the public, or

(b) facilitate the use by disabled persons of such a service, it is the duty of the provider of that service to take such steps as it is reasonable, in all the circumstances of the case, for him to have to take in order to provide that auxiliary aid or service.

The duty to make adjustments as described proscribes the circumstances in which discrimination might occur (by a breach of the duty) for the purposes of section 19 (goods, facilities, and services) and accordingly a breach of any such duty is not actionable as such.[393]

Section 21 contains wide regulation making powers and important regulations have been made supplementing the description of the reasonable adjustment duty contained in section 21.[394]

---

[392] Since 1 October 2004.

[393] Section 21(10), though depending on its context a breach may found an application in judicial review which is not excluded under the DDA: Schedule 3, Part 2, paragraph 5 DDA. See also *Roads v Central Trains Ltd* [2004] EWCA Civ 1541, at paragraph 12.

[394] See section 21(3), (5), (8), and (9) DDA. See also Disability Discrimination (Services and Premises) Regulations, SI 1999/1191 (made under section 21(5)(e), (h); Disability Discrimination (Providers of Services) (Adjustment of Premises) Regulations 2001, SI 2001/3253 (made under section 21(5)(a), (b); Disability Discrimination (Providers of Services) (Adjustment of Premises) (Amendment) Regulations 2004, SI 2004/1429 (made under section 21(5)(b) DDA).

As can be seen from section 21, the duty to make reasonable adjustments comprises three discrete main duties, as follows:

- changing practices, policies, and procedures;
- providing auxiliary aids and services;
- overcoming a physical feature by;
  —removing the feature; or
  —altering it; or
  —providing a reasonable means of avoiding it; or
  —providing the service by a reasonable alternative method.

These duties are each addressed in detail below.

5.7.1.1. *To whom and when is the duty to make reasonable adjustments owed?*
The duty to make reasonable adjustments that arises under the goods, services, and facilities provisions is a duty owed to disabled people at large. In this respect it can be distinguished from the narrower duty arising in the employment and related fields. It is not dependent upon a particular disabled person establishing disadvantage. The duty arises where the mere existence of a practice, policy, or procedure or physical feature makes it impossible or unreasonably difficult for disabled persons at large to make use of the service provided by the service provider. Accordingly, it is a duty owed to all disabled people, children, and adults and does not require a disabled person seeking to use such goods, facilities, or services to trigger its invocation. It is instead 'anticipatory' in nature.

This is an important distinction as compared to the duties arising under the employment and related fields. It obliges a service provider to plan in advance of the use of its services to ensure they are reasonably accessible to disabled customers. As the Goods, Facilities, Services and Premises Code of Practice observes:

Service providers should not wait until a disabled person wants to use a service which they provide before they give consideration to their duty to make reasonable adjustments. . . Failure to anticipate the need for an adjustment may render it too late to comply with the duty to make the adjustment. Furthermore, it may not of itself provide a defence to a claim that it was reasonable to have provided one.[395]

Necessarily, therefore, the duties are owed whether or not the service provider knows: that a particular member of the public is disabled, whether it currently has disabled customers, or whether there is a disabled person proposing to or seeking to use the services of that service provider. This again distinguishes the duties under the goods, facilities, and services provisions from those applicable in the context of employment and related fields.[396]

---

[395] Paragraph 4.14. [396] See 5.2 above.

The duties continue throughout the period during which the service provider provides services to members of the public. The Goods, Facilities, Services and Premises Code of Practice makes the following observation:

> Service providers should keep the duty under regular review in the light of their experience with disabled people wanting to access their services. In this respect it is an evolving duty, and not something that needs simply to be considered once and once only, and then forgotten. What was originally a reasonable step to take might no longer be sufficient and the provision of further or different adjustments might then have to be considered.[397]

In determining whether or not services are 'unreasonably difficult' for disabled people to use, so that a duty arises, service providers should take account of whether the following factors would be considered unreasonable by other people, if they had to endure similar difficulties:

- time;
- inconvenience;
- effort;
- discomfort; or
- loss of dignity.[398]

5.7.1.2. *Practices, policies, and procedures*

As can be seen, the duty to make reasonable adjustments extends to any 'practice, policy or procedure, which makes it impossible or unreasonably difficult for disabled persons to make use of a service provided to other members of the public'.[399]

Unlike the analogous provision under Part II (employment and related fields),[400] these expressions are not further defined under the DDA (except for the purposes of 'employment services'[401]). However, the Goods, Facilities, Services and Premises Code of Practice gives some guidance. It advises that such practices, policies, and procedures 'may be set out formally or may have become established informally or by custom'.[402] As described above, in relation to Part II, the concepts are clearly wider in scope than the words 'condition' and 'requirement' in the indirect discrimination provisions of the SDA and the RRA as originally enacted.[403]

Practices, policies, and procedures relate to the way in which a service provider operates its business or provides its services, as the Goods, Facilities, Services and Premises Code of Practice observes.[404] Thus, the expressions cover:

---

[397] Paragraph 4.19.
[398] Goods, Facilities, Services and Premises Code of Practice, paragraph 4.33.
[399] Section 21(1) DDA.   [400] Section 4A DDA and section 18D DDA.
[401] See 5.5 above and section 21A(6) DDA.
[402] Paragraph 5.4.   [403] See 5.2.2.2 above.
[404] Goods, Facilities, Services and Premises Code of Practice, paragraph 5.6.

- what a service provider actually does (its practices);
- what a service provider intends to do (its policy);
- how a service provider plans to go about it (its procedure).[405]

The three terms plainly overlap and, as the Code of Practice advises, it is not always sensible to treat them as separate concepts. The Goods, Facilities, Services and Premises Code of Practice gives the following example.

A DIY superstore has a policy of not allowing dogs onto its premises. Members of staff are instructed to prevent anyone with a dog from entering the superstore. The 'no dogs' policy is enforced in practice by this procedure. The policy makes it unreasonably difficult for disabled people accompanied by a guide or assistance dog to use the DIY superstore. The superstore has a duty to take such steps as are reasonable for it to have to take to avoid that effect and to make its services accessible to disabled people. It decides to amend its 'no dogs' policy by allowing an exception for disabled people accompanied by a guide or assistance dog. This is likely to be a reasonable step for the superstore to have to take.[406]

5.7.1.3. *Auxiliary aids and services*
As stated above, section 21(4) gives two examples of auxiliary aids or services:

- the provision of information on audio tape; and
- the provision of a sign language interpreter.

However, as is clear, these are examples only. The expressions 'auxiliary aids' and 'services' extend to aids other than those relating to communication, for example to a viewing platform[407] or a temporary ramp,[408] amongst other things.

An auxiliary aid or service may be temporary or permanent.[409] As observed above, since 1 October 2004 the limited exemption in relation to auxiliary aids and services which necessitate making a permanent alteration to the physical fabric of premises[410] is no longer in force.[411] Accordingly, auxiliary aids might be those necessitating permanent alterations to the fabric of a building or its furnishings as with, for example, an induction loop.

It is important to bear in mind that, whilst auxiliary aids or services might constitute equipment of one sort or another, the concepts also extend to services. Such a service may therefore constitute particular assistance to disabled customers (perhaps from specially trained staff).[412] The Goods, Facilities,

---

[405] Goods, Facilities, Services and Premises Code of Practice, paragraph 5.6.   [406] *Ibid.*

[407] *Baggley v Kingston upon Hull CC* [2002] (Kingston upon Hull County Court Claim Number KH101929), in which the Court accepted that the provision of a viewing platform was capable of amounting to an auxiliary aid or service, although on the facts of the case no breach of the duty was made out.

[408] See, Goods, Facilities, Services and Premises Code of Practice, paragraph 5.14.

[409] *Ibid.* paragraph 5.1.5.

[410] Including fixtures, fittings, furnishings, furniture, equipment, or materials.

[411] Disability Discrimination (Services and Premises) Regulations 1999, Regulation 4. See *supra* notes 386 and 388.

[412] Goods, Facilities, Services and Premises Code of Practice, paragraph 5.12.

Services and Premises Code of Practice gives the following (amongst other) examples.[413]

A large supermarket provides specially designed shopping baskets and trolleys which can be easily used by disabled shoppers in a wheelchair or with reduced mobility. It also provides electronic hand-held bar code readers with synthesised voice output which helps customers with a visual impairment to identify goods and prices. These are auxiliary aids which enable disabled shoppers to use the supermarket's services.

Disabled customers with a visual impairment or a learning disability may need assistance in a large supermarket to locate items on their shopping list. The supermarket instructs one of its employees to find the items for them. The supermarket is providing an auxiliary service which makes its goods accessible.

5.7.1.4. *Physical features*
The Disability Discrimination (Services and Premises) Regulations 1999 make provision for various matters to be treated as physical features.[414] These are:

- any feature arising from the design or construction of a building on the premises occupied by the provider of services;
- any feature on the premises occupied by the provider of services or any approach to, exit from, or access to such a building;
- any fixtures, fittings, furnishings, furniture, equipment, or materials in or on the premises occupied by the provider of services;
- any fixtures, fittings, furnishings, furniture, equipment, or materials:
    —brought onto premises other than those occupied by the provider of services by or on behalf of the provider of services;
    —in the course of providing services to the public or to a section of the public;
    —for the purpose of providing such services;
- any other physical element or quality or any land comprised in the premises occupied by the provider of services.

Such features are deemed to constitute 'physical features' for the purposes of section 21(2) DDA.[415] 'Building' in this context means an erection or structure of any kind.[416] This is an inclusive list of matters that may constitute physical features in that whilst these are deemed to be so they are not exclusively so defined. Accordingly, the expression 'physical feature' in section 21(2) DDA has a very wide meaning indeed.

Physical features will include steps, stairways, kerbs, exterior surfaces and paving, parking areas, building entrances and exits (including emergency escape

---

[413] *Ibid.* paragraph 5.12.
[414] SI 1999/1191, made under sections 21(5)(e)(h) and 67 DDA. See also *Ross v Ryanair* [2002] Claim No CL 209468, which illustrates the breadth of this concept.
[415] *Ibid.* Regulation 3.   [416] *Ibid.* Regulation 2.

routes), internal and external doors, gates, toilet and washing facilities, public facilities (such as telephones, counters, or service desks), lighting and ventilation, lifts and escalators, floor coverings, signs, furniture, and temporary or movable items (such as equipment and display racks); again, this is not an exhaustive list.[417] Physical features may be inside or outside a service provider's building but so long as they are within the boundaries of a service provider's premises, the duty to make adjustments (where such physical features make it impossible or unreasonably difficult for disabled people to use the service) will apply.[418]

It is likely that 'physical features' will include public footpaths, cycle ways, towpaths, footbridges, and the like, maintained by local and highway authorities. This has obvious ramifications for the duties of local and highway authorities in their management of such public passages.[419]

5.7.1.5. *How are the duties discharged?*

As described above, the duties are owed to disabled people at large and are, accordingly, anticipatory in nature. The duties are best met by a service provider endeavouring to anticipate the types of problems that might arise and by training its employees appropriately.[420]

The duties require service providers to take such steps as it is reasonable, in all the circumstances of the case, for them to have to take in order to achieve the result required by the three duties described above. What is a 'reasonable step' will depend on all the circumstances of the case. What is a reasonable step will vary according to:

- the type of service being provided;
- the nature of the service provider and its size and resources;
- the effect of the disability on the individual disabled person.[421]

Factors that must be taken into account when considering what is reasonable will include:

- whether taking any particular steps would be effective in overcoming the difficulty that disabled people face in accessing the service in question;
- the extent to which it is practicable for the service provider to take the step;
- the financial and other costs of making the adjustment;
- the extent of any disruption which taking the step would cause;
- the extent of the service provider's financial and other resources;
- the amount of any resources already spent on making adjustments; and
- the availability of financial or other assistance.[422]

---

[417] Goods, Facilities, Services and Premises Code of Practice, paragraph 5.45.
[418] *Ibid.* paragraph 5.46.   [419] *Ibid.* paragraph 2.14.
[420] *Ibid.* paragraph 5.1.6, and throughout Chapters 3–5.   [421] *Ibid.* paragraph 4.21.
[422] *Ibid.* paragraph 4.22.

Thus, for example, it is more likely to be reasonable for a service provider with substantial financial resources to have to make an adjustment with a significant cost attached than for a service provider with fewer resources.

As the Code advises, service providers must bear in mind that discharging the duties may not be simple. Action that may result in reasonable access to services being achieved for some disabled people may not do so for others. In addition, it is not enough for service providers to make some changes if their services remain impossible or unreasonably difficult for disabled people to use.[423] The Goods, Facilities, Services and Premises Code of Practice gives the following example (amongst others):[424]

The organiser of a large public conference provides qualified British Sign Language (BSL) interpreters to enable deaf delegates to follow and participate in the conference. However, this does not assist delegates with a mobility impairment or visual disabilities to access the conference, nor does it help delegates with a hearing impairment who do not use BSL but who can lipread. The conference organiser will need to consider the requirements of these delegates also.

Similarly, again as the Code observes, a service provider will not have taken reasonable steps if it attempts to provide an auxiliary aid or service which in practice does not help disabled people to access the services provided. Thus the way in which an auxiliary aid or service is provided may be just as important as the provision of the auxiliary aid or service itself:[425]

Despite providing qualified British Sign Language (BSL) interpreters for deaf delegates who use BSL, the conference organiser fails to ensure that those delegates have the option to be seated near and in full view of the interpreters (who are themselves in a well-lit area). As a result, not all those delegates are able to follow the interpretation. The auxiliary service provided has not been effective in making the conference fully accessible to those deaf delegates.

Service providers cannot, of course, 'be expected to anticipate the needs of every individual who may use their service, but what they are required to think about and provide for are features which may impede persons with particular kinds of disability—impaired vision, impaired mobility and so on'.[426]

Once a service provider has put in place a reasonable adjustment, it is important to make it known to disabled people: by appropriately placed notices, advertising, literature provided by the service provider about its services, and so on.[427] In so doing, the service provider must ensure that the means of communication selected is itself accessible to disabled people.[428] Failure to take these steps may itself constitute a breach of the duties. This is because any adjustments would lose much of their impact if disabled people did not know of them. If the

---

[423] *Ibid.* paragraph 4.24.   [424] *Ibid.*   [425] *Ibid.* paragraph 4.25.
[426] *Roads v Central Trains Ltd* [2004] EWCA Civ 1541 at paragraph 11, and see further below.
[427] See Goods, Facilities, Services and Premises Code of Practice, paragraph 4.26.
[428] *Ibid.*

effect of an absence of notice was such as to mean that the service provider's services were still impossible or unreasonably difficult for disabled people to make use of (because of a practice, policy, or procedure or physical feature) then the duty will not have been discharged.

The Goods, Facilities, Services and Premises Code of Practice observes that it is likely to be rare for a service provider genuinely and properly to conclude that there are no steps that it would be reasonable to take to make their services accessible. In such circumstances, of course, there would be no breach of the law but, as stated, such a situation would be very unusual.[429]

The duties do not require service providers to take any steps that would fundamentally alter the nature of the service in question or the nature of his trade, profession, or business.[430] Thus the duties do not extend to requiring a service provider to make adjustments in a way which would so alter the nature of his business that the service provider would effectively be providing a completely different kind of service. The Goods, Facilities, Services and Premises Code of Practice gives the following examples:[431]

A restaurant refuses to deliver a meal to the home of a disabled person with severe agoraphobia (a fear of public or open spaces) on the grounds that this would result in the provision of a different kind of service. This is unlikely to be against the law. However, if the restaurant already provides a home delivery service, it is likely to be discriminatory to refuse to serve the disabled person in this way.

A night club with low level lighting is not required to adjust the lighting to accommodate customers who are partially sighted if this would fundamentally change the atmosphere or ambience of the club.

However, this is not to say that, because a particular adjustment is not a reasonable step to take because of the effect it would otherwise have on the nature of the service provider's business, another adjustment ought not to be made where that adjustment would not have the same effect.[432] Thus the whole range of possible adjustments must be considered if the duty is to be properly discharged.

It is important to note that where an adjustment, by an additional service or the provision of an auxiliary aid or otherwise, is a reasonable step to take for the purposes of the duties under the DDA, disabled customers cannot be charged for the same.[433] The costs of discharging the duties under the DDA are to be borne by the service provider as part of their general expenses and, therefore, borne by customers across the board insofar as they are reflected in any charges

---

[429] Goods, Facilities, Services and Premises Code of Practice paragraph 4.27.

[430] Section 21(6) DDA.   [431] Paragraph 4.28.

[432] *Ibid.*, paragraph 4.29.

[433] Section 20(5) DDA: 'Any increase in the cost of providing a service to a disabled person which results from compliance by a provider of services with the section 21 duty shall be disregarded for the purposes of subsection (4)(e)' (conditions for establishing justification, see below) and so any attempt to charge would breach section 19(1)(d) DDA.

made.[434] The Goods, Facilities, Services and Premises Code of Practice gives the following examples:[435]

A guest house has installed an audio-visual fire alarm in one of its guest bedrooms in order to accommodate visitors with a sensory impairment. In order to recover the costs of this installation, the landlady charges disabled guests a higher daily charge for that room, although it is otherwise identical to other bedrooms. This is unlikely to be within the law.

A wine merchant runs an online shopping service and charges all customers for home delivery. Its customers include disabled people with mobility impairments. Since this online service is not impossible or unreasonably difficult for disabled people with mobility impairments to use, home delivery, in these circumstances, will not be a reasonable adjustment that the wine merchant has to make under the Act. Therefore, the wine merchant can charge disabled customers in the same way as other customers for this service.

However, another wine merchant has a shop which is inaccessible to disabled people with mobility impairments. Home delivery in these circumstances might be a reasonable adjustment for the wine merchant to have to make for such customers. The wine merchant could not then charge such customers for home delivery, even though it charges other customers for home delivery.

5.7.1.6. *Applying the reasonable adjustment duty*

As described above, the duty to make reasonable adjustments comprises duties falling under three main heads.[436] These duties work differently in practice and are considered separately below.

5.7.1.6.1. *Practices, policies, and procedures*   In determining what 'reasonable steps' are in relation to practices, policies, and procedures, guidance is given by the Goods, Facilities, Services and Premises Code of Practice.[437] There is no statutory definition or description of 'reasonable steps'. Unlike the duties arising in the employment field, Part III DDA does not give any guidance as to what factors will be relevant in determining whether a particular step is reasonable.[438] The factors which are likely to be relevant are those described above (at 5.7.1.5 above). In addition it should always be borne in mind that the purpose of taking a particular step is to ensure that the practice, policy, or procedure no longer has the effect of making it impossible or unreasonably difficult for disabled people to use the service and whether a step will be considered a 'reasonable' step will be measured against that benchmark in the first instance.[439] The Goods, Facilities, Services and Premises Code of Practice give the following examples:[440]

---

[434] See, for an example, *Ross v Ryanair* [2002] CLCC Claim No CL209468, in which Ryanair's policy of charging wheelchair users for the hire of a wheelchair was ruled unlawful: http://www.drc-gb.org/thelaw/judgementdetails.asp?id=11.

[435] Paragraphs 4.30 and 4.31.

[436] See 5.7.1 above.

[437] Paragraph 5.7 onwards.

[438] Compare section 18B DDA.

[439] Goods, Facilities, Services and Premises Code of Practice, paragraph 5.8.

[440] *Ibid.* paragraphs 5.8 and 5.9.

A medium-sized supermarket installs one extra-wide check-out lane intending it to be available to customers who are wheelchair users or accompanied by infants. However, that check-out lane is also designated as an express lane available only to shoppers with ten or less items. The effect of this practice is to exclude wheelchair-users from taking advantage of the accessible check-out unless they are making only a few purchases. It is likely to be a reasonable step for the supermarket to have to take to amend its practice by designating another check-out lane as the express lane.

A hotel refurbishes a number of rooms on each floor which are fully accessible to disabled guests. However, the hotel's reservations system allocates rooms on a first come, first served basis as guests arrive and register. The effect is that on some occasions the specially refurbished rooms are allocated to non-disabled guests and late-arriving disabled guests cannot be accommodated in those rooms. The hotel decides to change its reservation policy so that the accessible rooms are either reserved for disabled guests in advance or are allocated last of all. This is likely to be a reasonable step for the hotel to have to take.

Thus, practices, policies, and procedures should be scrutinized to ensure that they do not make it impossible or unreasonably difficult for disabled people to use the particular service and care must be taken to ensure that in making adjustments they are directed at removing the adverse effect.

5.7.1.6.2. *Auxiliary aids and services*   As has been seen above, the threshold at which the duty to provide an auxiliary aid or service is triggered is lower than that provided for under section 21(1) (practices, policies, and procedures) and (2) (physical features). It is only necessary that an auxiliary aid or service would either enable disabled persons to make use of the service or facilitate the use by disabled persons of such service.[441] Thus the duty is triggered where the provision of an auxiliary aid or service would facilitate the use by disabled persons of the service, even where such a service is not impossible or unreasonably difficult for disabled persons to make use of.

Apart from this, as with the other duties, there is no guidance in the DDA as to the factors which will be taken into account in determining whether or not a particular step is a reasonable step to take. The factors described above (in 5.7.1.5) will be relevant. As remarked upon above, the fact that one particular adjustment is not, in all the circumstances of the case, a reasonable adjustment to make, does not mean that the duty is necessarily discharged: it will always be necessary to consider the full range of possible adjustments. The Goods, Facilities, Services and Premises Code of Practice give the following examples:[442]

A large national museum has hourly guided tours of a popular major exhibition. It provides a radio microphone system for hearing aid users to accompany the tour and on one day a week has a BSL interpreter available. The museum advertises this service and encourages BSL users to book space with the interpreter on the tours on that day. These are likely to be reasonable steps for the museum to have to take.

---

[441] Section 21(4) DDA.   [442] Paragraph 5.17.

A small private museum with limited resources provides a daily guided tour of its exhibits. It investigates the provision of equipment for hearing aid users such as an induction loop in the main gallery or a radio microphone system to accompany the tour, but, after careful consideration, it rejects both options as too expensive and impracticable. Instead, with little effort or cost, the museum decides to provide good quality audio taped guides (with an option of plug-in neck loops) which can be used by people with hearing aids who want to follow the guided tour. This is likely to be a reasonable step for the museum to have to take.

5.7.1.6.2.1. Using auxiliary aids or services to improve communication When considering the need to provide auxiliary aids or services to improve communication, the type of aid or service will vary according to the importance, length, complexity or frequency of communication involved.[443]

In some cases, more than one type of auxiliary aid or service might be appropriate and account must be taken of people with multiple communication disabilities, such as deaf-blindness or combined speech and hearing disabilities.[444]

5.7.1.6.2.2. Provision for people with a hearing disability The auxiliary aids or services that it might be reasonable to provide for people with hearing disabilities include one of more of the following:

- written information (such as a leaflet or guide);
- a facility for taking and exchanging written notes;
- a verbatim speech-to-text transcription service;
- induction loop systems;
- subtitles;
- videos with BSL interpretation;
- information displayed on a computer screen;
- accessible websites
- textphones, telephone amplifiers, and inductive couplers;
- teletext displays;
- audio-visual telephones;
- audio-visual fire alarms; and
- qualified BSL interpreters or lip speakers.[445]

Where sign language interpretation is used, it is important to ensure that the interpreter is capable of communicating accurately and efficiently with both the disabled person and the other parties involved. Other interpretation services, such as lip speakers and Makaton communicators, should also be capable of communicating accurately and effectively.[446]

In all cases it is important to bear in mind that hearing impairments take many forms and are of varying degrees, and what might be a reasonable auxiliary aid or service for one person with a hearing impairment may not be for another.

---

[443] Goods, Facilities, Services and Premises Code of Practice, paragraph 5.22. [444] *Ibid.*
[445] *Ibid.* paragraph 5.23.
[446] *Ibid.* paragraph 5.24.

Thus, the Code gives the example of a person with tinnitus or reduced hearing in respect of whom a particular adjustment might be reasonable: such person is likely to have different requirements from somebody who is profoundly deaf and in respect of whom such a step might not be a reasonable adjustment.[447]

5.7.1.6.2.3. *Provision for people with a visual impairment*   The range of auxiliary aids or services that it might be reasonable to provide for people with visual impairments include:

• readers;
• documents in large or clear print, Moon, or Braille;
• information on computer disc or e-mail;
• information on audio tape;
• telephone services to supplement other information;
• spoken announcements or verbal communication;
• accessible web sites;
• assistance with guiding;
• audio description services;
• large print or tactile maps/plans and three-dimensional models;
• touch facilities (for example, interactive exhibits in a museum or gallery).[448]

Again, and as with other forms of sensory impairment, visual disabilities are of varying kinds and degrees. Service providers must consider what is the most appropriate auxiliary aid or service to provide; more than one may be necessary.[449]

5.7.1.6.2.4. *Provision for people with other disabilities or multiple disabilities* Service providers should consider how communication barriers might be overcome for people with other, non-sensory, disabilities. The Code gives the example of a customer with a learning disability who might be able to access a service by the provision of documents in large, clear print and plain language, or by the use of colour coding and illustrations.[450]

In addition services will not necessarily be made accessible to customers with multiple disabilities simply by providing auxiliary aids or services that are suitable for people with individual disabilities.[451] The Goods, Facilities, Services and Premises Code of Practice gives the example of deaf-blind people (that is individuals who have a severe combined sight and hearing impairment) who are not necessarily assisted in accessing services by the simple provision of communication aids designed for use by people with hearing disabilities or visual impairments. Such might assist deaf-blind people if appropriately used but what is appropriate will depend on the nature and extent of the individual sensory

---

[447] Goods, Facilities, Services and Premises Code of Practice, paragraph 5.25.
[448] *Ibid.* paragraph 5.26.
[449] *Ibid.* paragraph 5.27.   [450] *Ibid.* paragraph 5.28.
[451] *Ibid.* paragraphs 5.29–5.30.

impairment and the methods a particular disabled person uses to communicate and access information. The range of auxiliary aids or services that it might be reasonable to provide for people who are deaf-blind might include:

- engaging a deaf-blind manual interpreter for important meetings;
- having a member of staff trained in specific ways to help a deaf-blind person (such as guiding them safely and tracing capital letters and numbers on the palm of their hand).[452]

5.7.1.6.3. *Physical features*   As seen above, the duties to make adjustments to physical features which make it impossible or unreasonably difficult for disabled people to make use of any service provide for four alternatives:

- removing the feature; or
- altering it so that it no longer has that effect; or
- providing a reasonable means of avoiding the feature; or
- providing a reasonable alternative method of making the service available to disabled people.[453]

The DDA does not provide any further guidance as to what might constitute reasonable steps for the purposes of complying with the duty. It does not create any hierarchy insofar as the alternatives described above are concerned. The focus is on results, that is, achieving the aim of ensuring that the services are accessible to disabled people, rather than on how that aim is achieved.[454]

The Goods, Facilities, Services and Premises Code of Practice recommends an 'inclusive' approach. This means that whilst the different options are not placed in any hierarchy, a service provider should consider first whether a physical feature which creates a barrier to access for disabled people can be removed or altered.[455] This promotes an 'inclusive' approach to adjustments. It makes the services available to everyone in the same way, whereas complying with the duty by providing disabled people with an alternative method of accessing the service in question provides for a different form of service for disabled people than for non-disabled people.

In addition, addressing physical features that make it impossible or unreasonably difficult for a disabled person to make use of the service in question by removing them altogether helps maintain the dignity of disabled customers. It is also likely to be cost-effective because it avoids the ongoing costs of providing services by alternative means and may broaden the customer base. Only if it is not reasonable to remove the physical feature altogether or alter the physical feature so it no longer has the effect of making it impossible or unreasonably difficult for disabled people to use the services in question should alternative

---

[452] *Ibid.* paragraph 5.30.   [453] Section 21(2)(a)–(d) DDA.
[454] Goods, Facilities, Services and Premises Code of Practice, paragraphs 5.36–5.37.
[455] *Ibid.* paragraphs 5.38–5.41. See *Re Holy Cross, Pershore* [2002] Fam 1, at paragraph 105.

means of accessing the service be considered, by avoiding the feature or by providing an alternative method of making use of the service in question.

The Code recommends that service providers arrange for 'access audits' of their premises and to draw up access plans and strategies to enable them to comply with their duties to make adjustments.[456] In carrying out any audit, the Code recommends that service providers seek the views of people with different disabilities, or those representing them, to assist in identifying barriers and developing effective solutions.[457]

> Further, in determining whether a service provider has complied with its duties to make adjustments to physical features, though there was no obligation to do so before 1 October 2004, a court is likely to have regard to the long period that service providers had prior to that date to make preparations (a nine-year lead-in time).458 The duty arising in relation to physical features was contained within the original enactment (enacted in 1995) and detailed guidance on the meaning, scope, and compliance with the duty was contained in the revised Code of Practice which came into force in May 2002.459 A court is likely to expect, therefore, that service providers planned and prepared for the coming into force of the duty and might properly be expected to be ready for its coming into force in October 2004.460 Indeed, as the Code makes clear, it may well have been more cost-effective to make the necessary adjustments as part of a normal programme of work prior to October 2004 rather than waiting until then to secure proper accessibility only to have to apply for further consents and make further physical adjustments to premises that have already been the subject of, for example, refurbishment works.461

Examples of the sorts of steps that might be reasonable under each of the alternatives above include the following.[462]

• Removing the physical feature, which may be not merely a reasonable step but the most effective one:

> A countryside visitor centre includes, as an attraction, a lakeside walk. However, a stile prevents access to the lakeside walk for those with mobility difficulties. The park authority which runs the centre removes the stile and replaces it with an accessible gate. This is likely to be a reasonable step for the service provider to have to take.

• Altering the physical feature so that it no longer has the effect of making it impossible or unreasonably difficult for disabled people to use the services:

> A local religious group holds prayer meetings in a building entered by steps. The room in which the prayer meetings are held has a narrow entrance door. To ensure that its prayer meetings are accessible to disabled people, the religious group installs a permanent ramp at the entrance to the building. It also widens the door to the room. These

---

[456] *Ibid.* paragraph 5.42. [457] *Ibid.* paragraph 5.43. [458] *Ibid.* paragraph 5.34.
[459] Goods, Facilities, Services and Premises Code of Practice, commencement date 27 May 2002.
[460] *Ibid.* paragraphs 5.33–5.35.
[461] *Ibid.* paragraph 5.35. [462] *Ibid.* paragraph 5.48–5.52

are likely to be reasonable steps for the religious group to have to take.

• Providing reasonable means of avoiding the physical feature:

A public art gallery is accessible by a flight of stairs at its front entrance. It is housed in a listed building, and has not been able to obtain consent to install a ramped entrance to the gallery. A side entrance for staff use is fully accessible and always open. The gallery arranges for people with a mobility impairment to use this entrance. This is likely to be a reasonable step for the gallery to have to take. It could of course go further and adopt an inclusive approach by also making the side entrance available to everyone.

• Providing a reasonable alternative method of making services available:

A small self-service pharmacist's shop has goods displayed on high shelving separated by narrow aisles. It is not practicable to alter this arrangement. The goods are not easily accessible to many disabled people. The shop decides to provide a customer assistance service. On request, a member of staff locates goods and brings them to the cash till for a disabled customer. This is the provision of a service by an alternative method, which makes the service accessible for disabled people. This is likely to be a reasonable step for the shop to have to take.

Considerations that are relevant to the meaning of 'reasonable' in the context of providing a 'reasonable' method of avoiding the physical feature and providing a 'reasonable' alternative method of making services available, will include:

• whether the provision of the service in this way significantly offends the dignity of disabled people; and

• the extent to which it causes disabled people inconvenience.[463]

5.7.1.7. *Making reasonable adjustments to premises—legal ramifications* As observed in 5.6 above, there are obvious legal ramifications for occupiers of premises in seeking to comply with the duty to make adjustments to the physical features of premises.

Where adjustments are made to premises, building and planning regulations may be engaged; as described above, these not overridden by the provisions of the DDA.

5.7.1.7.1. *Building regulations* As stated above, the design and construction of new buildings, or a material alteration to an existing one, must comply with the Building Regulations.[464] Particular provision is made in relation to access for disabled people by 'Part M: Access and Facilities for Disabled People' (Schedule 1, Building Regulations). Buildings to which Part M applies should make reasonable provision for access and use by disabled people. Part M has been amended from time to time; the most recent version came into force in May

---

[463] *Ibid.* paragraphs 5.51–5.52.   [464] Building Regulations 2000, SI 2000/2531.

2004.[465] Importantly, the Regulations introducing the substituted Part M post-date the revised Goods, Facilities, Services and Premises Code of Practice.[466] Accordingly they are not referred to in the Code but they are important for reasons which will be seen below.

The most up-to-date version of Part M does not refer to disabled people (unlike its predecessors). Instead it requires that reasonable provision be made for 'people' to gain access to and use the building and its facilities so that the needs of disabled people are encompassed within the requirement, as are the needs (for example) of people who are experiencing a temporary impairment of mobility.[467] This is aimed at fostering a more 'inclusive' approach.[468]

Part M does not apply to material alterations of or extensions to dwellings. However, new requirements are introduced for extensions to buildings other than dwellings: these cover the provision, in certain circumstances, of independent access to the extension and of sanitary conveniences within the extension.

Guidance is issued to accompany the Building Regulations. For Part M of the Building Regulations in England and Wales, this is the 'Approved Document M'.[469] This sets out a number of 'objectives' to be met, 'design considerations' and technical details of design solutions (called 'provisions'). These provisions suggest some way in which the requirements of the Building Regulations might be met, but there is no obligation to adopt them. Some buildings will follow the guidance; others will instead have adopted other acceptable design solutions.

A building that complies with Part M of the Building Regulations should make reasonable provision for disabled people to gain access to and use the building. The building will comply with Part M if its physical features are consistent with those described in Approved Document M (although compliance with Part M can be achieved in other ways).[470] Even where a building complies with Part M, some disabled people might find it impossible or unreasonably difficult to use the services provided at that building. However, where a physical feature accords with the 1992, 1999, or 2004 edition of 'Approved Document M', an exemption is provided for by the Disability Discrimination (Providers of Services) (Adjustment of Premises) Regulations 2001 ('the 2001

---

[465] Building (Amendment) Regulations 2003, SI 2003/2692, Schedule 1, substituting the existing Part M of Schedule 1 to the Building Regulations 2000, SI 2000/2531. The substituted Part M is in force from 1 May 2004 (Regulation 1) with transitional provision made (Regulation 3).

[466] Commencement 27 date May 2002.

[467] See explanatory note to the Building (Amendment) Regulations 2003, SI 2003/2692.

[468] Approved Document M: Access to and Use of Buildings, 2004 Edition ISBN 0 11 753901 5 (as to which, see below), paragraph c.

[469] ISBN 0 11 752447 6; ISBN 0 11 753469 2 and, in relation to the most recent version of Part M, ISBN 0 11 753901 5 (2004 Edition). As stated, the Building (Amendment) Regulations 2003, SI 2003/2692 amend the Building Regulations to substitute a new Part M. A new Approved Document M: Access to and Use of Buildings, 2004 Edition ISBN 0 11 753901 5 has been published.

[470] See Goods, Facilities, Services and Premises Code of Practice, paragraphs 6.2–6.3.

Regulations').[471] These Regulations provide that if a physical feature accords with the 1992, 1999, or 2004 Approved Document M, the service provider will not have to make adjustments to that feature if ten years or less have passed since it was constructed or installed.[472]

The applicable Approved Document M will be whichever edition was the practical guidance that was relevant in relation to meeting the requirements of the Building Regulations which applied to the building work concerned. In any other case, the applicable Approved Document M is the last edition published at the time when the physical feature was provided in or in connection with the building.[473]

A building with physical features which do not accord with the relevant edition of the Approved Document M may have been accepted as meeting the requirements of Part M. According to the Goods, Facilities, Services and Premises Code of Practice,[474] if the physical feature is one which is covered by Approved Document M then, provided it enables any disabled person to access and use the building with the same degree of ease as would have been the case had the feature matched Approved Document M, it is unlikely to be reasonable for a service provider to have to make adjustments to that feature if ten years or less have passed since its installation or construction. This is because the Building Regulations and Approved Document M were not intended to deter people from adopting effective innovative alternative designs.

In addition, in England and Wales there are areas of development where Part M of the Building Regulations does not require that accessibility be improved. However, a service provider may choose to adopt the guidance in the Approved Document M and, where they do so, physical features that are included that accord with the objectives, design considerations, and provisions contained within Approved Document M will not have to be removed or altered if ten years or less have passed since their construction or installation, according to the Goods, Facilities, Services and Premises Code of Practice.[475] There is no statutory basis for this unequivocal guidance but it is likely to be very compelling given the objects of Approved Document M.

The Building Regulations just described and Part M and the Approved Document M, in particular, apply only to England and Wales. However, as observed above,[476] similar provision exists in relation to Scotland. From April 1991 until April 2000 the detailed requirements for compliance with the Building

---

[471] SI 2001/3253, as amended by the Disability Discrimination (Providers of Services) (Adjustment of Premises) (Amendment) Regulations 2004, SI 2004/1429 (which amends the 2001 Regulations to include the 2004 edition of Approved Document M). It should be noted, as remarked upon above, that the 2004 edition and indeed the 2004 amending regulations as just described are not referred to in the revised Code of Practice which pre-dates them.

[472] Regulation 3 and Schedule.

[473] 2001 Regulations, Schedule, paragraph 2(2) and (3).   [474] Paragraph 6.8.

[475] Goods, Facilities, Services and Premises Code of Practice, paragraph 6.14.

[476] Under the 'Employment' heading, paragraph 5.6.1 above.

Standards (Scotland) Regulations 1990 were set out in Part T of the Technical Standards. In April 2000 Part T was discontinued and its requirements were integrated into the general Technical Standards, applicable to buildings in Scotland.[477] From May 2005 the Building Standards (Scotland) Regulations 1990[478] were replaced by the Building (Scotland) Regulations 2004.[479] The 2001 Regulations[480] make similar provision for a limited exemption in relation to the reasonable adjustment duty insofar as it affects physical features in its application to Scotland, as it does to England and Wales. The differences are to take account of the fact that in Scotland requirements to provide access and facilities for disabled people are dispersed among general Technical Standards. However the effect of the Regulations is the same for Scotland as it is in England and Wales, so that for a period of ten years a service provider need not remove or alter any aspect of a physical feature of a building which accords with the relevant edition of Part T or the corresponding requirements included in other Technical Standards or Handbooks introduced in April 2000 and March 2002.

As with England and Wales, the relevant standard applicable in Scotland will be that relevant in relation to the particular physical feature[481] except that, importantly, they do not apply to work commenced before 30 June 1994 or after the Technical Standards 2001 (commencing as of 30 March 2002) ceased to have effect.[482] In such circumstances the feature is not deemed to satisfy the relevant design standard.

A physical feature is deemed to be provided in or in connection with a building on the day on which the works to install or construct the feature was commenced or, in the case of a physical feature provided as part of a larger building project, the day on which the work in relation to that project was commenced.[483] In Scotland, in a case where the physical feature is provided as part of building works in relation to which an application for a warrant for the construction or change of use of the building has been made and granted, the works are deemed to have commenced on the day upon which the application for the warrant was made.[484]

The 2001 Regulations do not stipulate, in the case of England and Wales or Scotland, when the date of completion is to be established for the purposes of determining when the period of ten years has elapsed.[485] However, according to the Goods, Facilities, Services and Premises Code of Practice, it is likely that in the majority of cases it will be the day on which the service provider was able to make use of the physical feature: or 'practical completion', as it is known in industry standard forms of contract.[486]

---

[477] SSI 1999/173.   [478] SI 1990/2179.   [479] SSI 2004/406.

[480] *Supra* note 471, Regulation 3(3), Schedule, paragraph 3.

[481] 2001 Regulations, *supra* note 471, Schedule, paragraph 1(2) and paragraph 2(4).

[482] *Ibid.*

[483] *Ibid.* In England, Scotland, and Wales, Schedule, paragraphs 2(4) and 3(2).

[484] *Ibid.* paragraph 3(3).   [485] *Ibid.* paragraph 1(3).

[486] Goods, Facilities, Services and Premises Code of Practice, paragraphs 6.15 and 6.20.

It is important to bear in mind that the exemption created by the 2001 Regulations relates only to the particular aspect of the physical feature in question that accords with the provision of Approved Document M in England and Wales or the relevant Technical Standard in Scotland, and not to the building as a whole.[487] In addition, physical features that fall outside Approved Document M or the relevant Technical Standards will be subject to the duty to make adjustments in the ordinary way. The Goods, Facilities, Services and Premises Code of Practice points to the fact that service providers can and are recommended to take account of the wealth of published advice on the principles and practice of 'inclusive design' so that, for example, though the Building Regulations do not cover the design of the external environments[488] or signage, advice and guidance on making the same inclusive is available.[489]

In addition, Approved Document M and the relevant Technical Standards describe how requirements might be met without certain physical features that would facilitate access. The exemption in the 2001 Regulations applies only to a physical feature that was in fact included (and which accords with the relevant Approved Document M or Technical Standard) and it does not apply to a physical feature that was not required and therefore not included on the premises. In such circumstances a service provider will still need to consider whether the provision of those features would be a reasonable adjustment to make. The Code gives the following example:[490]

The designer of a library built in Scotland in 1997 was careful to adopt all relevant provisions of Part T of the Technical Standards. A deaf person who uses a hearing aid cannot participate fully in seminars convened in the small meeting room because there is no induction loop in it. The exemption does not apply even though the Technical Standard states that induction loops need not be provided in meeting rooms of this size. The service provider would have to consider whether it would be reasonable under Part III of the DDA to provide an induction loop in this room.

In addition even where the exemption applies a service provider may still be required to provide:

• a reasonable means of avoiding the particular physical feature; or
• a reasonable alternative method of making services available.[491]

5.7.1.7.2. Statutory consents, historic buildings, conservation areas, etc Service providers may have to obtain statutory consent before making

---

[487] *Ibid.* paragraph 6.22.
[488] Except for those features which are needed to provide access to the building from the edge of the site and from car parking within the site.
[489] Goods, Facilities, Services and Premises Code of Practice, paragraph 6.24. For guidance on 'inclusive design', see for example Design Council http://www.design council.info/webdav/servlet/ XRM?Page/@id=6047&Session/@id=D_yhUoiPaw9BNKu33x7alE&Document[@id%3D2313]/C hapter /@id=2.
[490] Goods, Facilities, Services and Premises Code of Practice, paragraph 6.25.
[491] *Ibid.* paragraphs 6.13 and 6.19.

adjustments involving changes to the premises. As already discussed,[492] the DDA does not take precedence over planning law and other statutory regulation. Accordingly, consents including planning permission, Building Regulations approval, or building warrants in Scotland, listed building consents, scheduled monument consent, and fire regulations approval and the requirements in respect of the same are all unaffected by the DDA. Importantly, therefore, service providers should plan in advance for any adjustments that might be required and include in that planning the time and steps that might be necessary to obtain the requisite permissions.[493]

As to historic buildings, relevant guidance in respect of access to historic environments is provided by English Heritage in the:

• English Heritage, 'Disability Access Policy' (2001);[494] and
• English Heritage, 'Easy Access to Historic Buildings' (2004).[495]

The policies indicate that English Heritage aims to improve and enhance all forms of access to its properties and services, while bearing in mind the constraints contained within pre-existing legislation relating to the protection of historic monuments, listed buildings, and conservation areas.[496] As English Heritage observes, the DDA does not override such pre-existing legislation,[497] however:

[i]n most cases access can be improved without compromising the special interest of historic buildings. There are only rare occasions when nothing can be done to improve or facilitate access. By undertaking a careful process of research, brief-taking, consultation and creative exploration of alternatives, good quality solutions for adding a new layer of history to our historic buildings are usually possible.[498]

In addition, 'Planning Policy Guidance 15: Planning and the Historic Environment', issued by the Office of the Deputy Prime Minister, Planning Directorate, provides a statement of government policies for the identification and protection of historic buildings, conservation areas, and other elements of the historic environment. The guidance is provided for local authorities, public authorities, property owners, developers, amenity bodies, and all members of the public with an interest in the conservation of a historic environment.[499] It states that:

---

[492] See 5.6.1 above.
[493] Goods, Facilities, Services and Premises Code of Practice, paragraphs 6.28–6.29.
[494] http://www.english-heritage.org.uk/filestore/policy/pdf/accesslower_policy_revised 2004.pdf.
[495] English Heritage Customer Services (Product Code 50702) and at http://www.english-heritage.org.uk/filestore/publications/pdf/free/eh_easyaccess_2004.pdf.
[496] 2001 Policy, *supra* note 494 at paragraph 4.
[497] *Ibid.* See also 'Easy Access to Historic Buildings', *supra* note 495, page 9.
[498] 'Easy Access to Historic Buildings', *supra* note 495, page 8.
[499] Introduction, paragraphs 1 and 3: http://www.adpm.gov.uk/stellnet/groups/odpm-planning/documents/page/odpm_plan_606900.hcsp.

It is important in principle that disabled people should have dignified easy access to and within historic buildings. If it is treated as part of an integrated view of access requirements for all visitors or users and a flexible and pragmatic approach is taken, it should normally be possible to plan suitable access for disabled people without compromising the building's special interest. Alternative routes or reorganising the use of spaces may achieve the desired result without the need for damaging alterations.[500]

It should also be remembered that where a physical adjustment is pending approval, a provider of goods, facilities, or services may be required to make an interim or other adjustment pursuant to its obligations to make reasonable adjustments. Simply awaiting the outcome of an application for consent or approval is unlikely to be adequate.

5.7.1.7.3. *Leases and other binding obligations*   A service provider may be bound by the terms of an agreement or other legally binding obligation (for example, a mortgage, charge, or restrictive covenant or, in Scotland, a feu disposition) under which it cannot alter the premises without another's consent. As with discrimination arising in the employment field, there is specific statutory regulation addressing such a circumstance. The 2001 Regulations[501] make provision for the circumstances in which it is reasonable, and those in which it is not reasonable, for a provider of services to have to take certain specified steps. Where under any binding obligation a provider of services is required to obtain the consent of any person to an alteration of premises which he occupies and that alteration is one which, but for that requirement, it would be reasonable for the provider of services to have to make in order to comply with the duty under section 21 DDA, then:

• it is reasonable for the provider of services to have to request the consent; but

• it is not reasonable for him to have to make the alteration before that consent is obtained.[502]

Where the provider of services occupies premises under a lease and under the terms of the lease he would not be entitled to make a particular alteration to the premises which he proposes to make in order to comply with the section 21 duty, then the lease is deemed to have effect as if it provided:

• for the occupier to be entitled to make the alteration with the written consent of the lessor;

• for the occupier to have to make a written application to the lessor for consent if he wishes to make the alteration;

• if such an application is made, for the lessor not to withhold his consent unreasonably; and

---

[500] *Ibid.* paragraph 3.28.

[501] Disability Discrimination (Providers of Services) (Adjustment of Premises) Regulations 2001, SI 2001/3253, which came into force on 1 October 2004.

[502] *Ibid.* Regulation 3.

- for the lessor to be entitled to make his consent subject to reasonable conditions.[503]

On the other hand, where a service provider fails to make a written application he is not entitled to rely on any constraints attributable to the fact that he occupies the premises under a lease in defence of any claim that he has failed to comply with the section 21 duty.[504]

Where the lessor holds the premises himself under a lease (with a superior lessor), provision is also made under the 2001 Regulations for modifying the terms of any superior lease in relevant circumstances. Where any superior lease exists the same has effect as between the superior lessor and lessee as if it provided:

- for the superior lessee to be entitled to give consent to the alteration with the written consent of the superior lessor;
- for the superior lessee to have to make a written application to the superior lessor for consent if he wishes to give his consent to the alteration;
- if such an application is made, for the superior lessor not to withhold his consent unreasonably; and
- for the superior lessor to be entitled to make his consent subject to reasonable conditions.[505]

Thus similar provision is made affecting the relationship between the superior lessor and lessee as compared to that made in the case of the under-lessor and lessee, as described above.

The 2001 Regulations make provision for the obtaining of consent. By Regulation 5 the lessor has forty-two days to reply beginning on the day upon which he receives the application:

- consenting to or refusing the alteration; or
- consenting to the alteration subject to obtaining the consent of another person required under any superior lease (or pursuant to any binding obligation, for example, a mortgage).

Where he does not do so, or fails to seek a consent required under, for example, a superior lease,[506] he is taken to have withheld his consent to the alteration. In addition, a lessor who receives any consent required from another person, for example a superior lessor, will be taken to have withheld his consent if he fails within fourteen days to let the service provider, or any person who made the

---

[503] Section 27(1) and (2) DDA.   [504] Schedule 4, Part II, paragraph 5 DDA.

[505] 2001 Regulations, *supra* note 501, Regulation 9 inserting section 27(2A) DDA and making relevant modifications to the provisions of section 27 in cases where there is a superior lessor.

[506] The same would apply in respect of any other binding obligation, for example, a mortgage. As to the requirements for obtaining such consent, see 2001 Regulations, Regulation 5(7).

application on their behalf, know in writing that he has received such consent.[507] In such circumstances the lessee, or any interested disabled person, may refer the matter to a County Court (or in Scotland, to the Sheriff).[508]

This is addressed further below.

Where an application for consent has been made, the lessor is entitled to make a written request for any plans and specifications, so long as any such request is reasonable and they were not already included with the application. Such a request may be made at any time within the period of twenty-one days beginning with the date on which he receives the application.[509] Where the lessor makes such a request, the forty-two day period begins with the day on which he receives the plans and specifications.[510] As the Code observes,[511] it would plainly be sensible therefore, in order to ensure that any application for consent is dealt with as expeditiously as possible, for service providers to include any relevant plans and specifications with the application for consent.

As described above, a lessor may withhold consent save where it is unreasonable to do so.[512] The withholding of consent will always be unreasonable where the lease provides that consent will be given to the alterations in respect of which consent has been sought.[513] In addition, the Goods, Facilities, Services and Premises Code of Practice indicates that, unsurprisingly, a trivial or arbitrary reason would almost certainly be unreasonable.[514] On the other hand, where a particular adjustment is likely to result in a substantial permanent reduction in the value of a lessor's interest in the premises, the lessor is likely to be acting reasonably in withholding consent, although each case will depend very much on the specific circumstances.[515] Conversely, the 2001 Regulations provide that a lessor will always be taken to have acted reasonably in refusing consent where:

- there is a binding obligation requiring the consent of any other person for the alteration;
- the relevant lessor has taken steps to seek that consent; and
- consent has not been given, or has been given subject to a condition making it reasonable for him to withhold his consent.[516]

In addition, a lessor will be taken to have acted reasonably in withholding his consent where the relevant lessor does not know, and could not reasonably be expected to know, that the alteration in respect of which consent is sought is one which the occupier proposes to make in order to comply with the section 21 duty.[517]

---

[507] *Ibid.* Regulation 5(5).   [508] *Ibid.* Regulation 9.
[509] *Ibid.* Regulation 5(3).   [510] *Ibid.*
[511] Goods, Facilities, Services and Premises Code of Practice, paragraph 6.37.
[512] Section 27(2) DDA and Schedule 4, Part II, paragraph 6(3) and (4) DDA.
[513] 2001 Regulations, Regulation 6(2), *supra* note 501.
[514] Goods, Facilities, Services and Premises Code of Practice, paragraph 6.42.
[515] *Ibid.* paragraph 6.41.
[516] 2001 Regulations, Regulation 7, *supra* note 501.   [517] *Ibid.* Regulation 7(2)(b).

As stated above, a lessor may give consent subject to conditions. A condition will be taken to be reasonable, for the purposes of the DDA, where the condition is to the effect that:

- the occupier must obtain the necessary planning permission and any other consent or permission required by or under any enactment;
- the work must be carried out in accordance with the plans or specifications approved by the lessor;
- the lessor must be permitted a reasonable opportunity to inspect the works (whether before or after it is completed);
- the consent of another person required under the superior lease or a binding agreement must be obtained; and
- the occupier must repay to the lessor the costs reasonably incurred in connection with the giving of consent.[518]

Where a service provider has written to a lessor for consent to make an alteration and the lessor has refused consent, or is deemed to have refused consent in the circumstances described above, or has attached conditions to his consent, the service provider or an interested disabled person, may refer the matter to a County Court (or, in Scotland, the Sheriff Court). In such circumstances the court will decide whether the lessor's refusal or any conditions imposed are unreasonable. If it decides that they are, it may make a declaration accordingly or authorize the service provider to make the alteration specified in the order. Where there is a superior lessor, the same applies so that such a declaration or order may be made in respect of any refusal by or unreasonable conditions imposed by a superior lessor.[519] Any order may require the service provider to comply with conditions stated in the order.[520] This procedure may be contrasted with that applicable under Part II DDA (the employment field) which does not permit a free-standing complaint to be made to a court or Employment Tribunal but allows only for the issue of consent to alterations to be considered by an Employment Tribunal in the context of a complaint of discrimination.

In any legal proceedings in a claim under Part III DDA, involving a failure to make any adjustment to premises, the disabled person concerned or the service provider may apply for the lessor to be joined (or sisted in Scotland) as a party to proceedings.[521] Such an application:

- will be granted if it is made before the hearing of the claim begins;[522]
- may be refused if the request is made after the hearing of the claim begins;

---

[518] *Ibid.* Regulation 8

[519] *Ibid.* Regulation 9(5) and (6) and Schedule 4, Part II, paragraph 6 DDA.

[520] Schedule 4, paragraph 6(5) DDA.   [521] Schedule 4, paragraph 7 DDA.

[522] Unless it appears to the court that another lessor should be joined: 2001 Regulations, Regulation 9(7), *supra* note 501.

• may not be granted if it is made after the court has determined the claim.[523]

Where a lessor has been so joined as a party to the proceedings, the court may determine whether the lessor has (i) refused consent to the alteration or (ii) consented subject to one or more conditions and (iii) if so, whether the refusal or any of the conditions was unreasonable.[524] Where the court concludes that the refusal or any of the conditions was unreasonable it may make a declaration accordingly; it may make an order authorizing the occupier to make the alteration specified in the order and order the lessor to pay compensation to the complainant.[525] The same applies with appropriate modifications in respect of a superior lessor, who may be joined, and against whom such a declaration and/or order may be made.[526]

5.7.2. Disability-Related Discrimination

As with discrimination falling within the employment and related fields, discrimination in the context of the provision of goods, facilities, and services is defined so as to include less favourable treatment of a disabled person for a reason which relates to the disabled person's disability. Section 20(1) DDA provides as follows:

For the purposes of section 19, a provider of services discriminates against a disabled person if—

(a) for a reason which relates to the disabled persons' disability, he treats him less favourably than he treats or would treat others to whom that reason does not or would not apply; and
(b) he cannot show that the treatment in question is justified.

Thus the meaning given to disability-related discrimination under section 20 mirrors identically that provided for under section 3A DDA, addressed above.[527]

Accordingly, the principles described above apply equally to disability-related discrimination occurring in the context of the provision of goods, facilities, and services.

As with disability-related discrimination under section 3A DDA, disability-related discrimination occurring within the context of the provision of goods, facilities, and services may be justified. However, the defence of justification is somewhat different in this context and is addressed below.

There are many cases of disability-related discrimination. These include:

---

[523] Schedule 4, Part II, paragraph 7 DDA. [524] *Ibid.*
[525] Schedule 4, paragraph 7(6) DDA.
[526] 2001 Regulations, Regulation 9(7), *supra* note 501.
[527] See 5.2.3 above.

- 'no dogs' policies and refusals to permit access to disabled people with assistance dogs;[528]
- extra charges for wheelchair users.[529]

The Goods, Facilities, Services and Premises Code of Practice gives the following examples.

A football club admits visiting supporters to its stadium. However, one visiting supporter is refused entry because he has cerebral palsy and has difficulty controlling and co-ordinating his movements. No other visiting supporter is refused entry. This would amount to less favourable treatment for a reason related to disability and, unless the football club can justify its actions, would be an unlawful refusal of service contrary to the Act.[530]

A popular disco turns away prospective patrons who do not satisfy their 'image' in one respect or another. A woman with a severe facial disfigurement is not admitted by the doorman for this reason. Even though the club also does not allow entrance to many non-disabled people, for example, because it does not consider they are appropriately dressed, the woman with the severe disfigurement has been treated less favourably for a reason related to her disability. This is likely to be unlawful.[531]

A group of deaf people who use British Sign Language (BSL) is refused entry to a disco. The doorman assumes that other customers might mistake communication using BSL as threatening gestures. This refusal of service is for a reason related to disability. It is likely to be unlawful even though the disco would have refused entry to any person who made similar gestures.[532]

As to the proper comparator, the principles set out above[533] apply equally.[534] On the second reading of the Bill for the DDA, the Minister for Social Security and Disabled People, William Hague, stated (Hansard (HC Debates), 24 January 1995, col. 150): 'The Bill is drafted in such a way that indirect as well as direct discrimination can be dealt with . . . A situation where dogs were not admitted to a cafe, with the effect that blind people would be unable to enter it, would be a *prima facie* case of indirect discrimination against blind people and would be unlawful.'[535]

---

[528] *Purves v Joydisc Ltd* [2003] SC 694/01, a decision of the (Scottish) Court of Session that the claimant was discriminated against contrary to section 19 DDA when he was refused admission into a restaurant with his assistance dog. Compensation was increased on appeal from £350 to £1,000. *Glover v Lawford t/a Hannah's Café* [2003] MA 202533. And see '50 Key Cases from the DRC' (October 2002) DRC, 25, with a number of examples of discrimination within Part III.

[529] *Ibid.* And see *Ross v Ryanair, supra* note 434.

[530] Goods, Facilities, Services and Premises Code of Practice, paragraph 3.3.

[531] *Ibid.* paragraph 3.4. See too (for a similar case), '50 Key Cases from the DRC' (October 2002), DRC, 29.

[532] *Ibid.* paragraph 3.9.

[533] See 5.2.3.3 above. *R v Powys CC* ex parte *Hambidge (No 2)* [2000] TLR 196, [2000] 3 CCLR 231 should be regarded as wrongly decided. It has not been followed and the approach is inconsistent with the approach of the Codes of Practice.

[534] *Council of the City of Manchester v (1) Romano (2) Samari* [2004] EWCA Civ 834, paragraph 47.

[535] Cited in *Clark v Novacold Ltd* [1999] ICR 951 at 964.

Thus Parliament intended that the proper comparator would be a person to whom the reason for the treatment does not or would not apply: in the example given, that would be a customer who does not have a dog with him (see discussion in 5.2.3.3 above).

As with disability-related discrimination in the employment and related fields, it is not necessary for the service provider to know of the disabled person's disability for such discrimination to be established. If the treatment is caused by the fact that the person is disabled, that is treatment which 'relates to' the disability.[536] The Goods, Facilities, Services and Premises Code of Practice gives the following example.[537]

A pub employee orders a customer who is lying prone on a bench seat to leave the premises because he assumes she has had too much to drink. However, the customer is lying down as a result of a disability rather than alcoholic consumption. The refusal of further service is for 'a reason which relates to the disabled person's disability'. This will be unlawful unless the service provider is able to show that the treatment in question is justified, as defined by the Act.

This is not uncontroversial, particularly because of the impact of other legal regulation which may conflict, at a cursory glance, with the aspirations of the DDA. As observed by Lord Justice Brooke in *Council of the City of Manchester v (1) Romano (2) Samari* [2004], the above example does not address the impact of licensing law:

[P]ublicans and those who work for them commit criminal offences if they allow disorderly conduct on licensed premises [section 140 of the Licensing Act 2003] or sell alcohol to a person who is drunk [section 141]. (The 2003 Act is not yet in force, but is due to become so in 2005, and there are equivalent earlier provisions in force under the Licensing Act 1964.) There is a real possibility that the publican is bound to be in the wrong if he refuses to serve an apparently drunken person—if the person is in fact drunk then he will commit an offence (and may put his licence in jeopardy too); if that person is only apparently drunk due to a disability, then he will commit an unlawful act which may sound in damages for discrimination. If we are correct in this analysis, such a situation cries out for a fresh look by Parliament.[538]

The answer lies in the defence of justification, which permits the license holder to refuse alcohol if the conditions necessary to establish justification existed at the time of the discriminatory act (these are discussed in 5.7.3 below), and section 59 DDA, which was not addressed in *Council of the City of Manchester v (1) Romano (2) Samari* (as far as one can tell from the judgment) and which ensures that the DDA does not take precedence over other laws.[539] However, the real difficulties presented by this radical legislative scheme cannot be overlooked: there may be friction between the right of disabled people to dignified

---

[536] Goods, Facilities, Services and Premises Code of Practice, paragraph 3.4.
[537] *Ibid.* paragraph 3.11.   [538] *Supra* note 534, paragraph 123.
[539] See Chapter 10 below, at 10.3.

fair treatment and the laws regulating the activities in the context of which the discrimination has occurred. For this reason, training and planning for non-discriminatory service delivery is crucial if the law is to be properly complied with.

As with disability-related discrimination occurring in the employment and related fields, such discrimination might be inferred from all of the circumstances even in the absence of direct evidence in relation to the same.[540]

There is no prohibition against 'direct' discrimination in the context of the goods, facilities, and services provisions. However, less favourable treatment that is on the ground of a disabled person's disability will be caught by the disability-related provisions. The Goods, Facilities, Services and Premises Code of Practice gives the following example.[541]

A party of adults with learning disabilities has exclusively booked a restaurant for a special dinner. The restaurant staff spend most of the evening making fun of the party and provide it with worse service than normal. The fact that there are no other diners in the restaurant that evening does not mean that the disabled people have not been treated less favourably than other people. Other diners would not have been treated in this way.

In addition, there is no express prohibition against harassment in the context of the provision of goods, facilities, and services. Again, however, harassment that is grounded in or related to disability will constitute disability-related discrimination. As will be seen below, whilst it is technically possible to 'justify' and thus defend all disability-related discrimination under the goods, facilities, and services provisions, direct discrimination, especially harassment is extremely unlikely to be capable of justification.

5.7.3. Justification

As described above, both a failure to make reasonable adjustments and disability-related discrimination might be justified.

Section 20(3) DDA provides that:

treatment is justified only if—
(a) in the opinion of the provider of services, one or more of the conditions mentioned in subsection (4) are satisfied; and
(b) it is reasonable, in all the circumstances of the case, for him to hold that opinion.

The conditions set out in section 20(4) are as follows:

- in any case, the treatment is necessary in order not to endanger the health or safety of any person (which may include that of the disabled person);
- in any case, the disabled person is incapable of entering into an enforceable agreement, or of giving an informed consent, and for that reason the treatment is reasonable in that case;

---

[540] Goods, Facilities, Services and Premises Code, paragraph 3.5.   [541] *Ibid.* paragraph 3.7.

- in a case of a refusal to provide or deliberate failure to provide services, the treatment is necessary because the provider of the services would otherwise be unable to provide the service to members of the public;

- in a case of discrimination in the standard of service or the manner of service or in the terms of service, the treatment is necessary in order for the provider of services to be able to provide the service to the disabled person or to other members of the public;

- in a case of discrimination in the terms on which a service is provided, the difference in the terms on which the service is provided to the disabled person and those on which it is provided to other members of the pubic reflects the greater cost to the provider of the services in providing the service to the disabled person.

This is an exhaustive list of conditions, and any defence of 'justification' dependent upon an opinion based on some other consideration will fail. Similarly, as can be seen, some of the conditions apply only to certain of the discriminatory acts and reliance cannot be placed on a condition that does not apply to the particular discriminatory act. A refusal to supply services to a disabled person based only on the fact that there will be a greater cost to the provider of the services in providing the service to the disabled person cannot be justified on that ground.

This test therefore imposes a more rigorous test than the test of justification applicable in the employment and related fields.[542]

The test is a two-fold test, as has been seen. It requires:

- that the service provider believes that one or more of the relevant conditions are satisfied; and

- that it is reasonable in all the circumstances of the case for the service provider to hold that opinion.

There is then a necessity for a genuine belief that a relevant condition applies, as well as an objective scrutiny of the reasonableness of that belief. As the Goods, Facilities, Services and Premises Code of Practice makes clear, 'A service provider does not have to be an expert on disability, but it should take into account all the circumstances, including any information which is available, any advice which it would be reasonable to seek, and the opinion of the disabled person'.[543]

---

[542] See 5.2.3.5 above. Accordingly, some of the cases arising under the employment-related provisions will not be applicable (in particular *Jones v Post Office* [2001] EWCA Civ 558, [2001] ICR 805, [2001] IRLR 384, though recent developments in the employment field have limited the scope of this defence even in the employment and related fields).

[543] Paragraph 7.8.

Accordingly a service provider who relies on the adage 'ignorance is bliss' is unlikely to be able successfully in any attempt to avail himself of the justification defence. Similarly, opinion or beliefs which are based on generalizations and the stereotyping of disabled people would not satisfy the justification defence.[544]

Any justification must be tested at the time of the discriminatory act complained of. Accordingly, the question whether a service provider has established justification will depend on the opinion held by the service provider at that time and whether, at that time, it was reasonable in all the circumstances of the case for him to hold that opinion.[545]

In respect of a failure to make reasonable adjustments, recent case-law in the employment field (before the defence of justification was repealed for a failure to make adjustments in this field by the 2003 Regulations, see 5.2.2 above) indicates that the defence of justification should be regarded as 'heavily restricted'. In *Collins v Royal National Theatre Board Limited*, the Court of Appeal concluded that the only workable construction of the defence of justification to a claim of a failure to make reasonable adjustments in the employment field:

in the context of the DDA and its manifest objects, is that it does not permit justification of a breach of [such duty] to be established by reference to factors properly relevant to the establishment of a duty . . . [In relation to the defence of justification to a breach of such a duty] what is material and substantial for the purposes of justifying an established failure to take such steps as are reasonable to redress disadvantage cannot, consistencly with the statutory scheme, include elements which have already been or could already have been, evaluated in establishing that failure.[546]

Thus a respondent could not rely on the same factors as had been relied upon for determining *reasonableness*, for the purposes of establishing a breach of a duty, where such a duty was then established (and such factors therefore necessarily rejected) for the purposes of seeking to make out the defence of justification; such factors may not be resurrected (*per* Lord Justice Sedley, at paragraph 32). This conclusion was reached notwithstanding that the defence of justification was therefore to be given a different meaning depending on whether the claim was for a failure to comply with a duty to make reasonable adjustments or for disability-related discrimination, though the defence was in material terms identically expressed (albeit in different sub-sections). This case is likely to be important for understanding the defence of justification outside of the employment sphere. There are important differences in the way in which the defence is framed under section 20(3) DDA, as compared to the employment field (both currently and before the 2003 Regulations). However, the principle, namely that a respondent ought not to be entitled to rely on factors that have been found not to meet the threshold of 'reasonable' (in determining whether a breach of a duty has

---

[544] Goods, Facilities, Services and Premises Code of Practice, paragraph 7.12.
[545] *Rose v Bouchet* [1999] IRLR 463.   [546] [2004] EWCA Civ 144, [2004] IRLR 395.

occurred) for the purposes of making out the defence of justification, may prove to be equally applicable to the non-employment sphere (see 5.9.1.4.2 below for a fuller discussion).

5.7.3.1. *The conditions*   The Goods, Facilities, Services and Premises Code of Practice gives guidance on the circumstances in which the particular conditions set out in section 20(4) might apply so as to satisfy the defence of justification. Examples are given of the circumstances in which a service provider might justify discrimination and those in which he might not. Some broad observations can be made about the impact of the conditions as follows.

- *Health or safety* This condition might relate to the health and safety of the disabled person himself or the health and safety of another. 'Health' for these purposes might be interpreted in accordance with the World Health Organization definition of the word 'health': 'Health is a state of complete physical, mental and social well-being and not merely the absence of disease and infirmity'.[547] Health is endangered if it is 'put at risk'.[548] In addition, in appropriate circumstances, regard must be had to the Convention rights[549] of those persons whose 'health and safety' might be affected in the absence of the treatment complained of. (This is discussed further in 5.8.2 below.) 'Trivial risks' to a person's health should be disregarded.[550] In addition, health or safety considerations which are based on generalizations and the stereotyping of disabled people will not constitute reasonably held opinions. Thus, for example, Fire Regulations should not be used as an excuse to place unnecessary restrictions on wheelchair users based on the assumption that wheelchair users would automatically be a hazard in a fire.[551] Service providers must take advice from the relevant licensing authority or local fire officer to make appropriate provision. In addition, any action taken in relation to health or safety must be proportionate to the risk and in this respect there must be a balance between protecting against the risk and restricting disabled people from using the service provider's services. All of us are entitled to make the same choices and to take the same risks within the same limits.[552]

- *Incapacity to contract* If a disabled person is genuinely unable to understand a particular transaction, a service provider may refuse to enter into it with him. However, as the Code of Practice makes clear, service providers should assume that a disabled person is able to enter into a contract, not the converse.[553] In particular, simple transactions (for example, the purchase of a pair of earrings from a jeweller[554] or the handing over of money accompanied by a clear order) must not be assumed to be outwith the capacity of a person with

---

[547] *Council of the City of Manchester v (1) Romano (2) Sumari, supra* note 534, at paragraph 69.
[548] *Ibid.* paragraph 70.   [549] See Chapter 3 above.
[550] *Council of the City of Manchester v (1) Romano (2) Samari, supra* note 534, at paragraph 75.
[551] Goods, Facilities, Services and Premises Code of Practice, paragraph 7.12.
[552] *Ibid.*   [553] *Ibid.* paragraph 7.15.   [554] *Ibid.*

a learning disability, for example. In *Dexter v N Power* the claimant had a neurological condition that caused her to shake. Though she had full mental capacity, N Power, through its agents, refused to accept her signature to a contract for supply of gas and electricity without a counter-signature from a neighbour. There was no objective justification for imposing this requirement but instead it was apparently based on the supplier's mistaken belief that someone with the claimant's condition lacked mental capacity to enter into contractual arrangements. The defence of justification failed.[555] In addition, the Disability Discrimination (Services and Premises) Regulations 1996[556] provide that the condition in relation to capacity does not apply where a disabled person is acting through another person by virtue of: a power of attorney, functions conferred by or under Part VII of Mental Health Act 1983, or, in Scotland, powers exercisable in relation to the disabled person's property or affairs in consequence of the appointment of a *curator bonis*, tutor, or judicial factor.[557] In summary therefore, where another person is legally acting on behalf of the disabled person, a service provider cannot discriminate in the provision of services by reliance on the capacity condition. As the Code observes, in any event, before discriminating against a disabled person on the ground of capacity (or believed incapacity), reasonable adjustments should be considered. For example, it might be appropriate to prepare a contractual document in plain English to overcome an inability to give informed consent.[558]

- *Service provider is otherwise unable to provide the service to public* Refusing a service to a disabled person will only be justifiable based on this condition if other people would be effectively prevented from using the service at all unless the service provider treated the disabled person less favourably than other people. It would not be sufficient that other people would be merely inconvenienced or delayed. In this respect the interest of the disabled person has to be put in the balance. If the effect of the less favourable treatment is to deprive a disabled person of use of the service this cannot be outweighed by mere inconvenience that would otherwise be suffered by other people. The condition imposes a much stricter test than this.

- *To enable the service provider to provide the service to a disabled person and other members of the public* A service provider can justify the provision of an inferior service to a disabled person where it is necessary in order to be able to provide the service to the disabled person or other members of the public. This is so only where the treatment is *necessary* for the same. This again is a narrow condition and will not easily be met. Certainly mere prejudice by other service users will be insufficient to justify any discrimination based on this condition.

---

[555] Swindon County Court 23/4/01, Case No SN005348 (unreported), cited in Palmer, Gill, Monaghan, Moon, and Stacey, ed McColgan, *Discrimination Law Handbook* (LAG, 2002) 884.
[556] SI 1996/1836.   [557] Regulation 8.
[558] Goods, Facilities, Services and Premises Code of Practice, paragraph 7.17.

The Code gives an example of a hotel which restricts wheelchair users' choice of bedrooms to those with level access to the lifts although these rooms tend to be noisier and have restricted views. Where the disabled person would otherwise not be able to use the hotel, the restriction is necessary in order to provide the service to the disabled guest and is likely to be justified.[559] As with all other conditions, before a service provider seeks to rely on such justification, it should consider whether there are any reasonable adjustments that could be made to allow the disabled person to enjoy the service on a non-discriminatory basis.

• *Greater cost of providing a tailor-made service* Where a service provider charges more for services provided to a disabled person because the service is individually tailored to the requirements of that disabled person, it might justify the higher charge. For example, where a pedicurist charges clients a flat rate for certain foot treatments which generally take thirty minutes she may be justified in charging double the usual rate to a disabled customer who has a treatment which, due to arthritis in his feet, takes one hour.[560] Importantly, however, this ground cannot be relied upon to justify discriminatory treatment in relation to charging where the extra costs are attributable to the service provider discharging its duty to make reasonable adjustments.[561] This is therefore a very limited defence and is concerned with individually tailored services only.

A number of cases have arisen that have tested the boundaries of the justification defence under Part II DDA. However, cases under Part III DDA are still relatively rare. In *White v Clitheroe Grammar School*[562] a school sought to rely on health and safety grounds in refusing permission to a child to join a school water sports trip. The child had insulin-dependent diabetes and on a previous school trip had a hypoglycaemic attack which the school believed was because he had failed to manage his condition properly. The school relied upon the individual teacher supervising the trip to make the decision whether the child should attend. The school did not, the court found, have reasonable grounds for its stated belief either in the pupil's irresponsibility or in the risk to health and safety. The Court determined that 'if the opinion was to be reasonably held any underlying assumptions would have to be checked . . . [there would need to be] a reasoned assessment of the implications of any increased risk'. The school had not consulted the pupil, his parents, or his doctors nor made any further enquiries of the company organizing the trip before making the decision to refuse the child permission to attend. There was no serious attempt at a risk

---

[559] *Ibid* paragraph 7.21; see also paragraph 7.22.   [560] *Ibid.* paragraph 7.24.
[561] See 5.7.1.5 above.
[562] Preston County Court (District Judge Ashton) 29 April 2002, Case No BB002640 (unreported), cited in Palmer, Gill, Monaghan, Moon, and Stacey, ed McColgan, *Discrimination Law Handbook* (LAG, 2002) 886–7.

assessment taking into account the nature of the holiday and the medical realities. Accordingly the court concluded that justification was not made out.[563] *White* illustrates the narrowness of the specific conditions necessary to make out justification and the rigour that must be applied to the two-pronged test for justification under section 20(4) DDA.[564]

5.7.3.2. *Insurance, guarantees, and deposits* Special provision is made in relation to insurance, guarantees, and deposits. In summary, disability-related discrimination is taken to be justified where the less favourable treatment is:

• in connection with insurance business carried on by the provider of services;
• based upon information (for example, actuarial or statistical data or a medical report) that is relevant to the assessment of the risk to be insured and is from a source on which it is reasonable to rely;
• reasonable having regard to the information relied upon and any other relevant factors.[565]

The less favourable treatment must meet each of the conditions identified for justification to be taken as made out. The Goods, Facilities, Services and Premises Code of Practice gives the following illustration:[566]

A person with a diagnosis of manic depression applies for motor insurance. He is told that he will have to pay double the normal premium because of his condition. The insurer is relying on actuarial data relating to the risks posed by a person driving when in a manic episode. However, the applicant produces credible evidence that he has been stable on medication for some years and has an unblemished driving record. In these circumstances, the charging of a higher premium in this case is unlikely to be justified because not all of the conditions above have been fully satisfied.

In order to be relevant to the assessment, the information upon which the less favourable treatment is based must be current and from a source on which it is reasonable to rely.[567] A reliance upon untested assumptions, stereotyping, or generalizations in respect of a disabled person will not be sufficient.[568] Accordingly, an insurer should not adopt a general policy or practice of refusing to provide insurance to disabled people or people with particular disabilities

---

[563] The Court was concerned with 'a policy', being a policy that an individual teacher would make the decision as to whether a child should attend trips and the school would support that decision; this policy was one which made it unreasonably difficult for a disabled student to join a school trip because it created the potential for discrimination by the teacher which could then be routinely supported by the headmaster.

[564] See also *Rose v Bouchet* [1999] IRLR463 at paragraph 5.8.2 below for a case on justification (section 24 DDA) but which must be considered to be confined to its own facts.

[565] Disability Discrimination (Services and Premises) Regulations 1996, SI 1996/1836, Regulation 2.

[566] Paragraph 8.4.

[567] Goods, Facilities, Services and Premises Code of Practice, paragraph 8.5.

[568] *Ibid.*

unless this can be justified by reference to the four conditions set out above, nor should an insurer adopt a general policy or practice of insuring disabled people or people with particular disabilities on different terms.[569]

In relation to existing insurance policies, cover documents, and master policies, transitional arrangements are made so that in relation to insurance policies that existed before 2 December 1996[570] any less favourable treatment in respect of the same is to be treated as justified until the policy falls for review or renewal on or after 2 December 1996.[571]

In relation to guarantees, again special provision is made: where a disabled person whose disability is such as to result in higher than average wear or tear to goods or services supplied and where it is therefore appropriate to make differential provision in relation to guarantees, such differential provision will be justified.[572] A service provider provides a guarantee for these purposes where he provides a guarantee that:

- the purchase price of services that he has provided will be refunded if the services are not of satisfactory quality; or
- services in the form of goods that he has provided will be replaced or repaired if those goods are not of satisfactory quality.[573]

A 'guarantee' includes any documents having the effect just referred to, whether or not the document is described as a guarantee. Indeed there is nothing in the Regulations that requires the guarantee to be in documentary form at all.[574]

Disability-related discrimination in relation to the provision of a guarantee is to be treated as justified where:

- the provider refuses to provide a replacement, repair, or refund under the guarantee because damage has occurred for a reason that relates to the disabled person's disability, and the damage is above the level at which the provider would normally provide a replacement, repair, or refund under the guarantee; and
- it is reasonable in all the circumstances of the case for the provider to refuse to provide a replacement, repair, or refund under the guarantee.[575]

---

[569] *Ibid.* paragraph 8.6.

[570] When the Regulation *supra* note 565 *supra* came into force.

[571] Regulation 3. A review of an existing policy which is part of, or incidental to a general re-assessment by the provider of services of the pricing structure for a group of policies is not to be treated as a review for these purposes: *ibid.* Regulation 3(3). In relation to cover documents disability related discrimination is to be treated as justified where the relevant master policy was entered into a renewed before 2 December 1996 and the refusal to issue a cover document occurs before 2 December 1997 or related to a cover document which was accepted before 2 December 1997: *ibid.* Regulation 4.

[572] *Ibid.*

[573] *Ibid.* Regulation 5(2).

[574] *Ibid.* Regulation 5(3), it being inclusively described.

[575] *Ibid.* Regulation 5(2).

Each of these elements must be satisfied for the disability-related treatment to be deemed justified under the Regulations. It does not permit direct discrimination, so that a refusal to meet the terms of a guarantee in circumstances where the damage is not above the level at which a guarantee would normally be honoured will not be justified. In addition, the refusal must be reasonable in the circumstances of the particular case. Where a guarantee is provided which explicitly covers damage which might arise from ordinary use by the particular disabled person, having regard to their disability, it is likely to be unreasonable not to honour the guarantee and therefore likely not to be justified under the Regulations.[576]

As to deposits, special provision is made in relation to a refusal to return a deposit, or a refusal to return a deposit in full, where damage to the goods or facilities have occurred because of the customer's disability or for a reason related to it. Such treatment is treated as justified in the following circumstances:

• when the goods or facilities were provided, the disabled person was required to provide a deposit which was refundable if the goods or facilities were undamaged; and

• the provider refuses to refund some or all of the deposit because damage has occurred to the goods or facilities for a reason which relates to the disabled person's disability, and the damage is above the level at which the provider would normally refund the deposit in full; and

• it is reasonable in all the circumstances of the case for the provider to refuse to refund the deposit in full.

Again, each of these elements must be satisfied if disability-related discrimination is to be treated as justified. It does not permit direct discrimination: if a deposit would normally be refunded in full even having regard to the damage actually sustained then the fact that that damage occurred for a reason which relates to the disabled person's disability is irrelevant. In addition, the Regulations do not permit a service provider to charge a disabled person a higher deposit than it would normally charge other people or to pay a deposit at all in circumstances where the service provider would not ordinarily expect a deposit to be paid.[577] As the refusal to refund the deposit in full must be reasonable in all the circumstances of the case, a refusal to refund the whole or part of the deposit where such amount exceeds the value of the loss suffered by the service provider is very likely to be unreasonable and accordingly not justified under the Regulations.

The Regulations just described prescribe the circumstances in which disability-related discrimination is to be treated as justified without further scrutiny. However, even where treatment is outside the Regulations, a service

---

[576] Goods, Facilities, Services and Premises Code of Practice, paragraph 8.1–13.
[577] *Ibid.* paragraph 8.17.

provider might still justify such treatment under the ordinary test of justification provided for in section 20(3) and (4) DDA. This is because the Regulations are made[578] under section 20(8) DDA which provides that 'Regulations may make provision, for the purposes of this section, as to circumstances (other than those mentioned in subsection (4)) in which treatment is to be taken to be justified'. It does not substitute the justification defence under section 20(3) and (4) but rather supplements it. The Code does not address this issue. If treatment is not justified by reason of the Regulations, one of the conditions identified in section 20(4) would have to be met if justification were to be made out at all.[579]

5.7.4. Victimization

As described above, the protected act under section 55(2)(a)(iii) is modified for the purposes of Part II and to the extent that it relates to the provision of employment services under Part III (see 5.2.5.5.3 above).[580] This modification does not apply to Part III cases (except employment services). Thus for Part III cases section 55(2)(a)(iii) is to be read as: 'otherwise done anything under this Act in relation to A or any other person'.

This therefore has a narrower reach. The act must be done *under* the DDA, which might include serving a questionnaire or issuing proceedings under the DDA, for example. As discussed above, where a complainant relies on something done *under* the DDA, case-law indicates that a specific provision of the DDA (under which the act is done) must be capable of identification and be identified.[581]

Otherwise the victimization provisions apply equally to the field of goods, facilities and services as they do to the employment field and the guidance given above at in 5.2.5 applies equally.

5.8. DISPOSAL AND MANAGEMENT OF PREMISES

Discrimination in the disposal and management of premises is outlawed by section 22, in Part III, DDA. In short summary, discrimination in the terms upon which premises are disposed; or by a refusal to dispose of premises; or in relation to any list of persons in need of premises, and discrimination in the management of premises are all outlawed. It is also unlawful for a person whose

---

[578] Insofar as is material.

[579] See 5.7.3.1 above.

[580] For a full discussion of all the protected acts, see 5.2.5.5 above.

[581] *Kirby v Manpower Services Commission* [1980] ICR 420, [1980] 1 WLR 725, [1980] 3 All ER 334, [1980] IRLR 229. Note: the approach to the comparison exercise undertaken in this case was departed from by the House of Lords in *Khan, supra* note 19; see, for example, Lord Nicholls, paragraph 27.

licence or consent is required for the disposal of any leased or sub-let premises to discriminate against a disabled person by withholding that licence or consent.

These provisions are explained in Chapter 7 below.

'Discrimination' for these purposes is defined by sections 24 and 55 DDA.[582] It comprises:

- disability-related discrimination; and
- victimization.

There is no duty to make adjustments in the context of the disposal and management of premises.[583]

The Disability Discrimination Bill will when enacted insert new sections 24A–24J into Part III DDA. These will introduce duties to make reasonable adjustments in respect of all lettings of property. As a result, it will be unlawful for landlords and managers of rented premises to discriminate against a disabled tenant or prospective tenant by failing, without justification, to comply with a duty to provide certain forms of reasonable adjustments. A landlord or manager will, under specified conditions, be required to take reasonable steps to provide auxiliary aids and services for a disabled person and to change policies, practices, and procedures. Presently, however, no such duties exist.

5.8.1. Disability-Related Discrimination

Section 24 DDA provides that, for the purposes of the 'premises' provisions:

. . . a person ('A') discriminates against a disabled person if—
(a) for a reason which relates to the disabled person's disability, he treats him less favourably than he treats or would treat others to whom that reason does not or would not apply; and
(b) he cannot show that the treatment in question is justified.

Disability-related discrimination is therefore defined in the same way as under the goods, facilities, and services provisions[584] and the observations above apply equally. As with disability-related discrimination falling within the context of the other unlawful acts under the DDA, such discrimination may be justified. However, the defence of justification is differently defined in the context of the premises provisions and this is addressed below.

Examples of cases of disability-related discrimination falling within the scope of the premises 'provisions' include:

---

[582] On victimization see 5.2.5 and 5.7.4 above.

[583] Though see Clause 6 of the Disability Discrimination Bill, discussed in Chapter 13 below, at 13.7.

[584] See 5.7.2 above.

- a refusal to let a flat to a blind tenant because of a belief that it was unsafe by reason of the absence of a handrail on the stairs;[585]
- charging a tenant of a flat forming part of a residential block for damage assumed to be caused by his wheelchair (without evidence of the same);[586]
- asking a deaf person for a non-refundable deposit as a condition of him renting a flat in circumstances where other tenants are asked for a refundable deposit.[587]

However, relatively few cases are brought under the premises provisions of the DDA.

5.8.2. Justification

As mentioned above, disability-related discrimination might be justified. Section 24(2) DDA provides that:

... treatment is justified only if—
(a) in A's opinion, one or more of the conditions mentioned in subsection (3) are satisfied; and
(b) it is reasonable, in all the circumstances of the case, for him to hold that opinion.

The conditions mentioned in section 24(3) are as follows:

- in any case, the treatment is necessary in order not to endanger the health or safety of any person (which may include that of the disabled person);
- in any case, if the disabled person is incapable of entering into an enforceable agreement, or of giving an informed consent, and for that reason the treatment is reasonable in that case;
- in a case of discrimination in the way a disabled person is permitted to make use of any benefits or facilities, the treatment is necessary in order for the disabled person or the occupiers of other premises forming part of the building to make use of the benefits or facilities;
- in a case of a refusal or deliberate omission to permit the disabled person to make use of any benefit or facilities, the treatment is necessary in order for the occupiers of other premises forming part of the building to make use of the benefits or facilities.

This is an exhaustive list of conditions (as with section 20(4) DDA) and a defence of 'justification' dependent upon an opinion based on any other consideration will fail.

---

[585] *Rose v Bouchet* [1999] IRLR 463, though this discrimination was found to be justified on the facts, as to which see 5.8.2 below

[586] Ref DRC/00/006: http://www.drc-gb.org/the law/casedetailsAsp?id=277&category=partiii& subcat=premises.

[587] Goods, Facilities, Services and Premises Code of Practice, paragraph 9.5.

As with justification falling under the goods, facilities, and services provisions, the test of justification is a mixed subjective and objective test and the observations made above apply equally (see 5.7.3 above).

In *Rose v Bouchet*[588] Mr Rose, who was blind, complained of discrimination under section 22 DDA when the landlord of the premises, Mr Bouchet, refused to let him a flat on the ground that there was no handrail in place alongside the steps leading to the flat and as such it would be dangerous for Mr Rose. Mr Rose had telephoned Mr Bouchet seeking accommodation and when he mentioned he was blind Mr Bouchet explained that work on the outside of the building still had to be completed and that he thought the steps would be dangerous for a blind person without an adequate handrail. He consulted with his wife who agreed and on returning to the telephone he informed Mr Rose that he thought access to the flat would be unsafe for him and that it would not be suitable. Mr Rose then raised his voice and, shouting, accused Mr Bouchet of refusing to take his guide dog. The telephone conversation came to an end shortly afterwards. In the proceedings brought by Mr Rose, Mr Bouchet admitted discrimination but relied on justification and in particular the 'health or safety' condition (section 24(3)(a) DDA). The Edinburgh Sheriff Court[589] on appeal from a decision in favour of Mr Bouchet by the Sheriff dismissed Mr Rose's appeal. In so doing they made the following observations:

- the justification defence provided for requires an interpretation that is in part objective and in part subjective;[590]
- the manner in which the provisions ought to be applied in a particular case will depend to a large extent on the facts and circumstances of that case;[591]
- the subjective element of the test puts in issue the opinion of the person carrying out the discriminatory act and does not require that, as an objective fact, the treatment in question should have been necessary for the relevant person's health and safety;[592] what is required is that in the opinion of the discriminator the treatment was necessary;
- the objective element of the test requires an objective assessment of all the relevant circumstances. In determining what circumstances are relevant for this purpose regard must be had to those pertaining at the time of the less favourable treatment (reasonableness is not to be tested *ex post facto* by reference to evidence only heard at the trial or some later stage).[593]

The Court determined that *on the facts as then known to him* the opinion reached by Mr Bouchet was a reasonable one for him to reach. In so concluding, the Court had regard to the fact that:

- the claimant was blind and used a guide dog;

---

[588] [1999] IRLR 463.
[590] [1999] IRLR 463, paragraph 30.
[592] *Ibid.* paragraph 32.

[589] This was a Scottish case.
[591] *Ibid.*
[593] *Ibid.* paragraphs 34 and 35.

- Mr Bouchet knew that the steps leading up to the flat had no handrail, with the result that there was an unguarded drop each side;
- Mr Bouchet considered that that was a threat to safety and, importantly, the reasonableness of this view was subsequently confirmed by an inspector from the Environmental Health Department;
- Mr Bouchet sought the opinion of a second person, namely his wife, which confirmed his own.[594]

Looking objectively at those facts, the Court concluded that the Sheriff was fully entitled to hold that it was reasonable for Mr Bouchet to hold the opinion which he did.

In this respect the Court was asked to have regard to the fact that Mr Bouchet did not endeavour to obtain more information before finalizing his opinion. As the Court observed, the DDA does not impose any such duty, though the Code recommends it.[595] However, the Court concluded that the question whether further enquiries were required would depend very much on the facts and circumstances of a particular case.[596] In particular, the Court was influenced by the fact that Mr Rose 'himself gave [Mr Bouchet] no opportunity to pursue any further enquiries' and that 'it is not unreasonable to expect the disabled person himself to offer some further information which might influence the other person's opinion'.[597]

On analysis, this decision is difficult because it does appear that Mr Rose was not afforded an opportunity to proffer information before the less favourable treatment (the refusal to let the flat) occurred. It does indicate however that a lack of cooperation by the disabled person concerned may be a relevant factor in deciding whether or not the objective element of the test of justification is made out on the facts of a particular case. The decision itself might be reconciled with the statutory wording by, as must necessarily be implicit, reading the Court's conclusions as indicating that the actual refusal did not crystallize until the telephone call was brought to a conclusion, by which time Mr Rose had been uncooperative.

As can be seen, the health and safety condition is concerned with both the health and safety of the disabled person and the health and safety of others.[598] 'Health' for these purposes has a wide meaning, as discussed in paragraph 5.7.3.1 above, and where engaged, regard must be had to Convention rights.[599] In the context of housing this may be particularly important. In *Hatton v United Kingdom*[600] the European Court of Human Rights concluded that severe environmental pollution might prevent individuals from enjoying their homes in

---

[594] *Ibid.* paragraph 36. [595] *Ibid.* paragraph 33.

[596] *Ibid.* paragraph 37. [597] *Ibid.*

[598] See also *Council of the City of Manchester v (1) Romano (2) Samari, supra* note 534, paragraph 56.

[599] See Chapter 3 above. [600] [2003] 37 EHRR 28.

such a way as to affect their private and family life adversely, without, however, seriously endangering their health.[601] In addition, the State's responsibility under Article 8(1) of the European Convention may be engaged where a person is directly and seriously affected by noise pollution, even where the nuisance emanates from the activities of private individuals.[602] Accordingly, Article 8(1) might be infringed in these circumstances and section 24(3)(a) DDA must be read in a way which is compatible with those rights.[603] It is difficult to conceive of a case arising under section 22 where Article 8 will not be engaged.

Therefore where a belief is reasonably held that a person—the disabled person or another—might have their health, very broadly construed, 'put at risk' in the absence of the treatment complained of, the conditions in section 24(2) read with section 24(3)(a) are likely to be satisfied. In *Council of the City of Manchester v (1) Romano (2) Samari*[604] Ms Romano and Ms Samari were secure tenants of Manchester CC. Proceedings were brought against both of them for possession orders and they were granted by the County Court in consequence of anti-social behaviour. Both Ms Romano and Ms Samari had depressive illnesses[605] at material times. The extensive anti-social behaviour followed a breach of the terms of a suspended possession order in the first case and the terms of an injunction in the second. It was accepted by the Court of Appeal that the serving of a notice seeking possession was an act falling within section 22(3)(c) DDA,[606] even though eviction itself was mandated by the court, so that if the reason for it related to disability it required justification if it was to be lawful.[607] However, the Court of Appeal dismissed appeals against the possession orders based on the DDA, holding that on the evidence the court could properly conclude that the health of neighbours of Ms Romano and Ms Samari was endangered in the sense just described. In the first case they held that even if a section 22 DDA point had been taken at the trial (it had not) so that the Council's opinion to this effect had been tested at the trial, it would have been held to have been objectively reasonable. In addition, on the medical evidence, it was difficult to see how the bulk of the anti-social behaviour related to Ms Romano's mental impairment (the acts of anti-social behaviour were committed by her sons).[608] In the second case, the possession order was again justified having regard to section 24 DDA and the impact on Ms Samari's neighbours.

---

[601] *Hatton v United Kingdom, supra,* note 600, paragraph 96.

[602] *Ashworth v United Kingdom,* 20 January 2004, Application No 39561/98, the ECtHR, discussed in *Council of the City of Manchester v (1) Romano (2) Samari, supra* note 534, paragraph 74.

[603] See Chapter 3 above and *Council of the City of Manchester v (1) Romano (2) Samari, supra* note 534, paragraphs 70 and 73 for discussion.

[604] *Supra,* note 534.

[605] Though in Ms Romano's case there was an issue as to whether she was 'disabled' for the purposes of the DDA which was unresolved on appeal (*ibid.* paragraph 94).

[606] 'Eviction' or 'detriment', see Chapter 7 below.

[607] *Council of the City of Manchester v (1) Romano (2) Samari, supra* note 534, at paragraph 50.

[608] *Ibid.* at paragraph 93.

5.8.3. Deposits on Premises

Special provision is made in relation to requests for deposits on premises and justification. The Disability Discrimination (Services and Premises) Regulations 1996[609] provide that disability-related discrimination is to be treated as justified where:

- the provider grants a disabled person a right to occupy premises (whether by means of a formal tenancy agreement or otherwise);
- in respect of that occupation the disabled person is required to provide a deposit that is refundable at the end of the occupation provided that the premises and contents are not damaged;
- the provider refuses to refund some or all of the deposit because the premises or contents have been damaged for a reason which relates to the disabled person's disability, and the damage is above the level at which the provider would normally refund the deposit in full; and
- it is reasonable in all the circumstances of the case for the provider to refuse to refund the deposit in full.[610]

As with the provision made in relation to deposits under the goods, facilities, and services provisions, each of these elements must be satisfied if the treatment is to be treated as justified. This special provision does not justify a person with the power to dispose of the premises charging a disabled person a higher deposit than it would charge to other people; or charging a disabled person a deposit in circumstances where a deposit would not be required for non-disabled people.[611] In addition, the refusal to refund the deposit in full must be reasonable in all the circumstances of the case and so the sum withheld should properly reflect any damage to the premises and then only where sums would be withheld from non-disabled tenants who had caused comparable damage.[612]

5.8.4. Victimization

The victimization provisions apply in precisely the same way to those unlawful acts created under the 'premises' provisions (section 22 DDA) as they apply to the goods, facilities and services provisions. The observations at 5.7.4 above therefore apply to victimization falling within the scope of the unlawful acts created by section 22 DDA.

---

[609] SI 1996/1836. [610] *Ibid.* Regulation 7.
[611] Goods, Facilities, Services and Premises Code of Practice, paragraph 9.41.
[612] *Ibid.* paragraphs 9.42–9.43.

5.9. EDUCATION

Discrimination in education is outlawed by Part IV DDA, as amended by the Special Educational Needs and Disability Act 2001 (SENDA). In short summary, discrimination by a 'responsible' body against prospective pupils and existing pupils is outlawed by section 28A DDA in the case of schools; discrimination by a 'responsible' body against prospective students and existing students is outlawed by section 28R DDA in the case of further and higher educational institutions; and discrimination by local education authorities, including against users of certain statutory youth and community services, is outlawed by section 28U and Schedule 4C DDA. The 'responsible' bodies are defined by the DDA and discussed at Chapter 8 below.

In addition, discrimination by local education authorities in the exercising of their functions under the Education Acts is outlawed by section 28F DDA.

'Discrimination' is defined differently according to whether the discrimination occurs in the context of a school or local educational authority or further or higher educational institution, in material respects, and accordingly discrimination for the purposes of each is dealt with under separate headings below.

The DRC has issued two Codes of Practice addressing discrimination within the field of education:

• 'Disability Discrimination Act 1995 Part IV, Code of Practice for Schools' ('Schools Code of Practice');[613] and

• 'Disability Discrimination Act 1995 Part IV, Code of Practice for Providers of Post 16 Education and Related Services' ('Post 16 Code of Practice').[614]

These provide guidance on the meaning of discrimination and its impact and are addressed, as relevant, below.

5.9.1. Schools

'Discrimination' for the purposes of the schools provisions of the DDA is defined[615] by sections 28B and 55 DDA. It comprises:

• a failure to comply with a duty to make reasonable adjustments;
• disability-related discrimination; and
• victimization.

---

[613] Disability Rights Commission, COPSH July 2002. The Code came into force on 1 September 2002: Disability Discrimination Codes of Practice (Education) (Appointed Day) Order 2002, SI 2002/2216.

[614] Disability Rights Commission, COPP 16 July 2002. The Code came into force on 1 September 2002: Disability Discrimination Codes of Practice (Education) (Appointed Day) Order 2002, SI 2002/2216.

[615] Section 28A DDA.

As stated above, the DRC has prepared and issued a relevant Code of Practice: 'Disability Discrimination Act 1995 Part IV, Code of Practice for Schools' ('Schools Code of Practice').[616]

Direct discrimination and harassment are not outlawed explicitly. However, as discussed in paragraph 5.7.2 above, some instances of direct discrimination and harassment will constitute disability-related discrimination.

5.9.1.1. *Duty to make adjustments*
The duty to make reasonable adjustments in the context of school is addressed by section 28C DDA. This provides that:

(1) The responsible body[617] for a school must take such steps as it is reasonable for it to have to take to ensure that—
   (a) in relation to the arrangements it makes for determining the admission of pupils to the school, disabled persons are not placed at a substantial disadvantage[618] in comparison with persons who are not disabled; and
   (b) in relation to education and associated services provided for, or offered to, pupils at the school by it, disabled pupils are not placed at a substantial disadvantage in comparison with pupils who are not disabled.

As with the duties arising in other spheres, these duties determine the circumstances in which discrimination might occur and are not actionable as such.[619]

By section 28B(2) DDA discrimination against a disabled person occurs if the responsible body fails 'to his detriment' to comply with the duties under section 28C and cannot show that its failure to comply is justified. 'Detriment' has a very wide meaning[620] and any less favourable treatment or disadvantage is likely to constitute a 'detriment' for these purposes.

The duties explicitly do not require a responsible body to remove or alter a physical feature of premises or provide auxiliary aids or services.[621] The Schools Code of Practice explains the rationale behind these limitations. The 'Special Educational Needs' framework[622] is designed to identify, assess, and make provision for children with special educational needs and such provision will include, where necessary, educational aids and services.[623] For this reason, it is not necessary for the DDA to make additional provision. As to what constitutes an 'auxiliary aid' or 'service', regard should be had to the decision in *McAuley Catholic High School v (1) CC (2) PC and Special Educational Needs and*

---

[616] Disability Rights Commission, COPSH July 2002. The Code came into force on 1 September 2002: Disability Discrimination Codes of Practice (Education) (Appointed Day) Order 2002, SI 2002/2216.

[617] As to which see Chapter 8 below.

[618] Note that the same words appear in the reasonable adjustment duties in the employment field: see 5.2.2 above.

[619] Section 28C(8) DDA.   [620] See 5.2.4 above and 6.2.7.3 below.

[621] See exemption in section 28C(2) DDA.

[622] Discussed in Chapter 8 below.   [623] Schools Code of Practice, paragraph 6.20.

Disability Tribunal,[624] in which consideration was given to the question whether pastoral support might constitute an auxiliary service for the purposes of the exemption. In that case the Court upheld a finding of the Special Educational Needs and Disability Tribunal that in failing to make adjustments consisting of the provision of support for a child with autistic spectrum disorder during unstructured times and the making of arrangements to assist him in his transition from one year to the next, a school was in breach of their duty under section 28C DDA. The tribunal had concluded, in a decision upheld by the Court, that the school had failed to take reasonable steps by failing to give the pupil the necessary personal guidance and support within the context of the school's pastoral system.[625] No argument appears to have been mounted that such support might have constituted an auxiliary service and the Court (which can be taken to have had the exemption in mind because it is annexed to its judgment) treated the provision of such support as an issue of 'planning and organization' (and not 'resourcing').[626] This secures a purposive construction of the duty and ensures that the duty is engaged in relation to the planning, management, and support for disabled pupils and requires the provision of such support where it forms part of the usual school environment. Whilst the meaning given to auxiliary aids or services in particular is very wide in the field of goods, facilities, and services because the duty there extends to the provision of the same,[627] it should be given a narrower reading in the context of the schools provisions. This must be so if any real sense is to be made of the duty to make reasonable adjustments. The duty to make reasonable adjustments gives effect to the key purpose of Part IV DDA: to make mainstream education provision accessible for disabled pupils. This would be undermined if much provision could be characterized as a 'service' so as to fall outside the scope of the duty. The exemption is probably best viewed as covering exceptional or unusual and additional aids or services but not those that would ordinarily be provided as part of the ordinary school day or curriculum, even if differently according to the different needs of the particular child.

In the case of independent schools, a school may make specialist tuition available and can charge parents for this. Where they do so, however, such charges must properly reflect the cost of such provision—any effort to deter a disabled pupil or treat him or her less favourably for a reason relating to disability would remain unlawful (as disability-related discrimination) notwithstanding that there is no duty to provide auxiliary aids and services.[628]

As mentioned above, there is no duty under section 28C to remove or alter a physical feature (for example, one arising from the design or construction of the school premises or the location of resources).[629] However, the duty to make adjustments may require that other adjustments be made to mitigate the effects

---

[624] [2003] EWHC 3045 (Admin), [2001] 2 All ER 436.
[625] *Ibid.* paragraph 58.
[626] *Ibid.* paragraph 59.
[627] Section 21(4) DDA.
[628] Schools Code of Practice, paragraph 6.22.
[629] Section 28C(2)(a) DDA.

of a physical feature.[630] In addition, in England and Wales and in Scotland, there are planning duties requiring schools to secure accessibility for disabled pupils that may require adjustments to physical features, though a failure so to do does not give rise to an individual cause of action under the schools provisions of the DDA.[631]

The physical environment of schools, therefore, is addressed by the imposition of public law duties, rather than individual statutory causes of action.

As can be seen, the duties to make adjustments in the field of education are in some senses wider and some senses narrower than those provided for in relation to the goods, facilities, and services provisions. Whilst the duties do not extend to making adjustments to physical features or to the provision of auxiliary aids or services, they are not limited to practices, policies, or procedures but create anticipatory duties across the board in relation to the exercise of any function both in relation to the admission of pupils and in relation to the provision of education and associated services.[632] There is therefore no requirement to determine whether there is a practice, policy, or procedure in place which makes the enjoyment of any benefit impossible or unreasonably difficult for disabled pupils (cf the duties in the field of goods, facilities, and services); instead the focus is on the impact of *any* arrangements for disabled pupils and the management of those to ensure effective access and to eliminate disadvantage for such pupils. Thus the duties are very broad. 'Substantial' disadvantages for the purposes of determining whether a duty is engaged are those which are not 'minor' or 'trivial' (Schools Code of Practice, paragraph 6.9).

5.9.1.1.1. To whom is the duty to make reasonable adjustments owed? As described above, the duties are anticipatory in nature. They therefore apply to all disabled children at large. This means that a school must not wait until a disabled person seeks to gain admission or to use a service before considering what adjustments should be made. Instead schools must anticipate the requirements of disabled people and plan for their involvement.[633] A lack of notice alone would therefore not found a defence to a claim for a breach of the reasonable adjustment duty, though a lack of knowledge regarding a particular disabled person will be material; see paragraph 5.9.1.3 below.

5.9.1.1.2. How the duty is discharged As with the duties falling under the goods, facilities, and services provisions, the duties arising under the schools provisions of the DDA are anticipatory in nature. They are owed to disabled pupils at large and do not require disadvantage to be suffered by a particular disabled pupil for the imposition of the duties to be triggered. Thus while an unlawful act will only occur where a particular disabled person has suffered detriment in consequence

---

[630] Schools Code of Practice, paragraph 6.23.

[631] See section 28D DDA ('accessibility strategies and plans') and Education (Disability Strategies and Pupils' Educational Records) (Scotland) Act 2002. See Chapter 8 below.

[632] Section 28C DDA.   [633] Schools Code of Practice, paragraph 5.6.

of a breach of the duty, educational institutions must take steps in advance if they are to avoid a breach of the duty. A responsible body must take steps 'to ensure that' disabled persons are not placed at a substantial disadvantage. This will involve planning, and requires schools and other responsible bodies to be proactive about ensuring that the provision they make is accessible.

In determining whether any arrangements a responsible body makes for the purposes of admitting pupils to the school or any education and associated services it provides for pupils at the school are such as to place disabled pupils at a substantial disadvantage, regard might be had to the following factors:

- the time and effort that might need to be expended by a disabled child;
- the inconvenience, indignity, or discomfort a disabled child might suffer;
- the loss of opportunity or diminished progress that a disabled child might make, in comparison with his or her peers who are not disabled.[634]

In each case it is the potential for substantial disadvantage that triggers the duty, and accordingly schools cannot wait until a disabled pupils has arrived before considering whether adjustments ought to be made because by then it may be too late.[635] The Schools Code of Practice gives the following guidance:[636]

A selective school considers carefully how disabled children can take their entrance exams without being at a substantial disadvantage. The school sets up early 'admissions meetings' with the parents of disabled prospective pupils. The meetings are used to discuss any special arrangements for the exams. The particular arrangements for an individual child can then be put in place in time. This is likely to be a reasonable step that the school should take.

The planning necessary to ensure that such adjustments are properly made is likely to include discussions with the relevant local education authority in England or Wales, the relevant education authority in Scotland, and where appropriate the local health and social services bodies and parents.[637] The Schools Code of Practice gives the following example:[638]

A small rural primary school has little experience of disabled pupils. The school is going to admit a five-year-old girl with a rare syndrome involving moderate learning difficulties, poor muscle tone, and speech and language difficulties. The head teacher consults the child's mother and a local voluntary organisation and devises a series of short training events drawing on local expertise. The training enhances staff knowledge and confidence and the girl has a positive start to school. This is likely to be a reasonable step to take to prevent the pupil from being placed at a substantial disadvantage.

The impact of a failure in proper planning can be seen in *R (on the application of D) v Governing Body of Plymouth High School for Girls*[639] in which the Court

---

[634] Schools Code of Practice, paragraph 6.11.
[635] *Ibid.* paragraph 6.12.
[636] *Ibid.* paragraph 6.13(c).
[637] *Ibid.* paragraphs 6.16–6.17.
[638] *Ibid.* paragraph 6.17A.
[639] [2004] EWHC 1923.

held that a failure to provide a disabled pupil with one of the placements of her choice because the form in relation to the same did not disclose details of her 'medical' condition the school, which was responsible for organizing such placements, 'should have done a lot more in advance . . . to ensure that there was no substantial disadvantage to D, as compared with other pupils, because of her visual impairment'. In particular, 'there was absolutely no reason why the school, who after all knew about D's disability, should not in a covering letter or some other way have informed Trident [the placement organizer] that she had this relevant disability'. The school knew that work placements were a requirement of all pupils in the particular year and they knew that any disability was material and a potential employer would want to know about it, as would the placement organizers.[640]

The duty to make reasonable adjustments is a continuing one and therefore requires monitoring and, as appropriate, review, to ensure that it is at all times effectively discharged.[641]

Unlike the duties arising in other fields,[642] Part IV DDA does not give any guidance as to what factors will be relevant in determining whether a particular step is reasonable. Section 28C(4) DDA requires that 'in considering whether it is reasonable for it to have to take a particular step in order to comply with its duty under subsection (1) [the duty to make adjustments], a responsible body must have regard to any relevant provisions of a code of practice issued under section 53A'. This imposes a mandatory duty on a responsible body—and by implication, a court or tribunal—to have regard to the guidance in the Schools Code of Practice. The Schools Code of Practice provides guidance on the relevant factors to be taken into consideration as follows:[643]

• the need to maintain academic, musical, sporting, and other standards;
• the financial resources available to the responsible body;
• the cost of taking a particular step;
• the extent to which it is practicable to take a particular step;
• the extent to which aids and services will be provided to disabled pupils at the school under Part IV of the Education Act 1996 or sections 60 to 65G of the Education (Scotland) Act 1980;
• health and safety requirements;
• the interests of other pupils and persons who may be admitted to the schools as pupils.

The Code gives the following, amongst other, examples:[644]

---

[640] *Ibid.* paragraphs 47–51.
[642] Compare section 18B DDA.
[644] *Ibid.* paragraphs 6.34A and 6.34B.
[641] Schools Code of Practice, paragraph 6.18.
[643] Schools Code of Practice, paragraph 6.30.

The need to maintain standards

A secondary school, which includes a number of disabled pupils, plans a musical Christmas production. One of the disabled pupils has a powerful singing voice and is considered for a lead role. However, the stage is inaccessible.

The school goes through the following considerations:

- the need to maintain standards dictates that the show has to be up to the high standards that the school has set in the past;
- enabling the disabled pupil to participate will help to maintain the high standards;
- the school is not required to make physical alterations;
- it is possible to change round the proposed acting area and the auditorium. There would be no additional cost to this option but the audience might not get such a good view.

The school decides that, in order not to put the disabled pupil at a substantial disadvantage, and having considered the need to maintain standards, it will switch round the acting area and the auditorium.

The school has considered the factors and has identified a reasonable adjustment. In making this adjustment it is likely to be acting lawfully.

The interest of other pupils

An exchange trip is offered to pupils studying Italian in a secondary school. Accessible transport arrangements are made and a suitable host is identified who can accommodate a pupil who uses a wheelchair. At the last minute the Italian host drops out.

The school went through the following considerations:

- it was not practicable to take the disabled pupil without a host to go to;
- the school considered cancelling the trip, but if the other pupils did not go they would lose the opportunity of improving their Italian.

In the interests of other pupils the school decides to go ahead with the trip. The school has considered the factors and, whilst it has not been able to identify a reasonable adjustment that would enable the pupil to go on the trip, it is likely to be acting lawfully.

In addition, regard can be had to the overall purpose of the SENDA provisions. These were plainly designed to make schools more accessible to disabled pupils and mainstream the teaching of disabled pupils. The purposes are described in the Schools Code of Practice at paragraph 1.1 as follows: 'The principle behind this legislation is that wherever possible disabled people should have the same opportunities as non-disabled people in their access to education'.

The purpose of the SENDA provisions is exemplified by the duties under section 28D DDA to prepare accessibility strategies and plans. These are strategies for 'increasing the extent to which disabled pupils can participate in the schools' curricula, improving the physical environment of the school for the purpose of increasing the extent to which disabled pupils are able to take advantage of education and associated services provided or offered by the schools, and improving the delivery to disabled pupils . . . of information which is provided in writing for pupils who are not disabled'.[645] In all cases regard must also be had to the

---

[645] Section 28D(2) DDA.

object of the reasonable adjustment duty, which is to diminish, and if possible eliminate, any substantial disadvantage to which a disabled pupil may be subject by reason of any arrangements made or in relation to education and associated services provided.[646]

5.9.1.2. *Disability-related discrimination*
As with discrimination falling within the employment and related fields (amongst others), discrimination in the context of schools is defined so as to include disability-related discrimination. Section 28B DDA provides as follows:

A responsible body[647] discriminates against a disabled person if—
(a) for a reason which relates to his disability, it treats him less favourably than it treats or would treat others to whom that reason does not or would not apply; and
(b) it cannot show that the treatment in question is justified.

Thus the meaning given to disability-related discrimination under section 28B DDA mirrors in all material respects that provided for under section 3A DDA, addressed above.[648] Accordingly, the principles described above apply equally to disability-related discrimination occurring in the context of schools.

As in other fields, disability-related discrimination under section 28B DDA may be justified. The defence of justification is addressed in 5.9.1.4 below.

Cases of disability-related discrimination in the context of schools include:

• a failure to place a disabled child in a work placement of her choice because of her visual impairment and an absence of medical information relating to it;[649]

• a fixed-term exclusion for a reason relating to disability.[650]

The Schools Code of Practice gives the following, amongst other, examples:[651]

Example 5.7A
A father seeks admission to a primary school for his son, who has epilepsy. The school tells him that they cannot take the boy unless he stops having fits.

In effect, the school is placing conditions on the boy's admission because he might have fits. Having fits is an intrinsic part of the boy's epilepsy. The reason for the less favourable treatment is one that relates to the boy's disability.

---

[646] Section 28C(1) DDA.
[647] As to which see Chapter 8 below For the position in relation to 'knowledge', see 5.9.1.3 below.
[648] See 5.2.3 and 5.7.2 above.
[649] *R (on the application of D) v Governing Body of Plymouth High School for Girls*, *supra* note 639.
[650] *McAuley Catholic High School v (1) CC (2) PC and (3) Special Educational Needs and Disability Tribunal*, *supra* note 624.
[651] Paragraph 5.7.

Example 5.7B
An eleven-year-old girl is admitted to a secondary school. The school wants her to have all her lessons in a separate room in case she frightens other children with her muscle spasms and her involuntary noises.

The reasons for placing the girl in a separate room are the muscle spasms and the involuntary noises. These are an intrinsic part of her disability. The less favourable treatment proposed is for a reason that relates to the girl's disability.

As to the proper comparator, the principles set out above[652] apply equally. Accordingly, where a pupil is 'badly behaved' by reason of autistic spectrum disorder (a disability), the proper comparator is a child who is neither disabled nor badly behaved.[653] The Schools Code of Practice gives the following example:[654]

A pupil with Tourette's Syndrome is stopped from going on a school visit because he has used abusive language in class. The school has a policy of banning pupils from trips and after-school activities if they swear or are abusive to staff.
The reason for not allowing the pupil to go on the school visit is his use of abusive language. His involuntary swearing is a symptom of his Tourette's Syndrome. This is less favourable treatment for a reason that relates to the pupil's disability.

There must of course be a relationship between the disability and any disruptive or anti-social behaviour which is said to constitute a reason for the less favourable treatment, if disability-related discrimination is to be made out. The Schools Code of Practice illustrates this proposition by the following example:[655]

A school has received a number of complaints from local shopkeepers about the rowdy and disruptive behaviour of some of its pupils. It decides that the pupils in question should be banned from taking part in a school theatre visit because of their behaviour. One of the pupils has a hearing impairment. The rowdy and disruptive behaviour is not directly related to the pupil's impairment. The ban from the visit may be less favourable treatment, but it is not for a reason related to the pupil's disability.

5.9.1.3. *Knowledge of disability and confidentiality*
Where a responsible body does not know that a pupil, or prospective pupil, is disabled and could not reasonably have been expected to know, then the taking of any particular step will not amount to less favourable treatment.[656] As to whether a responsible body, including the school, might reasonably be expected to know that a particular child was disabled at material times, the guidance given

---

[652] See 5.2.3.3 above.
[653] *McAuley Catholic High School v (1) CC (2) PC and (3) Special Educational Needs and Disability Tribunal, supra* note 624.
[654] Paragraph 5.7C.   [655] Paragraph 5.8A.
[656] Section 28B(4) DDA. This can be contrasted with the position in the employment; goods, facilities, and services and premises provisions: see 5.2.3.4 and 5.7.2 above.

at 5.2.2.1 above is likely to be relevant. In particular, however, it should be borne in mind that in most cases schools will be aware of a child's disability because of the arrangements in place for the assessment of special educational needs through the Special Educational Needs framework.[657] Where a child presents as underachieving and behaviourly challenging this may indicate an underlying disability and where such indicators are present, a school is likely to find it difficult to discharge the burden of establishing lack of knowledge.[658] In addition, information given to a member of staff will be imputed to the responsible body and it is therefore unlikely that the responsible body would be able to rely on an absence of knowledge of which its staff ought to have been aware.[659] The Code of Practice gives the following example:[660]

A pupil tells the school secretary that she has diabetes and that she needs to carry biscuits to eat when her blood sugar levels fall. A teacher has no information about her diabetes and refuses to allow pupils to bring food into the class. The girl has a hypoglycaemic attack. In this case, the school is unlikely to be able to argue that it did not know about her condition. It is unlikely that the responsible body could rely on a lack of knowledge defence.

The Schools Code of Practice indicates that schools are therefore required to be proactive in seeking out information and that if they are not then they are unlikely to rely successfully on a lack of relevant knowledge. The Code of Practice suggests that responsible bodies may, for example:[661]

- want to establish an atmosphere and culture at the school that is open and welcoming, so that pupils and parents feel comfortable about disclosing information about a disability;
- ask parents, when they visit or during the admissions process, about the existence and nature of any disability that their child may have;
- provide continuing opportunities to share information, for example when seeking permission to go on a school trip or at points of transition within the school.

However, where a school does not know and could not reasonably have been expected to know, about the existence of a particular pupil's disability, no liability will arise for disability-related discrimination. The Schools Code of Practice gives the following example:[662]

A nursery school admits a four-year-old child with coeliac disease. All new parents are asked to complete a form and are encouraged to discuss with the school their child's general development and any special needs. However, the child's parents do not inform the school of the child's condition. On another child's birthday, all the pupils receive a piece of birthday cake. The cake makes the child with coeliac disease ill. The parents argue that

---

[657] Schools Code of Practice, paragraph 7.7. See also, Chapter 8 below.
[658] *Ibid.* paragraph 7.8.   [659] *Ibid.* paragraph 7.11.   [660] *Ibid.* paragraph 7.11A.
[661] *Ibid.* paragraph 7.9.   [662] *Ibid.* paragraph 7.10A.

the school has discriminated against their child because of his disability. He has eaten food which affects his health. They argue that none of the children should have been offered cake. The school says that it had no information about the child's special dietary needs and that staff would have offered appropriate alternatives to cake if they had been aware of the problem. There are other children in the nursery school with special dietary needs. These needs are met by the school. It is likely that the school has acted lawfully.

Similarly, in relation to a failure to take any particular step, for the purposes of the reasonable adjustments duty, a responsible body will not discriminate for the purposes of Part IV DDA where it can show:

• that, at the time in question, it did not know and could not reasonably have been expected to know, that the child was disabled; and

• that its failure to take the step was attributable to that lack of knowledge.[663]

This is a two-pronged test and both elements must be met. The first limb is self-explanatory but the second requires closer analysis.[664] Given that the duty to make reasonable adjustments is anticipatory, it will not be enough for a school simply to assert that they did not know that the particular pupil was disabled. In addition, they must establish that the reason for failing to take the step in question was the absence of knowledge of the disability, notwithstanding the anticipatory nature of the duty. Accordingly, where a school fails to plan, monitor, or review its policies, procedures and other arrangements to ensure that its admissions, education and associated provision are accessible, it is unlikely that it will be able to rely upon its lack of knowledge in relation to a particular child as a complete defence to the failure to comply with the duty. This might be contrasted with the situation where a school has proper measures in place, for example, to support disabled children but does not make them available to a specific child because it is ignorant of that particular child's disability. This is likely to be an important distinction in practice and, as can be seen, circumscribes the defence based on lack of knowledge.

In addition, in determining whether it is reasonable for a responsible body to have to take a particular step in relation to a disabled pupil in order to comply with its duty to make reasonable adjustments, regard must be had to the extent to which the taking of the step in question is consistent with compliance with any confidentiality request which has been made.[665] A 'confidentiality request' is a request that asks for the nature, or the existence, of a disabled person's disability to be treated as confidential.[666] Such a request must have been made by the disabled pupil's parent, or by the pupil himself in circumstances where the responsible body reasonably believes that the pupil has sufficient understanding of the nature of that request and of its effect.[667] This ensures that appropriate respect is given to any request for confidentiality.

---

[663] Section 28B(3) DDA.
[664] Though the Schools Code Practice says little about it, see 7.5.
[665] Section 28C(5) and (6) DDA.   [666] Section 28C(7) DDA.   [667] *Ibid.*

5.9.1.4. *Permitted forms of selection and justification*
Discrimination might be justified on two bases:

• where it is the result of a permitted form of selection;[668]

• where the reason for it is both material to the circumstances of the particular case and substantial.[669]

The first form of justification applies only to a case of disability-related discrimination. The second form applies both to a claim of disability-related discrimination and a failure to make reasonable adjustments; this is addressed below.

5.9.1.4.1. *Permitted forms of selection* 'Permitted forms of selection' for the purposes of the first form of justification (available only in a claim of disability-related discrimination) are:

• where the school is a maintained school which is not designated as a grammar school under section 104 of the School Standards and Framework Act 1998, any form of selection mentioned in section 99(2) or (4) of that Act;

• where the school is a maintained school which is so designated, any of its selective admission arrangements;

• where the school is an independent school, any arrangements which make provision for any or all of its pupils to be selected by reference to general or special ability or aptitude, with a view to admitting only pupils of high ability or aptitude.[670]

In Scotland, 'permitted forms of selection' are:

• where the school is managed by an education authority, such arrangements as have been approved by the Scottish Ministers for the selection of pupils for admission;

• where the school is an independent school or a self-governing school, any arrangements which make provision for any or all of its pupils to be selected by reference to general or special ability or aptitude with a view to admitting only pupils of high ability or aptitude.[671]

Section 99(2) of the Schools Standards and Framework Act 1998 provides, for example, that in general no admission arrangements for maintained schools may make provision for selection by ability. There is specific provision permitting exemptions to this general rule[672] and only where they apply will such arrangements constitute a 'permitted form of selection' for the purposes of the justification defence of the DDA (unless the school is designated as a grammar school).

---

[668] Section 28B(6) DDA.   [669] Section 28B(7) DDA.
[670] Section 28Q(9) DDA.   [671] Section 28Q(10) DDA.
[672] Sections 100–102, Schools Standards and Framework Act 1998.

An independent school may decide on its own selection criteria and may select on the grounds of ability and aptitude.

The Schools Code of Practice refers to the Code of Practice on School Admissions (1999) (which applied to England only) and the School Admissions Welsh Office Code of Practice (April 1999).[673] The English Code has been superseded and reference should now be made to the School Admissions Code of Practice (2003).[674]

The Schools Code of Practice gives the following examples:[675]

An eleven-year old girl with learning difficulties applies to go to a school that selects its intake on the basis of academic ability. She fails the entrance test. She is refused admission.

The refusal to admit the girl is based on her performance in the test. Her performance in the test is related to her learning difficulties, so this is less favourable treatment for a reason that relates to the child's disability. The treatment that she received has to be compared with the treatment that other children received who have passed the test. The treatment was less favourable as she was refused admission. However, the school has operated its selective criteria objectively and the less favourable treatment is likely to be justified because it is the result of a permitted form of selection. This is likely to be lawful.

The parents of a twelve-year-old boy apply for him to go to an independent school. He passes the entrance test, but when the school hears that he has learning and behaviour difficulties they refuse him admission.

This boy is turned down for admission because the school hears that he has learning difficulties and behaviour difficulties that are directly related to his disability. The reason is related to his disability. Because the treatment is less favourable than it is for someone who does not have learning and behaviour difficulties that are directly related to their disability, this is unlikely to be justified, as his treatment is not as a result of a permitted form of selection. The boy had already passed the entrance test.

5.9.1.4.2. *General justification*   Where a responsible body[676] can show that a failure to make adjustments or disability-related less favourable treatment is justified the same is not unlawful.[677] Section 28B(7) DDA provides that: '. . . less favourable treatment, or a failure to comply with section 28C,[678] is justified only if the reason for it is both material to the circumstances of the particularly case and substantial'.

The circumstances of the particular case may include those of both the school and the pupil.[679] A 'substantial reason' only requires that the reason is more

---

[673] Paragraphs 5.19 and 5.20.

[674] DfES/0031/2003, which came into force on 31 January 2003: The Education (School Admissions Code of Practice and School Admission Appeals Code of Practice) (Appointed Day) (England) Order 2003. Available at http://www.dfes.gov.uk/sacode/.

[675] Paragraphs 5.23A and B.   [676] See Chapter 8 below.

[677] Section 28B(1)(b) and (2)(b) DDA.   [678] The duty to make adjustments.

[679] *Baynton v Saurus Ltd* [2000] ICR 491, [1999] IRLR 604.

than minor or trivial.[680] 'Material' requires that there be a reasonably strong connection between the reason and the circumstances of the individual case.[681] This means that decisions based on general assumptions and stereotyping will not suffice.

The same defence was provided for (identically described in material respects) in the unamended employment provisions of the DDA (ex-section 5(3) and (4) DDA). Case-law under the unamended employment provisions indicates, controversially,[682] that the burden imposed upon the alleged discriminator by this justification defence is a 'very low' one.[683] In *Jones v Post Office*[684] the Court of Appeal concluded that the function of a court in this context is 'not very different from the task which they have to perform in cases of unfair dismissal.'[685] This means that, though the court might itself have come to a different conclusion on the evidence, it must respect the opinion of the employer (and by implication, the responsible body) if the reason given is material and substantial:

Upon a consideration of the wording of section 5(3) in context, I conclude that the Employment Tribunal are confined to considering whether the reason given for the less favourable treatment can properly be described as both material to the circumstances of the particular case and substantial. The less favourable treatment in the present case is the limit upon the hours of driving. The reason given for it is the risk arising from longer periods of driving. The respondent obtained what are admitted to be suitably qualified and expert medical opinions. Upon the basis of those opinions, the respondent decided that the risk was such as to require the less favourable treatment. In order to rely on section 5(3) it is not enough for the employer to assert that his conduct was reasonable in a general way; he has to establish that the reason given satisfies the statutory criteria. The respondent asserts in this case that the risk arising from the presence of diabetes is material to the circumstance of the particular case and is substantial. Where a properly conducted risk assessment provides a reason which is on its face both material and substantial, and is not irrational, the tribunal cannot substitute its own appraisal. The Employment Tribunal must consider whether the reason meets the statutory criteria; it does not have the more general power to make its own appraisal of the medical evidence and conclude that the evidence from admittedly competent medical witnesses was incorrect or make its own risk assessment.[686]

A court is not permitted to conclude that the reason is not material or substantial where the employer's decision (and by implication, that of a responsible body) is based on suitably qualified and competently expressed medical opinion because it is inferior to a different medical opinion expressed to the court.[687] The

---

[680] Schools Code of Practice, 6.36. And see *H J Heinz Co Ltd v Kenrick* [2000] ICR 491, [2000] IRLR 144.

[681] *Jones v Post Office* [2001] EWCA Civ 558, [2001] ICR 805, [2001] IRLR 384, *per* Lady Justice Arden at paragraph 37. And see Schools Code of Practice, paragraph 5.14.

[682] Industrial Relations Law Reports, 'Highlights' (2001) June; Palmer, Gill, Monaghan, Moon, and Stacey, ed McColgan, *Discrimination Law Handbook* (LAG, 2002) 872.

[683] *Heinz v Kenrick, supra* note 680, paragraph 16.   [684] *Supra* note 681.

[685] *Jones, supra* note 681, paragraph 29.   [686] *Ibid.* paragraph 25.

[687] *Ibid.* paragraph 27.

court's function therefore, as with a case in unfair dismissal, is to determine whether the employer's decision (and by implication, that of a responsible body) was irrational or (as the test is characterized in unfair dismissal case-law) outside 'the band of reasonable responses'.

The Schools Code of Practice gives the following (amongst other) examples:[688]

Some pupils from a special school are going to the theatre. The school does not offer the trip to a pupil with learning difficulties on the basis that he would not understand the play.

Is this less favourable treatment for a reason related to the pupil's disability?

The reason for not offering the boy the opportunity to go on the trip is his limited understanding which is directly related to his disability.

Is it less favourable treatment than someone gets if the reason does not apply to him or her?

The treatment that he was to receive has to be compared with the treatment that other pupils would receive who did not have limited understanding. They were being offered the trip.

Is it justified?

The reason for not offering the trip was an assumption that the boy would not understand the play. This was a general assumption and not a material reason.

This is likely to be unlawful discrimination.

A pupil with cerebral palsy who uses a wheelchair is on a trip with her class to an outdoor activity centre. The teachers arrange to take the class on a 12-mile hike over difficult terrain but, having carried out a risk assessment, they decide that the pupil who uses a wheelchair will be unable to accompany her class, for health and safety reasons.

Is the less favourable treatment for a reason that is related to the pupil's disability?

This is less favourable treatment for a reason that relates to the pupil's cerebral palsy, namely the use of a wheelchair.

Is it less favourable treatment than someone gets if the reason does not apply to him or her?

The treatment that she was to receive then has to be compared with the treatment that the others would receive who did not use a wheelchair. They were being offered the opportunity to go on the hike whereas this pupil was being denied it.

Is it justified?

The responsible body is likely to be able to justify the less favourable treatment for a material and substantial reason: a risk assessment, carried out in relation to this particular pupil in the particular setting in which she would have to travel, indicated that the health and safety of the pupil, and her classmates, could be jeopardized if she were to attempt the hike. This is likely to be lawful.

Where a duty to make reasonable adjustments arises and that duty has not been complied with, disability-related less favourable treatment will only be

---

[688] Paragraph 5.17.

justified if that treatment would have been justified even if the duty had been complied with. This significantly limits the scope of the defence.[689]

Particular controversy has arisen in relation to the application of the test of justification to a failure to make reasonable adjustments. The duty is to take 'reasonable' steps. This establishes that the threshold that must be passed before discrimination is made out and any defence engaged is that the responsible body has not acted reasonably. This requires objective scrutiny.[690] The defence of justification would appear to permit an unreasonable failure to be justified and vindicate a responsible body where the unreasonable failure satisfies the undemanding test set in *Jones*. In *Collins v Royal National Theatre Board Ltd*[691] the Court of Appeal considered the relationship between the justification defence and the duty to make reasonable adjustments in the employment and related fields. As stated above[692] the defence of justification is no longer available in a case of a failure to make adjustments in the employment and related fields, following the amendments made to the DDA in consequence of the Directive. The case of *Collins* pre-dated the amendments. Under the unamended DDA the defence of justification was in material respects identical to that provided for in section 28(7) DDA, save that the defence was provided for separately but (in substance) identically, for disability-related discrimination and a failure to make adjustments in two subsections.[693] No challenge was made to *Jones* in *Collins:* it was argued only that a different interpretation should be placed on the justification defence as it applied to a breach of the duty to make reasonable adjustments (*Jones* being a case of disability-related discrimination). In *Collins* the Court of Appeal concluded that 'the only workable construction of section 5(4), in the context of the DDA and its manifest objects, is that it does not permit justification of a breach of section 6 to be established by reference to factors properly relevant to the establishment of a duty under section 6'.[694] This means that the meaning of the closely similar words, in the two adjacent subsections as they were before amendment, was materially different. In the case of a failure to make reasonable adjustments, 'what is material and substantial for the purposes of justifying an established failure to take such steps as are reasonable to redress disadvantage cannot, consistently with the statutory scheme, include elements which have already been, or could already have been, evaluated in establishing that failure'.[695] As the Court of Appeal itself acknowledged, this departs significantly from the meaning and effect of justification in a case of disability-related discrimination but this is 'fully explained by the fact that justification under

---

[689] Section 28B(8) DDA. See *Nottinghamshire County Council v Meikle* [2004] ECWA Cov 859, [2004] IRLR 703, and 5.2.3.6 above.

[690] *Collins v Royal National Theatre Board Ltd* [2004] EWCA Civ 144, [2004] IRLR 395, paragraph 20.

[691] *Ibid.*   [692] See 5.2.2 above.

[693] Ex-section 5(3) and 5(4) DDA.   [694] *Supra,* note 690, paragraph 32.   [695] *Ibid.*

section 5(3) starts from a form of discrimination—less favourable treatment which is established without the need of any evaluative judgment'.[696] It is difficult to see how the justification defence could have had any real value in a case of a failure to make reasonable adjustments in the employment field having regard to *Collins*.

Relying on *Collins*, it would appear that the justification defence in section 28B(7) DDA should be construed otherwise than as the Court of Appeal held in *Jones*, particularly in a case of a failure to make adjustments. It would be difficult to argue that a different meaning should be afforded the defence depending on whether the case is of a failure to make adjustments or of a case of disability-related discrimination because the defence for both is singularly described in one subsection. If the *Collins* approach were to be followed it would mean that the very same words in the very same subsection should be given a different meaning depending on the nature of the claim. The *Jones* approach nevertheless creates its own difficulties, as the Court of Appeal in *Collins* observed. As stated above, the test of justification as described in *Jones* has proved controversial. It may be that a full frontal attack upon it has yet to happen and in this regard it can be noted that no argument was put in *Collins* that *Jones* was wrong despite the 'surprisingly low' threshold it set.[697] This may happen yet, particularly bearing in mind that in *Jones* the relationship between the defence of justification for a failure to make reasonable adjustments was not considered.[698] It can be properly noted in this respect that the defence of justification for a failure to make reasonable adjustments was a rather late addition to the DDA. It seems it was originally intended that the defence of justification would not exist for a breach of the duty to make reasonable adjustments[699] and the defence of justification for a failure to make adjustments in the employment field[700] was not in the initial Bill but entered it just prior to the report stage of its passage in the House of Lords.[701] It has now of course been repealed in the context of employment and related fields.

The *Collins* approach would appear preferable to *Jones* because it recognizes the need for an evaluative judgment in determining a breach of the duty to make adjustments before the defence is even triggered. Assuming *Collins* is followed, the impact of the defence of justification in a case of a failure to make adjustments should be regarded as minimal, having regard to the construction given to it by the Court of Appeal in *Collins*.

---

[696] *Collins, supra* note 690.
[697] *Ibid.* paragraphs 15 and 26.
[698] *Ibid.* paragraphs 15 and 16.
[699] White Paper, Cm 2729 (January 1995).
[700] The education provisions were introduced later by SENDA.
[701] *Collins, supra* note 690, paragraph 36.

5.9.1.5. *Victimization*

The victimization provisions are modified for the purposes of the schools provisions (Chapter 1, Part IV DDA), such that references to 'B' in section 55(2) (the 'victim') include references to B's parent and a sibling of B.[702] This means that a child's parents and siblings are equally protected but only in respect of protected acts done in the context of the education provisions.[703]

Otherwise the victimization provisions apply to the schools provisions just as they do to the employment field, and the guidance given above at 5.2.5 applies equally.

5.9.2. Local Education Authorities

Section 28F outlaws discrimination by education authorities when discharging their functions. Such an authority 'in discharging a function' must not discriminate against a disabled pupil or a disabled person who may be admitted to the school as a pupil.[704] This duty is described as a 'residual duty'.[705] The unlawful acts created by section 28F (and see section 28G) apply only where the discrimination complained of does not fall within one of the other provisions of Part IV, Chapter 1 (that is, discrimination in schools).[706]

'Discrimination' for these purposes is defined in materially the same way as it is in relation to schools. Thus disability-related discrimination is outlawed.[707] The defence of justification (as described above at 5.9.1.4) applies equally to the local education authorities provisions, as do the knowledge 'provisions' (as described above in 5.9.1.3[708]). A duty to make reasonable adjustments is imposed by section 28G(2) DDA, which requires that:

Each authority . . . take such steps as it is reasonable for it to have to take to ensure that, in discharging any function to which section 28F applies—

(a) disabled persons who may be admitted to a school as pupils are not placed at a substantial disadvantage in comparison with persons who are not disabled; and

(b) disabled pupils are not placed at a substantial disadvantage in comparison with pupils who are not disabled.

As with the duty arising in the context of schools, the duty is anticipatory in nature. The duty does not require authorities to remove or alter a physical feature or provide auxiliary aids or services.[709]

---

[702] Section 55(3A) DDA. [703] Section 55(3A)(b) DDA.

[704] Section 28F(3) DDA.

[705] See sidenote to section 28F DDA and Schools Code of Practice, Chapter 10.

[706] Section 28(F)(4) DDA. Discrimination in schools being addressed by sections 28A–28E DDA.

[707] Section 28G(1) read with section 28B DDA.

[708] Though no provision is made for 'confidentiality requests' and exceptions in relation to the same, in respect of the duty to make reasonable adjustments as it applies to local education authorities.

[709] Section 28G(3) DDA. See 5.9.1.1 above.

Again, the duty to make adjustments determines the circumstances in which discrimination might occur and is not actionable as such.[710]

The duty to make reasonable adjustments will be engaged in relation to all the functions of a local education authority, and such authorities are therefore required to consider proactively what adjustments ought to be made to the full range of their policies and practices so as to secure appropriate access for disabled pupils. The functions to which the duty applies include:

• policies (such as the authority's policies on special educational needs, capital building programmes, sports, cultural activities, transport, early years provision);

• the education authority's policy and arrangements on school admissions and exclusions and (in England and Wales) the schools admissions policy and arrangements;

• the deployment of the authority's non-delegated budget and any other arrangements which might directly affect disabled pupils;

• services to pupils (such as weekend or after-school leisure and sporting activities, school trips, cultural activities).[711]

The Schools Code of Practice gives the following example, amongst others:[712]

Home-school transport for disabled pupils in a local education authority (LEA) always leaves primary schools at 3.30pm. The LEA reviews its transport policy when it realises that disabled pupils who are dependent on taxis might be at a substantial disadvantage if they were not able to stay to after-school clubs. The LEA re-negotiates its contract with the taxi firm so that it is possible to specify later departure times. This is likely to be a reasonable adjustment that the LEA should make.

The duties apply to the whole range of education provision, including nursery education, arrangements for home and hospital tuition, and pupil referral units (in England and Wales) as well as the school stages of education.[713]

The victimization provisions apply in the same way to the unlawful acts created in relation to local education authorities as they do to schools (with the modification described above at 5.9.1.5).

5.9.3. Education: Post-16

Discrimination for the purposes of the post-16 provisions of the DDA is defined by section 28S and section 28T DDA[714] and section 55 DDA. It comprises:

• a failure to comply with the duty to make reasonable adjustments;

---

[710] Section 28G(4) DDA. [711] Schools Code of Practice, paragraph 10.3.
[712] *Ibid.* paragraph 10.3A. [713] Schools Code of Practice, paragraph 10.4.
[714] See also section 28U DDA and Schedule 4C DDA. The same applies, with some modification, to discrimination in the context of statutory youth and community services, see 5.9.4 above.

- disability-related discrimination; and
- victimization.

As mentioned above the DRC has prepared and issued a relevant code of practice: 'Code of Practice for Providers of Post 16 Education and Related Services' ('Post 16 Code of Practice').[715] This provides guidance on the meaning of discrimination for the purposes of the unlawful acts created by the DDA in relation to the post-16 education sector and relevant extracts are included below.

Direct discrimination and harassment are not outlawed explicitly. However, as discussed in 5.7.2 above, some instances of direct discrimination and harassment will constitute disability-related discrimination.

5.9.3.1. *Duty to make reasonable adjustments*

Section 28T(1) provides that the responsible body[716] for an educational institution:[717]

must take such steps as it is reasonable for it to have to take to ensure that
(a) in relation to the arrangements it makes for determining admission to the institution, disabled persons are not placed at a substantial disadvantage in comparison with persons who are not disabled; and
(b) in relation to student services provided for, or offered to, students by it, disabled students are not placed at a substantial disadvantage in comparison with students who are not disabled.

As with duties arising in other fields, the duties just described prescribe the circumstances in which discrimination might occur (by a breach of the duty) for the purposes of section 28R (discrimination by educational institutions) and accordingly a breach of any such duty is not actionable as such.[718]

By section 28S DDA, discrimination against a disabled person occurs if the responsible body fails 'to his detriment' to comply with the duties under section 28T and cannot show that its failure to comply is justified.[719] Justification is addressed below, in 5.9.3.3.1. 'Detriment' has a very wide meaning[720] and any less favourable treatment or disadvantage is likely to constitute a 'detriment' for these purposes.

The duties imposed by section 28T fall into two parts:

- those relating to the arrangements made for determining admission; and
- those relating to student services.

As with duties arising in other areas, these duties are anticipatory in nature. Thus while an unlawful act will only occur where a particular disabled person has suffered a detriment in consequence of a breach of the duty, educational

---

[715] *Supra* note 614.
[716] See Chapter 8 above, at 8.5.3.
[717] See Chapter 8 above, at 8.5.
[718] Section 28T(6) DDA
[719] Section 28S(2) DDA.
[720] See 5.2.4 above and 6.2.7.3 below.

institutions must plan in advance if they are to avoid breaching the duty which is owed to disabled persons at large.

In determining whether it is reasonable for an educational institution to have to take a particular step, Section 28T(2) DDA requires that regard must be had to any relevant provision of the Post 16 Code of Practice.

'Substantial' disadvantages for the purposes of determining whether a duty is engaged, are those which are not 'minor' or 'trivial'.

The Post 16 Code of Practice gives guidance as to the factors to which regard should be had in determining whether a disabled person is placed at a substantial disadvantage. Relevant factors include:

- inconvenience; and
- effort or discomfort.[721]

The Post 16 Code of Practice gives the following examples:[722]

A partially deaf student who lip reads is attending a Business Studies course. One of her lecturers continues to lecture while simultaneously writing on the whiteboard. The student asks him to stop speaking when he turns his back to use the whiteboard so that she can follow what he is saying. The student is likely to be at a substantial disadvantage if this adjustment is not made.

A student with restricted growth requests that all university student notice boards are lowered in height so that he can read the information more easily. He is, however, able to read the notices without significant difficulty or discomfort when the boards are placed at their regular height. The student's disadvantage compared to that of other students is unlikely to be found substantial.

There are no express exemptions in relation to auxiliary aids and services and physical features.[723] However, the duty to make reasonable adjustments does not require:

- the responsible body to provide auxiliary aids or services until after 31 August 2003;
- the responsible body to remove or alter a physical feature until after 31 August 2005.[724]

The fact that was some lead-in time was given (as with the duties arising in the context of goods, facilities, and services) means that educational institutions will be expected to have planned for their implementation. It would be no answer to a claim for breach of a reasonable adjustment duty arising immediately after the coming into force of these provisions that they had little time to plan when the fact of their implementation was known of in 2002.[725]

---

[721] Paragraph 5.2. [722] Paragraphs 5.2A and B.

[723] Compare the duty arising in the context of schools: section 28C(2) DDA.

[724] Special Educational Needs and Disability Act 2001 (Commencement No 5) Order 2002, SI 2002/2217, Article 6 and Schedule 2.

[725] *Ibid.*

Otherwise, the duties to make adjustments under section 28T(1) DDA came into force on 1 September 2002[726] from which date a relevant educational institution was required to make adjustments to, for example, its policies, practices, and procedures to comply with its duties under section 28T(1) DDA.

5.9.3.1.1. To whom is the duty to make reasonable adjustments owed? As described above, the duties are anticipatory in nature. They therefore apply to all disabled people at large. This means that an educational institution must not wait until a disabled person seeks to gain admission or use a service before considering what adjustments should be made. Instead educational institutions need to anticipate the requirements of disabled people and plan for their involvement.[727] A lack of notice alone will therefore not found a defence to a claim for a breach of the reasonable adjustment duty though a lack of knowledge regarding a particular disabled person will be material: see 5.9.3.3 below. The Post 16 Code of Practice gives the following examples:[728]

A university encourages its lecturers to put lecture notes on the institution intranet. It introduces new procedures to ensure that all notes put on the intranet meet established guidelines to ensure there is no conflict with specialist software or features that students with dyslexia may be using. It therefore anticipates reasonable adjustments that it might need to make for certain disabled students.

A university ensures that its Building Works Department is thoroughly briefed on all aspects of physical access. Each time building works are undertaken an assessment is made of how the building can be made more accessible, for example, when an area is repainted the department ensures it is using colour contrasts, which will help students with a visual impairment. It also carries out an acoustic audit to ensure it is responding appropriately to deaf students. The university is anticipating reasonable adjustments that might need to be made.

5.9.3.1.2. Discharging the reasonable adjustment duty The DDA does not give any guidance as to the steps that might be taken to discharge the duty under section 28T DDA. However, the object of the duty—to make educational institutions accessible and to eliminate any substantial disadvantage—identifies the aim of the duty and therefore what are reasonable steps can be measured against that central purpose. The Post 16 Code of Practice indicates that responsible bodies should consider a wide range of adjustments.[729] In some cases financial help may be available and that will be relevant to the question whether the taking of a step is a reasonable one.

The duty to make reasonable adjustments is a continuing one and therefore responsible bodies are obliged to keep under review any adjustments made and which might be made.[730]

---

[726] *Ibid.* Article 5.
[727] Post 16 Code of Practice, paragraph 5.6.
[728] *Ibid.* paragraphs 5.6A, 5.6E, and 5.7A.
[729] *Ibid.* paragraph 5.8.
[730] *Ibid.* paragraph 5.9.

In determining whether a particular step is reasonable, regard must be had to all the circumstances of the case. As the Post 16 Code of Practice observes, they will vary according to:

- the type of services being provided;
- the nature of the institution or service and its size and resources; and
- the effect of the disability on the individual disabled person or student.[731]

The sorts of relevant factors will include:

- the need to maintain academic and other prescribed standards;
- the financial resources available to the responsible body;
- grants or loans likely to be available to disabled students (for the purposes of enabling them to receive student services) such as disabled student's allowances;
- the cost of taking a particular step;
- the extent to which it is practicable to take a particular step;
- the extent to which aids or services will otherwise be provided to disabled people or students;
- health and safety requirements; and
- the relevant interests of other people including other students.[732]

The Post 16 Code of Practice gives examples under each of these heads.[733] The observations made above in relation to the duty to make adjustments in other fields are also relevant to the question of what might be a reasonable step in a particular case.

As observed above, the DDA does not require educational institutions to undermine their academic or other prescribed standards. Accordingly, this is relevant to the extent to which a particular adjustment may be required. The Post 16 Code of Practice gives the following example:[734]

A young man with moderate learning difficulties applies to study for an English A level. He has poor literacy skills and the college does not have sufficient evidence that he could sustain the reading and writing necessary to complete the course. It is unlikely to be reasonable to expect the college to adjust its entry requirements to accommodate the student.

5.9.3.1.3. *Auxiliary services and aids*   As noted above, the exemption in relation to the provision of auxiliary services and aids was removed from 31 August 2003. Auxiliary aids and services are not defined for these purposes but the guidance set out above in 5.7.1.3 applies equally. Little guidance is given by the Post 16 Code of Practice on the sorts of auxiliary aids and services that might be provided but they will involve equipment aids and services by individuals, as described in 5.7.1.3 above.

---

[731] Post 16 Code of Practice, paragraph 6.1.
[733] *Ibid.* paragraphs 6.3 onwards.

[732] *Ibid.* paragraph 6.2.
[734] *Ibid.* paragraph 6.3A.

5.9.3.1.4. *Physical features*   As described above, the duty to make adjustments does not extend to the removal or alteration of physical features before 31 August 2005. However, where a physical feature is such as to cause a substantial disadvantage to disabled people, it will be the duty of the responsible body to make other adjustments so as to reduce the disadvantage caused to disabled people, by providing an alternative route, for example, so that the particular physical feature can be avoided.

As to the obligation to make adjustments to physical features, the DDA gives little guidance about the impact of the duty in the post-16 educational field. The Post 16 Code of Practice also says little about the impact of the duty (it was published before the duty came into force). The guidance given in relation to the duty arising in the field of goods, facilities, and services will be instructive, however. (See 5.7.1.4 above.)

5.9.3.1.5. *Making reasonable adjustments to premises: legal ramifications*   As discussed above, there are obvious legal ramifications for occupiers of premises seeking to comply with the duty to make reasonable adjustments to the physical features of premises.[735] Specific provision is made in the field of goods, facilities, and services and this is discussed above in 5.7.1.7.

In the context of the duty arising in relation to the post-16 education field, the DDA makes specific provision in relation to leases and other binding obligations.

As with the duty arising in other fields, the DDA does not take precedence over planning law and regulation.[736] Thus an educational institution is required to obtain the normal permissions and consents for any adjustment to physical features and the observations about planning made above in 5.6 apply equally.

In addition, the DDA makes express provision for the making of adjustments to physical features where premises are occupied by an educational institution under a lease.[737] The provision it makes is similar to that made in relation to the goods, facilities, and services provisions. Thus, where an educational institution occupies premises under a lease and, but for the provision made by section 28W DDA, the responsible body would not be entitled to make a particular alteration to the premises and the alteration is one which the responsible body proposes to make in order to comply with its duty to make reasonable adjustments, then the lease is to be treated as modified.[738] In this respect where the terms and conditions of a lease impose conditions which are to apply to the responsible body or to the premises or entitle the lessor to impose conditions when consenting to the responsible body altering the premises, the responsible body is to be treated for the purposes of these provisions as not being entitled to make the alteration: section 28W(4) DDA. The lease is therefore to be treated as providing that the

---

[735] See 5.6 above.
[736] Section 59 DDA. See Chapter 10 below.
[737] Section 28W DDA.
[738] Section 28W(1) and (2) DDA.

responsible body is entitled to make the alteration with the written consent of the lessor; for the responsible body to have to make a written application to the lessor for consent if it wishes to make the alteration; if such an application is made, for the lessor not to withhold his consent unreasonably; and for the lessor to be entitled to make his consent subject to reasonable conditions.[739]

Regulations provide for the detailed requirements of notice and consent and reflect closely those made in the context of a duty arising in relation to the provision of goods, facilities, and services. The Disability Discrimination (Educational Institutions) (Alteration of Leasehold Premises) Regulations 2002[740] prescribe the circumstances in which a relevant lessor is to be taken to have withheld his consent for alterations to premises and the circumstances in which a lessor is deemed to have withheld his consent reasonably or unreasonably as the case may be.

Where complaint is made of a breach of the duty to make reasonable adjustments, the responsible body may make the lessor a party to the proceedings.[741] The court may determine in such proceedings whether the lessor has refused consent to the alteration or consented subject to one or more conditions and if so whether the refusal or conditions were unreasonable.[742] Where the court determines any refusal or conditions applied were unreasonable it may make such a declaration; make an order authorizing the responsible body to make the alteration specified in the order; and order the lessor to pay compensation to the complainant.[743] In addition, where the responsible body has applied in writing to the lessor for consent to the alteration and that consent has been refused or the lessor has made his consent subject to one or more conditions, that body or a disabled person who has an interest in the proposed alteration to the premises may refer the matter to the County Court or, in Scotland, to the Sheriff.[744] On such a reference the court must determine whether the lessor's refusal was unreasonable or whether any condition was unreasonable.[745] The court may then, if it determines that any refusal or conditions were unreasonable, make such declaration as it considers appropriate or make an order authorizing the responsible body to make the alteration specified in the order.[746]

5.9.3.2. *Disability-related discrimination*

'Discrimination' in the context of post-16 education provision is defined so as to include less favourable treatment of a disabled person for a reason which relates to the disabled person's disability. Section 28S(1) DDA provides as follows:

a responsible body[747] discriminates against a disabled person if—
(a) for a reason which relates to his disability, it treats him less favourably than it treats or would treat others to whom that reason does not or would not apply; and

---

[739] Section 28W(2) DDA. [740] SI 2002/1458.
[741] Section 28V, Schedule 4, Part III, paragraph 12 DDA.
[742] *Ibid.* paragraph 12(5). [743] *Ibid.* paragraph 12(6). [744] *Ibid.* paragraph 11(1).
[745] *Ibid.* paragraph 11(2). [746] *Ibid.* paragraph 12(6). [747] See Chapter 8 below.

(b) it cannot show that the treatment in question is justified.

The meaning given to disability-related discrimination under section 28S DDA mirrors that provided for under section 3A DDA (employment and related fields) and section 20(1) DDA (goods, facilities, and services) and the observations made in respect of the same apply equally.[748]

As with disability-related discrimination in other fields, such discrimination when it occurs within the context of post-16 education provision may be justified. However, the defence of justification is defined differently in this context and is addressed below.

The Post 16 Code of Practice gives some examples of disability-related discrimination, as follows:[749]

A dyslexic student applies to do a distance learning degree in English. The university tells her that it does not accept dyslexic students on English degrees. The treatment she receives is less favourable compared to other students, and the reason for the treatment relates to her disability. The university is likely to be acting unlawfully.

A student with a hearing impairment applies to do a course in Dentistry. He is turned down because he does not have the right entry qualifications. His rejection is not connected to his disability, and so is not likely to be unlawful.

A student with a facial disfigurement is taking an evening class in T'ai Chi. The tutor for the class spends time with all the students individually helping them with their technique. The tutor does not spend any time individually with the disabled student because he feels uncomfortable with her. Because no other student has been treated in this way, and because the less favourable treatment is related to her disability, the treatment is likely to be unlawful.

The less favourable treatment must, as observed above,[750] relate to a particular disabled person's disability. If it does not then the provisions governing disability-related discrimination are not engaged. The Post 16 Code of Practice gives the following example:[751]

A disabled student has been asked to leave the university's residential accommodation because of the number of noisy parties he has been holding which have been disturbing other students. The reason for asking him to leave is his disruptive behaviour and is not related to his disability, and so is likely to be lawful.

As to the proper comparator, the principles set out above apply.[752] This means that the proper comparator is a person to whom the *reason* for the treatment complained of would not apply, not a person who is not disabled but to whom such a reason would apply. The Post 16 Code of Practice gives the following example:[753]

---

[748] See 5.2.3 and 5.7.2 above.
[750] See 5.2.3.2 above.
[752] See 5.2.3 and 5.7.2 above.

[749] Paragraph 4.4.
[751] Paragraph 4.6A.
[753] Paragraph 4.5A.

A student's disability has caused her to take time off and miss three sessions of her course. A college requires all students who miss three lessons to take the course again, and several of the disabled students' classmates are told they must take the course again. However, but for the disability, the student would not have missed any lessons. In this case, therefore, the appropriate comparison is with someone who has not had to take time off. Removing her from the course because of her absence would probably be less favourable treatment for a reason relating to her disability, and would be likely to be unlawful. It may be the case, however, that the college could justify this treatment because of academic or other standards.

5.9.3.3. *Knowledge*

Unlike disability-related discrimination occurring in other fields, the question whether a responsible body knows of a disabled person's disability is material to the question whether such discrimination might occur. Thus section 28S(4) DDA provides that: 'The taking of a particular step by a responsible body in relation to a person does not amount to less favourable treatment if it shows that at the time in question it did not know, and could not reasonably have been expected to know, that he was disabled.'

In addition, where a responsible body does not know and could not reasonably have been expected to know that a person was disabled it does not discriminate against such person in relation to any failure to take a particular step, where the failure to take the steps was attributable to that lack of knowledge.[754]

This imposes a mixed subjective and objective test in relation to knowledge. The responsible body must not know, as a matter of fact, that the particular person was disabled but, importantly, it must also be the case that it could not reasonably have been expected to know. As the Post 16 Code of Practice makes clear, this does impose a proactive responsibility upon a responsible body.[755]

In this regard the Code of Practice points to guidance issued by the Government specifically to address the enquiries that ought to be made about people's disabilities: 'Finding Out about People's Disability: Good Practice Guide for Further and Higher Education Institutions'.[756] It will not be sufficient for an educational institution to simply adopt a position of 'ignorance is bliss': it must demonstrate that it has taken reasonable steps to find out about a person's disability. The Post 16 Code of Practice gives the following example:[757]

A student has a mental health problem and, because of the medication she is on, finds it difficult to get to her first morning class. After several weeks during which she has missed all her morning classes, and without approaching the student to find out why she has not turned up, the college decides to remove her from the course. The institution has not taken reasonable action to find out whether the student's failure to attend is due to a disability, and so is likely to be acting unlawfully.

---

[754] Section 28S(3) DDA.
[755] See the observations in relation to schools in 5.9.1.3 above.
[756] DES/0024/2002. [757] Paragraph 4.17A.

Thus an educational institution should consider asking people to disclose whether they have a disability in their application and enrolment forms and should publicize the provision it makes for disabled people generally, particularly confidentiality regarding disclosures of details of any disability.[758] The extent of enquiries that will be required before the objective limb of the lack of knowledge exemption is made out will vary depending on the particular educational provision engaged. As the Post 16 Code of Practice indicates, where for example in relation to a drop-in centre for young people, it is stated that it welcomes young disabled people, it will not necessarily be appropriate for each young person who visits to be asked whether they have a disability. This might be considered too intrusive and the absence of such enquiries might not deprive the drop-in centre of the ability to rely on an absence of knowledge in a particular case.[759]

As with 'knowledge' in other areas, where a member of staff or agent for the institution has been notified of the disabilities, such knowledge will be imputed to the responsible body.[760]

As to lack of knowledge and failure to comply with the duty to make adjustments, a failure to take the particular step must itself be attributable to that lack of knowledge if the lack of knowledge exemption is to be relied upon. This is important because, as observed above in 5.9.1.3, the duty is anticipatory in nature. Given that a responsible body is not entitled to wait for a disabled person before the duty is activated, mere ignorance of the existence of a particular disabled person may not be enough to justify a failure to take a particular step. However, where the step concerned relates to the specific needs of the disabled person concerned, it will be easier for a responsible body to show that its failure to take such step was attributable to a lack of knowledge about the disabled person's particular disability. The Post 16 Code of Practice gives the following examples:[761]

A man makes a written request to a college and asks for information about courses. He does not tell the college that he has no sight. Although the college produces its prospectus in electronic format, he is sent the print version, which he cannot access. The college's failure to make an adjustment for the enquirer is due to lack of knowledge about his disability. This is likely to be lawful.

A man with a visual impairment asks for information about courses at a college. He does not tell the college that he has a visual impairment. He can read type if it is of a reasonable size. He is sent a prospectus for the college, which is printed in very small type that he cannot read. The college does not produce information in any other format or even in reasonably sized type. The college's failure to make an adjustment for the enquirer with

---

[758] Post 16 Code of Practice, paragraph 4.18.

[759] *Ibid.* paragraph 4.19 and example 4.19A.

[760] Absent certain special circumstances, for example an independent, confidential counselling service: *ibid.* paragraph 4.21 and example 4.21A.

[761] Paragraphs 5.11A and 5.12A.

the visual impairment is not related to lack of knowledge about his disability, it is due to the college's failure to make anticipatory adjustments for disabled people. This is likely to be unlawful.

Provision is made for circumstances where a disabled person has made a confidentiality request. As with schools (see 5.9.1.3 above), in determining whether it is reasonable for a responsible body to have to take a particular step in relation to the disabled person in order to comply with the duty to make adjustments, regard must be had to the extent to which the taking of the step in question is consistent with compliance with that request.[762] A 'confidentiality request' means a request made by a disabled person, which asks for the nature, or the existence, of his disability to be treated as confidential.[763] The observations made in 5.9.1.3 above apply.

However, the fact that there has been a confidentiality request does not absolve the educational institution of the obligation to make adjustments. It may mean that reasonable adjustments have to be provided in an alternative way in order to preserve confidentiality.[764] The Post 16 Code of Practice gives the following example:[765]

A student with a visual impairment can only read clearly if he has text enlarged into 16-point type. He is very embarrassed by his disability and has requested strict confidentiality. Normally his tutors would give a visually impaired student large-print handouts at the beginning of each class. However, because he has requested confidentiality, they agree to give him his handouts in advance so that he can look at them before the lesson but does not have to be seen reading them during the class.

The Post 16 Code of Practice gives the following example:[766]

A college gives a disabled student a poor mark for his exam. The student experiences fatigue and cannot concentrate for long periods. The college is aware of this. The reason why he has performed badly in his examination is related to his disability and so he has been treated less favourably. The college tries to justify treating the student less favourably by arguing that this is necessary for maintaining academic standards. However, the college failed to make a reasonable adjustment for the student by allowing him short rest breaks. The college cannot use the justification, because they could have made an appropriate reasonable adjustment.

5.9.3.3.1. *Justification and academic standards* Disability-related discrimination and a failure to make reasonable adjustments may be justified, as discussed above. The justification defence falls into two parts:

- a specific defence of justification relating to academic or other prescribed standards (section 28S(6) DDA);

---

[762] Section 28T(4) DDA.
[763] Section 28T(5) DDA.
[764] Post 16 Code of Practice, paragraph 6.19.
[765] *Ibid.* paragraph 6.19A.
[766] Paragraph 4.25A.

- a general defence of justification where the reason for the failure is both material to the circumstances of the material case and substantial (section 28S(8) DDA).

The Post 16 Code of Practice suggests that the occasions upon which a failure to make reasonable adjustments will be justified are 'rare'.[767]

5.9.3.4. *Academic standards*

Less favourable treatment of a person is only justified (under the first limb above) if it is necessary in order to maintain academic standards.[768] The DDA permits other standards to be prescribed and other circumstances in which justification might be made out to be prescribed.[769] No such other standards or circumstances have yet been prescribed.

The specific defence of justification which pertains to the maintaining of academic standards makes clear that the DDA maintains a balance between protecting the rights of disabled students and maintaining proper academic standards. However, as the Post 16 Code of Practice makes clear, academic standards should not be used as a device to exclude disabled people from courses or services.[770] Any justification based on academic standards must pertain to the particular academic standards of the course concerned and to the abilities of the particular disabled person. The Post 16 Code of Practice gives the following examples:[771]

A severely dyslexic student applies to take a course in Journalism. She does not have the literacy necessary to complete the course because of her dyslexia. The college rejects her, using the justification of academic standards. This is likely to be lawful.

The college now introduces a policy of rejecting all dyslexic applicants to Journalism. The policy does not allow course selectors to consider different levels of dyslexia, the ability of individual applicants or the range of possible adjustments. This is likely to be unlawful.

5.9.3.4.1. *General justification* The general justification defence is defined in the same way as under the schools provisions and the observations made regarding the level of scrutiny required by the test (see 5.9.1.4.2 above) apply equally to the post-16 sector. The reason for the treatment must relate to the particular circumstances and thus generalizations and stereotypes will not found a defence. In addition, the reason must be 'substantial', which means more than 'minor' or 'trivial'.[772] The Post 16 Code of Practice gives the following examples:[773]

---

[767] Paragraph 5.16. See discussion in 5.9.1.4.2 above
[768] Section 28S(6) DDA.
[769] Section 28S(6) and (7) DDA.
[770] Paragraph 4.27.
[771] Paragraphs 4.27A and B.
[772] See 5.9.1.4.2 above.
[773] Paragraphs 4.31A and C.

A student with autistic spectrum disorder applies for a course. The student can be disruptive, and sometimes will talk inappropriately during classes. However, her interruptions are not much more than those made by other students, and when she has an assistant with her, her behaviour improves. There is unlikely to be any material and substantial reason to justify not admitting this student.

A deaf student applies to do a college course. She communicates through sign language and would need an interpreter for all her classes. The college approaches the interpreting service which provides support for its other deaf students, but because of high demand that year, the service is unable to support this additional student. The college makes wider enquiries, but is unable to find the services of an interpreter or communicator. Because it is not possible to make the necessary adjustments for her to gain access to the course, the college does not accept her application. This is likely to be a material and substantial reason for less favourable treatment.

Disability-related discrimination will only be justified where there has been a breach of the duty to make reasonable adjustments if that treatment would have been justified, even if the duty had been complied with. This significantly widens the scope of the defence.[774]

5.9.3.5. *Victimization*
The victimization provisions apply in the same was as they do to the unlawful acts in the field of goods, facilities, and services. The guidance in 5.7.4 above therefore applies equally.

5.9.4. Youth and Other Statutory Services

Discrimination by local education authorities in the provision of community and adult education and statutory youth services is outlawed by section 28U and Schedule 4C DDA. Discrimination is defined in the same way as is applicable to discrimination otherwise in the post 16 sector, save that the duty to make reasonable adjustments is modified. The duty is modified so that each responsible body:[775]

must take such steps as it is reasonable for it to have to take to ensure that—
(a) in relation to its arrangements for enrolling persons on a course of further or higher education provided by it and
(b) in relation to services provided, or offered by it, disabled persons are not placed at a substantial disadvantage in comparison with persons who are not disabled.

As with the duty to make adjustments otherwise in the post-16 sector, there are no express references to auxiliary aids, services, or physical features. However, the duty to make reasonable adjustments does not require:

---

[774] Section 28S(9) DDA. See *Nottinghamshire County Council v Meikle*, *supra* note 689, and at 5.2.3.6 above

[775] *Ibid.* Schedule 4C, paragraphs 2 and 6.

- the responsible body to provide auxiliary aids or services until 31 August 2003;
- the responsible body to remove or alter a physical feature until 31 August 2005.[776]

The observations made above[777] apply equally.

---

[776] Special Educational Needs and disability Act 2001 (Commencement No 5) Order 2002, Article 6 and Schedule 2.
[777] See 5.9.3.1.3–5.9.3.1.4.

6

EMPLOYMENT AND OCCUPATION

6.1. INTRODUCTION

Part II of the DDA regulates discrimination[1] in the employment and related fields. The Disability Discrimination Act 1995 (Amendment) Regulations 2003[2] ('the 2003 Regulations') have made significant changes to the scope of coverage provided by Part II DDA. In its original enactment the DDA contained only a limited number of unlawful acts in the employment field and a number of exemptions which would have been incompatible with the Directive,[3] had they remained in place. The gaps caused by the absence of specific legislative measures and the exemptions have been largely filled by the 2003 Regulations.

---

[1] As defined in Chapter 5 above, at 5.2–5.4.   [2] SI 2003/1673.
[3] 2000/78/EC. See Chapter 3 above

Part II DDA now outlaws 'discrimination'[4] by:

- employers, in respect of disabled applicants for employment and employees;[5]
- principals in respect of disabled applicants for contract work and contract workers;[6]
- relevant persons in relation to applicants for office and office holders;[7]
- firms in respect of applicants for partnership and partners;[8]
- barristers and barristers' clerks in relation to applicants for pupillage or tenancy and pupils and tenants;[9]
- advocates[10] in relation to applicants for pupillage and pupils;[11]
- work placement providers in respect of applicants for practical work experience or persons undertaking a work placement;[12]
- trade organizations in respect of applicants for membership and in respect of members;[13] and
- qualifications bodies in relation to professional or trade qualifications.[14]

The 2003 Regulations abolish exemptions for small employers, police officers, firefighters, prison officers, and statutory office holders. Barristers and partners in partnerships are brought within the scope of Part II DDA, leaving only the armed forces exempt.[15]

'Discrimination' for the purposes of Part II DDA is to be construed in accordance with its section 3A (Chapter 5 above, at 5.2–5.4)[16] and 'harassment' is to be construed in accordance with its section 3B (see Chapter 5 above, at 5.2.4).[17] Each of the unlawful acts created in respect of particular occupations address the duty to make reasonable adjustments, as explained in Chapter 5 above, at 5.2–5.4.

'Victimization' (a form of 'discrimination') of a person, whether disabled or not, is unlawful within the scope of each the unlawful acts described below.[18]

---

[4] As defined in Chapter 5 above, at 5.2–5.5.

[5] Section 4 DDA. Section 64(5)–(6) is repealed by the 2003 Regulations.

[6] Section 4B DDA.   [7] Section 4D DDA.   [8] Section 6A DDA.

[9] Section 7A DDA. This fills the gap identified in *Higham of 1 Pump Court Chambers v Horton* [2004] EWCA Civ 941.   [10] In Scotland.

[11] Section 7C DDA.   [12] Section 14C DDA.   [13] Section 13 DDA.

[14] Section 14A DDA. Note that in respect of each of the unlawful acts described above protection is also afforded to non-disabled applicants, employees, etc in the case of victimization only: see Chapter 5 above, at 5.2.5.

[15] Repealing sections 7 (exemption for small businesses); section 64(5) (Ministry of Defence Police, British Transport Police, Royal Parks Constabulary, United Kingdom Atomic Energy Authority Constabulary, Prison Officers, and Defence Firefighters); section 64(6) (firefighters); section 64(2)(a) (statutory office holders, including the police). See section 64(7) for the present exemption in relation to the armed forces.

[16] Section 18D(2) DDA.   [17] *Ibid.*

[18] Section 55, DDA. 'Victimization' is addressed at in Chapter 5 above, at 5.2.5.

In respect of all of the unlawful acts summarized above, it is also unlawful to discriminate after the relevant relationship has come to an end.[19]

A new Employment Code has been prepared by the DRC. This came into force on 1 October 2004 and has received Parliamentary approval pursuant to the negative resolution procedure: 'Code of Practice,[20] Employment and Occupation' ('the Employment Code'). Though the Employment Code is not binding in law, its provisions are important. Its issue followed a detailed consultation process.[21] The Code does not impose any legal obligations and a breach of any of its provision does not give rise to any legal liability.[22] However, courts and Employment Tribunals must take into account any provision of the Code if it appears to them relevant to any question arising in proceedings.[23] If employers and others who have duties under Part II DDA follow the guidance in the Code, it may help to avoid an adverse decision by a court or tribunal in any proceedings.[24]

Proceedings in respect of the unlawful acts created by Part II must be commenced in the Employment Tribunal. Enforcement and remedies are dealt with in Chapter 11 below.

This chapter should be read with Chapter 5 above, which addresses the definitions of 'discrimination' for the purposes of the unlawful acts.

6.2. EMPLOYMENT

The DDA now provides disabled employees and prospective employees with fairly comprehensive protection from discrimination by employers.

Section 4 DDA provides that:

(1) It is unlawful for an employer to discriminate against a disabled person—
    (a) in the arrangements which he makes for the purpose of determining to whom he should offer employment;
    (c) in the terms on which he offers that person employment; or
    (d) by refusing to offer, or deliberately not offering, him employment.

---

[19] Section 16A DDA. This is dealt with at 6.14 below.

[20] (2004) DRC ISBN 0 11 703419 3; Disability Discrimination Codes of Practice (Employment and Occupation, and Trade Organisations and Qualifications Bodies) Appointed Day Order 2004, SI 2004/2302.

[21] 'Disability Discrimination Act 1995: Part II, Employment Code on Employment and Occupation, Consultation Report: A report of the consultations conducted between 1 September and 30 November 2003 by the Disability Rights Commission on proposals for a Employment Code on Employment and Occupation' (2003) DRC, available at http://www.drc-gb.org/Uploaded_files/documents/DRC%20Final%20Draft%20Consultation%20Report%20-%20Employment%20Code.doc.

[22] Section 53A(8) DDA.   [23] Section 53(8) DDA.

[24] Employment Code, paragraph 1.6.

(2) It is unlawful for an employer to discriminate against a disabled person whom he employs—

(a) in the terms of employment which he affords him;

(b) in the opportunities which he affords him for promotion, a transfer, training or receiving any other benefit;

(c) by refusing to afford him, or deliberately not affording him, any such opportunity; or

(d) by dismissing him, or subjecting him to any other detriment.

In addition, section 4(3) makes it unlawful for an employer to subject to harassment:

• a disabled person whom he employs; or
• a disabled person who has applied to him for employment.

'Discrimination' and 'harassment' for the purposes of section 4 are described in Chapter 5 above, at 5.2.

6.2.1. Meanings of Employer, Employee, and Employment

Section 68(1) defines 'employment' for the purposes of the DDA. It provides that 'employment' means[25] 'employment under a contract of service or of apprenticeship or a contract personally to do any work, and related expressions are to be construed accordingly'. Thus employer and employee are to be construed in that context.

The concept of employment for the purposes of the DDA is wider than that at common law and under much of the employment rights legislation.[26]

The definition includes employees working under a contract of service but extends the definition to apprenticeships and, importantly, to any person:

• working under a contract,
• where that contract is personally to do work; or
• where the dominant purpose of that contract is to do work personally.[27]

This means that the relationship between employer and employee need not be solely for the provision of labour for a wage but that there must be some obligation to perform personally work or labour and the contract must contemplate that as its dominant purpose.[28] Thus, for example, it has been held that a Research Fellow, who had a contract both to study and to do research, fell within this wider definition of 'employee'.[29]

---

[25] Subject to any prescribed provision: there is none currently in force.

[26] See eg Employment Rights Act 1996, section 230.

[27] *Mirror Group Newspapers Ltd v Gunning* [1986] ICR 145, [1986] IRLR 27. [28] *Ibid.*

[29] *Hugh-Jones v St John's College, Cambridge* [1979] ICR 848, under the same provisions in the SDA, though the discrimination was exempt for other reasons.

A limited power to appoint substitutes may not be inconsistent with an obligation to do work personally.[30]

In addition, work tendered to a firm may be regarded as giving rise to an employment relationship for the purposes of the DDA where there is a sufficiently close nexus between the firm or business to whom the work is tendered and the person who will be performing the work. Thus in *Loughran and Kelly v Northern Ireland Housing Executive*[31] the House of Lords held that individual partners in a firm of solicitors could pursue claims under comparable provisions[32] as 'employees' in circumstances where they had applied for their firms to be appointed to a panel established by the respondents for the purposes of providing legal services to them. Ms Kelly was one of only two partners in her firm and Mr Loughran was the sole partner in his firm. In both cases they were identified as the designated solicitor who would be responsible for the work. The House of Lords held that the wider meaning of 'employment' in the anti-discrimination legislation was wide enough to afford protection to them. The Lords observed that having regard to the object of the anti-discrimination legislation and the wide definition of employment, 'personally' in that definition could include activity undertaken by a firm. Accordingly, where a firm undertook to do work, pursuant to a contract of appointment, and by one of its partners was responsible for and did that work, the contract was one 'personally to execute any work' and it was open to that partner, as well as the firm itself, to complain of discrimination when the firm was refused appointment.[33] This means that even where the contract is with a business rather than the individual worker, it may be possible to argue that there is a sufficiently close nexus between the business and the worker such that the requisite degree of 'personal' obligation is present.

In *Patterson v Legal Services Commission*,[34] on the other hand, the Court of Appeal concluded that the franchising arrangements between the Legal Services Commission and solicitors' firms and the contracts awarded to provide legal services were not such as to create an employment relationship between the Legal

---

[30] *Byrne Brothers (Formwork) Ltd v Baird* [2002] ICR 667, [2002] IRLR 96, in respect of claims brought under the analogous definition of 'worker' in the Working Time Regulations 1998. In that case, the applicants' claimed entitlement depended upon whether they were 'workers' within the definition in Regulation 2(1), which provides that: ' "worker" means an individual who has entered into or works under (or, where the employment has ceased, worked under)—(a) a contract of employment; or (b) any other contract, whether express or implied and (if it is express) whether oral or in writing, whereby the individual undertakes to do or perform personally any work or services for another party to the contract whose status is not by virtue of the contract that of a client or customer of any profession or business undertaking carried on by the individual'.

[31] [1998] ICR 828, [1998] IRLR 70.

[32] In the Fair Employment (Northern Ireland) Act 1976, section 57(1).

[33] [1998] ICR 828 at 835G–936A, 837C, 840E, 841A–B, 844H.

[34] [2004] EWCA Civ 1558, [2004] ICR 312, [2004] IRLR 153.

Services Commission and a sole principal in a solicitor's firm.[35] The Court of Appeal held that the proper questions were '(i) Who was the contracting party or who were the contracting parties? (ii) Was any obligation imposed under the contract upon a contracting party personally to carry out work or labour? (iii) If so, was that obligation personally to carry out work and labour the dominant purpose of the contract?' In the particular case, the contract as a whole did not impose personal obligations upon Ms Patterson, the sole practitioner, to carry out work personally. Although she was responsible legally, she could leave the work to be carried out by others. In those circumstances no employment relationship arose between her and the Legal Services Commission.[36]

In *Commissioners of Inland Revenue and others v Post Office Ltd*[37] the Employment Appeal Tribunal considered complaints by sub-postmasters brought under the Employment Rights Act 1996, the Working Time Regulations 1998, and the National Minimum Wage Act 1998, which (in material respects) applied to a 'worker'.[38] The Employment Appeal Tribunal held that sub-postmasters and mistresses were not 'employees' of the Post Office for the purposes of the unfair dismissal legislation (the application of which depends upon a narrower definition of employment than that contained in the anti-discrimination legislation[39]). In addition the Employment Appeal Tribunal concluded that the complainants were not 'workers' within the wider meaning of the legislation under which they made complaints. This was because they did not 'undertake to do or perform personally any work' under the contractual arrangements with the Post Office since they had the choice whether or not to do the work themselves. This was so notwithstanding that sub-postmasters and mistresses were required to certify that they had rendered on average not less than eighteen hours' personal service each week to qualify for 'holiday substitution allowance' because this was simply a statement of what was necessary in order to qualify for an extra payment.[40]

The fact that work undertaken personally pursuant to a contractual arrangement is provided to a third party is not inconsistent with an employment

---

[35] For the purposes of the RRA, in which 'employment' is defined in materially the same way as in the DDA: section 78 RRA.

[36] The Court of Appeal did however conclude that the arrangements fell within the scope of the 'qualifications' provisions. See 6.12 below.

[37] [2003] ICR 546, [2003] IRLR 199.

[38] Employment Rights Act 1996, sections 230(3), 54(3), National Minimum Wage Act 1998, and Regulation 2, Working Time Regulations 1998.

[39] Section 230(1) and (2), Employment Rights Act 1996.

[40] In the context of employment under the narrower meaning in section 230(1) of the Employment Rights Act 1996, which reflects the common law position, a term enabling provision of a substitute is inherently inconsistent with the existence of a contract of employment. Where a person who works for another is not required to perform his services personally, as a matter of law, the relationship between that person and the person for whom he works is not that of employer and employee: *Express and Echo Publications Ltd v Tanton* [1999] ICR 693, [1999] IRLR 367.

relationship (under section 68(1) DDA) between worker and 'employer'.[41] Thus persons 'on the books' of an employment agency who were engaged under a contract described as a 'temporary worker's contract' and sent to clients to provide work were 'employed' by the employment agency for the purposes of the DDA.[42]

6.2.2. Illegality

Though the meaning given to 'employment' in the DDA requires a contractual relationship, where a contract is tainted with illegality (for example, because the employee is implicated in tax evasion) a claim will still lie under the DDA, notwithstanding that at common law such a contract would be unenforceable.[43] This is because:

[T]he anti-discrimination Acts are not really concerned with employees' rights under their contracts of employment. So, for instance, where a contract of employment is tainted by illegality, an employee may nonetheless complain that her employer discriminated against her . . . since [the legislation is] designed to provide effective relief in respect of discriminatory conduct 'rather than in relief which reflects any contractual entitlement which may or may not exist': *Hall v Woolston Hall Leisure Ltd* [2000] IRLR 578, 586, paragraph 67 *per* Mance LJ. As Peter Gibson LJ put it, at page 584, paragraph 46: 'It is the . . . discrimination that is the core of the complaint, the fact of employment and the dismissal being the particular factual circumstances which Parliament has prescribed for the . . . discrimination complaint to be capable of being made'.[44]

Thus the complaint 'does not involve enforcing, relying on or founding a claim on the contract of employment'.[45] The position might be somewhat different if there is active participation in the illegality[46] or if the contract itself was entered into for an illegal purpose. However, mere illegality in performance will not deprive a complainant of the benefit of the protection afforded by the DDA.[47]

6.2.3. Police

The police are now expressly covered by the DDA. Because of their unusual constitutional position (they are office holders with an original jurisdiction and

---

[41] *Burton v Higham t/a Ace Appointments* [2003] IRLR 257, a case falling under the (now repealed) small-employer exemption in section 7 DDA but which remains good law for the purposes of section 68(1) DDA. See, however, *Dacas v Brook Street Bureau Ltd* [2004] IRLR 358.

[42] *Ibid.* See 'contract worker' provisions which would provide a remedy against the person for whom the employee was actually providing work.

[43] *Hall v Woolston Hall Leisure Ltd* [2001] ICR 99, [2000] IRLR 578, at 586, paragraph 67, *per* Lord Justice Mance. This case was referred to approvingly in *Rhys-Harper v Relaxion Group plc and others* [2003] UKHL 33, [2003] ICR 867, [2003] IRLR 484, at paragraph 210.

[44] *Rhys-Harper, supra* note 43, at paragraph 210.

[45] *Leighton v Michael* [1995] ICR 1091, [1996] IRLR 67, 69, paragraph 29, *per* Mummery J.

[46] *Hall, supra* note 43, paragraphs 46, 47 and 80.   [47] *Hall, supra*, note 43.

not employees at common law) special provision is made deeming them to be employees for the purposes of the DDA. Section 64A DDA provides that:

(1) For the purposes of Part 2, the holding of the office of constable shall be treated as employment—

(a) by the chief officer of police as respects any act done by him in relation to a constable or that office;

(c) by the police authority as respects any act done by them in relation to a constable or that office.

(2) For the purposes of section 58[48]—

(a) the holding of the office of constable shall be treated as employment by the chief officer of police (and as not being employment by any other persons); and

(c) anything done by a person holding such an office in the performance, or purported performance, of his functions shall be treated as done in the course of that employment.

This creates a statutory form of employment for the purposes of the DDA alone. It also makes the requisite amendments to the vicarious liability provisions in section 58 DDA[49] so as to ensure that vicarious liability arises against a Chief Constable where a person, including another police officer, complains of discrimination by a police officer.[50]

6.2.4. The Armed Forces

The armed forces remain exempt from the scope of Part II DDA: section 64(7) DDA.

The Joint Committee on the Draft Disability Discrimination Bill has recommended that the Disability Discrimination Bill should include a regulation making power enabling the Government to delete this exemption but the Government has not accepted this recommendation.[51] The exemption is, as the Government has observed, consistent with the Directive,[52] which provides that 'Member States may provide that this Directive, in so far as it relates to discrimination on the grounds of disability . . . , shall not apply to the armed forces'. There is therefore, no realistic prospect of legal challenge in this area.

---

[48] The vicarious liability provisions. See Chapter 10 below.

[49] See Chapter 10 below.

[50] The vicarious liability provision deals with the difficulty that would otherwise arise: see eg *Farah v Metropolitan Police Commissioner* [1998] QB 65; *Chief Constable of Kent Constabulary v Baskerville* [2003] EWCA Civ 1354, [2003] ICR 1463. Certain miscellaneous provisions are also introduced under section 64A to deal with the payment of compensation, costs and expenses, and other issues relating to the police.

[51] Joint Committee on the Draft Disability Discrimination Bill, First Report (May 2004), paragraph 121 and recommendation 18. 'The Government's response to the Report of the Joint Committee on the Draft Disability Discrimination Bill' DWP, presented to Parliament by the Minister for Disabled People, by command of Her Majesty, on 15 July 2004, response to recommendation 18. See Chapter 13 below.

[52] 2000/78/EC, Article 3(4). See Chapter 3 above.

6.2.5. Volunteers

Volunteers are not 'employees' within the meaning of section 68(1) of the DDA.[53] This is so even where there is some degree of commitment required by the volunteering arrangement and where expenses are paid.[54]

In determining whether an arrangement really is a volunteering arrangement 'at least one test which may help in this identification exercise is to consider whether, if the volunteer should decline without prior notice to perform any work for the employer, the latter would have any legal remedy against him; and similarly to consider whether, if the volunteer attends to do work and there is none, he has any legal remedy against the employer'.[55] In the absence of any contractual relationship founding the remedies that would flow from a breach there is not an employment relationship for the purposes of section 68(1).

The Joint Committee on the draft Disability Discrimination Bill has recommended that volunteers be brought within the scope of the DDA. First, they have recommended that the Government should consult on and produce an Employment Code on volunteers. Secondly, they have recommended that the Disability Discrimination Bill should include a regulation making power, enabling volunteers to be brought within coverage of the DDA, should the non-statutory Code prove ineffective. Thirdly, they have recommended that alongside the voluntary code the Disability Discrimination Bill should include a provision protecting disabled people who are volunteers, or who apply to volunteer, from direct discrimination.[56] The Joint Committee drew attention, in particular, to the importance of volunteering as a way of helping disabled people enter into the labour market, so that the impact of a lack of coverage in this sphere is significant. The Government in its response to the Joint Committee Report has indicated that, whilst it has invited the DRC to consider producing a Voluntary Employment Code on disabled volunteers, it does not consider that it would be right to legislate at this stage.[57]

---

[53] *South East Sheffield Citizens' Advice Bureau v Grayson* [2004] IRLR 353. This case concerned the exemption in the DDA under section 7(1), which provided that the employment provisions did not apply to an employer who had fewer than 15 employees. The question therefore was whether volunteers could be included for the purposes of that calculation. This exemption has now been repealed in consequence of the making of the 2003 Regulations but the meaning given to 'employee' remains the same and this case therefore remains relevant.

[54] *Ibid.*   [55] *Ibid.* paragraph 13.

[56] Joint Committee on the Draft Disability Discrimination Bill, First Report (May 2004), paragraphs 352–61.

[57] 'The Government's response to the Report of the Joint Committee on the Draft Disability Discrimination Bill' DWP, presented to Parliament by the Minister for Disabled People, by command of Her Majesty, on 15 July 2004, response to recommendations 63 and 64.

6.2.6. Prospective Employees

As can be seen from above (in 6.2), the DDA outlaws discrimination by employers against prospective disabled employees, including applicants for employment:

• in the arrangements made for the purpose of determining to whom to offer employment;

• in the terms on which employment is offered; and

• by refusing, or deliberately not offering, employment.

In addition, prospective disabled employees are protected against harassment.

Accordingly, discrimination or harassment in short-listing, interviewing, final selection, and offers of employment are all outlawed by section 4(1) DDA.

In addition the concept of 'arrangements' in section 4(1) DDA is very wide.[58] It is not confined to the arrangements an employer makes in deciding who should be offered a specific job, but also includes arrangements for deciding who should be offered employment more generally. For example, participation in a pre-employment training programme could be 'an arrangement' if its completion is a necessary step along the road to gaining an offer of employment.[59] The breadth of section 4(1) indicates that employers need to be proactive in ensuring discrimination does not occur in the recruitment process.

6.2.6.1. *Job descriptions and person specifications*

As for drawing up the job description or person specification, whilst an employer is of course entitled to specify that candidates for a job must have certain qualifications, employers must take great care to ensure that unnecessary or marginal requirements in a job description or person specification are not included where they might disadvantage disabled applicants.[60] The Employment Code gives the following example, amongst others.

An employer stipulates that employees must be 'good team players', when in fact the job in question does not involve working in a team. This requirement could unjustifiably exclude some people who have difficulty communicating, such as some people with autism.[61]

In addition, blanket exclusions which do not take account of individual circumstances might also constitute discrimination and as they are likely to amount to

---

[58] See *Archibald v Fife Council* [2004] UKHL 32, [2004] ICR 954, IRLR 651, for the wide meaning given to 'arrangements' under the unamended section 6(1)(a) DDA.

[59] Employment Code, paragraph 7.6.

[60] *Ibid.* paragraph 7.7. Regard must always be had to the duties to make reasonable adjustments, see Chapter 5 above, at 5.2.2, and 6.2.6.3 below.

[61] *Ibid.*

direct discrimination, it is unlikely that they would be capable of justification or excuse.[62] For example, a blanket exclusion on people with epilepsy from all driving jobs may be unlawful if, for example, one of the driving jobs in practice only requires a standard licence with standard insurance and a person with epilepsy who has such a licence and can obtain such insurance is turned down for the job.[63]

Apart from specific references to disabilities or impairments, job descriptions or personal specifications which call for characteristics which a disabled person with a particular impairment may be less likely to possess might be discriminatory, including characteristics such as 'active and energetic'.[64] A refusal to employ a disabled person because of a concern that they would not possess such characteristics may be directly discriminatory (and therefore not capable of justification) where such refusal is based upon an assumption that they are unlikely to possess such characteristics and without having regard to the particular disabled person's position. In addition, even if regard is had to the particular disabled person's position, a refusal to employ a disabled person because he or she does not possess those characteristics, if the reason why the disabled person lacks them is related to disability, will be unlawful unless justified, and may breach one of the duties to make reasonable adjustments.[65]

6.2.6.2. *Advertising the vacancy and the 'pool'*

As has been regularly observed, open recruitment from among the widest possible pool is most likely to result in the best candidate for the job and reduce the likelihood of unintentional discrimination occurring.[66] Discriminatory advertisements are addressed specifically by the DDA and this issue is addressed below (paragraph 6.16).

Informal recruitment methods are inherently more likely to result in discriminatory acts because the checks and balances that exist in an open, objective selection process are less likely to be present. Whilst the DDA does not prohibit indirect discrimination,[67] as has been seen[68] it does outlaw less favourable treatment of a disabled person for a reason that relates to his or her disability[69] and this meaning of discrimination is wide enough to catch some incidences of indirect discrimination. Recruitment that excludes schools, colleges, or graduates from vocational courses where disabled pupils and students are represented might in a particular case constitute disability discrimination and be

---

[62] *Ibid.* paragraph 7.8.   [63] *Ibid.*   [64] *Ibid.* paragraph 7.7.

[65] See Chapter 5 above, paragraph 5.2.3 and Employment Code, paragraph 7.10. See also the duties to make reasonable adjustments, paragraph 5.2.2 above.

[66] See *Anya v University of Oxford and another* [2001] EWCA Civ 405, [2001] ICR 847, 851–5, *per* Lord Justice Sedley, discussed at Chapter 5 above, paragraph 5.2.1.4.

[67] See Chapter 2 above, paragraph 2.4   [68] See Chapter 5 above, paragraph 5.2.3.

[69] *Ibid.*

unlawful.[70] Recruitment by word of mouth may result in unintended direct discrimination[71] or less favourable treatment of a disabled person for reasons relating to his or her disability.[72] In this regard the observations of the Court of Appeal in *Lord Chancellor v Coker and Osamor*[73] are relevant. This case concerned the indirect discrimination provisions of the SDA and the RRA.[74] The complainants argued that the Lord Chancellor's appointment of a special adviser without advertisement, or any transparent selection process, from amongst a group of people known to him was unlawfully discriminatory. It was contended by the complainants that because the Lord Chancellor's social circle was comprised largely of white men, such recruitment disadvantaged qualified black and ethnic minority candidates and women candidates. Though the claim was successful in the Employment Tribunal it was overturned on appeal. The appeal succeeded largely on the issue of disproportionate impact, which is not material to a disability discrimination case. Importantly, however, the Court of Appeal observed in a 'postscript' that:

For the reasons that we have given, the attack advanced in these proceedings on the practice of making appointments from a circle of family, friends and acquaintances has failed. We have held no breach of section 1(1)(b)[75] of the statutes has been made out. It does not follow, however, that this practice is unobjectionable. It will often be open to objection for a number of reasons. It may not produce the best candidate for the post. It may be likely to result in the appointee being of a particular gender or racial group. It may infringe the principle of equal opportunities.

In conclusion, we would emphasise that this judgment is not concerned with the practice of recruiting by word of mouth. The Employment Code issued by the Equal Opportunities Commission in 1985 under . . . the . . . [SDA], which contains valuable practical guidance for the elimination of discrimination in the field of employment and for the promotion of equality of opportunity between men and women, has this to say about that practice, at paragraph 19(c): 'Recruitment solely and primarily by word of mouth may unnecessarily restrict the choice of applicants available. The method should be avoided in a workforce predominantly of one sex, if in practice it precludes members of the opposite sex from applying'.

An Employment Code was also issued by the Commission for Racial Equality in 1983 under . . . the . . . [RRA] and nothing in this judgment detracts from the desirability of complying with the Codes of Practice.

. . .

---

[70] It is worth observing that such institutional barriers to recruitment would very likely fall within the scope of the concept of indirect discrimination, having regard to its meaning in the Directive (2000/78/EC), were it properly transposed, and this is an area where the Government's failure to introduce the concept into the DDA may be challengeable.

[71] See Chapter 5 above, at 5.2.1, and see *Anya, supra* note 66.

[72] See Chapter 5 above, at 5.2.3.

[73] [2001] EWCA Civ 1756, [2002] ICR 321, [2002] IRLR 80.

[74] Though with the wide meaning of less favourable treatment of a disabled person for a reason relating to his disability—see Chapter 5 above, at 5.2.3—the observations may be equally apt in a case in disability discrimination.

[75] The indirect discrimination provisions of the SDA and RRA.

It is possible that a recruitment exercise conducted by word of mouth, by personal recommendation or by other informal recruitment method will constitute indirect discrimination within the meaning of sections 1(1)(b) of the statutes. If the arrangement made for the purpose of determining who should be offered employment or promotion involves the application of a requirement or condition to an applicant that he or she should be personally recommended by a member of existing workforce that may, depending of course on all the facts, have the specified disproportionately adverse impact on one sex or on a particular ethnic group so infringing section 1(1)(b).[76]

For the same reasons in the context of disability discrimination, informal and word of mouth recruitment should be avoided because of its possible impact on disabled people and the risk that such recruitment will result in an unlawful act, particularly having regard to section 3A(1) and (5) (less favourable treatment on the ground of a disabled person's disability or for a reason which relates to the disabled person's disability) and section 4A DDA (duty on employers to make adjustments where a provision, criterion, or practice places the disabled person concerned at a substantial disadvantage in comparison with persons who are not disabled).[77]

The DDA permits discrimination in favour of disabled people (non-disabled persons are not protected by the DDA outside of the victimization provisions). Accordingly it is lawful to discriminate positively in favour of disabled candidates. In addition, and more particularly, it is entirely permissible to welcome explicitly applications from disabled applicants. Indeed the Employment Code recognizes that '[t]his would be a positive public statement of the employer's policy'.[78] In addition, where an organization recognizes that suitably qualified disabled people have not applied for work, it may want to, and can lawfully, contact local employment services, including job centres and specialist disability employment services, to encourage disabled people to apply.[79]

6.2.6.3. *Selection criteria*
Job requirements and qualifications or selection criteria that are set at a higher standard in the case of disabled applicants (by, for example, requiring that they 'prove' an unbroken attendance record in previous employment in circumstances where the same is not required of non-disabled applicants) will constitute direct discrimination and will not be justifiable.[80]

In addition, criteria that place a disabled person at a substantial disadvantage in comparison with persons who are not disabled will trigger the duty upon an employer to make reasonable adjustments.[81] The same will only apply where, in

---

[76] *Lord Chancellor v Coker and another* [2001] EWCA Civ 1756, [2002] ICR 321 at 339–40, paragraphs 53–7, *per* Lord Mummery.
[77] See Chapter 5 above, at 5.2. [78] Employment Code, paragraph 7.11.
[79] *Ibid.* paragraph 2.17.
[80] Section 3A(5) DDA. See Chapter 5 above, at 5.2.1.
[81] Section 4A DDA; see Chapter 5 above, at 5.2.2.

the case of a provision, criterion, or practice, the disabled person concerned is an applicant for the employment concerned or has notified the employer that he may be.[82] In addition, selection criteria that disadvantage a disabled person for a reason that relates to his or her disability will be unlawful unless justified.[83] Such treatment will not be capable of justification if the circumstances are such that a duty to make reasonable adjustments arises and there is a failure to comply with that duty, unless it would have been justified even if he had complied with that duty.[84]

This means that employers need to scrutinize their selection criteria with care. Many of the obstacles to equal access for disabled people arise from selection criteria and recruitment procedures that unintentionally disadvantage disabled people. Requirements that an applicant for employment be 'active and energetic', for example, when in fact the job concerned is largely sedentary, may unjustifiably exclude some people whose disabilities result in them getting tired more easily than others and may therefore be unlawful.[85] As stated above, blanket exclusions that do not have regard to individual circumstances may be unlawful.

In addition, acting on stereotypical assumptions about applicants, that persons with a history of mental illness would be unreliable, for example, will be unlawful.[86]

Requirements relating to previous experience or qualifications may also discriminate against a disabled person where for reasons relating to his or her disability they have been unable to obtain that experience. The Employment Code gives the following example:

An employer specifies that two GCSEs are required for a certain post. This is to show that a candidate has the general level of ability required. No particular subjects are specified. An applicant whose dyslexia prevented her from passing written examinations cannot meet this requirement. The employer would be unable to justify rejecting her on this account alone if she could show in some other way that she had the expertise called for in the post.[87]

Thus where a particular qualification imposed by the employer is such that a disabled person cannot meet it for a reason which relates to his or her disability, then an employer will have to show that it is justified if its imposition is to be lawful (and then only if any duty to make adjustments has been considered: see Chapter 5 above, 5.2.3.6).

---

[82] Section 4A(2)(a). Such knowledge is not required in the case of direct discrimination or disability-related discrimination.

[83] Section 3A(1) DDA. See Chapter 5 above, at 5.2.3.

[84] Section 3A(6) DDA. See Chapter 5 above, at 5.2.3.6.

[85] Employment Code, paragraph 7.7.   [86] Employment Code, paragraph 7.8.

[87] *Ibid.* paragraph 7.10.

As stated above, where an employer knows that a disabled person is an applicant for the employment concerned or has notified the employer that he may be, a duty to make adjustments will arise in respect of any provision, criterion, or practice that places the disabled person concerned at a substantial disadvantage in comparison with persons who are not disabled.[88] This may require adjustments to selection criteria and selection procedures, including the application process, the qualifications required, and testing procedures. Where an employer does not make such adjustments and the disabled person concerned is disadvantaged, then the employer will contravene section 4(1) DDA.[89] Adjustments may include: allowing more time to a candidate for interview or testing; providing and receiving applications or application forms in alternative formats (such as on disc, in large prints, in Braille, or on tape); adjustments to selection criteria; and accommodating assistance.

Criteria that relate to the health of an applicant for employment may particularly disadvantage disabled people. Health requirements therefore need to be very carefully reviewed to ensure that a disabled person is not less favourably treated for a reason relating to his or her disability in consequence and that the health requirement is truly being applied equally (that is, that it would be applied to a person without the disabled person's disability). Where a health requirement forms part of the criteria for selection and is applied to all candidates but which disadvantages a disabled person for a reason relating to his or her disability, then it will be unlawful unless justified. In addition, in such circumstances an employer may be under a duty to make adjustments to the criteria to prevent the particular health related criterion placing the disabled person at a substantial disadvantage in comparison with persons who are not disabled. Assumptions should not be made about 'health' in the case of disabled candidates. Such is likely to be direct discrimination and unlawful if a disabled person is treated less favourably in consequence. A disabled person, of course, may be as 'healthy' as a non-disabled person, and assumptions should not be made otherwise. Thus a requirement that a disabled person undertakes a medical examination or provides a medical report as to health may be discriminatory.

In *Hammersmith & Fulham LBC v Farnsworth*[90] the complainant applied for a post as a residential social worker in an Adolescent Service Unit. She was interviewed and given a provisional job offer but was referred to the Council's occupational health physician for 'medical clearance'. Her general practitioner and hospital doctor were consulted and it was found that the complainant had a history of mental illness. The occupational health physician informed the employers that the complainant had ill health over a number of years which at times had been severe and necessitated hospital admission. As a result the employers withdrew their provisional offer of appointment and the

---

[88] Section 4A(1) DDA. See Chapter 5 above, at 5.2.2.
[89] Read with sections 3A and 4A DDA.   [90] [2000] IRLR 691.

complainant brought proceedings against the employer claiming that she had been discriminated against by reason of her disability. The Employment Appeal Tribunal upheld the decision of the tribunal at first instance that the complainant had been treated less favourably for a reason that related to her disability. The treatment was not justified as the employers had failed to enquire further into the complainant's medical history having adopted a practice of denying itself information about the medical history on which the occupational health physician had based her report.[91]

Questioning in interviews may provide evidence of discrimination where the applicant for a post does not succeed. Further, words of discouragement at an interview may by themselves constitute 'arrangements' and amount to unlawful discrimination of the person discouraged.[92] Where a person of a different disability status would not have been asked the same questions or they relate to the disabled person's disability, they are likely to be unlawful. While questions relating to a person's disability may be relevant, not least to the question whether reasonable adjustments ought to be made, such questions ought to be asked sensitively and the purpose of such questions should be made clear. Any reliance upon such information to treat a disabled person less favourably is likely to be unlawful.

There is a considerable overlap between section 4(1)(a) and (c) DDA. In *Williams v Channel 5 Engineering Services Ltd*[93] the complainant, who had a hearing impairment, applied for a job as a Channel 5 re-tuner. He began a four-day training course and passed the test on the first two days. However, the third day involved a video with no subtitles. He was refused one-to-one training with the trainer and left without sitting the final day's test. Thereafter he was provided with one-to-one training and he passed the course. However, the training delay caused further delay during which time the need for re-tuners reduced and Mr Williams was never actually employed. An Employment Tribunal concluded that he had been unlawfully discriminated against by the failure to make adjustments to the training course at the outset and this led directly to the further delay. The tribunal rejected an argument by the employers that no duty to make reasonable adjustments arose until the applicant had passed his training course: 'The whole tenor of the Act read with the Employment Code is that employers should avoid discrimination and plan ahead by considering the needs of future disabled employees. Steps to obtain necessary equipment for training and deployment should have been initiated when Channel 5 embarked on the re-tuning programme including provision in the application form used by the recruitment agencies to state whether an applicant was in any way disabled and if so, in what respect.'

---

[91] See too *Paul v National Probation Service* [2004] IRLR 190.
[92] *Simon v Brimham Associates* [1987] ICR 596, [1987] IRLR 307.
[93] (ET Case No 2302136/97) EOR DCLD Number 34H, Winter 1997.

On the other hand where an applicant states that they have a disability but no particular needs, an employer may not be acting lawfully if he fails to make reasonable adjustments. In *Fozard v Greater Manchester Police Authority*[94] the complainant had a disability that caused reduced manual dexterity and learning difficulties. She applied for a temporary post of word processor operator with the respondent and indicated that she had a disability but that she did not have any special needs. One of the essential criteria for the job was accuracy in written work. The complainant's application form contained a number of errors and her application was rejected. The tribunal concluded that the treatment was justified in circumstances where the reason why the respondent was looking for accuracy in written work was 'that it was part of the job to create typed written records and minutes of meetings and other documents' and filling in the application form was a fair test of accuracy. This reason, concluded the tribunal, 'was material to the circumstances and substantial'. In addition, as the complainant did not suggest that she would be at a substantial disadvantage without a spelling text facility, the respondents did not know that she was likely to be affected in the way mentioned by the DDA (now see section 4A(3), discussed in Chapter 5 above, at 5.2.2.1).

6.2.6.4. *Terms*
In addition any discrimination in the terms upon which employment is offered will be discriminatory (section 4(1)(b) DDA). This pertains only to offers of employment to the particular disabled person. Once employment commences any complaint of discrimination in relation to the terms of employment fall within the scope of section 4(2) DDA, on which see below.

6.2.7. Existing Employees

As has been seen, the DDA outlaws discrimination by employers against existing disabled employees:

- in the terms of employment;
- in opportunities afforded for promotion, transfer, training, or receiving any other benefits;
- by a refusal to afford, or deliberately not affording, any such opportunity; and
- by a dismissal or by subjecting a disabled person to any other detriment.[95]

It is also unlawful for an employer to subject a disabled employee to harassment.[96]

---

[94] ET Case No 2401143/97, 33F,[6] Autumn 1997 EOR DCLD   [95] Section 4(2) DDA.
[96] Section 4(3) DDA.

6.2.7.1. *Terms*

The prohibition against discrimination in relation to 'terms' of employment is wide enough to cover all the main conditions and benefits attributable to work. These include pay, sick pay,[97] working hours, access to pension benefits, and the like.[98] Accordingly terms and conditions of service must not discriminate against disabled people and, where a duty arises, reasonable adjustments may have to be made to them. The Employment Code gives the following example:

An employer's terms and conditions state the hours an employee has to be in work. It might be a reasonable adjustment to change these hours for someone whose disability means that she has difficulty using public transport during rush hours.[99]

In addition, discrimination related to a disabled person's conditions of work might be unlawful. For example, where a disabled person was working part-time because of her disability and she was dismissed because her employer did not like employing part-timers, she was unlawfully discriminated against, such treatment being related to her disability and, on the facts, unjustified.[100]

Where performance-related pay is paid by an employer, the employer must ensure that the operation of the scheme does not discriminate against disabled employees. Such discrimination:

• may occur directly, where a disabled employee is excluded from the scheme on the ground of his or her disability;

• may occur for reasons related to disability where, for example, the scheme operates so as to reward a disabled employee at a lower level because of his or her inability to meet the targets under the scheme; and/or

• may give rise to a duty to make adjustments where such scheme places a disabled person at a substantial disadvantage in comparison with others.

A directly discriminatory scheme and a failure to make reasonable adjustments in respect of a scheme where a duty arises would both be unlawful, as would any unjustified less favourable treatment arising in consequence of the operation of such a scheme where it is related to disability.[101] Accordingly, employers have to be particularly careful about the operation of such schemes.[102] The Employment Code gives the following examples:[103]

---

[97] As to which a duty to make reasonable adjustments may arise: *Nottinghamshire County Council v Meikle* [2004] EWCA Civ 859, [2004] IRLR 703. In addition, a failure to pay sick pay—or full sick pay—may be unlawful if it is disability-related and unjustified: *ibid.*

[98] For limitations on the protection against discrimination in relation to 'benefits', see below.

[99] Employment Code, paragraph 8.4.

[100] *Ashmore v AMH Holdings Ltd* Case No 5208834/2001 [2003] EOR 122, 19. In such circumstances a duty to make adjustments would probably arise: see Chapter 5 above, at 5.2.2.

[101] Justification is only available in cases of disability-related discrimination: see Chapter 5 above, at 5.2.

[102] See Employment Code paragraphs, 8.5–8.6 for guidance.   [103] *Ibid.* paragraph 8.6.

A disabled man with arthritis works in telephone sales and is paid commission on the value of his sales. Because of a worsening of his impairment he is advised to switch to new computer equipment. This equipment slows his work down for a period of time while he gets used to it and consequently the value of his sales falls. It is likely to be a reasonable adjustment for his employer to continue to pay him his previous level of commission for the period in which he adjusts to the new equipment.

A woman who has recently become disabled because of diabetes works for an employer that operates a performance related bonus scheme. When she has her annual appraisal, the woman is unable to demonstrate that she has met all her objectives for the year, unlike in previous years when she had in fact exceeded her objectives. The reason why the woman has not met her objectives this year is that she has been adjusting to her disability (attending hospital appointments, paying careful attention to her diet, taking regular breaks, etc). The disabled woman's employer is likely to be discriminating against her if, because she has not met her objectives for the year, it refuses to pay her a bonus.

It is important to note that the partial exemption that existed in relation to performance-related pay schemes under the unamended DDA no longer applies.[104]

6.2.7.2. *Promotion, transfers, training, and other benefits*
As can be seen, discrimination is outlawed widely insofar as existing employees are concerned.

Section 4(2) DDA outlaws discrimination in the *opportunities* provided to disabled employees, as well as in the enjoyment of actual benefits (promotion, training, etc). Therefore discrimination is prohibited in access to possible benefits as well as in access to actual benefits. Such benefits may exist at the outset of the employment relationship and continue throughout.

Thus, employers must not discriminate in their induction procedures and may have to make adjustments to ensure a disabled person is introduced into a new working environment in an appropriate way. The Employment Code gives the following example:[105]

A small manufacturing company usually hands out written copies of all its policies by way of induction to new employees and gives them half a day to read the documentation and to raise any questions with their line manager. A new employee has dyslexia and the employer arranges for her supervisor to spend a morning with her talking through the relevant policies. This is likely to be a reasonable adjustment.

Employers must not discriminate in selection for training and must make reasonable adjustments in order to facilitate access for disabled people, where a duty arises. The Employment Code gives the following examples:[106]

---

[104] Regulation 3, Disability Discrimination (Employment) Regulations 1996, SI 1996/1456, repealed by Disability Discrimination (Employment Field) (Leasehold Premises) Regulations 2004, SI 2004/153. See also the Agricultural Wages (Abolition of Permits to Incapacitated Persons) Regulations 2004, SI 2004/2178, repealing the exception in the Agricultural Wages Act 1948 excluding the employment of certain disabled people from the minimum rates of pay set thereunder.
[105] Employment Code, paragraph 8.7.   [106] *Ibid.* paragraph 8.8.

Instead of taking an informed decision, an employer wrongly assumes that a disabled person will be unwilling or unable to undertake demanding training or attend a residential training course. This is likely to amount to direct discrimination.

An employer may need to alter the time or the location of the training for someone with a mobility problem, make training manuals, slides or other visual media accessible to a visually impaired employee (perhaps by providing Braille versions or having them read out), or ensure that an induction loop is available for someone with a hearing impairment.

The concept of 'benefits' encompasses the enjoyment of a wide range of opportunities, privileges, and tangible goods. It might include access to canteens, meal vouchers, social clubs and other recreational activities, dedicated car parking spaces, discounts on products, bonuses, share options, hairdressing, clothes allowances, financial services, healthcare, medical assistance/insurance, transport to work, company car, education assistance, workplace nurseries, and rights to special leave.[107] Indeed, any advantage will be caught.[108]

Whilst discrimination in the provision of benefits is widely outlawed, this relates only to benefits that are incidental to the employment relationship. Where an employer is concerned with the provision (whether or not for payment) of benefits to the public (or a section of the public) benefits of that description are not caught by section 4 of the DDA, unless: the provision of those benefits differs as between employees and members of the public; the provision of those benefits to employees is regulated by their contracts of employment; or the benefits relate to training.[109] This means that, for example, a leisure centre that provides swimming facilities to the public will not be discriminating against a disabled employee, under the employment provisions of the DDA,[110] if it treats that employee less favourably by denying him or her access to the swimming pool in the leisure centre, unless access to the swimming pool is regulated by the contract of employment or is differently provided (perhaps by special opening hours) to employees.

As to promotion and transfers, employers must ensure that arrangements for the same do not discriminate against disabled people. As stated, this relates not merely to existing opportunities but also to opportunities for potential advancement. Similar considerations to those involved in deciding whom to recruit and the arrangements for the same apply in respect of promotions and transfers. Reasonable adjustments may be required and criteria for promotion and transfer should be scrutinized carefully for any discriminatory impact.[111] Similarly,

---

[107] *Ibid.* paragraph 8.10.   [108] Subject to section 4(4) DDA, described below.

[109] Section 4(4) DDA.

[110] Though it may be under the goods, facilities, and services provisions, see Chapter 7 below.

[111] Employment Code, paragraphs 8.13–8.14. Of course, a transfer may well be required to *comply* with the duty to make adjustments: *Archibald, supra* note 58.

employers must not discriminate in relation to the provision of training and again reasonable adjustments may be required in respect of the same.[112]

6.2.7.3. *Detriment and dismissal*

Discrimination by subjecting a disabled person to a 'detriment' or 'dismissal' is outlawed.[113]

The concept of 'detriment' is very wide indeed. The conduct covered by the concept of 'detriment' has been somewhat narrowed by the amendments to the DDA. Harassment, which was previously not expressly outlawed by the DDA, was conduct which was caught by the 'detriment' provisions in the anti-discrimination legislation.[114] However, since the amendments to the DDA, express provision is made in relation to harassment (see Chapter 5 above, paragraph 5.2.4) and the concept of 'detriment' is now deemed not to include conduct of a nature falling within the meaning of 'harassment' in section 3B DDA.[115] To this extent the concept is somewhat narrower. Nevertheless, it covers a wide range of conduct and might be regarded as a residual provision in that any disadvantageous conduct which does not fall within the scope of one of the other unlawful acts is likely to fall within the concept of 'detriment'. Examples of cases in which a 'detriment' has been found include:

- a failure to investigate an employee's complaints that her work colleagues were harassing her: *Race v The University of York*;[116]
- a failure to tell a diabetic employee that he was only being removed from his job temporarily pending medical investigation and leading him to believe that he was being removed permanently: *Garrett v Brotherwood Automobility Ltd*;[117]
- inconsistent treatment by not automatically slotting a disabled employee into a new post when his job disappeared following a restructuring exercise: *Ludgate v London Borough of Brent*;[118]
- applying a sick pay scheme (half pay) to an employee who became ill while he was suspended on full pay: *Owen v Isle of Anglesea County Council*;[119] and
- insisting that an employee attend work five days a week when he was only fit for two or three days a week and sought to work at home on two days a week: *Brown v South Bank University*.[120]

---

[112] Employment Code, paragraph 8.88.

[113] Section 4(2)(d) DDA.

[114] The same concept is found in the SDA and the RRa, sections 6(2)(b) and 4(2)(c), respectively. See Chapter 5 above, at 5.2.4.2.

[115] Section 18D(2) DDA. The only exception to this is where the conduct complained of falls under section 16(C)(2)(b) (instructions and pressure to discriminate). See Chapter 5 above, at 5.2.4 for the meaning of 'harassment' under section 3B DDA.

[116] ET Case No 1806953/00, IDS, 'Disability Discrimination' (2002) 188.

[117] ET Case No 3101189/2000, *ibid.*   [118] ET Case No 2300069/00, *ibid.*

[119] ET Case No 2901076/00, *ibid.*   [120] ET Case No. 2305234/96, *ibid.*

Each case, however, will turn on its own facts. To establish 'detriment' it is only necessary to show that the disabled person has suffered a 'disadvantage'.[121] In particular, it is not necessary to show any financial or material disadvantage.[122] Nevertheless not all cases of subjectively felt hurt will constitute a 'detriment'. Thus, for example, in *Ellis v Suffolk County Council*[123] the Employment Tribunal concluded that no detriment had occurred where an employer arranged a seminar out of the office which an employee could not attend because of his agoraphobia. Although he was not required to attend, the employee felt excluded and depressed by the arrangements but did not, according to the tribunal, suffer a detriment. As stated, each case must be looked at on its own facts and decisions; in particular first instance decisions in other cases should not be regarded as setting any precedent for future cases.

A discriminatory dismissal is unlawful. Such a dismissal may occur in the usual way by termination of the contract by the employer. In addition, it may occur:

- where a person's employment terminates by the expiration of any period (including a period expiring by reference to an event or circumstance), not being a termination immediately after which the employment is renewed on the same terms.[124] Thus the expiry of a fixed-term contract or a fixed-project contract is to be regarded as a dismissal unless the contract is renewed immediately afterwards on the same terms; and

- on the termination of a person's employment by any act of his (including the giving of notice) in circumstances such that he is entitled to terminate it without notice by reason of the conduct of the employer.[125] Thus constructive dismissals are now expressly protected by the DDA. There had been some controversy about the extent to which the DDA protected against constructive dismissals, ironically only resolved in favour of the same after the enactment of the Regulations which eliminated any doubt.[126]

---

[121] *Ministry of Defence v Jeremiah* [1980] QB 87, [1979] IRLR 436, paragraph 27, in which the question of less favourable treatment and detriment were subsumed into one question by Lord Brandon. It is not necessary to know of the disadvantage for it to constitute a detriment: *Garry v London Borough of Ealing* [2001] IRLR 681.

[122] *Chief Constable of West Yorkshire v Khan* [2001] UKHL 48, [2001] ICR 1065, [2001] 1 WLR 1947, [2001] IRLR 830.

[123] ET Case No 1500019/01. See too *Smith v Vodafone UK Ltd* (EAT No: 0054/01) EOR DCLD Number 49D,[7].

[124] Section 4(5) DDA.   [125] *Ibid.*

[126] *Meikle, supra* note 97, in which the controversy over the two conflicting decisions of the Employment Appeal Tribunal was resolved: *Commissioner of Police of the Metropolis v Harley* [2001] ICR 927 (constructive dismissal *does not* fall within the scope of the word 'dismissal') and *Derby Specialist Fabrication Ltd v Burton* [2001] ICR 833 (constructive dismissal *does* fall within the scope of the word 'dismissal'). In *Meikle* the Court of Appeal concluded that *Derby* was to be preferred. *Derby* had by then been followed in *Catherall v Michelin Tyres plc* [2003] ICR 28.

All dismissals therefore fall to be considered under section 4(2)(d) DDA. This is so whatever the actual or purported reason for the dismissal (redundancy, misconduct, sickness,[127] retirement, compulsory ill-health retirement, expiry of a fixed term, etc). This means that employers must ensure that their arrangements for determining whom to dismiss, where a choice exists, or whether to dismiss in a particular case should be checked to ensure that they are not discriminatory.

Importantly, too, the duty to make reasonable adjustments now applies in relation to dismissals.[128] Thus, as the Employment Code advises:[129]

- when setting criteria for redundancy selection, employers should consider whether any proposed criterion would adversely impact upon a disabled employee. If so, it may be necessary for the employer to make reasonable adjustments. For example, it is likely to be a reasonable adjustment to discount disability-related sickness absence when assessing attendance as part of a redundancy selection scheme.[130] Some employers use 'flexibility' as a selection criterion for redundancy (for example, willingness to relocate or to work unpopular hours, or ability to carry out a wide variety of tasks). An employer should carefully consider how to apply such a criterion as it might be discriminatory in a particular case;

- where the dismissal of a disabled person is being considered for a reason relating to that person's conduct, the employer should consider whether any reasonable adjustments need to be made to the disciplinary or dismissal process. In addition, if the conduct in question is related to the employee's disability, that may be relevant in determining the sanction, if any, which it is appropriate to impose.

Where an employee becomes completely unable to do the job for which they were employed because of disability, an employer remains under a duty to make reasonable adjustments and these may include placing a disabled person in a new job without the need for competitive application.[131]

6.2.8. Managing Disability or Ill Health

The DDA does not make special provision for managing disability or ill health. Where an employer discriminates—either directly, or for a reason relating to disability, or by a failure to make adjustments when a duty arises—he will be acting unlawfully, whatever the context,[132] if his conduct falls within the scope of one of the unlawful acts described in section 4. However, the Employment Code

---

[127] See *Clark v TDG Ltd t/a Novacold* [1999] ICR 951, [1999] IRLR 318.
[128] Cf section 6(2) of the unamended DDA.   [129] Employment Code, paragraphs 8.25–8.26.
[130] See *Clark, supra* note 127.   [131] *Archibald v Fife Council, supra* note 58 .
[132] Subject to justification in the context of disability-related discrimination.

provides specific guidance in relation to managing disability and ill health and this reflects the fact that many discriminatory acts occur in this context, some probably unintentionally. This subject therefore warrants particular consideration.

The Employment Code gives the following important guidance. First, employers will often find that it is of benefit to their organization to retain a disabled employee, as this will prevent their knowledge and skills from being lost to the enterprise. In addition, the cost of retaining such an employee will frequently be less than the cost of recruiting and training a new member of staff.[133] If as a result of a disability an employer's arrangements or a physical feature of the premises give rise to a duty to make reasonable adjustments, then the following considerations will always be relevant:

• the first consideration in making reasonable adjustments should be to enable the disabled employee to continue in his present job if at all possible;

• the employer should consult the disabled person at appropriate stages about what his needs are and, where the employee has a progressive condition, what effect the disability might have on future employment, so that reasonable adjustments may be planned;

• in appropriate cases, the employer should also consider seeking extra advice on the extent of a disabled person's capabilities and on what might be done to change premises or working arrangements. Where an employee has been off work, a phased return might be appropriate;

• if there are no reasonable adjustments which would enable the disabled employee to continue in his present job, the employer must consider whether there are suitable alternative positions to which he could be deployed.[134]

In addition, it may be possible for the employer to modify the job to accommodate an employee's changing needs, by re-arranging working methods, giving another employee certain minor tasks that the disabled person can no longer do, providing practical aids or adaptions to premises or equipment, or allowing the disabled person to work at different times or from different places.[135] It might also be appropriate in particular cases to vary working hours.[136] Similarly, the duty to make reasonable adjustments may arise where an employee has a stable impairment but the nature of the job in which they are employed has changed.[137]

It should be remembered that the duty to make adjustments may require an employer to treat a disabled person apparently 'more favourably' than a non-disabled person, in order to remove the disadvantage arising from the disability. This may include transferring an employee to a suitable vacant position[138] where

---

[133] Employment Code, paragraph 8.15.
[134] *Ibid.* paragraph 8.16, and see *Archibald v Fife Council, supra* note 58.
[135] *Ibid.* paragraph 8.17.   [136] *Ibid.*   [137] *Ibid.* paragraph 8.18.
[138] *Archibald v Fife Council, supra* note 58.

a person becomes totally incapable of doing the job for which they were employed.[139] Such is the extent of the duty that it does not depend upon the disabled person undergoing competitive and open selection for a job that they may be capable of undertaking: the duty may require an employer to transfer an employee without such a process.[140]

In addition, an employer may be required to pay sick pay, or full sick pay, where a disabled employee is absent because of his or her disability. Where a reduction in sick pay amounts to less favourable treatment for a reason relating to disability (for example, length of absence) such a reduction will be unlawful unless justified. A corresponding duty to make reasonable adjustments might well arise.[141]

In addressing the question of continuing employment for a disabled employee, regard must be had by an employer to the assistance available from Job Centre Plus to the Access to Work scheme.[142] As the Employment Code observes, the purpose of the scheme is to provide practical support to disabled people in, or entering, paid employment to help overcome work-related obstacles resulting from disability. The scheme may provide a grant for additional employment costs and may assist an employer in deciding what steps it might take to facilitate the continuing employment of a disabled employee. The scheme does not diminish any of the employer's obligations under the DDA but where the scheme is able to provide assistance to facilitate the continuing employment of a disabled employee, it is likely to be unreasonable for an employer to refuse to accept it and make the corresponding adjustments. However, as the Employment Code points out, an employer may not rely upon the scheme as a defence to any challenge to a failure to comply with his own obligations under the DDA. The responsibility for making reasonable adjustments is the responsibility of the employer alone.

6.3. CONTRACT WORKERS

Section 4B of the amended DDA provides more extensive protection against disability discrimination in relation to contract workers than did the unamended DDA.[143]

It is unlawful for a principal, in relation to contract work, to discriminate against a disabled person who is a contract worker:

---

[139] *Ibid.*   [140] *Ibid.*

[141] *Nottinghamshire County Council v Meikle, supra* note 97. The controversy over the impact of section 6(11) DDA, and its impact on sick pay and similar benefits, is no longer live because section 6(11) has been repealed and substituted by the Disability Discrimination Act 1995 (Amendment) Regulations 2003, SI 2003/1673.

[142] For a description see Employment Code, paragraphs 8.19 *et seq.*

[143] As inserted by the 2003 Regulations. Section 12, which dealt with contract workers in the unamended DDA, is now repealed.

- in the terms on which he allows him to do that work;
- by not allowing him to do it or continue to do it;
- in the way he affords him access to any benefits or by refusing or deliberately omitting to afford him access to them; or
- by subjecting him to any other detriment.

These expressions mirror some of those contained within the employment provisions,[144] and where they do they will be interpreted in the same way.

It is also unlawful for a principal, in relation to contract work, to subject a disabled contract worker to harassment.[145]

A 'principal' is a person who makes work available for doing by individuals who are employed by another person who supplies them under a contract made with the principal. A 'contract worker' means any individual who is supplied to the principal under such a contract.[146]

A disabled person works for a computer software company which sometimes uses an employment business to deploy staff to work on projects for other companies. The employment business arranges for the disabled person to work on a project for a large supermarket chain. In this case the 'principal' is the supermarket chain.[147]

As with employment, section 4B DDA does not apply to benefits of any description if the principal is concerned with the provision (whether or not for payment) of benefits of that description to the public, or to a section of the public that includes the contract worker in question, unless that provision differs in a material respect from the provision of the benefits by the principal to contract workers.[148] This provision is therefore not concerned with those benefits which are not peculiarly incidental to the work relationship but are provided by the principal to the public generally (for example where a leisure centre allows members of the public to use its gym facilities and the disabled contract worker working there is discriminated against whilst using them[149]). The disabled person may have a claim under Part III of the DDA in such circumstances (see Chapter 7 below).

The effect of the contract worker provisions is that the contract worker is treated for all effective purposes as if he were employed by the principal. Accordingly the duty to make reasonable adjustments applies in the same way to the principal as it does to the contract worker's employer (who remains subject to the duty to make adjustments).[150] Where by reason of a provision,

---

[144] See 6.2 above.
[145] Section 4(2) DDA.
[146] Section 4B(9) DDA.
[147] Employment Code, paragraph 9.5.
[148] Section 4B(3) DDA.
[149] See also paragraph 8.12 of the Employment Code for an example in the context of employment.
[150] Section 4B(4)–(6) DDA. This is so except where the employer is required to make the adjustment concerned, section 4B(7) and Employment Code, paragraph 9.11. See Chapter 5 above, at 5.3.1.

criterion, or practice applied by or on behalf of all or most of the principals to whom a disabled contract worker is or might be supplied or by reason of a physical feature of premises occupied by such persons he or she is likely, on each occasion when he or she is supplied to a principal to do contract work, to be placed at a substantial disadvantage in comparison with persons who are not disabled which is the same or similar in each case, his *employer* is under a duty to make reasonable adjustments.[151]

A blind secretary is employed by an employment business which supplies her to other organizations for secretarial work. Her ability to access standard computer equipment places her at a substantial disadvantage at the offices of all or most of the principals to whom she might be supplied. The employment business provides her with a specially adapted portable computer and Braille keyboard.[152]

These arrangements also apply to the Workstep scheme[153] (formerly known as the Supported Placement Scheme) operated by Jobcentre Plus for severely disabled people. The 'contractor' under the scheme (usually a local authority or voluntary body) is the equivalent of the contract worker's own employer, and the 'host employer' is the equivalent of the principal. A local authority might even be the contractor and the host employer at the same time (as can a voluntary body).[154]

The prohibition of discrimination against contract workers applies if there is a contractual obligation to supply individuals to do what can properly be described as 'work for' the principal. There is no requirement that the supply of workers should be the dominant purpose of the contract between the principal and the employer. Thus staff employed by concessionaires at Harrods department store were 'contract workers' who worked 'for' Harrods for the purposes of section 7 RRA[155] in circumstances where Harrods' contractual arrangements required its concessionaires to ensure that the department was adequately staffed by suitably qualified employees. The work done by the staff members could properly be described as 'work for' Harrods, and the concessionaires were supplying employees under its contract with Harrods for the purposes of section 7 RRA.[156]

In addition, the contract worker provisions in the DDA do not require a direct contractual relationship between the employer and the principal. They apply equally where there is no direct contract between the person making the work available and the employer of the individual who is supplied to do that work. The statutory definition only requires that the supply of the individual be 'under a contract made with "A".' It does not expressly stipulate who is to be the party

---

[151] Section 4B(4) and (5) DDA.   [152] Employment Code, paragraph 9.10.
[153] For details see, http://www.jobcentreplus.gov.uk/cms.asp?Page=/Home/Customers/HelpForDisabledPeople.
[154] Employment Code, paragraph 9.13.
[155] Which is in materially the same terms as section 4B of the DDA.
[156] *Harrods Ltd v Remick* [1998] ICR 156, [1997] IRLR 583, CA.

who contracts with 'A'. Although in many cases the contract with the end-user will be made by the employer who supplies the individual, the definition does not require this. Accordingly, an applicant who was employed by a company that supplied him to an agency, which in turn supplied him to an end user, was a 'contract worker' who could present a claim against the end user as a 'principal'.[157]

The prohibition of discrimination against a contract worker appears not to be restricted to discrimination against a contract worker who is actually working. It prohibits discrimination in the selection by the principal from among workers supplied under an agency arrangement. Accordingly, a complaint could be brought under the SDA by a contract worker that she had been discriminated against by a principal by not permitting her to return to work after absence due to maternity.[158] By analogy it could be argued that a complaint could be brought by a disabled worker not permitted to return to work after a period of disability-related absence.

6.4. CROWN EMPLOYMENT AND OFFICE HOLDERS

The employment provisions of the DDA apply to service in a government department, for a Minister; to service for the Crown, and statutory bodies in the same way as they apply to employment by a private person.[159] The employment provisions also apply to staff at the House of Commons and the House of Lords.[160]

In addition, office holders are now protected by the DDA.[161] This change was necessary having regard to the comprehensive scope of the Directive.[162]

Sections 4C–4F DDA applies to an office holder or post holder.[163] Examples of office holders include some company directors, judges, and chairmen or members of non-departmental public bodies.[164] In each case the key characteristic is

---

[157] *Abbey Life Assurance Co Ltd v Tansell* [2000] ICR 789, [2000] IRLR 387, CA. See section 4B(9) DDA.

[158] *BP Chemicals Ltd v Gillick* [1995] IRLR 128, EAT, under section 9 SDA.

[159] Section 64 DDA.   [160] Section 65 DDA.

[161] Following their inclusion by the 2003 Regulations (now section 4D DDA). Prior to the amending Regulations any remedy for a discriminatory appointment to a statutory office lay only in judicial review: see section 66 DDA and CPR Pt 54. Staff employed in a statutory office holder's office have always been covered: section 64(2)(b) DDA.

[162] 2000/EC/78, Article 3. See by analogy for the impact of the Equal Treatment Directive 76/207/EEC: *Perceval-Price and others v Department of Economic Development and others* [2000] IRLR 380 (Court of Appeal in Northern Ireland ruled that Employment Tribunal chairmen are 'workers' who are in 'employment' within the meaning of European Community law, and are therefore entitled to bring equal pay and sex discrimination complaints, notwithstanding that they do not fall within the definition of 'employment' under domestic equal pay and sex discrimination legislation because they are holders of statutory office).

[163] Save where in relation to an appointment to the office or post one of the other 'employment' related provisions of the DDA applies: section 4C(1)(a).

[164] Employment Code, paragraph 9.14.

that they are not regarded as employees at common law or under the DDA[165] though the office or post must (for the purposes of the DDA) be:

- one which requires the office or post holder to discharge functions personally under the direction of another[166] in return for remuneration;[167] or

- one to which appointments are made by a Minister of the Crown, a Government department, the National Assembly for Wales, or any part of the Scottish Administration (or on the recommendation of, or subject to the approval of, such a person).

Holders of political office (including Members of Parliament) are not protected.[168]

Discrimination is outlawed against office and post holders in the same way as it is in relation to employees.[169] Section 4F(2) DDA describes the 'relevant' person for the purposes of determining against whom proceedings should be brought (see 5.3.2. above).

In relation to such an appointment to such an office or post, it is unlawful to discriminate against a disabled person:

- in the arrangements which are made to determine who should be offered the appointment;

- in the terms on which the appointment is offered; or

- by refusing to offer him the appointment.[170]

Where the appointment is made on the recommendation of a Minister of the Crown or Government department[171] (or is subject to their approval) it is unlawful to discriminate against a disabled person:

- in the arrangements which are made to determine who should be recommended or approved, or

- in making or refusing to make a recommendation, or in giving or refusing to give approval. The Employment Code gives the following example:

---

[165] And indeed given the exclusive nature of the protection of the office holder provisions, were such a person regarded as an employee then they would fall outside the office holder provision: section 4C(1)(a).

[166] A person is to be regarded as discharging his functions under the direction of another person if that other person is entitled to direct him as to when and where he discharges those functions: section 4C(4)(a) DDA.

[167] This means something more than mere expenses or compensation for the loss of income or benefits he would or might have received from any person had he not been carrying out the functions of the office or post: section 4C(4)(b) DDA.

[168] Section 4C(5) DDA.   [169] Section 3A DDA. As to reasonable adjustments, see below.

[170] Section 4D(1) DDA.

[171] Or the National Assembly for Wales or any part of the Scottish Administration: section 4D(2) DDA.

A deaf woman who communicates using British Sign Language applies for appointment as a member of a public body. Without interviewing her, the public body making the appointments writes to her saying that she would not be suitable as good communication skills are a requirement. This is likely to be unlawful.[172]

It is also unlawful, in relation to a disabled person who has been appointed to such an office or post, to discriminate against him:

• in the terms of the appointment;

• in the opportunities which are afforded (or refused) for promotion, transfer, training, or receiving any other benefit;

• by terminating the appointment; or

• by subjecting him to any other detriment in relation to the appointment.[173]

These expressions mirror some of those contained within the employment provisions[174] and where they do they will be interpreted in the same way.

As with employment, these provisions do not outlaw discrimination in the provision of benefits if the relevant person[175] is concerned with the provision (whether or not for payment) of benefits of that description to the public, or to a section of the public to which the disabled person belongs, unless that provision differs in a material respect from the provision of the benefits to persons appointed to offices or posts which are the same as, or not materially different from, that to which the disabled person has been appointed; or the provision of the benefits to the person appointed is regulated by the terms and conditions of his appointment or the benefits relate to training.[176]

In addition, it is unlawful to subject a disabled person to harassment if he is an office holder, or if he is seeking or being considered for an appointment (or a related Government recommendation or approval).

Section 4(E) DDA imposes a duty upon relevant persons[177] to make reasonable adjustments for disabled people holding relevant offices or posts, or seeking such appointments. The duty relates to any provision, criterion, or practice applied by or on behalf of the relevant person and to any physical feature of premises under the control of such a person where the functions of the office or post are performed. The effect of the duty is to provide a disabled person holding a relevant office or post, or seeking or being considered for appointment,

---

[172] Employment Code, paragraph 9.16.　　　　[173] Section 4D(3) DDA.

[174] See 6.2 above.

[175] Defined by section 4F(2) DDA. In summary: the person with power to make the appointment; the person or body with power to recommend or approve the appointment; the person with power to determine the terms or working conditions of the appointment (including any benefit or physical feature); or the person with power to terminate the appointment.

[176] Section 4D(5) DDA. See 6.2.7.2 above for comment. Such a complaint may be made under Part III DDA: see Chapter 7 below.

[177] Defined by section 4F(2) DDA: see Chapter 5 above, at 5.3.2.

rights similar to those of an employee or job applicant.[178] The disabled persons to whom the duty is owed are described in Chapter 5 above, at 5.3.2.

The extent of knowledge required to trigger the imposition of the duty upon a relevant person mirrors that applicable in the context of employment.[179]

The Employment Code gives the following example:

A selection process is carried out to appoint the chair of a public health body. The best candidate is found to be a disabled person with a progressive condition who is not able to work full-time because of her disability. Whoever makes or recommends the appointment should consider whether it would be a reasonable adjustment to appoint the disabled person on a job-share or part-time basis.[180]

6.5. PARTNERSHIPS

Section 6A DDA regulates discrimination in relation to 'partners'. This is a new addition and fills a gap in the DDA[181] not present in the SDA and RRA, both of which have always regulated discrimination against prospective and actual partners.[182]

It is unlawful for a firm, in relation to a position as a partner in the firm, to discriminate against a disabled person:

- in the arrangements it makes to determine who should be offered that position;
- in the terms on which it offers him that position;
- by refusing or deliberately omitting to offer him that position; or
- where the disabled person is already a partner in the firm:
  —in the way it affords him access to any benefits, or by refusing or deliberately omitting to afford him access to them; or
  —by expelling him from the partnership, or subjecting him to any other detriment.[183]

These expressions mirror some of those contained within the employment provisions,[184] and where they do they will be interpreted in the same way.

---

[178] Section 4E(2) DDA.

[179] Section 4E(3) DDA. See Chapter 5 above, at 5.3.2.

[180] Employment Code, paragraph 9.21.

[181] Salaried partners have always been able to bring proceedings under the employment provisions of the DDA.

[182] Section 11 SDA and section 10 RRA.

[183] Section 6A(1) DDA. The reference in this subsection to the expulsion from a partnership includes a reference to the termination of that person's partnership by the expiration of any period when it is not renewed on the same terms and to the termination of that person's partnership by any act of his (including the giving of notice) in circumstances such that he is entitled to terminate it without notice by reason of the conduct of the other partners (ie by reason of a fundamental breach of contract): section 6A(4) DDA.

[184] See 6.2 above.

In addition, it is unlawful to subject a disabled person to harassment if he is a partner in the firm or has applied for partnership.[185]

The effect of section 6A is to give a partner or applicant for partnership similar rights against the firm to those available to an employee or job applicant as against an employer.[186] The same applies where people are proposing to form themselves into a partnership and a disabled person is a prospective partner.[187] Limited liability partnerships are also covered.[188]

As with employment, discrimination in the provision of benefits is not outlawed if the partnership is concerned with the provision (whether or not for payment) of benefits of that description to the public, or to a section of the public that includes the partner in question, unless that provision differs in a material respect from the provision of the benefits to other partners.[189]

The duty to make reasonable adjustments applies in respect of any provision, criterion, or practice applied by or on behalf of the firm and to any physical feature of premises occupied by the firm.[190] The effect of the duty is to provide a disabled partner or prospective partner with similar rights to those of an employee or job applicant[191] (see Chapter 5 above, at 5.2.2[192]).

6.6. BARRISTERS AND ADVOCATES

Section 7A DDA regulates discrimination in relation to barristers (in England and Wales). Again, this is a new addition and fills a lacuna in the DDA[193] not found in the SDA and RRA, both of which have for some time regulated discrimination in relation to barristers and pupils.[194]

In England and Wales, it is unlawful for a barrister or a barrister's clerk, in relation to any offer of a pupillage or tenancy, to discriminate against a disabled person:

• in the arrangements which are made to determine to whom it should be offered;

• in respect of any terms on which it is offered; or

• by refusing or deliberately omitting to offer it to him.

It is also unlawful for a barrister or barrister's clerk, in relation to a disabled pupil or tenant in the set of chambers in question, to discriminate against him:

---

[185] Section 6A(2) DDA.
[186] Section 3A DDA. See also section 4 DDA.
[187] Section 6C(1) DDA.
[188] Section 6C(2) DDA.
[189] Section 6A(3) DDA. Such a complaint may be brought under Part III DDA. See 6.2.7.2 above for discussion.
[190] Section 6B DDA.
[191] Section 6B(3), DDA.
[192] Employment Code of Practice, paragraph 9.27.
[193] Identified, for example, in *Higham, 1 Pump Court Chambers v Horton*, *supra* note 9. (Note that by section 70(5A) DDA, this section does not extend to Scotland.)
[194] Sections 35A and 35B SDA and sections 26A and 26B RRA.

- in respect of any terms applicable to him as a pupil or tenant;
- in the opportunities for training, or gaining experience, which are afforded or denied to him;
- in the benefits which are afforded or denied to him;
- by terminating his pupillage or by subjecting him to any pressure to leave the chambers; or
- by subjecting him to any other detriment.

These expressions mirror some of those contained within the employment provisions[195] and where they do they will be interpreted in the same way.

The Employment Code gives the following example:

A solicitor telephones chambers to instruct a particular barrister, who is disabled, to appear in a particular Crown Court case. The clerk assumes that the court is not accessible and passes the brief to another barrister. This is likely to be unlawful.[196]

In addition, by section 7A(3) it is unlawful for a barrister or barrister's clerk to subject a disabled person who is a pupil or tenant in a set of chambers (or who has applied to be a pupil or tenant) to harassment. In effect discrimination against barristers and pupils is regulated in a similar way to discrimination against employees.[197]

It is also unlawful to discriminate against a disabled person or subject him or her to harassment in relation to the giving, withholding, or acceptance of instructions. Accordingly, it is unlawful for a solicitor to refuse to instruct a barrister or an advocate on the grounds of their disability and/or for a reason relating to it.[198]

As to the duty to make reasonable adjustments, this applies to barristers and barrister's clerks in the same way as it applies to an employer.[199] The duty applies to any provision, criterion, or practice applied by or on behalf of a barrister or barrister's clerk and to any physical feature of premises occupied by a barrister or by a barrister's clerk. A solicitor is not under a duty to make a reasonable adjustment in relation to a disabled barrister whom he instructs.[200]

Where a group of barristers practise together in a set of chambers, the duty to make reasonable adjustments applies to each and every individual barrister and the duty is a duty on each of them to take such steps as it is reasonable, in all of the circumstances of the case, for *him or her* to have to take (which may mean that management committee members or Heads of Chambers have a greater obligation).[201] The Employment Code gives the following example:

---

[195] See 6.2 above.   [196] Paragraph 9.33.   [197] Section 3A DDA. See also section 4 DDA.
[198] Sections 7A(4) and 3A DDA. However, no duty to make adjustments arises in these circumstances.
[199] See Chapter 5 above, at 5.2.2 and 5.3.4.
[200] Though see section 7A(4) DDA, referred to above.   [201] Section 7B(2) DDA.

The practice of writing messages on scrap paper is likely to disadvantage visually impaired members of chambers, and may need to be altered for individual disabled tenants and pupils.[202]

By section 7(5) DDA, barrister's clerk, pupil, etc have the meanings usually afforded those expressions.

These provisions apply to 'squatters' (barristers permitted to practice from a set of chambers though not members) just as they do to 'tenants'.[203]

'Advocates' in Scotland practise differently from barristers in England and Wales. They operate a 'library' rather than a 'chambers' system. This means that the provisions under the DDA have a somewhat narrower scope. However, the DDA does regulate discrimination (including reasonable adjustments) against disabled pupils and prospective pupils in much the same way as it does in respect of pupils and prospective pupils in England and Wales.[204] In addition, by section 7C(4) DDA, it is unlawful to discriminate against advocates in relation to the giving, withholding, or acceptance of instructions, though no duty to make adjustments arises.

6.7. PRACTICAL WORK EXPERIENCE

Section 14C of the DDA regulates discrimination in relation to practical work experience placements for the first time.

It is now unlawful for a placement provider to discriminate against a disabled person seeking or undertaking a work placement:

- in the arrangements which he makes for the purpose of determining who should be offered a work placement;
- in the terms on which he affords him access to any work placement or any facilities concerned with such a placement;
- by refusing or deliberately omitting to afford him such access;
- by terminating the placement; or
- by subjecting him to any other detriment in relation to the placement.

These expressions mirror some of those contained within the employment provisions,[205] and where they do they will be interpreted in the same way.

It is also unlawful to subject a disabled person to harassment where that disabled person is already undertaking work experience or has applied for a placement.[206]

---

[202] Paragraph 9.40.　　　　　　　　　　　　　[203] Section 7A(5) DDA.

[204] Section 7D DDA. This applies only in Scotland: section 70(5B) DDA. See Chapter 5 above, at 5.3.4.

[205] See 6.2 above.　　　　　　　　　　　　　　[206] Section 14C(2) DDA.

A 'work placement' means practical work experience undertaken for a limited period for the purposes of a person's vocational training and a 'placement provider' is any person who provides a work placement to a person whom he does not employ.[207]

It is always necessary to distinguish whether a work placement is in fact 'employment' for the purposes of section 4 DDA[208] because where it is, it will fall outside the work placement provisions.[209]

A duty to make reasonable adjustments in relation to a disabled person undergoing practical work experience is imposed upon a placement provider in the same circumstances and in the same way as it applies to an employer. As such, the duty applies in respect of any provision, criterion, or practice applied by or on behalf of the placement provider and to any physical feature of premises occupied by the provider and the requirement of knowledge to trigger the duty applies equally.[210] The Employment Code gives the following example, amongst others:

A disabled person who has a heart condition obtains a six-week placement at a computer company. Such placements are normally offered only on a full-time basis. However, because this would be too tiring for the disabled person, the placement provider allows him to work mornings only.[211]

In determining what adjustments it is reasonable to require a placement provider to make, regard can be had to the observations made in Chapter 5 above, at 5.2.2, which apply equally to work experience placements. However, as the Employment Code points out,[212] the length of the placement will be a relevant factor: 'Although many adjustments cost little or nothing to make, it is unlikely to be reasonable for a placement provider to spend significant sums on individually-tailored adjustments in respect of short placements'.[213]

Some disabled students undertaking work placements may be able to fund adjustments out of their Disabled Student's Allowance.[214] In addition, some disabled people may have their own equipment which they wish to use in the workplace. In that case, the placement provider may have to make reasonable adjustments in order to facilitate the use of that equipment (for example, by ensuring that it is transported and stored safely, and is adequately insured whilst at the workplace).[215]

An organization that sends a disabled person on a work placement may also have a duty to make reasonable adjustments in respect of that person. The Employment Code gives the following example:

---

[207] Section 14C(4) DDA.   [208] See at 6.2.1 above.

[209] Section 14C(3), as will anything which properly falls within Part III (as constituting a service made available to members of the public, for example) *ibid.*

[210] Section 14D DDA; see also Chapter 5, at 5.2.2 and 5.3.5.

[211] Paragraph 9.47.   [212] Paragraph 9.48.

[213] *Ibid.* See also Chapter 5 above, at 5.3.5.

[214] For details see: http://www.direct.gov.uk/Audiences/DisabledPeopleAndCarers/fs/en.

[215] Employment Code, paragraph 9.48.

Where a course provider[216] supplies a laptop computer for a visually impaired person to complete work, it would also be reasonable for it to supply the computer for that person to use during a related work placement.[217]

6.8. OCCUPATIONAL PENSION SCHEMES

The Disability Discrimination Act 1995 (Pensions) Regulations 2003[218] ('the Pensions Regulations') make specific provision (by amendment to the DDA) relating to occupational schemes. However, it is important to note that the prohibition in relation to discrimination in the terms of employment and the provision of benefits in the employment and related fields[219] makes no distinction between 'pay' (including pension) related terms and benefits and others.[220] Accordingly, an employer must not discriminate against a disabled person in relation to pension benefits and the duty to make reasonable adjustments applies to the manner in which employers make pensions available to a disabled employee.

In addition, the Pensions Regulations provide further regulation in relation to pension provision. They give effect to the requirements of the Directive which covers 'pay'.[221] 'Pay' has long been recognized in Community law as wide enough a concept to embrace occupational pensions and similar benefits.[222] The Pension Regulations create a number of unlawful acts in relation to the provision of pension benefits.[223] In short summary, the 2003 Regulations:

- insert a new non-discrimination rule into every occupational pension scheme, requiring trustees or managers to refrain from discriminating against a relevant disabled person in carrying out their functions in relation to the scheme or harassing such person in relation to the scheme. This includes functions relating to the admission and treatment of members of the scheme;[224]

- makes any act of discrimination or harassment by a trustee or manager contrary to the non-discrimination rule unlawful;[225]

- imposes a duty to make reasonable adjustments on trustees or managers of schemes in relation to provisions, criteria, or practices (including scheme rules) applied by them and physical features of premises occupied by them, where these place a relevant disabled person at a substantial disadvantage in comparison with persons who are not disabled;[226]

---

[216] On whom a duty to make reasonable adjustments would lie; see Chapter 5 above, at 5.9 and 5.7.
[217] Employment Code, paragraph 9.49.   [218] SI 2003/2770.   [219] See 6.2 above.
[220] *Ibid.*   [221] 2000/78/EC Article 3(c).
[222] Case 80/70, *Defrenne* [1971] ECR 445, paragraphs 7 and 8; Case C-109/91, *Ten Oever v Stichting Bedrijfspensioenfonds Voor Het Glazenwassers*-En Schoonmaakbedrijf (Case No: C-109/91) [1993] ECR I-4879; [1995] ICR 74; [1993] IRLR 601, *Pirkko Niemi* [2002] ECR I-07007, paragraph 41.
[223] By amendment to the DDA, see sections 4G–4K DDA.
[224] Section 4G(1) DDA.   [225] Section G(3) DDA.   [226] Section 4H DDA.

- ensures that where a relevant disabled person complains to an Employment Tribunal that trustees or managers of a scheme have acted in a way that is unlawful, the employer in relation to the scheme is to be treated as a party to the complaints;[227]
- makes provision in relation to remedies for a person discriminated against in the context of an occupational pension scheme;[228]
- identifies the classes of persons who are protected by various provisions of the Pensions Regulations.[229] A relevant disabled person in relation to an occupational pension scheme means a disabled person who is a member or prospective member of the scheme. However, certain protection extends to a disabled person who is entitled to present payment of dependants' or survivors' benefits under an occupational pension scheme or is a pension credit member of such a scheme.[230]

All other rules of the pension scheme take effect subject to the non-discrimination rule.[231] In addition, pension scheme trustees and managers have power to make alterations to the scheme in order to secure conformity with the non-discrimination rule.[232]

The duty to make reasonable adjustments applies to pension scheme trustees and managers in the same way as it applies to an employer. The duty is owed to disabled people who are members or prospective members of the scheme, and relates to any provision, criterion, or practice (including a scheme rule) applied by or on behalf of the trustees or managers and any physical feature of premises which they occupy.[233] Section 4H(2) DDA gives as an example of a reasonable adjustment the making of an alteration to the rules of the pension scheme.[234] The Employment Code gives the following example:

The rules of an employer's final salary scheme provide that the maximum pension receivable by a member is equivalent to 2/3 of salary in the last year of work. An employee becomes disabled and as a result has to reduce her working hours for the remainder of her working life, which will amount to two years. She has worked for twenty years full time prior to this. The scheme's rules put the disabled person at a substantial disadvantage because, regardless of her previous twenty years' service, her pension will only be calculated on her part-time salary as a result of her disability. The trustees decide in her case to average out her salary over a period of years prior to her retirement date, which will enable her full-time earnings to be taken into account. This is likely to be a reasonable adjustment to make.[235]

---

227 Section 4I(1) DDA.　　　228 Section 4J DDA.
229 Section 4K(1) and (2) DDA, as inserted by the Pensions Regulations.
230 Section 4K(1) DDA, as inserted by the Pensions Regulations.
231 Section 4G(2) DDA.　　　232 Section 4G(5) DDA.　　　233 Section 4H(1) DDA.
234 In addition to those examples given in section 18B(2) DDA, see 5.2.2.5.
235 Paragraph 10.8.

The non-discrimination rule does not apply in relation to rights accrued and benefits payable in respect of periods of service prior to 1 October 2004.[236] However, the rule does apply to communications about such rights or benefits with members or prospective members of the scheme.[237] So far as communications generally are concerned, both the non-discrimination rule and the duty to make reasonable adjustments apply in relation to disabled people who are entitled to, and presently receiving, dependants' or survivors' benefits under a pension scheme and credit members of the scheme, as they do in relation to disabled pensioner members of the scheme.[238] Communications include the provision of information and the operation of a dispute resolution procedure. Reasonable adjustments in respect of the same could include providing information in accessible formats (such as large print, Braille, tape, or disc) or providing a sign language interpreter for a meeting.[239] The Employment Code gives the following example:

A blind woman whose partner dies and who is in receipt of a survivor's pension asks for and receives information about the pension scheme on tape. The information relates to the period before October 2004 but nevertheless this is likely to be a reasonable adjustment to make.[240]

6.9. GROUP INSURANCE SERVICES

Section 18 of the DDA makes specific provision in relation to group insurers. As observed above in relation to occupational pension schemes, it is important to note that in the prohibition in relation to discrimination in the terms of employment and the provision of benefits in the employment and related fields[241] no distinction is made between insurance-related benefits and other benefits. Accordingly, an employer must not discriminate against a disabled person in relation to any insurance-related benefits and the duty to make reasonable adjustments applies to the manner in which employers make them available to a disabled employee.

However, some group insurance arrangements limit the employer's role to explaining the availability of the service and to proposing employees to the insurer for cover under such a policy.[242] By section 18 DDA, where an insurer agrees with the employer to provide insurance services to its employees, or to give its employees an opportunity to receive such services, it is unlawful for the insurer to discriminate against a disabled person:

- who is an employee of the employer in respect of whom the arrangements applies; or

- who has applied for, or is contemplating applying for, such employment.[243]

---

[236] Section 4(G)(4) DDA. [237] *Ibid.* [238] Section 4K(1) DDA.
[239] Employment Code, paragraph 10.10. [240] *Ibid.* paragraph 10.10.
[241] See 6.2 above. [242] Employment Code, paragraph 10.16.
[243] Section 18(3) and (4) DDA.

The insurance services to which section 18 applies are those in respect of:

- termination of service;
- retirement, old age, or death; and
- accident, injury, sickness, or invalidity.[244]

'Discrimination' is defined, for these purposes, in accordance with Part III DDA (goods, facilities, and services).[245] Thus in determining whether or not an insurance provider has discriminated against an employee within the meaning of section 18, the proper test is that provided for under section 20 DDA. This is addressed in Chapter 5 above, at 5.7.[246] However, where a disabled person considers that he has been discriminated against in relation to a group insurance service, any complaint must be brought before an Employment Tribunal. This is so whether the complaint relates to treatment by the employer or by the group insurer.[247]

6.10. EMPLOYMENT SERVICES

By section 21A DDA, discrimination in relation to employment services is regulated. This provision falls within Part III of the DDA. However, it incorporates certain concepts of discrimination that derive from Part II (direct discrimination[248] and harassment[249]) and the Employment Code addresses such discrimination. In addition claims of disability discrimination in respect of employment services are brought in the Employment Tribunal.[250] Given its obvious nexus to discrimination falling within the employment sphere it is dealt with in this chapter.

Section 21A was inserted by the 2003 Regulations[251] to give effect to the Directive.[252] Section 21A DDA now provides that it is unlawful for a provider of employment services[253] to discriminate against a disabled person:

- by refusing to provide (or deliberately not providing) to the disabled person any such services as it provides (or is prepared to provide) to members of the pubic;
- in the standard of service which it provides to the disabled person or the manner in which it provides the service;
- by failing to comply with a duty to make adjustments imposed on him;
- in the terms on which it provides the service to the disabled person.[254]

---

[244] Section 18(3) DDA, where the important conditions in the Disability Discrimination (Description of Insurance Services) Regulations 1999, SI 1999/2114, are met.

[245] See section 18(2) DDA and sections 19 and 20 DDA.　　[246] Section 18(2) DDA.

[247] Section 17A DDA. See also Chapter 13 below, at 13.9 for proposed changes.

[248] See Chapter 5 above, at 5.2.1 and 5.5.

[249] See Chapter 5 above, at 5.2.4 and 5.5.　　[250] Section 25(8) DDA.

[251] SI 2003/1673.　　[252] 2000/78/EC, Article 3. See Chapter 3 above.

[253] See below, section 21A(1) DDA.　　[254] Section 21A(4) read with section 19 DDA.

'Employment services' for the purposes of section 21A DDA comprise:

- vocational guidance;
- vocational training; and
- services to assist a person to obtain or retain employment, or to establish himself as self-employed.[255]

A number of acts will therefore constitute unlawful acts within the meaning of section 21A. The Employment Code gives the following examples:[256]

An employment agency refuses to allow a disabled person with a mobility impairment to register with the agency as it says that it does not have any posts which would be 'suitable' and on the ground floor. This is likely to be unlawful.

A disabled person with a speech impairment requests job advice from his local careers guidance service; he is asked to return next week when there is more time available to meet his needs, although other people, who do not have speech impairments, are being seen there and then. This is likely to be unlawful.

In addition, it is important to observe that the duty to make reasonable adjustments under Part III DDA[257] is anticipatory in nature. It is not a duty owed simply to individual disabled people but is owed to disabled people at large. Providers of employment services therefore (unlike other relevant persons operating within the employment field) are required to consider the need for reasonable adjustments in advance of any adverse impact upon a disabled person. This is discussed in Chapter 5 above, at 5.7.1 and 5.5.

6.11. TRADE ORGANIZATIONS

Section 13 of the DDA addresses discrimination by trade organizations. The unamended DDA addressed discrimination by trade organizations.[258] But amendments were introduced by the 2003 Regulations extending the scope of the unlawful acts created and the concept of discrimination, so as to give effect to the Directive.[259] Importantly too, the DRC has issued a 'Code of Practice, Trade Organisations and Qualifications Bodies' ('Trade and Qualifications Code') pursuant to its powers under section 53A DDA. This came into force on 1 October 2004.[260] As with the Employment Code, a breach of any provision of the Code does not of itself make a person liable to any proceedings or otherwise constitute an unlawful act. However, it contains extremely useful guidance and a court or

---

[255] Section 21A(1) DDA. [256] Paragraph 11.5.
[257] Which is discussed in Chapter 5 above, at 5.7.1.
[258] Sections 13–15 DDA. [259] 2000/78/EC. See Chapter 3 above.
[260] (2004) DRC, ISBN 0 11 703418 5; Disability Discrimination Codes of Practice (Employment and Occupation, and Trade Organisations and Qualifications Bodies) Appointed Day Order 2004, SI 2004/2302.

tribunal must take any relevant provision into account in determining any claim of disability discrimination.[261]

Sections 13 and 14 DDA now address discrimination by trade organizations. Section 13 DDA provides that:

(1) It is unlawful for a trade organisation to discriminate against a disabled person—in the arrangements which it makes for the purpose of determining who should be offered membership of the organisation;

    (a) in the terms on which it is prepared to admit him to membership of the organisation; or

    (c) by refusing to accept, or deliberately not accepting, his application for membership.

(2) It is unlawful for a trade organisation, in the case of a disabled person who is a member of the organisation, to discriminate against him—

    (a) in the way it affords him access to any benefits by refusing or deliberately omitting to afford him access to them;

    (c) by depriving him of membership, or varying the terms on which he is a member; or

    (d) by subjecting him to any other detriment.

It is also unlawful for a trade organization, in relation to membership of that organization, to subject to harassment a disabled member of the organization or a disabled person who has applied for membership.[262]

In addition, trade organizations are subject to a duty to make reasonable adjustments in certain circumstances.[263]

The unlawful acts are therefore very wide and will cover most acts of detrimental treatment by a trade organization to its existing or aspirant members.[264]

6.11.1. Meaning of 'Trade Organization'

'Trade organization' is defined by section 13(4) DDA, as follows:

'trade organisation' means
(a) an organisation of workers;
(c) an organisation of employers; or
(d) any other organisation whose members carry on a particular profession or trade for the purposes of which the organisation exists.

Thus trade unions and employers' organizations as well as organizations that have regulatory functions like the Bar Council and the Law Society will fall within the scope of section 13.

An organization does not have to have a membership comprised exclusively of employers or workers in order to fall within section 13 DDA. Thus in *National*

---

[261] Section 53A(8) and (8A) DDA.   [262] Section 13(3) DDA. See 5.4.
[263] See section 14 DDA, and Chapter 5 above, at 5.4.1.
[264] Examples are given in the Trade and Qualifications Code at paragraphs 7.5 *et seq.*

Federation of Self-employed and Small Businesses Ltd v Philpott[265] the Employment Appeal Tribunal concluded that the federation whose membership included individual self-employed people who had no employees as well as employers was nonetheless a 'trade organization' for the purposes of section 12 SDA.[266]

The Trade and Qualifications Code gives the following examples of organizations that are likely to be trade organizations for the purposes of section 13. These are:

• trade unions
• employers' associations
• chartered professional institutions
• the Law Society
• the Royal College of Nursing
• the Swimming Teachers' Association
• the Society of Floristry
• the British Computer Society and
• the Institute of Carpenters.[267]

As the Code observes, section 13 applies however many members the organization may have.

It should also be borne in mind that some trade organizations are also qualification bodies. These will include the Bar Council and the Law Society who have regulatory functions and confer 'qualifications' (within the broad meaning provided for in section 14A(5) DDA, see 6.12.2 below). This means that in determining whether a complaint falls within section 13 or 14A DDA, regard must be had to the particular function about which complaint is made. This may be particularly important where one is considering the application of a 'competence standard' which is of no relevance to the complaints under section 13 (trade organizations) but, as has been seen, may be very relevant to a claim under section 14A DDA.[268] Therefore, where an organization is carrying out functions that relate to its responsibilities as a qualifications body, complaint will have to be made under section 14A DDA. Where complaint is made about those functions which relate to its membership, the complaint will fall under section 13 DDA.

---

[265] [1997] ICR 518, [1997] IRLR 341.
[266] Which applies to trade organizations defined in the same way as in section 13 DDA.
[267] Paragraph 13.8.   [268] See Chapter 5 above, at 5.4.2.

6.12. QUALIFICATIONS BODIES

The 2003 Regulations have amended the DDA to provide protection against discrimination by qualifications bodies.[269] This brings the DDA into line with the SDA[270] and the RRA[271] and gives proper effect to the Directive.[272]

Section 14A makes it unlawful for a qualifications body to discriminate. It provides that:

(1) It is unlawful for a qualifications body to discriminate against a disabled person—

(a) in the arrangements which it makes for the purpose of determining upon whom to confer a professional or trade qualification;

(c) in the terms on which it is prepared to confer a professional or trade qualification on him;

(d) by refusing or deliberately omitting to grant any application by him for such a qualification; or

(e) by withdrawing such a qualification from him or varying the terms on which he holds it.

It is also unlawful for a qualifications body, in relation to a professional or trade qualification conferred by it, to subject a disabled person to harassment where that disabled person holds or applies for such a qualification.[273]

In addition, qualifications bodies are subject to a duty to make reasonable adjustments in certain circumstances.[274]

6.12.1. Meaning of Qualifications Bodies

Section 14A(5) defines 'qualifications body' for the purposes of section 14A and 14B DDA. A 'qualifications body':

- means any authority or body which can confer a professional or trade qualification;

- it does not include (a) a responsible body (within the meaning of Part 4 DDA[275]) (b) a local education authority in England and Wales or (c) an education authority (within the meaning of section 135(1) of the Education (Scotland) Act 1980).

Thus the qualifications bodies provisions are quite discrete from those addressing discrimination in the education field and care must be taken to ensure that any complaint is brought under the correct provisions because the enforcement

---

[269] Section 14A DDA. [270] Section 13 SDA. [271] Section 12 RDA.

[272] 2000/78/EC, Article 3. See Chapter 3 above.

[273] Section 14A(2) DDA. See Chapter 5 above, at 5.2.4, for the meaning of harassment.

[274] See Chapter 5, at 5.4.2 above.

[275] The education provisions. See Chapter 8 below.

mechanisms provided for under the DDA in respect of each set of provisions are quite distinct.[276]

'Confer', for these purposes, includes 'renew' or 'extend'.[277] Accordingly a body that has a facility to renew or extend a professional or trade qualification is equally covered.

As the Trade and Qualifications Code observes, certain professions and trades have arrangements with educational institutions or other bodies whereby such bodies devise, run, and examine their own courses for entry into certain professions or trades, whilst approval for entry into the particular profession or trade is controlled by an external body. In such circumstances those external bodies are likely to be qualifications bodies if they perform any of the following functions:

- maintaining a register of people who are qualified to practise in the profession or trade;

- conducting additional tests for people who have qualified, or who wish to qualify, into the profession or trade, such as basic skills tests or medical checks; or

- giving approval for a person's qualification to his course provider.[278]

Whilst in such circumstances, the educational institution is likely to be caught by the education provisions of the DDA (Part 4, Chapter 8) but not the qualifications bodies provisions.

There have been a number of cases under the comparable provisions in section 13 SDA and section 12 RRA which define qualifying bodies in materially the same way as the DDA defines qualifications bodies.[279] A fairly narrow reach has been given to those provisions. Thus in *Tattari v Private Patients Plan Ltd*[280] the Court of Appeal determined that a commercial provider of medical and health insurance, which stipulated in its commercial agreements that particular qualifications were necessary in order for doctors to be included on its list of specialist practitioners, was not a 'qualifying body' for the purposes of section 12 RRA. The Court of Appeal held that the insurance company did not confer any authorization or qualification itself, but merely stated what qualifications were required in order to include practitioners on its list. Further, in *Arthur v Attorney-General*,[281] the Attorney-General was held not to be a qualifying body for the purposes of section 12 RRA when carrying out functions relating to the appointment of magistrates. According to the Employment Appeal Tribunal, section 12 RRA 'is directed to circumstances in which A confers on B a qualification which will enable B to render services for C. Where A and C are the same

---

[276] See Chapter 11 below.
[277] Section 14A(5) DDA.
[278] Trade and Qualifications Code, paragraph 8.8.
[279] Sections 13(1) SDA and 12(1) RRA.
[280] [1998] ICR 106, [1997] IRLR 586.
[281] [1999] ICR 631 at 637.

entity, the section would appear to be inapplicable, otherwise it would apply to every selection panel.'

In *Triesman v Ali*[282] the Court of Appeal concluded that section 12 RRA did not extend to the Labour Party's selection procedures in respect of candidates for political office. Thus in failing to select and reselect the applicants as candidates for election as local councillors, the Labour Party were not acting as a qualifying body within the meaning of section 12 RRA. According to the Court of Appeal, the proper application of section 12 RRA was in relation to 'the employment field . . . in a wide or loose sense. The obvious application of the section is to cases where a body has among its functions that of granting some qualification to, or authorising, a person who has satisfied appropriate standards of competence, to practise a profession, calling or trade.'[283]

On the other hand, in *Patterson v Legal Services Commission*[284] the Court of Appeal concluded that the franchising arrangements imposed by the Legal Services Commission upon solicitors seeking contracts with the Legal Services Commission to provide legal services fell within the scope of section 12 RRA. In *Patterson* the Court of Appeal accepted that in granting a franchise and, in effect, the right to do publicly funded work on behalf of her clients, the Commission conferred an authorization on Ms Patterson, which facilitated her engagement in the solicitor's profession, within the meaning of section 12 RRA.[285] The Court of Appeal noted that the Commission was quite a different body from either the PPP (in *Tattari*) or the Labour Party and was charged with specific public functions under its establishing Act.[286] The Court of Appeal noted:

When it grants a franchise to a solicitor on the ground that LAFQAS has been satisfied and thus enables the franchisee to display the logo, it seems to us to grant an authorisation to do so. Further, since the grant of the franchise is an essential pre-condition to the making of a three year contract it can in our opinion again fairly be said to be conferring on the franchisee an authorisation to perform publicly funded legal services for its clients.[287]

In addition, such a franchise is sufficiently personal to constitute conferral upon Ms Patterson, as the applicant, of such authorization.[288]

6.12.2. Meaning of 'Professional or Trade Qualification'

'Professional or trade qualification' is defined in section 14A(5), as follows:

---

[282] [2002] EWCA Civ 93, [2002] ICR 1026, [2002] IRLR 489.

[283] *Ibid.* paragraph 28. In so holding they overruled the earlier case of *Sawyer v Ahsan* [2000] ICR 1, [1999] IRLR 609.

[284] *Supra* note 34.   [285] *Ibid.* paragraphs 62 and 63. See 6.12.2 below.

[286] Access to Justice Act 1999, see paragraph 71.   [287] *Supra* note 34, paragraph 72.

[288] *Ibid.* paragraph 79.

'Professional or trade qualification' means an authorisation, qualification, recognition, registration, enrolment, approval or certification which is needed for, or facilitates the engagement in, a particular profession or trade.[289]

This is a wide meaning but, as the case-law demonstrates, it has limits. It has been suggested by the courts that similar words of definition:

convey with reasonable clarity the idea of (a) some sort of status conferred on an employee or self-employed person in relation to his work, or the work which he proposes to do; and as respects the self-employed person, in relation to his trade, profession or calling or what he proposes to be his trade, profession or calling; (b) a status which relates only to a person carrying on that work or trade, profession or calling; and (c) is either necessary for the lawful carrying on thereof or making that carrying on more advantageous.[290]

Whilst Lord Slynn has remarked[291] that this emphasis on 'status' 'may be subject to further argument', the word 'status' may give some indication of the essence of a 'qualification'.[292] Some caution must be expressed about the emphasis on status because as has been observed, 'the reference . . . to the conferring of some sort of status may be dangerous as distracting one from the statutory requirement. Professional qualification within the section may give status, but the fact that status may follow upon an appointment does not necessarily mean that the appointment is one to which the section relates'.[293]

There has been some judicial indication that 'professions' and 'trades' for the purposes of the qualifications caught by section 12 RRA (and accordingly perhaps section 14A DDA) involve some engagement in remunerated occupation.[294] Thus in *Triesman*[295] the Court of Appeal observed that:

We own to having doubts as to whether being a local government councillor is being engaged in a profession or occupation within the meaning of the section, still more so if the profession or occupation is limited to being a Labour Party councillor. To our minds it is certainly not being engaged in a profession and, while being a councillor occupies some of the time of the councillor who is entitled to receive allowances, it is not an activity from which the councillors will earn his living or receive a salary, and we question whether it is within the intendment of the section.[296]

---

[289] See also section 68(1) DDA which defines 'profession' as including any 'vocation or occupation', and 'trade' as including any business.

[290] *Department of the Environment for Northern Ireland v Bone* [1993] 8NIJB 41 at 46 (regarding section 23, Fair Employment (Northern Ireland) Act 1976).

[291] In *Kelly v Northern Ireland Housing Executive* [1998] ICR 828; [1998] IRLR 593 at paragraph 34.

[292] *Ibid.*

[293] *Ibid.* paragraph 73, *per* Lord Clyde.

[294] *Triesman, supra* note 282, paragraph 33.

[295] *Ibid.*

[296] Paragraph 33, *per* Lord Justice Peter Gibson.

However, nothing in section 14A[297] requires the profession or trade concerned to be one which attracts remuneration. Indeed, in *British Judo Association v Petty*[298] the Employment Appeal Tribunal concluded that the granting or withholding of a certificate conferring status as a qualified referee by the British Judo Association fell within the scope of section 13 SDA,[299] notwithstanding that referees were not remunerated. This was because the National Referee Certificate facilitated the engagement by Miss Petty in her occupation as a paid instructor in judo. It was not necessary that the purpose of the certifying body in issuing the certificate was to facilitate the certificate holder's engagement in a particular profession or trade; if that were its effect then it was capable of falling within section 13 SDA.

The words 'is needed for' and 'facilitates' are disjunctive and therefore if the particular authorization 'facilitates engagement in' a particular profession or trade then that is sufficient.[300] Thus where the authorization or qualification is essential to engagement in the trade or profession in question then it is plainly covered but similarly, where it merely facilitates entry into or engagement in a particular trade or profession, irrespective of whether the qualifying body intended that it be so, it will also be covered.[301] Thus the Trade and Qualifications Code advises that the expressions 'professional or trade qualification' include qualifications etcetera which are conferred solely in anticipation of furthering a particular career but that they are 'also capable of including more general qualifications if attaining them facilitates engagement in a particular profession or trade'.[302] The Code advises that:

In order to decide whether a particular qualification is a professional or trade qualification for the purposes of the Act, it is necessary to address the following three questions:
• What is the profession or trade?
• What is the qualification?
• Does possession of that particular qualification make it easier to work in that particular profession or trade (rather than merely assisting general advancement in that or any other career)?[303]

The third point does not easily distinguish between merely assisting general advancement in a career and the making 'it easier to work' in that particular profession or trade and so regard must always be had to the case-law described above. The Code does make it clear, as is clear from the case-law, that 'qualification' should not be narrowly interpreted so as to include only the passing of formal examinations or tests. As the Code advises, simply being a member of an

---

[297] Or for that matter, Sections 13 SDA and 12 RRA.
[298] [1981] ICR 660, [1981] IRLR 484.   [299] The equivalent of section 14A DDA.
[300] *Patterson, supra* note 34, at paragraph 75.
[301] *Patterson, supra* note 34, and Petty *supra* note 298.
[302] Paragraph 8.5. This reflects the case-law including *Patterson, supra* note 34, and *Petty, supra* note 298.
[303] Trade and Qualifications Code, paragraph 8.5.

organization or body may amount to such a qualification if membership itself facilitates engagement in a particular profession or trade.[304] The Code gives the following examples of qualifications which would or could count as professional or trade qualifications for the purposes of section 14A:

- registration with the Nursing and Midwifery Council;
- certificate to practise as a solicitor issued by the Law Society;
- registration with the Council for Registered Gas Installers (CORGI);
- NVQs;
- BTECs;
- City and Guilds;
- Scottish Vocational Qualifications;
- HGV driving licences;
- membership, registration, or fellowship of trade or professional bodies (eg Fellow of the Institute of Linguists).[305]

6.12.3. Statutory Appeals

Where an appeal, or proceedings in the nature of an appeal, may be brought under 'any enactment' in respect of an act falling within the scope of section 14A(1) (discrimination by qualifications bodies) proceedings may not be brought in the Employment Tribunal.[306] 'Enactment' for these purposes includes an enactment comprised in, or in an instrument made under, an Act of the Scottish Parliament.[307]

Many professions are now regulated by statutory schemes. Some have statutory arrangements (either in primary or secondary legislation) addressing entry and practice in the professions with the provision of appeals against decisions affecting access to or continuation in a particular profession. This is particularly so in relation to the medical profession where a number of claims of discrimination have failed because appeals lie in respect of relevant decisions pursuant to statutory arrangements.[308] This exemption appears to apply even where the appeal process is limited and does not extend to reversing the original decision and where the appeal process itself is allegedly tainted by discrimination.[309]

However, it is possible to argue that unless

---

[304] See for example, *Zaidi v Financial Intermediaries' Managers' and Brokers' Regulatory Association (FIMBRA)* [1995] ICR 876.

[305] Trade and Qualifications Code, paragraph 8.7.   [306] Section 17A(1A).

[307] Section 17A(1B) DDA.

[308] Eg *Khan v General Medical Council* [1996] ICR 1032, [1993] IRLR 646.

[309] *Ibid.* under the analogous provisions in the RRA, section 54(2).

- the appeal process constitutes a proper investigation of the merits of any decision against the threshold of the DDA with the facility to overturn any discriminatory decision, and
- there is the possibility of addressing discrimination in the appeal process

then it does not provide an effective remedy. In those circumstances it may be possible to argue that such a process should not be regarded as an 'appeal' for the purpose of ousting the jurisdiction of the Employment Tribunal because otherwise such would not comply with the obligation under Article 9 of the Directive[310] to provide for the effective enforcement of obligations[311] created by the Directive.[312]

In addition, it might be possible to argue in an appropriate case that a statutory appeal which does not provide for a merits-based review of any alleged discriminatory decision with power to overturn it does not give proper effect to the obligations under Article 6, Schedule 1 HRA, which provides that 'in the determination of his civil rights and obligations . . . everyone is entitled to a fair and public hearing within a reasonable time by an independent and impartial tribunal established by law'[313] and in such circumstances the Employment Tribunal, which can effect an Article 6-compliant hearing, should not be treated as having its jurisdiction ousted by section 17A(1A). However, as far as the author is aware, no such argument has yet been pursued.[314]

It is important to remember that the exclusion of the Employment Tribunal's jurisdiction extends only to arrangements made under an 'enactment'. This covers subordinate legislation but not, for example, articles of association or other sets of non-statutory rules.[315]

---

[310] 2000/78/EC. See Chapter 3 above

[311] See arguments in *Khan, supra* note 308 at ICR 1039, IRLR paragraph 15, which were unsuccessful but predated a relevant Directive: the 'Race Directive' (2000/43/EC) was not enacted until 2000. The HRA is also relevant.

[312] See, by analogy, Article 6, in the unamended text of the Equal Treatment Directive 76/207/EC and in the amended Article 6 (amended pursuant to Council Directive 2002/73/EC, Article 1(5)). See also arguments in *Khan, supra* note 308 at 1039, paragraph 15.

[313] For a review of the impact of the HRA, see Chapter 3 above.

[314] In *R v Department of Health ex parte Gandhi* [1991] ICR 805; [1991] IRLR 431 the Divisional Court ruled that the Health Secretary, in exercising an appellate function in respect of the Medical Practices Committee of the NHS, was bound to consider the allegations of race discrimination upon which the appeal rested. However, even in that case, the obligations imposed by the Divisional Court as to the requirements of natural justice were not onerous. Thus the Secretary of State was not required to give reasons in respect of the dismissal of complaints of race discrimination made in the course of the appeal and nor was an oral hearing necessarily required. This case of course preceded the HRA. See now eg *Tehrani v UKCC* [2001] IRLR 208; *Preiss v General Dental Council* [2001] 1 WLR 1926, [2001] IRLR 696.

[315] *Zaidi Financial Intermediaries' Managers' and Brokers' Regulatory Association (FIMBRA)*, *supra* note 304.

In addition, a complainant may still have access to judicial review that is not excluded by the DDA.[316]

6.13. CONTRACTS, COLLECTIVE AGREEMENTS, AND RULES OF UNDERTAKING

Schedule 3A Parts 1 and 2 DDA[317] make provision for contracts, collective agreements, and rules of undertakings which contain discriminatory terms.

Any term in a contract is void where:

- the making of the contract is unlawful under Part II by reason of the inclusion of the term;
- the term is included in furtherance of an act which is itself unlawful under Part II; or
- the term provides for the doing of an act which is unlawful under Part II.

Where the inclusion of the term constitutes, provides for, or is in furtherance of unlawful discrimination or harassment of a party to the contract, it shall not be void but is unenforceable against that party. This means that that party can rely upon such terms himself including to support a complaint of disability discrimination.

Further, a term in a contract which purports to exclude or limit any provision of Part II or the jurisdiction of the Employment Tribunal is unenforceable by any person in whose favour the terms would operate. A limited exemption applies in relation to 'compromise agreements'. In short summary these are agreements made in settlement of a complaint or potential complaint under the DDA which comply with certain required formalities.[318] They are discussed further in Chapter 11 below.

In addition, collective agreements, employers' rules, and rules made by trade organizations and qualifications bodies are void where:

- the making of the collective agreement is, by reason of the inclusion of a term, unlawful;
- a term or rule is included in furtherance of an act which is unlawful under Part II;
- a term or rule provides for the doing of an act which is unlawful under Part II.

This ensures that discriminatory rules are not enforceable.

---

[316] Schedule 3, Part I, paragraph 2(2) DDA. See eg *Ghandi, supra* note 314.
[317] Read with section 17C DDA.   [318] Schedule 3A, Part 1, paragraphs 2–4.

A person or organization entering into a contract, constructing rules, or entering into any collective agreement with discriminatory terms might be liable for an unlawful discriminatory act under section 16C DDA (instructions and pressure to discriminate).

Where a disabled person has reason to believe that the discriminatory term or rule may at some time in the future affect him and (where the discriminatory term or rule provides for the doing of an act which is unlawful) the disabled person has reason to believe that the unlawful act may at some time be done in relation to him and the act will be unlawful if done in relation to him in present circumstances, that disabled person may present a complaint to an Employment Tribunal contending that the term or rule is void. Where such complaint is to be made:

- in the case of a complaint about the terms of a collective agreement made by or on behalf of an employer[319] the disabled person seeking to present a complaint to an Employment Tribunal must be one of the employer's employees or genuinely and actively seeking to be one;
- in the case of a complaint about a rule made by a trade organization, the disabled person seeking to make a complaint to an Employment Tribunal must be a member of the organization or genuinely or actively seeking to become one;
- in the case of a complaint about a rule made by a qualifications body, the disabled person seeking to make a complaint to an Employment Tribunal must be is a person upon whom the organization or body has conferred an authorization or qualification or a person who is genuinely and actively seeking an authorization or qualification which the organization or body has the power to confer.[320]

Where an Employment Tribunal finds that such a complaint presented to it is well founded, it may make an order declaring the term or rule void.[321]

6.14. RELATIONSHIPS THAT HAVE COME TO AN END

The potential for discriminatory treatment does not end with the termination of the relevant relationship. Many examples can be given of discriminatory acts occurring after the employment relationship has come to an end, and many such

---

[319] Or an organization of employers of which the employer is a member; or an association of such organizations, of one of which an employer is a member: Schedule 3A, Part 2, paragraph 6.

[320] Schedule 3A, Part 2, paragraph 7.

[321] This is without prejudice to the rights of the person who is to be discriminated against and the rights of any other persons who might be treated more favourably in consequence, as are conferred by or in respect of a contract made or modified wholly or partly in pursuance of, or by reference to, that term or rule: Schedule 3A, Part 2, paragraph 9.

examples are found scattered through the law reports. Examples include discriminatory refusals to provide references,[322] discrimination in the handling of an internal appeal against dismissal,[323] and discriminatory failures to reinstate.[324] Until the amendments made by the 2003 Regulations, the DDA did not contain any express provision protecting against discrimination after the formal relevant relationship had come to an end. However, by reason of an important House of Lords decision covering the SDA, RRA, and DDA, the employment provisions of the DDA[325] were to be read as protecting against discrimination occurring after formal termination of the employment relationship so long as there was a 'substantive connection' between the discriminatory conduct and the employment relationship.[326]

The Directive[327] makes specific provision in relation to discrimination occurring after a relevant relationship. It provides that Member States must ensure that appropriate measures are in place for the enforcement of obligations under the Directive to all persons 'who consider themselves wronged by failure to apply the principle of equal treatment to them, even after the relationship in which the discrimination is alleged to have occurred has ended'.[328] To give effect to this requirement, the DDA now contains express provision addressing discrimination after a relevant relationship has ended.[329]

Section 16A DDA applies to relationships which fall within the scope of Part II (that is employment and occupation)[330] and any relationship between a person providing employment services, within the meaning of Part III DDA,[331] and a person receiving such services. Section 16A provides that:

It is unlawful for the relevant person—
(a) to discriminate against a disabled person by subjecting him to a detriment, or
(b) to subject the disabled person to harassment,
where the discrimination or harassment arises out of and is closely connected to the relevant relationship.

In this way, it adopts a test very similar to that adopted by the House of Lords as described above.

---

[322] *Coote v Granada Hospitality Limited (No 2)* [1999] ICR 942, [1999] IRLR 452; *Kirker v British Sugar plc* [2003] UKHL 33, [2003] ICR 867, [2003] IRLR 484. On giving discriminatory references see *Metropolitan Police Service v Shoebridge* [2004] IRLB 15.

[323] *Adekeye v The Post Office (No 2)* [1997] ICR 110, [1997] IRLR 105; *Rhys-Harper v Relaxion Group plc, supra* note 43.

[324] *D'Souza v London Borough of Lambeth* [2003] UKHL 33, [2003] ICR 867, [2003] IRLR 484.

[325] And the SDA and RRA.

[326] *Rhys-Harper v Relaxion Group plc* and five other cases, *supra* note 43 at paragraph 215, *per* Lord Rodger. Their other Lordships adopted slightly different formulations but in essence the test was such as to ensure that there was a sufficiently close nexus between the employment relationship and the discrimination complained of, however long afterwards that occurred.

[327] 2000/78/EC. See Chapter 3 above.   [328] Article 9.

[329] Such change having been introduced by the 2003 Regulations.

[330] It does not apply to section 18 (insurance services): section 16A(2) (applying as it does to 'any preceding provision of this Part') DDA.   [331] See 6.10 above.

Importantly, section 16A also imposes a duty to make reasonable adjustments in the same circumstances as would apply were the relevant relationship still in place.[332] As with the duty in other contexts, it does not apply where the relevant person does not know, and could not reasonably be expected to know, that the disabled person has a disability and is likely to be affected in the way that would otherwise trigger the duty.[333] This means that the duty to make adjustments survives termination of the relevant relationship; this may have very important ramifications for employers and other bodies falling within the scope of Part II DDA. The Employment Code gives the following example:

A former employee with life-time membership of the works social club is no longer able to access the club because of a mobility impairment. Once the employer becomes aware of the problem, it will need to consider making reasonable adjustments.[334]

The victimization provisions apply equally after a relevant relationship has ended.[335]

It should be borne in mind that the proper comparator in a claim brought under section 16A will be *former* employees, members etc.

6.15. TERRITORIAL EXTENT

The employment provisions of the DDA apply only in relation to employment at an establishment in Great Britain.[336] The DDA provides a detailed description of when employment is to be regarded as at an establishment in Great Britain for these purposes. In particular, the employment provisions apply to all employers in respect of disabled people they employ wholly or partly at an establishment in Great Britain.[337] In addition, employment is to be regarded as at an establishment in Great Britain even where the employee does his work wholly outside Great Britain if:

- the employer has a place of business at an establishment in Great Britain;
- the work is for the purposes of the business carried on at the establishment; and
- the employee is ordinarily resident in Great Britain at the time when he applies for or is offered the employment or at any time during the course of the employment.[338]

Certain employment on board ships, hovercraft, and aircraft is also covered.[339]

---

[332] Section 16A(4) and (5) DDA.
[334] Employment Code, paragraph 8.30.
[336] Section 4(6) DDA.
[338] Section 68(2A) DDA.

[333] Section 16A(6).
[335] Sections 55 and 16A DDA.
[337] Section 68(2) DDA.
[339] See Section 68(2B)–(2D) DDA.

It should be noted that Article 39 EC (ex-Article 48) provides for freedom of movement for workers who are Community nationals. This has meant that geographical limitations in the anti-discrimination legislation have been dis-applied[340] where they have had the effect of discriminating against Community nationals exercising their right to freedom of movement by seeking work in other Member States.[341] Thus where the geographical limitation is relied upon in an attempt to exclude from the scope of the DDA a worker employed outside Great Britain (perhaps on an aircraft)[342] regard should always be had to Article 39 and the question whether that limitation should be disapplied.[343]

6.16. ADVERTISEMENTS

The DDA as originally enacted did not make it unlawful to publish an adver-tisement indicating an intention to discriminate on grounds of disability.[344] By section 11 of the unamended DDA, use of a discriminatory advertisement by an employer obliged an Employment Tribunal to assume, unless the contrary was proved, that the reason for a disabled applicant being refused a job was related to their disability.[345] This section therefore had the effect of reversing the burden of proof in cases where a disabled applicant had been refused employment and the employer has advertised for that employment in a dis-criminatory way.

The 2003 Regulations repealed section 11 and replaced it with a provision which specifically outlaws discriminatory advertisements. Section 16B makes it unlawful for a person intending to confer a relevant appointment or benefit to publish a discriminatory advertisement or cause such an advertisement to be published. An advertisement will be unlawful where it,

indicates, or might reasonably be understood to indicate, that an application will or may be determined to any extent by reference to—
(i)   the applicant not having any disability, or any particular disability, or

---

[340] Article 39 is directly effective: see Chapter 3 above.

[341] *Bossa v Nordstress Ltd* [1998] ICR 694, [1998] IRLR 284.

[342] See Section 68(2C)–(D) DDA.

[343] It should be noted that when *Bossa* was decided the geographical limitation in the RRA, under which the case was decided, was wider than that provided for in the DDA (and now in the amended RRA) but the point remains valid in those cases where the effect of the geographical limitation is to deprive Community nationals of the benefit of the DDA when they are exercising their right to freedom of movement.

[344] This might be contrasted with sections 38 SDA and 29 RRA, which make discriminatory advertisements unlawful.

[345] Section 11(1)–(3).

(ii) any reluctance of the person determining the application to comply with a duty to make reasonable adjustments or (in relation to employment services) with the duty imposed by section 21(1) as modified by section 21A(6).[346]

The Explanatory Memorandum attached to the Regulations gives as an example an advertisement: 'That only persons in perfect health need apply'. The Employment Code gives the following example:

An employer advertises a work placement for an office worker, stating 'We are sorry but because our offices are on the first floor, they are not accessible to disabled people'. This is likely to be unlawful. It would be better for the advertisement to state 'although our offices are on the first floor, we welcome applications from disabled people and are willing to make reasonable adjustments.'[347]

The 2003 Regulations, however, qualify the scope of the unlawful act by providing that an advertisement will not be unlawful where it would in fact be lawful to determine the application in the way indicated in the advertisement. According to the Explanatory Memorandum: 'For example, it would not be unlawful to say that persons applying for the position of train drivers must have a specific level of eyesight necessary for the performance of the essential functions of that post'.

Proceedings in respect of a breach of section 16B can only be brought by the Disability Rights Commission (DRC) in the Employment Tribunal. If the tribunal upholds the complaint and it appears to the DRC that, unless restrained, the person concerned is likely to do a further unlawful act, then the DRC can apply to a County Court for an injunction (or to a Sheriff Court in Scotland for an interdict)[348] otherwise the remedy is a declaration that the person concerned has done an act which is unlawful under section 16B.[349]

It is surprising that the new section 16B replaces the old section 11, rather than providing a remedy in addition to it. The statutory presumption created by section 11 ensured that individuals actually refused employment following an application in response to a discriminatory advertisement (or in respect of a post for which a discriminatory advertisement had been placed) could themselves secure a remedy. Now discriminatory advertisements will largely fall within the remit of the DRC which has limited resources. The burden of proof shift in the amended DDA to some extent compensates for the repeal of section 11[350] but this depends on a wide reading of the burden of proof provisions if equivalent protection is to be provided to an individual and the non-regression provision in the Directive[351] is not to be undermined.[352]

---

[346] Section 16B(1) DDA. For the meaning of 'relevant appointment or benefit' see section 16B(3) DDA.

[347] Employment Code, paragraph 7.12.

[348] Section 17B DDA.

[349] Section 17B(3) DDA.

[350] See Chapter 11 below.

[351] 2000/78/EC. See Chapter 3 above.

[352] For a discussion see EOR (2003) 122, 23.

6.17. PRESSURE AND INSTRUCTIONS TO DISCRIMINATE

The DDA now includes express provision relating to instructions and pressure to discriminate (in consequence of the 2003 Regulations). In its original enactment no such provision was made.[353] Section 16C(1) DDA now makes it unlawful for a person:

(a) who has authority over another person, or
(b) in accordance with whose wishes that other person is accustomed to act,
to instruct him to do any act which is unlawful under this Part or, to the extent that it relates to the provision of employment services, Part III, or to procure or attempt to procure the doing by him of any such act.

This requires that there be some relationship between the person giving the instructions or doing the procuring and the other person, and that the latter is accustomed to acting in accordance with the wishes of the first person. Since 'person', by reason of the Interpretation Act 1978,[354] includes 'a body of persons incorporate or unincorporate' then if there is evidence that the other person is accustomed to acting in accordance with the wishes of an employer, it would not matter that the other person had never before spoken to the particular person giving the instructions. However, it is unlikely that this provision will be interpreted as meaning that it is sufficient to show that the other person is merely accustomed to acting in accordance with the wishes of persons in the *same position* as the person giving the instructions.[355]

The words 'procure' and 'attempt to procure' have a wide meaning and include the use of words which bring about or attempt to bring about a certain course of action. Therefore an expression of preference for applicants from a particular racial group is 'an attempt to procure'.[356]

In addition, by section 16C(2) it is unlawful:

to induce, or attempt to induce, a person to do any act which contravenes this Part or, to the extent that it relates to the provision of employment services, Part III by—
(a) providing or offering to provide him with any benefit, or
(b) subjecting or threatening to subject him to any detriment.

The word 'induce' in section 16C(2) covers a mere request to discriminate. It does not necessarily imply an offer of some benefit or the threat of some detriment. The ordinary meaning of the word 'induce' is 'to persuade or to prevail upon or to bring about' and there is no reason to construe the word narrowly or in a restricted sense. Therefore a request by the respondent's secretary to a head

---

[353] Cf sections 39–40, SDA and 30–1 RRA.   [354] Schedule 1.
[355] *Commission for Racial Equality v Imperial Society of Teachers of Dancing* [1983] ICR 473, [1983] IRLR 315, EAT under the same provisions of the RRA, section 30.
[356] *Ibid.*

of careers at a school that 'she would rather the school did not send anyone coloured [*sic*]' to fill a job vacancy constituted an attempt to induce the head of careers not to send such applicants for interview.[357]

However, the additional words in sub-paragraphs (a) and (b) plainly require that such 'inducement' be accompanied by an actual, offered, or threatened 'benefit' or 'detriment' and in this respect section 16C(2) can be contrasted with section 31 RRA and section 40 SDA.

Importantly, an attempted inducement is not prevented from falling within subsection (2) because it is not made directly to the person in question if it is made in such a way that he is likely to hear of it.[358]

It appears that mere communication of information from a person other than the employer that an employer as a matter of fact operates a discriminatory policy is not likely to constitute an attempt to induce discrimination where there is no attempt to persuade another to do anything.[359]

As with discriminatory advertisements, section 16C is enforceable only by the DRC. Proceedings may only be brought by the DRC in the Employment Tribunal. If the tribunal upholds the complaint and it appears to the DRC that, unless restrained, the person concerned is likely to do a further unlawful act, then the DRC can apply to a County Court for an injunction (or to a Sheriff Court in Scotland for an interdict)[360] otherwise the remedy is a declaration that the person concerned has done an act which is unlawful under section 16C.[361]

6.18. CHARITIES

Nothing in Part II affects any charitable instrument that provides for conferring benefits on one or more categories of persons determined by reference to any physical or mental capacity or makes unlawful any act done by a charity or recognized body in pursuance of any of its charitable purposes, so far as those purposes are connected with persons so determined.[362] In addition, nothing in Part II prevents a person who provides supported employment from treating members of a particular group of disabled persons more favourably than other persons in providing such employment.[363] 'Supported employment' means facilities provided, or in respect of which payments are made, under section 15 of the Disabled Persons (Employment) Act 1944.

As already observed, nothing in the DDA prohibits more favourable treatment of disabled people in any event.

---

[357] *Ibid.* under section 31 RRA.   [358] Section 16C(3) DDA.

[359] *CRE v Powell and City of Birmingham District Council* (EAT, 10 September 1985) [1985] EOR 7B.

[360] Section 17B DDA.   [361] Section 17B(3) DDA.

[362] Section 18C (1) DDA.

[363] Further, nothing in Part II prevents the Secretary of State from agreeing to arrangements for the provision of supported employment which will, or may, have that effect: section 16C(2) DDA.

7

GOODS, FACILITIES, SERVICES, AND PREMISES

7.1. INTRODUCTION

Part III of the DDA regulates discrimination[1] in the provision of goods, facilities, services, and premises. In addition, the Disability Discrimination Act 1995 (Amendment) Regulations 2003[2] ('the 2003 Regulations') have included a new section 21A DDA regulating discrimination by providers of employment services.

Part III DDA now outlaws 'discrimination'[3] by:

- providers of goods, facilities, and services in respect of disabled members of the public;

- providers of employment services in respect of disabled persons to whom they are providing such services or who have requested them to provide such services;

- landlords and other persons with the power to dispose of any premises, in respect of disabled members of the public;

- landlords and other persons concerned with managing premises, in respect of disabled occupants of premises;

- landlords and other persons whose licence or consent is required for the disposal of any premises, in respect of disabled members of the public.

---

[1] As defined at Chapter 5 above, at 5.7.

[2] SI 2003/1673. Such services were previously covered by section 19 DDA but with a more limited concept of discrimination than that applicable to section 21A DDA; see Chapter 5 above, at 5.5.

[3] As defined at Chapter 5 above, at 5.7. And in the case of employment services, harassment: see Chapter 5 above, at 5.5.

'Discrimination' for the purposes of Part III DDA is to be construed in accordance with sections 20–21A and 24 (Chapter 5 above, at 5.7). Many of the unlawful acts created in Part III address the duty to make reasonable adjustments, as has been explained at Chapter 5 above, at 5.7.[4]

'Victimization' (a form of 'discrimination') of a person, whether disabled or not, is unlawful within the scope of each the unlawful acts described below.[5]

In respect of the unlawful acts created in relation to the provision of employment services, it is unlawful to discriminate after the relevant relationship has come to an end.[6] Otherwise no express provision addresses discrimination after the relevant relationship has been terminated. This issue is addressed further below (see 7.4).

Discrimination by providers of employment services is dealt with at Chapter 6 above, at 6.10, because of its close relationship with discrimination arising in the employment field.

A relevant Code of Practice has been issued by the DRC and has received Parliamentary approval pursuant to the negative resolution procedure:[7] the re-revised Code of Practice on 'Rights of Access, Goods, Facilities, Services and Premises'[8] ('Goods, Facilities, Services and Premises Code of Practice'). This replaces the first revised Code. The new Code takes account of the further duties on service providers to make adjustments to the physical features of their premises where they make it impossible or unreasonably difficult for disabled people to use their services. Although these remaining duties did not come into force until 1 October 2004, this Code was issued in May 2002 in order to encourage service providers to be proactive and to assist them in preparing for these significant extended obligations.[9]

Proceedings in respect of a breach of the unlawful acts created by Part III must be commenced in the County Court, or Sheriff Court in Scotland. Enforcement and remedies are dealt with at Chapter 11.

7.2. GOODS, FACILITIES, AND SERVICES

The DDA outlaws discrimination by providers of goods, facilities, and services. Section 19 DDA provides that:

(1) It is unlawful for a provider of services to discriminate against a disabled person—
    (a) in refusing to provide, or deliberately not providing, to the disabled person any service which he provides, or is prepared to provide, to members of the public;

---

[4] No such duty arises in respect of the 'premises' provisions.

[5] Section 55 DDA. 'Victimization' is addressed in Chapter 5 above, at 5.7.4.

[6] Section 16A DDA. This is dealt with at in Chapter 6 above, at 6.14.

[7] Section 53A DDA.   [8] ISBN 0 11 702860 6.

[9] Commencement date 27 May 2002, Disability Discrimination Code of Practice (Goods, Facilities, Services and Premises) (Appointed Day) Order 2002, SI 2002/720. See also 'Open 4 All, 2004' for further guidance from the DRC, available at www.open4all.org.

(b) in failing to comply with any duty imposed on him by section 21 in circumstances in which the effect of that failure is to make it impossible or unreasonably difficult for the disabled person to make use of any such service;

(c) in the standard of service which he provides to the disabled person or the manner in which he provides it to him; or

(d) in the terms on which he provides a service to the disabled person.

The meaning of 'discrimination' and the section 21 duty to make reasonable adjustments are described in Chapter 5 above, at 5.7. As can be seen, though the duty to make reasonable adjustments is anticipatory (see 5.7.1) an unlawful act is only committed in respect of a particular disabled person where they are personally disadvantaged in one of the ways described in section 19 DDA.[10]

7.2.1. 'Provider of Services'

A 'provider of services' for the purposes of section 19 DDA, is a person concerned with the provision:

• in the United Kingdom;
• of services to the public or to a section of the public;
• whether a service is provided on payment or without payment.[11]

There is then a geographical limitation on the reach of the DDA. It will not protect against discrimination arising in relation to services to be provided outside the United Kingdom. However, the fact that an end product is to be enjoyed outside the United Kingdom does not mean that services (the sale of airline tickets or the transporting of luggage, for example) are not provided in the United Kingdom. Given the wide meaning of 'goods, facilities, and services' discussed below, it is likely that any direct relationship between service provider and customer which itself occurs in the United Kingdom will fall within the scope of section 19 DDA.

As has been seen, the service provider must be 'concerned' with the provision of services to the public or a section of the public. The fact of services actually having been provided to members of the public, or a section thereof, is not material. The service provider simply must be concerned with providing such services to fall within the scope of section 19 DDA. The unsuccessful service provider and the first time service provider are covered equally.

---

[10] See *Roads v Central Trains Ltd* [2004] EWCA Civ 1541 at paragraph 12 in respect of section 19(1)(b) DDA, but by reason of section 20 (which defines 'discrimination' for the purposes of section 19 as including a breach of duty under section 21) a failure to comply with a duty under section 21 will be actionable under any limb of section 19 by a disabled person if it falls within the scope of one of the unlawful acts therein and causes the requisite degree of disadvantage to the particular disabled person thereby (eg by a 'refusal' to provide services or in the 'standard' or 'manner' of services etc).

[11] Section 19(2)(b) and (c) DDA.

It is irrelevant whether a service is provided on payment (for example, in a restaurant[12]) or without payment (for example, access to a park[13]).

The public to whom providers must provide services includes children as well as adults (and both children and adults may complain of discrimination under section 19 DDA) and therefore services to children are covered.

This means that all service providers, whether in the voluntary, statutory, or commercial sector are covered. This is so whatever the size of the service provider: 'It does not matter whether the services in question are being provided by a sole trader, firm, company or other organisation, or whether the person involved in providing the services is self-employed or an employee, volunteer, contractor or agent'.[14] The services that are covered are those provided to the public by, amongst others:

- local councils;
- Government departments and agencies;
- the emergency services;
- charities;
- voluntary organizations;
- hotels;
- restaurants;
- pubs;[15]
- post offices;
- banks;
- building societies;
- solicitors;
- accountants;
- telecommunications and broadcasting organizations;
- public utilities (such as gas, electricity, and water suppliers);
- national parks;
- sports stadia;
- leisure centres;[16]
- advice agencies;
- theatres;
- cinemas;
- hairdressers;
- shops;
- market stalls;
- petrol stations;
- telesales businesses;

---

[12] Goods, Facilities, Services and Premises Code of Practice, paragraph 2.13.
[13] *Ibid.*   [14] *Ibid.* paragraph 2.15.
[15] Eg *Gill v El Vinos Co Ltd* [1983] QB 425.
[16] Eg *James v Eastleigh Borough Council* [1990] 2 AC 751.

- places of worship;
- courts;[17] and
- hospitals and clinics.[18]

All those engaged in providing services are covered, from the most senior director or manager to the most junior employee, whether full or part-time, permanent or temporary.[19] More than one person may be ultimately responsible for providing particular services. The Code provides the following example:

A bank provides a cash machine facility inside a supermarket. Although the facility is located on the supermarket's premises, the service is being provided by the bank. The bank is likely to be responsible for any duties that may arise under the Act in respect of the cash machine. However, the supermarket is likely to be responsible for ensuring that the cash machine is physically accessible to disabled customers using its premises.[20]

7.2.2. Services Provided to 'Members of the Public'

Providers of services are only caught by section 19 DDA where the particular service is provided to, or is one which the service provider is prepared to provide to, members of the public. 'Members of the public' are not defined by the DDA but the term includes a 'section of the public'.[21] The DDA is not therefore concerned with purely private or one-off arrangements.

In *Dockers' Labour Club & Institute Limited v Race Relations Board*,[22] under comparable provisions in the RRA 1968, the Race Relations Board[23] sought a declaration that the Dockers' Labour Club, which operated a colour bar such that only white people were admitted into its club, was acting unlawfully.[24] The House of Lords upheld an earlier decision of the House[25] in holding that the club did not provide facilities or services to the public, or a section of it. The Club elected its members adopting a genuine process of selection and thus was not accessible to the public or a section of it but operated within the private sphere. The House of Lords also held that the same principle applied where clubs, operating under reciprocal arrangements with other clubs, offered hospitality or temporary membership to members of the other club. Even in such circumstances, so long as *each* club exercised 'a rigorous choice in electing their members', there

---

[17] See *Woodrup v London Borough of Southwark* [2002] EWCA Civ 1716, [2003] IRLR 111.

[18] Goods, Facilities, Services and Premises Code of Practice, paragraph 2.14.

[19] *Ibid.* paragraph 2.15.   [20] *Ibid.* paragraph 2.30.

[21] Section 19(2)(b) DDA.   [22] [1976] AC 285.

[23] The predecessor of the Commission for Racial Equality.

[24] The claim was brought under the Race Relations Act 1968, section 2(1), which is in similar terms to section 19 DDA.

[25] *Race Relations Board v Charter* [1973] AC 868.

would be no discrimination within the meaning of section 19 DDA because the clubs would truly be operating within the private sphere.[26]

Prisoners have been held to constitute a section of the public for the purposes of materially the same provisions of the RRA.[27] Children in the care of a local authority have been held to constitute a section of the public to whom foster parents provided services or facilities for the purposes of the RRA[28] (though foster arrangements have now been taken outside the scope of the RRA[29]).

As will be seen below, mere access to and use of a particular place may constitute a service or facility for the purpose of section 19 DDA, where the public are permitted to enter. Whether a place is one to which the public is permitted access will depend on the facts of each case. The Goods, Facilities, Services and Premises Code of Practice explains this as follows:

Members of the public are clearly permitted to enter some places. A shopping mall is an example. If the owner of a shopping mall leases shop units to individual retailers, the owner will be responsible for the common areas, such as access roads, pavements, car parks, toilets, lifts and stairs. By allowing members of the public to use these common parts, the owner is providing services to the public and is subject to the Act.[30]

In determining whether a person entering the premises is 'a member of the public' for the purposes of determining whether members of the public are permitted access, a number of factors may be relevant, including:

- whether tenants who are service providers are actually providing services in the building rather than from the building;
- whether those admitted to the building are there for the purposes of the occupier (such as employees or maintenance and service personnel) or whether they are there for purposes of their own (such as existing or potential clients or customers); and
- the nature and extent of the security and screening arrangements in place.[31]

The more regulated entry to a building or other place is, the less likely it will be that members of the public are permitted access. By analogy with clubs, if entry requires some particular status (employee, tenant, member) then it is unlikely to be a place to which members of the public are permitted access.

---

[26] The effect of the decision in the *Dockers' Labour Club* case has been limited by changes introduced by the RRA 1976. Discrimination by private members' clubs is now made expressly unlawful under the RRA. However, the same does not apply under the DDA. Thus membership policies by clubs which discriminate against disabled people are not made unlawful by the DDA. This will change with the enactment of the Disability Discrimination Bill which contains provision outlawing discrimination by clubs (Clause 5): see Chapter 13 below.

[27] *Alexander v Home Office* [1988] ICR 685, though apparently this point was not taken, at least on appeal.

[28] *Applin v Race Relations Board* [1975] AC 259.   [29] Section 23(2) RRA.

[30] Goods, Facilities, Services and Premises Code of Practice, paragraph 2.23.

[31] *Ibid.* paragraph 2.25.

7.2.3. Meaning of 'Goods, Facilities, and Services'

As stated above, section 19 outlaws discrimination in the provision of 'services'. However, the provision of 'services' for these purposes includes 'the provision of any goods or facilities'.[32]

A non-exhaustive list of examples of 'services' to which section 19 applies is given by section 19(3) DDA, as follows:

- access to and use of any place which members of the public are permitted to enter;
- access to and use of means of communication;
- access to and use of information services;
- accommodation in a hotel, boarding house, or similar establishment;
- facilities by way of banking or insurance or for grants, loans, credit, or finance;
- facilities for entertainment, recreation, or refreshment;
- facilities provided by employment agencies or under section 2 of Employment and Training Act 1973;
- the services of any profession or trade, or any local or other public authority.

'Profession' includes any vocation or occupation; 'trade' includes any business.[33] As stated this is an inclusive list. The words 'goods, facilities, or services' are not otherwise described in the DDA. They should be given their ordinary and natural meaning:

- 'goods' are any movable property, including merchandise or wares;
- 'facilities' include any opportunity for obtaining some benefit or for doing something;
- 'services' refer to any conduct tending to the welfare or advantage of other people, especially conduct which supplies their needs.[34]

Each of these expressions is deliberately vague and general; taken together, they cover a very wide range of human activity.[35]

Such services will include services provided by service providers that are incidental to their core or main services, for example in-store toilets, fire exits, and emergency escape procedures.[36]

Whether particular services are caught by section 19 will depend upon the particular circumstances. Some organizations may be providing services covered by section 19 for certain purposes but not for others. This may be so with membership clubs (discussed above at 7.2.2 and below at 7.2.6.4) when on an 'open

---

[32] Section 19(2) DDA.   [33] Section 68(1) DDA.
[34] Lester and Bindman, *Race and Law* (Penguin, 1972) 260.
[35] *Ibid.*   [36] Goods, Facilities, Services and Premises Code of Practice, paragraph 2.18.

day' to which the public are invited they will be covered by section 19, but when providing services exclusively to members they will not. Similarly, the police will be providing a service for the purposes of the DDA when giving advice and information about crime prevention, but are unlikely to be providing a service when arresting someone[37] (as to which, see paragraph 7.2.4 below).

Relevant 'services' include mere 'access to and use of any place which members of the public are permitted to enter'.[38] Thus there is no necessity for a product or tangible service to be provided. Such access may be to a building or other place, perhaps for the purposes of using another service.

The Code contemplates section 19 applying to 'roads', 'pavements', and 'parks' (when in private or public ownership). This has obvious ramifications for the duties of highway authorities, particularly having regard to the duty to make adjustments to physical features. This is discussed further below at paragraph 7.2.4.

Where a place is occupied by more than one service provider and the place concerned has common areas such as entrance halls, stairways, and lifts, difficult issues may arise. The Code advises as follows:

The Act does not expressly state whether or not the landlord (including any operator of the common parts) in such a case is a service provider for the purposes of the Act in respect of those common areas. Therefore, it does not make it explicit whether the landlord is under a duty to make reasonable adjustments to the common parts to make them accessible to disabled people.[39]

As the Code makes clear, however, where members of the public have access to those common parts, then the landlord or the occupier of those common parts will fall within the scope of section 19 DDA in respect of them. Disability-related discrimination will therefore be outlawed in respect of the use of them and a duty to make reasonable adjustments will arise in respect of them.[40]

Tenants providing services to the public from the premises will fall within section 19 DDA and will therefore have a duty to make reasonable adjustments to ensure that their services are accessible to disabled people.[41] Where the common parts make it impossible or unreasonably difficult for disabled people to use their services, asking the landlord to make such alterations as are required in order to make the premises accessible is likely to be a reasonable step for the tenant to have to take.[42]

---

[37] Goods, Facilities, Services and Premises Code of Practice, paragraph 2.14.
[38] Section 19(3)(a) DDA.
[39] Goods, Facilities, Services and Premises Code of Practice, paragraph 2.20.
[40] See Chapter 5 above, at 5.7 for an explanation of these terms.   [41] *Ibid.*
[42] Goods, Facilities, Services and Premises Code of Practice, paragraph 2.28.

7.2.4. Public Authorities

The DDA does not generally address discrimination by public authorities in the exercising of their functions. This can be contrasted with the RRA, which now outlaws discrimination by public authorities in exercising their functions.[43]

Section 19 DDA covers at least some of the functions of public authorities because sections 19(3)(h) provides as an example of the services to which section 19 applies 'the services of . . . any local or other public authority'. The Goods, Facilities, Services and Premises Code of Practice states that the DDA 'affects everyone concerned with the provision in the United Kingdom of services to the public, or to a section of the public, whether in the private, public or voluntary sectors'.[44]

The extent to which public functions are covered by the goods, facilities, and services provisions in the anti-discrimination legislation, however, has proved controversial. There has been important case-law testing the boundaries of the comparable provisions in the SDA and RRA. The RRA was eventually amended to cover the functions of public authorities[45] in the light of the recommendations of the Stephen Lawrence Inquiry Report, which recommended that: 'the full force of the Race Relations legislation should apply to all police officers'.[46]

However, the SDA and DDA have not been so amended, and discrimination by public authorities in the exercising of their public functions is not specifically outlawed. This will change with the enactment of the Disability Discrimination Bill (Clause 4) and any enactment creating a Single Equality and Human Rights Commission,[47] which will outlaw both disability and sex discrimination by public authorities in the exercising of their functions: See Chapters 12 and 13 below.

Such discrimination will therefore be unlawful only where it falls within the scope of one of the other unlawful acts. Public sector employers, public sector landlords, and 'responsible bodies' in the context of education all fall within the scope of the other unlawful acts created by the DDA when they discriminate against disabled employees,[48] tenants,[49] and pupils,[50] for example. Otherwise, discrimination by public authorities is outlawed[51] only where it occurs in the

---

[43] Section 19B RRA.   [44] Paragraph 2.13.   [45] Race Relations (Amendment) Act 2000.

[46] Recommendation 11 of the *Report of an Inquiry by Sir William McPherson of Cluny* (1999 Cmnd 4262), available on the Home Office website at http://www.archive.official-documents.co.uk/document/cm42/4262/4262.htm.

[47] White Paper 'Fairness for All: A New Commission for Equality and Human Rights', (2004) CM 6185, paragraph 3.3.

[48] Eg *Fu v London Borough of Camden* [2001] IRLR 186. See also, *Nottinghamshire County Council v Meikle* [2004] EWCA Civ 859, [2004] IRLR 703.

[49] Eg *Council of the City of Manchester v (1) Romano (2) Samari* [2004] EWCA Civ 834.

[50] Eg *McAuley Catholic High School v (1) CC (2) PC and Special Educational Needs and Disability Tribunal* [2003] EWHC 3045 (Admin), [2004] 2 All ER 436.

[51] So as to give rise to a private law remedy.

context of the provision of goods, facilities, or services[52] that the public author-ity concerned provides to the public or a section of it. Much of this type of discrimination has been placed beyond the scope of the goods, facilities, and services provisions in the anti-discrimination legislation by narrow judicial inter-pretation of its provisions. The case-law arising under the same provisions of the SDA and RRA is instructive.[53]

In *R v Immigration Appeal Tribunal ex parte Kassam*,[54] the Court of Appeal dismissed an appeal against a decision of the High Court refusing an application for judicial review against decisions of the Secretary of State and the Immigration Appeal Tribunal ordering the deportation of the applicant. The applicant had complained that he was subject to a deportation order in circum-stances where a woman in a comparable position would not have been subject to deportation and that accordingly section 29 SDA (which is in materially similar terms to section 19 DDA) was contravened. The Court of Appeal held that when giving leave to enter or remain in the United Kingdom in the exercise of powers under the Immigration Act 1971, or rules made under that Act, the Secretary of State was not 'any person concerned with the provision . . . of . . . facilities . . . to the public' for the purposes of section 29. The Court of Appeal concluded that read with their 'natural and ordinary meaning' the words in section 29 were not aimed at the Secretary of State when he was exercising powers concerned with giving leave to enter or remain under the Immigration Act 1971:

The word 'facilities' in that section is flanked on one side by the word 'goods' and on the other 'services'. This suggests to my mind that the word 'facilities' is not to be given a wholly unrestricted meaning but must be limited or confined to facilities that are akin to goods or services . . . When the Secretary of State allows an immigrant to enter and stay in this country, he is granting a permission, he is not providing a facility.[55]

In *Re Amin*[56] the House of Lords were concerned with the special voucher scheme under which certain Commonwealth citizens could apply to settle in the United Kingdom, so long as they were the head of a household. Ms Amin com-plained that this indirectly discriminated against women and, in judicial review proceedings, relied upon section 29 SDA. The House of Lords determined that section 29 was concerned with facilities and services that might be done by a private person and 'market place activities'.[57] As a result, the special voucher scheme was outside the scope of section 29 SDA.

---

[52] Eg *James v Eastleigh Borough Council, supra* note 16.
[53] Under sections 29 SDA and 20 RRA. In construing the three anti-discrimination statutes, gen-erally a broad and purposive construction is given (*Jones v Tower Boot Co Ltd* [1997] ICR 254 and *Anyanwu v South Bank Students' Union and Another* [2001] UKHL 14, [2001] ICR 391, [2001] IRLR 305) and a consistent meaning across the three Acts should be strived for (*Anyanwu, supra*, and *Rhys-Harper v Relaxion Group plc* and five other cases [2003] UKHL 33, [2003] ICR 867, [2003] IRLR 484.)
[54] [1980] 1 WLR 1037.
[56] [1983] 2 AC 818.
[55] *Ibid. per* Lord Justice Stephenson at 1044.
[57] At 835.

However, the courts have not been consistent in the approach they have taken to public authority functions and the exercising of executive discretion. Thus, in *Savjani v Inland Revenue Commissioners*[58] the Court of Appeal distinguished *Kassam*[59] in holding that the Inland Revenue provided a service under section 20 RRA (which is in materially the same terms as section 19 DDA and section 29 SDA) by the provision, dissemination, and implementation of regulations that enabled the taxpayer to know that he was entitled to a deduction or a repayment of tax and that might entitle him to know how to satisfy the Inspector or the Board if he was so entitled and that would enable him to obtain the actual deduction or repayment which Parliament said he was to have.[60] In *Alexander v The Home Office*[61] a prisoner complained about the allocation of work to him on racial grounds. He succeeded in his claim before a County Court and no point was apparently taken that his claim fell outside section 20 RRA.

In *Farah v Commissioner of Police of the Metropolis*[62] the Court of Appeal concluded that section 20 RRA[63] was wide enough to cover some activities of the police. In *Farah* a Somali refugee, claimed that she had been attacked in London by white youths who had set a dog on her and caused injury to her. When she had summoned the police, rather than taking action against the white youths, they had arrested her on no good ground. She had then been charged with various criminal offences including causing unnecessary suffering to a dog, but when she appeared to answer the summons no evidence was offered against her and she was acquitted. She commenced proceedings under section 20 of the RRA (amongst other things) contending that the police officers had deliberately omitted to provide her with services she sought or services on the like terms to those normally provided by the officers to other members of the public and that criminal proceedings had been brought against her on racial grounds. The police applied to strike out her complaints of race discrimination on the ground that they did not disclose complaints justiciable under section 20 RRA. On appeal, the Court of Appeal concluded that those parts of a police officer's duties involving assistance to or protection of members of the public amounted to the provision of services to the public for the purposes of section 20 RRA: 'What is said is that the service sought by the plaintiff was that of protection and that she did not, because of her race, obtain the protection that others would have been afforded. It seems to me that that is no less the provision of a service than is the giving of directions or other information to a member of the public who seeks them'.[64]

The Court of Appeal was particularly influenced by the words of Lord Fraser in *Amin*[65] that having regard to the Act as a whole it applies to acts done on

---

[58] [1981] QB 458. [59] [1980] 1 WLR 1037. [60] At 467 *per* Lord Justice Templeman.

[61] *Supra* note 27. [62] [1998] QB 65.

[63] And therefore sections 29 SDA and 19 DDA.

[64] *Farah, supra* note 62, at 78.

[65] *Supra* note 56 at 834–5.

behalf of the Crown but only where they are of a kind similar to acts that might be done by a private person. The Court of Appeal concluded that certain aspects of police officers' activities fell within the Act:

Lord Fraser . . . drew a distinction between acts done on behalf of the Crown which are of a kind similar to acts that might be done by a private person and acts done by a person holding statutory office in the course of formulating or carrying out government policy, the latter being quite different in kind from any act that would ever be done by a private person. The assertion in the pleading is that officers failed to react to the plaintiff's emergency telephone call, to investigate her account at the scene, and to afford her protection—all on account of her colour.

These acts (or services) which the plaintiff sought from the police were, to my mind, acts which might have been done by a private person. The second category envisaged by Lord Fraser covers those acts which a private person would never do, and would normally only ever be performed by the police, eg gaining forcible entry into a suspected drugs warehouse. Here the officers would be carrying out government policy to which the Act would not apply. Moreover, they would be performing duties in order to prevent and detect crime and exercising their powers to enable them to perform those duties.[66]

The claim in *Brooks v Commissioner of Police for the Metropolis*[67] arose out of the murder of Stephen Lawrence in a racist attack. Mr Brooks, a friend and witness to the attack, brought a claim against various police officers alleging that they had discriminated against him under section 20 RRA. The numerous allegations of discrimination fell into two broad categories, namely (1) allegations of failing to protect, assist, and support, and (2) allegations of failure to investigate crime with appropriate competence and vigour. The judge at first instance struck out parts of Mr Brooks' claim, in particular those parts which related to the investigation of the crime. The Court of Appeal allowed an appeal by Mr Brooks and permitted the complaints made regarding the investigation of the crime to proceed on the grounds that they were capable of falling within the scope of section 20. This followed a concession by counsel for the police officers that it would be 'technically possible' for an individual police officer to be asked to provide investigatory services by a member of the public, and to respond in a way which would fall foul of section 20(1)(a) or (b)'.[68] In addition, the Court of Appeal accepted that an express request for services is not necessary for an unlawful act to occur.

A number of points can be made about the case law in this area:

• Section 29 SDA and section 20 RRA (and by necessary implication section 19 DDA) have been given a wide meaning when the complaint is outside the immigration field.

---

[66] *Farah v Commissioner of Police, supra* note 62, at 84–5, *per* Lord Justice Otton.
[67] [2002] EWCA Civ 407; appeal to the House of Lords is pending.
[68] *Ibid.* at paragraph 36.

306

- The fact that an act is done pursuant to a statutory duty (*Savjani*) or a statutory power (*Farah*; *Brooks*; *Alexander*) does not necessarily take it outside the 'goods, facilities, and services' provisions of the SDA, the RRA, and, by necessary implication, the DDA.

- Many 'services' or 'facilities' which could barely be described as 'market place activities' have been held to fall within the 'goods, facilities, and services' provisions of the SDA, RRA, and DDA.

- Where the acts done are such that they might have been done by a private person they will not fall foul of the rulings in *Kassam* and *Amin* and are accordingly likely to fall within section 29 SDa, section 20 RRA, and section 19 DDA.

- An express request for services does not have to be made for section 20 RRA (and accordingly section 29 SDA and section 19 DDA) to become engaged. For example, a police officer who passes by a victim of crime without stopping to assist, protect, or investigate, on racial grounds, will be guilty of unlawful discrimination even if the victim did not request help.[69]

As to particular authorities, the following may be noted.

- *Policing functions* Those functions that involve assisting or protecting members of the public or investigating crime are likely to fall within section 19 DDA. The Goods, Facilities, Services and Premises Code of Practice states that: 'the police will be providing a service under the Act when giving advice and information about crime prevention, but are unlikely to be providing a service when arresting someone'.[70]

- *Functions of highway authorities* Highway authorities in providing paths, footways, and so on, are likely to be providing a service thereby and are likely to fall within section 19 DDA. Importantly, as described above, mere 'access' constitutes a service for section 19 DDA purposes. Such access may be provided by public or private institutions and, as has been seen above, no distinction is made between them by the DDA or the Goods, Facilities, Services and Premises Code of Practice. Indeed no rational distinction could be made as between, for example, private and public road owners, nor could any be made between open spaces and access routes held in private or public ownership. The Goods, Facilities, Services and Premises Code of Practice states that: 'A highway authority may be providing a service when assuring passage along the highway.'[71] This obviously has very significant consequences for highway authorities who might be under a duty to make adjustments to physical features including pavements, kerbs, etc.

---

[69] *Ibid.* paragraph 39; the same reasoning would apply to sections 29 SDA and 19 DDA. See also at 7.2.5 below.

[70] Goods, Facilities, Services and Premises Code of Practice, paragraph 2.14. See also section 64A DDA and Chapter 10 below on vicarious liability.

[71] Paragraph 2.14.

- *The functions of health authorities* Health authorities in providing health services will fall within section 19 DDA. Again such services may be provided by public or private institutions. The Goods, Facilities, Services and Premises Code of Practice states that: 'Among the services which are covered are those provided to the public by . . . hospitals and clinics'.[72]

- *The functions of the courts* Courts in exercising their functions may fall within section 19 DDA. The Goods, Facilities, Services and Premises Code of Practice states that: 'Among the services which are covered are those provided to the public by . . . courts'.[73] Courts, however, uniquely provide certain services which are not and cannot be replicated by private service providers. They administer justice on behalf of the State and at least when they are performing those functions the question whether they are providing a service for section 19 DDA purposes is controversial. In *Woodrup v London Borough of Southwark*[74] the Court of Appeal considered it unlikely that courts fell within section 19 DDA. Indeed Lord Justice Simon-Browne described the submission that an Employment Tribunal was 'providing a service to the public under Part III' as 'far-fetched'[75] and Lord Justice Clarke was 'not at present persuaded' of the same,[76] though it was not necessary in that case for the issue to be decided. Even if a court is not providing services for section 19 DDA purposes when carrying out justice functions, the court service will almost certainly be providing services when it provides physical access to courts, information services (leaflets etc) and other non-judicial services.

7.2.5. Seeking Services

Section 19 DDA does not expressly require that a disabled person is 'seeking' services before an unlawful act may be committed (this can be compared to the position under section 29 SDA and section 20 RRA: 'It is unlawful for any person concerned with the provision (for payment or not) of goods, facilities or services to the public or a section of the public to discriminate against a woman *who seeks to obtain or use* those goods, facilities or services'[77]).

Unlawful disability discrimination may therefore occur without a request having been made for particular services. A disabled person who cannot access a building or who is a victim of crime and not assisted by the police, for example, will have a claim under section 19 DDA without first having expressly asked the service provider to grant access or the police to assist.

---

[72] Goods, Facilities, Services and Premises Code of Practice, paragraph 2.14.

[73] *Ibid.* [74] *Supra* note 17. [75] *Ibid.* at paragraph 16.

[76] *Ibid.* at paragraph 24.

[77] Emphasis added. Even in the case of the SDA and RRA, unlawful discrimination might occur without an express request for services. That a person is seeking services can be inferred from the circumstances or a request can be implied (eg a victim of crime implicitly seeks the services of the police): *Brooks v Commissioner of Police for the Metropolis, supra* note 67.

7.2.6. Excluded Services

The DDA makes specific provision excluding certain services from section 19 DDA—in the fields of transport and education—and does not address indirect access to services, goods or facilities or outlaw discrimination by clubs. Section 19(5) DDA also excludes 'such other services as may be prescribed' but none have yet been prescribed.

7.2.6.1. *Transport*
Section 19(5) DDA provides that:

Except in such circumstances as may be prescribed, this section and sections 20 and 21 do not apply to—

. . .

(b) any service so far as it consists of the use of any means of transport.

Discrimination in the provision of any service insofar as it consists of the use of transport (only) is not outlawed by the DDA. Services related to transport use (ticket sales, customer services etc), and infrastructure,[78] though not the use of any transport itself, will be covered by section 19 DDA. This is discussed further in Chapter 9 below. The DDA does make specific provision in relation to transport and again this is addressed in Chapter 9 below.

7.2.6.2. *Education*
Further, any services which fall within the scope of the 'education' provisions are not outlawed by section 19 DDA. Thus section 19(5A) DDA provides that 'Nothing in this Part applies to the provision of a service in relation to which discrimination is made unlawful by section 28A, 28F or 28R'. This reflects the amendments made by SENDA to insert provision into the DDA outlawing discrimination in the education fields. Prior to these amendments, section 19 DDA excluded education provided in the public and voluntary sphere.[79] Importantly, however, some services provided in the context of education always fell within the scope of section 19 DDA and may continue to do so. These include:

• non-educational provision by schools and other bodies. In *White v Clitheroe Grammar School*,[80] a school sought to rely on the education exclusion in a claim brought by a disabled pupil who was refused permission to join two

---

[78] *Roads v Central Trains Ltd, supra* note 10.

[79] Ex-section 19(5) and (6) DDA. See Chapter 8 below on the position now.

[80] Preston County Court (District Judge Ashton) 29 April 2002, Case No BB002640 (unreported), cited in Palmer, Gill, Monaghan, Moon, and Stacey, ed McColgan, *Discrimination Law Handbook* (LAG, 2002) 872.

school trips: one a school exchange trip and the other a water sports holiday.[81] On a preliminary point the County Court held that 'education which is . . . provided at . . . the school' did not have to be physically provided at the school buildings but included systematic instruction provided as part of the services of the school. As the exchange trip emphasized the learning of a language in a contextual situation it was a substitute for attendance at school and thus excluded from section 19 DDA by the education exemption, even though attendance on the trip was voluntary and parents had to pay a contribution to its cost. The water sports holiday, however, was not excluded because it was essentially a holiday, albeit with some helpful instruction, and therefore it was covered by section 19 DDA. The Goods, Facilities, Services and Premises Code of Practice gives the following examples:

A parent-teacher association holds a fund-raising event in a school hall. This is a provision of a service which is likely to be subject to Part III of the Act.

A university puts on a conference which is not aimed wholly or mainly at students. Even if the majority of people who take up the places are students, the conference is still likely to be subject to Part III of the Act.[82]

• Educational services provided by private providers. The Goods, Facilities, Services and Premises Code of Practice gives the following example:

A privately-run college which provides typing courses is providing a service which is likely to be subject to Part III of the Act.[83]

After the changes made by SENDA and the much narrower exclusion from section 19 now provided for by section 19(5A) DDA, the above education-related services are likely to continue to fall within Section 19 DDA, as will other services previously excluded. These will be educational and related services that do not fall within the specific unlawful acts created by sections 28A, 28F, or 28R DDA, including non-statutory youth services, such as clubs and activities run by voluntary organizations, the Scouts, and church youth clubs.[84]

7.2.6.3. Indirect services

Both the SDA and RRA contain express provision addressing services that are indirectly provided.[85] Section 50 SDA provides that 'references in this Act to the affording by any persons of access to benefits, facilities or services are not

---

[81] See Chapter 8 below, at 8.2.4 for a discussion on the breadth of the unlawful acts in the education field now, and query whether a decision that such activities fall within the scope of section 19 would be the same now, having regard to section 19(5A) DDA.

[82] Paragraph 2.34.   [83] Ibid.

[84] The Goods, Facilities, Services and Premises Code of Practice, paragraph 2.35, though the line may be difficult to draw: see Chapter 8 below, at 8.2.2, 8.2.4 and 8.7, for further discussion.

[85] There are general exceptions which apply to the goods, services, and facilities provisions under the SDA and RRA to which regard should always be had (eg sections 35(3), 36(1), 44, 46, and 48 SDA; sections 23(1), 27(2), 35, and 38 RRA, amongst others).

limited to benefits, facilities or services provided by that person himself, but include any means by which it is in that person's power to facilitate access to benefits, facilities or services provided by any other person (the 'actual provider'). Section 40 RRA is in the same terms. The DDA contains no such provision.

Only persons actually engaged in providing services to the public are therefore covered. The Goods, Facilities, Services and Premises Code of Practice gives the following advice:

The manufacture and design of products are not in themselves covered by Part III of the Act because they do not involve the provision of services direct to the public. Nothing in the Act requires manufacturers or designers to make changes to their products, packaging or instructions. However, it makes good business sense for manufacturers and designers to make their goods (and user information) more accessible to disabled customers and they should consider doing so as a matter of good practice.[86]

However, if a manufacturer does provide services direct to the public, then section 19 DDA will apply. The Goods, Facilities, Services and Premises Code of Practice gives the following example:

A manufacturer of electrical goods provides a free guarantee. A purchaser of the goods is then entitled to have the goods replaced by the manufacturer if they are faulty within 6 months of purchase. For a fixed sum the manufacturer also provides an optional extended guarantee covering the goods against defects for up to 2 years after purchase. In both cases, the manufacturer is providing a service to the public (the guarantee) and is subject to the Act in relation to the provision of that service (but not in relation to the goods themselves).[87]

7.2.6.4. *Clubs*
The DDA does not outlaw discrimination by clubs. Genuine membership clubs do not provide services to the 'public' or a section thereof because access to them and any benefits they provide will be limited to members.[88]

Thus membership policies and other arrangements by clubs that discriminate against disabled people are not made unlawful by the DDA. This will change with the enactment of the Disability Discrimination Bill which contains provision outlawing discrimination by clubs (Clause 5) (see Chapter 13 below).

However, where the organization concerned, however described, does not truly regulate membership but in fact allows any member of the public access to its services and other benefits, it will fall within section 19 DDA. As described above (7.2.2), the House of Lords have concluded that where a club elects its members or adopts some other genuine process of selection it is not providing services to the public or a section of it. The same applies where a club, operating

---

[86] Paragraph 2.40.   [87] Paragraph 2.41.
[88] See *Dockers' Labour Club & Institute Limited v Race Relations Board*, *supra* note 22, discussed above in 7.2.2.

under reciprocal arrangements with another club, offers hospitality or temporary membership to members of the other club. Even in such circumstances, so long as *each* club exercised 'a rigorous choice in electing their members', there would be no discrimination within the meaning of section 19 DDA because the clubs would truly be operating within the private sphere.[89] The fact that an organization describes itself as a club does not mean it will necessarily fall outside section 19 DDA. It will be necessary for it genuinely to regulate admission and membership as described above if it is to fall outside section 19 DDA. The Goods, Facilities, Services and Premises Code of Practice gives the following example:

A health club in a hotel is open to the public. Club members pay an annual subscription and are provided with a membership card. Before using the club's fitness equipment, a member must undergo a fitness test. Although members have to satisfy certain requirements in order to use some of its facilities, compliance with a genuine selection procedure for membership is not a condition of using the club. The club is providing services to the public and is unlikely to be excluded from Part III of the Act.[90]

In addition, where a club provides particular services to members of the public it will fall within section 19 DDA for the purposes of those services. The Goods, Facilities, Services and Premises Code of Practice gives the following example:

A private golf club refuses to admit a disabled golfer to membership. This is not covered by the Act. However, if the golf club hires out its facilities for a wedding reception, the Act applies to this service. If the club allows non-members to use the course, a refusal to allow a disabled golfer to play is likely to be subject to the Act.[91]

7.2.7. Which Members of the Public are Protected?

Section 19 protects all disabled people (and, in the case of victimization, non-disabled people also[92]), both children and adults.

Usually the disabled person concerned will be acting as a customer or user of services in their own right. However, disabled people are equally protected when accessing services on behalf of another individual or organization.[93]

7.2.8. Unlawful Acts

As has been seen, section 19 DDA outlaws discrimination by:

• in refusing to provide, or deliberately not providing, to a disabled person any service that he provides, or is prepared to provide, to members of the public;

---

[89] The effect of the decision in the *Dockers' Labour Club* case has been limited by changes introduced by the RRA 1976. Discrimination by private members clubs is now expressly made unlawful under the RRA.

[90] Paragraph 2.39.   [91] Paragraph 2.38.   [92] Section 19(4) DDA.

[93] Goods, Facilities, Services and Premises Code of Practice, paragraph 2.16.

- in failing to comply with any duty imposed on him by section 21 in circumstances in which the effect of that failure is to make it impossible or unreasonably difficult for a disabled person to make use of any such service;
- in the standard of service which he provides to a disabled person or the manner in which he provides it to him; or
- in the terms on which he provides a service to a disabled person.

There is an overlap between each of the unlawful acts created. Discrimination by the provision of a service at a higher cost but without a comparable increase in standard may constitute discrimination in both the standard and terms on which the service is provided and may also, depending on the circumstances, constitute a breach of the duty to make adjustments.

Cases under section 19 DDA remain fairly rare. Such cases that have been successful at trial include:

- refusals to admit disabled people with assistance dogs into restaurants;[94]
- a refusal to serve drinks to a woman with learning difficulties and hearing and visual impairments and asking her to leave a pub shortly after arriving with a friend;[95]
- a refusal by a restaurant to take a booking from a wheelchair user (though wheelchair accessible);[96]
- a refusal to permit a disabled golfer to use a motorized golf cart on the turf (the golf club, though a private members' club, allowed non-members to use the course for a fee);[97]
- a refusal to accept a signature to a contract for supply of gas and electricity without a counter-signature from a neighbour from a disabled person who had a neurological condition that caused her to shake;[98]
- a breach of the duty to make adjustments by a failure to provide a suitably adapted taxi to transfer a wheelchair-using passenger between platforms at a railway station when the route between the platforms was such as to make it unreasonably difficult for wheelchair-using passengers to traverse (a footbridge or a difficult half-mile alternative route).[99]

---

[94] *Purves v Joydisc Ltd* [2003] SC 694/01; '50 Key Cases from the DRC' (October 2002) DRC, Case No 27.

[95] *Mary McKay v Bryn Thomas & Scottish and Newcastle plc* [2002] (Case No IG 100989). See DRC, 'Legal Bulletin' Issue 3, 13.

[96] *Caulfield v Sole Mio* (unreported) [2001] Case No A 579/01, Edinburgh Sheriff's Court, 2 December 2001 and *Sheldon v Taj Restaurant* [2001] Case No BF 103152.

[97] '50 Key Cases from the DRC' (October 2002) DRC, Case No 29.

[98] *Dexter v N Power*, Swindon County Court, 23 April 2001, Case No SN005348 (unreported), cited in Palmer, Gill, Monaghan, Moon, and Stacey, ed McColgan, *Discrimination Law Handbook* (LAG, 2002) 884.

[99] *Roads v Central Trains Ltd*, *supra* note 10.

The Goods, Facilities, Services and Premises Code of Practice gives the following, amongst other, examples:

A party of disabled children is on a visit to a zoo. Without giving any explanation, the manager refuses to allow the children to enter the zoo. This is a refusal of a service and is likely to be unlawful.

Bar staff in a pub pretend not to see a disabled person who is trying to be served at the bar. This is a non-provision of a service and is likely to be unlawful.

The manager of a fast food outlet tells a person with a severe facial disfigurement that he must sit at a table out of sight of other customers, despite other tables being free. This is likely to be against the law.

A person who has Usher's syndrome (and who, as a consequence, is deaf-blind) is booking a holiday. The travel agent asks her for a larger deposit than it requires from other customers. The travel agent believes, without good reason, that because of her disability she is more likely to cancel her holiday. This is likely to be against the law.[100]

As the Goods, Facilities, Services and Premises Code of Practice makes plain, service providers who have in place clear equality polices, backed up by proper training, are more likely to be able to comply with their duties under the DDA and prevent their employees from discriminating against disabled customers. They recommend that service providers take the following steps:

- establish a positive policy on the provision of services to ensure inclusion of disabled people, and communicating it to all staff;
- inform all staff dealing with the public that it is unlawful to discriminate against disabled people;
- train staff to understand the service provider's policy towards disabled people, their legal obligations, and the duty of reasonable adjustments;
- monitor the implementation and effectiveness of such a policy;
- provide disability awareness and disability etiquette training for all staff who have contact with the public;
- address acts of disability discrimination by staff as part of disciplinary rules and procedures;
- have a customer complaints procedure which is easy for disabled people to use;
- consult with disabled customers, disabled staff, and disability organizations;
- regularly review whether their services are accessible to disabled people;
- regularly review the effectiveness of reasonable adjustments made for disabled people in accordance with the DDA, and act on the findings of those reviews; and

---

[100] See paragraphs 3.17–3.22.

- provide regular training to staff which is relevant to the adjustments to be made.

As mentioned in previous chapters, the DDA does not outlaw more favourable treatment of disabled persons (and may require it). Accordingly, service providers who choose to make more favourable provision for its disabled customers will not be acting unlawfully. The Goods, Facilities, Services and Premises Code of Practice gives the following example:

A leisure park offers free entry to a communicator-guide accompanying a deaf-blind person. This allows the deaf-blind person to enjoy the park without having to pay two entrance fees. This is within the law.[101]

7.2.9. Territorial Extent

As described above at 7.2.1, section 19 DDA will not apply to goods, facilities, or services outside the United Kingdom. A provider of services for the purposes of section 19 must be a person concerned 'with the provision, in the United Kingdom, of services . . . '[102] Unlike the SDA[103] and RRA,[104] the DDA makes no specific provision regarding ships, and aeroplanes etc because transport is in any event excluded from the reach of section 19 DDA (see 7.2.6.1 above).

7.3. DISPOSAL AND MANAGEMENT OF PREMISES

The DDA outlaws discrimination by those who have the power to dispose of premised and those whose licence or consent is required for the disposal of premised and those who manage premises.

The meaning of 'discrimination' is described in Chapter 5 above, at 5.8. There is no duty to make reasonable adjustments in relation to the disposal and management of premises, as discussed above.

However, persons disposing of or managing premises may also be service providers (for example, estate agencies, accommodation bureaux, or management companies[105]) and in that capacity, be subject to the duty to make adjustments under section 21 DDA (see Chapter 5 above, at 5.7).

7.3.1. Meaning of 'Premises'

The term 'premises', for the purposes of the DDA, includes land of any description.[106] Thus commercial as well as domestic premises are covered.

---

[101] Paragraph 3.23.
[102] Section 19(2) DDA.
[103] Section 36(2), (3), and (5) SDA.
[104] Section 27(1)–(4) RRA.
[105] Goods, Facilities, Services and Premises Code of Practice, paragraph 9.6.
[106] Section 68(1) DDA.

7.3.2. Disposal of Premises

Section 22(1) DDA provides that:

It is unlawful for a person with power to dispose of any premises to discriminate against a disabled person—

(a) in the terms on which he offers to dispose of those premises to the disabled person;

(b) by refusing to dispose of those premises to the disabled person; or

(c) in his treatment of the disabled person in relation to any list of persons in need of premises of that description.

'Dispose' for these purposes includes granting a right to occupy the premises, and, in relation to premises comprised in, or (in Scotland) the subject of, a tenancy, includes (a) assigning the tenancy, and (b) subletting or parting with possession of the premises or any part of the premises.[107] A 'tenancy' for these purposes means a tenancy created:

• by a lease or sublease;
• by an agreement for a lease or sublease;
• by a tenancy agreement; or
• in pursuance of any enactment (for example a statutory tenancy).[108]

The meaning of 'dispose' is inclusively described and, having regard to this and the description which is provided, it can be taken to have a wide meaning. Any disposition of property, whether by a sale or the grant of a licence or tenancy, will be covered.

The mere hiring of premises or the booking of rooms in hotels or guest houses do not constitute 'disposal'. Such are the goods, facilities, and services provisions.

The unlawful acts provided for by Section 22(1) DDA are self-explanatory.[109] *Rose v Bouchet*[110] provides an illustration of disability discrimination in the housing context. In this case Mr Rose, who was blind, complained of discrimination under section 22 DDA when the landlord of the premises, Mr Bouchet, refused to let him a flat on the ground that there was no handrail in place alongside the steps leading to the flat and as such it would be dangerous for Mr Rose. Mr Rose had telephoned Mr Bouchet seeking accommodation and when he mentioned he was blind Mr Bouchet explained that work on the outside of the building still had to be completed and that he thought the steps would be dangerous for a blind person without an adequate handrail and refused to let the premises. On the facts of the case the court concluded that the discrimination, as

---

[107] Section 22(5) DDA. 'Disposal' is to be construed accordingly: *ibid.*   [108] *Ibid.*

[109] Illustrations of the circumstances in which treatment might be unlawful are provided for by the Goods, Facilities, Services and Premises Code of Practice at paragraphs 9.13–9.15.

[110] [1999] IRLR 463.

it plainly was being related to Mr Rose's disability, was justified.[111] This case is further discussed above at Chapter 5, at 5.8.

Section 22(1)(c) addresses discrimination in the treatment of disabled people in relation to a list of persons in need of premises. This would cover discrimination by local councils in the preparing of lists and prioritizing for council housing, as well as housing associations and agencies who create and maintain waiting lists for accommodation.

Where a person owns an estate or interest in premises and wholly occupies them, he is not covered by section 22(1) DDA and so any discrimination by him in the disposal of those premises is not made unlawful. However, if he uses the services of an estate agent or publishes an advertisement or causes an advertisement to be published, section 22(1) does apply and any discrimination is unlawful.[112] An 'estate agent' for these purposes is anyone carrying on a trade or profession providing services for the purpose of finding premises for people seeking to acquire them or assisting in the disposal of premises[113] (by letting, sale, or otherwise). Purely private sales and lettings of residential properties are not covered by the DDA. There is also a 'small premises' exemption which is addressed below (see 7.3.5).

7.3.3. Management of Premises

Section 22(3) DDA provides that:

It is unlawful for a person managing any premises to discriminate against a disabled person occupying those premises—
(a) in the way he permits the disabled person to make use of any benefits or facilities;
(b) by refusing or deliberately omitting to permit the disabled person to make use of any benefits or facilities; or
(c) by evicting the disabled person, or subjecting him to any other detriment.

A person 'managing' premises is not defined but will include property management agencies, accommodation bureaux, housekeepers, estate agents, rent collection services, and managing agents of commercial premises.[114]

7.3.3.1. *Benefits and facilities*
'Benefits' and 'facilities' are not defined but would include, for example, laundry facilities, access to a garden, and parking facilities.[115] The Goods, Facilities, Services and Premises Code of Practice gives the following example:[116]

A property management company manages and controls a residential block of flats on behalf of the landlord-owner. The block has a basement swimming pool and a communal garden for use by the tenants. A disabled tenant with a severe disfigurement is told by the

---

[111] *Ibid.* [112] Section 22(2) DDA. [113] Section 22(6) DDA.
[114] Goods, Facilities, Services and Premises Code of Practice, paragraph 9.24.
[115] *Ibid.* paragraph 9.25. [116] *Ibid.*

company that he can only use the swimming pool at restricted times because other tenants feel uncomfortable in his presence. This is likely to be unlawful.

7.3.3.2. *Eviction*

It is also unlawful for a person managing premises to discriminate against a disabled person occupying those premises by evicting him. The Goods, Facilities, Services and Premises Code of Practice gives the example 'A tenant of a house has recently been diagnosed with AIDS. His landlord gives him a week's notice to quit the house, although he is not in arrears of rent or otherwise in breach of his tenancy'.[117] This is an example described by Lord Justice Brooke as 'inept'.[118] This is because, though the Code makes passing reference to it, it does not pay proper regard to the significant statutory regulation of residential tenancies and evictions. A discussion of those statutory schemes is outside the scope of this work but should always be considered in an eviction case. In short summary, in England and Wales,[119] where a tenancy of residential property protected by the Rent Act 1977 comes to an end, a new statutory tenancy may arise in favour of the tenant or certain family members (where the tenant has died) and upon the expiration of an assured tenancy a statutory periodic tenancy arises in favour of the tenant or family members (where the tenant has died) by virtue of the Housing Act 1988. Where a tenancy of business premises reaches its contractual term date, the term continues by virtue of statute until a prescribed notice is served by the landlord on the tenant. Even where the landlord is entitled to possession, in that the lease has been determined in accordance with its contractual terms and the tenant does not enjoy any statutory protection, the landlord may still need the court's assistance in order to assert his right to possession.[120] An eviction from residential premises without an order of the court will always be unlawful and will give rise to a claim in damages under the Housing Act 1988[121] and may amount to a criminal offence.[122] The circumstances in which a possession order will be granted are limited. The example given by the Goods, Facilities, Services and Premises Code of Practice is therefore not very helpful.

The Code of Practice advises that section 22(3)(c) DDA does not 'prevent the eviction of a disabled tenant where the law allows it, for example, where he or she is in arrears of rent or has breached other terms of the tenancy, and where the reason for the eviction is not related to disability'. Of course, an eviction not related to disability will not be unlawful under the DDA because it will not be discriminatory within the meaning of the DDA. Thus the granting of a posses-

---

[117] *Ibid.* paragraph 9.26.

[118] *Council of the City of Manchester v (1) Romano (2) Samari, supra* note 49, paragraph 55.

[119] And see, for example, Housing (Scotland) Act 2001 for the position in relation to residential public sector tenancies in Scotland which might be terminated in limited circumstances.

[120] See *Halsbury's Law of England, 'Landlord and Tenant'* paragraph 500.

[121] Section 27 Housing Act 1998.   [122] Sections 1 and 2, Protection From Eviction Act 1977.

sion order for anti-social behaviour unrelated to disability will not engage section 22 DDA at all.[123] This area, however, has proved to be controversial. The case of *Council of the City of Manchester v (1) Romano (2) Samari*[124] is discussed in Chapter 5 above, at 5.8, and reference to that discussion should be made. In that case, Lord Justice Brooke expressed some concern about the impact of the DDA, and the housing provisions in particular (though not exclusively), and its relationship with other law. Lord Justice Brooke noted that:

Our attention was drawn to the fact that this judgment is of particular contemporary importance because by virtue of section 218A of the Housing Act 1996 (as inserted by section 12 of the Anti-Social Behaviour Act 2003) every local housing authority, housing action trust and registered social landlord must with effect from 1 July 2004 prepare a policy in relation to anti-social behaviour and also procedures for dealing with occurrences of anti-social behaviour, and they must also no later than 31 December 2003 publish a statement of their policy and procedures (see section 218A(1)–(3)). In preparing their policy and procedures such landlords must have regard to guidance issued in accordance with section 218(7). In the case of a local housing authority the Secretary of State is to issue the requisite guidance . . . [There are] difficulties in the statutory scheme contained in sections 22 and 24 of the 1995 Act. [D]ifficulties might arise from the fact that if a landlord obtains an injunction restraining a mentally disabled tenant from anti-social behaviour it will not be able to enforce that injunction by committal proceedings unless it can establish to the criminal standard of proof that it held an opinion on one of the matters specified in section 24(3) of the Act and that it was reasonable in all the circumstances of the case for it to hold that opinion. Simply by way of example, if complaints by a former council tenant of robust temperament who has bought his property under the 'right to buy' scheme have induced the local housing authority to seek and obtain an injunction against his neighbour in the council house next door restraining his anti-social behaviour, the council as the person managing the tenant's premises may not subsequently embark on enforcement proceedings unless it can establish statutory justification to the requisite standard of proof. In other words the owner-occupier whose health or safety is not endangered by his next door neighbour's breach of a court order will have to watch the value of his property deteriorating because the injunction cannot in these circumstances be enforced by the neighbour's landlord through the courts.

In fact, the court's concerns are probably largely groundless. In a situation such as that described by Lord Justice Brooke, the neighbour should bring the injunction proceedings. As he would not be the 'manager' of the disabled person's premises he would not fall within section 22(3) DDA and accordingly, even if the anti-social behaviour was related to disability, he would not be committing any unlawful act under the DDA. Secondly, the DDA would only bite at all if the tenant were 'disabled' within the meaning of section 1 DDA and certain impairments that might be characterized by anti-social behaviour are excluded

---

[123] *Council of the City of Manchester v (1) Romano (2) Samari, supra* note 49.
[124] *Supra* note 49.

(addiction to alcohol or any other substance;[125] a tendency to set fires; a tendency to steal; a tendency to physical or sexual abuse of other persons; exhibitionism; voyeurism[126]). Thirdly, for the most part a landlord will be able to rely on section 59 DDA (which was not referred to in *Council of the City of Manchester v (1) Romano (2) Samari*) in taking any action against an anti-social disabled tenant even if the anti-social behaviour is related to his disability. Section 59 is addressed briefly below and in more detail in Chapter 10 below but in short summary it ensures that the DDA does not take priority over other statutory law. A landlord who is acting pursuant to any statutory duties to address anti-social behaviour is likely to be able to rely on section 59 DDA. Fourthly, it is inherently unlikely that no evidence of an impact on the 'health' of a person could be found in a case of significant anti-social behaviour, such as to justify any action against a disabled tenant even if disability related.[127]

Further still, as remarked upon by Lord Justice Brooke, where discrimination may occur then there is a real duty to take extra care:

This judgment shows that landlords whose tenants hold secure or assured tenancies must consider the position carefully before they decide to serve a notice seeking possession or to embark on possession proceedings against a tenant who is or might be mentally impaired. This is likely to compel a local housing authority to liaise more closely with the local social services authority at an earlier stage of their consideration of a problem that might lead to an eviction than appears to be the case with many authorities, to judge from some of the papers the DRC placed before the court. To remove someone from their home may be a traumatic thing to do in the case of many who are not mentally impaired. It may be even more traumatic for the mentally impaired.[128]

This is, of course, sound guidance.

7.3.3.3. *Detriment and harassment*

'Detriment' is not defined in the DDA. However, it appears in the employment provisions of the DDA and in the unlawful acts created by the SDA and the RRA and has been the subject of a good deal of case-law, mainly in the employment field. The guidance given in Chapter 6 above, at 6.2.7.3 on the meaning of 'detriment' is therefore relevant.

In short summary, 'detriment' has a very wide meaning indeed. The test for determining whether particular treatment constitutes a 'detriment' has become largely subjective and any less favourable treatment is likely to satisfy the test. In *Council of the City of Manchester v (1) Romano (2) Samari*[129] the Court of Appeal observed that: 'To send a warning letter to a tenant about his conduct is

---

[125] The Disability Discrimination (Meaning of Disability) Regulations 1996, SI 1996/1455, Regulation 3(1). See Chapter 4, at 4.6.

[126] The Disability Discrimination (Meaning of Disability) Regulations 1996, SI 1996/1455, Regulation 4(1). See Chapter 4, at 4.6.

[127] Particularly given the wide meaning afforded to 'health': see Chapter 5 above, paragraph 5.8. See too *Council of the City of Manchester v (1) Romano (2) Samari, supra* note 49, paragraph 118.

[128] *Ibid.* paragraph 117.   [129] *Supra* note 49.

not to subject him to a detriment within the meaning of the Act'.[130] No author-ity was cited for this proposition and it does seem inconsistent with the broad meaning given to the expression 'detriment' in other fields. It is highly likely that a warning letter to an employee about conduct at work would be held to be a detriment.[131]

Of particular importance in the context of housing is harassment, which will constitute a detriment. Harassment covers a wide range of conduct and this is discussed in Chapter 5 above, at 5.2.4. No special provision is made in the DDA addressing harassment in the housing context (which might be contrasted with the position in the employment and related fields[132]) but, unlike harassment in the employment and related fields, harassment is not excluded from the detri-ment provision.[133] Accordingly, the 'detriment' provision must be relied upon in any disability-related harassment claim in the housing sphere. The meaning of harassment for the purposes of the 'detriment' provisions in the DDA are addressed above, in Chapter 5, at 5.2.4, and Chapter 6, at 6.2.7.3.

Because of the impact of recent case-law, for any harassment to be actionable under section 22(3) DDA, the landlord or the person managing the disabled per-son's premises, or an employee or agent[134] of such person, must himself do the acts complained of. A landlord or the person managing the premises will not otherwise be liable for the harassment. In particular, a landlord will not be liable for harassment done by other tenants, even where disability-related, and even where the harassers are tenants of the same landlord. In such circumstances, it is only where the landlord himself (or other person managing the premises, employee or agent) fails to take action to address the harassment and that fail-ure is for disability-related reasons will any liability arise.[135] The Goods, Facilities, Services and Premises Code of Practice states:

It is unlawful for a person managing any premises to discriminate against a disabled per-son occupying those premises by subjecting him or her to any other detriment. This includes subjecting disabled people to harassment (or failing to prevent them being sub-jected to harassment by others), for example, physical attack, damage to their property, verbal abuse and other similar behaviour, which deprives them of the peaceful enjoyment of their premises.

In the light of recent case-law,[136] this passage, insofar as it suggests that liability will arise for a failure to prevent the harassment, probably overstates the law unless the failure to prevent the harassment is to be read as requiring that it itself is for disability-related reasons.

---

[130] *Ibid.* paragraph 118.
[131] See Chapter 6 above, at 6.2.7.3.
[132] See Chapter 5 above, at 5.2.4.
[133] *Ibid.* and Chapter 6 above, at 6.2.7.3.
[134] Section 58 DDA, see Chapter 10.
[135] *MacDonald v Advocate General for Scotland* [2003] UKHL 34, [2003] ICR 937; *Pearce v Governing Body of Mayfield Secondary School* [2001] EWCA Civ 1347, [2002] ICR 198, [2003] IRLR 512 overruling *Burton and Rhule v De Vere Hotels Ltd* [1997] ICR 1, [1996] IRLR 596.
[136] *Ibid.*

The Goods, Facilities, Services and Premises Code of Practice gives the following example:

A block of flats is managed by a management committee of tenants. The members of the committee harass a disabled tenant who has sickle cell disease and who is mobility impaired. They believe that her use of a wheelchair causes above average wear and tear to the doors and carpets in communal areas, and that this will lead to an increase in their annual maintenance charges. This is likely to be unlawful.[137]

In this instance, because the harassers are themselves the persons managing the premises, their harassment would be actionable under section 22(3) DDA.

7.3.4. Licence or Consent

Section 22(4) DDA provides that:

It is unlawful for any person whose licence or consent is required for the disposal of any premises comprised in, or (in Scotland) the subject of, a tenancy to discriminate against a disabled person by withholding his licence or consent for the disposal of the premises to the disabled person.

This provision applies to tenancies created before as well as after the passing of the DDA.[138] The Goods, Facilities, Services and Premises Code of Practice gives the following example:

A tenant of a house occupies the premises under a tenancy agreement with a right to sub-let the house with the prior consent of the landlord-owner. The tenant is being posted to work abroad for a year. He wishes to sub-let the house to a disabled person who has partial paralysis as a result of polio. The owner of the house refuses to consent to the sub-letting. She wrongly assumes that the disabled person will be unable to keep up rent payments and may cause damage to the fabric of the house. This is likely to be unlawful.[139]

7.3.5. Small Premises and Other Exceptions

Section 23 DDA provides for an exception from the unlawful acts created by section 22 in the case of small premises. Premises fall outside section 22 DDA where:

• the relevant occupier (namely the person with power to dispose of the premises, or a near relative[140] of his or the person whose licence or consent is required for the disposal of the premises, or a near relative of his, as the case may be) resides, and intends to continue to reside, on the premises;

• the relevant occupier shares accommodation on the premises with persons who reside on the premises and are not members of his household;

---

[137] Paragraph 9.27.   [138] Section 22(5) DDA.   [139] Paragraph 9.29.
[140] 'Near relative' means a spouse, partner, parent, child, grandparent, grandchild, or brother or sister (whether of full or half blood or by affinity); and 'partner' means the other member of a

- the shared accommodation is not storage accommodation or a means of access; and
- the premises are small premises.[141]

Premises are 'small premises' if:

- only the relevant occupier and members of his household reside in the accommodation occupied by him;
- the premises comprise, in addition to the accommodation occupied by the relevant occupier, residential accommodation for at least one other household;
- the residential accommodation for each other household is let, or available for letting, on a separate tenancy or similar agreement;
- there are not normally more than two such other households.

Alternatively,

- there is not normally residential accommodation on the premises for more than six persons in addition to the relevant occupier and any members of his household.[142]

The Goods, Facilities, Services and Premises Code of Practice gives the following examples:

The basement and ground floor of a large Victorian house have been converted into two self-contained flats which are let to tenants under separate tenancies by the house owner. The house owner and her family continue to reside exclusively in the remaining floors of the house. The house satisfies the Act's definition of small premises [but the house may still not be exempt from the Act: see 9.22 below].

The owner of a four bedroomed detached house has converted two bedrooms into bed-sit accommodation for two people. He continues to live in the house with his family. The house satisfies the Act's definition of small premises.[143]

The converted Victorian house in the example in paragraph 9.20 above has a communal entrance door and hallway giving private access to the two flats and the remainder of the house. Although the house satisfies the definition of small premises, the small dwellings exemption does not apply. This is because the owner of the house resides on the premises but does not share any accommodation (other than means of access) with the tenants of the two self-contained flats.[144]

---

couple consisting of a man and a woman who are not married to each other but are living together as husband and wife: section 23(6) and (7) DDA. As for 'partners' query whether this meaning will have to give way to a Convention-compliant meaning, which includes same-sex partners" *S/S for Work and Pensions v M and Another* [2004] EWCA Civ 1343.

[141] Section 23(2) DDA. [142] Section 23(4) and (5) DDA.
[143] Paragraphs 9.20 and 9.21. [144] Paragraph 9.22.

Exceptions are provided for under Part III, which have been addressed under the relevant provisions. Importantly, section 59 also provides a general exemption where any act done has been done in pursuance of any enactment or instrument made by a Minister of the Crown under any enactment or to comply with any condition or requirement imposed by a Minister of the Crown by virtue of any enactment. This is addressed in Chapter 10 but in short summary its effect is that the DDA is not prioritized over other legislative measures.

7.3.6. Validity and Revision of Agreements

Section 26 DDA makes certain agreements void and provides for their modification by the courts.

Any term in a contract for the provision of goods, facilities or services or in any other agreement is void so far as it purports to:

- require someone to do something which would be unlawful under Part III DDA (services and premises);
- exclude or limit the operation of Part III; or
- prevent someone making a claim under Part III.

An agreement to settle a claim under Part III DDA is not affected by these provisions.

A party affected by such an agreement may make an application to a County Court (or Sheriff Court in Scotland) which may make an order modifying the agreement. In determining what if any modifications to order, the court will consider what is 'just' taking into account the provisions rendering void certain terms of any agreement, as described above.[145]

Employment services are not affected by these provisions. Instead, the question whether an agreement in relation to employment services is valid is addressed by the employment provisions which govern such contracts.[146]

7.3.7. Territorial Extent

Section 22 applies only to premises situated in the United Kingdom.[147]

7.4. DISCRIMINATION AFTER TERMINATION OF A RELEVANT RELATIONSHIP

Unlike discrimination occurring in the employment and related fields (see Chapter 6 above, at 6.14), no express provision is made for discrimination

---

[145] Section 26(3) DDA. Notice will usually be required: Section 26(5) DDA.
[146] See Chapter 6, at 6.13 and see Schedule 3A, paragraph 11.
[147] Section 22(8) DDA.

occurring after termination of any relevant formal relationship in the context of the provision of goods, facilities, and services and in the context of premises. This is unlikely to be problematic in the context of the unlawful acts created in relation to provision of goods, facilities, and services because the existence of a particular relationship is not a necessary precondition to their commission. As has been seen above, even the duty to make adjustments is anticipatory in nature (see 5.7).

However, the 'premises' provisions outlaw discrimination, against prospective and existing occupiers (see above, 7.3). They do not on their face cover discrimination occurring after those relationships have terminated. The potential for discrimination occurring after such relationships have ended is perhaps much less than that which might arise after termination of an employment relationship (see Chapter 6, at 6.14). However, such situations may arise, for example where an ex-tenant is entitled to remain a member of a management committee of a housing association in whose property he has resided; or to be consulted by such in respect of future developments; or to use certain communal services; or to be afforded the opportunity to make representations for fresh housing after an eviction, and so on. In such circumstances, regard should be had to the decision of the House of Lords in *Rhys-Harper v Relaxion Group plc* concerning the employment provisions of the SDA, RRA, and DDA (before the recent amendments)[148] in which it was held that they should be read as protecting against discrimination occurring after formal termination of the employment relationship so long as there was a 'substantive connection' between the discriminatory conduct and the employment relationship.[149] The arguments adopted in that case can be equally adopted to support a construction of section 22 which protects disabled persons who have occupied, but no longer occupy, the premises concerned.

---

[148] Discussed in Chapter 6, at 6.14.

[149] And five other cases [2003] UKHL 33, [2003] ICR 867, [2003] IRLR 484 at paragraph 215, *per* Lord Rodger. Their other Lordships adopted slightly different formulations but in essence the test was such as to ensure that there was a sufficiently close nexus between the employment relationship and the discrimination complained of, however long afterwards that occurred.

8

EDUCATION

8.1. INTRODUCTION

As originally enacted, the DDA did not outlaw discrimination against disabled pupils and students. In addition, the DDA excluded most 'education' from the goods, facilities, and services provisions.[1] No individual rights were conferred upon disabled pupils and students. Instead the DDA in its original form introduced reporting obligations on the governing bodies of schools, and further and higher education institutions, and local education authorities to publish information annually regarding their admission arrangements for disabled pupils and students and in respect of adult education and their arrangements for the provision of facilities for disabled pupils and students and the like.[2] With the enactment of the Special Educational Needs and Disability Act 2001 ('SENDA'[3]) the DDA was amended so as to outlaw discrimination in the field of education. Part IV, Chapter 1 DDA now regulates discrimination in relation to schools, and education authorities in relation to schooling, and Part IV Chapter 2 DDA regulates discrimination in relation to further and higher education.

---

[1] Section 19(5)(a) and (6) DDA.   [2] Sections 29–31 DDA, as unamended.

[3] For extent, see 8.9 below. SENDA does not, in the main, apply to Northern Ireland but see, Draft Special Educational Needs and Disability (Northern Ireland) Order for proposed similar provision in Northern Ireland. SENDA's provenance is described in Chapter 2 above, at 2.2.

Importantly, education is an area that is highly regulated outside the DDA and in all cases close attention must be paid in particular to the special educational needs framework that addresses the specific needs of children, who have particular educational requirements. The special educational needs framework is complex and is provided for in statute, a statutory Code of Practice, and a number of Statutory Instruments and DfES Circulars and Guidance. In England and Wales the Education Act 1996 is the main legislative source of the provision made in relation to special educational needs. It has been amended by SENDA.

The Education Act 1996 gives the Secretary of State for Education the power to issue and revise a Code of Practice giving practical advice and guidance to all those who have a responsibility to discharge legal functions regarding special educational needs.[4] The new 'Special Educational Needs Code of Practice' became effective in England on 1 January 2002[5] and in Wales on 1 April 2002.[6] This addresses certain of the amendments made by SENDA and is referred to as the Special Educational Needs Code of Practice ('the SEN Code of Practice').[7] The SEN Code of Practice gives detailed guidance which is informed by certain general principles and the guidance must 'be read with them clearly in mind'.[8] The general principles are as follows:

- a child with special educational needs should have their needs met;
- the special educational needs of children will normally be met in mainstream schools or settings;
- the views of the child should be sought and taken into account;
- parents have a vital role to play in supporting their child's education;
- children with special educational needs should be offered full access to a broad, balanced, and relevant education, including an appropriate curriculum for the foundation stage and national curriculum.

The Code gives detailed guidance on the identification and assessment of special educational needs.[9] The SEN Code of Practice makes clear that most special educational needs will be met effectively within mainstream settings and without the need for a statutory assessment. However, in some cases a statutory assessment will be required and the obligation for securing the same is on the local education authority. Where a local education authority is of the opinion that a child

---

[4] Section 313.

[5] The Special Educational Needs Code of Practice (Appointed Day) (England) Order 2001, SI 2001/3943.

[6] The Special Educational Needs Code of Practice (Appointed Day) (Wales) Order 2002, SI 2002/156.

[7] DfES 581/2001, Foreword, paragraphs 7 and 13. And see 'Disability Discrimination Act 1995 Part IV, Code of Practice for Schools', Disability Rights Commission, COPSH July 2002, referred to below.

[8] SEN Code of Practice, paragraph 1.5.   [9] Chapter 4.

for whom they are responsible has special educational needs and it is necessary for the authority to determine the special educational provision for which any learning difficulty he may have calls for, it must serve a notice on the child's parents informing them that they are considering whether to make an assessment and the procedure to be followed.[10] Where it remains of the opinion, having served the notice and taken into account any representations made, that the child has special educational needs and it is necessary for the authority to determine the special educational provision for which any learning difficulty he may have calls for, it must make an assessment of his educational needs.[11] If in the light of such assessment it is necessary for the local education authority to determine the special educational provision which any learning difficulty he may have calls for, the authority must make and maintain a 'statement of his special educational needs'.[12] As the SEN Code of Practice makes clear, where a school requests such a statutory assessment, the child will have demonstrated significant cause for concern.[13] A statutory assessment should only be undertaken if the local education authority believes that the child probably has special educational needs and that it needs or probably needs to determine the child's special educational provision itself by making a statement.[14] Further, a statutory assessment itself will not always lead to a statement.[15] Where a statement is made it will give details of the authority's assessment of the child's special educational needs and specify the special educational provision to be made for the purpose of meeting those needs, including specifying the type of school which the local education authority considers would be appropriate.[16]

A child has 'special educational needs' for the purposes of the special education needs framework if he has 'a learning difficulty which calls for special educational provision to be made for him'.[17] A child[18] has a 'learning difficulty' if he has a significantly greater difficulty in learning than the majority of children of his age, or he has a disability which either prevents or hinders him from making use of educational facilities of a kind generally provided for children of his age in schools, or he is under compulsory school age and would have such difficulties if provision were not made.[19]

Similar provision is made in Scotland through the Education (Scotland) Act 1980; the Standards in Scotland's Schools etc. Act 2000;[20] guidance from the Scottish Office Education and Industry Department, *Circular 4/96, Children and*

---

[10] Section 323, Education Act 1996.   [11] Section 323(1)–(3) Education Act 1996.

[12] Section 324, Education Act 1996.   [13] Paragraphs 5.62 and paragraph 6.71.

[14] SEN Code, paragraph 7.4.   [15] *Ibid.* paragraph 7.6.

[16] Education Act 1996, section 324.   [17] Education Act 1996, section 312.

[18] A child for the purposes of the Special Educational Needs provisions includes any person who has not attained the age of 19 and is a registered pupil at a school: Education Act 1996, section 312(5).

[19] Education Act 1996, section 312(2).

[20] See too the Education (Additional Support for Learning) (Scotland) Act 2004, not in force at the time of writing.

Young Persons with Special Educational Needs: Assessment and Recording (SOEID, 1996),[21] and guidance in the *Manual of Good Practice* (SOEID, 1998).[22]

Provision is made by the Education Act 1996 (in respect of England and Wales) permitting parents of a child to appeal to the Special Educational Needs and Disability Tribunal in relation to a decision not to make a statement or in relation to the contents of such a statement.[23]

It can be seen, therefore, that there is a close relationship between the DDA and the provision made by the special educational needs framework. However, the fact that a child has a 'special educational need' for the purposes of the special educational needs framework does not mean that they will be 'disabled' for the purposes of the DDA. A child may have special educational needs and no disability, or a disability and no special educational needs. Nevertheless where a child presents with a disability which does impact on its educational needs, regard must always be had to the special educational needs framework.

As can be seen, there is significant regulation applying to children's special needs outside of the DDA.

As stated above, Part IV (Chapters 1 and 2) DDA now regulates discrimination[24] in the field of education. This arises in consequence of the amendments made by SENDA which significantly increased the scope of the DDA. Part IV DDA now outlaws 'discrimination'[25] by:

- bodies responsible for schools, in respect of disabled prospective pupils and existing pupils;[26]

- local education authorities in England and Wales (and education authorities in Scotland), in respect of prospective and existing disabled pupils in respect of certain of their functions;[27]

- responsible bodies for educational institutions in the further and higher education spheres, in respect of prospective and existing disabled students;[28]

- certain providers of statutory youth and community services, including adult education, in respect of prospective and existing disabled students.[29]

In addition, the DDA imposes obligations on local education authorities to prepare 'accessibility strategies and plans'; these are addressed below at 8.3.

'Discrimination' for the purposes of the various unlawful acts created by Part IV DDA is separately defined according to the unlawful act concerned and its meaning is fully addressed in Chapter 5 above, at 5.9.

---

[21] Available at http://www.scotland.gov.uk/library3/education/csen-00.asp.
[22] Though there are differences that should be noted.
[23] Education Act 1996, sections 325, 326, 333, and 336ZA.
[24] As defined in Chapter 5 above, at 5.9.   [25] *Ibid.*
[26] Section 28A(1) DDA.   [27] Section 28F DDA.
[28] Section 28R DDA.   [29] Section 28U read with Schedule 4C DDA.

Two relevant Codes of Practice have been prepared by the DRC and have received parliamentary approval pursuant to the negative resolution procedure.[30] These are:

- 'Disability Discrimination Act 1995 Part IV, Code of Practice for Schools' ('Schools Code of Practice');[31] and

- 'Disability Discrimination Act 1995 Part IV, Code of Practice for Providers of Post 16 Education and Related Services' ('Post 16 Code of Practice').[32]

Though the Codes are not binding in law and do not impose any legal obligations, so that a breach of any provision will not give rise to any legal liability by itself,[33] their contents are very important indeed and will be taken into account by any court or tribunal determining any relevant matter under the DDA.[34]

Proceedings in respect of the unlawful acts created by Part IV must be commenced in the Special Educational Needs and Disability Tribunal[35] or in the County Court or Sheriff Court depending on the unlawful act concerned. Enforcement and remedies are dealt with in Chapter 11 below.

Cases brought under the education provisions of the DDA remain few. As the DRC describes it: 'The period around the advent of the new provisions on education in Part IV of the DDA was one of frenzied anticipation for disabled students, parents of disabled children and education and discrimination law practitioners'.[36] In fact, however, only one claim was lodged with the Special Educational Needs and Disability Tribunal in September 2002, on the coming into force of Part IV DDA. A small trickle followed. By September 2003 only seventy-eight claims had been registered with the Special Educational Needs and Disability Tribunal.[37] The first case reached the High Court, on appeal from the Special Educational Needs and Disability Tribunal, in December 2003.[38] There have been others, since but very few. In addition, cases before the Special Educational Needs and Disability Tribunal are, as a general rule, held in private and so the real impact of SENDA is difficult to judge.[39] However, examples of cases falling within the schools provisions of the DDA include:

---

[30] Section 53A DDA.

[31] Disability Rights Commission, COPSH July 2002. The Code came into force on 1 September 2002: Disability Discrimination Codes of Practice (Education) (Appointed Day) Order 2002, SI 2002/2216.

[32] Disability Rights Commission, COPP 16 July 2002. The Code came into force on 1 September 2002: Disability Discrimination Codes of Practice (Education) (Appointed Day) Order 2002, SI 2002/2216.

[33] Section 53A(8) DDA.   [34] Section 53A(8A), section 28C(4), and section 28T(2) DDA.

[35] Which has jurisdiction only in respect of complaints in England and Wales.

[36] 'Legal Bulletin' (April 2004) DRC, Issue 5, 18.

[37] *Ibid.*

[38] *McAuley Catholic High School v (1) CC (2) PC and Special Educational Needs and Disability Tribunal* [2003] EWHC 304 (Admin), [2004] 2 All ER 436.

[39] Special Educational Needs Tribunal Regulations 2001, SI 2001/600, Regulation 30, which provides that hearings shall be in private save where both the parent and the authority request that the hearing be in public or the President or the Tribunal at a hearing orders that the hearing should be in public.

- a failure to comply with the duty to make adjustments by providing a pupil with autistic spectrum disorder with the necessary personal guidance and support within the context of the school's pastoral system;[40]
- a fixed-term exclusion for a reason relating to disability;[41]
- a failure to place a disabled child in a work placement of her choice because of her visual impairment and an absence of medical information relating to it.[42]

The number of claims in the post-16 sector have probably been fewer. The DRC estimates that 'a generous estimate' would be less than twenty in the first year. By April 2004 no cases had reached trial or been reported.[43] However, it does appear that numerous settlements have been negotiated by DRC case workers and others resulting in agreed payments of compensation and agreements to review policies.[44] Thus, though there has been little by way of fully contested litigation, there have been significant developments in relation to negotiated settlements which is, of course, to be welcomed.

8.2. SCHOOLS

Section 28A DDA regulates discrimination by schools against disabled pupils and prospective pupils. Section 28A provides that:

(1) It is unlawful for the body responsible for a school to discriminate against a disabled person—

    (a) in the arrangements it makes for determining admission to the school as a pupil;

    (b) in the terms on which it offers to admit him to the school as a pupil; or

    (c) by refusing or deliberately omitting to accept an application for his admission to the school as a pupil.

(2) It is unlawful for the body responsible for a school to discriminate against a disabled pupil in the education or associated services provided for, or offered to, pupils at the school by that body

. . .

(4) It is unlawful for the body responsible for a school to discriminate against a disabled pupil by excluding him from the school, whether permanently or temporarily.

The meaning of 'discrimination' for the purposes of section 28A DDA is described in Chapter 5 above, at 5.9.

---

[40] *McAuley Catholic High School v (a) CC (2) PC and (3) Special Educational Needs and Disability Tribunal, supra* note 38.

[41] *Ibid.* though on the facts of the case that aspect of the claim was not successful, see paragraphs 47–9.

[42] *R (on the application of D) v Governing Body of Plymouth High School for Girls* [2004] EWHC 1923.

[43] 'Legal Bulletin' (April 2004) DRC, Issue 5, 20.   [44] *Ibid.*

8.2.1. Meanings of 'Pupil' and 'Responsible Body'

A 'pupil' and 'body responsible for a school' are defined by the DDA.
  A 'pupil':

- in relation to England and Wales, has the meaning given in section 3(1) of the Education Act 1996, namely a person for whom education is being provided at a school other than a person who has attained the age of 19 for whom further education is being provided or a person for whom part-time education suitable to the requirements of persons of any age over compulsory school age is being provided;
- in relation to Scotland, has the meaning given in section 135(1) of the Education (Scotland) Act 1980, namely a person for whom education is required to be provided.[45]

A 'disabled pupil' is a pupil who is a disabled person within the meaning of the DDA.[46]

A 'responsible body' for a school is determined by reference to Schedule 4A DDA. Schedule 4A provides that save in respect of independent schools and special schools not maintained by a local authority, in which case the proprietor is the responsible body, the local education authority or governing body will be the responsible body according to which has the function in question. Where the school is a pupil referral unit or a maintained nursery school it will always be the local education authority. As to Scotland, the education authority will be the responsible body in the case of a school managed by an education authority; the proprietor in the case of an independent school; the Board of Management in the case of a self-governing school; and the managers of the school where the school is one in respect of which the managers are for the time being receiving grants under section 73(c) or (d) of the Education (Scotland) Act 1980.[47]

Accordingly, proceedings in respect of discrimination arising in a school should usually be made against the local education authority in the case of a State school and against the proprietor in the case of an independent school, but care must be taken in each case to ensure that proceedings have been brought against the correct person and this will depend upon the type of school involved and, where relevant, the function involved.

8.2.2. Meaning of 'School'

'School' is defined by section 28Q(4) and (5) for the purposes of section 28A DDA. In short summary, education provided at all schools in England, Wales,

---

[45] Section 28Q(3) DDA. [46] Section 28Q(2) DDA.
[47] 'Local Education Authority'; 'Proprietor'; 'Board of Management'; 'Education Authority'; and 'Managers' are all defined by Schedule 4A DDA.

and Scotland is covered by section 28A DDA. This includes independent and publicly funded schools, mainstream and special schools. It includes primary and secondary schools, non-maintained special schools, and pupil referral units.[48]All local education authority and education authority maintained nursery schools, nursery classes, nursery provision at independent schools, and grant aided schools are also covered by section 28A DDA.[49] As the Schools Code of Practice observes, there are many private, voluntary, and statutory providers of nursery education that are not constituted as schools. Following the amendments made to the goods, facilities and services provisions of the DDA,[50] education provided by these bodies is covered by the unlawful acts created under Part III DDA.[51]

8.2.3. Prospective Pupils

As can be seen from the above[52] the DDA outlaws discrimination by schools[53] in relation to the admission of pupils.

The unlawful acts in relation to admissions are very widely drafted.[54] The Schools Code of Practice does not give any specific guidance in relation to the scope of these unlawful acts but they are likely to be given wide reach. The terms used are very similar to those used in the context of the employment provisions.[55] The discussion in relation to the same is likely to be instructive therefore, though plainly in a very different context. Regard must be had to the fact that the application of selection criteria based on 'ability' is generally not permissible in maintained schools.[56] Guidance has been issued by the DfES in relation to admissions.[57]

8.2.4. 'Education and Associated Services'

As can be seen above it is unlawful for a school to discriminate against a disabled pupil in education or the associated services provided for, or offered to, pupils at the school.[58]

---

[48] Schools Code of Practice, paragraph 4.11.　　[49] *Ibid.* paragraph 4.12.
[50] Section 19 DDA.　　[51] See Chapter 7 above, at 7.2.6.2.
[52] Section 28A DDA.
[53] For convenience the responsible body will be described as the school but care should always be taken to ensure that the correct responsible body is identified where proceedings are to be issued.
[54] Section 28A(1)(a)–(c) DDA.
[55] Section 4(1) DDA, see Chapter 6 above, at 6.2.6.
[56] Subject to exceptions: School Standards and Framework Act 1998, section 99(2). See Chapter 5 above, at 5.9.1.4.1.
[57] Schools Admissions Code (2003) and School Admissions Welsh Office Code of Practice (April 1999), see Chapter 5 above, at 5.9.1.4.1.
[58] Section 28A(2) DDA.

'Education and associated services' are not defined by the DDA. However, the Schools Code of Practice advises that the expressions cover 'all aspects of school life'.[59] The Schools Code of Practice gives a list which it says 'exemplifies the range of activities that may be covered' by the expression.[60] The list comprises:

- preparation for entry to the school;
- the curriculum;
- teaching and learning;
- classroom organization;
- timetabling;
- grouping of pupils;
- homework;
- access to school facilities;
- activities to supplement the curriculum, for example a drama group visiting the school;
- school sports;
- school policies;
- breaks and lunch times;
- the serving of school meals;
- interaction with peers;
- assessment and exam arrangements;
- school discipline and sanctions;
- exclusion procedures;
- school clubs and activities;
- school trips;
- the school's arrangements for working with other agencies;
- preparation of pupils for the next stage of education.[61]

As the Schools Code of Practice makes clear, this list is not exhaustive.[62]

In addition, where the school provides services which are available to the public, for example an open day, a car boot sale arranged by the Parent Teacher

---

[59] Schools Code of Practice, paragraph 4.23. [60] *Ibid.*

[61] Schools Code of Practice, paragraph 4.23. Cf the scope of the unlawful acts under section 19 DDA (Chapter 7 above, at 7.2.6.2). Activity which falls within the 'schools' provision will not also fall within section 19 (*ibid.*). Given that different enforcement provisions apply (see Chapter 11 below) great care must be taken when deciding whether a complaint falls within the 'schools' provision or under section 19 DDA.

[62] *Ibid.* paragraph 4.24.

Association, and so on, such activities will be covered by Part III DDA.[63] In addition, there may be activities in respect of which other bodies have responsibilities under other provisions of the DDA. The Code gives the example of providers of health services who may themselves fall within Part III DDA but in respect of whom, or in respect of which services, schools may have obligations under Part IV DDA.[64]

Section 28A(3) provides the Secretary of State with power to prescribe services (by regulation) which are, or services which are not, to be regarded for the purposes of section 28A DDA as being education or an associated service.[65] So far, no such regulations have been made.

8.2.5. Exclusions

Discrimination by excluding a disabled pupil from a school is unlawful. This is so whether the exclusion is permanent or temporary.[66] The DDA does not give any further guidance in relation to this unlawful act and the Code gives limited guidance. However, schools must ensure that exclusions based on behaviour that may itself be attributable to a disability are particularly carefully considered. Such exclusions will be unlawful unless justified. The Schools Code of Practice gives the following example:

A pupil with autism goes to the front of the dinner queue. A teacher standing nearby tells him not to 'barge in'. The pupil becomes anxious but does not move. The teacher insists that the pupil must not 'jump the queue'. The pupil becomes more anxious and agitated and hits the teacher. The pupil is excluded temporarily from the school.

Is the less favourable treatment for a reason related to the pupil's disability?

The reason for the exclusion, hitting the teacher, may be related to the pupil's disability. Particular features of his autism are that he has difficulty in managing social situations, he has difficulty in understanding the purpose of a queue, he has difficulty in understanding figurative language, such as 'barge in' and 'jump the queue', and he has difficulty in managing escalating levels of anxiety. If the hitting is related to these features of his autism, then the less favourable treatment, the exclusion, is for a reason related to the pupil's disability.

Is it less favourable treatment than someone gets if the reason does not apply to him or her?

It is less favourable treatment than someone would get if they had not hit the teacher. Is it justified?

The less favourable treatment is likely to be justified in terms of the order and discipline in the school. Any assault is likely to constitute a material and substantial reason justifying exclusion. However, there may be reasonable steps that might have been taken to prevent the incident happening in the first place. For staff there might have been training:

---

[63] See Chapter 7 above, at 7.2.6.2.
[64] Schools Code of Practice, paragraph 4.26.
[65] Section 28A(3) DDA.
[66] Section 28A(4) DDA.

- about autism and how the disability manifests itself;
- on strategies to avoid difficulties, for example, avoiding negative instructions and symbolic language such as 'barging in' and 'jumping the queue', and
- on strategies to overcome difficulties if they do arise.

For the pupil there might have been:

- particular training for social situations, such as queuing;
- the development of strategies for communicating that he is upset or confused.

If reasonable steps of this type could have been taken but were not, it may not be possible for the school to justify the exclusion. If steps of this type were taken but the incident still happened, the school is likely to be able to justify the exclusion.[67]

8.3. ACCESSIBILITY STRATEGIES AND PLANS

The DDA regulates discrimination by local education authorities by the imposition of what is described as a 'residual duty'.[68] This is described below. In addition, section 28D DDA imposes obligations on local education authorities (in England and Wales) to prepare, in relation to schools for which they are the responsible body:

- an accessibility strategy; and
- further such strategies at such times as may be prescribed.

In the case of Wales, such strategy must be prepared every three years.[69] In the case of England, no period has yet been prescribed for the preparation of further strategies.

An 'accessibility strategy' is a strategy for, over a prescribed period:

- increasing the extent to which disabled pupils can participate in the school's curriculums;
- improving the physical environment of the school for the purpose of increasing the extent to which disabled pupils are able to take advantage of education and associated services provided or offered by the school; and
- improving the delivery to disabled pupils—
  —within a reasonable time, and
  —in ways which are determined after taking account of their disabilities and any preferences expressed by them or their parents,
  of information which is provided in writing for pupils who are not disabled.[70]

---

[67] Paragraph 5.17E. See Chapter 5 above, at 5.9, for the concepts of discrimination identified in this example.

[68] Section 28F DDA.

[69] Disability Discrimination (Prescribed Periods for Accessibility Strategies and Plans for Schools) (Wales) Regulations 2003, SI 2003/2531 (W246).

[70] Section 28D(2) DDA.

An accessibility strategy must be in writing.[71] As to the prescribed period in respect of which the strategy is prepared, in England this is a period commencing 1 April 2003 and ending 31 March 2006 (that is, three years).[72] A local education authority is obliged to keep under review their accessibility strategies and revise them if necessary and it is its duty to secure their implementation.[73]

As observed above, the duty to make reasonable adjustments in the context of schools[74] explicitly does not require a responsible body to remove or alter a physical feature or provide auxilliary aids or services.[75] It is anticipated that the planning duties imposed by section 28D will secure such provision as is necessary to address these issues.

In addition to obligations on local education authorities, the responsible bodies of maintained schools,[76] independent schools, and special schools which are not maintained special schools, must prepare:

• an accessibility plan; and
• further such plans at such times as may be prescribed.

In the case of Wales, the period prescribed is three-yearly.[77] No periods have been prescribed in the case of England. An accessibility plan is a plan that addresses those matters required of an accessibility strategy and set out above. As with the duties of local education authorities, the responsible body must provide the accessibility plan in writing, review it, and if necessary revise it, and is under a duty to implement it.[78]

In addition, the governing body of a maintained school must publish information about its accessibility plan in its governors' annual report to parents.[79]

In Scotland, the Standards in Scotland's Schools etc Act 2000 requires educational authorities to produce annual statements of improvement objectives.[80] These are described as improvement plans and must state how authorities intend to improve education and support services in order to provide equal opportunities for disabled children. In addition, the Education (Disability Strategies and Pupils' Educational Records) (Scotland) Act 2002 requires responsible bodies in relation to schools, or schools where they are the responsible body, to prepare:

---

[71] Section 28D(3) DDA.

[72] Disability Discrimination (Prescribed Periods for Accessibility Strategies and Plans for Schools) (England) Regulations 2002, SI 2002/1981.

[73] Section 28D(4)–(6) DDA.

[74] Section 28C DDA.

[75] Section 28C(2) DDA. See Chapter 5 above, at 5.9.1.1, and see 5.7.1.3 for examples of auxiliary aids and services.

[76] As to maintained schools or maintained nursery schools the duties imposed are duties of the governing body: section 28D(14) DDA.

[77] Disability Discrimination (Prescribed Periods for Accessibility Strategies and Plans for Schools) (Wales) Regulations 2003, SI 2003/2531 (W246), Regulation 2.

[78] Section 28D(10)–(13) DDA.

[79] Education Act 1996, section 317(5) and (6) read with (7).

[80] Section 5, and see section 6 for school development plans.

- an accessibility strategy; and
- at such times as may by Regulations be prescribed, further such strategies.

A responsible body must prepare its first accessibility strategy by 1 April 2003 or no later than six months from the date a school is established, if later, and may be for a period of up to three years. Further accessibility strategies must be prepared not more than three years after the date of preparation of the previous strategy and must be for a period of three years to start immediately on the expiry of the period to which the previous strategy related.[81] An 'accessibility strategy' for these purposes is defined in materially the same way as for England and Wales, described above. As with accessibility strategies in England and Wales, a responsible body must keep the strategy under review, if necessary revise it, and has a duty to implement it.[82] The strategy must be in writing.[83]

Accessibility strategies must address, therefore, three discrete areas:

- access to the curriculum;
- the school environment; and
- school communication.

Section 28E DDA provides that guidance may be issued (for England by the Secretary of State, and for Wales by the National Assembly) as to: the contents of an accessibility strategy; the form in which it is to be produced; the persons to be consulted in its preparation and on implementing the obligation to review and, if necessary, to revise such strategy.[84] A local education authority must have regard to such guidance (and the need to allocate adequate resources for implementing the strategy[85]) in preparing its accessibility strategy and in complying with its obligation to keep under review and, if necessary, revise such strategy.[86]

Guidance has been issued, as follows:

- by the DfES, 'Accessible Schools: Planning to Increase Access to Schools for Disabled Pupils' (in respect of England only);[87]
- by the National Assembly for Wales, 'Planning to Increase Access to Schools for Disabled Pupils' (for Wales only).[88]

---

[81] Education (Disability Strategies) (Scotland) Regulations 2002, Regulation 2.

[82] Education (Disability Strategies and Pupils' Educational Records) (Scotland) Act 2002, section 1(2)–(5).

[83] *Ibid.* section 1(3).   [84] Section 28E(1)(b), (ii), and (iii) DDA.

[85] Section 28E(1)(a) DDA.   [86] Section 28E(1) and (2) read with section 28D(4) DDA.

[87] 8 July 2002, ref LEA/0168/2002, available at http://www.teachernet.gov.uk/_doc/2220/Access_Guide_.doc.

[88] March 2004, Circular No 15/2004, available at http://www.learning.wales.gov.uk/pdfs/access-disabled-pupils-e.pdf.

In Scotland the Education (Disability Strategies and Pupils Educational Records) (Scotland) Act 2002 permits the Scottish Ministers to prepare such guidance and they have done so. This guidance is applicable to Scotland only and is issued by the Scottish Executive: 'Planning to Improve Access to Education for Pupils with Disabilities: Guidance on Preparing Accessibility Strategies'.[89]

The provision made for accessibility strategies in Scotland requires that accessibility strategies be prepared by an education authority in relation to places other than schools at which the authority provides education for pupils who are under school age or who are of school age and are travelling people.[90]

Accessibility strategies form an important part of the overall scheme in the DDA for challenging disability discrimination. The guidance gives important examples of the steps that will be required to conform to the duties imposed in relation to accessibility strategies as follows.

- *The school curriculum* This will cover not only teaching and learning but the wider curriculum of the school, such as participation in after-school clubs, leisure, sporting and cultural activities, or school visits. Curriculum access must be considered at a 'whole school' level as many barriers to access to the curriculum will be similar for many groups of children and, as the guidance[91] observes, it is helpful to take a strategic approach to removing those barriers.[92] The guidance advises that local education authorities' accessibility strategies might focus on helping schools increase the accessibility of their curriculum to disabled children by securing appropriate staff training and encouraging schools to work together and share good practice.[93]

- *The physical environment of schools* This will cover improvements to the physical environment of the school and physical aids to access education. The physical environment includes steps, stairways, kerbs, exterior surfaces and paving, parking areas, building entrances and exits (including emergency escape routes), internal and external doors, gates, toilets and washing facilities, lighting, heating, ventilation, shifts, signs, interior surfaces, floor coverings, room decor, and furniture. Improvements to physical access might include ramps, handrails, lifts, widened doorways, electro-magnetic doors, adapted toilets and washing facilities, adjustable lighting, blinds, induction

---

[89] Available at http://www.scotland.gov.uk/libraryfive/5/education/gpas.pdf. The Scotland Act 2002 requires that accessibility strategies be made available in alternative forms where requested; alternative forms, for these purposes, are defined by the Education (Disability Strategies) (Scotland) Regulations 2002, SSI 2002/391 and the Education (Disability Strategies) (Scotland) Amendment Regulations 2003, SSI 2003/10, and they include orally, on audio tape, through sign language or lip speaking, and other formats.

[90] Education (Disability Strategies and Pupils Educational Records) (Scotland) Act 2002, section 2(2).

[91] In England.   [92] Paragraphs 3.2–3.3, England Guidance.

[93] Paragraph 3.4, England Guidance.

loops, well designed room acoustics, and way-finding systems. Physical aids to access education might include ICT equipment, enlarged computer screens and keyboards, concept keyboards, switches, photocopying enlargement facilities, specialist desks and chairs, and portable aids for children with motor coordination and poor hand/eye skills such as extra robust scientific glassware and specialist pens and pencils. In each case these lists are not exhaustive.[94]

• *Improving the delivery of information* This will cover planning to make written information normally provided by the school to its pupils available to its disabled pupils. The information should take account of pupils' disabilities, and pupils' and parents' preferred formats, and should be made available within a reasonable timeframe. The information might include handouts, timetables, and information about school events. The school might consider providing the information in alternative formats (such as large print and audio tape) using ICT, or providing the information orally.[95]

As can be seen, the strategic duties are extremely important to securing the delivery of accessible education to disabled children.

Provision is made in the DDA and the Education (Disability Strategies and Pupils Educational Records) (Scotland) Act 2002 for enforcing the obligations imposed in respect of accessibility strategies and plans. In the first place, where the Secretary of State asks for a copy of an accessibility strategy or accessibility plan it must be given to him.[96] Where a responsible body in Scotland prepares such a strategy, it must provide the Scottish Ministers with a copy of it and at any time after the body has revised its accessibility strategy, on being so required by the Scottish Ministers, it must provide them with a copy of the revised strategy.[97] In the second place, where the Secretary of State or the Welsh National Assembly is satisfied that a responsible body has acted or is proposing to act unreasonably in the discharge of its duties in respect of accessibility strategies and plans, or has failed to discharge a duty in respect of those matters, it may give the body such directions as to the discharge of those duties as appear to it to be expedient.[98] Thirdly, such directions may be enforced by the appropriate authority (the Secretary of State or the Welsh National Assembly) by a mandatory order in the High Court on an application for judicial review.[99]

In Scotland there is no such enforcement mechanism in place.

In England, Wales, and Scotland arrangements are in place to ensure that accessibility strategies are inspected as part of the inspection process. In England such inspections occur through the Office for Standards in Education (Ofsted),

---

[94] Paragraphs 3.10–3.11, England Guidance. Building regulations provide for making school premises accessible for disabled pupils and this is referred to in the Guidance. See also note 75 above.

[95] Paragraph 3.16, England Guidance.   [96] Section 28E(5) DDA.

[97] Education (Disability Strategies and Pupils Educational Records) (Scotland) Act 2002, section 3(4).

[98] Section 28M(1) DDA.   [99] Section 28M(7) DDA.

in Wales through HM Inspector of Education and Training in Wales, and in Scotland through Her Majesty's Inspectorate of Education.[100]

8.4. LOCAL EDUCATION AUTHORITIES' RESIDUAL DUTY

Section 28F DDA makes it unlawful for a local education authority in England or Wales, or an education authority in Scotland, to discriminate against a disabled pupil or prospective pupil in the exercising of certain of its statutory functions, in particular those falling under:

- the Education Acts;[101]
- the Education (Scotland) Act 1980;
- the Education (Scotland) Act 1996; and
- the Standards in Scotland's Schools etc Act 2000.

It is intended that the full range of education-related functions of education authorities that affect pupils or prospective pupils will be covered.[102] Such authorities will already fall within certain of the provisions under Part IV DDA (where it is the responsible body for a school or is required to prepare accessibility strategies). The obligations under section 28F are concerned with the more general functions of education authorities.[103] Such functions may include:

- policies (such as the authority's policies on special educational needs, capital building programmes, sports, cultural activities, transport, early years provision);
- the education authority's policy and arrangements on school admissions and exclusions and (in England and Wales) the school's admission policy and arrangements;
- the deployment of the authority's non-delegated budget and any other arrangements which might directly affect disabled pupils;
- services to pupils (such as weekend or after school-leisure and sporting activities, school trips, and cultural activities).

The Schools Code of Practice gives the following example:[104]

Home-school transport for disabled pupils in a local education authority (LEA) always leaves primary schools at 3.30pm. The LEA reviews its transport policy when it realizes

---

[100] See Schools Code of Practice, paragraphs 3.10–3.11 in the case of England and Wales, and in the case of Scotland see Guidance, ('Planning to Improve Access to Education for Pupils with Disabilities etc') referred to at note 89, paragraph 157.

[101] On the meaning of which see section 28F(7) DDA.

[102] Schools Code of Practice, paragraph 10.2. On the meanings of 'local education authority' and 'education authority' see section 28F(6) and (8) DDA.

[103] *Ibid.*   [104] Paragraph 10.3A.

that disabled pupils who are dependent on taxis might be at a substantial disadvantage if they were not able to stay to after-school clubs. The LEA renegotiates its contract with the taxi firm so that it is possible to specify later departure times. This is likely to be a reasonable adjustment that the LEA should make.

The duties apply to the full range of educational provision, including nursery education, arrangements for home and hospital tuition, and pupil referral units (in England and Wales) as well as the school stages of education.[105] The Schools Code of Practice therefore advises that education authorities may wish to review the full range of educational policies, practices, and procedures for current and prospective pupils to ensure that they do not discriminate against disabled children.[106]

The duty is described as 'residual'[107] because the unlawful acts created apply only where no other provision of Part IV, Chapter 1 applies to the act done in the discharge of the function concerned.[108] It will therefore always be necessary to consider whether the act complained of falls within one of the other provisions of Part IV before instituting proceedings under section 28F DDA, and where there is doubt, any claim should be framed in the alternative.

8.5. FURTHER AND HIGHER EDUCATION

Discrimination in the further and higher education sectors is addressed by Chapter 2 of Part IV DDA. Section 28R provides that:

(1) It is unlawful for the body responsible for an educational institution to discriminate against a disabled person—
   (a) in the arrangements it makes for determining admissions to the institution;
   (b) in the terms on which it offers to admit him to the institution; or
   (c) by refusing or deliberately omitting to accept an application for his admission to the institution.
(2) It is unlawful for the body responsible for an educational institution to discriminate against a disabled student in the student services it provides, or offers to provide.
(3) It is unlawful for the body responsible for an educational institution to discriminate against a disabled student by excluding him from the institution, whether permanently or temporarily.

As with discrimination occurring in the schools sphere, discrimination in further and higher education is therefore widely outlawed.

---

[105] Schools Code of Practice, paragraph 10.4.
[106] *Ibid.* paragraph 10.6. [107] See side note to sections 28F and 28G DDA.
[108] Section 28F(4) DDA.

8.5.1. Meaning of 'Educational Institution'

'Educational institution' for the purposes of section 28R DDA, in relation to England and Wales, means an institution:

• within the higher education sector;
• within the further education sector; or
• designated in an order made by the Secretary of State.[109]

'Educational institution', in relation to Scotland, means:

• an education within the higher education sector;[110]
• a College of Further Education with a Board of Management;[111]
• a Central Institution;[112]
• a College of Further Education maintained by an education authority;[113] or
• an institution designated in an order made by the Secretary of State.[114]

The Secretary of State has designated further institutions for the purposes of these provisions by order.[115] The institutions so designated are all named and are all wholly or partly funded from public funds, as is required for their designation.[116] Their 'responsible bodies' are also identified by name.[117]

8.5.2. Meanings of 'Student' and 'Disabled Student'

A 'student' means a person who is attending, or undertaking a course of study at, an educational institution. A 'disabled student' means a student who is a disabled person.[118] This plainly has a very wide meaning and does not actually require the student concerned to be studying at material times.

8.5.3. Meaning of 'Responsible Body'

A 'responsible body' for the purposes of an educational institution in the further and higher education sectors is to be determined in accordance with Schedule 4B DDA. In the case of England and Wales, this will be the governing body in the

---

[109] Section 28R(6) DDA, read with section 91 of the Further and Higher Education Act 1992; see section 28R(8) DDA.

[110] Within the meaning of section 56(2) of the Further and Higher Education (Scotland) Act 1992.

[111] Within the meaning of section 36 of the Further and Higher Education (Scotland) Act 1992.

[112] Within the meaning of section 135 of the Education (Scotland) Act 1980.

[113] In the exercise of their further education functions in providing courses of further education within the meaning of section 1(5)(b)(ii) of the Education (Scotland) Act 1980.

[114] Section 28R(7) DDA.

[115] The Disability Discrimination (Designation of Educational Institutions) Order 2002, SI 2002/1459.

[116] See section 28R(9) DDA.   [117] See below for responsible bodies.

[118] Section 31A DDA.

case of an institution within the further education sector, a university, or an institution other than a university within the higher education sector. Where the institution is one designated under order,[119] the responsible body is the one specified in the order.

In the case of Scotland, the responsible body of an institution within the higher education sector,[120] of a university, or of a central institution[121] will be the governing body. In the case of a College of Further Education with a Board of Management, it will be the Board of Management. In the case of an institution maintained by an education authority in the exercise of their further education functions, it will be the education authority. In the case of a school in respect of which the managers are for the time being receiving grants under section 73(c) or (d) of the Education (Scotland) Act 1980, it will be the managers of the school. Where the institution has been designated by order,[122] it will be the body specified in the order as the responsible body.

8.5.4. Prospective Students

As has been seen above, discrimination against prospective students is outlawed.[123] The unlawful acts created are wide and thus any discrimination in relation to prospective pupils is likely to be unlawful. The observations made in relation to prospective pupils and schools (see 8.2.3) apply equally.

The Post 16 Code of Practice gives examples of discriminatory acts which might occur against prospective students. These include, in the case of 'arrangements' made 'for determining admissions to the institution'[124] the following examples:

A 15-year-old with a disability attends an open day at his local adult education centre. He is covered by the legislation during the open day.

A university requires selected applicants to attend an interview. One applicant has a speech difficulty which gets worse when he is nervous. This means he needs more time to express himself. The university refuses to allow him any extra time at interview. This is likely to be unlawful.

In the case of discrimination 'in the terms on which it offers to admit' a disabled student 'to the institution' the Code gives the following example.[125]

An adult education centre informs a student with epilepsy that he may not enrol on a course unless he has an assistant with him at all times in case he has a seizure. In the past the student has only had seizures during the night. The centre's demand is likely to be unlawful.

---

[119] See 8.5.1 above.   [120] As defined, see 8.5.1 above.
[121] *Ibid.*   [122] *Ibid.*   [123] Section 28R(1) DDA.
[124] Paragraph 3.17B and 3.9B.   [125] Paragraph 3.9C.

In *Ford-Shubrook v St Dominic's Sixth Form College*[126] a wheelchair user was refused a place at his local Sixth Form College on health and safety grounds. The claimant proposed to access the classrooms on the first floor of the College by means of an innovative stair-climbing wheelchair. The College maintained that the claimant's presence at the College and in particular his use of a stair-climbing wheelchair would present a health and safety risk to the claimant and others. Despite the claimant and his parents approaching the College eighteen months before he was due to start his sixth form studies, the question of his admission was still not resolved very close to the date upon which he was due to commence his studies. The claimant was therefore in danger of losing a year of education. An interim injunction was applied for and granted so as to require the Sixth Form College to admit the claimant immediately.

8.5.5. Existing Students

Section 28R DDA outlaws discrimination in relation to the provision of student services that the institution provides or offers to provide.[127] 'Student services' mean services of any description that are provided wholly or mainly for students.[128] This plainly covers a whole range of student services and might include, for example:

- teaching, including classes, lectures, seminars, and practical sessions;
- curriculum design;
- examinations and assessments;
- field trips and outdoor education;
- arranging study abroad or work placements;
- outings and trips;
- research degrees and research facilities;
- informal/optional study skills sessions;
- short courses;
- day or evening adult education courses;
- training courses;
- distance learning;
- independent learning opportunities such as e-learning;
- learning facilities such as classrooms, lecture theatres, laboratories, studios, dark rooms, etc;

---

[126] 'Legal Bulletin' (April 2004), DRC, Issue 5, 21. [127] Section 28R(2) DDA.
[128] Section 28R(11) DDA. By section 28R(12) regulations may make provision as to services that are, or are not, to be regarded for these purposes as student services. However, no such regulations have been made, to date.

- learning equipment and materials such as laboratory equipment, computer facilities, class handouts, etc;
- libraries, learning centres and information centres and their resources;
- information and communication technology and resources;
- placement finding services;
- careers advice and training;
- careers libraries;
- job references;
- job shops and employment finding services;
- graduation and certificate ceremonies;
- leisure, recreation, entertainment, and sports facilities;
- the physical environment;
- chaplaincies and prayer areas;
- health services;
- counselling services;
- catering facilities;
- childcare facilities;
- campus and college shops;
- car parking;
- residential accommodation;
- accommodation finding services;
- financial advice; and
- welfare services.[129]

These are illustrative only. The unlawful acts cover the whole range of student services provided by, or offered by, an educational institution.

As the Post 16 Code of Practice observes, section 28R DDA covers students who are present at an educational institution for short periods as well as those undertaking a full course of study. The Post 16 Code of Practice gives the following example:[130]

A disabled student from the USA comes to a university in Britain to undertake a year's study for her junior year abroad. The British university has a duty not to discriminate against her during her period of study.

---

[129] Post 16 Code of Practice, paragraph 3.14.   [130] Paragraph 3.17A.

8.5.6. Exclusions

Section 28R DDA outlaws discriminatory exclusions whether they be permanent or temporary. The Post 16 Code of Practice gives the following example:[131]

A college learns that a student admitted himself to hospital during the holidays because of an ongoing mental health difficulty. The college excludes the student from the institution because staff fear he may be dangerous. The college has no evidence that the student will be dangerous; staff have simply made an assumption. This is likely to be unlawful.

8.6. STATUTORY YOUTH AND COMMUNITY SERVICES

Section 28U DDA read with Schedule 4C DDA outlaws discrimination by statutory youth and community services in the education field. These will include:

- clubs and activities;
- one-to-one counselling or guidance work;
- off-site and outreach work;
- outings and trips; and
- facilitated work with groups of people, such as support for a residents' association.[132]

The unlawful acts created are almost identical to those created under section 28R DDA (further and higher education). The modification to the unlawful acts is such that whereas section 28R(1)(b) DDA provides that it is unlawful for an educational institution to discriminate against a disabled person in the terms on which it offers to *admit* him to the institution, section 28U[133] makes it unlawful for a local education authority or governing body to discriminate against a disabled person in the terms on which they offer to *enrol* him on the course.[134] The duty to make adjustments is also modified and this is addressed in Chapter 5, at 5.9.4 above.

The responsible body in the case of statutory youth and community services is the local education authority or the governing body of a maintained school depending on the particular provision.[135] In Scotland the responsible body will be the education authority.[136]

---

[131] Paragraph 3.10A and see 8.2.5 above.   [132] Post 16 Code of Practice, paragraph 3.16.
[133] Read with section 28R, as modified by Schedule 4C DDA.
[134] Schedule 4C DDA.
[135] Section 28R(6) as substituted by Schedule 4C, Part 1, paragraph 1 DDA.
[136] Section 28R(6) as substituted by Schedule 4C, Part 2.

8.7. OTHER EDUCATIONAL PROVISION

As observed above (Chapter 7, at 7.2.6.2) the exemption relating to education in Part III DDA has been repealed following the coming into force of SENDA. This means that educational and related provision falling outside Part IV DDA will fall within Part III. The Codes of Practice give examples of the sorts of activities that will fall outside Part IV but within the scope of Part III. In the case of pre-16 provision, private, voluntary, and statutory providers of early years services that are not constituted as schools will not fall within the scope of Part IV but will fall within the scope of Part III.[137] If an early years establishment provides education and day care for children, all of these services will be covered by Part III.[138] In addition, non-statutory youth services, such as clubs and activities run by voluntary organizations, the Scouts, or church youth clubs, will not be covered by Part IV DDA but will be covered by Part III.[139]

Private providers of education (private universities and colleges, for example) and work-based training providers are not covered by Part IV of the DDA. They are covered by Part III DDA or Part II.[140]

In addition where an educational institution provides services to the public it may fall within Part III (for example, hiring out conference facilities; putting on a performance for the benefit of members of the public).[141]

8.8. VALIDITY AND REVISION OF AGREEMENTS

As with the provision made in other spheres[142] the DDA makes provision in relation to agreements which purport to limit the operation of the DDA and in particular makes such agreements void and provides for their modification by the courts.

Any term in a contract or other agreement made by or on behalf of a responsible body is void insofar as it purports to:

- require someone to do something which would contravene any provision of, or made under, Part IV DDA;

- exclude or limit the operation of any provision of, or made under, Part IV DDA; or

- prevent any person from making a claim under Part IV DDA.[143]

---

[137] Schools Code of Practice, paragraph 10.7.

[138] *Ibid.* paragraph 10.8. And see Table 1 under paragraph 10.09.

[139] Unless they are truly membership clubs: see Chapter 7 above, at 7.2.6.4. And see Post 16 Code of Practice, paragraph 3.3.

[140] The Post 16 Code of Practice advises that they will be covered by Part III, paragraph 3.4, but tsome work place training will be covered by Part II: see, for example Chapter 6 above, at 6.2.

[141] Post 16 Code of Practice, paragraph 3.20 and examples thereunder.

[142] See Chapters 6 and 7 above.   [143] Sections 28P and 28X DDA.

An agreement to settle a claim under Part IV DDA is not affected by these provisions.[144]

A person with an interest in such an agreement may apply to a County Court (or Sheriff Court in Scotland) which may make an order modifying the agreement. In determining what if any modifications to order, the court will consider what is 'just'.[145]

8.9. TERRITORIAL EXTENT

The schools or educational institutions to which Part IV applies are only those situated in England, Scotland, or Wales. The provisions do not extend to Northern Ireland.[146]

8.10. DISCRIMINATION AFTER TERMINATION OF A RELEVANT RELATIONSHIP

As discussed above in relation to goods, facilities, and services,[147] unlike discrimination occurring in the employment and related fields,[148] no express provision is made for discrimination occurring after termination of any relevant formal relationship in the education and other fields. This may be less significant than discrimination occurring in the employment field because many of the duties arising under Part IV are anticipatory in nature and so do not presuppose the existence of a particular relationship.[149] However, for example in relation to the provision of student services,[150] any complaint in relation to the same may only be made by a student who is attending, or undertaking a course of study at, the educational institution concerned.[151] Thus discrimination in relation to services that might be provided to ex-students appears to fall outside the scope of section 28R DDA. However, as observed above,[152] case-law suggests that it may be possible to argue that the unlawful acts, although framed in a way which suggests there must be a present protected relationship for unlawful discrimination to occur, might be read as covering discrimination after termination of such relationship.[153]

---

[144] Sections 28P(2) and 28X DDA.
[145] Sections 28P(4) and 28X DDA. Notice will usually be required: sections 28P(5) and (6) and 28X DDA.
[146] See Chapter 10, at 10.4.   [147] See Chapter 7 above, at 7.4.
[148] See Chapter 6 above, at 6.14.   [149] See Chapter 5 above, at 5.9.
[150] Section 28R DDA.   [151] See sections 31A DDA and 28R(2) DDA.
[152] See Chapter 6, at 6.14, and Chapter 7, at 7.4, both above.
[153] See *Rhys-Harper v Relaxion Group plc* [2003] UKHL 33, [2003] ICR 867, [2003] IRLR 484, and discussion in Chapter 6 above, at 6.14.

9

TRANSPORT

9.1. INTRODUCTION

The inaccessibility of the public transport system has a fundamental impact on the lives of disabled people. Leonard Cheshire has undertaken research showing that disabled people's access to employment and access to healthcare are limited because of a transport system which remains inaccessible. For example:

- 23 per cent of disabled people actively seeking employment have had to turn down a job offer because of inaccessible transport;
- 62 per cent of wheelchair users and 86 per cent of people with a visual impairment said inaccessible transport had restricted their choice of jobs.[1]

Inaccessible transport also affects leisure opportunities and all aspects of social and family life for disabled people of all ages.[2]

However, as noted in Chapter 7 above, at 7.2.6, the use of any means of transport is excluded from the goods, facilities, and services provisions of the DDA.[3] The draft Disability Discrimination Bill does contain provision bringing certain transport services within Part III DDA and allowing the Secretary of State to

---

[1] The Joint Committee on the Draft Disability Bill, First Report (May 2004), paragraph 122. See http://www.publications.parliament.uk/pa/jt200304/jtselect/jtdisab/82/8206.htm#n134. Not properly transcribed in the report, but see evidence from Leonard Cheshire, 'Memorandum from Leonard Cheshire (DDB 11)' available at http://www.publications.parliament.uk/pa/jt200304/jtselect/jtdisab/82/82we06.htm.

[2] 'An Overview of the Literature on Disability and Transport' (2004) DRC, available at http://www.drc-gb.org/uploaded_files/documents/10_548_Transport%20summary-final.pdf. And see Leonard Cheshire's evidence to the Joint Committee on the Draft Disability Bill, *supra* note 1.

[3] Section 19(5) DDA: see Chapter 7 above, at 7.2.6.1.

extend the requirements of Part III DDA to a broader range of transport services. This is addressed in Chapter 13 below. In the meantime, however, it should be kept in mind that transport-*related* activities (as contrasted with services consisting of the *use* of transport[4]) fall within Part III DDA (see Chapter 7, at 7.2.6.1). It is only the use of transport that is excluded, not related customer services or transport infrastructure. Thus, for example, assistance at a station for a visually impaired passenger and his dog was held not to fall within the transport exemption.[5] The Goods, Facilities, Services and Premises Code of Practice gives the following example:[6]

An airline company provides a flight reservation and booking service to the public on its website. This is a provision of a service and is subject to the Act.

The DDA does make relevant provision in relation to the use of transport. It does not, however, create any unlawful acts actionable by individuals. Instead the DDA imposes accessibility requirements on public transport providers under Part V DDA.

Part V confers regulation making powers on the Secretary of State for the purposes of securing accessible public transport and creates criminal liability in certain circumstances where there is a failure to comply with those regulations.

9.2. TAXIS

Sections 32–39 DDA provide the Secretary of State with the power to make 'taxi accessibility regulations' for the purpose of securing accessible taxis. Sections 32–6 have not been brought into force. This means that certain regulation-making powers designed to secure accessibility for disabled taxi users and certain duties requiring taxi drivers to carry wheelchair using passengers have not been brought into force.

Section 37 DDA imposes duties on the drivers of regulated taxis[7] (in England and Wales) in relation to disabled passengers accompanied by guide or hearing dogs (being dogs trained to guide blind persons or dogs trained to assist deaf persons[8]). Regulated taxis have a duty to carry such passengers with their dogs and to allow any dog to remain with the passenger. In addition they are under a duty not to make an additional charge for carrying such passengers and dogs.[9]

---

[4] Section 19(5) DDA.

[5] *McMurty v Virgin Trains* (Newcastle Upon Tyne County Court, NE 140154) (unreported), cited in Palmer, Gill, Monaghan, Moon, and Stacey, ed McColgan *Discrimination Law Handbook* (LAG, 2002) 901. See also *Roads v Central Trans Ltd* [2004] EWCA Civ 1541, and Chapter 7 above, at 7.2.8 and note 99.

[6] Paragraph 2.17.

[7] Taxis to which the regulations are expressed to apply: sections 32(5) and 68(1) DDA.

[8] Section 37(11) DDA.   [9] Section 37(3) DDA.

Regulations have been made extending section 37 DDA to include certain disabled people with other assistance dogs, namely those assisting disabled people with epilepsy or certain physical disabilities, where those dogs have been trained by specified charities and the disabled passenger is wearing a jacket on which is prominently inscribed the name of a specified charity.[10] Provision is made for exempting drivers of taxis from these requirements (on medical grounds).[11] Similar provision is made for Scotland.[12]

In addition, the Private Hire Vehicles (Carriage of Guide Dogs etc) Act 2002 amends the DDA to introduce duties on operators and drivers of private hire vehicles to carry guide and other assistance dogs at no additional charge.[13] Similar provision is made permitting exemptions on medical grounds.[14]

These transport duties are enforced by criminal sanctions.[15]

There is a considerable amount of non-statutory guidance, including:

• 'Carriage of Assistance Dogs in Taxis: Guidance to Licensing Authorities (2001)'.[16] This guidance is issued by the Department for Transport ('DfT') and informs licensing authorities about the duties on taxi drivers. It gives advice on the procedure for making applications for an exemption from the duties on medical grounds and sets out the framework for appeals against the refusal of licensing authorities to grant exemptions and the procedures for enforcing the duties.

• 'Carriage of Assistance Dogs in Private Hire Vehicles: Guidance for Licensing Authorities (2003)'.[17] As with the advice above in relation to taxis, this guidance is issued by the DfT and informs licensing authorities about the new duties. Again, it gives advice on the procedure for handling applications for exemption from the duties on medical grounds, sets out details of the exemption procedure,[18] and sets out the framework for appeals against the refusal of licensing authorities to grant exemptions and the procedures for enforcing the duties.

• 'Making Private Hire Services More Accessible to Disabled People: A Good Practice Guide for Private Hire Vehicle Operators and Drivers (2003)'.[19] This

---

[10] The Disability Discrimination Act 1995 (Taxis) (Carrying of Guide Dogs Etc) (England and Wales) Regulations 2000, SI 2000/2990.

[11] Section 37(3), (6), and (8) DDA and The Disability Discrimination Act 1995 (Private Hire Vehicles) (Carriage of Guide Dogs Etc) (England and Wales) Regulations 2003, SI 2003/3122. For appeals in respect of a refusal to grant an exemption certificate, see section 38 DDA.

[12] See Taxi Drivers' Licences (Carrying of Guide Dogs and Hearing Dogs) (Scotland) Regulations 2003, SI 2003/73.

[13] See Section 37 DDA.   [14] Section 37A(5)–(7) DDA.

[15] Sections 36(5), 37(4), 37A(4) DDA.

[16] Available at http://www.dft.gov.uk/stellent/groups/dft_mobility/documents/page/dft_mobility_503287.hcsp.

[17] Available at http://www.dft.gov.uk/stellent/groups/dft_mobility/documents/page/dft_mobility_026627.hcsp.

[18] *Ibid.* Appendix 1.   [19] Available at http://www.dptac.gov.uk/pubs/phv/index.htm.

guidance has been prepared by the Disabled Persons' Transport Advisory Committee ('DPTAC'). The DPTAC is a statutory body set up under the Transport Act 1985 to advise the Government on transport policy as it affects the mobility of disabled people. This non-statutory guide focuses on customer care and customer service, rather than on the types of vehicles used and their physical characteristics. It covers issues such as driver training and the responsibilities of booking staff.

9.3. PUBLIC SERVICE VEHICLES

Sections 40–45 DDA address accessibility and public service vehicles, principally by conferring regulation-making powers on the Secretary of State.

Regulations have been made pursuant to these powers. The Public Service Vehicles Accessibility Regulations 2000:[20]

- apply to prescribed single-deck and double-deck buses and coaches ('regulated public service vehicles');
- set out detailed accessibility requirements that are to be met by regulated public service vehicles (Schedules 1, 2, and 3);
- set out details of accessibility certificates (Part III, Part VII, and Schedule 4).

The Public Service Vehicles (Conduct of Drivers, Inspectors, Conductors and Passengers) Regulations 1990[21] prescribe certain conduct by requiring, for example, drivers and conductors of public service vehicles to allow wheelchair users to board if there is an unoccupied wheelchair space on the vehicle. The Public Service Vehicles (Conduct of Drivers, Inspectors, Conductors and Passengers) (Amendment) Regulations 2002[22] amend the Public Service Vehicles (Conduct of Drivers, Inspectors, Conductors and Passengers) Regulations 1990 to reflect the accessibility requirements of the Public Service Vehicles Accessibility Regulations 2000.

Again, there is relevant guidance. This includes the 'Public Service Vehicles Accessibility Regulations 2000: Guidance (2001)'.[23] This is issued by the DfT, and is non-statutory. It provides guidance for those in the manufacturing and operating industries on meeting the requirements of the Regulations. Importantly, it is expressly stated that this guidance does not replace or qualify the Regulations in any way and that, in every case, reference should be made to the relevant provisions of the Regulations to determine the extent of the legal

---

[20] SI 2000/1970, as amended by the Public Service Vehicles Accessibility (Amendment) Regulations 2000, SI 2000/3318, SI 2002/2981, SI 2003/1818, and SI 2004/1881 (mainly in relation to the fees payable for accessibility certificates).

[21] SI 1990/1020.   [22] SI 2002/1724.

[23] Available at http://www.dft.gov.uk/stellent/groups/dft_mobility/documents/page/dft_mobility_503298.hcsp.

requirements.[24] It is useful, however, in describing in straightforward terms: the scope of the Regulations; the purpose of the regulatory requirements; the application of the requirements of the Regulations; best practice (in particular, it specifies the provisions that should be followed wherever possible); how the special authorization procedure works; and the arrangements for the enforcement of the regulations and vehicle inspections.

The Public Service Vehicles (Conduct of Drivers, Inspectors, Conductors and Passengers) (Amendment) Regulations 2002: Guidance (2002)[25] is also issued by the DfT and is non-statutory. It describes the amendments to the Public Service Vehicles (Conduct of Drivers, Inspectors, Conductors and Passengers) Regulations 1990 and provides guidance on their application. In particular, it provides guidance on the proper conduct of:

• drivers, inspectors, and conductors of all public service vehicles with respect to certain dogs that may accompany a disabled person;
• passengers with respect to disabled people in general and to certain disabled people's dogs; and
• drivers and conductors of regulated public service vehicles with respect to wheelchair users and other disabled people.[26]

9.4. RAIL VEHICLES

Sections 46–47 DDA address accessibility and rail vehicles; as with public service vehicles, they do so principally by conferring regulation-making powers on the Secretary of State. The Rail Vehicle Accessibility Regulations 1998,[27] enacted pursuant to those powers, apply to rail vehicles used on railways, tramways, monorail systems, or magnetic levitation systems coming into service after 31 December 1998. They impose various accessibility requirements on these regulated rail vehicles.

Again there is a considerable amount of guidance. The Train and Station Services for Disabled Passengers: A Code of Practice (2002)[28] was prepared and

---

[24] Ibid.

[25] Available at http://www.dft.gov.uk/stellent/groups/dft_mobility/documents/page/dft_mobility_507586.pdf.

[26] See also, 'Wheelchair Boarding Ramps: A joint DfT/SMMT specification for a ramp fitted to a Regulated Public Service Vehicle and first used on or after 1 January 2004 (2003)', available at http://www.dft.gov.uk/stellent/groups/dft_mobility/documents/page/dft_mobility_507857.pdf

[27] SI 1998/2456, as amended by the Rail Vehicle Accessibility (Amendment) Regulations 2000, SI 2000/3215. And see the Rail Vehicle (Exemption Applications) Regulations 1998 that address applications for exemption from the requirements of The Rail Vehicle Accessibility Regulations 1998.

[28] Available at http://www.sra.gov.uk/publications/general/general_Train_and_Station_Services_for_Disabled_Passengers__A_Code_of_Practice_/code.

issued by the Strategic Rail Authority.[29] All passenger train and station opera-tors are now required, as a condition of their licence, to have due regard to the content of the Code when providing facilities or services for passengers with dis-abilities[30] (though compliance with the Code will not guarantee compliance with the requirements of the DDA[31]). The Code suggests that it will be difficult for operators to claim they are acting reasonably if they have not taken account of the Code.[32] The Code provides an overview of Part III of the DDA and the Rail Vehicle Accessibility Regulations 1998 as they relate to station and passenger train operators, along with practical guidance about the services and standards that operators are expected to provide for disabled passengers.

Further non-statutory guidance has been issued by the DfT in the 'Rail Vehicle Accessibility Regulations 1998: Guidance (2002)'.[33] This provides guidance for those in the rail vehicle industry on the requirements of the Regulations and the exemption procedure. The guidance covers: the scope of the Regulations; detailed advice on the requirements; best practice; how the exemp-tion procedure works; and enforcement of the Regulations.

9.5. AIR TRAVEL

Air travel is not expressly addressed by the DDA. The 'Access to Air Travel for Disabled People: Code of Practice (2003)',[34] however, provides guidance on compliance with the duties arising under Part III in respect of air travel services, such as booking services, and infrastructure, such as airport facilities. The voluntary Code is issued by the DfT.[35]

---

[29] Pursuant to Section 71B of the Railways Act 1993.
[30] Paragraph A4.3.
[31] Paragraph A1.
[32] Paragraph A4.5.
[33] Available at http://www.dft.gov.uk/stellent/groups/dft_mobility/documents/page/dft_mobility_503304.hcsp.
[34] Available at: http://www.dft.gov.uk/stellent/groups/dft_mobility/documents/page/dft_mobility_507855.pdf.
[35] See, for example, *Ross v Ryanair and Another* [2004] EWCA Civ 1751.

10

LIABILITY, EXEMPTIONS, AND TERRITORIAL EXTENT

10.1. INTRODUCTION

This chapter addresses the circumstances in which liability might arise under the DDA. It also addresses the general exemptions that apply to all unlawful acts. The specific exemptions applicable to particular unlawful acts have been dealt with as they arise in the subject-specific chapters above. In addition, this chapter deals with the territorial extent of the DDA. Again the territorial limitations of the particular unlawful acts have been dealt with as they arise in the subject-specific chapters above. However, some general points arise in relation to territorial extent and these are dealt with below (see 10.4).

10.2. LIABILITY

The unlawful acts under the DDA are framed so that the primary actor is made liable for his own discriminatory acts where that person is covered by the unlawful act concerned. Thus an employer will be liable for any discriminatory act he does that is caught by Part II DDA; the provider of goods, facilities, or services will be liable for any discriminatory act he does which is caught by Part III DDA; and so on. In addition, however, the DDA makes such persons liable for the discriminatory acts of their employees and agents, where those acts fall within the scope of the relevant unlawful acts created by the DDA, and makes those employees and agents jointly liable. A defence is available to an employer or a principal who would otherwise find himself so liable; this is addressed below (see 10.2.5).

Further, the DDA makes those who 'aid' the doing of unlawfully discriminatory acts jointly liable for such acts. This is addressed in 10.2.7 below.

In respect of some of the unlawful acts special provision enables the joinder of responsible parties (eg lessors, employers in relation to an occupational pension scheme) to the proceedings. This is discussed above in the chapters relating to the unlawful acts themselves.[1]

10.2.1. Vicarious Liability

Section 58(1) DDA provides that:

Anything done by a person in the course of his employment shall be treated for the purposes of this Act as also done by his employer, whether or not it was done with the employer's knowledge or approval.

This has the effect of making employers liable for the discriminatory acts of their employees[2] that are done in the course of their employment, whether or not they are done with the employer's knowledge or approval. Importantly, it is plain from section 58(1) DDA that employers may be liable for the acts of all their employees, not merely those of managerial status.[3]

An employer will have a defence to a claim based on vicarious liability where it can prove that it took such steps as were reasonably practicable to prevent the employee from doing the discriminatory act or from doing, in the course of his or her employment, acts of that description.[4] This is dealt with below (see 10.2.5).

10.2.2. In the Course of Employment

An employer will only be liable for discriminatory acts done by its employees *in the course of their employment*. In *Jones v Tower Boot Co Ltd*[5] the Court of Appeal gave a wide meaning to the expression 'course of employment' in this context. The case concerned the vicarious liability provision in the RRA, which is in all material respects identical to section 58(1) DDA.[6] The complainant, a sixteen-year-old boy, was subjected to horrific physical and verbal racial abuse by his co-workers. This included employees burning his arm with a hot screwdriver, whipping his legs with a welt, throwing bolts at him, and trying to put his arm in a lasting machine. The Employment Appeal Tribunal adopted the test of vicarious liability which at that time applied at common law, namely whether the

---

[1] See eg Chapter 5, at 5.6.2 (lessors in the employment and related fields); see 5.7.1.7.3 (lessors in claims concerning service providers); see 5.9.3.1.5 (lessors in the post-16 education sector; Chapter 6, at 6.8 (employers in relation to occupational pension schemes).

[2] Such expression is to be interpreted widely, see section 68(1) DDA and Chapter 6, at 6.2.1 above.

[3] *De Souza v Automobile Association* [1986] IRLR 103.   [4] Section 58(5) DDA.

[5] [1997] ICR 254, [1997] IRLR 168. *Irving v The Post Office* [1981] IRLR 289 (CA) must now be wrong. See the comments in *Waters v Commissioners of Police of the Metropolis* [1997] IRLR 589, CA.

[6] Section 32(1) RRA.

employees concerned were acting in a way which was authorized by the employer or acting in a way which could be described as a mode, albeit an improper mode, of acting in an authorized way. The Employment Appeal Tribunal concluded (by a majority) that the employer was not liable because the acts could not be described as an improper mode of performing authorized tasks. The Court of Appeal robustly rejected this test, together with the implicit assumption that the more heinous the acts of harassment, the less likely the employer would be liable under the discrimination legislation.

The Court of Appeal held in *Jones v Tower Boot* that the 'course of employment' test in the RRA (and therefore the SDA and DDA) was not the same as the test for vicarious liability at common law. The purpose of the vicarious liability provisions in the discrimination legislation was, according to the Court of Appeal:

[T]o deter racial and sexual harassment in the workplace through a widening of the net of responsibility beyond the guilty employees themselves by making all employers additionally liable for such harassment, and then supplying them with the reasonable steps defence under section 32(3) [RRA[7]] which will exonerate the conscientious employer who has used his best endeavours to prevent such harassment, and will encourage all employers who have not yet undertaken such endeavours to take the steps necessary to make the same defence available in their own workplace.[8]

The effect of the Court of Appeal's decision in *Jones v Tower Boot* is to make employers liable for a wide range of discriminatory actions even if they do not occur as part of work duties or indeed do not occur in the context of the working environment (subject only to the employer making out the statutory defence). See 10.2.3 below.

The fact that an employer expressly prohibits an employee from carrying out the act complained of does not necessarily take the act outside the 'course of employment', although it may assist the employer in making out the statutory defence (see 10.2.5 below).

The House of Lords in *Lister v Helsey Hall*[9] has now brought the common law test of vicarious liability closer to the *Tower Boot* test. In *Lister* the warden of a boarders' house in a school sexually abused a number of pupils, who brought a County Court action some years later. On appeal the House of Lords held that the respondent school was vicariously liable for the warden's actions, ruling that the correct approach to vicarious liability was to concentrate on the closeness of the connection between the nature of the employment and the employee's wrongdoing, and to ask whether it would be fair and just to hold the employer vicariously liable. The House of Lords concluded that the fact that the warden's actions were an abuse of his position did not sever the connection

---

[7] See section 58(5) DDA.   [8] *Supra* note 5 at 263–4; paragraph 38.
[9] [2001] UKHL 22, [2001] IRLR 472.

with his employment.[10] This means that in cases in which more than one cause of action is relied upon (particularly outside the employment field, where disability discrimination claims will often be pursued alongside other complaints) questions of vicarious liability which arise under the DDA and at common law are likely to be determined on similar principles.

10.2.3. Discrimination Outside Working Hours

Section 58(1) DDA recognizes that discrimination may occur as between persons employed by the same employer in circumstances where their mutual employer is not liable for it. The 'in the course of employment' requirement draws the line between those incidents for which an employer will be liable and those for which he will not. However, that line is sometimes difficult to discern.

Discrimination may occur during a rest break, just before going home, or outside the workplace altogether, and in some such cases discrimination might be found to have been 'in the course of employment' so as to make the employer liable for it. There are, as the Court of Appeal said in *Jones v Tower Boot*, an infinite variety of circumstances and in each case it will be a question of fact for the court or tribunal to resolve, having regard to the broad test set down in that case. A court or tribunal might find an employer liable for acts of discrimination notwithstanding that they were done outside working hours and outside the workplace altogether. Each case will, however, turn very much on its own facts.

In *Sidhu v Aerospace Composite Technology*[11] the complainant was subjected to racial abuse by a fellow employee during a family day out at a theme park. The day out had been organized by the employer and participants were told to report any problems to a senior manager who was also there. The Court of Appeal upheld the Employment Tribunal's decision that the harassment did not fall within the course of the harasser's employment, although it recognized that another Employment Tribunal could properly have reached the opposite conclusion.

The Court of Appeal in *Sidhu* did not consider its decision to be incompatible with *Chief Constable of the Lincolnshire Police v Stubbs*,[12] in which a woman police officer had been subjected to sexual harassment by a male officer while drinking in a pub after her shift. The Employment Appeal Tribunal in that case found that the harassment did fall within the course of employment.

10.2.4. Employees' Liability

An employee who does a discriminatory act made unlawful by the DDA 'in the course of his employment' such that his employer is liable for it (or would be but

---

[10] See too *Mattis v Pollock (t/a Flamingo's Nightclub)* [2003] EWCA Civ 887, [2003] 1 WLR 2158, [2003] IRLR 603.

[11] [2000] ICR 167, [2000] IRLR 602.   [12] [1999] ICR 547, [1999] IRLR 81.

for the statutory defence described below) is personally liable under the DDA for that discrimination in whichever field it occurs (whether it relates to employment, education, housing, etc). This is because the perpetrator is deemed to 'aid' his or her employer's vicarious liability for his or her actions.[13] This applies even where the employer makes out the statutory defence (see 10.2.5), in which case the guilty employee will find himself solely liable.[14] In any case where an employer might make out such defence, a complainant should consider bringing proceedings against the employee as well as the employer.[15]

If the acts of discrimination complained of are not done in the course of employment the employee will not be liable under the DDA, nor will any liability attach to the employer.

10.2.5. The Employer's Defence

An employer has a defence to a claim based on vicarious liability by reason of section 58(5) DDA. Section 58(5) DDA provides that:

> In proceedings under this Act against any person in respect of an act alleged to have been done by an employee of his, it shall be a defence for that person to prove that he took such steps as were reasonably practicable to prevent the employee from—
> (a) doing that act; or
> (b) doing, in the course of his employment, acts of that description.

This defence is only available to an employer where the claim is one of vicarious liability against the employer. It is not available to the employee who is said to have done the discriminatory act.

The defence depends upon an employer establishing that it took steps *before* the relevant discriminatory act occurred.[16] In *Canniffe v East Riding of Yorkshire Council*[17] the Employment Appeal Tribunal concluded that the proper approach to determining whether the defence is made out is, first, to identify whether the employer took any steps at all to prevent the employee from doing the act or acts complained of in the course of his employment; and second (having identified what steps, if any, the employer took) to consider whether

---

[13] *AM v (1) WC (2) SPV* [1999] IRLR 410. An employer is vicariously liable for an employee's act of discrimination by virtue of Section 58(1). The employee who perpetrated the act of discrimination is deemed to have aided his/her employer's vicarious liability by section 57(2) DDA. Liability for knowingly aiding unlawful acts of discrimination arises under section 57(1) DDA, see 10.2.7 below.

[14] For an example of the same, see *Yeboah v Crofton* [2002] EWCA Civ 794, [2002] IRLR 634.

[15] Where liability is joint, the court or employment tribunal will apportion compensation between the employer and individual discriminator. Thus in *HM Prison Service and Others v Johnson* [1997] ICR 275, [1997] IRLR 162, £500 was awarded against each of the individual respondents as well as £27,500 against the Prison Service. See Chapter 11 below

[16] See for example *Martins v Marks & Spencer plc* [1998] ICR 1005, IRLR 326, CA. The burden is on the employer: section 58(5) DDA.

[17] [2000] IRLR 555.

there were any further steps the employer could have taken that were reasonably practicable. Whether the taking of any such steps would have been successful in preventing the acts of discrimination in question is not determinative. An employer will not be exculpated if it has not taken reasonably practicable steps simply because, if it had done so, it would not have prevented the discrimination from occurring. In this regard, the Employment Appeal Tribunal recognized that, if it were otherwise, the more serious the act of discrimination, the more likely that the employer would escape liability.

The question whether an employer has adopted an equal opportunities policy and otherwise followed the recommendations in any relevant Codes of Practice issued by the DRC will be very significant in determining whether it has made out the statutory defence. All the DRC Codes themselves emphasize the importance of compliance with the Codes and the developing of proper equal opportunities policies. The size of the employer will also be a relevant consideration, so that the larger the employer the greater the expectation that it will properly implement and observe an equal opportunities policy.[18]

In *Balgobin and Francis v London Borough of Tower Hamlets*[19] an alleged harasser was suspended pending the outcome of an inquiry after a complaint by two women. The inquiry was inconclusive and the harasser was returned to work. The majority of the Employment Appeal Tribunal held that the employer had made out the statutory defence in circumstances where there was proper and adequate staff supervision and the employer had made known its equal opportunities policy. The Employment Appeal Tribunal found that 'it was very difficult to see what steps in practical terms the employers could reasonably have taken to prevent that which had occurred from occurring'.

If an employer had only to establish that a system was in place for supervising staff and an equal opportunities policy was observed in order successfully to make out the statutory defence then it would be all too easy to avoid liability, and the policy behind the discrimination legislation would be undermined. There are in fact many other steps that might be taken to avoid discriminatory harassment. As was pointed out by the complainant in *Balgobin*, these might include the provision of training for all staff, clear guidelines for dealing with harassment, categorizing harassment as gross misconduct, and so on. It is likely that, in the light of the strong policy statements made by the Court of Appeal in *Jones v Tower Boot* and the formulation of the two-stage test in *Canniffe*, the decision in *Balgobin* would not be the same now.

In other cases, employers have not avoided liability so easily. In *Earlam v VMP Ltd & Andrews*,[20] for example, an Employment Tribunal concluded that a large company should take the following steps to avoid harassment:

---

[18] See *A v Civil Aviation Authority* [1996] DCLD 27.   [19] [1987] ICR 829, [1987] IRLR 401.
[20] [1995] DCLD 25. See also *Hurtley v Halfords & Leach*; *Wilson v J Sainsbury plc*; and *Dias v Avon County Council*, all reported in [1995] DCLD 25.

- issue a policy statement about harassment, defining it and stating that it will not be permitted or condoned;
- establish a complaints procedure, specifying to whom complaints should be made and setting out the consequences for perpetrators;
- provide training; and
- ensure that managers and supervisors are aware of the factors that contribute to a working environment free of harassment.

10.2.6. Liability for Acts of Third Parties

There have been cases holding that a person covered by the unlawful acts created by the DDA (an employer, provider of goods, facilities, and services, etc) might be liable for the discriminatory acts of third parties, that is persons who are not the employer's employees or agents. In *Burton and Rhule v De Vere Hotels*[21] the Employment Appeal Tribunal held that an employer had subjected its employees to racial harassment when a third party (an 'entertainer' at the employer's hotel[22]) racially and sexually harassed them. In reaching this conclusion, the Employment Appeal Tribunal held that an employer might be held to have subjected an employee to the detriment of racial harassment if the event in question was sufficiently under the control of the employer that it could, by the application of good employment practice, have prevented the harassment or reduced the extent of it.[23] There are numerous examples of the application of the principle in *Burton and Rhule* in the case-law. However, *Burton and Rhule* and the principle expounded in it were overruled by the House of Lords in *Pearce v Governing Body of Mayfield School.*[24] Now liability will only be established for the acts of third parties where a person covered by the unlawful acts (employer, provider of goods, facilities, or service etc) has themself failed to take action for reasons relating to disability or in consequence of a failure to comply with a duty to make adjustments. The effect of *Burton and Rhule* in the meantime was to compel bodies falling within the scope of the unlawful acts to take positive measures to prevent harassment and those consequences are now well known to us (notices in public buildings, railway stations, doctors' surgeries etc that harassment of staff will not be tolerated, and so on). Many regret the passing of *Burton and Rhule.*

---

[21] [1997] ICR 1, [1996] IRLR 596.

[22] For whose actions the employer would not be vicariously liable under the Acts.

[23] There are many illustrations of the application of the principle in *Burton and Rhule*; see, eg *Thompson v Black Country Housing Association Ltd* [1999] DCLD 39; *Bennett v Essex County Council* and others (EAT No. 1447/98) EOR DCLD No. 42B,[2] Winter 1999; *Bhimji v Wigan and Leigh College* (ET Case No. 2400202/00) EOR DCLD Number 48S,[3] Summer 2001; *Ado-Jingwa v Connex South Eastern Ltd* [2001] DCLD 48; *Motcho v Greene King Retail Services Ltd* [2001] DCLD 49; *Anthony v Marlows Ltd t/a Marlows Restaurant* [2001] DCLD 49.

[24] [2003] ICR 937, [2003] UKHL 34, [2003] IRLR 512. The new meaning of 'harassment' under section 3B DDA and its potential in respect of third party harassment remains untested.

Some of the DRC Codes of Practice were prepared and issued before the House of Lords decision in *Pearce* and are in terms which suggest that the guidance depends upon the principle in *Burton and Rhule*.[25] This guidance now needs to be treated with some care.

10.2.7. 'Aiders'

Section 57(1) DDA provides that:

A person who knowingly aids another person to do an unlawful act is to be treated for the purposes of this Act as himself doing the same kind of unlawful act.

Thus a person who knowingly aids another to do an unlawfully discriminatory act will be liable for that act.

A person aids another if he helps, assists, cooperates, or collaborates with him.[26] It is not necessary for the person's help to be substantial or productive, so long as it is not so insignificant as to be negligible.[27] The aid must be knowingly given, so a general attitude of helpfulness and cooperation will not be enough. An aider must know that the person he is aiding is doing an act made unlawful or that he is about to do so or is thinking of doing so.[28] In most cases there will be little doubt that aid was given 'knowingly' if it is found to have been given at all.[29]

A person who aids a discriminator is not liable if, in so doing, he was acting in reliance on the discriminator's claim that the act was not unlawful.[30] Such a case would be very unusual: the author has not come across a single one.

'Aiding' cases in which the alleged aider is not an employee are rare. Examples of claims include a complaint that a person has complained about a person to their professional body, on racial grounds, thereby knowingly aiding that body to bring disciplinary proceedings on racial grounds.[31]

---

[25] For example, the Goods, Facilities, Services and Premises Code of Practice, paragraph 9.27 ('It is unlawful for a person managing any premises to discriminate against a disabled person occupying those premises by subjecting him or her to any other detriment. This includes subjecting disabled people to harassment (or failing to prevent them being subjected to harassment by others), for example, physical attack, damage to their property, verbal abuse and other similar behaviour, which deprives them of the peaceful enjoyment of their premises.').

[26] *Anyanwu and another v South Bank Students' Union and South Bank University* [2001] ICR 391, 1 WLR 638, [2001] IRLR 305, *per* Lord Steyn.

[27] *Ibid. per* Lord Bingham.

[28] *Hallam v Avery* [2001] ICR 408, [2001] 1 WLR 655, [2001] IRLR 312, HL.

[29] *Ibid.* paragraph 11.   [30] Section 57(3) DDA.

[31] *Herbert v (1) Bar Council (2) Lord Laming* [2004] (ET Case No 2200381/04) (at the date of writing, this case had not been determined); see also *Anyanwu, supra* note 26.

10.2.8. Vicarious Liability of Chief Constables

Before the amendments made to the DDA by the 2003 Regulations, a Chief Officer of Police could not be vicariously liable for any act of discrimination perpetrated by his police officers. Vicarious liability only arises in respect of the actions of employees. Prior to the making of the 2003 Regulations the DDA did not extend vicarious liability to the actions of police officers who, at common law, are not employees but officer holders with original authority.[32] Section 64A DDA now provides that:

(1) For the purposes of Part 2, the holding of the office of constable shall be treated as employment—
  (a) by the chief officer of police as respects any act done by him in relation to a constable or that office;
  (b) by the police authority as respects any act done by them in relation to a constable or that office.
(2) For the purposes of section 58—
  (a) the holding of the office of constable shall be treated as employment by the chief officer of police (and as not being employment by any other person); and
  (b) anything done by a person holding such an office in the performance, or purported performance, of his functions shall be treated as done in the course of that employment.

This ensures that police officers are treated as employees for Part II purposes and that for the purposes of all the unlawful acts created by the DDA (including those under Part III), a chief officer of police (or chief constable in Scotland) will be vicariously liable for the actions of his police officers.

Section 64A DDA was inserted by the 2003 Regulations that were made to give effect to the Directive, which applies in the employment and related fields only.[33] As noted above, section 64A(2) nevertheless applies across the board so that chief officers are vicariously liable in relation to unlawful acts under both Part II and Part III.[34]

The same provision is made in respect of police cadets.[35]

10.2.9. Liability of Principals for Agents

Section 58(2) DDA makes principals liable for the discriminatory acts of their agents.[36] It provides that:

---

[32] *Farah* v *Commissioner of Police for the Metropolis* [1998] QB 65. This case arose under the RRA but the principle applies equally to the DDA.

[33] See Chapter 3 above.   [34] There are no relevant unlawful acts outside Parts II and III.

[35] Section 64A(6) DDA.

[36] Section 58(2) of the DDA is somewhat differently worded but this does not seem significant in practice.

Anything done by a person as agent for another person with the authority of that other person shall be treated for the purposes of this Act as also done by that other person.

The relationship of principal and agent arises where one person, the principal, consents to another person, the agent, acting on his or her behalf. Where an agent has authority (either express or implied, and whether given before or after the act in question[37]) to act for the principal, both principal and agent will be liable for the discriminatory acts of the agent.

In *Lana v Positive Action Training in Housing (London) Ltd*[38] the complainant was placed by the respondent as a trainee with another company, WM. Very soon after she announced that she was pregnant, WM informed the respondent that it wished to dispense with her services. The respondent terminated its training contract with the complainant on the basis that it did not have any work to offer her. The Employment Appeal Tribunal allowed an appeal against a finding that Ms Lana had not been discriminated against by Positive Action Training, holding that WM was the agent of the respondent and that, accordingly, the respondent was liable for any discriminatory acts done by it.

The Employment Appeal Tribunal in *Lana* concluded that liability arises not only where authority had been given to do a discriminatory act (which will rarely if ever be authorized) but also where authority had been given to do an act which was capable of being done in a discriminatory manner, as well as in a lawful manner. The agents in this case had authority to terminate the placement and, if they did so in a discriminatory way, Positive Action Training was liable under section 41(2) SDA (which is in the same material terms as section 58(2) DDA).

10.3. EXEMPTIONS

A number of exemptions are provided for in relation to the particular unlawful acts created by the DDA. These are dealt with in the subject-specific chapters above. In addition, there are some general exemptions. These relate to acts done under statutory authority and those which may engage national security issues.

10.3.1. Acts Done Under Statutory Authority

Importantly, section 59 DDA provides that the unlawful acts created by the DDA do not make unlawful discriminatory acts done in pursuance of any enactment or in pursuance of any instrument made under any enactment by a Minister of the Crown, or in order to comply with any condition or requirement imposed by a Minister of the Crown (whether before or after the passing of the DDA) by virtue of any enactment. This means that the DDA is not prioritized over other legislative measures.

---

[37] Section 58(2) and (3) DDA.   [38] [2001] IRLR 501.

The equivalent provision in the RRA[39] has been narrowly interpreted. In *Hampson v Department of Education and Science*[40] the House of Lords considered the effect of section 41(1) RRA (which is in materially the same terms as section 59 DDA) upon a claim by a teacher from Hong Kong who had sought, and been refused, approval of her teaching qualification so as to enable her to teach in a State school in Britain. It was conceded by the defendants that their decision was indirectly discriminatory. However, the defendants contended that the action was taken in pursuance of an instrument (regulations) made under an enactment (the Education Act 1980) by a Minister of the Crown. The House of Lords concluded that section 41(1) RRA did not apply so as to exempt from the RRA acts done in the exercise of a power or discretion conferred by a relevant instrument. In this case the Secretary of State was under a duty to make a decision under the Regulations as to whether to withhold approval or not but was not obliged by statute to withhold approval to the complainant. The House of Lords concluded that the words 'in pursuance of any instrument' are confined to acts done in the *necessary* performance of an express obligation contained in the instrument under consideration, and do not include acts done in the exercise of a power or discretion conferred by the instrument.

Many acts are done pursuant to a statutory power, particularly by public authorities (although sometimes by private actors too). The DDA would lose much of its force if *all* such acts were excluded, indeed some of its provisions would be rendered largely ineffective. This is because the activities covered are highly regulated by other legislative measures[41] pursuant to which the discriminatory actions caught by the DDA are likely to be done. Section 59 is therefore likely to be construed narrowly, consistent with the opinions of the House of Lords in *Hampson*. This ensures that appropriate respect is afforded to other statutory measures which might truly conflict with the DDA but that the DDA retains its effectiveness in those areas that are otherwise highly regulated.[42]

10.3.2. National Security

Prior to the coming into force of the 2003 Regulations, the DDA excluded, without qualification, acts 'done for the purposes of safeguarding national security'.[43] That exclusion has been modified in its application to the unlawful acts created under Part II DDA (employment and related fields) and under Part III insofar as its applies to the provision of employment services.[44] Section 59(2A) DDA now provides that Part II DDA and the employment services provisions

---

[39] Section 41(1) RRA.   [40] [1991] 1 AC 171, [1990] ICR 511, [1990] IRLR 302.

[41] For example, the unlawful acts caught by the education provisions: Part IV DDA.

[42] See too discussion at Chapter 7, at 7.3.3.2.   [43] Section 59(3) DDA.

[44] Section 21A DDA. This was necessary to give proper effect to the Directive: see Article 9 and *Johnston v Chief Constable of the RUC* Case 222/84 [1986] ECR 1651, [1986] IRLR 263 (on the impact of the comparable provisions of the Equal Treatment Directive 76/207/EEC).

do not make unlawful any act done 'for the purpose of safeguarding national security if the doing of the act was justified by that purpose'. Thus in each case, if reliance is to be place on 'national security', proof that the discriminatory acts complained of were justified for that purpose must be demonstrated. This represents a considerable shift from the position before the Regulations.

Discriminatory acts falling under Part III DDA (save for those falling under the employment services provisions) are still subject to the blanket exclusion in section 59(3) DDA, described above. In addition, Schedule 3, paragraph 8(1)(b) DDA provides that a certificate signed by or on behalf of a Minister of the Crown[45] that an act specified in the certificate was done for the purpose of safeguarding national security shall be conclusive evidence of the matters certified. A document purporting to be such a certificate shall be received in evidence and, unless the contrary is proved, be deemed to be such a certificate.[46] This means there can be no challenge to the substance of such certificate (that is, that the act done was for the purpose of safeguarding national security) and in any challenge to the veracity of the certificate itself, it will be presumed that it is genuine unless the contrary is proved. No procedure is in place for challenging the contents of a certificate (this may be contrasted with the position now under the RRA[47]). Whether this is compatible with Article 6, Schedule 1 HRA[48] must be seriously doubted.[49]

10.4. TERRITORIAL EXTENT

The territorial extent of the particular unlawful acts has been dealt with in the subject-specific Chapters above. Generally, the DDA applies to England, Scotland, and Wales[50] and where there are differences these have been addressed under the unlawful acts concerned above.

In addition, section 70(6) DDA extends the application of the DDA to Northern Ireland. The provisions of the DDA in their application to Northern Ireland are subject to the modifications set out in Schedule 8 DDA. These modifications are concerned with acknowledging and accommodating the particular bodies, constitutional arrangements,[51] and legislative context that exists in Northern Ireland.

Subject to Sections 5, 6, and 7, Northern Ireland Act 1998, the Northern Ireland Assembly has legislative powers in matters which have been devolved to it by Parliament, including those relating to equality. Section 5(6), Northern Ireland Act 1998 provides that 'an Act of the Assembly may modify any

---

[45] The Secretary of State in Northern Ireland.   [46] Schedule 3, paragraph 8(2) DDA.
[47] Section 67A RRA.   [48] See Chapter 3.
[49] *Tinnelly & Sons Ltd and Others v UK* (1998) 27 EHRR 249.
[50] Section 70(6) DDA. See, for an exception, section 70(5A) and (5B) DDA.
[51] See, in particular, the Northern Ireland Act 1998 and the Northern Ireland Assembly.

provision made by or under an Act of Parliament in so far as it is part of the law of Northern Ireland'. Amendments now made to the DDA by Parliament do not extend to Northern Ireland. Accordingly the 2003 Regulations[52] and the 2003 Pensions Regulations do not apply to Northern Ireland (though the Disability Discrimination Act 1995 (Amendment) Regulations (Northern Ireland) 2004 make substantively identical provision to that made by the 2003 Regulations and the 2003 Pensions Regulations[53]).

In addition, the Special Education Needs and Disability Act 2001 only applies to Northern Ireland to the extent that it does not encroach upon the powers of the Assembly, and accordingly its substantive provisions do not apply to Northern Ireland.[54] There is currently no comparable provision in Northern Ireland although a Draft Order has been published.[55]

As the Assembly is currently suspended, arrangements have been put in place to try and ensure that any legislative measures that are required are still being adopted.[56]

Numerous Regulations have been adopted to give effect in Northern Ireland to changes to the DDA adopted by Parliament.[57] The major exception to this is the Special Education Needs and Disability Act 2001, as stated. Otherwise, measures by and large identical to those applicable in the rest of the UK have been adopted, though some time later, usually coming into force on the same date.[58]

The arrangements for promoting and enforcing the legislation in Northern Ireland differ from those elsewhere in the UK and these are addressed in Chapter 12, at 12.14.

---

[52] Regulation 1(4), Disability Discrimination Act 1995 (Amendment) Regulations 2003, SI 2003/1673.

[53] Statutory Rule 2004, No 55.

[54] Section 43(12), Special Education Needs and Disability Act 2001, states that Parts 2 and 3 of the Act do not apply to Northern Ireland.

[55] A Draft Special Educational Needs and Disability (Northern Ireland) Order 2004 to give effect to those parts of the Special Education Needs and Disability Act 2001, which do not apply to Northern Ireland, was published in March 2004. Available at: http://www.deni.gov.uk/about/consultation/SEN_consultation/SEN_draft_order.htm.

[56] Northern Ireland Act 2000.

[57] A search of the HMSO webpage reveals that, to date, 54 such measures have been adopted.

[58] For example, the Disability Discrimination (Services and Premises) Regulations (Northern Ireland) 1996, Statutory Rule 1996, No 557, and Disability Discrimination (Services and Premises) Regulations 1996, SI 1996/836, were adopted at different times but both came into force on the same date. These measures have subsequently been amended. The Disability Discrimination Act 1995 (Amendment) Regulations (Northern Ireland) 2004 were made later than the 2003 Regulations but come into force on the same day (see Regulation 1(3)).

11

ENFORCEMENT AND REMEDIES

11.1. INTRODUCTION

The DDA is a self-contained code. Proceedings in respect of the unlawful acts created may only be brought in accordance with the enforcement mechanisms provided for in the DDA itself. The enforcements mechanisms differ, as do the remedies available, according to the class of unlawful act concerned, and accordingly they are addressed under discrete heads below.

The unlawful acts are statutory torts and in general terms the courts and tribunals have addressed enforcement and remedies issues arising in relation to them in much the same way as any other statutory tort. Thus, where an award of compensation is made in respect of joint tortfeasors, the award will be distributed according to what is just and equitable having regard to the extent of that person's responsibility for the damage in question.[1] Further, where a person has a cause of action under the DDA, that cause of action survives his death for the benefit of his estate.[2]

The DRC's powers in relation to enforcement (including conciliation) are addressed at Chapter 12.

---

[1] Civil Liability (Contribution) Act 1978 and see *Prison Service and Others v Johnson* [1997] ICR 275 and *Ross v Ryanair and Another* [2004] EWCA Civ 1751.

[2] Law Reform (Miscellaneous Provisions) Act 1934; *Lewisham and Guy's Mental Health NHS Trust v Harris (Personal Representative of Andrews (Deceased)* [2000] ICR 707, [2000] IRLR 320.

11.2. EMPLOYMENT AND RELATED FIELDS

11.2.1. The Employment Tribunals

Claims arising under Part II DDA in England, Scotland, and Wales are instituted and heard in the Employment Tribunals.[3]

The rules relating to the institution, management, and hearing of such claims
are dealt with by the Employment Tribunals (Constitution and Rules of
Procedure Regulations 2004.[4] These came into force on 1 October 2004. They
are extremely important and contain stringent rules governing the contents of an
Originating Application and the steps that must be taken in certain cases before
proceedings are even instituted (particularly in the case of employees, that they
have first raised the relevant complaint as a grievance with their employer[5]). A
full study of the rules is outside the scope of this work but close attention must
be paid to them before proceedings are issued. Importantly these new rules
make specific provision for making restricting reporting orders in disability
discrimination cases.[6]

11.2.2. Statutory Appeals

Where an appeal, or proceedings in the nature of an appeal, may be brought
under 'any enactment' in respect of an act falling within the scope of section
14A(1) or (2) DDA (discrimination by qualifications bodies), proceedings may
not be brought in the Employment Tribunal.[7] This is addressed fully above in
Chapter 6, at 6.12.3.

11.2.3. Burden of Proof and Questionnaires

The DDA makes specific provision in relation to the proving of disability
discrimination.

Section 17A(1C) DDA provides that:

Where, on the hearing of a complaint under subsection (1), the complainant proves facts
from which the tribunal could, apart from this subsection, conclude in the absence of an
adequate explanation that the respondent has acted in a way which is unlawful under this
Part, the tribunal shall uphold the complaint unless the respondent proves that he did not
so act.

---

[3] Section 17A DDA.   [4] SI 2004/1861.   [5] See also Employment Act 2002.
[6] Employment Tribunals (Constitution and Rules of Procedure) Regulations 2004, SI 2004/1861,
Employment Tribunals Rules of Procedure, Rule 50.
[7] Section 17A(1A).

This provision applies to a complaint presented to an Employment Tribunal before this regulation came into force as well as one presented after that date, as long as the complaint has not been determined by an Employment Tribunal.[8]

This reflects the requirements of the Directive.[9] The impact of this provision is as yet unclear. As can be seen, the burden shifts to a respondent where an Employment Tribunal could conclude in the absence of an adequate explanation that the respondent has acted in a way which is unlawful. The key issue is what a complainant is required to show before a tribunal *could* so conclude. In the case of direct discrimination, at least (Chapter 5 above, paragraph 5.2.1) case-law indicated even prior to these changes that a tribunal *could* infer that an act of direct discrimination had occurred where there was a proven difference in treatment, a difference in status, and no adequate explanation for the same. It would therefore seem that in such circumstances, following the change in the burden of proof, a tribunal would be bound to so conclude. However, the position remains unclear. In *Barton v Investec Henderson Crosthwaite Securities Ltd*,[10] the Employment Appeal Tribunal gave the following guidance on the comparable provision in the SDA (section 63A).

(1) Pursuant to section 63A of the 1975 Act, it is for the applicant who complains of sex discrimination to prove on the balance of probabilities facts from which the tribunal could conclude, in the absence of an adequate explanation, that the employer has committed an act of discrimination against the applicant which is unlawful by virtue of Part 2 . . . These are referred to below as 'such facts'.

(2) If the applicant does not prove such facts he or she will fail.

(3) It is important to bear in mind in deciding whether the applicant has proved such facts that it is unusual to find direct evidence of sex discrimination. Few employers would be prepared to admit such discrimination, even to themselves. In some cases the discrimination will not be an intention but merely based on the assumption that 'he or she would not have fitted in'.

(4) In deciding whether the applicant has proved such facts, it is important to remember that the outcome at this stage of the analysis by the tribunal will therefore usually depend on what inferences it is proper to draw from the primary facts found by the tribunal.

(5) It is important to note the word is 'could'. At this stage the tribunal does not have to reach a definitive determination that such facts would lead it to the conclusion that there was an act of unlawful discrimination. At this stage a tribunal is looking at the primary facts proved by the applicant to see what inferences of secondary fact could be drawn from them.

(6) These inferences can include, in appropriate cases, any inferences that it is just and equitable to draw . . . from an evasive or equivocal reply to a questionnaire . . .

(7) Likewise, the tribunal must decide whether any provision of any relevant code of practice is relevant, and if so take it into account in determining such facts. . . . This means that inferences may also be drawn from any failure to comply with any relevant code of practice.

---

[8] In this respect it has some limited retroactive effect: Regulation 2(1), 2003 Regulations.

[9] 2000/78/EC, Article 10.   [10] [2003] ICR 1205, [2003] IRLR 332.

(8) Where the applicant has proved facts from which inferences could be drawn that the employer has treated the applicant less favourably on the grounds of sex, then the burden of proof moves to the employer.

(9) It is then for the employer to prove that he did not commit, or, as the case may be, is not to be treated as having committed, that act.

(10) To discharge that burden it is necessary for the employer to prove, on the balance of probabilities, that the treatment was in no sense whatsoever on the grounds of sex, since 'no discrimination whatsoever' is compatible with the Burden of Proof Directive 97/80.

(11) That requires a tribunal to assess not merely whether the employer has proved an explanation for the facts from which such inferences can be drawn, but further that it is adequate to discharge the burden of proof on the balance of probabilities that sex was not any part of the reasons for the treatment in question.

(12) Since the facts necessary to prove an explanation would normally be in the possession of the employer, a tribunal would normally expect cogent evidence to discharge that burden of proof. In particular, the tribunal will need to examine carefully explanations for failure to deal with the questionnaire procedure and/or code of practice.[11]

This guidance sets a relatively low threshold for a complainant. The burden shifts—and accordingly discrimination is proved, absent the respondent proving an explanation otherwise—where inferences *might* be drawn that discrimination has occurred. As can be seen, it is a *could* test and not a *would* test at this stage. Thereafter, according to the Employment Appeal Tribunal in this case, the burden is on the respondent to show that the treatment was in no sense whatsoever on the ground of sex, or as is material to this work, disability. It appears from subsequent authority that it will not be sufficient for an Employment Tribunal to find only that there is a difference in treatment and a difference in status[12] if the burden is to shift. They must be satisfied that they *could* draw an inference of discrimination within the meaning of the DDA. Nevertheless, a difference in treatment and a difference in status allied with a failure to follow proper equal opportunities procedures or a failure properly to reply to the questionnaire or follow the Code of Practice should be enough to shift the burden of proof from the complainant to the respondent in a direct discrimination case or a disability-related discrimination case.[13] In the case of a failure to comply with the duty to make adjustments, it is likely that the complainant would have to show that the duty is at least triggered (by reason that he as a disabled person is at a substantial disadvantage) before the burden is shifts and perhaps more. As stated, the impact of the shift is still being felt and at the time of writing the impact of it is not entirely clear.

---

[11] Barton, *supra* note 10, paragraph 25.

[12] *University of Huddersfield v Wolff* [2004] ICR 828, [2004] IRLR 534. And see *Chamberlin Solicitors and another v Emokpae* [2004] IRLR 592.

[13] *Igen Ltd (formerly Leeds Careers Guidance) and others v Wong* [2004] UKEAT 0944/03 which, at the time of writing, is expected to be heard by the Court of Appeal in January 2005.

11.2.4. Questionnaire

Section 56 DDA provides for the questionnaire procedure, which is now well known[14] of in discrimination cases. Section 56 DDA permits a person who considers that he may have been discriminated against, or subjected to harassment, in contravention of any provision of Part II or, to the extent that it relates to the provision of employment services, of Part III to serve a questionnaire in the prescribed form[15] asking the respondent questions which explore the facts relating to the treatment complained of and the reasons for it. This is an extremely important tool. The questionnaire procedure is not available in Part III cases (except in the case of employment services).[16] The reply to any such questionnaire is admissible as evidence in any proceedings under Part II DDA (or Part III to the extent that it relates to the provision of employment services).[17] In addition, where it appears to an Employment Tribunal that either the respondent has deliberately, and without reasonable excuse, omitted to reply within a period of eight weeks beginning with the day on which the questionnaire was served on him or the respondent's reply is evasive or equivocal, it may draw any inference which it considers it just and equitable to draw, including an inference that the respondent has done a relevant unlawful act.[18] This procedure is very important indeed.[19] Carefully crafted questions can assist a complainant in properly identifying his complaints and in proving them, as can be seen from the guidance in *Barton* in 11.2.3 above and see Chapter 5 above, at 5.2.1.4.

11.2.5. Remedies

By section 17A(2) DDA, where an Employment Tribunal finds a complaint of discrimination well founded, it:

shall take such of the following steps as it considers just and equitable—
(a) making a declaration as to the rights of the complainant and the respondent in relation to the matters to which the complaint relates;
(c) ordering the respondent to pay compensation to the complainant;
(d) recommending that the respondent take, within a specified period, action appearing to the tribunal to be reasonable, in all the circumstances of the case, for the purpose of obviating or reducing the adverse effect on the complainant of any matter to which the complaint relates.

---

[14] See sections 74 SDA and 65 RRA.
[15] Disability Discrimination (Questions and Replies) Order 2004, SI 2004/1168 (revoking the Disability Discrimination (Questions and Replies) Order 1996).
[16] Though see discussion on the Draft Disability Discrimination Bill, Chapter 13 below.
[17] Section 56(3) DDA.
[18] Ie under Part II or Part III as it relates to employment services: section 56(3) DDA, as amended by the 2003 Regulations.
[19] See eg *West Midlands Passenger Transport Executive v Singh* [1988] IRLR 186.

11.2.5.1. *Declarations*

An Employment Tribunal has power to make a 'declaration'. A declaration is a statement declaring the rights of the complainant and respondent. This will simply reflect the findings in the judgment of the Employment Tribunal but acknowledges that a finding of discrimination is important in its own right and loss need not have been sustained or claimed.

11.2.5.2. *Compensation*

In practice the most important remedy is compensation. Where compensation is ordered 'the amount of the compensation shall be calculated by applying the principles applicable to the calculation of damages in claims in tort or (in Scotland) in reparation for beach of statutory duty'.[20] An award of compensation may include compensation for injury to feelings.[21]

Awards of compensation are unlimited, and on average awards are growing.[22] The average award in disability cases in 2000 was just over £13,000, an increase over the year before of 31 per cent.[23] In 2003 the average award of compensation in disability discrimination cases was £15,634 (the highest average across all discrimination cases).[24] In addition, in disability cases, future loss of earnings accounted for one-fifth of the £1,429,972 total amount awarded, reflecting the Employment Tribunals' view that where a complainant has been dismissed on the ground of their disability, it would be difficult for them to gain other employment.[25] Compensation may be awarded in respect of past financial losses (for example loss of earnings and benefits, cost of moving house, school, or obtaining alternative services up to the date of the hearing, less any earnings received or financial savings made) and future financial losses (for example loss of earnings, pension losses and benefits, additional accommodation costs, etc). In addition compensation may be awarded in respect of personal injury and injury to feelings. An award of aggravated damages can also be made. Further, there is a strong argument that an award of exemplary damages could be awarded in an appropriate case (see further below).

As noted above, in respect of remedies an Employment Tribunal shall take such steps in relation to the same, as 'it considers just and equitable'. However, this does not confer on the Employment Tribunals a general discretion as to the amount to award in compensation. Once an Employment Tribunal has decided that it is 'just and equitable' to make an order for compensation, then it must do so having regard to the normal tort principles.[26] Thus the conduct of a complainant is not usually relevant to the amount of compensation that might

---

[20] Section 17A(3) DDA.   [21] Section 17A(4) DDA.
[22] At least in the Employment Tribunals where such analysis has been undertaken: *Equal Opportunities Review* (2001) 100, 12.
[23] *Ibid.*   [24] *Equal Opportunities Review* (2004), 133, 10, though the median was only £5,310.
[25] *Ibid.*   [26] *Hurley v Mustoe (No 2)* [1983] ICR 422.

be ordered.[27] In determining whether any particular losses are recoverable the test is whether such losses are caused by (or arise naturally and directly from) the discrimination found proved.[28]

Calculating financial losses can be complex in all but the most straightforward of cases. The most complex cases may require expert evidence on, for example, the impact of particular discriminatory treatment on the complainant's position in the labour market or actuarial evidence relating to pension losses. Guidance can be obtained from *Kemp and Kemp, The Quantum of Damages*.[29]

A complainant is under a duty to 'mitigate' his losses. This means that a complainant must take reasonable steps to keep his losses to a minimum (usually by finding alternative employment).[30] The question whether a complainant has properly mitigated is a question of fact in each case. Where a complainant has not acted reasonably, an Employment Tribunal will deduct from any award of compensation a sum equivalent to that which would have been saved had he properly mitigated. This is necessarily so because it cannot be said that such loss has been truly caused by the discriminatory treatment as opposed to the complainant's conduct.[31]

As mentioned above, an award may be made in respect of injury to feelings. In 2003[32] nearly two-thirds of awards (65 per cent) of injury to feelings in discrimination cases fell between £1,000 and £10,000, but they can be much higher. In *Prison Service & others v Johnson*[33] the Employment Appeal Tribunal gave the following general guidance:

(i) Awards for injuries to feelings are compensatory. They should be just to both parties. They should compensate fully without punishing the tortfeasor. Feelings of indignation at the tortfeasor's conduct should not be allowed to inflate the award. (ii) Awards should not be too low, as that would diminish respect for the policy of the anti-discrimination legislation. Society has condemned discrimination and awards must ensure that it is seen to be wrong. On the other hand, awards should be restrained, as excessive awards could ... be seen as the way to 'untaxed riches'. (iii) Awards should bear some broad general similarity to the range of awards in personal injury cases. We do not think this should be done by reference to any particular type of personal injury award; rather to the whole range of such awards. (iv) In exercising their discretion in assessing a sum, Tribunals should remind themselves of the value in everyday life of the sum they have in mind. This

---

[27] See 'mitigation' below for the circumstances in which the conduct of the complainant might be relevant. Conduct may also be relevant to an award of aggravated damages.

[28] *Essa v Laing Ltd* [2004] ICR 746, [2004] IRLR 313.

[29] For an introduction to the issues, see Palmer, Gill, Monaghan, Moon and Stacey, ed MCColgan, *Discrimination Law Handbook* (*LAG*, 2002) Chapter 33.

[30] *Fougére v Phoenix Motor Co Ltd* [1996] ICR 495.

[31] As to circumstances where there is a claim in compensation for 'loss of a chance' and a failure to mitigate, see *Ministry of Defence v Wheeler* [1998] ICR 242, [1998] IRLR 23. See also *HM Prison v Beart* [2004] UKEAT 0279/04.

[32] Equal Opportunities Review (2002) 133, 10.

[33] [1997] ICR 275 at 283, [1997] IRLR 162, paragraph 27, *per* Smith J.

may be done by reference to purchasing power or by reference to earnings. Finally, Tribunals should bear in mind . . . the need for public respect for the level of awards made.

As to the size of such awards, recent guidance from the Court of Appeal indicates that there are, in general terms, three bands of compensation for injury to feelings:

(i) The top band should normally be between £15,000 and £25,000. Sums in this range should be awarded in the most serious cases, such as where there has been a lengthy campaign of discriminatory harassment. . . Only in the most exceptional case should an award of compensation for injury to feelings exceed £25,000. (ii) The middle band of between £5,000 and £15,000 should be used for serious cases, which do not merit an award in the highest band. (iii) Awards of between £500 and £5,000 are appropriate for less serious cases, such as where the act of discrimination is an isolated or one off occurrence. In general, awards of less than £500 are to be avoided altogether, as they risk being regarded as so low as not to be a proper recognition of injury to feelings.[34]

Within each band there is 'considerable flexibility, allowing tribunals to fix what is considered to be fair, reasonable and just compensation in the particular circumstances of the case'.[35]

An award of compensation for injury to feelings does not automatically flow from a finding of unlawful discrimination. Injury to feelings, like other loss and damage, must be proved.[36] In appropriate cases, an award for injury to feelings may include a sum for loss of enjoyable or congenial employment[37] and may reflect the hurt caused by damage to reputation in appropriate cases.[38] In looking at comparable awards regard should be had to the change in the value of money. Increases should be accounted for by reference to the impact of inflation. An inflation table can be found in *Kemp and Kemp, The Quantum of Damages*, volume 2.

An award of compensation in respect of personal injury (including awards for pain, suffering, and loss of amenity and pecuniary losses caused) may be made.[39] Most commonly personal injury claims, in the context of discrimination complaints, arise either out of assaults or comprise claims in respect of psychiatric injury. In the case of injury caused by assault, eg bruising, abrasions, and so on, issues of causation are unlikely to be problematic.[40] Where a complainant claims

---

[34] *Vento v Chief Constable of West Yorkshire Police* [2003] ICR 318, paragraph 65, [2003] IRLR 102, paragraph 65, *per* Lord Justice Mummery.

[35] *Ibid.* [36] *Coleman v Sky Rail Oceanic Ltd (t/a Goodmos Tours)* [1981] IRLR 398.

[37] *Ministry of Defence v Cannock* [1994] ICR 918, [1994] IRLR 509.

[38] *Yeboah v (1) L.B. Hackney and (2) B. Crofton* [1998] Case No 56617/94 and Others and see *ibid.* at [2002] IRLR 634. Indeed, damages for loss of reputation may in an appropriate case comprise a separate head, though the author is not aware of such an award being made in a discrimination case.

[39] *Sheriff v Klyne Tugs (Lowestoft) Ltd* [1999] IRLR 481; *Essa v Laing Ltd* [2004] ICR 746, [2004] IRLR 313.

[40] For an illustration of a complainant who was the subject of racially discriminatory assaults in the course of his employment, see *Jones v Tower Boot Co Ltd* [1997] IRLR 168.

compensation for psychiatric injury in consequence of unlawful discrimination, issues of causation are usually more complex. This is because, in part, psychiatrists are undecided or not in agreement about the specific causes of psychiatric illness. However, in the context of a claim for compensation a complainant need only demonstrate, upon reliable psychiatric evidence, that the unlawful discrimination caused or materially contributed to the psychiatric injury.[41] This is important because a psychiatrist will ordinarily suggest that there is more than one cause for the onset of psychiatric injury. Guidance on the size of awards for non-pecuniary personal injury losses (pain, suffering, and loss of amenity) can be found in the latest edition of the *Judicial Studies Board's Guidelines for the Assessment of General Damages in Personal Injury Cases*. There may be an overlap between an award in compensation for personal injury and injury to feelings and this must be taken into account to ensure that there is no double recovery:

Common sense requires that regard should also be had to the overall magnitude of the sum total of the awards of compensation for non-pecuniary loss made under the various headings of injury to feelings, psychiatric damage and aggravated damage. In particular, double recovery should be avoided by taking appropriate account of the overlap between the individual heads of damage. The extent of overlap will depend on the facts of each particular case.[42]

As a matter of principle an award of aggravated damages might be made in a discrimination case.[43] An award of compensation for aggravated damages may be made where 'the [complainant's] . . . sense of injury resulting from the wrongful . . . act is justifiably heightened by the manner in which or motive for which the Defendant did it'.[44] This may include conduct after the discrimination has occurred up until the hearing.[45] There is authority indicating that where an award of aggravated damages is made it should not be an extra sum over and above compensation for injury to feelings.[46] Instead, any element of aggravation ought to be taken into account in determining the extent of the injury to feelings. In practice, the element of aggravated damages is often separately determined.

Exemplary damages are unlike compensatory damages because they do not operate so as to *compensate* a victim for loss or hurt, but rather punish the wrongdoer. Until recently, such damages were not available in discrimination cases because the law had developed in such a way that they were only available

---

[41] See *Winfield and Jolowicz on Tort*, 15th edn, 199 *et seq.*

[42] *Vento v Chief Constable of West Yorkshire Police* [2003] ICR 318, paragraph 68, [2003] IRLR 102, paragraph 68, *per* Lord Justice Mummery.

[43] *HM Prison Service & Others v Johnson* [1997] ICR 275 at 283, [1997] IRLR 162.

[44] *Broome v Cassell* [1972] AC 1027 at 1124, *per* Lord Diplock.

[45] *HM Prison Service & Others v Johnson supra* note 43. And see *Hussain v Resourcing Solution (Edinburgh) Ltd and Matsell* [2000] DCLD No 44, 7 for an example of an award of aggravated damages higher than the award for the act of discrimination itself.

[46] *McConnell v Police Authority for Northern Ireland* [1997] IRLR 625 NICA; *Richardson v Howie* [2004] EWCA Civ 1127 (a decision of a two-judge court that is widely regarded as inconsistent with other authority and wrong in principle).

in respect of a limited number of causes of action (or types of claims).[47] However, the House of Lords has now held that such damages are not restricted to certain causes of action but are available in any case where the criteria for awarding exemplary damages are met.[48] The criteria for awarding exemplary damages are: that the conduct complained of constitutes oppressive, arbitrary, or unconstitutional actions by servants of the government; or that the defendant's conduct is calculated to make a profit for himself that may exceed the compensation payable to the complainant; and that the compensation awarded is inadequate to punish the wrongdoer.[49] Thus in all serious cases of discrimination, particularly where the actual loss is limited and so compensation is likely to be small, exemplary damages should be considered. There is little guidance as to the appropriate level of exemplary damages. However, in *Thompson & Hsu v Commissioner of Police for the Metropolis*[50] the Court of Appeal indicated, in the context of civil claims against the police for false imprisonment and so on, that where exemplary damages are appropriate they are unlikely to be less than £5,000, otherwise the case is probably not one which justifies an award of exemplary damages at all, and the figure of £50,000 should be regarded as the absolute maximum. These figures should be adjusted to take account of inflation.

An Employment Tribunal has the power to award interest on losses calculated to the date of the tribunal hearing.[51] Interest compensates a complainant for loss of use of the money that he is eventually awarded in compensation. It therefore only attaches to compensation in respect of losses which accrue before the 'date of calculation', which in practice is the date of the remedies hearing.[52] Interest may be awarded by an Employment Tribunal in respect of compensation for injury to feelings for the period beginning when the act complained of was done and ending on the day of calculation. In respect of compensation for other losses (arising before the date of calculation), interest is awarded for the period beginning on the mid-point date (ie halfway through the period beginning when the act complained of was done and ending on the day of the calculation) and ending on the day of the calculation. This takes account of the fact that, where

---

[47] *Broome v Cassell & Co* [1972] AC 1027; *Deane v London Borough of Ealing* [1993] IRLR 209, EAT.

[48] *Kuddus (AP) v Chief Constable of Leicestershire Constabulary* [2001] UKHL 29; [2002] AC 122.

[49] Exemplary damages may also be awarded where the awarding of exemplary damages is expressly authorized by statute (the DDA does *not* expressly authorize the awarding of exemplary damages).

[50] [1998] QB 498.

[51] Employment Tribunals (Interest on Awards in Discrimination Cases) Regulations 1996, SI 1996/2803. At the time of writing the rate is 6% though it does vary. Interest will also accrue on an award of compensation made by a tribunal or court where it is not paid: Employment Tribunals (Interest) Order 1990, SI 1990/479. At the time of writing the rate is 8%. Interest is usually assessed at the rate of 2% flat per annum from the date of presentation of the claim to the date of computation on personal injury awards for pain, suffering, and loss of amenity.

[52] Employment Tribunals (Interest on Awards in Discrimination Cases) Regulations 1996, *supra* note 51. Regulation 5.

there is a continuing loss, not all of the loss arises on the date on which the act occurred and awarding interest from halfway through the period of loss gives appropriate credit for that. An Employment Tribunal may award interest in respect of a different period than that prescribed by the Regulations or for such different periods in respect of various sums where it considers that in the circumstances serious injustice would otherwise be caused.[53]

Some compensation is taxable. The rules relating to taxation are very complex and outside the scope of this book. As a very general guide, compensation in respect of lost money which would have been taxable in the hands of a complainant is taxable. If any sum in compensation will be taxable in the hands of the complainant, it should be 'grossed' up to take account of any tax that will need to paid upon it.

11.2.5.3. *Recommendations*

The DDA permits an Employment Tribunal to make recommendations upon a finding of unlawful discrimination.[54] The power is limited in that any recommendation must be for the purpose of obviating or reducing the adverse effect on the complainant of any matter to which the complaint relates.[55] Whilst a recommendation under the DDA must therefore be directed at obviating or reducing the adverse effects on the complainant, those adverse effects need only be *related* to the complaint made, not necessarily consequent upon it. This might permit an Employment Tribunal to recommend a change to a policy or rule even if the policy or rule was not itself the subject of complaint.

Where an Employment Tribunal makes a recommendation and 'without reasonable justification' the respondent fails to comply with it, then 'if it thinks it just and equitable to do so', the Employment Tribunal may increase the amount of any compensatory award or, if an order of compensation was not made, make such an order.[56]

11.2.5.4. *Settlements*

As stated above, a term in a contract which purports to exclude or limit any provision of Part II or the jurisdiction of the Employment Tribunal in respect of a Part II claim, is unenforceable by any person in whose favour the term would operate (Chapter 6 above, at 6.13). A limited exemption, however, applies in relation to 'compromise agreements'. Such agreements are agreements made in settlement of a complaint or potential complaint under the DDA that comply

---

[53] *Ibid.* Regulation 6(3).

[54] Section 17A(2)(c) DDA.

[55] This is somewhat wider (*'any matter to which the complaint* relates') than the comparable power in the SDA and RRA (SDA section 65(1)(c); RRA section 56(1)(c)). *British Gas v Sharma* [1991] IRLR 101, *Noone v NW Thames Regional Health Authority [1998] IRLR 195* and *Noone v NW Thames Regional Health Authority (No 2)* [1988] IRLR 530, must be viewed in that light.

[56] Section 17A(5) DDA.

with certain required formalities.[57] These formalities are set out in Schedule 3A DDA and are as follows:

- the contract must be in writing;
- the contract must relate to the particular complaint;
- the complainant must have received advice from a relevant independent adviser as to the terms and effect of the proposed contract and in particular its effect on his ability to pursue a complaint before an Employment Tribunal;
- there must be in force, when the adviser gives the advice, a contract of insurance, or an indemnity provided for members of a profession or professional body, covering the risk of a claim by the complainant in respect of loss arising in consequence of the advice;
- the contract must identify the adviser; and
- the contract must state that the conditions regulating compromise contracts under Schedule 3A DDA are satisfied.

A relevant independent adviser for these purposes is a qualified lawyer; or an officer, official, employee, or member of an independent trade union who has been certified in writing by the trade union as competent to give advice and as authorized to do so on behalf of the trade union; or works at an advice centre (whether as an employee or a volunteer) and has been certified in writing by the centre as competent to give advice and as authorized to do so on behalf of the centre. However, employees or other persons acting for or connected to the opposing party are not qualified for these purposes. Any other 'settlements' even if otherwise contractual will not exclude the jurisdiction of the Employment Tribunal.

11.3. GOODS, FACILITIES, SERVICES, AND PREMISES

Claims under Part III DDA must be instituted in a County Court, in England and Wales, and in a Sheriff Court, in Scotland.[58] This may be done by way of a claim under the DDA (in the small claims court where any award of compensation will be small) or by way of a counter-claim (as, for example, in possession proceedings where a landlord seeks to evict a tenant in breach of the DDA[59]).

The questionnaire procedure is not available in Part III cases (except in the case of employment services). This is addressed by the Draft Disability

---

[57] Schedule 3A, Part 1, paragraphs 2–4.

[58] Section 25(3) and (4) DDA. Note the Draft Disability Discrimination Bill will, when enacted, remove claims in respect of 'employment services' to the jurisdiction of the employment tribunals: Disability DiscriminationBill, Schedule, paragraph 11. See further Chapter 13 below.

[59] *Council of the City of Manchester v (1) Romano (2) Samari* [2004] EWCA Civ 834, paragraphs 63–4.

Discrimination Bill (Clause 10), which will extend the procedure to Part III cases (see Chapter 13 below).

The remedies available in a County or Sheriff Court action are those which are available in the High Court (in England and Wales) and the Court of Session (in Scotland). In particular, awards of compensation[60] and declarations may be made. Unlike in the Employment Tribunals there is no power to make recommendations but there is power to grant mandatory and prohibitory injunctions (including interim injunctions).[61] Compensation may be awarded and the same principles as set out above apply equally.

Awards of interest in the County Court are regulated by section 69 of the County Courts Act 1984 and in Scotland by the Act of Sederunt (Interest in Sheriff Court Decrees or Extracts) 1975.[62] Interest on financial losses is likely to be calculated on the same basis as in the Employment Tribunals, though it is unclear what rate would apply on awards for injury to feelings.[63]

11.4. EDUCATION

Claims under Part IV, Chapter 1 (schools and local authorities' residual duties[64]) in England and Wales,[65] must be brought in the Special Educational Needs and Disability Tribunals[66] ('SENDIST') (for England and for Wales), subject to the exceptions described below. Such a claim may only be brought against the responsible body[67] and only by the child's parent.[68]

The Special Educational Needs and Disability Tribunal (General Provisions and Disability Claims Procedure) Regulations 2002[69] govern the procedure in relation to such claims. As to the remedies available, section 28I DDA provides that the tribunal may 'declare' that the complainant (pupil or prospective pupil) has been discriminated against and, if it does so, it may make 'such order as it considers reasonable in all the circumstances of the case'.[70] Such orders may, in

---

[60] The same principles would apply as are set out above in relation to employment tribunal claims: see 11.2

[61] See Part 25, Civil Procedure Rules. See generally Bean QC, *Injunctions* (Sweet & Maxwell, 2003). For an example under the DDA, see *Anthony Ford-Shubrook v Governing Body of St Dominic's Sixth Form College* [2003] Case No MA315699, Manchester County Court, 27 August 2003.

[62] And the Act of Sederunt (Interest in Sheriff Court Decrees and Extracts) 1993.

[63] By comparison, interest is usually assessed at the flat rate of 2% per annum from the date of presentation of the claim to the date of computation on personal injury awards for pain, suffering and loss of amenity.

[64] See Chapter 8 above.   [65] Section 28I(5) DDA.   [66] Section 28I(1) DDA.

[67] Ie not the individual for whom a responsible might be liable: section 28I(1) DDA (though the liability provisions apply to liability against the responsible body: section 58(1)).

[68] *Ibid.*

[69] SI 2002/1985 (as amended by the Special Educational Needs Tribunal (Amendment) Regulations 2002, SI 2002/2787).

[70] Section 28I(3) DDA.

particular, be made with a view to obviating or reducing the adverse effect on the person concerned of any matter to which the claim relates.[71] These powers, then, are similar to those available to an Employment Tribunal upon a finding under Part II DDA (see 11.2 above). SENDA has no power to make an award of compensation in respect of a claim under the DDA.[72] If a claim of unlawful discrimination is successful, SENDIST can make a declaration that a child has been unlawfully discriminated against, and it can order any remedy it thinks reasonable against the responsible body, with the exception of financial compensation. Examples of the kind of orders that SENDIST might make include:

- disability training for staff;
- the preparation of guidance for staff on combating disability discrimination;
- meetings between an LEA equal opportunities officer, parents, the pupil, and the school to review what reasonable adjustments (short of adjustments to the physical premises or provision of auxiliary aids) might be required;
- the review or alteration of school or LEA policies, for example those that prevent visually impaired pupils going into the science laboratory, those that prevent disabled pupils going on certain school trips, and anti-bullying policies so that they deal with bullying on the grounds of disability;
- additional tuition to compensate for missed lessons (such as science lessons in the example above);
- the relocation of facilities (short of requiring an adjustment to the physical premises);
- the admission of a disabled pupil to an independent school (where the school had previously refused) or their admission on the same terms as pupils who are not disabled;
- additional tuition for a temporarily excluded pupil to enable the pupil to catch up on education missed due to discrimination;
- a formal written apology to a child.[73]

Claims under Part IV, Chapter 1 in Scotland must be brought in the Sheriff Courts in the same way as Part III claims.[74] The remedies available are the same as those available in a claim under Part III, save that an award of damages may not be made.[75] The Education (Additional Support for Learning) (Scotland) Act 2004 makes provision for specialist tribunals similar to SENDIST. However, at the time of writing this Act has not been brought into force.

Where the claim relates to admissions or exclusions where prescribed appeal arrangements are in place, such claims can only be made through those appeal arrangements.[76]

---

[71] Section 28I(4)(a) DDA.
[72] Section 28I(4)(b) DDA.
[73] Schools Code of Practice, paragraph 9.11.
[74] Section 28N DDA.
[75] Section 28N(3) DDA.
[76] Sections 28K and 28L DDA.

As for the enforcement of the duties arising in respect of accessibility strategies and plans, see Chapter 8 above, at 8.3.

Claims under Part IV, Chapter 2 (further and higher education) in England, Wales, and Scotland must be brought in the County Court of Sheriff Court in precisely the same way as a claim under Part III, and all the same remedies, including compensation for injury to feelings,[77] are available.[78]

11.5. TIME LIMITS

The time limits for instituting proceedings in the Employment Tribunal, County or Sheriff Court, or SENDIST are prescribed by Schedule 3 of the DDA, as follows:

- within three months in the case of Employment Tribunal cases;[79]
- within six months in the case of Part III County Court and Sheriff Court cases;[80]
- within six months in the case of Part IV, Chapter 1 (schools) claims in SENDIST or the Sheriff Court;[81]
- within six months in the case of Part IV, Chapter 2 (further and higher education) claims in the County Court or Sheriff Court.[82]

As to when time begins to run:

- where an unlawful act of discrimination is attributable to a term in a contract, that act is to be treated as extending throughout the duration of the contract;
- any act extending over a period shall be treated as done at the end of that period; and
- a deliberate omission shall be treated as done when the person in question decided upon it.[83]

A person is to be taken to have decided upon an omission when he does an act inconsistent with doing the omitted act; or if he has done no such inconsistent act, when the period expires within which he might reasonably have been expected to do the omitted act if it was to be done.[84]

The circumstances in which an act might be said to 'extend over a period' for the purposes of the time limit has proved problematic and controversial. A policy, rule, or practice, in accordance with which decisions are taken from time

---

[77] Section 28V(2) and (5) DDA.   [78] Section 28V DDA.

[79] Schedule 3, Part I, paragraph 3(1) DDA.   [80] Schedule 3, Part II, paragraph 10 DDA.

[81] Schedule 3, Part III, paragraph 9 read with section 28N(5) DDA.

[82] Schedule 3, Part IV, paragraph 13 DDA.

[83] Schedule 3, Part I, paragraph 3(3); Part II, paragraph 6(4); Part III, paragraph 10(5); Part IV, paragraph 13(4) DDA.

[84] Schedule 3, Part I, paragraph 3(4); Part II, paragraph 6(5); Part III, paragraph 10(6); Part IV, paragraph 13(5) DDA.

to time, might constitute a 'continuing act' for these purposes, even where such policy is unwritten and informal.[85] Likewise a continuing state of affairs may constitute a continuing act for these purposes[86] even where the individual acts relied upon are done by different persons and are done at different places.

In a claim of discriminatory constructive dismissal time begins to run from the termination of employment (not from the discriminatory act founding the breach of contract).[87]

In addition, in each case, a claim may be considered notwithstanding that it has been instituted outside of the time limit where it would be 'just and equitable' to do so.[88] This confers a wide discretion to hear a claim notwithstanding that it has been presented out of time. Relevant factors will include:

• the length of time and the reasons for the delay;
• the extent to which the cogency of the evidence is likely to be affected by the delay;
• the extent to which the party sued had cooperated with any requests for information;
• the promptness with which the plaintiff acted once he or she knew of the facts giving rise to the cause of action;
• the steps taken by the plaintiff to obtain the appropriate professional advice once he or she knew of the possibility of taking action.[89]

However, in all cases, in determining whether to exercise its discretion to extend time, a court or tribunal should consider the general justice of a decision either way.[90] The fact that proceedings have been instituted very far outside of the statutory time limits will not necessarily mean that it will be inappropriate to extend time (see, for example, *London Borough of Southwark v Afolabi*[91] presented nearly nine years after the expiry of the statutory time limit). Each case will turn on its own facts.

11.6. JUDICIAL REVIEW

Nothing in any of the provisions of the DDA prevents an application being made in judicial review in respect of a relevant matter.[92]

---

[85] *Owusu v London Fire and Civil Defence Authority* [1995] IRLR 574; *Cast v Croydon College* [1998] ICR 500, [1998] IRLR 318.

[86] *Hendricks v MPC* [2003] IRLR 96.

[87] *Nottinghamshire County Council v Meikle* [2004] EWCA Civ 859, [2004] IRLR 703.

[88] Schedule 3, Part I, paragraph 3(2); Part II, paragraph 6(3); Part III, paragraph 10(3); Part IV, paragraph 13(3) DDA.

[89] *Anderson v Rover Group* (1999) EAT 1426/99; *British Coal Corporation v Keeble and others* [1997] IRLR 336 at 338

[90] *Anderson v Rover Group* (1999) EAT 1426/99.   [91] [2003] IRLR 220.

[92] Schedule 3, Part 1, paragraph 2(2) (or the pensions ombudsman); Part II, paragraph 5(2); Part III, paragraph 9(2); Part IV, paragraph 12(2) DDA.

12

DISABILITY RIGHTS COMMISSION

12.1. INTRODUCTION

The DDA did not create for disability a body comparable to the Commission for Racial Equality ('CRE') or the Equal Opportunities Commission ('EOC'). Instead the DDA established the National Disability Council[1] whose main duty was to advise the Secretary of State. Whether on its own initiative or when asked to do so by the Secretary of State, the National Disability Council was expected to advise the Secretary of State:

• on matters relevant to the elimination of discrimination against disabled persons and persons who had had a disability;

• on measures which were likely to reduce or eliminate such discrimination; and

---

[1] Section 50(1) DDA.

- on matters related to the operation of the DDA or of provisions made under the DDA.[2]

The National Disability Council was required to consult before giving any relevant advice to the Secretary of State.[3] In addition the National Disability Council was required, when asked to do so by the Secretary of State, to prepare proposals for Codes of Practice under the Act.[4]

The National Disability Council was a body corporate[5] and consisted of a membership appointed by the Secretary of State.[6] The powers of the National Disability Council were very limited. It had no power to support individual complainants; no law enforcement powers, and no investigative powers.[7] Overall it was a much weaker institution than the EOC and the CRE.

12.2. THE DISABILITY RIGHTS TASK FORCE AND THE DISABILITY RIGHTS COMMISSION

The Labour Government in its pre-election manifesto committed itself to securing 'comprehensive and enforceable civil rights for disabled people'.[8] As part of that commitment the Government established the Disability Rights Task Force in December 1997.[9] Their role was to advise the Government on what further action it should take to promote comprehensive and enforceable civil rights for disabled people. In April 1998 the Task Force produced an interim report on the role and functions of a proposed Disability Rights Commission. This highlighted the problems caused by the lack of an enforcement body responsible for ensuring compliance with the DDA. In response, the Government issued a White Paper for consultation in July 1998: 'Promoting Disabled People's Rights: Creating a Disability Rights Commission fit for the 21st Century'.[10] The White Paper identified that there was clear evidence that discrimination against disabled people continued[11] and that a Disability Rights Commission was essential if the rights of disabled people were truly to be recognized and if business and the public and voluntary sectors were to have the consistent and central support

---

[2] Section 50(2) DDA. In discharging such duties, the National Disability Council was required to have regard to the extent and nature of the benefits which would be likely to result from the implementation of any recommendation it made and the likely cost of implementing any such recommendation and where reasonably practicable it was required to make an assessment of the likely cost and likely financial benefits which would result from implementing any recommendation: section 50(5) and (6) DDA.

[3] Section 50(7) DDA.   [4] Section 51(1) DDA.
[5] Schedule 5, paragraph 1(1) DDA.   [6] Schedule 5, paragraph 3(1), (3) DDA.
[7] See Section 50 and, in particular, section 50(3) and (4) DDA.
[8] See reference to the same in the Introduction to the White Paper 'Promoting Disabled Peoples Rights, Creating a Disability Rights Commission fit for the 21st Century' (July 1998) CM 3977.
[9] Discussed in Chapter 2 above.
[10] CM 3977.   [11] White Paper, *supra* note 8, paragraph 1.5.

they needed to act in accordance with, and fulfil the spirit of, the legislation.[12] The White Paper proposed eight key principles upon which a Disability Rights Commission would be based:

- it should be truly effective in helping disabled people secure their rights in eliminating discrimination;
- it should be able to work effectively with business, the public, and the voluntary sector;
- it should be even-handed between the legitimate interests of all stakeholders, notably disabled people, employers, and service providers;
- it should be a central source of information and advice and a means through which to spread good practice;
- it should promote conciliation in cases of dispute, but also, when necessary, the development of case-law which would clarify the rights and responsibilities of all concerned;
- it should operate effectively, keeping red tape to a minimum;
- it should work in partnership with existing bodies; and
- it should provide value for money to the community.[13]

The White Paper identified the key duties and powers that the Government viewed as essential to give effect to those underpinning principles.

The following year the Disability Rights Commission Act 1999 ('DRCA') was enacted establishing the Disability Rights Commission ('DRC').

The DRC has more extensive powers compared to the National Disability Council which it replaced, and is much more like the EOC and the CRE. It has the power to support individual complainants, it has law enforcement powers, and it has formal investigation powers.

12.3. THE DUTIES AND POWERS OF THE DRC

As a statutory corporation,[14] the duties and powers of the DRC are as prescribed in its establishing Act. Section 2(1) of the DRCA provides that the DRC has the following duties:

- to work towards the elimination of discrimination against disabled persons;
- to promote the equalization of opportunities for disabled persons;
- to take such steps as it considers appropriate with a view to encouraging good practice in the treatment of disabled persons; and

---

[12] *Ibid.* paragraph 1.6.   [13] *Ibid.* paragraph 2.1.
[14] Schedule 1, paragraph 1(1) Disability Rights Commission Act 1999.

- to keep under review the working of the Disability Discrimination Act 1995 and the DRCA.

Under section 2(2):

The Commission may, for any purpose connected with the performance of its functions—
(a) make proposals or give other advice to any Minister of the Crown as to any aspect of the law or a proposed change to the law;
(b) make proposals or give other advice to any Government agency or other public authority as to the practical application of any law;
(c) undertake, or arrange for or support (whether financially or otherwise), the carrying out of research or the provision of advice or information.

However, section 2(2) also provides that '[n]othing in this subsection is to be regarded as limiting the Commission's powers'. The powers of the DRC are therefore not closely prescribed but are to be deduced from and will be incidental to its duties. The limits on the DRC's powers will be determined by reference to the scope of its functions. Its functions are prescribed by the duties imposed upon it as set out above. Its implicit powers under the DRCA have justified the DRC intervening in litigation on occasions to make representations to the Court, in accordance with its duties under section 2(1) of the DRCA.[15]

In addition the DRCA gives the DRC a number of specific powers. These are:

- the power to conduct formal investigations;
- the power to enter into binding agreements;
- the power to bring injunction proceedings in cases of persistent discrimination;
- the power to provide assistance to individuals who have brought or propose to bring proceedings under the DDA;
- the power to issue Codes of Practice; and
- the power to make arrangements with another person for the provision of conciliation services.

These are addressed below. The 2003 Regulations also give the DRC powers to bring proceedings in respect of discriminatory advertisements and pressure and instructions to discriminate. These unlawful acts and the DRC's powers in respect of the same are addressed fully in Chapter 6 above, paragraphs 6.16 and 6.17.

---

[15] *Essa v Laing Ltd* [2004] ICR 746, IRLR 313; *R (A, B, X and Y) v East Sussex CC and the Disability Rights Commission (No 2)* [2003] EWHC 167 (Admin), (2003) 6 CCLR 194 (see, paragraphs 178–85); *R (Burke) v (1) General Medical Council (2) The Disability Rights Commission (3) The Official Solicitor* [2004] EWHC 1879 (Admin) (see paragraph 23).

12.4. CONSTITUTION OF THE DRC

As stated, the DRC is a statutory corporation.[16] It consists of a membership of not less than ten and not more than fifteen Commissioners who are appointed by the Secretary of State.[17] There is a statutory requirement that the majority of the Commissioners will be disabled persons or persons who have had a disability.[18] The Secretary of State is empowered to appoint as a Commissioner a person who is not disabled or has not had a disability but only if he is satisfied that after that appointment more than half of the Commissioners will still be disabled persons or persons who have had a disability.[19] This ensures that the representation of disabled people in the governance of the DRC is mandatory and institutionalised.

The period in respect of which a Commissioner might hold office and provisions for termination are set out in Schedule 1.[20] In addition, the Secretary of State may appoint one Commissioner as Chairman of the Commission[21] and one or two other Commissioners as deputy Chairmen.[22]

12.5. FORMAL INVESTIGATIONS

Section 3(1) of the DRCA makes provision for formal investigations, in particular it gives the DRC power to conduct a formal investigation 'for any purpose connected with the performance of its duties under section 2(1)'.

Formal investigation powers are extremely important. They permit the DRC, and the other Commissions, to address institutional discrimination and widespread discriminatory practices without the requirement for an individual complainant or the burden of individual litigation. They enable the DRC to use coercive powers to obtain documentary and other evidence that may be relevant in exposing unlawful practices. Individual litigation, whilst a useful model for providing redress to victims of specific acts of discrimination, is an unwieldy and unreliable tool for challenging entrenched discriminatory practices. Often individual litigants settle cases, sometimes with confidentiality clauses, and usually

---

[16] Section 1(1) and Schedule 1, paragraph 1(1) DRCA.

[17] Schedule 1, paragraph 2(1) DRCA. Schedule 1, paragraph 8 addresses remuneration, pensions, etc of Commissioners. Incidental provision is made in relation to the Commission for staffing, the regulation of its proceedings and accounts, and so on under Schedule 1.

[18] Schedule 1, paragraph 2(2) DRCA.

[19] *Ibid.* This requirement does not apply in respect of the first 3 appointments of Commissioners but applies thereafter and in particular to the balance of appointments made to achieve the minimum number of Commissioners being between ten and fifteen in total, Schedule 1, paragraph 2(3) DRCA.

[20] See, Schedule 1, paragraphs 3–5.   [21] Currently Bert Massie.

[22] Schedule 1, paragraph 6. See too paragraph 8 for remuneration, pensions, etc of Commissioners. Incidental provision is made in relation to the Commission for staffing, the regulation of its proceedings and accounts, and so on under Schedule 1.

without admission of liability. Individual litigation can be expensive and carries the risk that the facts relied on to support the particular complaint may not, on the evidence, be made out. The White Paper recognized and acknowledged the significance of formal investigations.[23]

In addition, the DRC's formal investigation powers have been drafted in such a way as to address some of the weaknesses seen in the formal investigation powers of the EOC and the CRE. In particular, the DRCA appears to avoid some of the problems that had developed for the CRE and the EOC following the decision of the House of Lords in *Re Prestige Group plc.* Under the RRA the CRE has powers to conduct what are, in effect, two different types of formal investigations: 'named person' investigations, based on suspicion of unlawful acts by one or more named persons, and 'general' investigations, for which the RRA specified different procedural requirements at various stages. In *Re Prestige* the House of Lords held that it is 'a condition precedent to the exercise by the CRE of its power to conduct named persons investigations that the CRE should in fact have already formed a suspicion that the persons named may have committed some unlawful act of discrimination and had at any rate *some* grounds for so suspecting'.[24]

The test for determining whether there are sufficient grounds to propose a 'named person' investigation was described by the House of Lords in *R v Commission for Racial Equality, ex parte Hillingdon London Borough Council*:[25]

To entitle the Commission to embark upon the full investigation it is enough that there should be material before the Commission sufficient to raise in the minds of reasonable men, possessed of the experience of covert racial discrimination that has been acquired by the Commission, a suspicion that there may have been acts by the person named of racial discrimination of the kind that it is proposed to investigate.[26]

This means that for a named person investigation, the exercise of the investigative powers of the EOC and CRE, including the power to obtain information and disclosure of documents,[27] are dependent upon there first being some suspicion, based on some grounds, that an unlawful act has been committed. The difficulty with this interpretation is that it requires some evidence founding a suspicion as a precondition to the exercising of the formal investigation powers. However, it is plain that the very purpose of the investigative powers is to provide the Commissions with the evidence necessary to determine whether there are any unlawful acts occurring. It therefore undermines the role of the Commissions in tackling particularly covert or institutional discrimination. It also prohibits the Commissions from uncovering and addressing unlawful acts

---

[23] 'Promoting Disabled Peoples Rights: Creating a Disability Rights Commission fit for the 21st Century', *supra* at notes 8 and 10, at paragraph 4.23.

[24] [1984] 1 WLR 335, *per* Lord Diplock at 342 and see *R v Commission for Racial Equality, ex parte Hillingdon London Borough Council* [1982] QB 276.

[25] [1982] QB 276.   [26] *Hillingdon, supra* note 25, *per* Lord Diplock at 791.

[27] Sections 59(1) SDA and 50(1) RRA.

by named persons during the course of a general investigation and from acting upon them, and it risks drawing the Commissions into prolonged and expensive litigation about whether or not a particular investigation of a named person falls within or outwith their powers (as exemplified by the *Hillingdon* and *Prestige* cases, which both went to the House of Lords). It appears that this interpretation of the Commission's powers is not consistent with Parliament's intention[28] but reflects the courts' hostility to Parliament's chosen model.[29]

The DRCA contains a broad power to conduct formal investigations in section 3(1) DRCA, as set out above. In addition, the DRC must conduct a formal investigation if directed to do so by the Secretary of State (section 3(2) DRA).

As with the SDA and the RRA, it is plainly envisaged that the DRC might conduct a general or a named investigation as the DRCA provides for different forms of notice. Thus, '[w]here the terms of reference confine the investigation to activities of one or more named persons, notice of the holding of the investigation and the terms of reference shall be served on each of those persons'.[30] However, '[w]here the terms of reference do not confine the investigation to activities of one or more named persons, notice of the holding of the investigation and the terms of reference shall be published in such manner as appears to the Commission appropriate to bring it to the attention of persons likely to be affected by it'.[31]

In addition, reflecting the case-law described above, where the DRC proposes to investigate whether a person has committed or is committing any unlawful act[32] during the course of a formal investigation, the DRC may not do so unless:

• the investigation is a named person investigation and such persons are named within the terms of reference;

• the DRC 'has reason to believe that the person concerned may have committed or may be committing the acts in question'. The 'unlawful acts' are acts made unlawful by any provision of Parts II, III, or IV of the DDA.[33]

---

[28] See observations of the CRE in their first review of the Race Relations Act 1976, 'Review of the Race Relations Act 1976: Proposals for Change' (1985), CRE.

[29] See for example the comments of Lord Denning in *Science Research Council v Nassé* [1979] QB144, 172: '[The CRE] can conduct "formal investigations" by which they can interrogate employers and educational authorities up to the hilt and compel disclosure of documents on a massive scale. . . . No plea is available to the accused that they are not bound to incriminate themselves. You might think that we were back in the days of the Inquisition.'

[30] Schedule 3, Part 1, paragraph 2(3) DRCA.   [31] *Ibid.* at (4).

[32] Meaning an act made unlawful by Parts II–IV DDA, Schedule 3, paragraph 3(10), DRCA. (The same meaning is given to references elsewhere to 'unlawful acts' in the context of formal investigations: see eg section 4(5) DRCA in relation to non-discrimination notices; section 5(11) in relation to agreements in lieu.

[33] Save where that matter is to be investigated in the course of a formal investigation into the named person's compliance with any requirement of a non-discrimination notice or any undertaking given in lieu: Schedule 3, Part 1, paragraph 3(1), (2), and (3) DRCA.

This puts the *Prestige* test described above in a statutory form where an 'accusatory' investigation into a named person is to take place. In such a case the DRC must serve a notice on the person concerned offering him the opportunity to make written or oral representations about the matters being investigated.[34] In such notice the DRC is required to include a statement informing the named person that it has reason to believe that he may have committed or may be committing an unlawful act.[35] However, importantly, where the DRC does not propose to investigate whether a person has committed or is committing any unlawful act, it is still entitled to commence a formal investigation into a named person.

Section 3(1) of the DDA plainly envisages that a 'non-accusatory' investigation (that is, one which is not proposing to investigate whether an unlawful act has been committed and not predicated upon such belief) may take place into a named person. This means that the DRC has at its disposal powers to obtain information, documents, etc[36] without any necessary precondition of the sort described in the case-law above. If evidence founding an appropriate belief thereafter emerges the requisite notice must be served before the DRC can investigate whether such an unlawful act has occurred.[37] But, as indicated, an investigation may be commenced even into a named person—with all the information gathering powers then available (see below)—without such a belief having been formulated and notices being given. This is contrary to the approach taken by the RRA (and by necessary implication the EOC) at least as it has been interpreted by the House of Lords in *Re Prestige*.

In addition, the DRC may conduct a formal investigation into whether any requirement imposed by a non-discrimination notice served on a person (including a requirement to take action specified in an action plan) has been or is being complied with or any undertaking given by a person in an agreement made with the Commission under section 5 (see below) is being or has been complied but (as with 'unlawful acts') only where the investigation is a named person investigation and such persons are named within the terms of reference.[38]

In summary, the powers of the DRC to conduct formal investigations, and their obligations in respect of the same, are as follows.

- The DRC may decide to conduct a formal investigation for any purpose connected with the performance of its duties under section 2(1) DRCA.[39]

- The DRC shall conduct a formal investigation if directed to do so by the Secretary of State for any such purpose.[40]

---

[34] Schedule 3, Part 1, paragraph 3(4), DRCA.　　[35] Schedule 3, Part 1, paragraph 3(5) DRCA.
[36] Schedule 3, paragraph 4 DRCA.　　[37] Schedule 3, paragraph 3 DRCA.
[38] Schedule 3, Part 1, paragraph 3 DRCA.　　[39] Section 3 DRCA.
[40] Section 3(2) DRCA.

- The DRC may at any time decide to stop or suspend the conduct of a formal investigation (but only with the approval of the Secretary of State if the investigation is being conducted at his direction).[41]

- The DRC may nominate one or more Commissioners to conduct the investigation on their behalf and authorize those persons to exercise such of its functions in relation to the investigation as it may determine.[42]

- The DRC may not take any steps in the conduct of a formal investigation until terms of reference for the investigation have been drawn up and notice of the holding of the investigation has been given:
  —where the terms of reference confine the investigation to the activities of one or more named persons, to such persons;
  —where the terms of reference do not confine the investigation to activities of one or more named persons, by the publication in such manner as appears to the Commission appropriate to bring it to the attention of persons likely to be affected by it.[43]

- Such notice must contain notice of the formal investigation and the terms of reference.[44]

- The DRC has power to obtain information, including documents, from persons named in a named person investigation and from others with the authority of the Secretary of State.[45]

- The DRC must give persons against whom findings may be made (of an unlawful act, a failure to comply with a non-discrimination notice, or a breach of an agreement in lieu[46]) an opportunity to make oral and written representations before any such findings are made.[47]

The importance of the power to obtain information cannot be overstated. It provides a real opportunity for reviewing compliance with the DDA and the DRCA. The power permits the DRC to serve a notice on any person requiring specific written information to be given, documents to be produced, or witnesses to attend to give oral evidence.[48] Unless the terms of reference confine the investigation to activities of one or more named persons and the person being served is one of those named persons, the DRC must first obtain the written authority of the Secretary of State.[49] The power is enforceable by order of a County Court and supported by penal measures.[50]

---

[41] Section 3(3) DRCA. [42] Section 3(5) DRCA.

[43] Schedule 3, Part 1, paragraph 2(1)(b) and (iii) and (iv) DRCA

[44] *Ibid.* Where the terms of reference are revised, the notice requirements apply to the revised investigation and its terms of reference: Schedule 3, Part 1, paragraph 2(5) DRCA.

[45] Schedule 3, Part 1, paragraph 4 DRCA. [46] See below.

[47] Schedule 3, Part 1, paragraph 3(6)–(8) DRCA.

[48] Schedule 3, Part 1, paragraph 4(1) DRCA.

[49] Schedule 3, Part 1, paragraph 4(2) DRCA.

[50] Schedule 3, Part 1, paragraph 5(1) and Part IV, paragraph 24(1) DRCA. Given the breadth of the power to undertake a formal investigation in section 3(1) as set out above, the powers to obtain

At the conclusion of an investigation the DRC must prepare a report of its findings.[51] However, the DRC must exclude from such report any matter which relates to an individual's private affairs or a person's business interests if in the DRC's opinion it might prejudicially affect that individual or person and its exclusion is consistent with the DRC's duties and the object of the report.[52] Such a report must be published.[53]

Unlike formal investigations conducted by the EOC and CRE, there are statutory time limits for a DRC formal investigation. The DRC must publish the report of a formal investigation within eighteen months (subject to the Secretary of State granting extensions) of the notice of the investigation and its terms of reference being served or published, failing which:

- any requirement contained in a non-discrimination notice served by the Commission in relation to the formal investigation ceases to have effect;

- any requirement contained in an information notice served in relation to the formal investigation which has not yet been complied with ceases to have effect; and

- no steps or further steps may be taken by the Commission in the conduct of the formal investigation.[53a]

In the light of its findings, the DRC has power to:

- make recommendations[54] and/or
- serve a non-discrimination notice.

The DRC has power to make recommendations to any person for changes in their policies or procedures, or as to any other matter, with a view to promoting the equalization of opportunities for disabled persons or persons who have had a disability. In addition it may make recommendations to the Secretary of State, for changes in the law or otherwise. This power arises before the conclusion of the investigation concerned.[55]

The DRC may issue a 'non-discrimination notice'[56] where in the course of a formal investigation the DRC becomes satisfied that a person has committed or is committing an unlawful act. The notice is required to give details of the unlawful act and requires the person on whom it is served not to commit any further unlawful acts of the same kind or to cease so doing.[57] Such a notice may include

---

information will be particularly useful when the DDA is amended so as to impose a statutory duty upon public authorities to promote equality for disabled people: see Chapter 13 below, and see 'Delivering Equality for Disabled People, A Consultation on the Extension of the Disability Discrimination Act to Functions of Public Authorities, and the Introduction of a Duty to Promote Equality for Disabled People' (2004), CM 6255. Such powers will provide the DRC with a mechanism for auditing compliance with the statutory duty.

[51] Schedule 3, Part 1, paragraph 7 DRCA.   [52] *Ibid.*   [53] *Ibid.*
[53a] Disability Rights Commission (Time Limits) Regulations 2000, SI 2000/879.
[54] Schedule 3, paragraph 6 DRCA.   [55] Schedule 3, Part I, paragraph 6(3) DRCA.
[56] Section 4 DRCA.   [57] *Ibid.*

a recommendation to the person concerned as to action which the DRC considers they could reasonably be expected to take so as to comply with the requirements not to commit any further unlawful acts or to cease so doing.[58] The notice may require the person concerned to propose an adequate action plan (see below) and, once such an action plan has become final, to take any action specified in the plan which he has not already taken at times specified.[59]

An action plan is a document drawn up by the person concerned specifying action, including action he has already taken, intended to change anything in his practice, policies, procedures, or other arrangements that caused or contributed to the commission of the unlawful act concerned or is liable so to do.[60] Such a plan is adequate if the action specified is sufficient to ensure within a reasonable time that the person concerned is not prevented from complying with the requirement not to commit any further unlawful acts or to cease so doing.[61] Inadequate action plans can be addressed by the DRC in the first place by requesting a revised plan and then by application to the County Court for an order that the person concerned provide an adequate plan.[62]

Action plans become final twelve weeks after a draft is served on the DRC[63] or eight weeks after a revised plan is served where the same has been served.[64] Additional time limits apply following an order by the court.[65]

A person to whom a non-discrimination notice is addressed may appeal the same[66] to an Employment Tribunal or County or Sheriff Court (depending on the requirements imposed by it). A court or tribunal may quash any requirement in a non-discrimination notice if it considers it unreasonable or based on an incorrect finding of fact.[67] In addition the court or tribunal may make modifications as it considers appropriate.[68] Further provision is made in relation to action plans so that if within a period of five years, beginning on the date on which an action plan became final, the DRC considers that the person concerned has failed to comply with the requirements to carry out any action specified in the action plan, it may apply to the County Court or Sheriff Court for an order requiring the person to comply with the requirement.[69]

Once an action plan is in force, then the person concerned is bound to comply with it. This position might be distinguished from the position under the SDA

---

[58] *Ibid.*   [59] *Ibid.*   [60] *Ibid.*   [61] *Ibid.*

[62] Schedule 3, Part III, paragraphs 16 and 17 DRCA. See Disability Rights Commission (Time Limits) Regulations 2000, SI 2000/879, for the time at which such plans come into force.

[63] Disability Rights Commission (Time Limits) Regulations 2000, SI 2000/879, Regulation 3(1).

[64] *Ibid.* Regulation 3(2). Where a revised plan has been sought and not served, the original plan becomes final four weeks from the date given by the DRC for service of the revised plan or four weeks from any extended period provided by the DRC: Regulation 3(3) and (4).

[65] Disability Rights Commission (Time Limits) Regulations 2000, Regulation 3(5) and (6) and Schedule 3, Part III DRCA.

[66] Schedule 3, Part II, paragraph 10 DRCA.   [67] *Ibid.*   [68] *Ibid.*

[69] Schedule 3, Part III, paragraph 20 DRCA. The DRCA makes provision for obtaining information in relation to whether a person has complied or is complying with a requirement to take action specified: see Schedule 3, Part III, paragraph 21.

and RRA. The EOC and the CRE do not have power to require enforceable action plans. Such action plans have the obvious attribute of requiring persons subject to investigations to themselves consider and adopt plans for addressing institutionalized disability discrimination.

The DRC has so far conducted one formal investigation. This was an investigation into the worldwide web: 'The Web, Access and Inclusion for Disabled People, a Formal Investigation conducted by the Disability Rights Commission'.[70] The investigation found that most web sites (81 per cent) failed to satisfy even the most basic Web Accessibility Initiative category. Less than one in five of the over 1,000 company web sites that the formal investigation looked into met even minimal levels of accessibility. In addition, they found those web sites had characteristics that made it very difficult, if not impossible, for people with certain impairments, especially those who were blind, to make use of the services provided.[71] The DRC has made a number of recommendations in respect of the same.[72] The DRC has developed plans for their next formal investigation into health inequalities faced by people with learning disabilities and users of mental health services.[73] The DRC has also indicated that they plan an increased use of formal investigations and other strategic legal powers.[74] In particular, they aim to have at least two investigations under way each year focusing on key systemic barriers to participation faced by disabled people.[75]

12.6. BINDING AGREEMENTS

Unlike the EOC and CRE, the DRC may enter into agreements in lieu of enforcement action.

Where the DRC has reason to believe that a person has committed or is committing an unlawful act it may enter into an agreement in writing with that person on the assumption that the belief is well founded (whether or not it is admitted).[76] Such an agreement requires the DRC to undertake not to take any enforcement action and requires the person concerned not to commit any further unlawful acts, or to cease the same, and to take such action as may be specified in the agreement.[77] Such 'action' will be that which is intended to change anything in the policies, practices, or procedures of the person that caused or

---

[70] (2004) DRC ISBN 0 11 703287 5. [71] *Ibid.* finding 1.

[72] See for report: http://www.drc-gb.org/publicationsandreports/2.pdf.

[73] 2003–2004 Annual Report of the Disability Rights Commission, as submitted to the Secretary of State for Work and Pensions: http://www.drc-gb.org/uploaded_files/documents/20_697_Annual%20Reportfinal16june.doc.

[74] *Ibid.*   [75] *Ibid.*   [76] Section 5(1) DRCA.

[77] Section 5 DRCA.

contributed to the unlawful act, or that is likely to cause or contribute to a failure by that person to honour his undertaking not to do a similar thing.[78]

These agreements are binding so that the DRC may apply to a County Court or a Sheriff Court for an order requiring the other party to comply with the undertaking or with directions for the purpose of ensuring compliance with the undertaking.[79] In addition, a belief that a party has failed to comply may form the basis of an 'accusatory' formal investigation (see above).

Importantly, such an agreement only stops the DRC commencing or continuing a formal investigation[80] and taking steps to issue a non-discrimination notice in relation to the particular unlawful act in question.[81] It does not prevent the DRC supporting individual cases or (although unlikely) commencing or continuing a formal investigation on other grounds or entering into a second agreement on a different issue.

The model presented by section 5 therefore offers real potential for securing expeditious and cost-effective strategic change. It allows the DRC to insist upon change against an agreed timetable without the need to prove harassment or discrimination or to embark upon, or continue, an expensive formal investigation. However, so far little use appears to have been made of these powers.[82]

12.7. PERSISTENT DISCRIMINATION

In addition to its formal investigation powers and its power to enter into agreements in lieu of enforcement action, the DRC has power to take action in cases of 'persistent discrimination'. By section 6 of the DRCA the DRC may apply to a County Court for an injunction[83] where it appears to the DRC that unless restrained a person is likely to do one or more unlawful acts.[84] The power exists only where in the previous five years the person concerned has been:

- served with a non-discrimination notice;

- the subject of a finding by a court or tribunal in proceedings under Part II, III, or IV of the DDA that they have committed an act of unlawful discrimination; or

---

[78] 'DRC Legal Strategy: 2003–2006' (2003) DRC, paragraph 40 at http://www.drc-gb.org/thelaw/lawdetails.asp?id=496&title=ls.

[79] As in relation to non-discrimination notices, an 'unlawful act' for these purposes is one made unlawful by Part II to 4 of the DDA: section 5(11) DRCA.

[80] Section 5(4)(a)–(c) DRCA.

[81] Section 5(4)(a)–(c) DRCA.

[82] Though the DRC has stated that it plans to make more extensive use of their special legal powers, in particular to reach voluntary agreements with key organizations in lieu of enforcement action: 2003–2004 Annual Report of the Disability Rights Commission, as submitted to the Secretary of State for Work and Pensions: http://www.drc-gb.org/uploaded_files/documents/20_697_Annual%20Reportfinal16june.doc.

[83] Or to the sheriff for an interdict.   [84] Section 6(2) DDA.

- the subject of a finding by a court or tribunal in any other proceedings that they have committed an act of unlawful discrimination.[85]

In addition, the DRC has powers described in Chapter 6 above, at 6.16 and 6.17, to take action in their own name (exclusively) in the case of discriminatory advertisements and in cases of pressure and instructions to discriminate.[86]

12.8. INDIVIDUAL ASSISTANCE

The DRCA empowers the DRC to assist individuals who have brought or propose to bring proceedings under Parts II–IV of the DDA.[87]

Where an application for assistance is made, the DRC may grant such assistance where:

- the case raises a question of principle;
- it is unreasonable to expect the applicant to deal with the case unaided (because of its complexity, because of the applicant's position in relation to another party, or for some other reason); or
- there is some other special consideration which makes it appropriate for the DRC to provide assistance.[88]

If the DRC grants an application, it may,

- provide or arrange for the provision of legal advice;
- arrange for legal or other representation (which may include any assistance usually given by a solicitor or counsel);
- seek to procure the settlement of any dispute; and
- provide or arrange for the provision of any other assistance which it thinks appropriate.[89]

The powers to support individuals are of course important and the DRC has funded more than 213 cases since April 2000.[90] The importance of representation in disability discrimination cases cannot be overstated. Such cases are legally complex and often evidentially so.[91] Recent research demonstrates that having a legally qualified representative in a disability discrimination case in the Employment Tribunal makes a significant difference to an applicant's chance of success. The overall success rate for an applicant at an Employment Tribunal hearing between the period 2 December 1996 and 1 September 2000 was 19.5 per

---

[85] Section 6(1) DRCA. [86] Sections 16B and 16C DDA.
[87] Section 7 DRCA.
[88] Section 7(2) DRCA. [89] Section 7(3) DRCA.
[90] See Annual Report 2003–2004, *supra* note 73.
[91] Particularly where 'disability' is in issue or the question of reasonable adjustments arises.

cent. However, applicants who were represented by a friend or relative had an 11.8 per cent chance of success; an applicant who represented him or herself had a 13.7 per cent chance of success; whilst those represented by a Law Centre representative had a 27.3 per cent chance of success and those represented by a barrister a 28.9 per cent chance of success.[92]

The DRC, of course, is not bound to grant such assistance. As long as the DRC exercises its discretion lawfully[93] and compatibly with the Convention rights[94] a refusal to grant assistance is likely to be unchallengeable. Article 6, Schedule 1 HRA requires the State and public authorities to secure a fair trial.[95] Where a fair trial would be jeopardized by the lack of provision of representation or funding for the same, a refusal by the DRC to provide it is likely to be unlawful. The DRC appears to recognize this.[96] The DRC has stated that it will prioritize for legal representation cases that highlight areas in which the DDA has hitherto been under-used or which clarify a point of legal principle.[97]

The power to provide assistance is narrowly drawn. The White Paper[98] recognized that it was likely that individual disabled people would want to test their Convention rights following the enactment of the Human Rights Bill[99] by reliance on Article 14. The White Paper indicated that '[g]iving the DRC powers to provide assistance in Article 14 cases where discrimination prevents individuals enjoying the other rights provided for in the ECHR would seem to fall within the DRC's duty to eliminate discrimination'.[100] The White Paper therefore proposed that the DRC should have power to assist individuals bringing cases under the Human Rights Act in cases where a breach of Article 14 was an issue.[101] However, the power to provide assistance does not reflect this recommendation. Instead regulation-making powers were included under section 7(1) DRCA for the purposes of authorizing support in other proceedings 'being proceedings in which an individual who has or has had a disability relies or proposes to rely on a matter relating to that disability'. However, no regulations have been made under this provision and accordingly the DRC's powers remain limited. It is possible to argue that there is an implicit power to support individuals bringing cases under the Human Rights Act having regard to the DRC's general

---

[92] S Leverton, 'Monitoring the Disability Discrimination Act 1995 (Phase 2), Final Report' (2001) IDS, 97.

[93] By ensuring it has had regard to all relevant factors, ignored irrelevant factors and reached a conclusion that cannot be characterized as legally perverse, etc. For a discussion on the limits on the exercising of a statutory discretion, see Fordham, *Judicial Review Handbook* (Hart, 2003) 39.

[94] See Chapter 3 above.

[95] Article 6: 'In the determination of his civil rights and obligations or of any criminal charge against him, everyone is entitled to a fair and public hearing within a reasonable time by an independent and impartial tribunal established by law.'

[96] 'DRC Legal Strategy: 2003–2006' (2003) DRC, paragraphs 8 and 9 at http://www.drc-gb.org/thelaw/lawdetails.asp?id=496&title=ls.

[97] *Ibid.*   [98] *Supra* at notes 8 and 10

[99] As it was at the time of publication of the White Paper.

[100] *Supra*, note 8 at paragraph 4.11.   [101] *Ibid.*

duties[102] but given that Parliament has provided express powers to provide assistance to individuals in a limited range of circumstances it may be difficult to deduce greater powers by implication.

All three Commissions nevertheless regularly support complainants who have claims in proceedings in addition to discrimination, as is very common indeed, without challenge. A very narrow reading of the powers to assist individuals is likely to be unworkable because it is unusual in practice to find a discrimination claim being pursued without any other causes of action attached to it.[103] It would be disproportionate and impractical to hive off the discrimination claims from the other claims and have separate representation for each of them. A pragmatic construction of the DRCA therefore requires a sufficiently broad meaning to be given to the powers of the DRC so as to permit them to provide assistance at least in cases where one of the claims is a DDA claim even if other causes of action are attached.

Apart from funding cases, the DRC are empowered to and do in fact provide advice and assistance outside of litigation.[104]

Provision is made under the DRCA for recouping costs and expenses incurred by the DRC in providing assistance to an individual by the creation of a statutory charge over any costs or expenses awarded to such an individual.[105]

12.9. CODES OF PRACTICE

As has been referred to in earlier chapters, the DRC has power to prepare and issue Codes of Practice giving practical guidance on how to avoid discrimination or on any other relevant matter to:

• employers;

• service providers;

• bodies which are responsible bodies for the purposes of Part IV DDA (education); and

• other persons to whom the provisions of Parts II–IV DDA apply.[106]

In addition the DRC is empowered to prepare and issue Codes of Practice giving practical guidance to any persons on any other matter with a view to promoting the equalization of opportunities for disabled persons and persons

---

[102] Section 2(1) DRCA.

[103] For example, commonly in an employment-related disability discrimination claim there will be claims for unfair dismissal, unlawful deduction from wages, etc. Similarly in goods and services claims, there may be a claim for breach of contract or, where the claim is against, for example, the police, for unlawful arrest etc. Research indicates, for example, that 51.6% of DDA claims instituted in the Employment Tribunal include a claim in unfair dismissal: S Leverton, 'Monitoring the Disability Discrimination Act 1995 (Phase 2), Final Report' (2001) IDS, iii.

[104] For most recent details see DRC *Annual Report 2003–2004, supra* note 73.

[105] Section 8 DRCA.   [106] Section 53A(1) DDA.

who have had a disability or encouraging good practice in the way such persons are treated in any field of activity regulated by Parts II–IV DDA.[107]

The DRC has issued Codes of Practice in each of the areas covered by the DDA. These were referred to above in earlier chapters.

The DRC is required to carry out consultations in preparing any Code of Practice. Before issuing such a Code it must be submitted to and approved by the Secretary of State and laid by him before both Houses of Parliament and forty days must elapse without either House resolving not to approve the draft before the DRC are empowered to issue it.[108] This process is described as the 'negative resolution procedure' and ensures that the Codes have Parliamentary approval.

As described in earlier chapters, a failure to observe any provision of a Code of Practice does not of itself make a person liable in any proceedings but if a provision of a Code of Practice appears to a court, tribunal, or other body hearing any proceedings under Parts II–IV DDA to be relevant, it must take that provision into account.[109]

12.10. CONCILIATION

By section 28 DDA, the DRC has power to make arrangements with any other person for the provision of conciliation services. The DRC has made such arrangements for the purposes of conciliating claims under Part III (goods and services) DDA. The 'Disability Conciliation Service' (DCS) liaises between disabled people and providers of goods and services within the meaning of Part III of the DDA. The DCS is an independent service, funded by the DRC and run by Mediation UK. Its purpose is to resolve disputes by assisting those involved to reach agreement with the help of an impartial third-party conciliator.[110] Section 28 applies only in relation to arrangements under Part III DDA.

By section 31B DDA, the DRC may make arrangements with any other person for the provision of conciliation services in relation to disputes arising under the education provisions. The DRC has made arrangements for the provision of conciliation services in the education field. The DCS, as referred to above, provides conciliation services in this field as well as in relation to disputes arising under Part III DDA.[111]

[107] Section 53A(1A) DDA.   [108] Section 53A(4) DDA.
[109] Section 53A(8) and (8A) DDA.
[110] See http://www.drc-gb.org/publicationsandreports/publicationhtml.asp?id=108&docsect=0&s.
[111] See http://www.drc-gb.org/whatwedo/conciliation.asp.

12.11. TIME LIMITS

It is important to note that, unlike the RRA and applications for assistance to the CRE, time limits are not extended where applications for assistance are made to the DRC.[112] However, where a dispute arising under Part III or Part IV (goods, facilities, services, and education) is referred for conciliation in pursuance of the statutory arrangements described above, the time limit for instituting proceedings is extended from six months to eight months.[113]

12.12. INTERVENTIONS

It has become increasingly common for the statutory Commissions (EOC, CRE, and DRC) to intervene in litigation. There is no express power in the DRCA (as with the SDA and RRA) permitting the DDA to intervene in litigation. However, as described above, the DRC's powers, are non-exclusively defined and can properly be determined by reference to its duties under section 2(1) DRCA.

The Commissions have regarded their powers as being broadly enough defined to include an implicit power to intervene in litigation where a matter of general interest relating to the anti-discrimination legislation is likely to be determined, or where the purpose of any proposed intervention would be connected with one or more of their duties. As for the DRC, such a situation is likely to arise where the DRC wishes to argue that the DDA or the DRCA ought to be interpreted in a particular way, that interpretation being, in the DRC's view, more conducive than other possible interpretations to the 'elimination of discrimination against disabled persons', the promotion of the 'equalization of opportunities for disabled persons', or the encouragement of 'good practice in the treatment of disabled persons'.[114] The DRC intervened in *Essa v Laing*[115] for example, to argue that the proper test to be applied in determining compensation in respect of the statutory tort of unlawful discrimination[116] was a causation, rather than a reasonably foreseeable, test. In addition, such an intervention may

---

[112] See sections 68(3) and 66(4) RRA, by comparison.

[113] Schedule 3, Part II, paragraph 6(2) and Part III, paragraph 10(2) and Part IV, paragraph 13(2) DDA.

[114] Section 2(1) DRCA. Examples of cases in which there have been interventions by the CRE and the EOC, whose powers do not expressly include the power to intervene either, include *Anyanwu v South Bank Student Union* [2000] ICR 221 and [2001] ICR 391 in the Court of Appeal and House of Lords respectively; *Essa v Laing Ltd* [2004] ICR 746; [2004] IRLR 313.

[115] *Supra*, note 114.

[116] Including under the DDA.

be regarded as appropriate where the legal argument contended for promotes or encourages good practice in the treatment of disabled persons.[117]

There is no entitlement to intervene in litigation. In each case an interest must be shown and the court retains a discretion as to whether to grant leave so to do. The question whether interventions are appropriate is not uncontroversial.[118] Proceedings in this jurisdiction are largely adversarial and the idea of permitting a third party to intervene to make representations has not always proved welcome. Nevertheless, interventions are now part of the jurisprudential landscape. Where the DRC has intervened, on occasions those interventions have been expressly welcomed by the court.[119]

The procedures for applying to intervene vary according to the court in which the proceedings are being heard. A detailed survey of the various procedural rules that might be relevant is outside the scope of this work.[120]

The Government is proposing that any new Commission for Equality and Human Rights (see 12.15 below) should be enabled to intervene in proceedings (although still at the discretion of the court). The Government has indicated that it believes this would give a positive signal to the courts about the potential value of the CEHR's involvement. It anticipates that the CEHR would be able to seek leave to intervene in support of the full breadth of its remit, covering both equality and human rights cases.[121]

12.13. PROCEEDINGS IN THE DRC'S OWN NAME

As observed above, the DRC has power to bring proceedings in respect of certain unlawful acts created by the DDA, as amended by the 2003 Regulations (unlawful advertisements and pressure and instructions to discriminate[122]) and in the case of persistent discrimination.

---

[117] Section 2(1) DRCA. See, *R (A, B, X and Y) v East Sussex CC and the Disability Rights Commission (No 2)* [2003] EWHC 167 (Admin), (2003) 6 CCLR 194 (see paragraphs 178–85); *R (Burke) v (1) General Medical Council (2) Disability Rights Commission (3) Official Solicitor* [2004] EWHC 1879 (Admin), paragraph 23.

[118] See discussion in Hannett, 'Third Party Interventions: In the Public Interest' (2003) PL, 128.

[119] *R (A, B, X and Y) v East Sussex CC and the DRC (No 2)* [2003] EWHC 167 (Admin), (2003) 6 CCLR 194 (see paragraphs 178–85); *R (Burke) v (1) General Medical Council (2) Disability Rights Commission (3) Official Solicitor* [2004] EWHC 1879 (Admin), see paragraph 23.

[120] The usual method is to apply to be joined as a party, albeit an intervening party. Rule 18 of the Employment Appeal Tribunal Rules (SI 1993/2854) applies in respect of the same in the Employment Appeal Tribunal; rule 19.2 of the Civil Procedure Rules 1998 apply in respect of the same in the County Courts, the High Court, and the Court of Appeal. Rule 54.17 of the Civil Procedure Rules 1998 applies in respect of the same in relation to judicial review proceedings where a person may apply for permission to file evidence or make representations at the hearing of a judicial review. Direction 36 of the House of Lords Practice Directions and Standing Orders Applicable to Civil Appeals (November 2003) regulates interventions in the House of Lords, although little guidance is given.

[121] White Paper, 'Fairness for All: A New Commission for Equality and Human Rights' (2004) CM 6185, paragraphs 4.11–4.13.

[122] See Chapter 6 above, at 6.16 and 6.17.

In addition, although the DRC is not provided with express powers to bring proceedings in its own name, it appears that where proceedings are instigated in pursuance of its statutory duties, the taking of such proceedings would fall within the scope of its implied powers. By analogy, the House of Lords in *R v Secretary of State for Employment, ex parte Equal Opportunities Commission*[123] accepted that the EOC had standing to bring legal proceedings on its own behalf, despite the absence of any express statutory power so to do, in pursuance of its duty to work towards the elimination of discrimination.[124]

12.14. NORTHERN IRELAND

The arrangements for promoting and enforcing the DDA in Northern Ireland differ from GB. Northern Ireland has a single equality commission, the Equality Commission for Northern Ireland (ECNI). This was established by section 73 of the Northern Ireland Act 1998. By section 74(2), Northern Ireland Act 1998 the ECNI exercises the functions previously exercised by, amongst others, the Northern Ireland Disability Council. The Disability Rights Commission Act 1999 does not extend to Northern Ireland.[125] The Equality (Disability, Etc) (Northern Ireland) Order 2000,[126] however, endows the ECNI with the same powers as the Disability Rights Commission, for Northern Ireland.

Section 75, Northern Ireland Act 1998 imposes a duty on public authorities (including most Northern Ireland public authorities and UK-wide public authorities with functions in the Province and other designated authorities[127]), to have due regard to the need to promote equality of opportunity between (amongst others) 'persons with a disability and persons without'.[128] 178 public authorities have been designated for this purpose and 162 of them have had equality schemes approved by the ECNI (pursuant to Schedule 9, Northern Ireland Act 1998).[129] Implementation of the schemes has meant that public authorities must, *inter alia*:

• mainstream equality of opportunity considerations into policy development, implementation, monitoring, and review;

---

[123] [1995] 1 AC 1, [1994] IRLR 176.

[124] See also *R v Birmingham City Council, ex parte EOC* [1989] IRLR 173; *R v Secretary of State for Social Security,* ex parte *EOC* [1992] IRLR 376. Note too that the statutory provisions governing the manner in which proceedings must be brought in respect of an unlawful act are without prejudice to any entitlement to bring proceedings in judicial review: Schedule 3, paragraphs 2(2), 5(2), and 9(2).

[125] Section 16(5) DRCA 1999. See section 16(4) for the very limited exceptions to this rule.

[126] SI 2000 No 1110 (NI2).

[127] Section 75(3), Northern Ireland Act 1998.

[128] Section 75(1)(c), Northern Ireland Act 1998.

[129] See section 3, Memorandum from the ECNI to the Joint Committee on the Draft Disability Discrimination Bill, Minutes of Evidence (DDB 112) Session 2003–2004.

- strategically implement the duty, through their strategic and corporate objectives and plans;
- screen their policies, existing and new, to identify those which have significant implications for promoting equality of opportunity, and consult with affected groups to validate their decisions;
- assess policies which have significant impact; consider available data and research (quantitative and qualitative); assess the impact of the policy on people in the nine categories covered by the Act; consider measures to mitigate adverse impacts or better promote equality of opportunity; formally consult on their assessment of impacts and steps to mitigate; following consultation, decide the revised policy and provide feedback on consultation to consultees; publish the Equality Impact Assessment (EQIA); and monitor the implementation of the revised policy to verify that it is effectively promoting equality of opportunity for people in the nine categories;
- make staff aware, at all levels, of section 75 requirements and the need to effectively promote equality;
- provide training on section 75 processes and skills for eg screening, EQIA, consultation, ensuring accessibility of information, and accessibility to services;
- collect data to improve policy and services for people in the nine categories;
- provide information in a way which is more accessible than in the past, including by the use of a range of formats;
- deal with complaints that the authority has breached its approved equality scheme;
- consult in a way that is meaningful and inclusive, including giving feedback and taking on board views and suggestions of people from the nine categories.

The Disability Discrimination Bill, when enacted, will introduce a similar duty upon public authorities in England, Scotland, and Wales (see Chapter 13 below). Something of its likely impact can be deduced from the impact of the section 75 duty in Northern Ireland.

12.15. A COMMISSION FOR EQUALITY AND HUMAN RIGHTS

On 30 October 2003 the Government announced its intention to establish a single Commission for Equality and Human Rights (CEHR). In May 2004 the Government published a White Paper 'Fairness for All: A New Commission for Equality and Human Rights'[130] in which it outlined its proposals for a single

---

[130] (2004) CM 6185.

Commission. It is proposed that the existing Commissions will be replaced by a single Commission with enhanced powers, including:

- a new duty on the CEHR to consult stakeholders on its strategic plans;
- regional arrangements to promote tailored delivery of the CEHR's work;
- powers to promote human rights, including powers to undertake general enquiries; and
- powers to promote good practice and enforce the law in the new areas of discrimination legislation covering sexual orientation, religion or belief, and age.[131]

There have been some objections in principle to the establishment of a CEHR.[132] In addition there are concerns about the limited vision of the White Paper. Its proposals on the investigation powers of the CEHR offer a more restricted model than that provided for by the SDA, RRA, and DRCA. Rather than adopting the DRCA model of permitting the institution of an investigation either into the activities of one or more named persons or into the operation of a policy or practice more generally without an initial suspicion of discrimination, the White Paper envisages only general investigations or 'inquiries'. These would not 'target' individuals.[133] There would be more limited powers to compel parties to provide information. Such restrictions are unexplained and do not appear justified having regard to the very important role for formal investigations. These recommendations have not received support from the Joint Committee on Human Rights[134] nor from the Discrimination Law Association.[135]

In addition, the White Paper indicates that the Government does not propose to pursue certain suggestions made in response to its Consultation Paper 'Equality and Diversity: Making it Happen'.[136] These include suggestions that the CEHR has the facility to take class or representative actions. The Directive[137] addresses such possibilities by providing that:

Member States shall ensure that associations, organisations or other legal entities which have, in accordance with the criteria laid down by their national law, a legitimate interest in ensuring that the provisions of this Directive are complied with, may engage, either on

---

[131] White Paper, paragraph 1.5.

[132] See, for example, the observations of Trevor Phillips, Chair of the CRE, who has indicated that the CRE are adamantly opposed to a merger of the Commissions. See, for example, *Guardian* report, Friday 23 July 2004 'Battle Lines Drawn for Equality Body'. See also submissions of the Discrimination Law Association that such a body should not precede the enactment of a Single Equality Act, 'Discrimination Law Association Response to "Fairness For All: A New Commission for Equality and Human Rights"' (2004) DLA.

[133] Paragraphs 4.3–4.6.

[134] House of Lords Paper 156/House of Commons Paper 998, Sixteenth Report of Session 2003–04, 'Commission for Equality and Human Rights: The Government's White Paper' (2004) 11.

[135] Discrimination Law Association, *supra* note 132.

[136] DTI, October 2002: http://164.36.253.98/equality/project/making_it_happen/cons_doc.htm.

[137] 2000/78/EC.

behalf or in support of the complainant, with his or her approval, in any judicial and/or administrative procedure provided for the enforcement of obligations under this Directive.[138]

However, though this requirement is mandatory, it only requires Member States to permit organizations to engage in legal proceedings where the same is 'in accordance with the criteria laid down by . . . national law'. There is no national legal requirement requiring or indeed permitting the statutory Commissions or any CEHR (absent legislation on the point) to engage in legal proceedings on behalf of litigants, in representative actions or otherwise. The Directive therefore does not compel such engagement.

---

[138] Article 9(2).

13

THE DRAFT DISABILITY DISCRIMINATION BILL

13.1. INTRODUCTION

The draft Disability Discrimination Bill, published on 3 December 2003, contains a number of provisions that, when enacted, will significantly amend the DDA. The Bill takes forward a number of the recommendations contained within the Disability Rights Task Force Report, 'From Exclusion to Inclusion'.[1] Some of the Task Force's recommendations have already been brought into force, in particular by the creation of the Disability Rights Commission[2] and the enactment of the Special Educational Needs and Disability Act 2001.[3] The provisions in the draft Disability Discrimination Bill are, taken together, at least as significant as these changes already made. At the time of writing it is expected that the Bill will be enacted at some time in 2005.

In short summary, the Disability Discrimination Bill when enacted will amend the DDA in the following respects:

---

[1] 'From Exclusion to Inclusion, Final Report of the Disability Rights Task Force', November 1999. Available at http://www.disability.gov.uk/drtf/full_report/.

[2] Disability Rights Commission Act 1999. See Chapter 2 above.

[3] See Chapters 8 and 2 above.

- the scope of the prohibition on discriminatory advertisements will be extended so as to make publishers liable for publishing discriminatory advertisements;
- the coverage by the DDA of group insurance will be simplified;
- the coverage in relation to transport will be extended and improved;
- the scope of the DDA will be extended so as to cover the 'functions' of public authorities not already covered (subject to some exceptions);
- clubs and associations with twenty-five or more members will be brought within the scope of the DDA;
- the DDA's duties on landlords and managers of premises will be extended to include a duty to make reasonable adjustments to policies, practices, and procedures and to provide auxiliary aids and services, where reasonable, to enable a disabled person to rent a property and facilitate a disabled tenant's enjoyment of the premises;
- a new duty will be placed upon public authorities to have due regard to the need to eliminate discrimination against and harassment of disabled people, and to promote equality of opportunity and the DRC will be given power to enforce specific duties imposed by Order and to issue Codes of Practice in relation to such duties.
- the definition of disability will be extended so as to deem people with HIV infection, cancer, or multiple sclerosis 'disabled' from the point of diagnosis;
- the questionnaire procedure[4] will be extended to cover non-employment claims; and
- additional clauses will prohibit local authorities from discriminating against disabled councillors.[5]

In addition other miscellaneous changes to the DDA are proposed by the Bill (including, for example, transferring claims in respect of 'employment services' from the jurisdiction of the County and Sheriff Courts to the Employment Tribunals).[6]

By motions of the House of Commons on 15 January 2004 and the House of Lords on 21 January 2004 a Joint Committee was established to scrutinize the draft Disability Discrimination Bill ('the Joint Committee on the draft Disability Discrimination Bill'). This Parliamentary Scrutiny Committee reported on 27 May 2004 and made a number of important recommendations relating to the contents of the Bill.[7] In general terms, the Joint Committee observed that the

---

[4] See Chapter 11 above.

[5] Introduced in February 2004, after the draft Bill was published: see Joint Committee on the Draft Disability Discrimination Bill (May 2004), paragraph 18.

[6] Schedule, paragraph 11. By Clause 11 some minor additional provision is made in respect of actions against the police: see 13.11 below.

[7] Joint Committee on the Draft Disability Discrimination Bill, *First Report* (May 2004) available at http://www.publications.parliament.uk/pa/jt200304/jtselect/jtdisab/82/8202.

draft Disability Discrimination Bill is in some respects 'a skeleton Bill'.[8] It contains numerous provisions authorizing the Secretary of State to make regulations on nearly every aspect of the draft Bill. While such an approach allows for flexibility so that unexpected decisions from the courts or changes in our understanding of certain conditions and the like can be addressed speedily without the need to wait for primary legislation, it does create uncertainty. It is not clear from the draft Bill precisely what the legislative scheme will look like in its final form. Much of the final shape of the new legislative provisions will be determined by regulations. In addition, the Committee has emphasized the need to ensure consistency across the anti-discrimination legislation, in particular between the DDA, the SDA, and the RRA *and* between the DDA and other new legislation touching upon disability (the Mental Incapacity Bill and the Mental Health Bill, in particular).[9]

The Government has responded to the Report of the Joint Committee on the draft Disability Discrimination Bill.[10] They have accepted certain of the recommendations of the Joint Committee, as discussed below. In broad terms they express the view that,

too much change that affects the fundamental concepts underpinning the DDA is likely to lead to confusion and uncertainty at precisely the time that employers, service providers and disabled people themselves are already trying to come to terms with wide-ranging change. . . Our response to the Committee is informed by the view that allowing the current and anticipated duties to bed down fully, and allowing disabled people, employers, business and others to have ample time to apply them in practice is of paramount importance.[11]

This Chapter addresses the clauses in the Bill in the same order as the Joint Committee on the draft Disability Discrimination Bill.

13.2. MEANING OF DISABILITY

The draft Disability Discrimination Bill contains provision affecting the meaning of 'disability' for the purposes of the DDA. Clause 12 of the Bill provides that:

(1) In Schedule 1 to the [DDA] . . . there is inserted—
'6A (1) Subject to sub-paragraph (2), a person who has cancer, HIV infection of multiple sclerosis is to be deemed to have a disability, and hence to be a disabled person.

---

[8] *Ibid.* paragraph 28.   [9] *Ibid.* paragraph 26.

[10] 'The Government's Response to the Report of the Joint Committee on the draft Disability Discrimination Bill', 15 July 2004 ('The Government's Response'). Available at http://www.disability.gov.uk/legislation/ddb/response.asp.

[11] *Ibid.* section 1.

(2) Regulations may provide for sub-paragraph (1) not to apply in the case of a person who has cancer if he has cancer of a prescribed description.

(3) A description of cancer prescribed under sub-paragraph (2) may (in particular) be framed by reference to consequences for a person of his having it.'

(2) In that Schedule, at the end there is inserted—

'*Interpretation*

9. In this Schedule, "HIV infection" means infection by a virus capable of causing the Acquired Immune Deficiency Syndrome.'

Accordingly, certain conditions will be deemed to constitute a disability for the purposes of the DDA. Schedule 1 DDA already provides that people with progressive conditions which already have (or have had) an effect on their ability to carry out normal day-to-day activities,[12] and which are likely in the future to produce a substantial adverse effect, are to be treated as disabled. Cancer, multiple sclerosis, and muscular dystrophy are listed as such conditions.[13] The DDA, however, presently requires that some effect is caused by the condition; mere diagnosis is not sufficient. The draft Disability Discrimination Bill containing the proposed amendments to the DDA just described will remove the requirement to show that the protected progressive conditions have a present or have had a past effect on normal day-to-day activities. As can be seen, this will not affect the position of persons who have a progressive condition of a sort not covered by the amendments (that is, not HIV infection, multiple sclerosis, or cancer). In addition, the draft Disability Discrimination Bill makes provision for excluding certain types of cancer from the proposed deeming provision, by regulations.

This proposed change emanates from the report of the Disability Rights Task Force.[14] The Disability Rights Task Force considered that the current definition of disability in the DDA had 'significant flaws'.[15] They recommended that HIV infection should be deemed a disability from the point at which it is diagnosed.[16] In relation to persons with cancer, the draft Disability Discrimination Bill goes further than the Disability Rights Task Force, which recommended that people with cancer 'should also be deemed to be disabled from the point at which it has significant consequences on their lives'.[17] As can be seen, Clause 12 proposes that protection be afforded from the moment of diagnosis, even if asymptomatic, subject only to the power to exclude certain cancers by regulations.[18]

The Joint Committee on the draft Disability Discrimination Bill recommends that the Government should not take a power to exclude certain types of cancer.[19]

---

[12] See Chapter 4 above.

[13] *Ibid.*

[14] 'From Exclusion to Inclusion', *supra* note 1.

[15] *Ibid.* chapter 3, paragraph 3.

[16] *Ibid.* paragraph 3.2.

[17] *Ibid.* Recommendation 3.3.

[18] It can be noted that the Task Force Recommendations in relation to blind and partially sighted people (Recommendation 3.4) have already been given effect by the Disability Discrimination (Blind and Partially Sighted Persons) Regulations 2003, SI 2003/712; see Chapter 4, at 4.4.

[19] Joint Committee on the draft Disability Discrimination Bill, First Report, *supra* note 7, at paragraph 55.

They noted that the regulation-making powers in Clause 12 'were criticised by all respondents who addressed this point'.[20] The Government, however, in its response[21] has rejected this recommendation. It has indicated that its view 'remains that there is still a need for such a power given that quick and effective treatment is available for a range of very minor cancers, which would not normally be considered as disabilities'.[22] This does not address the concerns identified by the Joint Committee about the draft Disability Discrimination Bill arising from evidence received by them. Macmillan Cancer Relief, for example, gave evidence that people with cancer had a particular problem in accessing financial products, particularly travel insurance, and that the fact that treatment is more effective, far from being a factor which reduces the likelihood of discrimination occurring, increases the problem 'as improvements in treatments and demographic changes meant people were living longer with cancer'.[23]

In addition, the Joint Committee recommended that all progressive conditions should be deemed disabilities for the purposes of the DDA from the point of diagnosis, noting, the evidence given that the inclusion of some progressive conditions and not others appeared inconsistent and itself discriminatory.[24] The Joint Committee recommended 'that all progressive conditions which are currently covered under the DDA when they begin to have an effect, should be included from the point of diagnosis'.[25] That recommendation has not been accepted by the Government.[26] The Government has indicated that whilst it accepts the 'principle' of the recommendation, it is not persuaded that there are any additional progressive conditions in respect of which protection would be inadequate once the Bill is enacted. This does not meet the concerns expressed and identified in the evidence to the Joint Committee.[27] However, the Government has indicated that it will ensure that there are sufficient powers (presumably regulation-making powers) in the DDA to enable the definition of disability to be amended so as to allow further progressive conditions to be covered more effectively and to address any concerns that might arise from case-law should this prove necessary.[28] The latter proposal is consistent with another of the Joint Committee's recommendations which proposes that the Government should retain a regulation-making power to address any surprising decisions from the courts on the definition of disability.[29] The difficulty with the extensive regulation-making powers has been described above.

The Joint Committee has also made recommendations on the protection afforded to persons with mental health problems. The Committee received

---

[20] *Ibid.*   [21] The Government's Response, *supra* note 10.   [22] *Ibid.* R10.

[23] Joint Committee on the draft Disability Discrimination Bill, First Report, *supra* note 7, at paragraph 54.

[24] *Ibid.* paragraphs 56–7.   [25] *Ibid.* paragraph 63.

[26] The Government's Response, *supra* note 10, R11.   [27] *Supra* notes 23–5.

[28] The Government's Response, *supra* note 10, R11.

[29] Joint Committee on the draft Disability Discrimination Bill, First Report, *supra* note 7, paragraph 64.

evidence indicating that many people with mental health problems were inadequately protected by the DDA.[30] There was substantial evidence that people with mental health problems have had major difficulties in establishing that they meet the definition of disability.[31] The Joint Committee recommended the removal of the requirement that mental illnesses be 'clinically well recognized' and that instead there should be a requirement that medical evidence must establish the effect of the condition on the person.[32] Importantly, this recommendation has been accepted by the Government.[33] Accordingly, the focus will be on the effect of the mental impairment on the person's ability to carry out normal day-to-day activities, rather than a classification or identification of the condition.

The Joint Committee also recommended that further additions should be made to the list of 'activities' described as 'day-to-day activities' for the purposes of determining whether a person is disabled within the meaning of the DDA.[34] They recommended, in particular, that 'ability to care for oneself', 'ability to communicate and interact with others', and 'perception of reality' be included in the list.[35] That recommendation has not been accepted by the Government[36] but the Government has indicated that the statutory guidance[37] will be revised to ensure that developments in case-law and legislative changes are covered. The Committee's recommendation that people experiencing separate periods of depression totalling six months over a two-year period should be considered to meet the 'long term' requirement in the test of 'disability' has been rejected by the Government.[38]

The Joint Committee recommended that the DDA be amended so as to protect persons associated with disabled people against discrimination and harassment and to protect persons who are perceived to be disabled against such discrimination and harassment.[39] This would bring the protection into line with the protection, for example, afforded under the RRA (section 1(1)(a))[40] and make it consistent with Community law, in particular the requirements of the Directive.[41] It is highly likely that the failure to protect persons against less favourable treatment 'on grounds of disability' (which would include both discrimination by association and discrimination based on a misperception that

---

[30] Joint Committee on the draft Disability Discrimination Bill, First Report, *supra* note 7, paragraph 65.

[31] *Ibid.* at paragraph 70. [32] *Ibid.* at paragraph 69.

[33] The Government's Response, *supra* note 10, R13. [34] See Chapter 4 above.

[35] Joint Committee on the draft Disability Discrimination Bill, First Report, *supra* note 7, paragraph 88.

[36] The Government's Response, *supra* note 10, R14.

[37] 'Guidance on Matters to be Taken into Account in Determining Questions Relating to the Definition of Disability', SI 1996/1996; see Chapter 4.

[38] The Government's Response, *supra* note 10, R15.

[39] Joint Committee on the draft Disability Discrimination Bill, First Report, *supra* note 7, paragraph 109.

[40] See eg *Weathersfield (t/a Van and Truck Rentals) v Sargent* [1999] IRLR 94.

[41] 2000/78/EC, see Chapter 3 above.

a particular person is disabled) does not meet the requirements of the Directive. However, the Government has rejected this recommendation, relying on the asymmetrical nature of the protection afforded by the DDA:

The DDA is unique because it does not generally prohibit discrimination against non-disabled people. Indeed, it actively requires positive action to be taken to ensure a disabled person has a quality of access or outcome. This contrasts with the approach taken in other anti-discrimination legislation . . . extending the Act to cover people who associate with disabled people who are perceived to be disabled would fundamentally alter the approach taken in the DDA.[42]

As observed above, the model adopted by the DDA is principally a medical model (Chapters 2 and 4 above). Whilst there are certain, minimal, aspects that might be described as reflecting a social model,[43] in the main it is concerned with the clinical effect of an impairment upon a person rather than its social impact. The recommendations made by the Joint Committee go some way further towards acknowledging a social model which would, as the Government rightly acknowledges, significantly change the focus of the DDA, but this would be consistent with a progressive concept of disability and Community law.[44] Nevertheless, the Government has rejected these recommendations.[45]

13.3. TRANSPORT

Clause 3 of the draft Disability Discrimination Bill addresses transport by bringing transport services within the scope of Part III DDA. It does this by replacing the existing exemption in relation to the use of transport in Part III DDA[46] with a more limited exemption permitting a transport provider to discriminate against a disabled person by 'not providing, or in providing, him with a vehicle or in not providing, or in providing, him with services when he is travelling in a vehicle provided in the course of the transport service'.[47] In addition, a regulation-making power is included so that provision may be made excluding the operation of the exemption or providing that it applies only to a prescribed extent, in relation to vehicles of a prescribed description.[48] This makes it clear that services allied to transport, such as customer-related services,[49] which are already covered by Part III DDA, will continue to be covered. In addition, transport services by the use of a vehicle may be covered where the regulations so provide. The draft Disability Discrimination Bill also makes

---

[42] The Government's Response, *supra* note 10, R16.
[43] For example, the treating of severe disfigurements as having a substantial adverse effect on a person's ability to carry out normal day-to-day activities, paragraph 3(1), Schedule 1 DDA.
[44] See Chapters 2 and 3 above.
[45] The Government's Response, *supra* note 10, R16.
[46] Section 19(5)(b) DDA.   [47] Clause 3, inserting a new 21ZA into the DDA.
[48] Clause 3(3).   [49] See Chapter 7 above, at 7.2, and Chapter 9.

it clear that it will never be reasonable for a provider of services who is a provider of a transport service to have to take steps which would involve the alteration or removal of a physical feature of a vehicle used in providing the service; or to have to take steps which would affect whether vehicles are provided in the course of the service; what vehicles are so provided; or where a vehicle is provided in the course of the service, what happens in it while someone is travelling in it.[50] Again therefore the principal provision made, the exclusion of the exemption in relation to the use of transport, is to be shaped principally by regulations which are not yet made and their contents not known. This has been the source of concern expressed by those giving evidence to the Joint Committee and by the Joint Committee themselves.[51]

As to aviation and shipping, the Government has indicated that it does not propose to use its regulation-making powers to legislate against disability discrimination in these fields unless a voluntary approach (supported by Codes of Practice) proves ineffective.[52] The Joint Committee recommends that following an evaluation of the impact of the Codes, if this indicates that a voluntary approach is not working satisfactorily, the Government should consult without delay on the desirability of the statutory approach. In the meantime it seems plain that there will be no legislative action in the fields of aviation and shipping.

13.4. DISCRIMINATION BY PUBLIC AUTHORITIES

The draft Disability Discrimination Bill contains provision addressing discrimination by public authorities.[53] As stated above[54] the DDA regulates discrimination by public authorities in certain spheres. However, there is no general prohibition against discrimination by public authorities. This might be compared to the RRA which, after the Stephen Lawrence Inquiry Report,[55] was amended to make it unlawful for public authorities to racially discriminate and so as to introduce certain statutory duties upon public authorities in respect of the same.

Clause 4 of the draft Disability Discrimination Bill will introduce a new section 21B in the DDA (if enacted) making it 'unlawful for a public authority to discriminate against a disabled person in carrying out its functions'.[56] 'Public authority' is defined in the same way as in the RRA.[57] Certain public authorities

---

[50] Draft Bill, Clause 3(2).

[51] Joint Committee on the draft Disability Discrimination Bill, First Report, *supra* note 7, paragraphs 132–4.

[52] *Ibid.* paragraph 151.   [53] Clause 4.

[54] Chapter 7 above, at 7.2.   [55] Cm 4262 (February 1999).

[56] As with the RRA, this unlawful act will apply only where the act concerned does not fall within one of the other unlawful acts in the DDA (new Clause 21B(6)) or would do so but for any provision made under the DDA, ie a specific exclusion. This means this unlawful act is exclusive.

[57] Section 19B(2) RRA.

are excluded, including the Houses of Parliament and the Security Services. Where the body is a 'hybrid' body, that is a body certain of whose functions are of a public nature but which is not a pure public authority, then the unlawful act does not apply to acts the nature of which are private.[58] In addition, 'judicial acts' are excluded so that no complaints of disability discrimination could be made in relation to a decision or other act done by a court or tribunal. Decisions not to institute criminal proceedings are excluded (though decisions *to* institute criminal proceedings are covered). In addition, there is a specific exclusion such that the unlawful act does not apply to an act done in carrying out a function of allocating prisoners to a prison or allocating prisoners to accommodation within a prison.[59] This provision is unique: it does not appear in the RRA. Objection has been made to this exclusion and particular reference has been made to the decision of the European Court of Human Rights in *Price v United Kingdom*.[60] In addition there is some evidence that the Prison Service already manages itself in a way which assumes that the DDA applies to prison allocation.[61] Indeed there is some case-law indicating that prison allocation might fall within Part 3 DDA.[62] It therefore seems particularly retrograde to introduce an express exclusion in relation to prison allocation when the Prison Service presently considers that it ought to comply. The rationale for the exclusion seems particularly unclear. According to the Joint Committee Report, the Minister for Disabled People told the Committee that the Home Office had sought the exemption 'because they have other constraints . . . like security classification or medical rehabilitative things to bear in mind when they are thinking about the allocation of prisoners to particular prisons'.[63] The same considerations obviously apply in the context of the RRA and presently apply, though the Prison Service appears to be managing the Prison Service on the assumption that the DDA covers it. The Joint Committee, for its part, recommended that prisoners should be fully protected under the DDA and that the exemption should be removed.[64] The Government has now accepted that this exemption in relation to the allocation of prisoners should be removed. All such activities will therefore be covered when the Bill is enacted.[65]

As with other of the unlawful acts created under the draft Disability Discrimination Bill, regulation-making powers permit the exclusion of certain bodies (so as to treat them as not being public authorities for the purposes of the

---

[58] For example, entering into employment relationships.

[59] Clause 4 of the draft Disability Discrimination Bill, inserting section 21B(5) into the DDA.

[60] See Chapter 3 above.

[61] See Joint Committee on the draft Disability Discrimination Bill, First Report, *supra* note 7, paragraph 198.

[62] See Chapter 7, at 7.2.4.

[63] Joint Committee on the draft Disability Discrimination Bill, First Report, *supra* note 7, paragraph 200.

[64] *Ibid.* paragraph 201.   [65] Government Response, *supra* note 10, R34.

unlawful act) and the exclusion of certain types of acts.[66] The Committee recommend that these regulation-making powers should not form part of any final Bill: if there are good reasons for such exclusions they should be evident from the face of the Bill. The Government has not, however, accepted this recommendation[67] and so the final and precise scope of the new unlawful act is as yet unknown.

'Discrimination' for the purposes of the new unlawful act is defined by a proposed new section 21D DDA and includes disability-related discrimination and a duty to make adjustments, though defined quite differently (confusingly) from the other parts of the DDA. The Government appears to have accepted that the duty requires redrafting.[68]

Importantly, the draft Disability Discrimination Bill will, if enacted, place a new positive statutory duty upon public authorities in carrying out their functions to have due regard to:

• the need to eliminate discrimination against disabled persons;

• the need to eliminate unlawful harassment of disabled persons; and

• the need to promote equality of opportunity between disabled persons and other persons by improving opportunities for disabled persons.[69]

The duty places a proactive obligation on public authorities to mainstream disability equality in the exercising of all their functions and activities. Similar provision is made in section 71 RRA. Clause 9 of the draft Disability Discrimination Bill provides the DRC with power to issue Codes of Practice in relation to the performance of those duties. 'Public authority' is defined in the same way as it is in relation to the unlawful act created under Clause 4, and similar exclusions are provided for. In addition a proposed new section 49D DDA gives the Secretary of State power to impose by regulations 'such duties as the Secretary of State considers appropriate for the purpose of ensuring the better performance by that authority of its [general statutory] duty'.[70] The Scottish Ministers are provided with similar regulation-making powers in respect of Scotland; in respect of Wales, the Secretary of State would be required to consult the National Assembly for Wales and obtain its consent before making any regulations in respect of Wales. Before making any such regulations, the Secretary of State would be required to consult with the DRC.

The definition of 'public authority', as observed above, matches that contained within the unlawful act. This diverges from the approach taken by the RRA, and indeed the Northern Ireland Act 1998, which both impose statutory duties upon public authorities but do so by scheduling a list of named public authorities (to which might be added others by regulation). This has the

---

[66] Proposed sections 21B(5) and 28C(6).   [67] Government Response, *supra* note 10, R35.

[68] Government Response, *supra* note 10, R31 and 32.

[69] Clause 8 inserting a new section 49A into the DDA.   [70] See new section 49D DDA.

advantage of ensuring that those to whom the duty applies can be in no doubt about its application, and those with responsibility for enforcing the duty can be in no doubt about who they have power to enforce the duty against. The Joint Committee received submissions on the different approaches and recommended that the approach taken by the RRA and the Northern Ireland Act 1998 be adopted.[71] In so concluding they had regard to the evidence of the CRE and the Equality Commission (Northern Ireland) both of whom stated a preference for the 'list' model which provided 'clarity' and was 'most likely to have an impact in terms of equality . . . rather than a blanket overall approach'.[72] The obvious downside of such an approach is that it is necessarily exclusive and there may be authorities which ought properly to be subject to the duty but which, by deliberate omission, accident, or oversight, are excluded. Nevertheless, it does have the virtues of certainty and clarity which is important in ensuring that a positive duty is effective. The Government, however, has rejected this recommendation on the basis that the Bill ensures that all public authorities are covered and that a list is likely to become out of date quickly.[73] The Government has accepted the Joint Committee's recommendation that the Bill must ensure that a public authority is responsible for compliance with its duty even where its functions are contracted out to a private or voluntary body, but believes that the Clause as drafted achieves this (notwithstanding that it does not say so on its face).[74]

As to the content of the duties, the Joint Committee notes that, unlike the comparable duty under the RRA, the duty to promote equality of opportunity between disabled persons and other persons arises only where 'opportunities for disabled persons are not as good as those for other persons'.[75] The Welsh LGA describes the wording of the duty as 'confusing in terminology and negative in focus in comparison to the race equality duty'.[76] This appears to be a well-founded complaint. The drafting is unclear and inelegant. (Though that is the least of its faults.) It creates the real danger that the focus upon public authorities will be first to determine whether opportunities are not 'as good' before determining what they might do to secure and promote equality of opportunity. This would be a waste of resources. Both the statutory Commissions, the CRE and the Equality Commission (Northern Ireland), who have experience of such statutory duties, gave evidence to the Joint Committee that this requirement should be removed and that there should be no requirement to wait for disadvantage or discrimination before action is taken.[77] The Joint Committee

---

[71] Joint Committee on the draft Disability Discrimination Bill, First Report, *supra* note 7, paragraph 220.

[72] Joint Committee on the draft Disability Discrimination Bill, First Report, *supra* note 7, paragraph 213.

[73] Government's Response, *supra* note 10, R36.   [74] *Ibid.* R38.

[75] See proposed section 49A(c).

[76] Joint Committee on the draft Disability Discrimination Bill, First Report, *supra* note 7, paragraph 224.

[77] *Ibid.* paragraph 225.

recommends that the precondition should be removed.[78] The Government has accepted that there should be no such pre-condition and has agreed to reconsider the drafting of the duty.[79]

The duty also excludes any requirement to 'promote good relations' such as is seen in the RRA. This is apparently because, so far as the Minister for Disabled People is concerned, it is not 'at all obvious that there are not good relations between disabled people and other people'.[80] This presents an unjustifiably rosy picture of relations between disabled people and non-disabled people. As the Joint Committee observed, it heard much evidence that disabled people do in fact suffer widespread harassment and bullying in their communities.[81] In the circumstances, the Joint Committee recommended that the Bill include a duty on public authorities to have due regard to the need to promote good relations between disabled and non-disabled people. The Disability Charities Consortium and the DRC identified four main strands of activity which have been undertaken with a view to promoting good race relations, and which they considered could be useful in the context of addressing disability discrimination. These include building community cohesion, addressing harassment and violence outside the workplace, promoting general understanding and awareness in the community and improving civic participation, and combating social exclusion and deprivation.[82] However, the Government have rejected this recommendation on the incomprehensible basis that it 'might have a negative impact on public authorities' ability to take positive steps for disabled people'.[83]

13.5. COUNCILLORS

Clause 15 of the Draft Disability Discrimination Bill was published in February 2004, three months after the publication of the rest of the draft Bill. If enacted, it will make it unlawful for locally elected authorities to discriminate against councillors in the carrying out of their official business. Councillors are currently excluded from Part II of the DDA.[84] It is proposed that this new provision will be inserted into Part II DDA. Clause 15A(1) lists the authorities to be covered by the new provisions, including all local authorities in England, Wales, and Scotland and the Greater London Authority. Clause 15 responds to the recommendation of the Disability Rights Task Force that 'local councils should be

---

[78] *Ibid.* paragraph 228. [79] Government's Response, *supra* note 10, R39.

[80] Joint Committee on the draft Disability Discrimination Bill, First Report, *supra* note 7, paragraph 231.

[81] *Ibid.*

[82] Joint Committee on the draft Disability Discrimination Bill, First Report, *supra* note 7, paragraph 230.

[83] Government's Response, *supra* note 10, R40. [84] Section 4C(5) DDA.

placed under a duty not to discriminate against disabled councillors, including a duty to make reasonable adjustments'.[85]

The Government rejected the Joint Committee's recommendations that the Clause be extended to cover all statutory elected and appointed office- and post-holders.[86]

13.6. PRIVATE MEMBERS' CLUBS

As discussed above (Chapter 7, at 7.2) the goods, facilities, and services provisions in Part III DDA do not cover private members' clubs. Clause 5 of the Draft Disability Discrimination Bill does address discrimination by private clubs. It will insert a new section 21E into the DDA making it unlawful for any club or association, operating either open or selective membership, to discriminate against disabled people in relation to membership and use of the club's facilities. Private clubs are defined as any association of persons with twenty-five or more members, which is not a trade association, and where admission is regulated by a constitution. This would include social clubs, working men's clubs, sports clubs that operate membership selection, and political parties. The draft Bill provides a regulation-making power which could be used to extend the provisions of Clause 5 to guests of private club members.[87] Discrimination is defined to include disability-related discrimination and imposes an anticipatory duty to make reasonable adjustments.[88] The Joint Committee has recommended that members' guests be included immediately under the new provisions and the Government has accepted this.[89]

13.7. HOUSING

Clause 6 of the Draft Disability Discrimination Bill makes further provision addressing disability discrimination in the letting of premises. It will insert new sections 24A–24J into Part III of the DDA. The new provisions introduce a duty to make reasonable adjustments in the letting of property. As a result, it will be unlawful for landlords and managers of rented premises to discriminate against a disabled tenant or prospective tenant by failing, without justification, to comply with a duty to provide certain forms of reasonable adjustments for the disabled person. A landlord or manager will, under specified conditions, be

---

[85] 'From Exclusion to Inclusion', *supra* note 1, recommendation 5.18.

[86] Joint Committee on the draft Disability Discrimination Bill, First Report, *supra* note 7, paragraph 262 and Government's Response, *supra* note 10, R44.

[87] Proposed section 21H DDA.   [88] Proposed sections 21F and 21G DDA.

[89] Joint Committee on the draft Disability Discrimination Bill, First Report, *supra* note 7, paragraph 91 and Government's Response, *supra* note 10, R51.

required to take reasonable steps to provide auxiliary aids and services for a disabled person and to change policies, practices, and procedures. The small premises exemption remains, and the new provisions inserted by Clause 6 of the draft Bill will therefore not apply to small dwellings. However, Clause 7 provides a power to the Secretary of State to amend or repeal that exemption by statutory instrument.

According to the Joint Committee, the evidence it received on this aspect of the Bill 'generally welcomed' the proposed changes.[90] However, there was 'widespread uncertainty concerning the meaning and scope of the concept of 'reasonable adjustments', and exactly what auxiliary aids and services landlords might be expected to provide'.[91] Accordingly, they recommended that the DRC Code of Practice on housing should, following consultation, clarify the extent of the duty on controllers of premises to provide reasonable adjustments under the draft Bill, and explain exactly how the duties will work in practice.[92]

The Committee also recommended, in line with the recommendations of the Disability Rights Task Force's report,[93] that landlords should not be able to unreasonably withhold consent for a disabled person to make, at the disabled person's expense, physical changes to their premises. The Government has rejected this proposal.[94]

13.8. DISCRIMINATORY ADVERTISEMENTS

As from 1 October 2004 section 16B DDA, inserted by the 2003 Regulations,[95] makes it unlawful for a prospective employer to publish a job advertisement that indicates an intention to discriminate against an applicant because of their disability (Chapter 6 above, at 6.16). The DRC is given the exclusive power to enforce these provisions. However, section 16B does not currently prohibit third parties (eg newspaper and magazine proprietors) from publishing discriminatory advertisements. This gap will be filled by the Draft Disability Discrimination Bill, which provides at Clause 1(1) for a new section 16B DDA which will ensure that third parties are held liable for any discriminatory job advertisements published by them, subject only to limited exemptions. Thus a third-party publisher will be exempt from liability where they did not know, and could not have known, that the advert was prohibited (new subsection (2A)) and where they relied upon a statement made by the person placing the advert that it

---

[90] Joint Committee on the draft Disability Discrimination Bill, First Report, *supra* note 7, paragraph 308.

[91] *Ibid.*   [92] *Ibid.*

[93] 'From Exclusion to Inclusion', *supra* note 1, chapter 8.

[94] Joint Committee on the draft Disability Discrimination Bill, First Report, *supra* note 7, paragraphs 311–21 and Government's Response, *supra* note 10, R56.

[95] SI 2003/1673.

was not unlawful and it was reasonable for them to do so (new subsection (2B)).

As the Joint Committee has observed, it is unclear why a defence of 'ignorance' should exist (they do not in the case of discriminatory advertisements under the SDA and RRA) and they have recommended that it be removed.[96] The Government has accepted this recommendation.[97]

13.9. GROUP INSURANCE

Clause 2 of the Draft Disability Discrimination Bill makes provision in relation to group insurance arrangements. This is currently dealt with explicitly under section 18 DDA but is also addressed by Part III (goods, facilities, and services, which concepts are wide enough to include insurance services: see Chapter 7 above, at 7.2). Clause 2 proposes to clarify the position by repealing section 18 and making clear that group insurance providers should be treated as service providers and be subject to provisions under Part III of the DDA, though it is intended that Employment Tribunals will continue to hear any cases brought against group insurers and employers (see Clause 2(2)).

13.10. QUESTIONNAIRES

The Draft Disability Discrimination Bill extends the questionnaire procedure to Part III DDA claims (Clause 10). The questionnaire procedure is discussed above at Chapter 11.

13.11. POLICE

As mentioned in earlier chapters, chief police officers are now vicariously liable for the actions of police officers in claims falling under Parts II and III, following the amendments made by the 2003 Regulations (see Chapter 10 above and see section 64A(2) read with section 58 DDA). Provision is also made for payments out of police funds and for other miscellaneous matters where a claim falls under Part II. The Draft Disability Discrimination Bill makes further such provision in relation to claims made under Part III (Clause 11).

---

[96] Joint Committee on the draft Disability Discrimination Bill, First Report, *supra* note 7 paragraph 338.
[97] Government's Response, R60, *supra* note 10.

APPENDIX 1

Disability Discrimination Act 1995, as amended (c 50)

An Act to make it unlawful to discriminate against disabled persons in connection with employment, the provision of goods, facilities and services or the disposal or management of premises; to make provision about the employment of disabled persons; and to establish a National Disability Council.

[8 November 1995]

BE IT ENACTED by the Queen's most Excellent Majesty, by and with the advice and consent of the Lords Spiritual and Temporal, and Commons, in this present Parliament assembled, and by the authority of the same, as follows:

PART I
DISABILITY

1. Meaning of 'disability' and 'disabled person'

(1) Subject to the provisions of Schedule 1, a person has a disability for the purposes of this Act if he has a physical or mental impairment which has a substantial and long-term adverse effect on his ability to carry out normal day-to-day activities.

(2) In this Act 'disabled person' means a person who has a disability.

2. Past disabilities

(1) The provisions of this Part and Parts II [to 4][1] apply in relation to a person who has had a disability as they apply in relation to a person who has that disability.

(2) Those provisions are subject to the modifications made by Schedule 2.

(3) Any regulations or order made under this Act may include provision with respect to persons who have had a disability.

(4) In any proceedings under Part II[, 3 or 4][2] of this Act, the question whether a person had a disability at a particular time ('the relevant time') shall be determined, for the purposes of this section, as if the provisions of, or made under, this Act in force when the act complained of was done had been in force at the relevant time.

(5) The relevant time may be a time before the passing of this Act.

---

[1] Amended by the Special Educational Needs and Disability Act 2001.   [2] See n 1 above.

3. Guidance

(1) The Secretary of State may issue guidance about the matters to be taken into account in determining—

    (a) whether an impairment has a substantial adverse effect on a person's ability to carry out normal day-to-day activities; or

    (b) whether such an impairment has a long-term effect.

(2) The guidance may, among other things, give examples of—

    (a) effects which it would be reasonable, in relation to particular activities, to regard for purposes of this Act as substantial adverse effects;

    (b) effects which it would not be reasonable, in relation to particular activities, to regard for such purposes as substantial adverse effects;

    (c) substantial adverse effects which it would be reasonable to regard, for such purposes, as long-term;

    (d) substantial adverse effects which it would not be reasonable to regard, for such purposes, as long-term.

(3) [An adjudicating body][3] determining, for any purpose of this Act, whether an impairment has a substantial and long-term adverse effect on a person's ability to carry out normal day-to-day activities, shall take into account any guidance which appears to it to be relevant.

[(3A) 'Adjudicating body' means—

    (a) a court;

    (b) a tribunal; and

    (c) any other person who, or body which, may decide a claim under Part 4.][4]

(4) In preparing a draft of any guidance, the Secretary of State shall consult such persons as he considers appropriate.

(5) Where the Secretary of State proposes to issue any guidance, he shall publish a draft of it, consider any representations that are made to him about the draft and, if he thinks it appropriate, modify his proposals in the light of any of those representations.

(6) If the Secretary of State decides to proceed with any proposed guidance, he shall lay a draft of it before each House of Parliament.

(7) If, within the 40-day period, either House resolves not to approve the draft, the Secretary of State shall take no further steps in relation to the proposed guidance.

(8) If no such resolution is made within the 40-day period, the Secretary of State shall issue the guidance in the form of his draft.

(9) The guidance shall come into force on such date as the Secretary of State may appoint by order.

(10) Subsection (7) does not prevent a new draft of the proposed guidance from being laid before Parliament.

(11) The Secretary of State may—

    (a) from time to time revise the whole or part of any guidance and re-issue it;

    (b) by order revoke any guidance.

(12) In this section—

'40-day period', in relation to the draft of any proposed guidance, means—

    (a) if the draft is laid before one House on a day later than the day on which it is laid before the other House, the period of 40 days beginning with the later of the two days, and

    (b) in any other case, the period of 40 days beginning with the day on which the draft is laid before each House,

---

[3] Amended by the Special Educational Needs and Disability Act 2001.   [4] See n 3 above.

no account being taken of any period during which Parliament is dissolved or prorogued or during which both Houses are adjourned for more than 4 days; and 'guidance' means guidance issued by the Secretary of State under this section and includes guidance which has been revised and re-issued.

PART II
[THE EMPLOYMENT FIELD[5]

Meaning of 'discrimination' and 'harassment'

3A. Meaning of 'discrimination'

(1) For the purposes of this Part, a person discriminates against a disabled person if—
  (a) for a reason which relates to the disabled person's disability, he treats him less favourably than he treats or would treat others to whom that reason does not or would not apply, and
  (b) he cannot show that the treatment in question is justified.
(2) For the purposes of this Part, a person also discriminates against a disabled person if he fails to comply with a duty to make reasonable adjustments imposed on him in relation to the disabled person.
(3) Treatment is justified for the purposes of subsection (1)(b) if, but only if, the reason for it is both material to the circumstances of the particular case and substantial.
(4) But treatment of a disabled person cannot be justified under subsection (3) if it amounts to direct discrimination falling within subsection (5).
(5) A person directly discriminates against a disabled person if, on the ground of the disabled person's disability, he treats the disabled person less favourably than he treats or would treat a person not having that particular disability whose relevant circumstances, including his abilities, are the same as, or not materially different from, those of the disabled person.
(6) If, in a case falling within subsection (1), a person is under a duty to make reasonable adjustments in relation to a disabled person but fails to comply with that duty, his treatment of that person cannot be justified under subsection (3) unless it would have been justified even if he had complied with that duty.

3B. Meaning of 'harassment'

(1) For the purposes of this Part, a person subjects a disabled person to harassment where, for a reason which relates to the disabled person's disability, he engages in unwanted conduct which has the purpose or effect of—
  (a) violating the disabled person's dignity, or
  (b) creating an intimidating, hostile, degrading, humiliating or offensive environment for him.
(2) Conduct shall be regarded as having the effect referred to in paragraph (a) or (b) of subsection (1) only if, having regard to all the circumstances, including in particular the perception of the disabled person, it should reasonably be considered as having that effect.]

---

[5] Part heading substituted, and ss 3A, 3B inserted, by the Disability and Discrimination Act 1995 (Amendment) Regulations, SI 2003/1673.

[Employment[6]

4. Employers: discrimination and harassment

(1) It is unlawful for an employer to discriminate against a disabled person—

    (a) in the arrangements which he makes for the purpose of determining to whom he should offer employment;

    (b) in the terms on which he offers that person employment; or

    (c) by refusing to offer, or deliberately not offering, him employment.

(2) It is unlawful for an employer to discriminate against a disabled person whom he employs—

    (a) in the terms of employment which he affords him;

    (b) in the opportunities which he affords him for promotion, a transfer, training or receiving any other benefit;

    (c) by refusing to afford him, or deliberately not affording him, any such opportunity; or

    (d) by dismissing him, or subjecting him to any other detriment.

(3) It is also unlawful for an employer, in relation to employment by him, to subject to harassment—

    (a) a disabled person whom he employs; or

    (b) a disabled person who has applied to him for employment.

(4) Subsection (2) does not apply to benefits of any description if the employer is concerned with the provision (whether or not for payment) of benefits of that description to the public, or to a section of the public which includes the employee in question, unless—

    (a) that provision differs in a material respect from the provision of the benefits by the employer to his employees;

    (b) the provision of the benefits to the employee in question is regulated by his contract of employment; or

    (c) the benefits relate to training.

(5) The reference in subsection (2)(d) to the dismissal of a person includes a reference—

    (a) to the termination of that person's employment by the expiration of any period (including a period expiring by reference to an event or circumstance), not being a termination immediately after which the employment is renewed on the same terms; and

    (b) to the termination of that person's employment by any act of his (including the giving of notice) in circumstances such that he is entitled to terminate it without notice by reason of the conduct of the employer.

(6) This section applies only in relation to employment at an establishment in Great Britain.

4A. Employers: duty to make adjustments

(1) Where—

    (a) a provision, criterion or practice applied by or on behalf of an employer, or

    (b) any physical feature of premises occupied by the employer,

places the disabled person concerned at a substantial disadvantage in comparison with persons who are not disabled, it is the duty of the employer to take such steps as it is reasonable, in all the circumstances of the case, for him to have to take in order to prevent the provision, criterion or practice, or feature, having that effect.

---

[6] Cross-heading and ss 4, 4A–4F substituted for original ss 4–6 by the Disability and Discrimination Act 1995 (Amendment) Regulations, SI 2003/1673.

(2) In subsection (1), 'the disabled person concerned' means—

    (a) in the case of a provision, criterion or practice for determining to whom employment should be offered, any disabled person who is, or has notified the employer that he may be, an applicant for that employment;

    (b) in any other case, a disabled person who is—

        (i) an applicant for the employment concerned, or

        (ii) an employee of the employer concerned.

(3) Nothing in this section imposes any duty on an employer in relation to a disabled person if the employer does not know, and could not reasonably be expected to know—

    (a) in the case of an applicant or potential applicant, that the disabled person concerned is, or may be, an applicant for the employment; or

    (b) in any case, that that person has a disability and is likely to be affected in the way mentioned in subsection (1).

Contract workers

4B. Contract workers

(1) It is unlawful for a principal, in relation to contract work, to discriminate against a disabled person who is a contract worker (a 'disabled contract worker')—

    (a) in the terms on which he allows him to do that work;

    (b) by not allowing him to do it or continue to do it;

    (c) in the way he affords him access to any benefits or by refusing or deliberately omitting to afford him access to them; or

    (d) by subjecting him to any other detriment.

(2) It is also unlawful for a principal, in relation to contract work, to subject a disabled contract worker to harassment.

(3) Subsection (1) does not apply to benefits of any description if the principal is concerned with the provision (whether or not for payment) of benefits of that description to the public, or to a section of the public which includes the contract worker in question, unless that provision differs in a material respect from the provision of the benefits by the principal to contract workers.

(4) This subsection applies to a disabled contract worker where, by virtue of—

    (a) a provision, criterion or practice applied by or on behalf of all or most of the principals to whom he is or might be supplied, or

    (b) a physical feature of premises occupied by such persons,

he is likely, on each occasion when he is supplied to a principal to do contract work, to be placed at a substantial disadvantage in comparison with persons who are not disabled which is the same or similar in each case.

(5) Where subsection (4) applies to a disabled contract worker, his employer must take such steps as he would have to take under section 4A if the provision, criterion or practice were applied by him or on his behalf or (as the case may be) if the premises were occupied by him.

(6) Section 4A applies to any principal, in relation to contract work, as if he were, or would be, the employer of the disabled contract worker and as if any contract worker supplied to do work for him were an employee of his.

(7) However, for the purposes of section 4A as applied by subsection (6), a principal is not required to take a step in relation to a disabled contract worker if under that section the disabled contract worker's employer is required to take the step in relation to him.

(8) This section applies only in relation to contract work done at an establishment in Great Britain (the provisions of section 68 about the meaning of 'employment at an establish-

ment in Great Britain' applying for the purposes of this subsection with the appropriate modifications).

(9) In this section—
'principal' means a person ('A') who makes work available for doing by individuals who are employed by another person who supplies them under a contract made with A;
'contract work' means work so made available; and
'contract worker' means any individual who is supplied to the principal under such a contract.

Office-holders

4C. Office-holders: introductory

(1) Subject to subsection (5), sections 4D and 4E apply to an office or post if—
    (a) no relevant provision of this Part applies in relation to an appointment to the office or post; and
    (b) one or more of the conditions specified in subsection (3) is satisfied.

(2) The following are relevant provisions of this Part for the purposes of subsection (1)(a): section 4, section 4B, section 6A, section 7A, section 7C and section 14C.

(3) The conditions specified in this subsection are that—
    (a) the office or post is one to which persons are appointed to discharge functions personally under the direction of another person, and in respect of which they are entitled to remuneration;
    (b) the office or post is one to which appointments are made by a Minister of the Crown, a government department, the National Assembly for Wales or any part of the Scottish Administration;
    (c) the office or post is one to which appointments are made on the recommendation of, or subject to the approval of, a person referred to in paragraph (b).

(4) For the purposes of subsection (3)(a) the holder of an office or post—
    (a) is to be regarded as discharging his functions under the direction of another person if that other person is entitled to direct him as to when and where he discharges those functions;
    (b) is not to be regarded as entitled to remuneration merely because he is entitled to payments—
        (i) in respect of expenses incurred by him in carrying out the functions of the office or post, or
        (ii) by way of compensation for the loss of income or benefits he would or might have received from any person had he not been carrying out the functions of the office or post.

(5) Sections 4D and 4E do not apply to—
    (a) any office of the House of Commons held by a member of it,
    (b) a life peerage within the meaning of the Life Peerages Act 1958, or any office of the House of Lords held by a member of it,
    (c) any office mentioned in Schedule 2 (Ministerial offices) to the House of Commons Disqualification Act 1975,
    (d) the offices of Leader of the Opposition, Chief Opposition Whip or Assistant Opposition Whip within the meaning of the Ministerial and other Salaries Act 1975,
    (e) any office of the Scottish Parliament held by a member of it,
    (f) a member of the Scottish Executive within the meaning of section 44 of the Scotland Act 1998, or a junior Scottish Minister within the meaning of section 49 of that Act,
    (g) any office of the National Assembly for Wales held by a member of it,

(h) in England, any office of a county council, a London borough council, a district council or a parish council held by a member of it,

(i) in Wales, any office of a county council, a county borough council or a community council held by a member of it,

(j) in relation to a council constituted under section 2 of the Local Government etc (Scotland) Act 1994 or a community council established under section 51 of the Local Government (Scotland) Act 1973, any office of such a council held by a member of it,

(k) any office of the Greater London Authority held by a member of it,

(l) any office of the Common Council of the City of London held by a member of it,

(m) any office of the Council of the Isles of Scilly held by a member of it, or

(n) any office of a political party.

4D. Office-holders: discrimination and harassment

(1) It is unlawful for a relevant person, in relation to an appointment to an office or post to which this section applies, to discriminate against a disabled person—

(a) in the arrangements which he makes for the purpose of determining who should be offered the appointment;

(b) in the terms on which he offers him the appointment; or

(c) by refusing to offer him the appointment.

(2) It is unlawful for a relevant person, in relation to an appointment to an office or post to which this section applies and which satisfies the condition set out in section 4C(3)(c), to discriminate against a disabled person—

(a) in the arrangements which he makes for the purpose of determining who should be recommended or approved in relation to the appointment; or

(b) in making or refusing to make a recommendation, or giving or refusing to give an approval, in relation to the appointment.

(3) It is unlawful for a relevant person, in relation to a disabled person who has been appointed to an office or post to which this section applies, to discriminate against him—

(a) in the terms of the appointment;

(b) in the opportunities which he affords him for promotion, a transfer, training or receiving any other benefit, or by refusing to afford him any such opportunity;

(c) by terminating the appointment; or

(d) by subjecting him to any other detriment in relation to the appointment.

(4) It is also unlawful for a relevant person, in relation to an office or post to which this section applies, to subject to harassment a disabled person—

(a) who has been appointed to the office or post;

(b) who is seeking or being considered for appointment to the office or post; or

(c) who is seeking or being considered for a recommendation or approval in relation to an appointment to an office or post satisfying the condition set out in section 4C(3)(c).

(5) Subsection (3) does not apply to benefits of any description if the relevant person is concerned with the provision (for payment or not) of benefits of that description to the public, or a section of the public to which the disabled person belongs, unless—

(a) that provision differs in a material respect from the provision of the benefits to persons appointed to offices or posts which are the same as, or not materially different from, that to which the disabled person has been appointed;

(b) the provision of the benefits to the person appointed is regulated by the terms and conditions of his appointment; or

(c) the benefits relate to training.

(6) In subsection (3)(c) the reference to the termination of the appointment includes a reference—

(a) to the termination of the appointment by the expiration of any period (including a period expiring by reference to an event or circumstance), not being a termination immediately after which the appointment is renewed on the same terms and conditions; and

(b) to the termination of the appointment by any act of the person appointed (including the giving of notice) in circumstances such that he is entitled to terminate the appointment by reason of the conduct of the relevant person.

(7) In this section—

    (a) references to making a recommendation include references to making a negative recommendation; and

    (b) references to refusal include references to deliberate omission.

4E. Office-holders: duty to make adjustments

(1) Where—

    (a) a provision, criterion or practice applied by or on behalf of a relevant person, or

    (b) any physical feature of premises—

        (i) under the control of a relevant person, and

        (ii) at or from which the functions of an office or post to which this section applies are performed,

places the disabled person concerned at a substantial disadvantage in comparison with persons who are not disabled, it is the duty of the relevant person to take such steps as it is reasonable, in all the circumstances of the case, for him to have to take in order to prevent the provision, criterion or practice, or feature, having that effect.

(2) In this section, 'the disabled person concerned' means—

    (a) in the case of a provision, criterion or practice for determining who should be appointed to, or recommended or approved in relation to, an office or post to which this section applies, any disabled person who—

        (i) is, or has notified the relevant person that he may be, seeking appointment to, or (as the case may be) seeking a recommendation or approval in relation to, that office or post, or

        (ii) is being considered for appointment to, or (as the case may be) for a recommendation or approval in relation to, that office or post;

    (b) in any other case, a disabled person—

        (i) who is seeking or being considered for appointment to, or a recommendation or approval in relation to, the office or post concerned, or

        (ii) who has been appointed to the office or post concerned.

(3) Nothing in this section imposes any duty on the relevant person in relation to a disabled person if the relevant person does not know, and could not reasonably be expected to know—

    (a) in the case of a person who is being considered for, or is or may be seeking, appointment to, or a recommendation or approval in relation to, an office or post, that the disabled person concerned—

        (i) is, or may be, seeking appointment to, or (as the case may be) seeking a recommendation or approval in relation to, that office or post, or

        (ii) is being considered for appointment to, or (as the case may be) for a recommendation or approval in relation to, that office or post; or

    (b) in any case, that that person has a disability and is likely to be affected in the way mentioned in subsection (1).

4F. Office-holders: supplementary

(1) In sections 4C to 4E, appointment to an office or post does not include election to an office or post.

(2) In sections 4D and 4E, 'relevant person' means—

   (a) in a case relating to an appointment to an office or post, the person with power to make that appointment;

   (b) in a case relating to the making of a recommendation or the giving of an approval in relation to an appointment, a person or body referred to in section 4C(3)(b) with power to make that recommendation or (as the case may be) to give that approval;

   (c) in a case relating to a term of an appointment, the person with power to determine that term;

   (d) in a case relating to a working condition afforded in relation to an appointment—

      (i) the person with power to determine that working condition; or

      (ii) where there is no such person, the person with power to make the appointment;

   (e) in a case relating to the termination of an appointment, the person with power to terminate the appointment;

   (f) in a case relating to the subjection of a disabled person to any other detriment or to harassment, any person or body falling within one or more of paragraphs (a) to (e) in relation to such cases as are there mentioned.

(3) In subsection (2)(d), 'working condition' includes—

   (a) any opportunity for promotion, a transfer, training or receiving any other benefit; and

   (b) any physical feature of premises at or from which the functions of an office or post are performed.]

[Occupational pension schemes[7]

4G. Occupational pension schemes: non-discrimination rule

(1) Every occupational pension scheme shall be taken to include a provision ('the non-discrimination rule') containing the following requirements—

   (a) a requirement that the trustees or managers of the scheme refrain from discriminating against a relevant disabled person in carrying out any of their functions in relation to the scheme (including in particular their functions relating to the admission of members to the scheme and the treatment of members of the scheme);

   (b) a requirement that the trustees or managers of the scheme do not subject a relevant disabled person to harassment in relation to the scheme.

(2) The other provisions of the scheme are to have effect subject to the non-discrimination rule.

(3) It is unlawful for the trustees or managers of an occupational pension scheme—

   (a) to discriminate against a relevant disabled person contrary to requirement (a) of the non-discrimination rule; or

   (b) to subject a relevant disabled person to harassment contrary to requirement (b) of the non-discrimination rule.

(4) The non-discrimination rule does not apply in relation to rights accrued, or benefits payable, in respect of periods of service prior to the coming into force of this section (but it does apply to communications with members or prospective members of the scheme in relation to such rights or benefits).

---

[7] Cross-heading and ss 4G–4K inserted by the Disability Discrimination Act 1995 (Pensions) Regulations 2003, SI 2003/2770.

(5) The trustees or managers of an occupational pension scheme may, if—
   (a) they do not (apart from this subsection) have power to make such alterations to the scheme as may be required to secure conformity with the non-discrimination rule, or
   (b) they have such power but the procedure for doing so—
      (i) is liable to be unduly complex or protracted, or
      (ii) involves the obtaining of consents which cannot be obtained, or can only be obtained with undue delay or difficulty,
   by resolution make such alterations to the scheme.
(6) The alterations referred to in subsection (5) may have effect in relation to a period before the alterations are made (but may not have effect in relation to a period before the coming into force of this section).

4H. Occupational pension schemes: duty to make adjustments

(1) Where—
   (a) a provision, criterion or practice (including a scheme rule) applied by or on behalf of the trustees or managers of an occupational pension scheme, or
   (b) any physical feature of premises occupied by the trustees or managers,
   places a relevant disabled person at a substantial disadvantage in comparison with persons who are not disabled, it is the duty of the trustees or managers to take such steps as it is reasonable, in all the circumstances of the case, for them to have to take in order to prevent the provision, criterion or practice, or feature, having that effect.
(2) The making of alterations to scheme rules is (in addition to the examples set out in section 18B(2)) an example of a step which trustees or managers may have to take in order to comply with the duty set out in subsection (1).
(3) Nothing in subsection (1) imposes any duty on trustees or managers in relation to a disabled person if they do not know, and could not reasonably be expected to know—
   (a) that the disabled person is a relevant disabled person; or
   (b) that that person has a disability and is likely to be affected in the way mentioned in subsection (1).

4I. Occupational pension schemes: procedure

(1) Where under section 17A a relevant disabled person presents a complaint to an employment tribunal that the trustees or managers of an occupational pension scheme have acted in relation to him in a way which is unlawful under this Part, the employer in relation to that scheme shall, for the purposes of the rules governing procedure, be treated as a party and be entitled to appear and be heard in accordance with those rules.
(2) In this section, 'employer', in relation to an occupational pension scheme, has the meaning given by section 124(1) of the Pensions Act 1995 as at the date of coming into force of this section.

4J. Occupational pension schemes: remedies

(1) This section applies where—
   (a) under section 17A a relevant disabled person presents to an employment tribunal a complaint that—
      (i) the trustees or managers of an occupational pension scheme have acted in relation to him in a way which is unlawful under this Part; or
      (ii) an employer has so acted in relation to him;
   (b) the complaint relates to—
      (i) the terms on which persons become members of an occupational pension scheme, or

      (ii) the terms on which members of the scheme are treated;

(c) the disabled person is not a pensioner member of the scheme; and

(d) the tribunal finds that the complaint is well-founded.

(2) The tribunal may, without prejudice to the generality of its power under section 17A(2)(a), make a declaration that the complainant has a right—

    (a) (where subsection (1)(b)(i) applies) to be admitted to the scheme in question; or

    (b) (where subsection (1)(b)(ii) applies) to membership of the scheme without discrimination.

(3) A declaration under subsection (2)—

    (a) may be made in respect of such period as the declaration may specify (but may not be made in respect of any period before the coming into force of this section);

    (b) may make such provision as the tribunal considers appropriate as to the terms upon which, or the capacity in which, the disabled person is to enjoy such admission or membership.

(4) The tribunal may not award the disabled person any compensation under section 17A(2)(b) (whether in relation to arrears of benefits or otherwise) other than—

    (a) compensation for injury to feelings;

    (b) compensation pursuant to section 17A(5).

4K. Occupational pension schemes: supplementary

(1) In their application to communications, sections 4G to 4J apply in relation to a disabled person who is—

    (a) entitled to the present payment of dependants' or survivors' benefits under an occupational pension scheme; or

    (b) a pension credit member of such a scheme,

as they apply in relation to a disabled person who is a pensioner member of the scheme.

(2) In sections 4G to 4J and in this section—

'active member', 'deferred member', 'managers', 'pension credit member', 'pensioner member' and 'trustees or managers' have the meanings given by section 124(1) of the Pensions Act 1995 as at the date of coming into force of this section;

'communications' includes—

    (i) the provision of information, and

    (ii) the operation of a dispute resolution procedure;

'member', in relation to an occupational pension scheme, means any active, deferred or pensioner member;

'non-discrimination rule' means the rule in section 4G(1);

'relevant disabled person', in relation to an occupational pension scheme, means a disabled person who is a member or prospective member of the scheme; and

'prospective member' means any person who, under the terms of his contract of employment or the scheme rules or both—

    (i)   is able, at his own option, to become a member of the scheme,

    (ii) will become so able if he continues in the same employment for a sufficiently long period,

    (iii) will be admitted to it automatically unless he makes an election not to become a member, or

    (iv) may be admitted to it subject to the consent of his employer.]

5, 6. . . .[8]

---

[8] See n 6 above.

[Partnerships[9]

6A. Partnerships: discrimination and harassment

(1) It is unlawful for a firm, in relation to a position as partner in the firm, to discriminate against a disabled person—
    (a) in the arrangements which they make for the purpose of determining who should be offered that position;
    (b) in the terms on which they offer him that position;
    (c) by refusing or deliberately omitting to offer him that position; or
    (d) in a case where the person already holds that position—
        (i) in the way they afford him access to any benefits or by refusing or deliberately omitting to afford him access to them; or
        (ii) by expelling him from that position, or subjecting him to any other detriment.

(2) It is also unlawful for a firm, in relation to a position as partner in the firm, to subject to harassment a disabled person who holds or has applied for that position.

(3) Subsection (1) does not apply to benefits of any description if the firm are concerned with the provision (whether or not for payment) of benefits of that description to the public, or to a section of the public which includes the partner in question, unless that provision differs in a material respect from the provision of the benefits to other partners.

(4) The reference in subsection (1)(d)(ii) to the expulsion of a person from a position as partner includes a reference—
    (a) to the termination of that person's partnership by the expiration of any period (including a period expiring by reference to an event or circumstance), not being a termination immediately after which the partnership is renewed on the same terms; and
    (b) to the termination of that person's partnership by any act of his (including the giving of notice) in circumstances such that he is entitled to terminate it without notice by reason of the conduct of the other partners.

6B. Partnerships: duty to make adjustments

(1) Where—
    (a) a provision, criterion or practice applied by or on behalf of a firm, or
    (b) any physical feature of premises occupied by the firm,
places the disabled person concerned at a substantial disadvantage in comparison with persons who are not disabled, it is the duty of the firm to take such steps as it is reasonable, in all the circumstances of the case, for them to have to take in order to prevent the provision, criterion or practice, or feature, having that effect.

(2) In this section, 'the disabled person concerned' means—
    (a) in the case of a provision, criterion or practice for determining to whom the position of partner should be offered, any disabled person who is, or has notified the firm that he may be, a candidate for that position;
    (b) in any other case, a disabled person who is—
        (i) a partner, or
        (ii) a candidate for the position of partner.

(3) Nothing in this section imposes any duty on a firm in relation to a disabled person if the firm do not know, and could not reasonably be expected to know—
    (a) in the case of a candidate or potential candidate, that the disabled person concerned is, or may be, a candidate for the position of partner; or

---

[9] Cross-heading and ss 6A–6C inserted by the Disability and Discrimination Act 1995 (Amendment) Regulations, SI 2003/1673.

(b) in any case, that that person has a disability and is likely to be affected in the way mentioned in subsection (1).

(4) Where a firm are required by this section to take any steps in relation to the disabled person concerned, the cost of taking those steps shall be treated as an expense of the firm; and the extent to which such cost should be borne by that person, where he is or becomes a partner in the firm, shall not exceed such amount as is reasonable, having regard in particular to the proportion in which he is entitled to share in the firm's profits.

6C. Partnerships: supplementary

(1) Sections 6A(1)(a) to (c) and (2) and section 6B apply in relation to persons proposing to form themselves into a partnership as they apply in relation to a firm.

(2) Sections 6A and 6B apply to a limited liability partnership as they apply to a firm; and, in the application of those sections to a limited liability partnership, references to a partner in a firm are references to a member of the limited liability partnership.

(3) In the case of a limited partnership, references in sections 6A and 6B to a partner shall be construed as references to a general partner as defined in section 3 of the Limited Partnerships Act 1907.

(4) In sections 6A and 6B and in this section, 'firm' has the meaning given by section 4 of the Partnership Act 1890.]

7. ...[10]

[Barristers and advocates[11]

7A. Barristers: discrimination and harassment

(1) It is unlawful for a barrister or a barrister's clerk, in relation to any offer of a pupillage or tenancy, to discriminate against a disabled person—
(a) in the arrangements which are made for the purpose of determining to whom it should be offered;
(b) in respect of any terms on which it is offered; or
(c) by refusing, or deliberately omitting, to offer it to him.

(2) It is unlawful for a barrister or a barrister's clerk, in relation to a disabled pupil or tenant in the set of chambers in question, to discriminate against him—
(a) in respect of any terms applicable to him as a pupil or tenant;
(b) in the opportunities for training, or gaining experience, which are afforded or denied to him;
(c) in the benefits which are afforded or denied to him;
(d) by terminating his pupillage or by subjecting him to any pressure to leave the chambers; or
(e) by subjecting him to any other detriment.

(3) It is unlawful for a barrister or barrister's clerk, in relation to a pupillage or tenancy, to subject to harassment a disabled person who is, or has applied to be, a pupil or tenant in the set of chambers in question.

(4) It is also unlawful for any person, in relation to the giving, withholding or acceptance of instructions to a barrister, to discriminate against a disabled person or to subject him to harassment.

---

[10] Repealed by the Disability and Discrimination Act 1995 (Amendment) Regulations, SI 2003/1673.

[11] Cross-heading and ss 7A–7D inserted by the Disability and Discrimination Act 1995 (Amendment) Regulations, SI 2003/1673.

(5) In this section and in section 7B—

'barrister's clerk' includes any person carrying out any of the functions of a barrister's clerk;

'pupil', 'pupillage' and 'set of chambers' have the meanings commonly associated with their use in the context of barristers practising in independent practice; and

'tenancy' and 'tenant' have the meanings commonly associated with their use in the context of barristers practising in independent practice, but they also include reference to any barrister permitted to practise from a set of chambers.

7B. Barristers: duty to make adjustments

(1) Where—

    (a) a provision, criterion or practice applied by or on behalf of a barrister or barrister's clerk, or

    (b) any physical feature of premises occupied by a barrister or a barrister's clerk,

places the disabled person concerned at a substantial disadvantage in comparison with persons who are not disabled, it is the duty of the barrister or barrister's clerk to take such steps as it is reasonable, in all the circumstances of the case, for him to have to take in order to prevent the provision, criterion or practice, or feature, having that effect.

(2) In a case where subsection (1) applies in relation to two or more barristers in a set of chambers, the duty in that subsection is a duty on each of them to take such steps as it is reasonable, in all of the circumstances of the case, for him to have to take.

(3) In this section, 'the disabled person concerned' means—

    (a) in the case of a provision, criterion or practice for determining to whom a pupillage or tenancy should be offered, any disabled person who is, or has notified the barrister or the barrister's clerk concerned that he may be, an applicant for a pupillage or tenancy;

    (b) in any other case, a disabled person who is—

        (i) a tenant;

        (ii) a pupil; or

        (iii) an applicant for a pupillage or tenancy.

(4) Nothing in this section imposes any duty on a barrister or a barrister's clerk in relation to a disabled person if he does not know, and could not reasonably be expected to know—

    (a) in the case of an applicant or potential applicant, that the disabled person concerned is, or may be, an applicant for a pupillage or tenancy; or

    (b) in any case, that that person has a disability and is likely to be affected in the way mentioned in subsection (1).

7C. Advocates: discrimination and harassment

(1) It is unlawful for an advocate, in relation to taking any person as his pupil, to discriminate against a disabled person—

    (a) in the arrangements which he makes for the purpose of determining whom he will take as his pupil;

    (b) in respect of any terms on which he offers to take the disabled person as his pupil; or

    (c) by refusing, or deliberately omitting, to take the disabled person as his pupil.

(2) It is unlawful for an advocate, in relation to a disabled person who is a pupil, to discriminate against him—

    (a) in respect of any terms applicable to him as a pupil;

    (b) in the opportunities for training, or gaining experience, which are afforded or denied to him;

    (c) in the benefits which are afforded or denied to him;

    (d) by terminating the relationship or by subjecting him to any pressure to leave; or

(e) by subjecting him to any other detriment.

(3) It is unlawful for an advocate, in relation to taking any person as his pupil, to subject to harassment a disabled person who is, or has applied to be taken as, his pupil.

(4) It is also unlawful for any person, in relation to the giving, withholding or acceptance of instructions to an advocate, to discriminate against a disabled person or to subject him to harassment.

(5) In this section and section 7D—

'advocate' means a member of the Faculty of Advocates practising as such; and

'pupil' has the meaning commonly associated with its use in the context of a person training to be an advocate.

7D. Advocates: duty to make adjustments

(1) Where—

(a) a provision, criterion or practice applied by or on behalf of an advocate, or

(b) any physical feature of premises occupied by, and under the control of, an advocate,

places the disabled person concerned at a substantial disadvantage in comparison with persons who are not disabled, it is the duty of the advocate to take such steps as it is reasonable, in all the circumstances of the case, for him to have to take in order to prevent the provision, criterion or practice, or feature, having that effect.

(2) In this section, 'the disabled person concerned' means—

(a) in the case of a provision, criterion or practice for determining whom he will take as his pupil, any disabled person who has applied, or has notified the advocate that he may apply, to be taken as a pupil;

(b) in any other case, a disabled person who is—

(i) an applicant to be taken as the advocate's pupil, or

(ii) a pupil.

(3) Nothing in this section imposes any duty on an advocate in relation to a disabled person if he does not know, and could not reasonably be expected to know—

(a) in the case of an applicant or potential applicant, that the disabled person concerned is, or may be, applying to be taken as his pupil; or

(b) in any case, that that person has a disability and is likely to be affected in the way mentioned in subsection (1).]

8. . . .[12]

9. . . .[13]

10. . . .[14]

11, 12. . . .[15]

---

[12] Renumbered as s 17A, amended and moved, with the cross-heading that preceded, it by the Disability and Discrimination Act 1995 (Amendment) Regulations, SI 2003/1673.

[13] Repealed by the Disability and Discrimination Act 1995 (Amendment) Regulations, SI 2003/1673.

[14] Renumbered as s 18C and moved by the Disability and Discrimination Act 1995 (Amendment) Regulations, SI 2003/1673.

[15] Repealed by the Disability and Discrimination Act 1995 (Amendment) Regulations, SI 2003/1673.

[Trade and professional bodies[16]

13. Trade organisations: discrimination and harassment

(1) It is unlawful for a trade organisation to discriminate against a disabled person—
  (a) in the arrangements which it makes for the purpose of determining who should be offered membership of the organisation;
  (b) in the terms on which it is prepared to admit him to membership of the organisation; or
  (c) by refusing to accept, or deliberately not accepting, his application for membership.
(2) It is unlawful for a trade organisation, in the case of a disabled person who is a member of the organisation, to discriminate against him—
  (a) in the way it affords him access to any benefits or by refusing or deliberately omitting to afford him access to them;
  (b) by depriving him of membership, or varying the terms on which he is a member; or
  (c) by subjecting him to any other detriment.
(3) It is also unlawful for a trade organisation, in relation to membership of that organisation, to subject to harassment a disabled person who—
  (a) is a member of the organisation; or
  (b) has applied for membership of the organisation.
(4) In this section and section 14 'trade organisation' means—
  (a) an organisation of workers;
  (b) an organisation of employers; or
  (c) any other organisation whose members carry on a particular profession or trade for the purposes of which the organisation exists.

14. Trade organisations: duty to make adjustments

(1) Where—
  (a) a provision, criterion or practice applied by or on behalf of a trade organisation, or
  (b) any physical feature of premises occupied by the organisation,
  places the disabled person concerned at a substantial disadvantage in comparison with persons who are not disabled, it is the duty of the organisation to take such steps as it is reasonable, in all the circumstances of the case, for it to have to take in order to prevent the provision, criterion or practice, or feature, having that effect.
(2) In this section 'the disabled person concerned' means—
  (a) in the case of a provision, criterion or practice for determining to whom membership should be offered, any disabled person who is, or has notified the organisation that he may be, an applicant for membership;
  (b) in any other case, a disabled person who is—
    (i) a member of the organisation, or
    (ii) an applicant for membership of the organisation.
(3) Nothing in this section imposes any duty on an organisation in relation to a disabled person if the organisation does not know, and could not reasonably be expected to know—
  (a) in the case of an applicant or potential applicant, that the disabled person concerned is, or may be, an applicant for membership of the organisation; or
  (b) in any case, that that person has a disability and is likely to be affected in the way mentioned in subsection (1).

---

[16] Cross-heading and ss 13, 14, 14A–4D substituted for original ss 13–15 by the Disability and Discrimination Act 1995 (Amendment) Regulations, SI 2003/1673.

14A. Qualifications bodies: discrimination and harassment

(1) It is unlawful for a qualifications body to discriminate against a disabled person—
   (a) in the arrangements which it makes for the purpose of determining upon whom to confer a professional or trade qualification;
   (b) in the terms on which it is prepared to confer a professional or trade qualification on him;
   (c) by refusing or deliberately omitting to grant any application by him for such a qualification; or
   (d) by withdrawing such a qualification from him or varying the terms on which he holds it.

(2) It is also unlawful for a qualifications body, in relation to a professional or trade qualification conferred by it, to subject to harassment a disabled person who holds or applies for such a qualification.

(3) In determining for the purposes of subsection (1) whether the application by a qualifications body of a competence standard to a disabled person constitutes discrimination within the meaning of section 3A, the application of the standard is justified for the purposes of section 3A(1)(b) if, but only if, the qualifications body can show that—
   (a) the standard is, or would be, applied equally to persons who do not have his particular disability; and
   (b) its application is a proportionate means of achieving a legitimate aim.

(4) For the purposes of subsection (3)—
   (a) section 3A(2) (and (6)) does not apply; and
   (b) section 3A(4) has effect as if the reference to section 3A(3) were a reference to subsection (3) of this section.

(5) In this section and section 14B—
   'qualifications body' means any authority or body which can confer a professional or trade qualification, but it does not include—
   (a) a responsible body (within the meaning of Chapter 1 or 2 of Part 4),
   (b) a local education authority in England or Wales, or
   (c) an education authority (within the meaning of section 135(1) of the Education (Scotland) Act 1980);
   'confer' includes renew or extend;
   'professional or trade qualification' means an authorisation, qualification, recognition, registration, enrolment, approval or certification which is needed for, or facilitates engagement in, a particular profession or trade;
   'competence standard' means an academic, medical or other standard applied by or on behalf of a qualifications body for the purpose of determining whether or not a person has a particular level of competence or ability.

14B. Qualifications bodies: duty to make adjustments

(1) Where—
   (a) a provision, criterion or practice, other than a competence standard, applied by or on behalf of a qualifications body; or
   (b) any physical feature of premises occupied by a qualifications body,
   places the disabled person concerned at a substantial disadvantage in comparison with persons who are not disabled, it is the duty of the qualifications body to take such steps as it is reasonable, in all the circumstances of the case, for it to have to take in order to prevent the provision, criterion or practice, or feature, having that effect.

(2) In this section 'the disabled person concerned' means—
   (a) in the case of a provision, criterion or practice for determining on whom a professional

or trade qualification is to be conferred, any disabled person who is, or has notified the qualifications body that he may be, an applicant for the conferment of that qualification;

(b) in any other case, a disabled person who—
   (i) holds a professional or trade qualification conferred by the qualifications body, or
   (ii) applies for a professional or trade qualification which it confers.

(3) Nothing in this section imposes a duty on a qualifications body in relation to a disabled person if the body does not know, and could not reasonably be expected to know—
   (a) in the case of an applicant or potential applicant, that the disabled person concerned is, or may be, an applicant for the conferment of a professional or trade qualification; or
   (b) in any case, that that person has a disability and is likely to be affected in the way mentioned in subsection (1).

Practical work experience

14C. Practical work experience: discrimination and harassment

(1) It is unlawful, in the case of a disabled person seeking or undertaking a work placement, for a placement provider to discriminate against him—
   (a) in the arrangements which he makes for the purpose of determining who should be offered a work placement;
   (b) in the terms on which he affords him access to any work placement or any facilities concerned with such a placement;
   (c) by refusing or deliberately omitting to afford him such access;
   (d) by terminating the placement; or
   (e) by subjecting him to any other detriment in relation to the placement.

(2) It is also unlawful for a placement provider, in relation to a work placement, to subject to harassment—
   (a) a disabled person to whom he is providing a placement; or
   (b) a disabled person who has applied to him for a placement.

(3) This section and section 14D do not apply to—
   (a) anything made unlawful by section 4 or any provision of Part 3 or 4; or
   (b) anything which would be unlawful under that section or any such provision but for the operation of any other provision of this Act.

(4) In this section and section 14D—
   'work placement' means practical work experience undertaken for a limited period for the purposes of a person's vocational training;
   'placement provider' means any person who provides a work placement to a person whom he does not employ.

(5) This section and section 14D do not apply to a work placement undertaken in any of the naval, military and air forces of the Crown.

14D. Practical work experience: duty to make adjustments

(1) Where—
   (a) a provision, criterion or practice applied by or on behalf of a placement provider, or
   (b) any physical feature of premises occupied by the placement provider,
   places the disabled person concerned at a substantial disadvantage in comparison with persons who are not disabled, it is the duty of the placement provider to take such steps as it is reasonable, in all the circumstances of the case, for him to have to take in order to prevent the provision, criterion or practice, or feature, having that effect.

(2) In this section, 'the disabled person concerned' means—
  (a) in the case of a provision, criterion or practice for determining to whom a work placement should be offered, any disabled person who is, or has notified the placement provider that he may be, an applicant for that work placement;
  (b) in any other case, a disabled person who is—
    (i) an applicant for the work placement concerned, or
    (ii) undertaking a work placement with the placement provider.
(3) Nothing in this section imposes any duty on a placement provider in relation to the disabled person concerned if he does not know, and could not reasonably be expected to know—
  (a) in the case of an applicant or potential applicant, that the disabled person concerned is, or may be, an applicant for the work placement; or
  (b) in any case, that that person has a disability and is likely to be affected in the way mentioned in subsection (1).]

15. ...[17]

16. ...[18]

[Other unlawful acts[19]

16A. Relationships which have come to an end

(1) This section applies where—
  (a) there has been a relevant relationship between a disabled person and another person ('the relevant person'), and
  (b) the relationship has come to an end.
(2) In this section a 'relevant relationship' is—
  (a) a relationship during the course of which an act of discrimination against, or harassment of, one party to the relationship by the other party to it is unlawful under any preceding provision of this Part; or
  (b) a relationship between a person providing employment services (within the meaning of Part 3) and a person receiving such services.
(3) It is unlawful for the relevant person—
  (a) to discriminate against the disabled person by subjecting him to a detriment, or
  (b) to subject the disabled person to harassment,
  where the discrimination or harassment arises out of and is closely connected to the relevant relationship.
(4) This subsection applies where—
  (a) a provision, criterion or practice applied by the relevant person to the disabled person in relation to any matter arising out of the relevant relationship, or
  (b) a physical feature of premises which are occupied by the relevant person,
  places the disabled person at a substantial disadvantage in comparison with persons who are not disabled, but are in the same position as the disabled person in relation to the relevant person.

---

[17] See n 16 above.

[18] Renumbered as s 18A, amended and moved, and the cross-heading that preceded it repealed, by the Disability and Discrimination Act 1995 (Amendment) Regulations, SI 2003/1673.

[19] Cross-heading and ss 16A–16C inserted by the Disability and Discrimination Act 1995 (Amendment) Regulations, SI 2003/1673.

(5) Where subsection (4) applies, it is the duty of the relevant person to take such steps as it is reasonable, in all the circumstances of the case, for him to have to take in order to prevent the provision, practice or criterion, or feature, having that effect.

(6) Nothing in subsection (5) imposes any duty on the relevant person if he does not know, and could not reasonably be expected to know, that the disabled person has a disability and is likely to be affected in the way mentioned in that subsection.

(7) In subsection (2), reference to an act of discrimination or harassment which is unlawful includes, in the case of a relationship which has come to an end before the commencement of this section, reference to such an act which would, after the commencement of this section, be unlawful.

16B. Discriminatory advertisements

(1) It is unlawful for a person, in relation to a relevant appointment or benefit which he intends to make or confer, to publish or cause to be published an advertisement which—
   (a) invites applications for that appointment or benefit; and
   (b) indicates, or might reasonably be understood to indicate, that an application will or may be determined to any extent by reference to—
      (i) the applicant not having any disability, or any particular disability, or
      (ii) any reluctance of the person determining the application to comply with a duty to make reasonable adjustments or (in relation to employment services) with the duty imposed by section 21(1) as modified by section 21A(6).

(2) Subsection (1) does not apply where it would not in fact be unlawful under this Part or, to the extent that it relates to the provision of employment services, Part 3 for an application to be determined in the manner indicated (or understood to be indicated) in the advertisement.

(3) In subsection (1), 'relevant appointment or benefit' means—
   (a) any employment, promotion or transfer of employment;
   (b) membership of, or a benefit under, an occupational pension scheme;
   (c) an appointment to any office or post to which section 4D applies;
   (d) any partnership in a firm (within the meaning of section 6A);
   (e) any tenancy or pupillage (within the meaning of section 7A or 7C);
   (f) any membership of a trade organisation (within the meaning of section 13);
   (g) any professional or trade qualification (within the meaning of section 14A);
   (h) any work placement (within the meaning of section 14C);
   (i) any employment services (within the meaning of Part 3).

(4) In this section, 'advertisement' includes every form of advertisement or notice, whether to the public or not.

16C. Instructions and pressure to discriminate

(1) It is unlawful for a person—
   (a) who has authority over another person, or
   (b) in accordance with whose wishes that other person is accustomed to act,
   to instruct him to do any act which is unlawful under this Part or, to the extent that it relates to the provision of employment services, Part 3, or to procure or attempt to procure the doing by him of any such act.

(2) It is also unlawful to induce, or attempt to induce, a person to do any act which contravenes this Part or, to the extent that it relates to the provision of employment services, Part 3 by—
   (a) providing or offering to provide him with any benefit, or
   (b) subjecting or threatening to subject him to any detriment.

(3) An attempted inducement is not prevented from falling within subsection (2) because it is not made directly to the person in question, if it is made in such a way that he is likely to hear of it.]

17. . . .[20]

[Enforcement etc [21]

17A. Enforcement, remedies and procedure

(1) A complaint by any person that another person—

    (a) has discriminated against him[, or subjected him to harassment,][22] in a way which is unlawful under this Part, or

    (b) is, by virtue of section 57 or 58, to be treated as having [done so],[23]

may be presented to an [employment tribunal].[24]

[(1A) Subsection (1) does not apply to a complaint under section 14A(1) or (2) of an act in respect of which an appeal, or proceedings in the nature of an appeal, may be brought under any enactment.

(1B) In subsection (1A), 'enactment' includes an enactment comprised in, or in an instrument made under, an Act of the Scottish Parliament.

(1C) Where, on the hearing of a complaint under subsection (1), the complainant proves facts from which the tribunal could, apart from this subsection, conclude in the absence of an adequate explanation that the respondent has acted in a way which is unlawful under this Part, the tribunal shall uphold the complaint unless the respondent proves that he did not so act.][25]

(2) Where an [employment tribunal][26] finds that a complaint presented to it under this section is well-founded, it shall take such of the following steps as it considers just and equitable—

    (a) making a declaration as to the rights of the complainant and the respondent in relation to the matters to which the complaint relates;

    (b) ordering the respondent to pay compensation to the complainant;

    (c) recommending that the respondent take, within a specified period, action appearing to the tribunal to be reasonable, in all the circumstances of the case, for the purpose of obviating or reducing the adverse effect on the complainant of any matter to which the complaint relates.

(3) Where a tribunal orders compensation under subsection (2)(b), the amount of the compensation shall be calculated by applying the principles applicable to the calculation of damages in claims in tort or (in Scotland) in reparation for breach of statutory duty.

(4) For the avoidance of doubt it is hereby declared that compensation in respect of discrimination in a way which is unlawful under this Part may include compensation for injury to feelings whether or not it includes compensation under any other head.

(5) If the respondent to a complaint fails, without reasonable justification, to comply with a recommendation made by an [employment tribunal][27] under subsection (2)(c) the tribunal may, if it thinks it just and equitable to do so—

---

[20] Repealed (with the cross-heading that preceded it) by the Disability Discrimination Act 1995 (Pensions) Regulations 2003, SI 2003/2770.

[21] See n 12 above.

[22] Amended by the Disability and Discrimination Act 1995 (Amendment) Regulations, SI 2003/1673.

[23] See n 22 above.

[24] Amended by the Employment Rights (Dispute Resolution) Act 1998.

[25] See n 22 above.   [26] See n 24 above.   [27] See n 24 above.

(a) increase the amount of compensation required to be paid to the complainant in respect of the complaint, where an order was made under subsection (2)(b); or

(b) make an order under subsection (2)(b).

(6) Regulations may make provision—

(a) for enabling a tribunal, where an amount of compensation falls to be awarded under subsection (2)(b), to include in the award interest on that amount; and

(b) specifying, for cases where a tribunal decides that an award is to include an amount in respect of interest, the manner in which and the periods and rate by reference to which the interest is to be determined.

(7) Regulations may modify the operation of any order made under [section 14 of [the Employment Tribunals Act 1996][28]][29] (power to make provision as to interest on sums payable in pursuance of [employment tribunal][30] decisions) to the extent that it relates to an award of compensation under subsection (2)(b).

(8) Part I of Schedule 3 makes further provision about the enforcement of this Part and about procedure.]

[17B. Enforcement of sections 16B and 16C[31]

(1) Only the Disability Rights Commission may bring proceedings in respect of a contravention of section 16B (discriminatory advertisements) or section 16C (instructions and pressure to discriminate).

(2) The Commission shall bring any such proceedings in accordance with subsection (3) or (4).

(3) The Commission may present to an employment tribunal a complaint that a person has done an act which is unlawful under section 16B or 16C; and if the tribunal finds that the complaint is well-founded it shall make a declaration to that effect.

(4) Where—

(a) a tribunal has made a finding pursuant to subsection (3) that a person has done an act which is unlawful under section 16B or 16C,

(b) that finding has become final, and

(c) it appears to the Commission that, unless restrained, he is likely to do a further act which is unlawful under that section,

the Commission may apply to a county court for an injunction, or (in Scotland) to a sheriff court for an interdict, restraining him from doing such an act; and the court, if satisfied that the application is well-founded, may grant the injunction or interdict in the terms applied for or in more limited terms.

(5) A finding of a tribunal under subsection (3) in respect of any act shall, if it has become final, be treated as conclusive by a county court or sheriff court upon an application under subsection (4).

(6) A finding of a tribunal becomes final for the purposes of this section when an appeal against it is dismissed, withdrawn or abandoned or when the time for appealing expires without an appeal having been brought.

(7) An employment tribunal shall not consider a complaint under subsection (3) unless it is presented before the end of the period of six months beginning when the act to which it relates was done; and a county court or sheriff court shall not consider an application under subsection (4) unless it is made before the end of the period of five years so beginning.

---

[28] See n 24 above.   [29] Amended by the Employment Tribunals Act 1996.

[30] See n 24 above.

[31] Inserted with s 17C by the Disability and Discrimination Act 1995 (Amendment) Regulations, SI 2003/1673.

(8) A court or tribunal may consider any such complaint or application which is out of time if, in all the circumstances of the case, it considers that it is just and equitable to do so.

(9) The provisions of paragraph 3(3) and (4) of Schedule 3 apply for the purposes of subsection (7) as they apply for the purposes of paragraph 3(1) of that Schedule.

17C. Validity of contracts, collective agreements and rules of undertakings

Schedule 3A shall have effect.

[Supplementary and general[32]

18. Insurance services

(1) This section applies where a provider of insurance services ('the insurer') enters into arrangements with an employer under which the employer's employees, or a class of his employees—
(a) receive insurance services provided by the insurer; or
(b) are given an opportunity to receive such services.

(2) The insurer is to be taken, for the purposes of this Part, to discriminate unlawfully against a disabled person who is a relevant employee if he acts in relation to that employee in a way which would be unlawful discrimination for the purposes of Part III if—
(a) he were providing the service in question to members of the public; and
(b) the employee was provided with, or was trying to secure the provision of, that service as a member of the public.

(3) In this section—
'insurance services' means services of a prescribed description for the provision of benefits in respect of—
(a) termination of service;
(b) retirement, old age or death;
(c) accident, injury, sickness or invalidity; or
(d) any other prescribed matter; and
'relevant employee' means—
(a) in the case of an arrangement which applies to employees of the employer in question, an employee of his;
(b) in the case of an arrangement which applies to a class of employees of the employer, an employee who is in that class.

(4) For the purposes of the definition of 'relevant employee' in subsection (3), 'employee', in relation to an employer, includes a person who has applied for, or is contemplating applying for, employment by that employer or (as the case may be) employment by him in the class in question.

[18A. Alterations to premises occupied under leases[33]

(1) This section applies where—
(a) [a person to whom a duty to make reasonable adjustments applies][34] ('the occupier') occupies premises under a lease;

---

[32] Cross-heading inserted by the Disability and Discrimination Act 1995 (Amendment) Regulations, SI 2003/1673.

[33] See n 18 above.

[34] Amended by the Disability and Discrimination Act 1995 (Amendment) Regulations, SI 2003/1673.

(b) but for this section, the occupier would not be entitled to make a particular alteration to the premises; and

(c) the alteration is one which the occupier proposes to make in order to comply with [that duty].[35]

(2) Except to the extent to which it expressly so provides, the lease shall have effect by virtue of this subsection as if it provided—

(a) for the occupier to be entitled to make the alteration with the written consent of the lessor;

(b) for the occupier to have to make a written application to the lessor for consent if he wishes to make the alteration;

(c) if such an application is made, for the lessor not to withhold his consent unreasonably; and

(d) for the lessor to be entitled to make his consent subject to reasonable conditions.

(3) In this section—

'lease' includes a tenancy, sub-lease or sub-tenancy and an agreement for a lease, tenancy, sub-lease or sub-tenancy; and

'sub-lease' and 'sub-tenancy' have such meaning as may be prescribed.

(4) If the terms and conditions of a lease—

(a) impose conditions which are to apply if the occupier alters the premises, or

(b) entitle the lessor to impose conditions when consenting to the occupier's altering the premises,

the occupier is to be treated for the purposes of subsection (1) as not being entitled to make the alteration.

(5) Part I of Schedule 4 supplements the provisions of this section.]

[18B. Reasonable adjustments: supplementary[36]

(1) In determining whether it is reasonable for a person to have to take a particular step in order to comply with a duty to make reasonable adjustments, regard shall be had, in particular, to—

(a) the extent to which taking the step would prevent the effect in relation to which the duty is imposed;

(b) the extent to which it is practicable for him to take the step;

(c) the financial and other costs which would be incurred by him in taking the step and the extent to which taking it would disrupt any of his activities;

(d) the extent of his financial and other resources;

(e) the availability to him of financial or other assistance with respect to taking the step;

(f) the nature of his activities and the size of his undertaking;

(g) where the step would be taken in relation to a private household, the extent to which taking it would—

(i) disrupt that household, or

(ii) disturb any person residing there.

(2) The following are examples of steps which a person may need to take in relation to a disabled person in order to comply with a duty to make reasonable adjustments—

(a) making adjustments to premises;

(b) allocating some of the disabled person's duties to another person;

(c) transferring him to fill an existing vacancy;

---

[35] See n 34 above.

[36] Inserted by the Disability and Discrimination Act 1995 (Amendment) Regulations, SI 2003/1673.

    (d) altering his hours of working or training;

    (e) assigning him to a different place of work or training;

    (f) allowing him to be absent during working or training hours for rehabilitation, assessment or treatment;

    (g) giving, or arranging for, training or mentoring (whether for the disabled person or any other person);

    (h) acquiring or modifying equipment;

    (i) modifying instructions or reference manuals;

    (j) modifying procedures for testing or assessment;

    (k) providing a reader or interpreter;

    (l) providing supervision or other support.

(3) For the purposes of a duty to make reasonable adjustments, where under any binding obligation a person is required to obtain the consent of another person to any alteration of the premises occupied by him—

    (a) it is always reasonable for him to have to take steps to obtain that consent; and

    (b) it is never reasonable for him to have to make that alteration before that consent is obtained.

(4) The steps referred to in subsection (3)(a) shall not be taken to include an application to a court or tribunal.

(5) In subsection (3), 'binding obligation' means a legally binding obligation (not contained in a lease (within the meaning of section 18A(3)) in relation to the premises, whether arising from an agreement or otherwise.

(6) A provision of this Part imposing a duty to make reasonable adjustments applies only for the purpose of determining whether a person has discriminated against a disabled person; and accordingly a breach of any such duty is not actionable as such.]

[18C. Charities and support for particular groups of persons[37]

(1) Nothing in this Part—

    (a) affects any charitable instrument which provides for conferring benefits on one or more categories of person determined by reference to any physical or mental capacity; or

    (b) makes unlawful any act done by a charity or recognised body in pursuance of any of its charitable purposes, so far as those purposes are connected with persons so determined.

(2) Nothing in this Part prevents—

    (a) a person who provides supported employment from treating members of a particular group of disabled persons more favourably than other persons in providing such employment; or

    (b) the Secretary of State from agreeing to arrangements for the provision of supported employment which will, or may, have that effect.

(3) In this section—

'charitable instrument' means an enactment or other instrument (whenever taking effect) so far as it relates to charitable purposes;

'charity' has the same meaning as in the Charities Act 1993;

'recognised body' means a body which is a recognised body for the purposes of Part I of the Law Reform (Miscellaneous Provisions) (Scotland) Act 1990; and

'supported employment' means facilities provided, or in respect of which payments are made, under section 15 of the Disabled Persons (Employment) Act 1944.

---

[37] See n 14 above.

(4) In the application of this section to England and Wales, 'charitable purposes' means purposes which are exclusively charitable according to the law of England and Wales.

(5) In the application of this section to Scotland, 'charitable purposes' shall be construed in the same way as if it were contained in the Income Tax Acts.]

[18D. Interpretation of Part 2[38]

(1) Subject to any duty to make reasonable adjustments, nothing in this Part is to be taken to require a person to treat a disabled person more favourably than he treats or would treat others.

(2) In this Part—

'benefits'[, except in sections 4G to 4K,][39] includes facilities and services;

'detriment', except in section 16C(2)(b), does not include conduct of the nature referred to in section 3B (harassment);

'discriminate', 'discrimination' and other related expressions are to be construed in accordance with section 3A;

'duty to make reasonable adjustments' means a duty imposed by or under section 4A, 4B(5) or (6), 4E, [4H,][40] 6B, 7B, 7D, 14, 14B, 14D or 16A(5);

'employer' includes a person who has no employees but is seeking to employ another person;

'harassment' is to be construed in accordance with section 3B;

'physical feature', in relation to any premises, includes any of the following (whether permanent or temporary)—

(a) any feature arising from the design or construction of a building on the premises,

(b) any feature on the premises of any approach to, exit from or access to such a building,

(c) any fixtures, fittings, furnishings, furniture, equipment or material in or on the premises,

(d) any other physical element or quality of any land comprised in the premises;

'provision, criterion or practice' includes any arrangements.]

PART III
DISCRIMINATION IN OTHER AREAS

Goods, facilities and services

19. Discrimination in relation to goods, facilities and services

(1) It is unlawful for a provider of services to discriminate against a disabled person—

(a) in refusing to provide, or deliberately not providing, to the disabled person any service which he provides, or is prepared to provide, to members of the public;

(b) in failing to comply with any duty imposed on him by section 21 in circumstances in which the effect of that failure is to make it impossible or unreasonably difficult for the disabled person to make use of any such service;

(c) in the standard of service which he provides to the disabled person or the manner in which he provides it to him; or

---

[38] Inserted by the Disability and Discrimination Act 1995 (Amendment) Regulations, SI 2003/1673.

[39] Amended by the Disability Discrimination Act 1995 (Pensions) Regulations 2003, SI 2003/2770.

[40] See n 39 above.

   (d) in the terms on which he provides a service to the disabled person.

(2) For the purposes of this section and sections 20 and 21—

   (a) the provision of services includes the provision of any goods or facilities;

   (b) a person is 'a provider of services' if he is concerned with the provision, in the United Kingdom, of services to the public or to a section of the public; and

   (c) it is irrelevant whether a service is provided on payment or without payment.

(3) The following are examples of services to which this section and sections 20 and 21 apply—

   (a) access to and use of any place which members of the public are permitted to enter;

   (b) access to and use of means of communication;

   (c) access to and use of information services;

   (d) accommodation in a hotel, boarding house or other similar establishment;

   (e) facilities by way of banking or insurance or for grants, loans, credit or finance;

   (f) facilities for entertainment, recreation or refreshment;

   (g) facilities provided by employment agencies or under section 2 of the Employment and Training Act 1973;

   (h) the services of any profession or trade, or any local or other public authority.

(4) In the case of an act which constitutes discrimination by virtue of section 55, this section also applies to discrimination against a person who is not disabled.

(5) Except in such circumstances as may be prescribed, this section and sections 20 and 21 do not apply to—

   (a), (aa), (ab) . . .[41]

   (b) any service so far as it consists of the use of any means of transport; or

   (c) such other services as may be prescribed.

[(5A) Nothing in this Part applies to the provision of a service in relation to which discrimination is made unlawful by section 28A, 28F or 28R.][42]

(6) . . .[43]

20. Meaning of 'discrimination'

(1) For the purposes of section 19, a provider of services discriminates against a disabled person if—

   (a) for a reason which relates to the disabled person's disability, he treats him less favourably than he treats or would treat others to whom that reason does not or would not apply; and

   (b) he cannot show that the treatment in question is justified.

(2) For the purposes of section 19, a providers of services also discriminates against a disabled person if—

   (a) he fails to comply with a section 21 duty imposed on him in relation to the disabled person; and

   (b) he cannot show that his failure to comply with that duty is justified.

(3) For the purposes of this section, treatment is justified only if—

   (a) in the opinion of the provider of services, one or more of the conditions mentioned in subsection (4) are satisfied; and

   (b) it is reasonable, in all the circumstances of the case, for him to hold that opinion.

(4) The conditions are that—

   (a) in any case, the treatment is necessary in order not to endanger the health or safety of any person (which may include that of the disabled person);

---

   [41] Amended by the Learning and Skills Act 2000 and repealed by the Special Educational Needs and Disability Act 2001.

   [42] Inserted by the Special Educational Needs and Disability Act 2001.

   [43] Repealed by the Special Educational Needs and Disability Act 2001.

    (b) in any case, the disabled person is incapable of entering into an enforceable agreement, or of giving an informed consent, and for that reason the treatment is reasonable in that case;

    (c) in a case falling within section 19(1)(a), the treatment is necessary because the provider of services would otherwise be unable to provide the service to members of the public;

    (d) in a case falling within section 19(1)(c) or (d), the treatment is necessary in order for the provider of services to be able to provide the service to the disabled person or to other members of the public;

    (e) in a case falling within section 19(1)(d), the difference in the terms on which the service is provided to the disabled person and those on which it is provided to other members of the public reflects the greater cost to the provider of services in providing the service to the disabled person.

(5) Any increase in the cost of providing a service to a disabled person which results from compliance by a provider of services with a section 21 duty shall be disregarded for the purposes of subsection (4)(e).

(6) Regulations may make provision, for purposes of this section, as to circumstances in which—

    (a) it is reasonable for a provider of services to hold the opinion mentioned in subsection (3)(a);

    (b) it is not reasonable for a provider of services to hold that opinion.

(7) Regulations may make provision for subsection (4)(b) not to apply in prescribed circumstances where—

    (a) a person is acting for a disabled person under a power of attorney;

    (b) functions conferred by or under Part VII of the Mental Health Act 1983 are exercisable in relation to a disabled person's property or affairs; or

    (c) powers are exercisable in Scotland in relation to a disabled person's property or affairs in consequence of the appointment of a curator bonis, tutor or judicial factor.

(8) Regulations may make provision, for purposes of this section, as to circumstances (other than those mentioned in subsection (4)) in which treatment is to be taken to be justified.

(9) In subsections (3), (4) and (8) 'treatment' includes failure to comply with a section 21 duty.

21. Duty of providers of services to make adjustments

(1)   Where a provider of services has a practice, policy or procedure which makes it impossible or unreasonably difficult for disabled persons to make use of a service which he provides, or is prepared to provide, to other members of the public, it is his duty to take such steps as it is reasonable, in all the circumstances of the case, for him to have to take in order to change that practice, policy or procedure so that it no longer has that effect.

(2)   Where a physical feature (for example, one arising from the design or construction of a building or the approach or access to premises) makes it impossible or unreasonably difficult for disabled persons to make use of such a service, it is the duty of the provider of that service to take such steps as it is reasonable, in all the circumstances of the case, for him to have to take in order to—

    (a) remove the feature;

    (b) alter it so that it no longer has that effect;

    (c) provide a reasonable means of avoiding the feature; or

    (d) provide a reasonable alternative method of making the service in question available to disabled persons.

(3)   Regulations may prescribe—

    (a) matters which are to be taken into account in determining whether any provision of a kind mentioned in subsection (2)(c) or (d) is reasonable; and

    (b) categories of providers of services to whom subsection (2) does not apply.

(4) Where an auxiliary aid or service (for example, the provision of information on audio tape or of a sign language interpreter) would—
    (a) enable disabled persons to make use of a service which a provider of services provides, or is prepared to provide, to members of the public, or
    (b) facilitate the use by disabled persons of such a service,
it is the duty of the provider of that service to take such steps as it is reasonable, in all the circumstances of the case, for him to have to take in order to provide that auxiliary aid or service.

(5) Regulations may make provision, for the purposes of this section—
    (a) as to circumstances in which it is reasonable for a provider of services to have to take steps of a prescribed description;
    (b) as to circumstances in which it is not reasonable for a provider of services to have to take steps of a prescribed description;
    (c) as to what is to be included within the meaning of 'practice, policy or procedure';
    (d) as to what is not to be included within the meaning of that expression;
    (e) as to things which are to be treated as physical features;
    (f) as to things which are not to be treated as such features;
    (g) as to things which are to be treated as auxiliary aids or services;
    (h) as to things which are not to be treated as auxiliary aids or services.

(6) Nothing in this section requires a provider of services to take any steps which would fundamentally alter the nature of the service in question or the nature of his trade, profession or business.

(7) Nothing in this section requires a provider of services to take any steps which would cause him to incur expenditure exceeding the prescribed maximum.

(8) Regulations under subsection (7) may provide for the prescribed maximum to be calculated by reference to—
    (a) aggregate amounts of expenditure incurred in relation to different cases;
    (b) prescribed periods;
    (c) services of a prescribed description;
    (d) premises of a prescribed description; or
    (e) such other criteria as may be prescribed.

(9) Regulations may provide, for the purposes of subsection (7), for expenditure incurred by one provider of services to be treated as incurred by another.

(10) This section imposes duties only for the purpose of determining whether a provider of services has discriminated against a disabled person; and accordingly a breach of any such duty is not actionable as such.

[21A. Employment services[44]

(1) In this Part, 'employment services' means—
    (a) vocational guidance;
    (b) vocational training; or
    (c) services to assist a person to obtain or retain employment, or to establish himself as self-employed.

(2) It is unlawful for a provider of employment services, in relation to such services, to subject to harassment a disabled person—
    (a) to whom he is providing such services, or
    (b) who has requested him to provide such services;

---

[44] Inserted by the Disability and Discrimination Act 1995 (Amendment) Regulations, SI 2003/1673.

and section 3B (meaning of 'harassment') applies for the purposes of this subsection as it applies for the purposes of Part 2.

(3) In their application to employment services, the preceding provisions of this Part have effect as follows.

(4) Section 19 has effect as if—

    (a) after subsection (1)(a), there were inserted the following paragraph—

        '(aa) in failing to comply with a duty imposed on him by subsection (1) of section 21 in circumstances in which the effect of that failure is to place the disabled person at a substantial disadvantage in comparison with persons who are not disabled in relation to the provision of the service;';

    (b) in subsection (1)(b), for 'section 21' there were substituted 'subsection (2) or (4) of section 21';

    (c) in subsection (2), for 'sections 20 and 21' there were substituted 'sections 20, 21 and 21A'.

(5) Section 20 has effect as if—

    (a) after subsection (1), there were inserted the following subsection—

        '(1A) For the purposes of section 19, a provider of services also discriminates against a disabled person if he fails to comply with a duty imposed on him by subsection (1) of section 21 in relation to the disabled person.';

    (b) in subsection (2)(a), for 'a section 21 duty imposed' there were substituted 'a duty imposed by subsection (2) or (4) of section 21';

    (c) after subsection (3), there were inserted the following subsection—

        '(3A) But treatment of a disabled person cannot be justified under subsection (3) if it amounts to direct discrimination falling within section 3A(5).'.

(6) Section 21 has effect as if—

    (a) in subsection (1), for 'makes it impossible or unreasonably difficult for disabled persons to make use of' there were substituted 'places disabled persons at a substantial disadvantage in comparison with persons who are not disabled in relation to the provision of';

    (b) after subsection (1), there were inserted the following subsection—

        '(1A) In subsection (1), 'practice, policy or procedure' includes a provision or criterion.'.]

22. Discrimination in relation to premises

(1) It is unlawful for a person with power to dispose of any premises to discriminate against a disabled person—

    (a) in the terms on which he offers to dispose of those premises to the disabled person;

    (b) by refusing to dispose of those premises to the disabled person; or

    (c) in his treatment of the disabled person in relation to any list of persons in need of premises of that description.

(2) Subsection (1) does not apply to a person who owns an estate or interest in the premises and wholly occupies them unless, for the purpose of disposing of the premises, he—

    (a) uses the services of an estate agent, or

    (b) publishes an advertisement or causes an advertisement to be published.

(3) It is unlawful for a person managing any premises to discriminate against a disabled person occupying those premises—

    (a) in the way he permits the disabled person to make use of any benefits or facilities;

    (b) by refusing or deliberately omitting to permit the disabled person to make use of any benefits or facilities; or

    (c) by evicting the disabled person, or subjecting him to any other detriment.

(4) It is unlawful for any person whose licence or consent is required for the disposal of any

premises comprised in, or (in Scotland) the subject of, a tenancy to discriminate against a disabled person by withholding his licence or consent for the disposal of the premises to the disabled person.

(5) Subsection (4) applies to tenancies created before as well as after the passing of this Act.

(6) In this section—

'advertisement' includes every form of advertisement or notice, whether to the public or not;

'dispose', in relation to premises, includes granting a right to occupy the premises, and, in relation to premises comprised in, or (in Scotland) the subject of, a tenancy, includes—

(a) assigning the tenancy, and

(b) sub-letting or parting with possession of the premises or any part of the premises; and 'disposal' shall be construed accordingly;

'estate agent' means a person who, by way of profession or trade, provides services for the purpose of finding premises for persons seeking to acquire them or assisting in the disposal of premises; and

'tenancy' means a tenancy created—

(a) by a lease or sub-lease,

(b) by an agreement for a lease or sub-lease,

(c) by a tenancy agreement, or

(d) in pursuance of any enactment.

(7) In the case of an act which constitutes discrimination by virtue of section 55, this section also applies to discrimination against a person who is not disabled.

(8) This section applies only in relation to premises in the United Kingdom.

23. Exemption for small dwellings

(1) Where the conditions mentioned in subsection (2) are satisfied, subsection (1), (3) or (as the case may be) (4) of section 22 does not apply.

(2) The conditions are that—

(a) the relevant occupier resides, and intends to continue to reside, on the premises;

(b) the relevant occupier shares accommodation on the premises with persons who reside on the premises and are not members of his household;

(c) the shared accommodation is not storage accommodation or a means of access; and

(d) the premises are small premises.

(3) For the purposes of this section, premises are 'small premises' if they fall within subsection (4) or (5).

(4) Premises fall within this subsection if—

(a) only the relevant occupier and members of his household reside in the accommodation occupied by him;

(b) the premises comprise, in addition to the accommodation occupied by the relevant occupier, residential accommodation for at least one other household;

(c) the residential accommodation for each other household is let, or available for letting, on a separate tenancy or similar agreement; and

(d) there are not normally more than two such other households.

(5) Premises fall within this subsection if there is not normally residential accommodation on the premises for more than six persons in addition to the relevant occupier and any members of his household.

(6) For the purposes of this section 'the relevant occupier' means—

(a) in a case falling within section 22(1), the person with power to dispose of the premises, or a near relative of his;

(b) in a case falling within section 22(4), the person whose licence or consent is required for the disposal of the premises, or a near relative of his.

(7) For the purposes of this section—

'near relative' means a person's spouse, partner, parent, child, grandparent, grandchild, or brother or sister (whether of full or half blood or by affinity); and

'partner' means the other member of a couple consisting of a man and a woman who are not married to each other but are living together as husband and wife.

24. Meaning of 'discrimination'

(1) For the purposes of section 22, a person ('A') discriminates against a disabled person if—

    (a) for a reason which relates to the disabled person's disability, he treats him less favourably than he treats or would treat others to whom that reason does not or would not apply; and

    (b) he cannot show that the treatment in question is justified.

(2) For the purposes of this section, treatment is justified only if—

    (a) in A's opinion, one or more of the conditions mentioned in subsection (3) are satisfied; and

    (b) it is reasonable, in all the circumstances of the case, for him to hold that opinion.

(3) The conditions are that—

    (a) in any case, the treatment is necessary in order not to endanger the health or safety of any person (which may include that of the disabled person);

    (b) in any case, the disabled person is incapable of entering into an enforceable agreement, or of giving an informed consent, and for that reason the treatment is reasonable in that case;

    (c) in a case falling within section 22(3)(a), the treatment is necessary in order for the disabled person or the occupiers of other premises forming part of the building to make use of the benefit or facility;

    (d) in a case falling within section 22(3)(b), the treatment is necessary in order for the occupiers of other premises forming part of the building to make use of the benefit or facility.

(4) Regulations may make provision, for purposes of this section, as to circumstances in which—

    (a) it is reasonable for a person to hold the opinion mentioned in subsection 2(a);

    (b) it is not reasonable for a person to hold that opinion.

(5) Regulations may make provision, for purposes of this section, as to circumstances (other than those mentioned in subsection (3)) in which treatment is to be taken to be justified.

Enforcement, etc

25. Enforcement, remedies and procedure

(1) A claim by any person that another person—

    (a) has discriminated against him in a way which is unlawful under this Part; or

    (b) is by virtue of section 57 or 58 to be treated as having discriminated against him in such a way,

may be made the subject of civil proceedings in the same way as any other claim in tort or (in Scotland) in reparation for breach of statutory duty.

(2) For the avoidance of doubt it is hereby declared that damages in respect of discrimination in a way which is unlawful under this Part may include compensation for injury to feelings whether or not they include compensation under any other head.

(3) Proceedings in England and Wales shall be brought only in a county court.

(4) Proceedings in Scotland shall be brought only in a sheriff court.

(5) The remedies available in such proceedings are those which are available in the High Court or (as the case may be) the Court of Session.

(6) Part II of Schedule 3 makes further provision about the enforcement of this Part and about procedure.

[(7) Subsection (1) does not apply in relation to a claim by a person that another person—

(a) has discriminated against him or subjected him to harassment in relation to the provision of employment services in a way which is unlawful under this Part; or

(b) is by virtue of section 57 or 58 to be treated as having discriminated against him or subjected him to harassment in such a way.

(8) A claim of the kind referred to in subsection (7) may be presented as a complaint to an employment tribunal.

(9) Section 17A(1A) to (7) and paragraphs 3 and 4 of Schedule 3 apply in relation to a complaint under subsection (8) as if it were a complaint under section 17A(1) (and paragraphs 6 to 8 of Schedule 3 do not apply in relation to such a complaint).][45]

26. Validity and revision of certain agreements

(1) Any term in a contract for the provision of goods, facilities or services or in any other agreement is void so far as it purports to—

(a) require a person to do anything which would contravene any provision of, or made under, this Part,

(b) exclude or limit the operation of any provision of this Part, or

(c) prevent any person from making a claim under this Part.

[(1A) Subsection (1) does not apply to any term in a contract, or other agreement, for the provision of employment services.][46]

(2) Paragraphs (b) and (c) of subsection (1) do not apply to an agreement settling a claim to which section 25 applies.

(3) On the application of any person interested in an agreement to which subsection (1) applies, a county court or a sheriff court may make such order as it thinks just for modifying the agreement to take account of the effect of subsection (1).

(4) No such order shall be made unless all persons affected have been—

(a) given notice of the application; and

(b) afforded an opportunity to make representations to the court.

(5) Subsection (4) applies subject to any rules of court providing for that notice to be dispensed with.

(6) An order under subsection (3) may include provision as respects any period before the making of the order.

27. Alterations to premises occupied under leases

(1) This section applies where—

(a) a provider of services ('the occupier') occupies premises under a lease;

(b) but for this section, he would not be entitled to make a particular alteration to the premises; and

(c) the alteration is one which the occupier proposes to make in order to comply with a section 21 duty.

---

[45] Inserted by the Disability and Discrimination Act 1995 (Amendment) Regulations, SI 2003/1673.

[46] Inserted by the Disability and Discrimination Act 1995 (Amendment) Regulations, SI 2003/1673.

(2) Except to the extent to which it expressly so provides, the lease shall have effect by virtue of this subsection as if it provided—

    (a) for the occupier to be entitled to make the alteration with the written consent of the lessor;

    (b) for the occupier to have to make a written application to the lessor for consent if he wishes to make the alteration;

    (c) if such an application is made, for the lessor not to withhold his consent unreasonably; and

    (d) for the lessor to be entitled to make his consent subject to reasonable conditions.

(3) In this section—

'lease' includes a tenancy, sub-lease or sub-tenancy and an agreement for a lease, tenancy, sub-lease or sub-tenancy; and

'sub-lease' and 'sub-tenancy' have such meaning as may be prescribed.

(4) If the terms and conditions of a lease—

    (a) impose conditions which are to apply if the occupier alters the premises, or

    (b) entitle the lessor to impose conditions when consenting to the occupier's altering the premises,

the occupier is to be treated for the purposes of subsection (1) as not being entitled to make the alteration.

(5) Part II of Schedule 4 supplements the provisions of this section.

[28. Conciliation of disputes[47]

(1) The Commission may make arrangements with any other person for the provision of conciliation services by, or by persons appointed by, that person in relation to disputes arising under this Part.

(2) In deciding what arrangements (if any) to make, the Commission shall have regard to the desirability of securing, so far as reasonably practicable, that conciliation services are available for all disputes arising under this Part which the parties may wish to refer to conciliation.

(3) No member or employee of the Commission may provide conciliation services in relation to disputes arising under this Part.

(4) The Commission shall ensure that any arrangements under this section include appropriate safeguards to prevent the disclosure to members or employees of the Commission of information obtained by a person in connection with the provision of conciliation services in pursuance of the arrangements.

(5) Subsection (4) does not apply to information relating to a dispute which is disclosed with the consent of the parties to that dispute.

(6) Subsection (4) does not apply to information which—

    (a) is not identifiable with a particular dispute or a particular person; and

    (b) is reasonably required by the Commission for the purpose of monitoring the operation of the arrangements concerned.

(7) Anything communicated to a person while providing conciliation services in pursuance of any arrangements under this section is not admissible in evidence in any proceedings except with the consent of the person who communicated it to that person.

(8) In this section 'conciliation services' means advice and assistance provided by a conciliator to the parties to a dispute with a view to promoting its settlement otherwise than through the courts.]

---

[47] Substituted by the Disability Rights Commission Act 1999.

PART IV
EDUCATION
[CHAPTER 1[48]
SCHOOLS

Duties of responsible bodies

28A. Discrimination against disabled pupils and prospective pupils

(1) It is unlawful for the body responsible for a school to discriminate against a disabled person—
    (a) in the arrangements it makes for determining admission to the school as a pupil;
    (b) in the terms on which it offers to admit him to the school as a pupil; or
    (c) by refusing or deliberately omitting to accept an application for his admission to the school as a pupil.

(2) It is unlawful for the body responsible for a school to discriminate against a disabled pupil in the education or associated services provided for, or offered to, pupils at the school by that body.

(3) The Secretary of State may by regulations prescribe services which are, or services which are not, to be regarded for the purposes of subsection (2) as being—
    (a) education; or
    (b) an associated service.

(4) It is unlawful for the body responsible for a school to discriminate against a disabled pupil by excluding him from the school, whether permanently or temporarily.

(5) The body responsible for a school is to be determined in accordance with Schedule 4A, and in the remaining provisions of this Chapter is referred to as the 'responsible body'.

(6) In the case of an act which constitutes discrimination by virtue of section 55, this section also applies to discrimination against a person who is not disabled.

28B. Meaning of 'discrimination'

(1) For the purposes of section 28A, a responsible body discriminates against a disabled person if—
    (a) for a reason which relates to his disability, it treats him less favourably than it treats or would treat others to whom that reason does not or would not apply; and
    (b) it cannot show that the treatment in question is justified.

(2) For the purposes of section 28A, a responsible body also discriminates against a disabled person if—
    (a) it fails, to his detriment, to comply with section 28C; and
    (b) it cannot show that its failure to comply is justified.

(3) In relation to a failure to take a particular step, a responsible body does not discriminate against a person if it shows—
    (a) that, at the time in question, it did not know and could not reasonably have been expected to know, that he was disabled; and
    (b) that its failure to take the step was attributable to that lack of knowledge.

(4) The taking of a particular step by a responsible body in relation to a person does not amount to less favourable treatment if it shows that at the time in question it did not know, and could not reasonably have been expected to know, that he was disabled.

---

[48] Chapter 1 (ss 28A–28X) inserted by the Special Educational Needs and Disability Act 2001.

(5) Subsections (6) to (8) apply in determining whether, for the purposes of this section—
    (a) less favourable treatment of a person, or
    (b) failure to comply with section 28C,
is justified.

(6) Less favourable treatment of a person is justified if it is the result of a permitted form of selection.

(7) Otherwise, less favourable treatment, or a failure to comply with section 28C, is justified only if the reason for it is both material to the circumstances of the particular case and substantial.

(8) If, in a case falling within subsection (1)—
    (a) the responsible body is under a duty imposed by section 28C in relation to the disabled person, but
    (b) it fails without justification to comply with that duty,
its treatment of that person cannot be justified under subsection (7) unless that treatment would have been justified even if it had complied with that duty.

28C. Disabled pupils not to be substantially disadvantaged

(1) The responsible body for a school must take such steps as it is reasonable for it to have to take to ensure that—
    (a) in relation to the arrangements it makes for determining the admission of pupils to the school, disabled persons are not placed at a substantial disadvantage in comparison with persons who are not disabled; and
    (b) in relation to education and associated services provided for, or offered to, pupils at the school by it, disabled pupils are not placed at a substantial disadvantage in comparison with pupils who are not disabled.

(2) That does not require the responsible body to—
    (a) remove or alter a physical feature (for example, one arising from the design or construction of the school premises or the location of resources); or
    (b) provide auxiliary aids or services.

(3) Regulations may make provision, for the purposes of this section—
    (a) as to circumstances in which it is reasonable for a responsible body to have to take steps of a prescribed description;
    (b) as to steps which it is always reasonable for a responsible body to have to take;
    (c) as to circumstances in which it is not reasonable for a responsible body to have to take steps of a prescribed description;
    (d) as to steps which it is never reasonable for a responsible body to have to take.

(4) In considering whether it is reasonable for it to have to take a particular step in order to comply with its duty under subsection (1), a responsible body must have regard to any relevant provisions of a code of practice issued under section 53A.

(5) Subsection (6) applies if, in relation to a person, a confidentiality request has been made of which a responsible body is aware.

(6) In determining whether it is reasonable for the responsible body to have to take a particular step in relation to that person in order to comply with its duty under subsection (1), regard shall be had to the extent to which taking the step in question is consistent with compliance with that request.

(7) 'Confidentiality request' means a request which asks for the nature, or asks for the existence, of a disabled person's disability to be treated as confidential and which satisfies either of the following conditions—
    (a) it is made by that person's parent; or
    (b) it is made by that person himself and the responsible body reasonably believes that he has sufficient understanding of the nature of the request and of its effect.

(8) This section imposes duties only for the purpose of determining whether a responsible body has discriminated against a disabled person; and accordingly a breach of any such duty is not actionable as such.

28D. Accessibility strategies and plans

(1) Each local education authority must prepare, in relation to schools for which they are the responsible body—
  (a) an accessibility strategy;
  (b) further such strategies at such times as may be prescribed.

(2) An accessibility strategy is a strategy for, over a prescribed period—
  (a) increasing the extent to which disabled pupils can participate in the schools' curriculums;
  (b) improving the physical environment of the schools for the purpose of increasing the extent to which disabled pupils are able to take advantage of education and associated services provided or offered by the schools; and
  (c) improving the delivery to disabled pupils—
    (i) within a reasonable time, and
    (ii) in ways which are determined after taking account of their disabilities and any preferences expressed by them or their parents,
  of information which is provided in writing for pupils who are not disabled.

(3) An accessibility strategy must be in writing.

(4) Each local education authority must keep their accessibility strategy under review during the period to which it relates and, if necessary, revise it.

(5) It is the duty of each local education authority to implement their accessibility strategy.

(6) An inspection under section 38 of the Education Act 1997 (inspections of local education authorities) may extend to the performance by a local education authority of their functions in relation to the preparation, review, revision and implementation of their accessibility strategy.

(7) Subsections (8) to (13) apply to—
  (a) maintained schools;
  (b) independent schools; and
  (c) special schools which are not maintained special schools but which are approved by the Secretary of State, or by the National Assembly, under section 342 of the Education Act 1996.

(8) The responsible body must prepare—
  (a) an accessibility plan;
  (b) further such plans at such times as may be prescribed.

(9) An accessibility plan is a plan for, over a prescribed period—
  (a) increasing the extent to which disabled pupils can participate in the school's curriculum;
  (b) improving the physical environment of the school for the purpose of increasing the extent to which disabled pupils are able to take advantage of education and associated services provided or offered by the school; and
  (c) improving the delivery to disabled pupils—
    (i) within a reasonable time, and
    (ii) in ways which are determined after taking account of their disabilities and any preferences expressed by them or their parents,
  of information which is provided in writing for pupils who are not disabled.

(10) An accessibility plan must be in writing.

(11) During the period to which the plan relates, the responsible body must keep its accessibility plan under review and, if necessary, revise it.

(12) It is the duty of the responsible body to implement its accessibility plan.

(13) An inspection under the School Inspections Act 1996 may extend to the performance by the responsible body of its functions in relation to the preparation, publication, review, revision and implementation of its accessibility plan.

(14) For a maintained school [or maintained nursery school],[49] the duties imposed by subsections (8) to (12) are duties of the governing body.

(15) Regulations may prescribe services which are, or services which are not, to be regarded for the purposes of this section as being—

    (a) education; or

    (b) an associated service.

(16) In this section and in section 28E, 'local education authority' has the meaning given in section 12 of the Education Act 1996.

(17) In relation to Wales—

    'prescribed' means prescribed in regulations; and

    'regulations' means regulations made by the National Assembly.

(18) 'Disabled pupil' includes a disabled person who may be admitted to the school as a pupil.

(19) 'Maintained school' and 'independent school' have the meaning given in section 28Q(5).

28E. Accessibility strategies and plans: procedure

(1) In preparing their accessibility strategy, a local education authority must have regard to—

    (a) the need to allocate adequate resources for implementing the strategy; and

    (b) any guidance issued as to—

        (i) the content of an accessibility strategy;

        (ii) the form in which it is to be produced; and

        (iii) the persons to be consulted in its preparation.

(2) A local education authority must have regard to any guidance issued as to compliance with the requirements of section 28D(4).

(3) Guidance under subsection (1)(b) or (2) may be issued—

    (a) for England, by the Secretary of State; and

    (b) for Wales, by the National Assembly.

(4) In preparing an accessibility plan, the responsible body must have regard to the need to allocate adequate resources for implementing the plan.

(5) If the Secretary of State asks for a copy of—

    (a) the accessibility strategy prepared by a local education authority in England, or

    (b) the accessibility plan prepared by the proprietor of an independent school (other than [an Academy][50]) in England,

the strategy or plan must be given to him.

(6) If the National Assembly asks for a copy of—

    (a) the accessibility strategy prepared by a local education authority in Wales, or

    (b) the accessibility plan prepared by the proprietor of an independent school [(other than an Academy)][51] in Wales,

the strategy or plan must be given to it.

(7) If asked to do so, a local education authority must make a copy of their accessibility strategy available for inspection at such reasonable times as they may determine.

(8) If asked to do so, the proprietor of an independent school which is not [an Academy][52] must make a copy of his accessibility plan available for inspection at such reasonable times as he may determine.

---

[49] Amended by the Education Act 2002, not yet in force in relation to Wales.

[50] Amended by the Education Act 2002.   [51] See n 50 above.

[52] See n 50 above.

Residual duty of education authorities

28F. Duty of education authorities not to discriminate

(1) This section applies to—
  (a) the functions of a local education authority under the Education Acts; and
  (b) the functions of an education authority under—
    (i) the Education (Scotland) Act 1980;
    (ii) the Education (Scotland) Act 1996; and
    (iii) the Standards in Scotland's Schools etc Act 2000.
(2) But it does not apply to any prescribed function.
(3) In discharging a function to which this section applies, it is unlawful for the authority to discriminate against—
  (a) a disabled pupil; or
  (b) a disabled person who may be admitted to a school as a pupil.
(4) But an act done in the discharge of a function to which this section applies is unlawful as a result of subsection (3) only if no other provision of this Chapter makes that act unlawful.
(5) In the case of an act which constitutes discrimination by virtue of section 55, this section also applies to discrimination against a person who is not disabled.
(6) In this section and section 28G, 'local education authority' has the meaning given in section 12 of the Education Act 1996.
(7) 'The Education Acts' has the meaning given in section 578 of the Education Act 1996.
(8) In this section and section 28G, 'education authority' has the meaning given in section 135(1) of the Education (Scotland) Act 1980.

28G. Residual duty: supplementary provisions

(1) Section 28B applies for the purposes of section 28F as it applies for the purposes of section 28A with the following modifications—
  (a) references to a responsible body are to be read as references to an authority; and
  (b) references to section 28C are to be read as references to subsections (2) to (4).
(2) Each authority must take such steps as it is reasonable for it to have to take to ensure that, in discharging any function to which section 28F applies—
  (a) disabled persons who may be admitted to a school as pupils are not placed at a substantial disadvantage in comparison with persons who are not disabled; and
  (b) disabled pupils are not placed at a substantial disadvantage in comparison with pupils who are not disabled.
(3) That does not require the authority to—
  (a) remove or alter a physical feature; or
  (b) provide auxiliary aids or services.
(4) This section imposes duties only for the purpose of determining whether an authority has discriminated against a disabled person; and accordingly a breach of any such duty is not actionable as such.
(5) A reference in sections 28I, 28K(1), 28M(6) and 28P to a responsible body is to be read as including a reference to a local education authority in relation to a function to which section 28F applies.
(6) A reference in section 28N and 28P to a responsible body is to be read as including a reference to an education authority in relation to a function to which section 28F applies.
(7) 'Authority' means—
  (a) in relation to England and Wales, a local education authority; and
  (b) in relation to Scotland, an education authority.

Enforcement: England and Wales

[28H. Tribunals[53]

(1) The Special Educational Needs Tribunal—
  (a) is to continue to exist; but
  (b) after the commencement date is to be known as the Special Educational Needs and Disability Tribunal.

[(2) In this Chapter—
  'the Tribunal' means the Special Educational Needs and Disability Tribunal, and
  'the Welsh Tribunal' means the Special Educational Needs Tribunal for Wales.

(3) In addition to the jurisdiction of those tribunals under Part 4 of the Education Act 1996, each of them is to exercise the jurisdiction conferred on it by this Chapter.][54]

(4) 'Commencement date' means the day on which section 17 of the Special Educational Needs and Disability Act 2001 comes into force.

28I. Jurisdiction and powers of the Tribunal

(1) A claim that a responsible body—
  (a) has discriminated against a person ('A') in a way which is made unlawful under this Chapter, or
  (b) is by virtue of section 58 to be treated as having discriminated against a person ('A') in such a way,
  may be made to the [appropriate tribunal][55] by A's parent.

(2) But this section does not apply to a claim to which section 28K or 28L applies.

(3) If the [appropriate tribunal][56] considers that a claim under subsection (1) is well founded—
  (a) it may declare that A has been unlawfully discriminated against; and
  (b) if it does so, it may make such order as it considers reasonable in all the circumstances of the case.

(4) The power conferred by subsection (3)(b)—
  (a) may, in particular, be exercised with a view to obviating or reducing the adverse effect on the person concerned of any matter to which the claim relates; but
  (b) does not include power to order the payment of any sum by way of compensation.

[(5) Subject to regulations under section 28J(8), the appropriate tribunal—
  (a) for a claim against the responsible body for a school in England, is the Tribunal,
  (b) for a claim against the responsible body for a school in Wales, is the Welsh Tribunal.][57]

28J. Procedure

(1) Regulations may make provision about—
  (a) the proceedings of the Tribunal on a claim of unlawful discrimination under this Chapter; and
  (b) the making of a claim.

(2) The regulations may, in particular, include provision—
  (a) as to the manner in which a claim must be made;
  (b) if the jurisdiction of the Tribunal is being exercised by more than one tribunal—
    (i) for determining by which tribunal any claim is to be heard, and
    (ii) for the transfer of proceedings from one tribunal to another;

---

[53] Amended by the Education Act 2002.   [54] See n 53 above.
[55] Amended by the Education Act 2002.   [56] See n 55 above.
[57] See n 55 above.

(c)　for enabling functions which relate to matters preliminary or incidental to a claim (including, in particular, decisions under paragraph 10(3) of Schedule 3) to be performed by the President, or by the chairman;

(d)　enabling hearings to be conducted in the absence of any member other than the chairman;

(e)　as to the persons who may appear on behalf of the parties;

(f)　for granting any person such disclosure or inspection of documents or right to further particulars as might be granted by a county court;

(g)　requiring persons to attend to give evidence and produce documents;

(h)　for authorising the administration of oaths to witnesses;

(i)　for the determination of claims without a hearing in prescribed circumstances;

(j)　as to the withdrawal of claims;

(k)　for enabling the Tribunal to stay proceedings on a claim;

(l)　for the award of costs or expenses;

(m)　for taxing or otherwise settling costs or expenses (and, in particular, for enabling costs to be taxed in the county court);

(n)　for the registration and proof of decisions and orders; and

(o)　for enabling prescribed decisions to be reviewed, or prescribed orders to be varied or revoked, in such circumstances as may be determined in accordance with the regulations.

[(2A) If made with the agreement of the National Assembly, the regulations apply to the Welsh Tribunal as they apply to the Tribunal, subject to such modifications as may be specified in the regulations.][58]

(3)　Proceedings before the Tribunal [or the Welsh Tribunal][59] are to be held in private, except in prescribed circumstances.

(4)　. . .[60]

(5)　The Secretary of State may pay such allowances for the purpose of or in connection with the attendance of persons at the Tribunal [or the Welsh Tribunal][61] as he may, with the consent of the Treasury, determine.

(6)　In relation to [the Welsh Tribunal],[62] the power conferred by subsection (5) may be exercised only with the agreement of the National Assembly.

(7)　Part 1 of the Arbitration Act 1996 does not apply to proceedings before the Tribunal [or the Welsh Tribunal][63] but regulations may make provision, in relation to such proceedings, corresponding to any provision of that Part.

(8)　The regulations may make provision for a claim under this Chapter to be heard, in prescribed circumstances, with an appeal under Part 4 of the Education Act 1996[, including provision—

(a)　for determining the appropriate tribunal for the purposes of section 28I for such a claim, and

(b)　for the transfer of proceedings between the Tribunal and the Welsh Tribunal.][64]

(9)　A person who without reasonable excuse fails to comply with—

(a)　a requirement in respect of the disclosure or inspection of documents imposed by the regulations by virtue of subsection (2)(f), or

(b)　a requirement imposed by the regulations by virtue of subsection (2)(g),

is guilty of an offence.

---

[58] Amended by the Education Act 2002.　　[59] See n 58 above.
[60] See n 58 above.　　[61] See n 58 above.　　[62] See n 58 above.
[63] See n 58 above.　　[64] See n 58 above.

(10) A person guilty of an offence under subsection (9) is liable on summary conviction to a fine not exceeding level 3 on the standard scale.

(11) Part 3 of Schedule 3 makes further provision about enforcement of this Chapter and about procedure.

28K. Admissions

(1) If the condition mentioned in subsection (2) is satisfied, this section applies to a claim in relation to an admissions decision that a responsible body—
   (a) has discriminated against a person ('A') in a way which is made unlawful under this Chapter; or
   (b) is by virtue of section 58 to be treated as having discriminated against a person ('A') in such a way.

(2) The condition is that arrangements ('appeal arrangements') have been made—
   (a) under section 94 of the School Standards and Framework Act 1998, or
   (b) under an agreement entered into between the responsible body for [an Academy][65] and the Secretary of State under section 482 of the Education Act 1996,
   enabling an appeal to be made against the decision by A's parent.

(3) The claim must be made under the appeal arrangements.

(4) The body hearing the claim has the powers which it has in relation to an appeal under the appeal arrangements.

(5) 'Admissions decision' means—
   (a) a decision of a kind mentioned in section 94(1) or (2) of the School Standards and Framework Act 1998;
   (b) a decision as to the admission of a person to [an Academy][66] taken by the responsible body or on its behalf.

28L. Exclusions

(1) If the condition mentioned in subsection (2) is satisfied, this section applies to a claim in relation to an exclusion decision that a responsible body—
   (a) has discriminated against a person ('A') in a way which is made unlawful under this Chapter; or
   (b) is by virtue of section 58 to be treated as having discriminated against a person ('A') in such a way.

(2) The condition is that arrangements ('appeal arrangements') have been made—
   (a) under [section 52(3)(c) of the Education Act 2002],[67] or
   (b) under an agreement entered into between the responsible body for [an Academy][68] and the Secretary of State under section 482 of the Education Act 1996,
   enabling an appeal to be made against the decision by A or by his parent.

(3) The claim must be made under the appeal arrangements.

(4) The body hearing the claim has the powers which it has in relation to an appeal under the appeal arrangements.

(5) 'Exclusion decision' means—
   (a) a decision of a kind mentioned in [section 52(3)(c) of the Education Act 2002];[69]
   (b) a decision not to reinstate a pupil who has been permanently excluded from [an Academy][70] by its head teacher, taken by the responsible body or on its behalf.

---

[65] Amended by the Education Act 2002.
[67] Amended by the Education Act 2002.
[69] See n 67 above.

[66] See n 65 above.
[68] See n 67 above.
[70] See n 67 above.

(6) 'Responsible body', in relation to a maintained school, includes the discipline committee of the governing body if that committee is required to be established as a result of regulations made under [section 19 of the Education Act 2002].[71]

(7) 'Maintained school' has the meaning given in section 28Q(5).

28M. Roles of the Secretary of State and the National Assembly

(1) If the appropriate authority is satisfied (whether on a complaint or otherwise) that a responsible body—

    (a) has acted, or is proposing to act, unreasonably in the discharge of a duty imposed by or under section 28D or 28E, or

    (b) has failed to discharge a duty imposed by or under either of those sections,

it may give that body such directions as to the discharge of the duty as appear to it to be expedient.

(2) Subsection (3) applies in relation to—

    (a) special schools which are not maintained special schools but which are approved by the Secretary of State, or by the National Assembly, under section 342 of the Education Act 1996; and

    (b) city academies.

(3) If the appropriate authority is satisfied (whether on a complaint or otherwise) that a responsible body—

    (a) has acted, or is proposing to act, unreasonably in the discharge of a duty which that body has in relation to—

        (i) the provision to the appropriate authority of copies of that body's accessibility plan, or

        (ii) the inspection of that plan, or

    (b) has failed to discharge that duty,

it may give that body such directions as to the discharge of the duty as appear to it to be expedient.

(4) Directions may be given under subsection (1) or (3) even if the performance of the duty is contingent upon the opinion of the responsible body.

(5) Subsection (6) applies if the Tribunal [or the Welsh Tribunal][72] has made an order under section 28I(3).

(6) If the Secretary of State is satisfied (whether on a complaint or otherwise) that the responsible body concerned—

    (a) has acted, or is proposing to act, unreasonably in complying with the order, or

    (b) has failed to comply with the order,

he may give that body such directions as to compliance with the order as appear to him to be expedient.

(7) Directions given under subsection (1), (3) or (6)—

    (a) may be varied or revoked by the directing authority; and

    (b) may be enforced, on the application of the directing authority, by a mandatory order obtained in accordance with section 31 of the Supreme Court Act 1981.

(8) 'Appropriate authority' means—

    (a) in relation to England, the Secretary of State; and

    (b) in relation to Wales, the National Assembly.

---

[71] Substituted for the words 'paragraph 4 of Schedule 11 to the School Standards and Framework Act 1998' by the Education Act 2002, not yet in force in relation to Wales.

[72] Amended by the Education Act 2002.

(9) 'Directing authority' means—
- (a) the Secretary of State in relation to a direction given by him; and
- (b) the National Assembly in relation to a direction given by it.

[Enforcement: Scotland[73]

28N. Civil proceedings

(1) A claim that a responsible body in Scotland—
- (a) has discriminated against a person in a way which is unlawful under this Chapter, or
- (b) is by virtue of section 58 to be treated as having discriminated against a person in such a way,

may be made the subject of civil proceedings in the same way as any other claim for the enforcement of a statutory duty.

(2) Proceedings in Scotland may be brought only in a sheriff court.

(3) The remedies available in such proceedings are those which are available in the Court of Session other than an award of damages.

(4) Part 3 of Schedule 3 makes further provision about the enforcement of this Chapter and about procedure.

(5) In relation to civil proceedings in Scotland, in that Part of that Schedule—
- (a) references to sections 28I, 28K and 28L, or any of them, are to be construed as a reference to this section;
- (b) references to the Tribunal are to be construed as references to the sheriff court.

Agreements relating to enforcement

28P. Validity and revision of agreements of responsible bodies[74]

(1) Any term in a contract or other agreement made by or on behalf of a responsible body is void so far as it purports to—
- (a) require a person to do anything which would contravene any provision of, or made under, this Chapter;
- (b) exclude or limit the operation of any provision of, or made under, this Chapter; or
- (c) prevent any person from making a claim under this Chapter.

(2) Paragraphs (b) and (c) of subsection (1) do not apply to an agreement settling a claim—
- (a) under section 28I or 28N; or
- (b) to which section 28K or 28L applies.

(3) On the application of any person interested in an agreement to which subsection (1) applies, a county court or a sheriff court may make such order as it thinks just for modifying the agreement to take account of the effect of subsection (1).

(4) No such order may be made unless all persons affected have been—
- (a) given notice of the application; and
- (b) afforded an opportunity to make representations to the court.

(5) Subsection (4) applies subject to any rules of court providing for notice to be dispensed with.

(6) An order under subsection (3) may include provision as respects any period before the making of the order.

---

[73] Inserted with ss 28N, 28P–28X by the Special Educational Needs and Disability Act 2001.
[74] See n 73 above.

Interpretation of Chapter 1

28Q. Interpretation[75]

(1) This section applies for the purpose of interpreting this Chapter.

(2) 'Disabled pupil' means a pupil who is a disabled person.

(3) 'Pupil'—

(a) in relation to England and Wales, has the meaning given in section 3(1) of the Education Act 1996; and

(b) in relation to Scotland, has the meaning given in section 135(1) of the Education (Scotland) Act 1980.

(4) Except in relation to Scotland (when it has the meaning given in section 135(1) of the Education (Scotland) Act 1980) 'school' means—

(a) a maintained school;

(b) a maintained nursery school;

(c) an independent school;

(d) a special school which is not a maintained special school but which is approved by the Secretary of State, or by the National Assembly, under section 342 of the Education Act 1996;

(e) a pupil referral unit.

(5) In subsection (4)—

'maintained school' has the meaning given in section 20(7) of the School Standards and Framework Act 1998;

'maintained nursery school' has the meaning given in section 22(9) of the School Standards and Framework Act 1998;

'independent school' has the meaning given in section 463 of the Education Act 1996; and

'pupil referral unit' has the meaning given in section 19(2) of the Education Act 1996.

(6) 'Responsible body' has the meaning given in section 28A(5).

(7) 'Governing body', in relation to a maintained school, means the body corporate (constituted in accordance with [regulations under section 19 of the Education Act 2002][76]) which the school has as a result of [that section].[77]

(8) 'Parent'—

(a) in relation to England and Wales, has the meaning given in section 576 of the Education Act 1996; and

(b) in relation to Scotland, has the meaning given in section 135(1) of the Education (Scotland) Act 1980.

(9) In relation to England and Wales 'permitted form of selection' means—

(a) if the school is a maintained school which is not designated as a grammar school under section 104 of the School Standards and Framework Act 1998, any form of selection mentioned in section 99(2) or (4) of that Act;

(b) if the school is a maintained school which is so designated, any of its selective admission arrangements;

(c) if the school is an independent school, any arrangements which make provision for any or all of its pupils to be selected by reference to general or special ability or aptitude, with a view to admitting only pupils of high ability or aptitude.

---

[75] See n 73 above.

[76] Substituted for the words 'Schedule 9 to the School Standards and Framework Act 1998' by the Education Act 2002, not yet in force in relation to Wales.

[77] Substituted for the words 'section 36 of that Act' by the Education Act 2002, not yet in force in relation to Wales.

(10) In relation to Scotland, 'permitted form of selection' means—
(a) if the school is managed by an education authority, such arrangements as have been approved by the Scottish Ministers for the selection of pupils for admission;
(b) if the school is an independent school or a self-governing school, any arrangements which make provision for any or all of its pupils to be selected by reference to general or special ability or aptitude, with a view to admitting only pupils of high ability or aptitude.

(11) In subsection (10), 'education authority', 'independent school' and 'self-governing school' have the meaning given in section 135(1) of the Education (Scotland) Act 1980.

(12) ...[78]

(13) 'Accessibility strategy' and 'accessibility plan' have the meaning given in section 28D.

(14) 'The National Assembly' means the National Assembly for Wales.

CHAPTER 2
FURTHER AND HIGHER EDUCATION

Duties of responsible bodies

28R. Discrimination against disabled students and prospective students[79]

(1) It is unlawful for the body responsible for an educational institution to discriminate against a disabled person—
(a) in the arrangements it makes for determining admissions to the institution;
(b) in the terms on which it offers to admit him to the institution; or
(c) by refusing or deliberately omitting to accept an application for his admission to the institution.

(2) It is unlawful for the body responsible for an educational institution to discriminate against a disabled student in the student services it provides, or offers to provide.

(3) It is unlawful for the body responsible for an educational institution to discriminate against a disabled student by excluding him from the institution, whether permanently or temporarily.

(4) In the case of an act which constitutes discrimination by virtue of section 55, this section also applies to discrimination against a person who is not disabled.

(5) The body responsible for an educational institution is to be determined in accordance with Schedule 4B, and in the remaining provisions of this Chapter is referred to as the 'responsible body'.

(6) 'Educational institution', in relation to England and Wales, means an institution—
(a) within the higher education sector;
(b) within the further education sector; or
(c) designated in an order made by the Secretary of State.

(7) 'Educational institution', in relation to Scotland, means—
(a) an institution within the higher education sector (within the meaning of section 56(2) of the Further and Higher Education (Scotland) Act 1992);
(b) a college of further education with a board of management within the meaning of section 36 of that Act;
(c) a central institution within the meaning of section 135 of the Education (Scotland) Act 1980;

---

[78] Repealed by the Education Act 2002. [79] See n 73 above.

(d) a college of further education maintained by an education authority in the exercise of their further education functions in providing courses of further education within the meaning of section 1(5)(b)(ii) of that Act;

(e) an institution designated in an order made by the Secretary of State.

(8) Subsection (6) is to be read with section 91 of the Further and Higher Education Act 1992.

(9) The Secretary of State may not make an order under subsection (6)(c) or (7)(e) unless he is satisfied that the institution concerned is wholly or partly funded from public funds.

(10) Before making an order under subsection (7)(e), the Secretary of State must consult the Scottish Ministers.

(11) 'Student services' means services of any description which are provided wholly or mainly for students.

(12) Regulations may make provision as to services which are, or are not, to be regarded for the purposes of subsection (2) as student services.

28S. Meaning of 'discrimination'[80]

(1) For the purposes of section 28R, a responsible body discriminates against a disabled person if—
   (a) for a reason which relates to his disability, it treats him less favourably than it treats or would treat others to whom that reason does not or would not apply; and
   (b) it cannot show that the treatment in question is justified.

(2) For the purposes of section 28R, a responsible body also discriminates against a disabled person if—
   (a) it fails, to his detriment, to comply with section 28T; and
   (b) it cannot show that its failure to comply is justified.

(3) In relation to a failure to take a particular step, a responsible body does not discriminate against a person if it shows—
   (a) that, at the time in question, it did not know and could not reasonably have been expected to know, that he was disabled; and
   (b) that its failure to take the step was attributable to that lack of knowledge.

(4) The taking of a particular step by a responsible body in relation to a person does not amount to less favourable treatment if it shows that at the time in question it did not know, and could not reasonably have been expected to know, that he was disabled.

(5) Subsections (6) to (9) apply in determining whether, for the purposes of this section—
   (a) less favourable treatment of a person, or
   (b) failure to comply with section 28T,
   is justified.

(6) Less favourable treatment of a person is justified if it is necessary in order to maintain—
   (a) academic standards; or
   (b) standards of any other prescribed kind.

(7) Less favourable treatment is also justified if—
   (a) it is of a prescribed kind;
   (b) it occurs in prescribed circumstances; or
   (c) it is of a prescribed kind and it occurs in prescribed circumstances.

(8) Otherwise less favourable treatment, or a failure to comply with section 28T, is justified only if the reason for it is both material to the circumstances of the particular case and substantial.

---

[80] See n 73 above.

(9) If, in a case falling within subsection (1)—
    (a) the responsible body is under a duty imposed by section 28T in relation to the disabled person, but
    (b) fails without justification to comply with that duty,
its treatment of that person cannot be justified under subsection (8) unless that treatment would have been justified even if it had complied with that duty.

28T. Disabled students not to be substantially disadvantaged[81]

(1) The responsible body for an educational institution must take such steps as it is reasonable for it to have to take to ensure that—
    (a) in relation to the arrangements it makes for determining admissions to the institution, disabled persons are not placed at a substantial disadvantage in comparison with persons who are not disabled; and
    (b) in relation to student services provided for, or offered to, students by it, disabled students are not placed at a substantial disadvantage in comparison with students who are not disabled.
(2) In considering whether it is reasonable for it to have to take a particular step in order to comply with its duty under subsection (1), a responsible body must have regard to any relevant provisions of a code of practice issued under section 53A.
(3) Subsection (4) applies if a person has made a confidentiality request of which a responsible body is aware.
(4) In determining whether it is reasonable for the responsible body to have to take a particular step in relation to that person in order to comply with its duty under subsection (1), regard shall be had to the extent to which taking the step in question is consistent with compliance with that request.
(5) 'Confidentiality request' means a request made by a disabled person, which asks for the nature, or asks for the existence, of his disability to be treated as confidential.
(6) This section imposes duties only for the purpose of determining whether a responsible body has discriminated against a disabled person; and accordingly a breach of any such duty is not actionable as such.

Other providers of further education or training facilities

28U. Further education etc provided by local education authorities and schools[82]

(1) Part 1 of Schedule 4C modifies this Chapter for the purpose of its application in relation to—
    (a) higher education secured by a local education authority;
    (b) further education—
        (i) secured by a local education authority; or
        (ii) provided by the governing body of a maintained school;
    (c) recreational or training facilities secured by a local education authority.
(2) Part 2 of that Schedule modifies this Chapter for the purpose of its application in relation to—
    (a) further education, within the meaning of section 1(5)(b)(iii) of the Education (Scotland) Act 1980;
    (b) facilities whose provision is secured by an education authority under section 1(3) of that Act.

---

[81] See n 73 above.   [82] See n 73 above.

Enforcement, etc

28V. Enforcement, remedies and procedure[83]

(1) A claim by a person—

    (a) that a responsible body has discriminated against him in a way which is unlawful under this Chapter,

    (b) that a responsible body is by virtue of section 57 or 58 to be treated as having discriminated against him in such a way, or

    (c) that a person is by virtue of section 57 to be treated as having discriminated against him in such a way,

may be made the subject of civil proceedings in the same way as any other claim in tort or (in Scotland) in reparation for breach of statutory duty.

(2) For the avoidance of doubt it is hereby declared that damages in respect of discrimination in a way which is unlawful under this Chapter may include compensation for injury to feelings whether or not they include compensation under any other head.

(3) Proceedings in England and Wales may be brought only in a county court.

(4) Proceedings in Scotland may be brought only in a sheriff court.

(5) The remedies available in such proceedings are those which are available in the High Court or (as the case may be) the Court of Session.

(6) The fact that a person who brings proceedings under this Part against a responsible body may also be entitled to bring proceedings against that body under Part 2 is not to affect the proceedings under this Part.

(7) Part 4 of Schedule 3 makes further provision about the enforcement of this Part and about procedure.

28W. Occupation of premises by educational institutions[84]

(1) This section applies if—

    (a) premises are occupied by an educational institution under a lease;

    (b) but for this section, the responsible body would not be entitled to make a particular alteration to the premises; and

    (c) the alteration is one which the responsible body proposes to make in order to comply with section 28T.

(2) Except to the extent to which it expressly so provides, the lease has effect, as a result of this subsection, as if it provided—

    (a) for the responsible body to be entitled to make the alteration with the written consent of the lessor;

    (b) for the responsible body to have to make a written application to the lessor for consent if it wishes to make the alteration;

    (c) if such an application is made, for the lessor not to withhold his consent unreasonably; and

    (d) for the lessor to be entitled to make his consent subject to reasonable conditions.

(3) In this section—

'lease' includes a tenancy, sub-lease or sub-tenancy and an agreement for a lease, tenancy, sub-lease or sub-tenancy; and

'sub-lease' and 'sub-tenancy' have such meaning as may be prescribed.

(4) If the terms and conditions of a lease—

    (a) impose conditions which are to apply if the responsible body alters the premises, or

---

[83] See n 73 above.   [84] See n 73 above.

(b) entitle the lessor to impose conditions when consenting to the responsible body's altering the premises,

the responsible body is to be treated for the purposes of subsection (1) as not being entitled to make the alteration.

(5) Part 3 of Schedule 4 supplements the provisions of this section.

28X. Validity and revision of agreements[85]

Section 28P applies for the purposes of this Chapter as it applies for the purposes of Chapter 1, but with the substitution, for paragraphs (a) and (b) of subsection (2), of 'under section 28V'.]

29. ...[86]

Duties of funding councils

30. Further and higher education of disabled persons[87]

31. Further and higher education of disabled persons: Scotland[88]

[Interpretation of Chapter 2[89]

31A. Interpretation

(1) Subsections (2) to (4) apply for the purpose of interpreting this Chapter.

(2) 'Disabled student' means a student who is a disabled person.

(3) 'Student' means a person who is attending, or undertaking a course of study at, an educational institution.

(4) 'Educational institution', 'responsible body' and 'student services' have the meaning given in section 28R.

CHAPTER 3
SUPPLEMENTARY

31B. Conciliation for disputes

(1) The Disability Rights Commission may make arrangements with any other person for the provision of conciliation services by, or by persons appointed by, that person in connection with disputes.

(2) In deciding what arrangements (if any) to make, the Commission must have regard to the desirability of securing, so far as reasonably practicable, that conciliation services are available for all disputes which the parties may wish to refer to conciliation.

(3) No member or employee of the Commission may provide conciliation services in connection with disputes.

(4) The Commission must ensure that arrangements under this section include appropriate safeguards to prevent the disclosure to members or employees of the Commission of

---

[85] See n 73 above.

[86] Repealed by the Special Educational Needs and Disability Act 2001.

[87] Amends the Further and Higher Education Act 1992; otherwise repealed by the Education Act 1996, the Learning and Skills Act 2000 and the Special Educational Needs and Disability Act 2001.

[88] Amends the Further and Higher Education (Scotland) Act 1992; otherwise repealed by the Special Educational Needs and Disability Act 2001.

[89] Inserted with ss 31A–31C by the Special Educational Needs and Disability Act 2001.

information obtained by any person in connection with the provision of conciliation services in accordance with the arrangements.

(5) Subsection (4) does not apply to information which is disclosed with the consent of the parties to the dispute to which it relates.

(6) Subsection (4) does not apply to information which—
    (a) does not identify a particular dispute or a particular person; and
    (b) is reasonably required by the Commission for the purpose of monitoring the operation of the arrangements concerned.

(7) Anything communicated to a person providing conciliation services in accordance with arrangements under this section is not admissible in evidence in any proceedings except with the consent of the person who communicated it.

(8) 'Conciliation services' means advice and assistance provided to the parties to a dispute, by a conciliator, with a view to promoting its settlement otherwise than through a court, tribunal or other body.

(9) 'Dispute' means a dispute arising under Chapter 1 or 2 concerning an allegation of discrimination.

(10) 'Discrimination' means anything which is made unlawful discrimination by a provision of Chapter 1 or 2.

31C. Application to Isles of Scilly

This Part applies to the Isles of Scilly—
    (a) as if the Isles were a separate non-metropolitan county (and the Council of the Isles of Scilly were a county council), and
    (b) with such other modifications as may be specified in an order made by the Secretary of State.]

PART V
PUBLIC TRANSPORT

Taxis

32. Taxi accessibility regulations

(1) The Secretary of State may make regulations ('taxi accessibility regulations') for the purpose of securing that it is possible—
    (a) for disabled persons—
        (i) to get into and out of taxis in safety;
        (ii) to be carried in taxis in safety and in reasonable comfort; and
    (b) for disabled persons in wheelchairs—
        (i) to be conveyed in safety into and out of taxis while remaining in their wheelchairs; and
        (ii) to be carried in taxis in safety and in reasonable comfort while remaining in their wheelchairs.

(2) Taxi accessibility regulations may, in particular—
    (a) require any regulated taxi to conform with provisions of the regulations as to—
        (i) the size of any door opening which is for the use of passengers;
        (ii) the floor area of the passenger compartment;
        (iii) the amount of headroom in the passenger compartment;
        (iv) the fitting of restraining devices designed to ensure the stability of a wheelchair while the taxi is moving;

(b) require the driver of any regulated taxi which is plying for hire, or which has been hired, to comply with provisions of the regulations as to the carrying of ramps or other devices designed to facilitate the loading and unloading of wheelchairs;

(c) require the driver of any regulated taxi in which a disabled person who is in a wheelchair is being carried (while remaining in his wheelchair) to comply with provisions of the regulations as to the position in which the wheelchair is to be secured.

(3) The driver of a regulated taxi which is plying for hire, or which has been hired, is guilty of an offence if—

(a) he fails to comply with any requirement imposed on him by the regulations; or

(b) the taxi fails to conform with any provision of the regulations with which it is required to conform.

(4) A person who is guilty of such an offence is liable, on summary conviction, to a fine not exceeding level 3 on the standard scale.

(5) In this section—

'passenger compartment' has such meaning as may be prescribed;

'regulated taxi' means any taxi to which the regulations are expressed to apply;

'taxi' means a vehicle licensed under—

(a) section 37 of the Town Police Clauses Act 1847, or

(b) section 6 of the Metropolitan Public Carriage Act 1869,

but does not include a taxi which is drawn by a horse or other animal.

33. Designated transport facilities

(1) In this section 'a franchise agreement' means a contract entered into by the operator of a designated transport facility for the provision by the other party to the contract of hire car services—

(a) for members of the public using any part of the transport facility; and

(b) which involve vehicles entering any part of that facility.

(2) The Secretary of State may by regulations provide for the application of any taxi provision in relation to—

(a) vehicles used for the provision of services under a franchise agreement; or

(b) the drivers of such vehicles.

(3) Any regulations under subsection (2) may apply any taxi provision with such modifications as the Secretary of State considers appropriate.

(4) In this section—

'designated' means designated for the purposes of this section by an order made by the Secretary of State;

'hire car' has such meaning as may be prescribed;

'operator', in relation to a transport facility, means any person who is concerned with the management or operation of the facility;

'taxi provision' means any provision of—

(a) this Act, or

(b) regulations made in pursuance of section 20(2A) of the Civic Government (Scotland) Act 1982,

which applies in relation to taxis or the drivers of taxis; and

'transport facility' means any premises which form part of any port, airport, railway station or bus station.

34. New licences conditional on compliance with taxi accessibility regulations

(1) No licensing authority shall grant a licence for a taxi to ply for hire unless the vehicle conforms with those provisions of the taxi accessibility regulations with which it will be required to conform if licensed.

(2) Subsection (1) does not apply if such a licence was in force with respect to the vehicle at any time during the period of 28 days immediately before the day on which the licence is granted.

(3) The Secretary of State may by order provide for subsection (2) to cease to have effect on such date as may be specified in the order.

(4) Separate orders may be made under subsection (3) with respect to different areas or localities.

35. Exemption from taxi accessibility regulations

(1) The Secretary of State may make regulations ('exemption regulations') for the purpose of enabling any relevant licensing authority to apply to him for an order (an 'exemption order') exempting the authority from the requirements of section 34.

(2) Exemption regulations may, in particular, make provision requiring a licensing authority proposing to apply for an exemption order—
   (a) to carry out such consultations as may be prescribed;
   (b) to publish the proposal in the prescribed manner;
   (c) to consider any representations made to it about the proposal, before applying for the order;
   (d) to make its application in the prescribed form.

(3) A licensing authority may apply for an exemption order only if it is satisfied—
   (a) that, having regard to the circumstances prevailing in its area, it would be inappropriate for the requirements of section 34 to apply; and
   (b) that the application of section 34 would result in an unacceptable reduction in the number of taxis in its area.

(4) After considering any application for an exemption order and consulting the Disabled Persons Transport Advisory Committee and such other persons as he considers appropriate, the Secretary of State may—
   (a) make an exemption order in the terms of the application;
   (b) make an exemption order in such other terms as he considers appropriate; or
   (c) refuse to make an exemption order.

(5) The Secretary of State may by regulations ('swivel seat regulations') make provision requiring any exempt taxi plying for hire in an area in respect of which an exemption order is in force to conform with provisions of the regulations as to the fitting and use of swivel seats.

(6) The Secretary of State may by regulations make provision with respect to swivel seat regulations similar to that made by section 34 with respect to taxi accessibility regulations.

(7) In this section—
'exempt taxi' means a taxi in relation to which section 34(1) would apply if the exemption order were not in force;
'relevant licensing authority' means a licensing authority responsible for licensing taxis in any area of England and Wales other than the area to which the Metropolitan Public Carriage Act 1869 applies; and
'swivel seats' has such meaning as may be prescribed.

36. Carrying of passengers in wheelchairs

(1) This section imposes duties on the driver of a regulated taxi which has been hired—
   (a) by or for a disabled person who is in a wheelchair; or
   (b) by a person who wishes such a disabled person to accompany him in the taxi.

(2) In this section—
'carry' means carry in the taxi concerned; and

'the passenger' means the disabled person concerned.
(3) The duties are—
    (a) to carry the passenger while he remains in his wheelchair;
    (b) not to make any additional charge for doing so;
    (c) if the passenger chooses to sit in a passenger seat, to carry the wheelchair;
    (d) to take such steps as are necessary to ensure that the passenger is carried in safety and in reasonable comfort;
    (e) to give such assistance as may be reasonably required—
        (i) to enable the passenger to get into or out of the taxi;
        (ii) if the passenger wishes to remain in his wheelchair, to enable him to be conveyed into and out of the taxi while in his wheelchair;
        (iii) to load the passenger's luggage into or out of the taxi;
        (iv) if the passenger does not wish to remain in his wheelchair, to load the wheelchair into or out of the taxi.
(4) Nothing in this section is to be taken to require the driver of any taxi—
    (a) except in the case of a taxi of a prescribed description, to carry more than one person in a wheelchair, or more than one wheelchair, on any one journey; or
    (b) to carry any person in circumstances in which it would otherwise be lawful for him to refuse to carry that person.
(5) A driver of a regulated taxi who fails to comply with any duty imposed on him by this section is guilty of an offence and liable, on summary conviction, to a fine not exceeding level 3 on the standard scale.
(6) In any proceedings for an offence under this section, it is a defence for the accused to show that, even though at the time of the alleged offence the taxi conformed with those provisions of the taxi accessibility regulations with which it was required to conform, it would not have been possible for the wheelchair in question to be carried in safety in the taxi.
(7) If the licensing authority is satisfied that it is appropriate to exempt a person from the duties imposed by this section—
    (a) on medical grounds, or
    (b) on the ground that his physical condition makes it impossible or unreasonably difficult for him to comply with the duties imposed on drivers by this section,
it shall issue him with a certificate of exemption.
(8) A certificate of exemption shall be issued for such period as may be specified in the certificate.
(9) The driver of a regulated taxi is exempt from the duties imposed by this section if—
    (a) a certificate of exemption issued to him under this section is in force; and
    (b) the prescribed notice of his exemption is exhibited on the taxi in the prescribed manner.

37. Carrying of guide dogs and hearing dogs

(1) This section imposes duties on the driver of a taxi which has been hired—
    (a) by or for a disabled person who is accompanied by his guide dog or hearing dog, or
    (b) by a person who wishes such a disabled person to accompany him in the taxi.
(2) The disabled person is referred to in this section as 'the passenger'.
(3) The duties are—
    (a) to carry the passenger's dog and allow it to remain with the passenger; and
    (b) not to make any additional charge for doing so.
(4) A driver of a taxi who fails to comply with any duty imposed on him by this section is guilty of an offence and liable, on summary conviction, to a fine not exceeding level 3 on the standard scale.

(5) If the licensing authority is satisfied that it is appropriate on medical grounds to exempt a person from the duties imposed by this section, it shall issue him with a certificate of exemption.

(6) In determining whether to issue a certificate of exemption, the licensing authority shall, in particular, have regard to the physical characteristics of the taxi which the applicant drives or those of any kind of taxi in relation to which he requires the certificate.

(7) A certificate of exemption shall be issued—

    (a) with respect to a specified taxi or a specified kind of taxi; and

    (b) for such period as may be specified in the certificate.

(8) The driver of a taxi is exempt from the duties imposed by this section if—

    (a) a certificate of exemption issued to him under this section is in force with respect to the taxi; and

    (b) the prescribed notice of his exemption is exhibited on the taxi in the prescribed manner.

(9) The Secretary of State may, for the purposes of this section, prescribe any other category of dog trained to assist a disabled person who has a disability of a prescribed kind.

(10) This section applies in relation to any such prescribed category of dog as it applies in relation to guide dogs.

(11) In this section—

'guide dog' means a dog which has been trained to guide a blind person; and

'hearing dog' means a dog which has been trained to assist a deaf person.

[37A. Carrying of assistance dogs in private hire vehicles[90]

(1) It is an offence for the operator of a private hire vehicle to fail or refuse to accept a booking for a private hire vehicle—

    (a) if the booking is requested by or on behalf of a disabled person, or a person who wishes a disabled person to accompany him; and

    (b) the reason for the failure or refusal is that the disabled person will be accompanied by his assistance dog.

(2) It is an offence for the operator of a private hire vehicle to make an additional charge for carrying an assistance dog which is accompanying a disabled person.

(3) It is an offence for the driver of a private hire vehicle to fail or refuse to carry out a booking accepted by the operator of the vehicle—

    (a) if the booking was made by or on behalf of a disabled person, or a person who wishes a disabled person to accompany him; and

    (b) the reason for the failure or refusal is that the disabled person is accompanied by his assistance dog.

(4) A person who is guilty of an offence under this section is liable on summary conviction to a fine not exceeding level 3 on the standard scale.

(5) If the licensing authority is satisfied that it is appropriate on medical grounds to issue a certificate of exemption to a driver in respect of subsection (3) it must do so.

(6) In determining whether to issue a certificate of exemption, the licensing authority shall, in particular, have regard to the physical characteristics of the private hire vehicle which the applicant drives or those of any kind of private hire vehicle in relation to which he requires the certificate.

(7) A certificate of exemption shall be issued—

    (a) with respect to a specified private hire vehicle or a specified kind of private hire vehicle; and

---

[90] Inserted by the Private Hire Vehicles (Carriage of Guide Dogs etc) Act 2002.

(b) for such period as may be specified in the certificate.

(8) No offence is committed by a driver under subsection (3) if—

(a) a certificate of exemption issued to him under this section is in force with respect to the private hire vehicle; and

(b) the prescribed notice is exhibited on the private hire vehicle in the prescribed manner.

(9) In this section—

'assistance dog' means a dog which—

(a) has been trained to guide a blind person;

(b) has been trained to assist a deaf person;

(c) has been trained by a prescribed charity to assist a disabled person who has a disability which—

(i) consists of epilepsy; or

(ii) otherwise affects his mobility, manual dexterity, physical co-ordination or ability to lift, carry or otherwise move everyday objects;

'driver' means a person who holds a licence granted under—

(a) section 13 of the Private Hire Vehicles (London) Act 1998 (c 34) ('the 1998 Act');

(b) section 51 of the Local Government (Miscellaneous Provisions) Act 1976 (c 57) ('the 1976 Act'); or

(c) an equivalent provision of a local enactment;

'licensing authority', in relation to any area of England and Wales, means the authority responsible for licensing private hire vehicles in that area;

'operator' means a person who holds a licence granted under—

(a) section 3 of the 1998 Act;

(b) section 55 of the 1976 Act; or

(c) an equivalent provision of a local enactment;

'private hire vehicle' means a vehicle licensed under—

(a) section 6 of the 1998 Act;

(b) section 48 of the 1976 Act; or

(c) an equivalent provision of a local enactment.]

38. Appeal against refusal of exemption certificate

(1) Any person who is aggrieved by the refusal of a licensing authority to issue an exemption certificate under [section 36, 37 or 37A][91] may appeal to the appropriate court before the end of the period of 28 days beginning with the date of the refusal.

(2) On an appeal to it under this section, the court may direct the licensing authority concerned to issue the appropriate certificate of exemption to have effect for such period as may be specified in the direction.

(3) 'Appropriate court' means the magistrates' court for the petty sessions area in which the licensing authority has its principal office.

39. Requirements as to disabled passengers in Scotland[92]

. . .

Public service vehicles

40. PSV accessibility regulations

(1) The Secretary of State may make regulations ('PSV accessibility regulations') for the purpose of securing that it is possible for disabled persons—

---

[91] Amended by the Private Hire Vehicles (Carriage of Guide Dogs etc) Act 2002.

[92] Amends the Civic Government (Scotland) Act 1982.

    (a) to get on to and off regulated public service vehicles in safety and without unreason-
able difficulty (and, in the case of disabled persons in wheelchairs, to do so while
remaining in their wheelchairs); and

    (b) to be carried in such vehicles in safety and in reasonable comfort.

(2) PSV accessibility regulations may, in particular, make provision as to the construction, use
and maintenance of regulated public service vehicles including provision as to—

    (a) the fitting of equipment to vehicles;

    (b) equipment to be carried by vehicles;

    (c) the design of equipment to be fitted to, or carried by, vehicles;

    (d) the fitting and use of restraining devices designed to ensure the stability of wheelchairs
while vehicles are moving;

    (e) the position in which wheelchairs are to be secured while vehicles are moving.

(3) Any person who—

    (a) contravenes or fails to comply with any provision of the PSV accessibility regulations,

    (b) uses on a road a regulated public service vehicle which does not conform with any
provision of the regulations with which it is required to conform, or

    (c) causes or permits to be used on a road such a regulated public service vehicle,

    is guilty of an offence.

(4) A person who is guilty of such an offence is liable, on summary conviction, to a fine not
exceeding level 4 on the standard scale.

(5) In this section—

    'public service vehicle' means a vehicle which is—

    (a) adapted to carry more than eight passengers; and

    (b) a public service vehicle for the purposes of the Public Passenger Vehicles Act 1981;

    'regulated public service vehicle' means any public service vehicle to which the PSV acces-
sibility regulations are expressed to apply.

(6) Different provision may be made in regulations under this section—

    (a) as respects different classes or descriptions of vehicle;

    (b) as respects the same class or description of vehicle in different circumstances.

(7) Before making any regulations under this section or section 41 or 42 the Secretary of State
shall consult the Disabled Persons Transport Advisory Committee and such other representative organisations as he thinks fit.

41. Accessibility certificates

(1) A regulated public service vehicle shall not be used on a road unless—

    (a) a vehicle examiner has issued a certificate (an 'accessibility certificate') that such pro-
visions of the PSV accessibility regulations as may be prescribed are satisfied in respect
of the vehicle; or

    (b) an approval certificate has been issued under section 42 in respect of the vehicle.

(2) The Secretary of State may make regulations—

    (a) with respect to applications for, and the issue of, accessibility certificates;

    (b) providing for the examination of vehicles in respect of which applications have been
made;

    (c) with respect to the issue of copies of accessibility certificates in place of certificates
which have been lost or destroyed.

(3) If a regulated public service vehicle is used in contravention of this section, the operator of
the vehicle is guilty of an offence and liable on summary conviction to a fine not exceeding level 4 on the standard scale.

(4) In this section 'operator' has the same meaning as in the Public Passenger Vehicles Act
1981.

42. Approval certificates

(1) Where the Secretary of State is satisfied that such provisions of the PSV accessibility regulations as may be prescribed for the purposes of section 41 are satisfied in respect of a particular vehicle he may approve the vehicle for the purposes of this section.

(2) A vehicle which has been so approved is referred to in this section as a 'type vehicle'.

(3) Subsection (4) applies where a declaration in the prescribed form has been made by an authorised person that a particular vehicle conforms in design, construction and equipment with a type vehicle.

(4) A vehicle examiner may, after examining (if he thinks fit) the vehicle to which the declaration applies, issue a certificate in the prescribed form ('an approval certificate') that it conforms to the type vehicle.

(5) The Secretary of State may make regulations—
  (a) with respect to applications for, and grants of, approval under subsection (1);
  (b) with respect to applications for, and the issue of, approval certificates;
  (c) providing for the examination of vehicles in respect of which applications have been made;
  (d) with respect to the issue of copies of approval certificates in place of certificates which have been lost or destroyed.

(6) The Secretary of State may at any time withdraw his approval of a type vehicle.

(7) Where an approval is withdrawn—
  (a) no further approval certificates shall be issued by reference to the type vehicle; but
  (b) any approval certificate issued by reference to the type vehicle before the withdrawal shall continue to have effect for the purposes of section 41.

(8) In subsection (3) 'authorised person' means a person authorised by the Secretary of State for the purposes of that subsection.

43. Special authorisations

(1) The Secretary of State may by order authorise the use on roads of—
  (a) any regulated public service vehicle of a class or description specified by the order, or
  (b) any regulated public service vehicle which is so specified,
  and nothing in section 40, 41 or 42 prevents the use of any vehicle in accordance with the order.

(2) Any such authorisation may be given subject to such restrictions and conditions as may be specified by or under the order.

(3) The Secretary of State may by order make provision for the purpose of securing that, subject to such restrictions and conditions as may be specified by or under the order, provisions of the PSV accessibility regulations apply to regulated public service vehicles of a description specified by the order subject to such modifications or exceptions as may be specified by the order.

44. Reviews and appeals

(1) Subsection (2) applies where—
  (a) the Secretary of State refuses an application for the approval of a vehicle under section 42(1); and
  (b) before the end of the prescribed period, the applicant asks the Secretary of State to review the decision and pays any fee fixed under section 45.

(2) The Secretary of State shall—
  (a) review the decision; and
  (b) in doing so, consider any representations made to him in writing, before the end of the prescribed period, by the applicant.

(3) A person applying for an accessibility certificate or an approval certificate may appeal to the Secretary of State against the refusal of a vehicle examiner to issue such a certificate.

(4) An appeal must be made within the prescribed time and in the prescribed manner.

(5) Regulations may make provision as to the procedure to be followed in connection with appeals.

(6) On the determination of an appeal, the Secretary of State may—

    (a) confirm, vary or reverse the decision appealed against;

    (b) give such directions as he thinks fit to the vehicle examiner for giving effect to his decision.

45. Fees

(1) Such fees, payable at such times, as may be prescribed may be charged by the Secretary of State in respect of—

    (a) applications for, and grants of, approval under section 42(1);

    (b) applications for, and the issue of, accessibility certificates and approval certificates;

    (c) copies of such certificates;

    (d) reviews and appeals under section 44.

(2) Any such fees received by the Secretary of State shall be paid by him into the Consolidated Fund.

(3) Regulations under subsection (1) may make provision for the repayment of fees, in whole or in part, in such circumstances as may be prescribed.

(4) Before making any regulations under subsection (1) the Secretary of State shall consult such representative organisations as he thinks fit.

Rail vehicles

46. Rail vehicle accessibility regulations

(1) The Secretary of State may make regulations ('rail vehicle accessibility regulations') for the purpose of securing that it is possible—

    (a) for disabled persons—

        (i) to get on to and off regulated rail vehicles in safety and without unreasonable difficulty;

        (ii) to be carried in such vehicles in safety and in reasonable comfort; and

    (b) for disabled persons in wheelchairs—

        (i) to get on to and off such vehicles in safety and without unreasonable difficulty while remaining in their wheelchairs, and

        (ii) to be carried in such vehicles in safety and in reasonable comfort while remaining in their wheelchairs.

(2) Rail vehicle accessibility regulations may, in particular, make provision as to the construction, use and maintenance of regulated rail vehicles including provision as to—

    (a) the fitting of equipment to vehicles;

    (b) equipment to be carried by vehicles;

    (c) the design of equipment to be fitted to, or carried by, vehicles;

    (d) the use of equipment fitted to, or carried by, vehicles;

    (e) the toilet facilities to be provided in vehicles;

    (f) the location and floor area of the wheelchair accommodation to be provided in vehicles;

    (g) assistance to be given to disabled persons.

(3) If a regulated rail vehicle which does not conform with any provision of the rail vehicle accessibility regulations with which it is required to conform is used for carriage, the operator of the vehicle is guilty of an offence.

(4) A person who is guilty of such an offence is liable, on summary conviction, to a fine not exceeding level 4 on the standard scale.

(5) Different provision may be made in rail vehicle accessibility regulations—

    (a) as respects different classes or descriptions of rail vehicle;

    (b) as respects the same class or description of rail vehicle in different circumstances;

    (c) as respects different networks.

(6) In this section—

'network' means any permanent way or other means of guiding or supporting rail vehicles or any section of it;

'operator', in relation to any rail vehicle, means the person having the management of that vehicle;

'rail vehicle' means a vehicle—

    (a) constructed or adapted to carry passengers on any railway, tramway or prescribed system; and

    (b) first brought into use, or belonging to a class of vehicle first brought into use, after 31st December 1998;

'regulated rail vehicle' means any rail vehicle to which the rail vehicle accessibility regulations are expressed to apply; and

'wheelchair accommodation' has such meaning as may be prescribed.

(7) In subsection (6)—

'prescribed system' means a system using a prescribed mode of guided transport ('guided transport' having the same meaning as in the Transport and Works Act 1992); and

'railway' and 'tramway' have the same meaning as in that Act.

(8) The Secretary of State may by regulations make provision as to the time when a rail vehicle, or a class of rail vehicle, is to be treated, for the purposes of this section, as first brought into use.

(9) Regulations under subsection (8) may include provision for disregarding periods of testing and other prescribed periods of use.

(10) For the purposes of this section and section 47, a person uses a vehicle for carriage if he uses it for the carriage of members of the public for hire or reward at separate fares.

(11) Before making any regulations under subsection (1) or section 47 the Secretary of State shall consult the Disabled Persons Transport Advisory Committee and such other representative organisations as he thinks fit.

47. Exemption from rail vehicle accessibility regulations

(1) The Secretary of State may by order (an 'exemption order') authorise the use for carriage of any regulated rail vehicle of specified accessibility description, or in specified circumstances, even though that vehicle does not conform with the provisions of the rail vehicle accessibility regulations with which it is required to conform.

(2) Regulations may make provision with respect to exemption orders including, in particular, provision as to—

    (a) the persons by whom applications for exemption orders may be made;

    (b) the form in which such applications are to be made;

    (c) information to be supplied in connection with such applications;

    (d) the period for which exemption orders are to continue in force;

    (e) the revocation of exemption orders.

(3) After considering any application for an exemption order and consulting the Disabled

Persons Transport Advisory Committee and such other persons as he considers appropriate, the Secretary of State may—

    (a) make an exemption order in the terms of the application;

    (b) make an exemption order in such other terms as he considers appropriate;

    (c) refuse to make an exemption order.

(4) An exemption order may be made subject to such restrictions and conditions as may be specified.

(5) In this section 'specified' means specified in an exemption order.

Supplemental

48. Offences by bodies corporate etc

(1) Where an offence under section 40 or 46 committed by a body corporate is committed with the consent or connivance of, or is attributable to any neglect on the part of, a director, manager, secretary or other similar officer of the body, or a person purporting to act in such a capacity, he as well as the body corporate is guilty of the offence.

(2) In subsection (1) 'director', in relation to a body corporate whose affairs are managed by its members, means a member of the body corporate.

(3) Where, in Scotland, an offence under section 40 or 46 committed by a partnership or by an unincorporated association other than a partnership is committed with the consent or connivance of, or is attributable to any neglect on the part of, a partner in the partnership or (as the case may be) a person concerned in the management or control of the association, he, as well as the partnership or association, is guilty of the offence.

49. Forgery and false statements

(1) In this section 'relevant document' means—

    (a) a certificate of exemption issued under [section 36, 37 or 37A];[93]

    (b) a notice of a kind mentioned in section [36(9)(b), 37(8)(b) or 37A(8)(b)];[94]

    (c) an accessibility certificate; or

    (d) an approval certificate.

(2) A person is guilty of an offence if, with intent to deceive, he—

    (a) forges, alters or uses a relevant document;

    (b) lends a relevant document to any other person;

    (c) allows a relevant document to be used by any other person; or

    (d) makes or has in his possession any document which closely resembles a relevant document.

(3) A person who is guilty of an offence under subsection (2) is liable—

    (a) on summary conviction, to a fine not exceeding the statutory maximum;

    (b) on conviction on indictment, to imprisonment for a term not exceeding two years or to a fine or to both.

(4) A person who knowingly makes a false statement for the purpose of obtaining an accessibility certificate or an approval certificate is guilty of an offence and liable on summary conviction to a fine not exceeding level 4 on the standard scale.

---

[93] Amended by the Private Hire Vehicles (Carriage of Guide Dogs etc) Act 2002.

[94] See n 93 above.

PART VI

THE NATIONAL DISABILITY COUNCIL

50. . . .[95]

51. Codes of practice prepared by the Council

(1), (2) . . .[96]

(3) A failure on the part of any person to observe any provision of a code does not of itself make that person liable to any proceedings.

(4) A code is admissible in evidence in any proceedings under this Act before an [employment tribunal],[97] a county court or a sheriff court.

(5) If any provision of a code appears to a tribunal or court to be relevant to any question arising in any proceedings under this Act, it shall be taken into account in determining that question.

(6) In this section and section 52 'code' means a code issued by the Secretary of State under this section and includes a code which has been altered and re-issued.

52. Further provision about codes issued under section 51

(1)—(10) . . .[98]

(11) The Secretary of State may by order revoke a code.

(12) . . .[99]

PART VII

SUPPLEMENTAL

[53A. Codes of practice[100]

[(1) The Disability Rights Commission may prepare and issue codes of practice giving practical guidance on how to avoid [acts which are unlawful under Part 2, 3 or 4],[101] or on any other matter relating to the operation of any provision of [those Parts],[102] to—

(a) employers;

(b) service providers;

(c) bodies which are responsible bodies for the purposes of Chapter 1 or 2 of Part 4; or

(d) other persons to whom the provisions of Parts 2 or 3 or Chapter 2 of Part 4 apply.

(1A) The Commission may also prepare and issue codes of practice giving practical guidance to any persons on any other matter with a view to—

(a) promoting the equalisation of opportunities for disabled persons and persons who have had a disability; or

(b) encouraging good practice in the way such persons are treated,

in any field of activity regulated by any provision of Part 2, 3 or 4.

---

[95] Repealed by the Disability Rights Commission Act 1999.

[96] Repealed by the Disability Rights Commission Act 1999.

[97] Amended by the Employment Rights (Dispute Resolution) Act 1998.

[98] Repealed by the Disability Rights Commission Act 1999.   [99] See n 98 above.

[100] Inserted by the Disability Rights Commission Act 1999.

[101] Amended by the Disability and Discrimination Act 1995 (Amendment) Regulations, SI 2003/1673.

[102] See n 101 above.

(1B) Neither subsection (1) nor (1A) applies in relation to any duty imposed by or under sections 28D or 28E.][103]

(2) The Commission shall, when requested to do so by the Secretary of State, prepare a code of practice dealing with the matters specified in the request.

(3) In preparing a code of practice the Commission shall carry out such consultations as it considers appropriate (which shall include the publication for public consultation of proposals relating to the code).

(4) The Commission may not issue a code of practice unless—

(a) a draft of it has been submitted to and approved by the Secretary of State and laid by him before both Houses of Parliament; and

(b) the 40 day period has elapsed without either House resolving not to approve the draft.

(5) If the Secretary of State does not approve a draft code of practice submitted to him he shall give the Commission a written statement of his reasons.

(6) A code of practice issued by the Commission—

(a) shall come into effect on such day as the Secretary of State may by order appoint;

(b) may be revised in whole or part, and re-issued, by the Commission; and

(c) may be revoked by an order made by the Secretary of State at the request of the Commission.

(7) Where the Commission proposes to revise a code of practice—

(a) it shall comply with subsection (3) in relation to the revisions; and

(b) the other provisions of this section apply to the revised code of practice as they apply to a new code of practice.

(8) Failure to observe any provision of a code of practice does not of itself make a person liable to any proceedings . . .[104]

[(8A) But if a provision of a code of practice appears to a court, tribunal or other body hearing any proceedings under Part 2, 3 or 4 to be relevant, it must take that provision into account.][105]

(9) In this section—

'code of practice' means a code of practice under this section;

. . .[106] and

'40 day period' has the same meaning in relation to a draft code of practice as it has in section 3 in relation to draft guidance.]

53. Codes of practice prepared by the Secretary of State

(1)–(3) . . .[107]

(4) A failure on the part of any person to observe any provision of a code does not of itself make that person liable to any proceedings.

(5) A code is admissible in evidence in any proceedings under this Act before an [employment tribunal],[108] a county court or a sheriff court.

(6) If any provision of a code appears to a tribunal or court to be relevant to any question arising in any proceedings under this Act, it shall be taken into account in determining that question.

(7) In this section and section 54 'code' means a code issued by the Secretary of State under this section and includes a code which has been revised and re-issued.

(8), (9) . . .[109]

---

[103] Amended by the Special Educational Needs and Disability Act 2001.

[104] See n 103 above.   [105] See n 103 above.   [106] See n 101 above.

[107] Repealed by the Disability Rights Commission Act 1999.

[108] Amended by the the Employment Rights (Dispute Resolution) Act 1998.

[109] See n 107 above.

54. Further provision about codes issued under section 53

(1)–(7) ...[110]

(8) The Secretary of State may by order revoke a code.

(9) ...[111]

55. Victimisation

(1) For the purposes of Part II[, Part 3 or Part 4],[112] a person ('A') discriminates against another person ('B') if—
  (a) he treats B less favourably than he treats or would treat other persons whose circumstances are the same as B's; and
  (b) he does so for a reason mentioned in subsection (2).

(2) The reasons are that—
  (a) B has—
    (i) brought proceedings against A or any other person under this Act; or
    (ii) given evidence or information in connection with such proceedings brought by any person; or
    (iii) otherwise done anything under this Act in relation to A or any other person; or
    (iv) alleged that A or any other person has (whether or not the allegation so states) contravened this Act; or
  (b) A believes or suspects that B has done or intends to do any of those things.

(3) Where B is a disabled person, or a person who has had a disability, the disability in question shall be disregarded in comparing his circumstances with those of any other person for the purposes of subsection (1)(a).

[(3A) For the purposes of Chapter 1 of Part 4—
  (a) references in subsection (2) to B include references to—
    (i) a person who is, for the purposes of that Chapter, B's parent; and
    (ii) a sibling of B; and
  (b) references in that subsection to this Act are, as respects a person mentioned in sub-paragraph (i) or (ii) of paragraph (a), restricted to that Chapter.][113]

(4) Subsection (1) does not apply to treatment of a person because of an allegation made by him if the allegation was false and not made in good faith.

[(5) In the case of an act which constitutes discrimination by virtue of this section, sections 4, 4B, 4D, [4G,][114] 6A, 7A, 7C, 13, 14A, 14C and 16A also apply to discrimination against a person who is not disabled.

(6) For the purposes of Part 2 and, to the extent that it relates to the provision of employment services, Part 3, subsection (2)(a)(iii) has effect as if there were inserted after 'under' or 'by reference to'.][115]

---

[110] Repealed by the Disability Rights Commission Act 1999.   [111] See n 110 above.

[112] Amended by the Special Educational Needs and Disability Act 2001.

[113] See n 112 above.

[114] Amended by the Disability Discrimination Act 1995 (Pensions) Regulations 2003, SI 2003/2770.

[115] Amended by the Disability and Discrimination Act 1995 (Amendment) Regulations, SI 2003/1673.

56. Help for persons suffering discrimination

(1) For the purposes of this section—

    (a) a person who considers that he may have been discriminated against [or subjected to harassment],[116] in contravention of any provision of Part II [or, to the extent that it relates to the provision of employment services, Part 3],[117] is referred to as 'the complainant'; and

    (b) a person against whom the complainant may decide to make, or has made, a complaint under Part II or, to the extent that it relates to the provision of employment services, Part 3 is referred to as 'the respondent'.

(2) The Secretary of State shall, with a view to helping the complainant to decide whether to make a complaint against the respondent and, if he does so, to formulate and present his case in the most effective manner, by order prescribe—

    (a) forms by which the complainant may question the respondent on his reasons for doing any relevant act, or on any other matter which is or may be relevant; and

    (b) forms by which the respondent may if he so wishes reply to any questions.

(3) Where the complainant questions the respondent in accordance with forms prescribed by an order under subsection (2)—

    (a) the question, and any reply by the respondent (whether in accordance with such an order or not), shall be admissible as evidence in any proceedings under Part II [or, to the extent that it relates to the provision of employment services, Part 3];[118]

    (b) if it appears to the tribunal in any such proceedings—

        (i) that the respondent deliberately, and without reasonable excuse, omitted to reply within [the period of eight weeks beginning with the day on which the question was served on him],[119] or

        (ii) that the respondent's reply is evasive or equivocal,

it may draw any inference which it considers it just and equitable to draw, including an inference that the respondent has contravened a provision of Part II [or, to the extent that it relates to the provision of employment services, Part 3].[120]

(4) The Secretary of State may by order prescribe—

    (a) the period within which questions must be duly served in order to be admissible under subsection (3)(a); and

    (b) the manner in which a question, and any reply by the respondent, may be duly served.

(5) This section is without prejudice to any other enactment or rule of law regulating interlocutory and preliminary matters in proceedings before an [employment tribunal],[121] and has effect subject to any enactment or rule of law regulating the admissibility of evidence in such proceedings.

57. Aiding unlawful acts

(1) A person who knowingly aids another person to do an [unlawful act][122] is to be treated for the purposes of this Act as himself doing the same kind of unlawful act.

(2) For the purposes of subsection (1), an employee or agent for whose act the employer or principal is liable under section 58 (or would be so liable but for section 58(5)) shall be taken to have aided the employer or principal to do the act.

---

[116] Amended by the Disability and Discrimination Act 1995 (Amendment) Regulations, SI 2003/1673.

[117] See n 116 above.   [118] See n 116 above.   [119] See n 116 above.

[120] See n 116 above.

[121] Amended by the Employment Rights (Dispute Resolution) Act 1998.

[122] Amended by the Special Educational Needs and Disability Act 2001.

(3) For the purposes of this section, a person does not knowingly aid another to do an unlawful act if—

(a) he acts in reliance on a statement made to him by that other person that, because of any provision of this Act, the act would not be unlawful; and

(b) it is reasonable for him to rely on the statement.

(4) A person who knowingly or recklessly makes such a statement which is false or misleading in a material respect is guilty of an offence.

(5) Any person guilty of an offence under subsection (4) shall be liable on summary conviction to a fine not exceeding level 5 on the standard scale.

[(6) 'Unlawful act' means an act made unlawful by any provision of this Act other than a provision contained in Chapter 1 of Part 4.][123]

58. Liability of employers and principals

(1) Anything done by a person in the course of his employment shall be treated for the purposes of this Act as also done by his employer, whether or not it was done with the employer's knowledge or approval.

(2) Anything done by a person as agent for another person with the authority of that other person shall be treated for the purposes of this Act as also done by that other person.

(3) Subsection (2) applies whether the authority was—

(a) express or implied; or

(b) given before or after the act in question was done.

(4) Subsections (1) and (2) do not apply in relation to an offence under section 57(4).

(5) In proceedings under this Act against any person in respect of an act alleged to have been done by an employee of his, it shall be a defence for that person to prove that he took such steps as were reasonably practicable to prevent the employee from—

(a) doing that act; or

(b) doing, in the course of his employment, acts of that description.

59. Statutory authority and national security etc

(1) Nothing in this Act makes unlawful any act done—

(a) in pursuance of any enactment; or

(b) in pursuance of any instrument made by a Minister of the Crown under any enactment; or

(c) to comply with any condition or requirement imposed by a Minister of the Crown (whether before or after the passing of this Act) by virtue of any enactment.

(2) In subsection (1) 'enactment' includes one passed or made after the date on which this Act is passed and 'instrument' includes one made after that date.

[(2A) Nothing in—

(a) Part 2 of this Act, or

(b) Part 3 of this Act to the extent that it relates to the provision of employment services, makes unlawful any act done for the purpose of safeguarding national security if the doing of the act was justified by that purpose.][124]

(3) Nothing in [any other provision of][125] this Act makes unlawful any act done for the purpose of safeguarding national security.

---

[123] See n 122 above.

[124] Amended by the Disability and Discrimination Act 1995 (Amendment) Regulations, SI 2003/1673.

[125] See n 124 above.

PART VIII
MISCELLANEOUS

60. Appointment by Secretary of State of advisers

(1) The Secretary of State may appoint such persons as he thinks fit to advise or assist him in connection with matters relating to the employment of disabled persons and persons who have had a disability.

(2) Persons may be appointed by the Secretary of State to act generally or in relation to a particular area or locality.

(3) The Secretary of State may pay to any person appointed under this section such allowances and compensation for loss of earnings as he considers appropriate.

(4) The approval of the Treasury is required for any payment under this section.

(5) In subsection (1) 'employment' includes self-employment.

(6) The Secretary of State may by order—

    (a) provide for section 17 of, and Schedule 2 to, the Disabled Persons (Employment) Act 1944 (national advisory council and district advisory committees) to cease to have effect—

        (i) so far as concerns the national advisory council; or

        (ii) so far as concerns district advisory committees; or

    (b) repeal that section and Schedule.

(7) At any time before the coming into force of an order under paragraph (b) of subsection (6), section 17 of the Act of 1944 shall have effect as if in subsection (1), after 'disabled persons' in each case there were inserted ', and persons who have had a disability,' and as if at the end of the section there were added—

    '(3) For the purposes of this section—

        (a) a person is a disabled person if he is a disabled person for the purposes of the Disability Discrimination Act 1995; and

        (b) 'disability' has the same meaning as in that Act.'

(8) At any time before the coming into force of an order under paragraph (a)(i) or (b) of subsection (6), section 16 of the Chronically Sick and Disabled Persons Act 1970 (which extends the functions of the national advisory council) shall have effect as if after 'disabled persons' in each case there were inserted ', and persons who have had a disability,' and as if at the end of the section there were added—

    '(2) For the purposes of this section—

        (a) a person is a disabled person if he is a disabled person for the purposes of the Disability Discrimination Act 1995; and

        (b) 'disability' has the same meaning as in that Act.'

61. Amendment of Disabled Persons (Employment) Act 1944

(1)–(7) . . .[126]

(8) Any provision of subordinate legislation in which 'disabled person' is defined by reference to the Act of 1944 shall be construed as if that expression had the same meaning as in this Act.

(9) Subsection (8) does not prevent the further amendment of any such provision by subordinate legislation.

---

[126] Amends the Disabled Persons (Employment) Act 1944.

62. . . .[127]

63. . . .[128]

64. Application to Crown etc

(1) This Act applies—
    (a) to an act done by or for purposes of a Minister of the Crown or government depart-
        ment, or
    (b) to an act done on behalf of the Crown by a statutory body, or a person holding a statu-
        tory office,
    as it applies to an act done by a private person.

(2) . . .[129] Part II applies to service—
    (a) for purposes of a Minister of the Crown or government department, other than ser-
        vice of a person holding a statutory office, or
    (b) on behalf of the Crown for purposes of a person holding a statutory office or purposes
        of a statutory body,
    as it applies to employment by a private person.

[(2A) Subsections (1) and (2) have effect subject to section 64A.][130]

(3) The provisions of Parts II to IV of the 1947 Act apply to proceedings against the Crown
    under this Act as they apply to Crown proceedings in England and Wales; but section 20
    of that Act (removal of proceedings from county court to High Court) does not apply.

(4) The provisions of Part V of the 1947 Act apply to proceedings against the Crown under
    this Act as they apply to proceedings in Scotland which by virtue of that Part are treated
    as civil proceedings by or against the Crown; but the proviso to section 44 of that Act
    (removal of proceedings from the sheriff court to the Court of Session) does not apply.

(5), (6) . . .[131]

(7) . . .[132] Part II does not apply to service in any of the naval, military or air forces of the
    Crown.

(8) In this section—
    'the 1947 Act' means the Crown Proceedings Act 1947;
    . . .[133]
    'Crown proceedings' means proceedings which, by virtue of section 23 of the 1947 Act, are
    treated for the purposes of Part II of that Act as civil proceedings by or against the Crown;
    . . .[134]
    'service for purposes of a Minister of the Crown or government department'
    does not include service in any office for the time being mentioned in Schedule 2
    (Ministerial offices) to the House of Commons Disqualification Act 1975;
    'statutory body' means a body set up by or under an enactment;
    'statutory office' means an office so set up; . . .
    . . . .[135]

---

[127] Repealed in relation to England, Wales and Scotland by the Employment Tribunals Act 1996, and in relation to Northern Ireland by the Industrial Tribunals (Northern Ireland) Order 1996, SI 1996/1921.

[128] Repealed in relation to England, Wales and Scotland by the Employment Tribunals Act 1996.

[129] Amended by the Disability and Discrimination Act 1995 (Amendment) Regulations, SI 2003/1673.

[130] See n 129 above.   [131] See n 129 above.   [132] See n 129 above.
[133] See n 129 above.   [134] See n 129 above.   [135] See n 129 above.

[64A. Police[136]

(1) For the purposes of Part 2, the holding of the office of constable shall be treated as employment—

    (a) by the chief officer of police as respects any act done by him in relation to a constable or that office;

    (b) by the police authority as respects any act done by them in relation to a constable or that office.

(2) For the purposes of section 58—

    (a) the holding of the office of constable shall be treated as employment by the chief officer of police (and as not being employment by any other person); and

    (b) anything done by a person holding such an office in the performance, or purported performance, of his functions shall be treated as done in the course of that employment.

(3) There shall be paid out of the police fund—

    (a) any compensation, costs or expenses awarded against a chief officer of police in any proceedings brought against him under Part 2, and any costs or expenses incurred by him in any such proceedings so far as not recovered by him in the proceedings; and

    (b) any sum required by a chief officer of police for the settlement of any claim made against him under Part 2 if the settlement is approved by the police authority.

(4) Any proceedings under Part 2 which, by virtue of subsection (1), would lie against a chief officer of police shall be brought against—

    (a) the chief officer of police for the time being, or

    (b) in the case of a vacancy in that office, against the person for the time being performing the functions of that office;

and references in subsection (3) to the chief officer of police shall be construed accordingly.

(5) A police authority may, in such cases and to such extent as appear to it to be appropriate, pay out of the police fund—

    (a) any compensation, costs or expenses awarded in proceedings under Part 2 of this Act against a person under the direction and control of the chief officer of police;

    (b) any costs or expenses incurred and not recovered by such a person in such proceedings; and

    (c) any sum required in connection with the settlement of a claim that has or might have given rise to such proceedings.

(6) Subsections (1) and (2) apply to a police cadet and appointment as a police cadet as they apply to a constable and the office of constable.

(7) Subject to subsection (8), in this section—

'chief officer of police'—

    (a) in relation to a person appointed, or an appointment falling to be made, under a specified Act, has the same meaning as in the Police Act 1996,

    (b) in relation to a person appointed, or an appointment falling to be made, under section 9(1)(b) or 55(1)(b) of the Police Act 1997 (police members of the National Criminal Intelligence Service and the National Crime Squad) means the Director General of the National Criminal Intelligence Service or, as the case may be, the Director General of the National Crime Squad,

    (c) in relation to a person appointed, or an appointment falling to be made, under the Police (Scotland) Act 1967, means the chief constable of the relevant police force,

---

[136] Inserted by the Disability and Discrimination Act 1995 (Amendment) Regulations, SI 2003/1673.

(d) in relation to any other person or appointment means the officer or other person who has the direction and control of the body of constables or cadets in question;

'police authority'—

(a) in relation to a person appointed, or an appointment falling to be made, under a specified Act, has the same meaning as in the Police Act 1996,

(b) in relation to a person appointed, or an appointment falling to be made, under section 9(1)(b) or 55(1)(b) of the Police Act 1997, means the Service Authority for the National Criminal Intelligence Service or, as the case may be, the Service Authority for the National Crime Squad,

(c) in relation to a person appointed, or an appointment falling to be made, under the Police (Scotland) Act 1967, has the meaning given in that Act,

(d) in relation to any other person or appointment, means the authority by whom the person in question is or on appointment would be paid;

'police cadet' means any person appointed to undergo training with a view to becoming a constable;

'police fund'—

(a) in relation to a chief officer of police within paragraph (a) of the above definition of that term, has the same meaning as in the Police Act 1996,

(b) in relation to a chief officer of police within paragraph (b) of that definition, means the service fund established under section 16 or (as the case may be) section 61 of the Police Act 1997, and

(c) in any other case means money provided by the police authority;

'specified Act' means the Metropolitan Police Act 1829, the City of London Police Act 1839 or the Police Act 1996.

(8) In relation to a constable of a force who is not under the direction and control of the chief officer of police for that force, references in this section to the chief officer of police are references to the chief officer of the force under whose direction and control he is, and references in this section to the police authority are references to the relevant police authority for that force.]

65. Application to Parliament

(1) This Act applies to an act done by or for purposes of the House of Lords or the House of Commons as it applies to an act done by a private person.

(2) For the purposes of the application of Part II in relation to the House of Commons, the Corporate Officer of that House shall be treated as the employer of a person who is (or would be) a relevant member of the House of Commons staff for the purposes of [section 195 of the Employment Rights Act 1996].[137]

(3) Except as provided in subsection (4), for the purposes of the application of sections 19 to 21, the provider of services is—

(a) as respects the House of Lords, the Corporate Officer of that House; and

(b) as respects the House of Commons, the Corporate Officer of that House.

(4) Where the service in question is access to and use of any place in the Palace of Westminster which members of the public are permitted to enter, the Corporate Officers of both Houses jointly are the provider of that service.

(5) Nothing in any rule of law or the law or practice of Parliament prevents proceedings being instituted before an [employment tribunal][138] under Part II or before any court under Part III.

---

[137] Amended by the the Employment Rights Act 1996.

[138] Amended by the Employment Rights (Dispute Resolution) Act 1998.

66. ...[139]

67. Regulations and orders

(1) Any power under this Act to make regulations or orders shall be exercisable by statutory instrument.

(2) Any such power may be exercised to make different provision for different cases, including different provision for different areas or localities.

(3) Any such power includes power—
   (a) to make such incidental, supplemental, consequential or transitional provision as appears to the Secretary of State to be expedient; and
   (b) to provide for a person to exercise a discretion in dealing with any matter.

(4) No order shall be made under section 50(3) unless a draft of the statutory instrument containing the order has been laid before Parliament and approved by a resolution of each House.

(5) Any other statutory instrument made under this Act, other than one made under section 3(9), [53A(6)(a)][140] or 70(3), shall be subject to annulment in pursuance of a resolution of either House of Parliament.

(6) Subsection (1) does not require an order under section 43 which applies only to a specified vehicle, or to vehicles of a specified person, to be made by statutory instrument but such an order shall be as capable of being amended or revoked as an order which is made by statutory instrument.

(7) Nothing in section 34(4), 40(6) or 46(5) affects the powers conferred by subsections (2) and (3).

68. Interpretation

(1) In this Act—
   'accessibility certificate' means a certificate issued under section 41(1)(a);
   'act' includes a deliberate omission;
   'approval certificate' means a certificate issued under section 42(4);
   ...[141]
   'conciliation officer' means a person designated under section 211 of the Trade Union and Labour Relations (Consolidation) Act 1992;
   'employment' means, subject to any prescribed provision, employment under a contract of service or of apprenticeship or a contract personally to do any work, and related expressions are to be construed accordingly;
   ['employment at an establishment in Great Britain' is to be construed in accordance with subsections (2) to (4A);][142]
   'enactment' includes subordinate legislation and any Order in Council[, and (except in section 56(5)) includes an enactment comprised in, or in an instrument made under, an Act of the Scottish Parliament];[143]
   ['Great Britain' includes such of the territorial waters of the United Kingdom as are adjacent to Great Britain;][144]

---

[139] Repealed by the Disability and Discrimination Act 1995 (Amendment) Regulations, SI 2003/1673.

[140] Amended by the Disability Rights Commission Act 1999.

[141] Amended by the Disability and Discrimination Act 1995 (Amendment) Regulations, SI 2003/1673.

[142] See n 141 above.

[143] Amended by the Scotland Act 1998 (Consequential Modifications) Order 2000, SI 2000/2040.

[144] See n 141 above.

'licensing authority'[, except in section 37A,][145] means—

(a) in relation to the area to which the Metropolitan Public Carriage Act 1869 applies, the Secretary of State or the holder of any office for the time being designated by the Secretary of State; or

(b) in relation to any other area in England and Wales, the authority responsible for licensing taxis in that area;

'mental impairment' does not have the same meaning as in the Mental Health Act 1983 or the Mental Health (Scotland) Act 1984 but the fact that an impairment would be a mental impairment for the purposes of either of those Acts does not prevent it from being a mental impairment for the purposes of this Act;

['Minister of the Crown' includes the Treasury and the Defence Council;][146]

'occupational pension scheme' has the same meaning as in the Pension Schemes Act 1993;

'premises' includes land of any description;

'prescribed' means prescribed by regulations;

'profession' includes any vocation or occupation;

'provider of services' has the meaning given in section 19(2)(b);

'public service vehicle' and 'regulated public service vehicle' have the meaning given in section 40;

'PSV accessibility regulations' means regulations made under section 40(1);

'rail vehicle' and 'regulated rail vehicle' have the meaning given in section 46;

'rail vehicle accessibility regulations' means regulations made under section 46(1);

'regulations' means regulations made by the Secretary of State;

. . .[147]

'section 21 duty' means any duty imposed by or under section 21;

'subordinate legislation' has the same meaning as in section 21 of the Interpretation Act 1978;

'taxi' and 'regulated taxi' have the meaning given in section 32;

'taxi accessibility regulations' means regulations made under section 32(1);

'trade' includes any business;

'trade organisation' has the meaning given in section 13;

'vehicle examiner' means an examiner appointed under section 66A of the Road Traffic Act 1988.

[(2) Employment (including employment on board a ship to which subsection (2B) applies or on an aircraft or hovercraft to which subsection (2C) applies) is to be regarded as being employment at an establishment in Great Britain if the employee—

(a) does his work wholly or partly in Great Britain; or

(b) does his work wholly outside Great Britain and subsection (2A) applies.

(2A) This subsection applies if—

(a) the employer has a place of business at an establishment in Great Britain;

(b) the work is for the purposes of the business carried on at the establishment; and

(c) the employee is ordinarily resident in Great Britain—

(i) at the time when he applies for or is offered the employment, or

(ii) at any time during the course of the employment.

(2B) This subsection applies to a ship if—

(a) it is registered at a port of registry in Great Britain; or

(b) it belongs to or is possessed by Her Majesty in right of the Government of the United Kingdom.

---

[145] Amended by the Private Hire Vehicles (Carriage of Guide Dogs etc) Act 2002.

[146] See n 141 above.   [147] See n 141 above.

(2C) This subsection applies to an aircraft or hovercraft if—
    (a) it is—
        (i) registered in the United Kingdom, and
        (ii) operated by a person who has his principal place of business, or is ordinarily resident, in Great Britain; or
    (b) it belongs to or is possessed by Her Majesty in right of the Government of the United Kingdom.
(2D) The following are not to be regarded as being employment at an establishment in Great Britain—
    (a) employment on board a ship to which subsection (2B) does not apply;
    (b) employment on an aircraft or hovercraft to which subsection (2C) does not apply.][148]
(4) Employment of a prescribed kind, or in prescribed circumstances, is to be regarded as not being employment at an establishment in Great Britain.
[(4A) For the purposes of determining if employment concerned with the exploration of the sea bed or sub-soil or the exploitation of their natural resources is outside Great Britain, subsections (2)(a) and (b), (2A) and (2C) of this section each have effect as if 'Great Britain' had the same meaning as that given to the last reference to Great Britain in section 10(1) of the Sex Discrimination Act 1975 by section 10(5) of that Act read with the Sex Discrimination and Equal Pay (Offshore Employment) Order 1987.][149]
(5) . . .[150]

69. Financial provisions

There shall be paid out of money provided by Parliament—
    (a) any expenditure incurred by a Minister of the Crown under this Act;
    (b) any increase attributable to this Act in the sums payable out of money so provided under or by virtue of any other enactment.

70. Short title, commencement, extent etc

(1) This Act may be cited as the Disability Discrimination Act 1995.
(2) This section (apart from subsections (4), (5) and (7)) comes into force on the passing of this Act.
(3) The other provisions of this Act come into force on such day as the Secretary of State may by order appoint and different days may be appointed for different purposes.
(4) Schedule 6 makes consequential amendments.
(5) The repeals set out in Schedule 7 shall have effect.
[(5A) Sections 7A and 7B extend to England and Wales only.
(5B) Sections 7C and 7D extend to Scotland only.][151]
(6) [Subject to subsections (5A) and (5B), this Act extends to England and Wales, Scotland and Northern Ireland;][152] but in their application to Northern Ireland the provisions of this Act mentioned in Schedule 8 shall have effect subject to the modifications set out in that Schedule.
(7) . . .[153]

---

[148] See n 141 above.   [149] See n 141 above.   [150] See n 141 above.
[151] Amended by the Disability and Discrimination Act 1995 (Amendment) Regulations, SI 2003/1673.
[152] See n 151 above.
[153] Amends the House of Commons Disqualification Act 1975 and the Northern Ireland Assembly Disqualification Act 1975; partly repealed by the Disability Rights Commission Act 1999.

(8) Consultations which are required by any provision of this Act to be held by the Secretary of State may be held by him before the coming into force of that provision.

SCHEDULE 1
PROVISIONS SUPPLEMENTING SECTION 1

Section 1(1)

Impairment

1.—(1) 'Mental impairment' includes an impairment resulting from or consisting of a mental illness only if the illness is a clinically well-recognised illness.
(2) Regulations may make provision, for the purposes of this Act—
(a) for conditions of a prescribed description to be treated as amounting to impairments;
(b) for conditions of a prescribed description to be treated as not amounting to impairments.
(3) Regulations made under sub-paragraph (2) may make provision as to the meaning of 'condition' for the purposes of those regulations.

Long-term effects

2.—(1) The effect of an impairment is a long-term effect if—
(a) it has lasted at least 12 months;
(b) the period for which it lasts is likely to be at least 12 months; or
(c) it is likely to last for the rest of the life of the person affected.
(2) Where an impairment ceases to have a substantial adverse effect on a person's ability to carry out normal day-to-day activities, it is to be treated as continuing to have that effect if that effect is likely to recur.
(3) For the purposes of sub-paragraph (2), the likelihood of an effect recurring shall be disregarded in prescribed circumstances.
(4) Regulations may prescribe circumstances in which, for the purposes of this Act—
(a) an effect which would not otherwise be a long-term effect is to be treated as such an effect; or
(b) an effect which would otherwise be a long-term effect is to be treated as not being such an effect.

Severe disfigurement

3.—(1) An impairment which consists of a severe disfigurement is to be treated as having a substantial adverse effect on the ability of the person concerned to carry out normal day-to-day activities.
(2) Regulations may provide that in prescribed circumstances a severe disfigurement is not to be treated as having that effect.
(3) Regulations under sub-paragraph (2) may, in particular, make provision with respect to deliberately acquired disfigurements.

Normal day-to-day activities

4.—(1) An impairment is to be taken to affect the ability of the person concerned to carry out normal day-to-day activities only if it affects one of the following—
(a) mobility;

(b) manual dexterity;

(c) physical co-ordination;

(d) continence;

(e) ability to lift, carry or otherwise move everyday objects;

(f) speech, hearing or eyesight;

(g) memory or ability to concentrate, learn or understand; or

(h) perception of the risk of physical danger.

(2) Regulations may prescribe—

    (a) circumstances in which an impairment which does not have an effect falling within sub-paragraph (1) is to be taken to affect the ability of the person concerned to carry out normal day-to-day activities;

    (b) circumstances in which an impairment which has an effect falling within sub-paragraph (1) is to be taken not to affect the ability of the person concerned to carry out normal day-to-day activities.

Substantial adverse effects

5.—Regulations may make provision for the purposes of this Act—

    (a) for an effect of a prescribed kind on the ability of a person to carry out normal day-to-day activities to be treated as a substantial adverse effect;

    (b) for an effect of a prescribed kind on the ability of a person to carry out normal day-to-day activities to be treated as not being a substantial adverse effect.

Effect of medical treatment

6.—(1) An impairment which would be likely to have a substantial adverse effect on the ability of the person concerned to carry out normal day-to-day activities, but for the fact that measures are being taken to treat or correct it, is to be treated as having that effect.

(2) In sub-paragraph (1) 'measures' includes, in particular, medical treatment and the use of a prosthesis or other aid.

(3) Sub-paragraph (1) does not apply—

    (a) in relation to the impairment of a person's sight, to the extent that the impairment is, in his case, correctable by spectacles or contact lenses or in such other ways as may be prescribed; or

    (b) in relation to such other impairments as may be prescribed, in such circumstances as may be prescribed.

Persons deemed to be disabled

7.—(1) Sub-paragraph (2) applies to any person whose name is, both on 12th January 1995 and on the date when this paragraph comes into force, in the register of disabled persons maintained under section 6 of the Disabled Persons (Employment) Act 1944.

(2) That person is to be deemed—

    (a) during the initial period, to have a disability, and hence to be a disabled person; and

    (b) afterwards, to have had a disability and hence to have been a disabled person during that period.

(3) A certificate of registration shall be conclusive evidence, in relation to the person with respect to whom it was issued, of the matters certified.

(4) Unless the contrary is shown, any document purporting to be a certificate of registration shall be taken to be such a certificate and to have been validly issued.

(5) Regulations may provide for prescribed descriptions of person to be deemed to have disabilities, and hence to be disabled persons, for the purposes of this Act.

(6) Regulations may prescribe circumstances in which a person who has been deemed to be a disabled person by the provisions of sub-paragraph (1) or regulations made under sub-paragraph (5) is to be treated as no longer being deemed to be such a person.

(7) In this paragraph—

'certificate of registration' means a certificate issued under regulations made under section 6 of the Act of 1944; and

'initial period' means the period of three years beginning with the date on which this paragraph comes into force.

Progressive conditions

8.—(1) Where—

(a) a person has a progressive condition (such as cancer, multiple sclerosis or muscular dystrophy or infection by the human immunodeficiency virus),

(b) as a result of that condition, he has an impairment which has (or had) an effect on his ability to carry out normal day-to-day activities, but

(c) that-effect is not (or was not) a substantial adverse effect,

he shall be taken to have an impairment which has such a substantial adverse effect if the condition is likely to result in his having such an impairment.

(2) Regulations may make provision, for the purposes of this paragraph—

(a) for conditions of a prescribed description to be treated as being progressive;

(b) for conditions of a prescribed description to be treated as not being progressive.

SCHEDULE 2
PAST DISABILITIES

Section 2(2)

1. The modifications referred to in section 2 are as follows.

2. References in Parts II [to 4][154] to a disabled person are to be read as references to a person who has had a disability.

[2A. References in Chapter 1 of Part 4 to a disabled pupil are to be read as references to a pupil who has had a disability.

2B. References in Chapter 2 of Part 4 to a disabled student are to be read as references to a student who has had a disability.][155]

[2C. In section 3A(5), after 'not having that particular disability' insert 'and who has not had that particular disability'.][156]

[3. In sections 4A(1), 4B(4), 4E(1), [4H(1),][157] 6B(1), 7B(1), 7D(1), 14(1), 14B(1), 14D(1) and 16A(4), section 21A(4)(a) (in the words to be read as section 19(1)(aa)) and section 21A(6)(a) (in the words to be substituted in section 21(1)), after 'not disabled' (in each place it occurs) insert 'and who have not had a disability'.][158]

---

[154] Amended by the Special Educational Needs and Disability Act 2001.

[155] See n 154 above.

[156] Amended by the Disability and Discrimination Act 1995 (Amendment) Regulations, SI 2003/1673.

[157] Amended by the Disability Discrimination Act 1995 (Pensions) Regulations 2003, SI 2003/2770.

[158] See n 156 above.

[4.   In sections 4A(3)(b), 4E(3)(b), [4H(3)(b),]¹⁵⁹ 6B(3)(b), 7B(4)(b), 7D(3)(b), 14(3)(b), 14B(3)(b), 14D(3)(b) and 16A(6), for 'has' (in each place it occurs) substitute 'has had'.]¹⁶⁰

[4A. In section 28B(3)(a) and (4), after 'disabled' insert 'or that he had had a disability'.

4B. In section 28C(1), in paragraphs (a) and (b), after 'not disabled' insert 'and who have not had a disability'.

4C. In section 28S(3)(a) and (4), after 'disabled' insert 'or that he had had a disability'.

4D. In subsection (1) of section 28T, after 'not disabled' insert 'and who have not had a disability'.

4E. In that subsection as substituted by paragraphs 2 and 6 of Schedule 4C, after 'not disabled' insert 'and who have not had a disability'.]¹⁶¹

5.   For paragraph 2(1) to (3) of Schedule 1, substitute—

'(1) The effect of an impairment is a long-term effect if it has lasted for at least 12 months.

(2) Where an impairment ceases to have a substantial adverse effect on a person's ability to carry out normal day-to-day activities, it is to be treated as continuing to have that effect if that effect recurs.

(3) For the purposes of sub-paragraph (2), the recurrence of an effect shall be disregarded in prescribed circumstances.'

SCHEDULE 3
ENFORCEMENT AND PROCEDURE

Sections [17A(8)],¹⁶² 25(6)

PART I
EMPLOYMENT

Conciliation

1. . . .¹⁶³

Restriction on proceedings for breach of Part II

2.—[(1) Except as provided by Part 2, no civil or criminal proceedings may be brought against any person in respect of an act merely because the act is unlawful under that Part.]¹⁶⁴

(2) Sub-paragraph (1) does not prevent the making of an application for judicial review [or the investigation or determination of any matter in accordance with Part 10 (investigations) of the Pension Schemes Act 1993 by the Pensions Ombudsman].¹⁶⁵

---

¹⁵⁹ See n 157 above.   ¹⁶⁰ See n 156 above.   ¹⁶¹ See n 154 above.
¹⁶² Amended by the Disability and Discrimination Act 1995 (Amendment) Regulations, SI 2003/1673.
¹⁶³ Amended by the Employment Tribunals Act 1996.   ¹⁶⁴ See n 162 above.
¹⁶⁵ Amended by the Disability Discrimination Act 1995 (Pensions) Regulations 2003, SI 2003/2770.

Period within which proceedings must be brought

3.—(1) An [employment tribunal][166] shall not consider a complaint under [section 17A or 25(8)][167] unless it is presented before the end of the period of three months beginning when the act complained of was done.

(2) A tribunal may consider any such complaint which is out of time if, in all the circumstances of the case, it considers that it is just and equitable to do so.

(3) For the purposes of sub-paragraph (1)—

(a) where an unlawful act . . .[168] is attributable to a term in a contract, that act is to be treated as extending throughout the duration of the contract;

(b) any act extending over a period shall be treated as done at the end of that period; and

(c) a deliberate omission shall be treated as done when the person in question decided upon it.

(4) In the absence of evidence establishing the contrary, a person shall be taken for the purposes of this paragraph to decide upon an omission—

(a) when he does an act inconsistent with doing the omitted act; or

(b) if he has done no such inconsistent act, when the period expires within which he might reasonably have been expected to do the omitted act if it was to be done.

Evidence

4.—(1) In any proceedings under [section 17A or 25(8)],[169] a certificate signed by or on behalf of a Minister of the Crown and certifying—

(a) that any conditions or requirements specified in the certificate were imposed by a Minister of the Crown and were in operation at a time or throughout a time so specified, . . .[170]

(b) . . .[171]

shall be conclusive evidence of the matters certified.

(2) A document purporting to be such a certificate shall be received in evidence and, unless the contrary is proved, be deemed to be such a certificate.

PART II
DISCRIMINATION IN OTHER AREAS

Restriction on proceedings for breach of Part III

5.—(1) Except as provided by section 25 no civil or criminal proceedings may be brought against any person in respect of an act merely because the act is unlawful under Part III.

(2) Sub-paragraph (1) does not prevent the making of an application for judicial review.

Period within which proceedings must be brought

6.—(1) A county court or a sheriff court shall not consider a claim under section 25 unless proceedings in respect of the claim are instituted before the end of the period of six months beginning when the act complained of was done.

(2) Where, in relation to proceedings or prospective proceedings under section 25, [the dispute concerned is referred for conciliation in pursuance of arrangements under section 28][172]

---

[166] Amended by the Employment Rights (Dispute Resolution) Act 1998.

[167] See n 162 above.   [168] See n 162 above.   [169] See n 162 above.

[170] Amended by the Employment Relations Act 1999.   [171] See n 170 above.

[172] Amended by the Disability Rights Commission Act 1999.

before the end of the period of six months mentioned in sub-paragraph (1), the period allowed by that sub-paragraph shall be extended by two months.

(3) A court may consider any claim under section 25 which is out of time if, in all the circumstances of the case, it considers that it is just and equitable to do so.

(4) For the purposes of sub-paragraph (1)—

    (a) where an unlawful act of discrimination is attributable to a term in a contract, that act is to be treated as extending throughout the duration of the contract;

    (b) any act extending over a period shall be treated as done at the end of that period; and

    (c) a deliberate omission shall be treated as done when the person in question decided upon it.

(5) In the absence of evidence establishing the contrary, a person shall be taken for the purposes of this paragraph to decide upon an omission—

    (a) when he does an act inconsistent with doing the omitted act; or

    (b) if he has done no such inconsistent act, when the period expires within which he might reasonably have been expected to do the omitted act if it was to be done.

Compensation for injury to feelings

7. In any proceedings under section 25, the amount of any damages awarded as compensation for injury to feelings shall not exceed the prescribed amount.

Evidence

8.—(1) In any proceedings under section 25, a certificate signed by or on behalf of a Minister of the Crown and certifying—

    (a) that any conditions or requirements specified in the certificate were imposed by a Minister of the Crown and were in operation at a time or throughout a time so specified, or

    (b) that an act specified in the certificate was done for the purpose of safeguarding national security,

shall be conclusive evidence of the matters certified.

(2) A document purporting to be such a certificate shall be received in evidence and, unless the contrary is proved, be deemed to be such a certificate.

[PART 3]
DISCRIMINATION IN SCHOOLS[173]

Restriction on proceedings for breach of Part 4, Chapter 1

9.—(1) Except as provided by sections 28I, 28K and 28L, no civil or criminal proceedings may be brought against any person in respect of an act merely because the act is unlawful under Chapter 1 of Part 4.

(2) Sub-paragraph (1) does not prevent the making of an application for judicial review.

Period within which proceedings must be brought

10.—(1) The Tribunal [or the Welsh Tribunal][174] shall not consider a claim under section 28I

---

[173] Parts 3 (paras 9–11) and 4 (paras 12–15) inserted by the Special Educational Needs and Disability Act 2001.

[174] Amended by the Education Act 2002.

unless proceedings in respect of the claim are instituted before the end of the period of six months beginning when the act complained of was done.

(2) If, in relation to proceedings or prospective proceedings under section 28I, the dispute concerned is referred for conciliation in pursuance of arrangements under section 31B before the end of the period of six months mentioned in sub-paragraph (1), the period allowed by that sub-paragraph shall be extended by two months.

(3) The Tribunal [or the Welsh Tribunal][175] may consider any claim under section 28I which is out of time if, in all the circumstances of the case, it considers that it is just and equitable to do so.

(4) But sub-paragraph (3) does not permit the Tribunal [or the Welsh Tribunal][176] to decide to consider a claim if a decision not to consider that claim has previously been taken under that sub-paragraph.

(5) For the purposes of sub-paragraph (1)—
   (a) if an unlawful act of discrimination is attributable to a term in a contract, that act is to be treated as extending throughout the duration of the contract;
   (b) any act extending over a period shall be treated as done at the end of that period; and
   (c) a deliberate omission shall be treated as done when the person in question decided upon it.

(6) In the absence of evidence establishing the contrary, a person shall be taken for the purposes of this paragraph to decide upon an omission—
   (a) when he does an act inconsistent with doing the omitted act; or
   (b) if he has done no such inconsistent act, when the period expires within which he might reasonably have been expected to do the omitted act if it was to be done.

Evidence

11.—(1) In any proceedings under section 28I, 28K or 28L, a certificate signed by or on behalf of a Minister of the Crown and certifying that any conditions or requirements specified in the certificate—
   (a) were imposed by a Minister of the Crown, and
   (b) were in operation at a time or throughout a time so specified,
shall be conclusive evidence of the matters certified.

(2) A document purporting to be such a certificate shall be received in evidence and, unless the contrary is proved, be deemed to be such a certificate.

PART 4
DISCRIMINATION IN FURTHER AND HIGHER EDUCATION INSTITUTIONS

Restriction on proceedings for breach of Part 4, Chapter 2

12.—(1) Except as provided by section 28V, no civil or criminal proceedings may be brought against any person in respect of an act merely because the act is unlawful under Chapter 2 of Part 4.

(2) Sub-paragraph (1) does not prevent the making of an application for judicial review.

---

[175] See n 174 above.   [176] See n 174 above.

Period within which proceedings must be brought

13.—(1) A county court or a sheriff court shall not consider a claim under section 28V unless proceedings in respect of the claim are instituted before the end of the period of six months beginning when the act complained of was done.

(2) If, in relation to proceedings or prospective proceedings under section 28V—

(a) the dispute concerned is referred for conciliation in pursuance of arrangements under section 31B before the end of the period of six months mentioned in sub-paragraph (1), or

(b) in England and Wales, in a case not falling within paragraph (a), the dispute concerned relates to the act or omission of a qualifying institution and is referred as a complaint under the student complaints scheme before the end of that period,

the period of six months allowed by sub-paragraph (1) shall be extended by two months.

(2A) In sub-paragraph (2)(b)—

'qualifying institution' has the meaning given by section 11 of the Higher Education Act 2004;

'the student complaints scheme' means a scheme for the review of qualifying complaints, as defined by section 12 of that Act, that is provided by the designated operator, as defined by section 13(5)(b) of that Act.

(3) A court may consider any claim under section 28V which is out of time if, in all the circumstances of the case, it considers that it is just and equitable to do so.

(4) For the purposes of sub-paragraph (1)—

(a) if an unlawful act of discrimination is attributable to a term in a contract, that act is to be treated as extending throughout the duration of the contract;

(b) any act extending over a period shall be treated as done at the end of that period; and

(c) a deliberate omission shall be treated as done when the person in question decided upon it.

(5) In the absence of evidence establishing the contrary, a person shall be taken for the purposes of this paragraph to decide upon an omission—

(a) when he does an act inconsistent with doing the omitted act; or

(b) if he has done no such inconsistent act, when the period expires within which he might reasonably have been expected to do the omitted act if it was to be done.

Compensation for injury to feelings

14. In any proceedings under section 28V, the amount of any damages awarded as compensation for injury to feelings shall not exceed the prescribed amount.

Evidence

15.—(1) In any proceedings under section 28V, a certificate signed by or on behalf of a Minister of the Crown and certifying that any conditions or requirements specified in the certificate—

(a) were imposed by a Minister of the Crown, and

(b) were in operation at a time or throughout a time so specified,

is conclusive evidence of the matters certified.

(2) A document purporting to be such a certificate is to be—

(a) received in evidence; and

(b) deemed to be such a certificate unless the contrary is proved.]

[SCHEDULE 3A
VALIDITY OF CONTRACTS, COLLECTIVE AGREEMENTS AND RULES OF
UNDERTAKINGS[177]

Section 17C

PART 1
VALIDITY AND REVISION OF CONTRACTS

1.—(1) A term of a contract is void where—
- (a) the making of the contract is, by reason of the inclusion of the term, unlawful by virtue of this Part of this Act;
- (b) it is included in furtherance of an act which is unlawful by virtue of this Part of this Act; or
- (c) it provides for the doing of an act which is unlawful by virtue of this Part of this Act.

(2) Sub-paragraph (1) does not apply to a term the inclusion of which constitutes, or is in furtherance of, or provides for, unlawful discrimination against, or harassment of, a party to the contract, but the term shall be unenforceable against that party.

(3) A term in a contract which purports to exclude or limit any provision of this Part of this Act is unenforceable by any person in whose favour the term would operate apart from this paragraph.

(4) Sub-paragraphs (1), (2) and (3) apply whether the contract was entered into before or after the date on which this Schedule comes into force; but in the case of a contract made before that date, those sub-paragraphs do not apply in relation to any period before that date.

2.—(1) Paragraph 1(3) does not apply—
- (a) to a contract settling a complaint to which section 17A(1) or 25(8) applies where the contract is made with the assistance of a conciliation officer (within the meaning of the Trade Union and Labour Relations (Consolidation) Act 1992); or
- (b) to a contract settling a complaint to which section 17A(1) or 25(8) applies if the conditions regulating compromise contracts under this Schedule are satisfied in relation to the contract.

(2) The conditions regulating compromise contracts under this Schedule are that—
- (a) the contract must be in writing;
- (b) the contract must relate to the particular complaint;
- (c) the complainant must have received advice from a relevant independent adviser as to the terms and effect of the proposed contract and in particular its effect on his ability to pursue a complaint before an employment tribunal;
- (d) there must be in force, when the adviser gives the advice, a contract of insurance, or an indemnity provided for members of a profession or professional body, covering the risk of a claim by the complainant in respect of loss arising in consequence of the advice;
- (e) the contract must identify the adviser; and
- (f) the contract must state that the conditions regulating compromise contracts under this Schedule are satisfied.

---

[177] Inserted by the Disability and Discrimination Act 1995 (Amendment) Regulations, SI 2003/1673.

(3) A person is a relevant independent adviser for the purposes of sub-paragraph (2)(c)—

(a) if he is a qualified lawyer;

(b) if he is an officer, official, employee or member of an independent trade union who has been certified in writing by the trade union as competent to give advice and as authorised to do so on behalf of the trade union; or

(c) if he works at an advice centre (whether as an employee or a volunteer) and has been certified in writing by the centre as competent to give advice and as authorised to do so on behalf of the centre.

(4) But a person is not a relevant independent adviser for the purposes of sub-paragraph (2)(c) in relation to the complainant—

(a) if he is, is employed by or is acting in the matter for the other party or a person who is connected with the other party;

(b) in the case of a person within sub-paragraph (3)(b) or (c), if the trade union or advice centre is the other party or a person who is connected with the other party; or

(c) in the case of a person within sub-paragraph (3)(c), if the complainant makes a payment for the advice received from him.

(5) In sub-paragraph (3)(a) 'qualified lawyer' means—

(a) as respects England and Wales, a barrister (whether in practice as such or employed to give legal advice), a solicitor who holds a practising certificate, or a person other than a barrister or solicitor who is an authorised advocate or authorised litigator (within the meaning of the Courts and Legal Services Act 1990); and

(b) as respects Scotland, an advocate (whether in practice as such or employed to give legal advice), or a solicitor who holds a practising certificate.

(6) In sub-paragraph (3)(b) 'independent trade union' has the same meaning as in the Trade Union and Labour Relations (Consolidation) Act 1992.

(7) For the purposes of sub-paragraph (4)(a) any two persons are to be treated as connected—

(a) if one is a company of which the other (directly or indirectly) has control; or

(b) if both are companies of which a third person (directly or indirectly) has control.

(8) An agreement under which the parties agree to submit a dispute to arbitration—

(a) shall be regarded for the purposes of sub-paragraph (1)(a) and (b) as being a contract settling a complaint if—

(i) the dispute is covered by a scheme having effect by virtue of an order under section 212A of the Trade Union and Labour Relations (Consolidation) Act 1992, and

(ii) the agreement is to submit it to arbitration in accordance with the scheme; but

(b) shall be regarded as neither being nor including such a contract in any other case.

3.—(1) On the application of a disabled person interested in a contract to which paragraph 1(1) or (2) applies, a county court or a sheriff court may make such order as it thinks fit for—

(a) removing or modifying any term rendered void by paragraph 1(1), or

(b) removing or modifying any term made unenforceable by paragraph 1(2);

but such an order shall not be made unless all persons affected have been given notice in writing of the application (except where under rules of court notice may be dispensed with) and have been afforded an opportunity to make representations to the court.

(2) An order under sub-paragraph (1) may include provision as respects any period before the making of the order (but after the coming into force of this Schedule).

PART 2
COLLECTIVE AGREEMENTS AND RULES OF UNDERTAKINGS

4.—(1) This Part of this Schedule applies to—
  (a) any term of a collective agreement, including an agreement which was not intended, or is presumed not to have been intended, to be a legally enforceable contract;
  (b) any rule made by an employer for application to all or any of the persons who are employed by him or who apply to be, or are, considered by him for employment;
  (c) any rule made by a trade organisation (within the meaning of section 13) or a qualifications body (within the meaning of section 14A) for application to—
    (i) all or any of its members or prospective members; or
    (ii) all or any of the persons on whom it has conferred authorisations or qualifications or who are seeking the authorisations or qualifications which it has power to confer.
(2) Any term or rule to which this Part of this Schedule applies is void where—
  (a) the making of the collective agreement is, by reason of the inclusion of the term, unlawful by virtue of this Part of this Act;
  (b) the term or rule is included in furtherance of an act which is unlawful by virtue of this Part of this Act; or
  (c) the term or rule provides for the doing of an act which is unlawful by virtue of this Part of this Act.
(3) Sub-paragraph (2) applies whether the agreement was entered into, or the rule made, before or after the date on which this Schedule comes into force; but in the case of an agreement entered into, or a rule made, before the date on which this Schedule comes into force, that sub-paragraph does not apply in relation to any period before that date.
5. A disabled person to whom this paragraph applies may present a complaint to an employment tribunal that a term or rule is void by virtue of paragraph 4 if he has reason to believe—
  (a) that the term or rule may at some future time have effect in relation to him; and
  (b) where he alleges that it is void by virtue of paragraph 4(2)(c), that—
    (i) an act for the doing of which it provides, may at some such time be done in relation to him, and
    (ii) the act would be unlawful by virtue of this Part of this Act if done in relation to him in present circumstances.
6. In the case of a complaint about—
  (a) a term of a collective agreement made by or on behalf of—
    (i) an employer,
    (ii) an organisation of employers of which an employer is a member, or
    (iii) an association of such organisations of one of which an employer is a member, or
  (b) a rule made by an employer within the meaning of paragraph 4(1)(b),
paragraph 5 applies to any disabled person who is, or is genuinely and actively seeking to become, one of his employees.
7. In the case of a complaint about a rule made by an organisation or body to which paragraph 4(1)(c) applies, paragraph 5 applies to any disabled person—
  (a) who is, or is genuinely and actively seeking to become, a member of the organisation or body;
  (b) on whom the organisation or body has conferred an authorisation or qualification; or
  (c) who is genuinely and actively seeking an authorisation or qualification which the organisation or body has power to confer.

8.—(1) When an employment tribunal finds that a complaint presented to it under paragraph 5 is well-founded the tribunal shall make an order declaring that the term or rule is void.

(2) An order under sub-paragraph (1) may include provision as respects any period before the making of the order (but after the coming into force of this Schedule).

9. The avoidance by virtue of paragraph 4(2) of any term or rule which provides for any person to be discriminated against shall be without prejudice to the following rights (except in so far as they enable any person to require another person to be treated less favourably than himself), namely—

(a) such of the rights of the person to be discriminated against, and

(b) such of the rights of any person who will be treated more favourably in direct or indirect consequence of the discrimination,

as are conferred by or in respect of a contract made or modified wholly or partly in pursuance of, or by reference to, that term or rule.

PART 3
INTERPRETATION

10. In this Schedule 'collective agreement' means any agreement relating to one or more of the matters mentioned in section 178(2) of the Trade Union and Labour Relations (Consolidation) Act 1992 (meaning of trade dispute), being an agreement made by or on behalf of one or more employers or one or more organisations of employers or associations of such organisations with one or more organisations of workers or associations of such organisations.

11. Any reference in this Schedule to a contract or act which is unlawful by virtue of this Part of this Act shall be taken to include a reference to a contract or act which is unlawful by virtue of Part 3 of this Act to the extent that it relates to the provision of employment services.]

[SCHEDULE 4
PREMISES OCCUPIED UNDER LEASES

Sections [18A(5)],[178] 27(5)

PART I
OCCUPATION BY [EMPLOYER ETC][179]

Failure to obtain consent to alteration

1. If any question arises as to whether the occupier has failed to comply with [any duty to make reasonable adjustments],[180] by failing to make a particular alteration to the premises, any constraint attributable to the fact that he occupies the premises under a lease is to be ignored unless he has applied to the lessor in writing for consent to the making of the alteration.

---

[178] Amended by the Disability and Discrimination Act 1995 (Amendment) Regulations, SI 2003/1673.

[179] See n 178 above.   [180] See n 178 above.

Joining lessors in proceedings under [section 17A or 25(8)][181]

2.—(1) In any proceedings under [section 17A or 25(8)],[182] in a case to which [section 18A][183] applies, the complainant or the occupier may ask the tribunal hearing the complaint to direct that the lessor be joined or sisted as a party to the proceedings.

(2) The request shall be granted if it is made before the hearing of the complaint begins.

(3) The tribunal may refuse the request if it is made after the hearing of the complaint begins.

(4) The request may not be granted if it is made after the tribunal has determined the complaint.

(5) Where a lessor has been so joined or sisted as a party to the proceedings, the tribunal may determine—
   (a) whether the lessor has—
      (i) refused consent to the alteration, or
      (ii) consented subject to one or more conditions, and
   (b) if so, whether the refusal or any of the conditions was unreasonable.

(6) If, under sub-paragraph (5), the tribunal determines that the refusal or any of the conditions was unreasonable it may take one or more of the following steps—
   (a) make such declaration as it considers appropriate;
   (b) make an order authorising the occupier to make the alteration specified in the order;
   (c) order the lessor to pay compensation to the complainant.

(7) An order under sub-paragraph (6)(b) may require the occupier to comply with conditions specified in the order.

(8) Any step taken by the tribunal under sub-paragraph (6) may be in substitution for, or in addition to, any step taken by the tribunal under [section 17A(2)].[184]

(9) If the tribunal orders the lessor to pay compensation it may not make an order under [section 17A(2)][185] ordering the occupier to do so.

Regulations

3. Regulations may make provision as to circumstances in which—
   (a) a lessor is to be taken, for the purposes of [section 18A][186] and this Part of this Schedule to have—
      (i) withheld his consent;
      (ii) withheld his consent unreasonably;
      (iii) acted reasonably in withholding his consent;
   (b) a condition subject to which a lessor has given his consent is to be taken to be reasonable;
   (c) a condition subject to which a lessor has given his consent is to be taken to be unreasonable.

Sub-leases etc

4. The Secretary of State may by regulations make provision supplementing, or modifying, the provision made by [section 18A][187] or any provision made by or under this Part of this Schedule in relation to cases where the occupier occupies premises under a sub-lease or sub-tenancy.

---

[181] See n 178 above.   [182] See n 178 above.   [183] See n 178 above.
[184] See n 178 above.   [185] See n 178 above.   [186] See n 178 above.
[187] See n 178 above.

PART II
OCCUPATION BY PROVIDER OF SERVICES

Failure to obtain consent to alteration

5. If any question arises as to whether the occupier has failed to comply with the section 21 duty, by failing to make a particular alteration to premises, any constraint attributable to the fact that he occupies the premises under a lease is to be ignored unless he has applied to the lessor in writing for consent to the making of the alteration.

Reference to court

6.—(1) If the occupier has applied in writing to the lessor for consent to the alteration and—
    (a) that consent has been refused, or
    (b) the lessor has made his consent subject to one or more conditions,
the occupier or a disabled person who has an interest in the proposed alteration to the premises being made, may refer the matter to a county court or, in Scotland, to the sheriff.
(2) In the following provisions of this Schedule 'court' includes 'sheriff'.
(3) On such a reference the court shall determine whether the lessor's refusal was unreasonable or (as the case may be) whether the condition is, or any of the conditions are, unreasonable.
(4) If the court determines—
    (a) that the lessor's refusal was unreasonable, or
    (b) that the condition is, or any of the conditions are, unreasonable,
it may make such declaration as it considers appropriate or an order authorising the occupier to make the alteration specified in the order.
(5) An order under sub-paragraph (4) may require the occupier to comply with conditions specified in the order.

Joining lessors in proceedings under section 25

7.—(1) In any proceedings on a claim under section 25, in a case to which this Part of this Schedule applies, the plaintiff, the pursuer or the occupier concerned may ask the court to direct that the lessor be joined or sisted as a party to the proceedings.
(2) The request shall be granted if it is made before the hearing of the claim begins.
(3) The court may refuse the request if it is made after the hearing of the claim begins.
(4) The request may not be granted if it is made after the court has determined the claim.
(5) Where a lessor has been so joined or sisted as a party to the proceedings, the court may determine—
    (a) whether the lessor has—
        (i) refused consent to the alteration, or
        (ii) consented subject to one or more conditions, and
    (b) if so, whether the refusal or any of the conditions was unreasonable.
(6) If, under sub-paragraph (5), the court determines that the refusal or any of the conditions was unreasonable it may take one or more of the following steps—
    (a) make such declaration as it considers appropriate;
    (b) make an order authorising the occupier to make the alteration specified in the order;
    (c) order the lessor to pay compensation to the complainant.
(7) An order under sub-paragraph (6)(b) may require the occupier to comply with conditions specified in the order.

(8) If the court orders the lessor to pay compensation it may not order the occupier to do so.

Regulations

8. Regulations may make provision as to circumstances in which—
    (a) a lessor is to be taken, for the purposes of section 27 and this Part of this Schedule to have—
        (i)   withheld his consent;
        (ii) withheld his consent unreasonably;
        (iii) acted reasonably in withholding his consent;
    (b) a condition subject to which a lessor has given his consent is to be taken to be reasonable;
    (c) a condition subject to which a lessor has given his consent is to be taken to be unreasonable.

Sub-leases etc

9. The Secretary of State may by regulations make provision supplementing, or modifying, the provision made by section 27 or any provision made by or under this Part of this Schedule in relation to cases where the occupier occupies premises under a sub-lease or sub-tenancy.

[PART 3
OCCUPATION BY EDUCATIONAL INSTITUTIONS[188]

Failure to obtain consent

10. If any question arises as to whether a responsible body has failed to comply with the duty imposed by section 28T, by failing to make a particular alteration to premises, any constraint attributable to the fact that the premises are occupied by the educational institution under a lease is to be ignored unless the responsible body has applied to the lessor in writing for consent to the making of the alteration.

Reference to court

11.—(1) If the responsible body has applied in writing to the lessor for consent to the alteration and—
    (a) that consent has been refused, or
    (b) the lessor has made his consent subject to one or more conditions,
    that body or a disabled person who has an interest in the proposed alteration to the premises being made, may refer the matter to a county court or, in Scotland, to the sheriff.
(2) On such a reference the court must determine whether the lessor's refusal was unreasonable or (as the case may be) whether the condition is, or any of the conditions are, unreasonable.

---

[188] Inserted by the Special Educational Needs and Disability Act 2001.

(3) If the court determines—
    (a) that the lessor's refusal was unreasonable, or
    (b) that the condition is, or any of the conditions are, unreasonable,
it may make such declaration as it considers appropriate or an order authorising the responsible body to make the alteration specified in the order.

(4) An order under sub-paragraph (3) may require the responsible body to comply with conditions specified in the order.

Joining lessors in proceedings under section 28V

12.—(1) In proceedings on a claim under section 28V, in a case to which this Part of this Schedule applies, the claimant, the pursuer or the responsible body concerned may ask the court to direct that the lessor be joined or sisted as a party to the proceedings.

(2) The request must be granted if it is made before the hearing of the claim begins.

(3) The court may refuse the request if it is made after the hearing of the claim begins.

(4) The request may not be granted if it is made after the court has determined the claim.

(5) If a lessor has been so joined or sisted as a party to the proceedings, the court may determine—
    (a) whether the lessor has—
        (i) refused consent to the alteration, or
        (ii) consented subject to one or more conditions, and
    (b) if so, whether the refusal or any of the conditions was unreasonable.

(6) If, under sub-paragraph (5), the court determines that the refusal or any of the conditions was unreasonable it may take one or more of the following steps—
    (a) make such a declaration as it considers appropriate;
    (b) make an order authorising the responsible body to make the alteration specified in the order;
    (c) order the lessor to pay compensation to the complainant.

(7) An order under sub-paragraph (6)(b) may require the responsible body to comply with conditions specified in the order.

(8) If the court orders the lessor to pay compensation it may not order the responsible body to do so.

Regulations

13. Regulations may make provision as to circumstances in which—
    (a) a lessor is to be taken, for the purposes of section 28W and this Part of this Schedule to have—
        (i) withheld his consent;
        (ii) withheld his consent unreasonably;
        (iii) acted reasonably in withholding his consent;
    (b) a condition subject to which a lessor has given his consent is to be taken to be reasonable;
    (c) a condition subject to which a lessor has given his consent is to be taken to be unreasonable.

Sub-leases etc

14. Regulations may make provision supplementing, or modifying, section 28W or any provision made by or under this Part of this Schedule in relation to cases where the premises of the educational institution are occupied under a sub-lease or sub-tenancy.]

[SCHEDULE 4A
RESPONSIBLE BODIES FOR SCHOOLS[189]

Section 28A

1.—(1) The bodies responsible for schools in England and Wales are set out in the following table.

(2) In that Table—

'the local education authority' has the meaning given by section 22(8) of the School Standards and Framework Act 1998; and

'proprietor' has the meaning given by section 579 of the Education Act 1996.

Table

Type of school	Responsible body
1. Maintained school [or maintained nursery school].[190]	The local education authority. or governing body, according to which has the function in question.
2. Pupil referral unit.	The local education authority.
3. . . .[191]	The local education authority.
4. Independent school.	The proprietor.
5. Special school not maintained by a local education authority.	The proprietor.

2.—(1) The bodies responsible for schools in Scotland are set out in the following table.

(2) In that Table 'board of management', 'education authority', 'managers' and 'proprietor' each have the meaning given in section 135(1) of the Education (Scotland) Act 1980.

Table

Type of school	Responsible body
1. School managed by an education authority.	The education authority.
2. Independent school.	The proprietor.
3. Self-governing school.	The board of management.
4. School in respect of which the managers are for the time being receiving grants under section 73(c) or (d) of the Education (Scotland) Act 1980.	The managers of the school.]

---

[189] Inserted by the Special Educational Needs and Disability Act 2001.

[190] Inserted by the Education Act 2002, not yet in force in relation to Wales.

[191] Paragraph 3 ('Maintained nursery school') repealed by the Education Act 2002, not yet in force in relation to Wales.

[SCHEDULE 4B
RESPONSIBLE BODIES FOR EDUCATIONAL INSTITUTIONS[192]

Section 28R

1.—(1) The bodies responsible for educational institutions in England and Wales are set out in the following table.

(2) In that Table 'governing body' has the meaning given by section 90 of the Further and Higher Education Act 1992.

Table

Type of institution	Responsible body
1. Institution within the further education sector.	The governing body.
2. University.	The governing body.
3. Institution, other than a university, within the higher education sector.	The governing body.
4. Institution designated under section 28R(6)(c).	The body specified in the order as the responsible body.

2.—(1) The bodies responsible for relevant institutions in Scotland are set out in the following table.

(2) In that Table—

'board of management' has the meaning given in section 36(1) of the Further and Higher Education (Scotland) Act 1992 ('the 1992 Act');

'central institution', 'education authority' and 'managers' have the meaning given in section 135(1) of the Education (Scotland) Act 1980; and

'governing body' has the meaning given in section 56(1) of the 1992 Act.

Table

Type of institution	Responsible body
1. Designated institution within the meaning of Part 2 of the 1992 Act.	The governing body.
2. University.	The governing body.
3. College of further education with a board of management.	The board of management.
4. Institution maintained by an education authority in the exercise of their further education functions.	The education authority.
5. Central institution.	The governing body.

---

[192] Inserted by the Special Educational Needs and Disability Act 2001.

Type of institution	Responsible body
6. School in respect of which the managers are for the time being receiving grants under section 73(c) or (d) of the Education (Scotland) Act 1980.	The managers of the school.
7. Institution designated under section 28R(7)(e).	The body specified in the order as the responsible body.]

[SCHEDULE 4C
MODIFICATIONS OF CHAPTER 2 OF PART 4[193]

Section 28U

PART 1
MODIFICATIONS FOR ENGLAND AND WALES

1. For section 28R, substitute—

'28R. Further education etc provided by local education authorities and schools

(1) Subsections (2) and (3) apply in relation to—
   (a) any course of higher education secured by a local education authority under section 120 of the Education Reform Act 1988;
   (b) any course of further education—
      (i) secured by a local education authority; or
      (ii) provided by the governing body of a maintained school under section 80 of the School Standards and Framework Act 1998.

(2) It is unlawful for the local education authority or the governing body to discriminate against a disabled person—
   (a) in the arrangements they make for determining who should be enrolled on the course;
   (b) in the terms on which they offer to enrol him on the course; or
   (c) by refusing or deliberately omitting to accept an application for his enrolment on the course.

(3) It is unlawful for the local education authority or the governing body to discriminate against a disabled person who has enrolled on the course in the services which they provide, or offer to provide.

(4) 'Services', in relation to a course, means services of any description which are provided wholly or mainly for persons enrolled on the course.

(5) It is unlawful for a local education authority to discriminate against a disabled person in the terms on which they provide, or offer to provide, recreational or training facilities.

(6) In this Chapter 'responsible body' means—
   (a) a local education authority, in relation to—
      (i) a course of further or higher education secured by them;

---

[193] Inserted by the Special Educational Needs and Disability Act 2001.

           (ii) recreational or training facilities; and

    (b) the governing body of a maintained school, in relation to a course of further education provided under section 80 of the School Standards and Framework Act 1998.

(7) 'Further education'—

    (a) in relation to a course secured by a local education authority, has the meaning given in section 2(3) of the Education Act 1996; and

    (b) in relation to a course provided under section 80 of the School Standards and Framework Act 1998 means education of a kind mentioned in subsection (1) of that section.

(8) In relation to further education secured by a local education authority—
'course' includes each of the component parts of a course of further education if, in relation to the course, there is no requirement imposed on persons registered for any component part of the course to register for any other component part of that course; and 'enrolment', in relation to such a course, includes registration for any one of those parts.

(9) 'Higher education' has the meaning given in section 579(1) of the Education Act 1996.

(10) 'Local education authority' has the meaning given in section 12 of the Education Act 1996.

(11) 'Governing body' and 'maintained school' have the same meaning as in Chapter 1.

(12) 'Recreational or training facilities' means any facilities secured by a local education authority under subsection (1), or provided by it under subsection (1A), of section 508 of the Education Act 1996 (recreation and social and physical training).'

2.   For subsection (1) of section 28T, substitute—

    '(1) Each responsible body must take such steps as it is reasonable for it to have to take to ensure that—

        (a) in relation to its arrangements for enroling persons on a course of further or higher education provided by it, and

        (b) in relation to services provided, or offered by it,

    disabled persons are not placed at a substantial disadvantage in comparison with persons who are not disabled.'

3.   In section 28W(1)(a) for 'by an educational institution' substitute 'by a responsible body wholly or partly for the purpose of its functions'.

4.   Omit section 31A.

PART 2
MODIFICATIONS FOR SCOTLAND

5.   For section 28R, substitute—

28R. Further education etc provided by education authorities in Scotland

(1) Subsections (2) and (3) apply to any course of further education secured by an education authority.

(2) It is unlawful for the education authority to discriminate against a disabled person—

    (a) in the arrangements they make for determining who should be enrolled on the course;

    (b) in the terms on which they offer to enrol him on the course; or

    (c) by refusing or deliberately omitting to accept an application for his enrolment on the course.

(3) It is unlawful for the education authority to discriminate against a disabled person who has enrolled on the course in the services which they provide, or offer to provide.

(4) 'Services', in relation to a course, means services of any description which are provided wholly or mainly for persons enrolled on the course.

(5) It is unlawful for an education authority to discriminate against a disabled person in the terms on which they provide, or offer to provide, recreational or training facilities.

(6) In this Chapter 'responsible body' means an education authority.

(7) 'Further education' has the meaning given in section 1(5) of the Education (Scotland) Act 1980.

(8) 'Education authority' has the meaning given in section 135(1) of that Act.'

6. For subsection (1) of section 28T, substitute—

'(1) Each responsible body must take such steps as it is reasonable for it to have to take to ensure that—

(a) in relation to its arrangements for enroling persons on a course of further education provided by it, and

(b) in relation to services provided or offered by it,

disabled persons are not placed at a substantial disadvantage in comparison with persons who are not disabled.'

7. In section 28W(1)(a) for 'by an educational institution' substitute 'by a responsible body wholly or partly for the purpose of its functions'.

8. Omit section 31A.]

SCHEDULE 5[194]

. . .

SCHEDULE 6[195]

. . .

SCHEDULE 7
REPEALS

Section 70(5)

Chapter	Short title	Extent of repeal
7 & 8 Geo 6 c 10	The Disabled Persons (Employment) Act 1944	Section 1
		Sections 6 to 14
		Section 19
		Section 21
		Section 22(4)
6 & 7 Eliz 2 c 33	The Disabled Persons (Employment) Act 1958	Section 2
1970 c 44	The Chronically Sick and Disabled Persons Act 1970	Section 16
1978 c 44	The Employment Protection (Consolidation) Act 1978	In Schedule 13, in paragraph 20(3), the word 'or' in the definitions of 'relevant complaint of dismissal' and 'relevant conciliation powers'

[194] Repealed by the Disability Rights Commission Act 1999.

[195] Amends the Employment and Training Act 1973; the Employment Protection (Consolidation) Act 1978; the Companies Act 1985; the Local Government and Housing Act 1989; and the Enterprise and New Towns (Scotland) Act 1990. Repealed in part by the Employment Rights Act 1996; the Employment Tribunals Act 1996; and the Employment Rights (Northern Ireland) Order 1996, SI 1996/1919 (NI 16).

Chapter	Short title	Extent of repeal
1989 c 42	The Local Government and Housing Act 1989	In section 7(2), paragraph (a) and the word 'and' at the end of paragraph (d)
1993 c 62	The Education Act 1993	In section 161(5), the words from 'and in this subsection' to the end

SCHEDULE 8
MODIFICATIONS OF THIS ACT IN ITS APPLICATION TO NORTHERN IRELAND

Section 70(6)

1.   In its application to Northern Ireland this Act shall have effect subject to the following modifications.

2.—(1) In section 3(1) for 'Secretary of State' substitute 'Department'.

(2) In section 3 for subsections (4) to (12) substitute—

'(4)   In preparing a draft of any guidance, the Department shall consult such persons as it considers appropriate.

(5)   Where the Department proposes to issue any guidance, the Department shall publish a draft of it, consider any representations that are made to the Department about the draft and, if the Department thinks it appropriate, modify its proposals in the light of any of those representations.

(6)   If the Department decides to proceed with any proposed guidance, the Department shall lay a draft of it before the Assembly.

(7)   If, within the statutory period, the Assembly resolves not to approve the draft, the Department shall take no further steps in relation to the proposed guidance.

(8)   If no such resolution is made within the statutory period, the Department shall issue the guidance in the form of its draft.

(9)   The guidance shall come into force on such date as the Department may by order appoint.

(10)   Subsection (7) does not prevent a new draft of the proposed guidance being laid before the Assembly.

(11)   The Department may—

(a)   from time revise the whole or any part of any guidance and re-issue it;

(b)   by order revoke any guidance.

(12)   In this section—

"the Department" means the Department of Economic Development;

"guidance" means guidance issued by the Department under this section and includes guidance which has been revised and re-issued;

"statutory period" has the meaning assigned to it by section 41(2) of the Interpretation Act (Northern Ireland) 1954.'

3.   In section 4(6) for 'Great Britain' substitute 'Northern Ireland'.

4.—(1) In section 7(2) for 'Secretary of State' substitute 'Department of Economic Development'.

(2) In section 7(4) to (10) for 'Secretary of State' wherever it occurs substitute 'Department of Economic Development', for 'he' and 'him' wherever they occur substitute 'it' and for 'his' wherever it occurs substitute 'its'.

(3) In section 7(9) for 'Parliament' substitute 'the Assembly'.

5.—(1) In section 8(3) omit 'or (in Scotland) in reparation'.

(2) In section 8(7) for 'paragraph 6A of Schedule 9 to the Employment Protection (Consolidation) Act 1978' substitute '[Article 16 of the Industrial Tribunals (Northern Ireland) Order 1996]'.[196]

6.—(1) In section 9(2)(a) for 'a conciliation officer' substitute 'the Agency'.

(2) In section 9(4) in the definition of 'qualified lawyer' for the words from 'means' to the end substitute 'means a barrister (whether in practice as such or employed to give legal advice) or a solicitor of the Supreme Court who holds a practising certificate.'.

7.—(1) In section 10(1)(b) omit 'or recognised body'.

(2) In section 10(2)(b) for 'Secretary of State' substitute 'Department of Economic Development'.

(3) In section 10(3) in the definition of 'charity' for '1993' substitute '(Northern Ireland) 1964', omit the definition of 'recognised body' and in the definition of 'supported employment' for 'Act 1944' substitute 'Act (Northern Ireland) 1945'.

(4) In section 10(4) for 'England and Wales' where it twice occurs substitute 'Northern Ireland'.

(5) Omit section 10(5).

8. In section 12(5) for 'Great Britain' where it twice occurs substitute 'Northern Ireland'.

9.—(1) In section 19(3)(g) for 'section 2 of the Employment and Training Act 1973' substitute 'sections 1 and 2 of the Employment and Training Act (Northern Ireland) 1950'.

(2) In section 19(5) for paragraph (a) substitute—

'(a) Meducation which is funded, or secured, by a relevant body or provided at—

  (i) an establishment which is funded by such a body or by the Department of Education for Northern Ireland; or

  (ii) any other establishment which is a school within the meaning of the Education and Libraries (Northern Ireland) Order 1986;'.

(3) For section 19(6) substitute—

'(6) In subsection (5) "relevant body" means—

  (a) an education and library board;

  (b) a voluntary organisation; or

  (c) a body of a prescribed kind.'.

10. In section 20(7) for paragraphs (b) and (c) substitute

'; or

  (b) functions conferred by or under Part VIII of the Mental Health (Northern Ireland) Order 1986 are exercisable in relation to a disabled person's property or affairs.'.

11. In section 22(4) and (6) omit 'or (in Scotland) the subject of'.

12.—(1) In section 25(1) omit 'or (in Scotland) in reparation'.

(2) In section 25(3) for 'England and Wales' substitute 'Northern Ireland'.

(3) Omit section 25(4).

(4) In section 25(5) omit the words from 'or' to the end.

13. In section 26(3) omit 'or a sheriff court'.

14.—(1) In section 28 for 'Secretary of State' wherever it occurs substitute 'Department of Health and Social Services'.

(2) In section 28(3) and (4) for 'he' substitute 'it'.

(3) In section 28(5) for 'Treasury' substitute 'Department of Finance and Personnel in Northern Ireland'.

15. Omit sections 29, 30 and 31.

---

[196] Amended by the Industrial Tribunals (Northern Ireland) Order 1996, SI 1996/1921.

16.—(1) In section 32(1) for 'Secretary of State' substitute 'Department of the Environment'.

(2) In section 32(5) for the definition of 'taxi' substitute—

"taxi" means a vehicle which—

(a) is licensed under Article 61 of the Road Traffic (Northern Ireland) Order 1981 to stand or ply for hire; and

(b) seats not more than 8 passengers in addition to the driver'.

17. In section 33, for 'Secretary of State', wherever it occurs, substitute 'Department of the Environment'.

18. For section 34 substitute—

'34. New licences conditional on compliance with accessibility taxi regulations

(1) The Department of the Environment shall not grant a public service vehicle licence under Article 61 of the Road Traffic (Northern Ireland) Order 1981 for a taxi unless the vehicle conforms with those provisions of the taxi accessibility regulations with which it will be required to conform if licensed.

(2) Subsection (1) does not apply if such a licence was in force with respect to the vehicle at any time during the period of 28 days immediately before the day on which the licence is granted.

(3) The Department of the Environment may by order provide for subsection (2) to cease to have effect on such date as may be specified in the order.'.

19. Omit section 35.

20. In section 36(7) for 'licensing authority' substitute 'Department of the Environment'.

21.—(1) In section 37(5) and (6) for 'licensing authority' substitute 'Department of the Environment'.

(2) In section 37(9) for 'Secretary of State' substitute 'Department of the Environment'.

22.—(1) In section 38(1) for 'a licensing authority' substitute 'the Department of the Environment'.

(2) In section 38(2) for 'licensing authority concerned' substitute 'Department of the Environment'.

(3) In section 38(3) for the words from 'the magistrates' court' to the end substitute 'a court of summary jurisdiction acting for the petty sessions district in which the aggrieved person resides'.

23. Omit section 39.

24.—(1) In section 40 for 'Secretary of State' wherever it occurs substitute 'Department of the Environment'.

(2) In section 40(5) for the definition of 'public service vehicle' substitute—

' "public service vehicle" means a vehicle which—

(a) seats more than 8 passengers in addition to the driver; and

(b) is a public service vehicle for the purposes of the Road Traffic (Northern Ireland) Order 1981;'.

(3) In section 40(7) for the words from 'the Disabled' to the end substitute 'such representative organisations as it thinks fit'.

25.—(1) In section 41(2) for 'Secretary of State' substitute 'Department of the Environment'.

(2) In section 41 for subsections (3) and (4) substitute—

'(3) Any person who uses a regulated public service vehicle in contravention of this section is guilty of an offence and liable on summary conviction to a fine not exceeding level 4 on the standard scale.'.

26.—(1) In section 42 for 'Secretary of State' wherever it occurs substitute 'Department of the Environment'.

(2) In section 42(1) for 'he' substitute 'it'.

(3) In section 42(6) for 'his' substitute 'its'.

27. In section 43 for 'Secretary of State' wherever it occurs substitute 'Department of the Environment'.

28.—(1) In section 44 for 'Secretary of State' wherever it occurs substitute 'Department of the Environment'.

(2) In section 44(2) for 'him' substitute 'it'.

(3) In section 44(6) for 'he' substitute 'it' and for 'his' substitute 'its'.

29.—(1) In section 45 for 'Secretary of State' wherever it occurs substitute 'Department of the Environment'.

(2) In section 45(2) for 'him' substitute 'it' and at the end add 'of Northern Ireland'.

(3) In section 45(4) for 'he' substitute 'it'.

30.—(1) In section 46 for 'Secretary of State' wherever it occurs substitute 'Department of the Environment'.

(2) In section 46(6) in the definition of 'rail vehicle' for the words 'on any railway, tramway or prescribed system' substitute 'by rail'.

(3) Omit section 46(7).

(4) In section 46(11) for the words from 'the Disabled' to the end substitute 'such representative organisations as it thinks fit'.

31.—(1) In section 47 for 'Secretary of State' wherever it occurs substitute 'Department of the Environment'.

(2) In section 47(3) for the words 'the Disabled Persons Transport Advisory Committee and such other persons as he' substitute 'such persons as it' and for 'he' substitute 'it'.

32. Omit section 48(3).

33.—[(1) In sections 50 to 52, for 'the Council' substitute, in each place, the 'Equality Commission for Northern Ireland'.

(1A) Section 50(1) shall have no effect.][197]

(2) In section 50(2) for 'the Secretary of State' in the first place where it occurs substitute 'a Northern Ireland department' and in the other place where it occurs substitute 'that department'.

(3) In section 50(3) for 'Secretary of State' substitute 'Department of Health and Social Services'.

(4) In section 50(7) for 'the Secretary of State' substitute 'a Northern Ireland department' and after 'Crown' insert 'or a Northern Ireland department'.

(5) In section 50(9)(a) for sub-paragraphs (i) to (iv) substitute—
    '(i) the Disabled Persons (Employment) Act (Northern Ireland) 1945;
    (ii) the Contracts of Employment and Redundancy Payments Act (Northern Ireland) 1965;
    (iii) the Employment and Training Act (Northern Ireland) 1950;
    (iv) [the Employment Rights (Northern Ireland) Order 1996];[198] or'.

(6) In section 50(10) for the words from 'time when' to the end substitute—
    'time when—
    (a) there are no committees in existence under section 17 of the Disabled Persons (Employment) Act (Northern Ireland) 1945; and
    (b) there is no person appointed to act generally under section 60(1) of this Act.'.

34.—(1) In section 51(1) for 'the Secretary of State' substitute 'any Northern Ireland department' and for 'the Secretary of State's' substitute 'that department's'.

(2) In section 51(2) for 'The Secretary of State' substitute 'A Northern Ireland department'.

---

[197] Amended by the Northern Ireland Act 1998.

[198] Amended by the Employment Rights (Northern Ireland) Order 1996, SI 1996/1919 (NI 16).

(3) In section 51(4) for 'a county court or a sheriff court' substitute 'or a county court'.

(4) In section 51(6) for 'the Secretary of State' substitute 'a Northern Ireland department'.

35. For section 52 substitute—

'52. Further provisions about codes issued under section 51

(1) In this section—

"proposal" means a proposal made by [the Equality Commission for Northern Ireland][199] to a Northern Ireland department under section 51;

"responsible department"—

(a) in relation to a proposal, means the Northern Ireland department to which the proposal is made,

(b) in relation to a code, means the Northern Ireland department by which the code is issued; and

"statutory period" has the meaning assigned to it by section 41(2) of the Interpretation Act (Northern Ireland) 1954.

(2) In preparing any proposal, [the Equality Commission for Northern Ireland][200] shall consult—

(a) such persons (if any) as the responsible department has specified in making its request to [the Equality Commission for Northern Ireland][201]; and

(b) such other persons (if any) as [the Equality Commission for Northern Ireland][202] considers appropriate.

(3) Before making any proposal [the Equality Commission for Northern Ireland][203] shall publish a draft, consider any representations made to it about the draft and, if it thinks it appropriate, modify its proposal in the light of any of those representations.

(4) Where [the Equality Commission for Northern Ireland][204] makes any proposal, the responsible department may—

(a) approve it;

(b) approve it subject to such modifications as that department thinks appropriate; or

(c) refuse to approve it.

(5) Where the responsible department approves any proposal (with or without modifications) that department shall prepare a draft of the proposed code and lay it before the Assembly.

(6) If, within the statutory period, the Assembly resolves not to approve the draft, the responsible department shall take no further steps in relation to the proposed code.

(7) If no such resolution is made within the statutory period, the responsible department shall issue the code in the form of its draft.

(8) The code shall come into force on such date as the responsible department may appoint by order.

(9) Subsection (6) does not prevent a new draft of the proposed code from being laid before the Assembly.

(10) If the responsible department refuses to approve a proposal, that department shall give [the Equality Commission for Northern Ireland][205] a written statement of the department's reasons for not approving it.

(11) The responsible department may by order revoke a code.'.

---

[199] See n 197 above. [200] See n 197 above. [201] See n 197 above.

[202] See n 197 above. [203] See n 197 above. [204] See n 197 above.

[205] See n 197 above.

36.—(1) In section 53 for 'Secretary of State' wherever it occurs substitute 'Department of Economic Development'.

(2) In section 53(1) for 'he' substitute 'it'.

(3) In section 53(5) for 'a county court or a sheriff court' substitute 'or a county court'.

37. For section 54 substitute—

'54. Further provisions about codes issued under section 53

(1) In preparing a draft of any code under section 53, the Department shall consult such organisations representing the interests of employers or of disabled persons in, or seeking, employment as the Department considers appropriate.

(2) Where the Department proposes to issue a code, the Department shall publish a draft of the code, consider any representations that are made to the Department about the draft and, if the Department thinks it appropriate, modify its proposals in the light of any of those representations.

(3) If the Department decides to proceed with the code, the Department shall lay a draft of it before the Assembly.

(4) If, within the statutory period, the Assembly resolves not to approve the draft, the Department shall take no further steps in relation to the proposed code.

(5) If no such resolution is made within the statutory period, the Department shall issue the code in the form of its draft.

(6) The code shall come into force on such date as the Department may appoint by order.

(7) Subsection (4) does not prevent a new draft of the proposed code from being laid before the Assembly.

(8) The Department may by order revoke a code.

(9) In this section—
"the Department" means the Department of Economic Development; and
"statutory period" has the meaning assigned to it by section 41(2) of the Interpretation Act (Northern Ireland) 1954.'.

38. In section 56(2) and (4) for 'Secretary of State' substitute 'Department of Economic Development'.

39. In section 59(1) after 'Crown' where it twice occurs insert 'or a Northern Ireland department'.

40.—(1) In section 60(1) to (3) for 'Secretary of State' wherever it occurs substitute 'Department of Economic Development' and for 'he' and 'him' wherever they occur substitute 'it'.

(2) In section 60(4) for 'Treasury' substitute 'Department of Finance and Personnel in Northern Ireland'.

(3) For section 60(6) substitute—
'(6) The Department of Economic Development may by order repeal section 17 of, and Schedule 2 to, the Disabled Persons (Employment) Act (Northern Ireland) 1945 (district advisory committees).'.

(4) In section 60(7) omit 'paragraph (b) of', for '1944' substitute '1945' and omit 'in each case'.

(5) In section 60, omit subsection (8).

41. For section 61 substitute—

'61. Amendments of Disabled Persons (Employment) Act (Northern Ireland) 1945

(1) Section 15 of the Disabled Persons (Employment) Act (Northern Ireland) 1945 (which gives the Department of Economic Development power to make arrangements for the provision of supported employment) is amended as set out in subsections (2) to (5).

(2) In subsection (1)—

   (a) for "persons registered as handicapped by disablement" substitute "disabled persons";

   (b) for "their disablement" substitute "their disability"; and

   (c) for "are not subject to disablement" substitute "do not have a disability".

(3) In subsection (2) for the words from "any of one or more companies" to "so required and prohibited" substitute "any company, association or body".

(4) After subsection (2) insert—

"(2A) The only kind of company which the Department itself may form in exercising its powers under this section is a company which is—

(a) required by its constitution to apply its profits, if any, or other income in promoting its objects; and

(b) prohibited by its constitution from paying any dividend to its members.".

(5) After subsection (5) insert—

"(5A) For the purposes of this section—

(a) a person is a disabled person if he is a disabled person for the purposes of the Disability Discrimination Act 1995; and

(b) 'disability' has the same meaning as in that Act.".

(6) The provisions of section 16 of the Act of 1945 (preference to be given under section 15 of that Act to ex-service men and women) shall become subsection (1) of that section and at the end insert—

"and whose disability is due to that service.

(2) For the purposes of subsection (1) of this section, a disabled person's disability shall be treated as due to service of a particular kind only in such circumstances as may be prescribed."

(7) The following provisions of the Act of 1945 shall cease to have effect—

(a) section 1 (definition of "disabled person");

(b) sections 2 to 4 (training for disabled persons);

(c) sections 6 to 8 (the register of disabled persons);

(d) sections 9 to 11 (obligations on employers with substantial staffs to employ quota of registered persons);

(e) section 12 (the designated employment scheme for persons registered as handicapped by disablement);

(f) section 13 (interpretation of provisions repealed by this Act);

(g) section 14 (records to be kept by employer);

(h) section 19 (proceedings in relation to offences);

(j) sections 21 and 22 (supplementary).

(8) Any statutory provision in which 'disabled person' is defined by reference to the Act of 1945 shall be construed as if that expression had the same meaning as in this Act.'.

42. . . .[206]

43. Omit section 63.

44.—(1) In section 64(3) for 'England and Wales' substitute 'Northern Ireland'.

(2) Omit section 64(4).

(3) In section 64(5)(a) omit the words from ', the British' to the end.

(4) In section 64(8)—

(a) omit the definitions of 'British Transport Police', 'Royal Parks Constabulary' and 'United Kingdom Atomic Energy Authority Constabulary';

(b) in the definition of 'the 1947 Act' at the end add 'as it applies both in relation to the Crown in right of Her Majesty's Government in Northern Ireland and in relation to the Crown in right of Her Majesty's Government in the United Kingdom';

---

[206] See n 196 above.

(c) in the definition of 'fire brigade' for the words from 'means' to the end substitute 'has the same meaning as in the Fire Services (Northern Ireland) Order 1984';

(d) in the definition of 'prison officer' for the words from 'means' to the end substitute 'means any individual who holds any post, otherwise than as a medical officer, to which he has been appointed under section 2(2) of the Prison Act (Northern Ireland) 1953 or who is a prison custody officer within the meaning of Chapter III of Part VIII of the Criminal Justice and Public Order Act 1994';

(e) in the definition of 'service for purposes of a Minister of the Crown or government department' at the end add 'or service as the head of a Northern Ireland department'.

45. Omit section 65.

46. For section 67 substitute—

'67. Regulations and orders etc

(1) Any power under this Act to make regulations or orders shall be exercisable by statutory rule for the purposes of the Statutory Rules (Northern Ireland) Order 1979.

(2) Any such power may be exercised to make different provision for different cases, including different provision for different areas or localities.

(3) Any such power, includes power—

(a) to make such incidental, supplementary, consequential or transitional provision as appears to the Northern Ireland department exercising the power to be expedient; and

(b) to provide for a person to exercise a discretion in dealing with any matter.

(4) No order shall be made under section 50(3) unless a draft of the order has been laid before and approved by a resolution of the Assembly.

(5) Any other order made under this Act, other than an order under section 3(9), 52(8), 54(6) or 70(3), and any regulations made under this Act shall be subject to negative resolution within the meaning of section 41(6) of the Interpretation Act (Northern Ireland) 1954 as if they were statutory instruments within the meaning of that Act.

(6) Section 41(3) of the Interpretation Act (Northern Ireland) 1954 shall apply in relation to any instrument or document which by virtue of this Act is required to be laid before the Assembly as if it were a statutory instrument or statutory document within the meaning of that Act.

(7) Subsection (1) does not require an order under section 43 which applies only to a specified vehicle, or to vehicles of a specified person, to be made by statutory rule.

(8) Nothing in section 40(6) or 46(5) affects the powers conferred by subsections (2) and (3).'

47.—(1) For section 68(1) substitute—

'(1) In this Act—

"accessibility certificate" means a certificate issued under section 41(1)(a);

"act" includes a deliberate omission;

"the Agency" means the Labour Relations Agency;

"approval certificate" means a certificate issued under section 42(4);

"the Assembly" means the Northern Ireland Assembly;

"benefits", in Part II, has the meaning given in section 4(4);

"the Department of Economic Development" means the Department of Economic Development in Northern Ireland;

"the Department of the Environment" means the Department of the Environment for Northern Ireland;

"the Department of Health and Social Services" means the Department of Health and Social Services for Northern Ireland;

"employment" means, subject to any prescribed provision, employment under a contract of service or of apprenticeship or a contract personally to do work and related expressions are to be construed accordingly;

"employment at an establishment in Northern Ireland" is to be construed in accordance with subsections (2) to (5);

"enactment" means any statutory provision within the meaning of section 1(f) of the Interpretation Act (Northern Ireland) 1954;

"government department" means a Northern Ireland department or a department of the Government of the United Kingdom;

"Minister of the Crown" includes the Treasury;

"Northern Ireland department" includes (except in sections 51 and 52) the head of a Northern Ireland department;

"occupational pension scheme" has the same meaning as in the Pension Schemes (Northern Ireland) Act 1993;

"premises", includes land of any description;

"prescribed" means prescribed by regulations;

"profession" includes any vocation or occupation;

"provider of services" has the meaning given in section 19(2)(b);

"public service vehicle" and "regulated public service vehicle" have the meaning given in section 40;

"PSV accessibility regulations" means regulations made under section 40(1);

"rail vehicle" and "regulated rail vehicle" have the meaning given in section 46;

"rail vehicle accessibility regulations" means regulations made under section 46(1);

"regulations" means—

(a) in Parts I and II of this Act, section 66, the definition of "employment" above and subsections (3) and (4) below, regulations made by the Department of Economic Development;

(b) in Part V of this Act, regulations made by the Department of the Environment;

(c) in any other provision of this Act, regulations made by the Department of Health and Social Services;

"section 6 duty" means any duty imposed by or under section 6;

"section 15 duty" means any duty imposed by or under section 15;

"section 21 duty" means any duty imposed by or under section 21;

"taxi" and "regulated taxi" have the meaning given in section 32;

"taxi accessibility regulations" means regulations made under section 32(1);

"trade" includes any business;

"trade organisation" has the meaning given in section 13;

"vehicle examiner" means an officer of the Department of the Environment authorised by that Department for the purposes of sections 41 and 42.'.

[(2) In section 68—

(a) for subsection (2) substitute—

'(2) Where an employee does his work wholly outside Northern Ireland, his employment is not to be treated as being work at an establishment in Northern Ireland.'; and

(b) in subsections (3) and (4) for 'Great Britain' wherever it occurs substitute 'Northern Ireland'.][207]

48.—(1) In section 70(3) for 'Secretary of State' substitute 'Department of Health and Social Services'.

---

[207] Amended by the Equal Opportunities (Employment Legislation) (Territorial Limits) Regulations (Northern Ireland) 2000, SR 2000/8.

(2) In section 70(8) for 'the Secretary of State' substitute 'a Northern Ireland department' and for 'him' substitute 'it'.

49.—(1) In Schedule 1 in paragraph 7(1) for 'Act 1944' substitute 'Act (Northern Ireland) 1945'.

(2) In Schedule 1 in paragraph 7(7) for '1944' substitute '1945'.

50.—(1) . . .[208]

(2) In Schedule 3 for paragraph 4(1) substitute—

'(1) In any proceedings under section 8—

(a) a certificate signed by or on behalf of a Minister of the Crown or a Northern Ireland department and certifying that any conditions or requirements specified in the certificate were imposed by that Minister or that department (as the case may be) and were in operation at a time or throughout a time so specified; or

(b) a certificate signed by or on behalf of the Secretary of State and certifying that an act specified in the certificate was done for the purpose of safeguarding national security,

shall be conclusive evidence of the matters certified.'.

(3) In Schedule 3 in paragraph 6(1) omit 'or a sheriff court'.

(4) In Schedule 3 for paragraph 8(1) substitute—

'(1) In any proceedings under section 25—

(a) a certificate signed by or on behalf of a Minister of the Crown or a Northern Ireland department and certifying that any conditions or requirements specified in the certificate were imposed by that Minister or that department (as the case may be) and were in operation at a time or throughout a time so specified; or

(b) a certificate signed by or on behalf of the Secretary of State and certifying that an act specified in the certificate was done for the purpose of safeguarding national security,

shall be conclusive evidence of the matters certified.'.

51.—(1) In Schedule 4 in paragraphs 2(1) and (5) and 7(1) and (5) omit 'or sisted'.

(2) In Schedule 4 in paragraph 4 for 'Secretary of State' substitute 'Department of Economic Development'.

(3) In Schedule 4 in paragraph 6(1) omit 'or, in Scotland, to the sheriff'.

(4) In Schedule 4 omit paragraph 6(2).

(5) In Schedule 4 in paragraph 9 for 'Secretary of State' substitute 'Department of Health and Social Services'.

[52.—(1) Schedule 5, except paragraph 7(a) to (c), shall have no effect.

(2) In paragraph 7(a) to (c), for 'Secretary of State' wherever it occurs substitute 'Department of Health and Social Services.][209]

53. For Schedules 6 and 7 substitute—

'SCHEDULE 6
CONSEQUENTIAL AMENDMENTS

The Industrial Relations (Northern Ireland) Order 1976 (NI 16)

1. In Article 68(6) of the Industrial Relations (Northern Ireland) Order 1976 (reinstatement or re-engagement of dismissed employees—

---

[208] See n 196 above. [209] See n 197 above.

(a) in the definition of "relevant complaint of dismissal", omit "or" and at the end insert "or a complaint under section 8 of the Disability Discrimination Act 1995 arising out of a dismissal";

(b) in the definition of "relevant conciliation powers", omit "or" and at the end insert "or paragraph 1 of Schedule 3 to the Disability Discrimination Act 1995";

(c) in the definition of "relevant compromise contract" for "or Article" substitute "Article" and at the end insert "or section 9(2) of the Disability Discrimination Act 1995".

The Companies (Northern Ireland) Order 1986 (NI 6)

3. In paragraph 9 of Schedule 7 to the Companies (Northern Ireland) Order 1986 (disclosure in directors' report of company policy in relation to disabled persons) in the definition of "disabled person" in sub-paragraph (4)(b) for "Disabled Persons (Employment) Act (Northern Ireland) 1945" substitute "Disability Discrimination Act 1995".

SCHEDULE 7
REPEALS

Chapter	Short title	Extent of repeal
1945 c 6 (NI)	The Disabled Persons (Employment) Act (Northern Ireland) 1945	Sections 1 to 4
		Sections 6 to 14
		In section 16 the words 'vocational training and industrial rehabilitation courses and', the words 'courses and' and the words from 'and in selecting' to 'engagement'
		Section 19
		Section 21
		Section 22
1960 c 4 (NI)	The Disabled Persons (Employment) Act (Northern Ireland) 1960	The whole Act
1976 NI 16	The Industrial Relations (Northern Ireland) Order 1976	In Article 68(6) the word 'or' in the definitions of 'relevant complaint of dismissal' and 'relevant conciliation powers'.'

Extracts from the Disability Discrimination Act 1995 Codes of Practice

CODE OF PRACTICE ON EMPLOYMENT AND OCCUPATION[1]

2. How can discrimination be avoided?

Introduction

2.1. Prevention is better than cure. There are various actions which employers can take in order to avoid discriminating against disabled people. By doing so, employers are not only likely to minimise the incidence of expensive and time-consuming litigation, but will also improve their general performance and the quality of their business operations. This chapter sets out some guidance on ways to help ensure that disabled people are not discriminated against.

Understanding the social dimension of disability

2.2. The concept of discrimination in the Act reflects an understanding that functional limitations arising from disabled people's impairments do not inevitably restrict their ability to participate fully in society. Rather than the limitations of an impairment, it is often environmental factors (such as the structure of a building, or an employer's working practices) which unnecessarily lead to these social restrictions. This principle underpins the duty to make reasonable adjustments described in Chapter 5. Understanding this will assist employers and others to avoid discrimination. It is as important to consider which aspects of employment and occupation create difficulties for a disabled person as it is to understand the particular nature of an individual's disability.

Recognising the diverse nature of disability

2.3. There are around ten million disabled adults in our society. The nature and extent of their disabilities vary widely, as do their requirements for overcoming any difficulties they may face. If employers are to avoid discriminating, they need to understand this, and to be aware of the effects their decisions and actions—and those of their agents and employees—may have on disabled people. The evidence shows that many of the steps that can be taken to avoid discrimination cost little or nothing and are easy to implement.

---

[1] (2004) DRC ISBN 0 11 703419 3; Disability Discrimination Codes of Practice (Employment and Occupation, and Trade Organisations and Qualifications Bodies) Appointed Day Order 2004, SI 2004/2302.

Avoiding making assumptions

2.4.   It is advisable to avoid making assumptions about disabled people. Disabilities will often affect different people in different ways and their needs may be different as well. The following suggestions may help to avoid discrimination:

- Do not assume that because a person does not look disabled, he is not disabled.

- Do not assume that because you do not know of any disabled people working within an organisation there are none.

- Do not assume that most disabled people use wheelchairs.

- Do not assume that people with learning disabilities cannot be valuable employees, or that they can only do low status jobs.

- Do not assume that a person with a mental health problem cannot do a demanding job.

- Do not assume that all blind people read Braille or have guide dogs.

- Do not assume that all deaf people use sign language.

- Do not assume that because a disabled person may have less employment experience (in paid employment) than a non-disabled person, he has less to offer.

Finding out about disabled people's needs

2.5.   As explained later in the Code (see paragraphs 7.22 and 8.16 for example), the Act requires employers to think about ways of complying with their legal duties. Listening carefully to disabled people and finding out what they want will help employers to meet their obligations by identifying the best way of meeting disabled people's needs. There is a better chance of reaching the best outcome if discussions are held with disabled people at an early stage.

2.6.   Often, discussing with disabled people what is required to meet their needs will reassure an employer that suitable adjustments can be carried out cheaply and with very little inconvenience.

2.7.   Evidence shows that in meeting the needs of disabled employees an organisation learns how to meet the needs of disabled customers, and vice versa. By consulting with disabled employees, an organisation can therefore improve the service it provides to its disabled customers and enhance its business.

2.8.   There are various ways in which the views of disabled people can be obtained. Many larger employers have established formal structures for seeking and representing the views of disabled people. Small employers can also consult with disabled employees, although the methods may be less formal.

A large employer sets up a network through which disabled employees can discuss their concerns and make recommendations to management, either directly or via a recognised trade union.

A small employer asks a disabled employee if he has any concerns about how a reorganisation of the business will impact upon him.

Seeking expert advice

2.9.   It may be possible to avoid discrimination by using personal or in-house knowledge and expertise—particularly if information or views are obtained from the disabled person concerned. However, although the Act does not specifically require anyone to obtain expert advice about meeting the needs of disabled people with regard to employment, in practice it may sometimes be necessary to do so in order to comply with the principal duties set out in the Act. Expert advice might be especially useful if a person is newly disabled or if the effects of a person's disability become more marked. Expert advice about meeting the needs of disabled people may be available from local Jobcentre Plus offices, or from local and national disability organisations.

Planning ahead

2.10. The duties which the Act places on employers are owed to the individual disabled people with whom they have dealings. There is no duty owed to disabled people in general. Nevertheless, it is likely to be cost effective for employers to plan ahead. Considering the needs of a range of disabled people when planning for change (such as when planning a building refurbishment, a new IT system, or the design of a website) is likely to make it easier to implement adjustments for individuals when the need arises.

2.11. It is good practice for employers to have access audits carried out to identify any improvements which can be made to a building to make it more accessible. Access audits should be carried out by suitably qualified people, such as those listed in the National Register of Access Consultants (see Appendix C for details). Websites and intranet sites can also be reviewed to see how accessible they are to disabled people using access software.

The owner of a small shop is planning a refit of her premises. As part of the refit she asks the designers to comply with British Standard 8300 to ensure that the shop has a good standard of access for a variety of disabled people, whether customers or employees. BS 8300 is a code of practice on the design of buildings and their approaches to meet the needs of disabled people (see Appendix C for details).

An employer is re-designing its website, which it uses to promote the company as well as to advertise vacancies. The employer ensures that the new design for the website is easy to read for people with a variety of access software; has the website checked for accessibility; and invites disabled readers of the website to let the employer know if they find any part of it inaccessible.

Implementing anti-discriminatory policies and practices

2.12. Employers are more likely to comply with their duties under the Act, and to avoid the risk of legal action being taken against them, if they implement anti-discriminatory policies and practices. These are often referred to as equality policies or diversity policies. Additionally, in the event that legal action is taken, employers may be asked to demonstrate to an employment tribunal that they have effective policies and procedures in place to minimise the risk of discrimination. Although large and small employers are likely to have different kinds of anti-discriminatory policies and practices, it is advisable for all employers to take the following steps:

- Establish a policy which aims to prevent discrimination against disabled people and which is communicated to all employees and agents of the employer.
- Provide disability awareness and equality training to all employees. In addition, train employees and agents so that they understand the employer's policy on disability, their obligations under the Act and the practice of reasonable adjustments. People within the organisation who have responsibility for managing, recruiting or training employees are likely to need more specialist training.

- Inform all employees and agents that conduct which breaches the policy will not be tolerated, and respond quickly and effectively to any such breaches.
- Monitor the implementation and effectiveness of such a policy.
- Address acts of disability discrimination by employees as part of disciplinary rules and procedures.
- Have complaints and grievance procedures which are easy for disabled people to use and which are designed to resolve issues effectively.
- Have clear procedures to prevent and deal with harassment for a reason related to a person's disability.
- Establish a policy in relation to disability-related leave, and monitor the implementation and effectiveness of such a policy.
- Consult with disabled employees about their experiences of working for the organisation.
- Regularly review the effectiveness of reasonable adjustments made for disabled people in accordance with the Act, and act on the findings of those reviews.
- Keep clear records of decisions taken in respect of each of these matters.

When a large company introduces a new disability policy, it might ask an external training company to run training sessions for all staff, or it might ask a human resources manager to deliver training to staff on this policy. The external training company might be one run by disabled people.

A small employer introducing a similar policy asks the managing director to devote a team meeting to explaining the policy to her staff and to discuss why it is important and how it will operate.

A large employer trains all its employees in disability equality, the organisation's disability policy and the Disability Discrimination Act. It also trains all occupational health advisers with whom it works to ensure that they have the necessary expertise about the Act and the organisation's disability policy.

A small employer only uses occupational health advisers who can demonstrate that they have knowledge of the Act.

A large employer issues a questionnaire to employees about the organisation's attitude to disability, inviting suggestions for improvements.

A small employer asks disabled employees to feed back views on the employer's approach to disability issues.

Auditing policies and procedures

2.13. Although there is no duty under Part 2 to anticipate the needs of disabled people in general, it is a good idea for employers to keep all their policies under review, and to consider the needs of disabled people as part of this process. It is advisable for employers to do this in addition to having a specific policy to prevent discrimination. Employers are likely to have policies about matters such as:

- flexible working arrangements
- appraisal and performance-related pay systems
- sickness absence
- redundancy selection criteria

- emergency evacuation procedures
- procurement of equipment, IT systems, software and websites
- information provision
- employee training and development
- employee assistance schemes offering financial or emotional support.

An organisation has a policy to ensure that all employees are kept informed about the organisation's activities through an intranet site. The policy says that the intranet site should be accessible to all employees, including those who use access software (such as synthetic speech output) because of their disabilities.

An employer has a policy of having annual appraisal interviews for all employees. The policy says that during the interviews, disabled employees should be asked whether they need any (further) reasonable adjustments. This could equally apply to a large or small employer.

An employer introduces a system for performance-related pay. It takes advice on performance-related pay systems from an employers' organisation, to ensure that the system it introduces is an effective tool for improving performance and is fair to all employees. It also ensures that every year the system is monitored to ensure that disabled people do not, on average, get lower awards.

A redundancy policy that has sickness absence as a selection criterion is amended to exclude disability-related absence. The sickness absence policy is also changed so that disability-related sickness is recorded separately.

A new procurement policy requires a number of factors to be taken into account in procuring equipment and IT systems. These factors include cost and energy efficiency. It is good practice for such factors to include accessibility for disabled people as well.

Emergency evacuation policies and procedures are reviewed to ensure that there are individual evacuation plans for any disabled people who need them.

Monitoring

2.14. Monitoring of employees is an important way of determining whether anti-discrimination measures taken by an organisation are effective, and ensuring that disability equality is a reality within that organisation. Information must be gathered sensitively, with appropriately worded questions, and confidentiality must be ensured. Knowing the proportion of disabled people at various levels of the organisation, and at various stages in relation to the recruitment process, can help an organisation determine where practices and policies need to be improved. The extent to which formal monitoring can be carried out will depend on the size of the organisation.

2.15. Monitoring will be more effective if employees (or job applicants) feel comfortable about disclosing information about their disabilities. This is more likely to be the case if the employer explains the purpose of the monitoring and if employees or job applicants believe that the employer genuinely values disabled employees and is using the information gathered to create positive change.

Through monitoring of candidates at the recruitment stage an employer becomes aware that, although several disabled people applied for a post, none was short-listed for interview. It uses this information to review the essential requirements for the post.

2.16. Some organisations, especially large ones, choose to monitor by broad type of disability to understand the barriers faced by people with different types of impairment.

A large employer notices through monitoring that the organisation has been successful at retaining most groups of disabled people, but not people with mental health problems. It acts on this information by contacting a specialist organisation for advice about good practice in retaining people with mental health problems.

Ensuring good practice in recruitment

Attracting disabled applicants

2.17. An organisation which recognises that suitably qualified disabled people have not applied to work for it may want to make contact with local employment services, including Jobcentre Plus and specialist disability employment services, to encourage disabled people to apply. It is normally lawful for an employer to advertise a vacancy as open only to disabled people (see paragraph 7.5).

By monitoring the recruitment process a small employer notices that very few disabled people apply to work for it. In the light of this information, it decides to notify local disability employment projects of its vacancies.

A retailer has a number of vacancies to fill. It contacts Jobcentre Plus and arranges an open morning for local disabled people to find out more about working for this employer.

Through its monitoring process, a medium-sized employer becomes aware of the fact that disabled people are under-represented in its workforce. It is looking for people to fill 3 work experience placements and decides to offer these placements to disabled people only.

A museum wants to understand the needs of its disabled visitors better. It decides to change its person specifications for posts in the visitor services department to include a requirement to have knowledge of disability access issues. It notifies local employment services for disabled people of these posts.

2.18. It is good practice to consider carefully what information should be included in advertisements and where they should be placed.

An advertisement which specifies that flexible working is available may encourage more disabled applicants to apply.

An advertisement that appears in the disability press and a local talking newspaper may encourage disabled applicants to apply.

Promoting a positive image

2.19. It is good practice for an employer to consider its image to ensure that it gives an impression of itself as an organisation that is aware of the needs of disabled people and is striving to create a more diverse workforce.

A large employer ensures that its recruitment brochure includes images of disabled employees, and contains information about its disability policy.

A small employer advertises in a local newspaper. The advertisement states that disabled people are encouraged to apply.

Use of the Disability Symbol

2.20. The Disability Symbol is a recognition given to employers by Jobcentre Plus. An employer displaying the Disability Symbol must commit itself to a number of measures concerning the recruitment, development and retention of disabled people, including offering a guaranteed interview to any disabled person who meets the essential requirements of the job. It is important that employers make clear what those essential requirements are. For more information about the Disability Symbol see Appendix C.

Resolving disputes

2.21. Having policies and practices to combat discrimination, together with regular consultation with employees, is likely to minimise disputes about disability discrimination. But when such disputes do occur, it is in the interests of employers to attempt wherever possible to resolve them as they arise. Grievance procedures can provide an open and fair way for employees to make their concerns known, and can enable grievances to be resolved quickly before they become major problems. Use of the procedures may highlight areas in which the duty to make reasonable adjustments has not been observed, and can prevent misunderstandings leading to complaints to tribunals. It is important to ensure that grievance procedures are accessible to disabled people.

2.22. In certain circumstances, employers and employees are required by law to comply with internal dispute resolution procedures before making a complaint to a tribunal. Chapter 13 contains further information about grievance procedures and about resolving disputes under the Act. Whether or not an attempt at internal resolution of a dispute is made as a result of a legal requirement, it should be carried out in a non-discriminatory way to comply with the Act.

. . .

Appendix A: Changes to the Act

The table below summarises the main changes to the Act's provisions on employment and occupation taking effect on 1 October 2004. It does not include all the changes occurring on that date, and is not a full explanation of the law.

	Position before 1 October 2004	**Position after 1 October 2004**
Scope	• DDA covered employers with 15 or more employees. • Some occupations (e.g. police & firefighters) were not covered	• All employers are covered by the DDA except for the Armed Forces. • New occupations such as police and partners in firms are covered. • Practical work experience, whether paid or unpaid, is covered. • There are new provisions on discriminatory advertisements. • Employment services are covered.
Types of discrimination	*Three kinds of discrimination:* • Less favourable treatment. • Failure to make reasonable adjustments. • Victimisation.	*Four kinds of discrimination:* • Direct discrimination. • Failure to make reasonable adjustments. • 'Disability-related discrimination'. • Victimisation.

	Position before 1 October 2004	Position after 1 October 2004
When is justification relevant?	*Justification was of relevance in cases about:* • Less favourable treatment. • Failure to make reasonable adjustments.	*Justification is NOT relevant in cases about:* • Direct discrimination. • Failure to make reasonable adjustments. *Justification is relevant in cases about:* • Disability-related discrimination.
Harassment	Covered, but no separate provisions on this.	New provisions on harassment.
Claims	Most claims covered by the Code were brought in the employment tribunal apart from those involving trustees and managers of occupational pension schemes and claims about employment services.	All claims covered by this Code are brought in the employment tribunal.

. . .

CODE OF PRACTICE ON TRADE ORGANISATIONS AND QUALIFICATIONS BODIES[2]

Who has obligations under the Act?

Trade organisations

3.8. **[s 13(4)]** The Act defines a trade organisation as an organisation of workers or of employers, or any other organisation whose members carry on a particular profession or trade for the purposes of which the organisation exists. Bodies like trade unions, employers' associations, chartered professional institutions are all trade organisations because they exist for the purposes of the profession or trade which their members carry on. Examples of trade organisations include the Law Society, the Royal College of Nursing, the Swimming Teachers' Association, the Society of Floristry, the British Computer Society, and the Institute of Carpenters. The Act applies to all trade organisations, no matter how many (or how few) members they may have.

Qualifications bodies

3.9. **[s 14A(5)]** The Act defines a qualifications body as an authority or body which can confer, renew or extend a professional or trade qualification. For this purpose a professional or trade qualification is an authorisation, qualification, recognition, registration, enrolment, approval or certification which is needed for, or which facilitates engagement in, a particular profession or trade. What this means in practice is considered in paragraphs

---

[2] (2004) DRC ISBN 0 11 703418 5; Disability Discrimination Codes of Practice (Employment and Occupation, and Trade Organisations and Qualifications Bodies) Appointed Day Order 2004, SI 2004/2302.

8.5 to 8.7. Qualifications bodies include examination boards, the General Medical Council, the Nursing and Midwifery Council, and the Driving Standards Agency. Other examples are City and Guilds, the Institute of the Motor Industry, the Hospitality Awarding Body and the Guild of Cleaners and Launderers.

3.10. **[s 14A(5)]** Nevertheless, certain bodies are not regarded as qualifications bodies for the purposes of Part 2, even though they may perform some of the functions mentioned in paragraph 3.9. These are listed in the Act. Broadly speaking, they comprise local education authorities in England and Wales, education authorities in Scotland, and other bodies having responsibility for schools and colleges. This is because discrimination by such bodies is the concern of Part 4 of the Act, which relates to discrimination in the provision of education. The DRC has issued two separate codes of practice giving guidance on the operation of Part 4 (see Appendix C for details).

3.11. Clearly, certain trade organisations (such as the Law Society) also confer professional or trade qualifications. Consequently, the same organisation or body can be both a trade organisation and a qualifications body. Where this is the case, the application of the Act's provisions depends upon the capacity in which the organisation or body is acting at the time in question. For example, if an alleged act of discrimination relates to conferring, renewing or extending a professional or trade qualification, the relevant provisions are those relating to discrimination by qualifications bodies—the fact that the body is also a trade organisation is irrelevant in this context.

. . .

CODE OF PRACTICE ON 'RIGHTS OF ACCESS, GOODS, FACILITIES, SERVICES AND PREMISES'[3]

5. Reasonable adjustments in practice

Introduction

5.1. In **Chapter 4** the Code outlines the concept of the duty to make reasonable adjustments and provides an overview of the legal principles which underpin it. In this chapter the Code explains and illustrates how the duty works in practice.

5.2. As explained in **Chapter 4**, the duty to make reasonable adjustments comprises a series of duties falling into three main areas:

• changing practices, policies and procedures;
• providing auxiliary aids and services;
• overcoming a physical feature by
 —removing the feature; or
 —altering it; or
 —providing a reasonable means of avoiding it; or
 —providing the service by a reasonable alternative method.

A physical feature includes, for example, a feature arising from the design or construction of a building or the approach or access to premises (and see paragraph 5.44 below).

5.3. These duties are being introduced in two stages.
Since 1 October 1999 the duties in respect of:

• changing practices, policies and procedures;
• providing auxiliary aids and services;

---

[3] Disability Discrimination Code of Practice (Goods, Facilities, Services and Premises) (Appointed Day) Order 2002, SI 2002/720. ISBN 0 11 702860 6.

- overcoming a physical feature by providing services by reasonable alternative methods,

have been in force.

From 1 October 2004 the duties in respect of:

- overcoming a physical feature by
- removing the feature; or
- altering it; or
- providing a reasonable means of avoiding it

will also apply.

This chapter considers each in turn.

Practices, policies and procedures

What is the duty to change a practice, policy or procedure?

5.4.   When a service provider is providing services to its customers, it will have established a particular way of doing this. Its practices (including policies and procedures) may be set out formally or may have become established informally or by custom. A service provider might have a practice which—perhaps unintentionally—makes it impossible or unreasonably difficult for disabled people to make use of its services.

s 21(1)

5.5.   In such a case, the service provider must take such steps as it is reasonable for it to have to take, in all the circumstances, to change the practice so that it no longer has that effect. This may simply mean instructing staff to waive a practice or amending a policy to allow exceptions or abandoning it altogether. Often, such a change involves little more than an extension of the courtesies which most service providers already show to their customers.

A restaurant has a policy of refusing entry to male diners who do not wear a collar and tie. A disabled man who wishes to dine in the restaurant is unable to wear a tie because he has psoriasis (a severe skin complaint) of the face and neck. Unless the restaurant is prepared to waive its policy, its effect is to exclude the disabled customer from the restaurant. This is likely to be unlawful.

A video rental shop allows only people who can provide a driving licence as proof of their identity to become members. This automatically excludes some disabled people from joining because the nature of their disabilities prevents them from obtaining a driving licence (for example blind people or some people with epilepsy or mental health problems). The shop would be required to take reasonable steps to change this practice. It does so by being prepared to accept alternative forms of identification from its customers. This is likely to be a reasonable step for the shop to have to take.

What are practices, policies and procedures?

5.6.   Practices, policies and procedures relate to the way in which a service provider operates its business or provides its services. This includes any requirements that it makes of its customers. In principle, the terms cover:

- what a service provider actually does (its **practice**);
- what a service provider intends to do (its **policy**);
- how a service provider plans to go about it (its **procedure**).

However, the three terms overlap and it is not always sensible to treat them as separate concepts.

A DIY superstore has a policy of not allowing dogs onto its premises. Members of staff are instructed to prevent anyone with a dog from entering the superstore. The 'no dogs' policy is enforced in practice by this procedure. The policy makes it unreasonably difficult for disabled people accompanied by a guide or assistance dog to use the DIY superstore. The superstore has a duty to take such steps as are reasonable for it to have to take to avoid that effect and to make its services accessible to disabled people. It decides to amend its 'no dogs' policy by allowing an exception for disabled people accompanied by a guide or assistance dog. This is likely to be a reasonable step for the superstore to have to take.

What are 'reasonable steps' in relation to practices, policies and procedures?

5.7. The Act does not define what are 'reasonable steps' for a service provider to have to take in order to change its practices. The kinds of factors which may be relevant are described in paragraphs 4.21 to 4.27 above.

5.8. The purpose of taking the steps is to ensure that the practice no longer has the effect of making it impossible or unreasonably difficult for disabled people to use a service. Where there is an adjustment that the service provider could reasonably put in place and which would make the service accessible, it is not sufficient for the service provider to take some lesser step which would not result in the service being accessible.

A medium-sized supermarket installs one extra-wide check-out lane intending it to be available to customers who are wheelchair users or accompanied by infants. However, that check-out lane is also designated as an express lane available only to shoppers with 10 or less items. The effect of this practice is to exclude wheelchair-users from taking advantage of the accessible check-out unless they are making only a few purchases. It is likely to be a reasonable step for the supermarket to have to take to amend its practice by designating another check-out lane as the express lane.

5.9. A practice may have the effect of excluding or screening out disabled people from enjoying access to services. Or the practice may create a barrier or hurdle which makes it unreasonably difficult for disabled people to access the services. In such cases, unless the practice can be justified, a reasonable step for a service provider to have to take might be to abandon it entirely or to amend or modify it so that it no longer has that effect.

A town hall has procedures for the evacuation of the building in the event of a fire or emergency. Visitors are required to leave the building by designated routes. The emergency procedures are part of the way in which the town hall provides services to its visitors. It modifies the procedures (with the agreement of the local fire authority) to allow visitors with mobility impairments or sensory disabilities to be evacuated safely. This is likely to be a reasonable step for the town hall to have to take.

A hotel refurbishes a number of rooms on each floor which are fully accessible to disabled guests. However, the hotel's reservations system allocates rooms on a first come, first served basis as guests arrive and register. The effect is that on some occasions the specially refurbished rooms are allocated to non- disabled guests and late-arriving disabled guests cannot be accommodated in those rooms. The hotel decides to change its reservation policy so that the accessible rooms are either reserved for disabled guests in advance or are allocated last of all. This is likely to be a reasonable step for the hotel to have to take.

Auxiliary aids and services

What is the duty to provide auxiliary aids or services?

s 21(4)

5.10. A service provider must take reasonable steps to provide auxiliary aids or services if this would enable (or make it easier for) disabled people to make use of any services which it offers to the public.

What is an auxiliary aid or service?

s 21(4)

5.11. The Act gives two examples of auxiliary aids or services: the provision of information on audio tape and the provision of a sign language interpreter.

A building society provides information on an audio tape about its savings accounts. A customer with a visual impairment can use the audio tape at home or in a branch to decide whether to open an account. This is an auxiliary aid.

A department store has a member of staff able to communicate with deaf clients who use British Sign Language. This is an auxiliary service.

5.12. But these are only illustrations of the kinds of auxiliary aids or services which a service provider might need to consider. An auxiliary aid or service might be the provision of a special piece of equipment or simply extra assistance to disabled people from (perhaps specially trained) staff. In some cases a technological solution might be available.

A large supermarket provides specially designed shopping baskets and trolleys which can be easily used by disabled shoppers in a wheelchair or with reduced mobility. It also provides electronic hand-held bar code readers with synthesised voice output which helps customers with a visual impairment to identify goods and prices. These are auxiliary aids which enable disabled shoppers to use the supermarket's services.

Disabled customers with a visual impairment or a learning disability may need assistance in a large supermarket to locate items on their shopping list. The supermarket instructs one of its employees to find the items for them. The supermarket is providing an auxiliary service which makes its goods accessible.

A petrol station decides that an assistant will help disabled people use the petrol pumps on request. It places a prominent notice at the pumps advertising this. This is an auxiliary service.

5.13. In any event, service providers should ensure that any auxiliary aids they provide are carefully chosen and properly maintained.

A person with a hearing impairment is attending a performance at a theatre. When booking the tickets he is told that the theatre auditorium has an induction loop. However, the theatre does not check that the loop is working and on the day of the performance the system is not working properly. Although the theatre has provided an auxiliary aid, its failure to check that the loop is working properly means that the theatre is unlikely to have taken reasonable steps to enable disabled people to make use of its services.

5.14. What is an appropriate auxiliary aid or service will vary according to the type of service provider, the nature of the services being provided, and the requirements of the disabled customers or potential customers. Auxiliary aids and services are not limited to aids to communication.

A community centre is accessible by two raised steps. It provides a suitably chosen portable ramp which helps disabled people with a mobility impairment to enter the premises safely. This is an auxiliary aid which is suited to the requirements of those people.

A new cinema complex has deep airline-style seats. A disabled patron with restricted growth finds it difficult to see the screen when using such a seat. The cinema provides a bolster cushion on request which enables him to enjoy the film. This is an auxiliary aid appropriate to the circumstances.

A museum provides a written guide to its exhibits. It wants to make the exhibits accessible to visitors with learning disabilities. The museum produces a version of the guide which uses plain language, text and pictures to explain the exhibits. This is an auxiliary aid suited to visitors with learning disabilities and may also benefit other people.

s 21(4)
SI 1999/1191
reg 4

5.15. From 1 October 2004 auxiliary aids and services could be any kind of aid or service (whether temporary or permanent). Until 1 October 2004 the Disability Discrimination (Services and Premises) Regulations 1999 temporarily restrict their meaning so as not to require the provision of auxiliary aids or services which involve a permanent alteration to the physical fabric of premises (or fixtures, fittings, furnishings, furniture, equipment or materials). There is nothing in the Act, however, to prevent such provision in anticipation of 1 October 2004 and service providers should take note of paragraphs 5.33 to 5.35 below.

5.16. Nothing in the Act requires a service provider to provide an auxiliary aid or service to be used for personal purposes unconnected to the services being provided or to be taken away by the disabled person after use.

A solicitors' firm lends an audio tape recorder to a client with multiple disabilities who is unable to communicate in writing or to attend the firm's office. The client uses this auxiliary aid in order to record his instructions or witness statement. The client would be expected to return the recorder after use.

What are 'reasonable steps' in relation to auxiliary aids or services?

5.17. The duty to provide auxiliary aids or services requires the service provider to take such steps as it is reasonable for it to have to take in all the circumstances of the case to make its services accessible to disabled people. What might be reasonable for a large service provider (or one with substantial resources) might not be reasonable for a smaller service provider. The size of the service provider, the resources available to it and the cost of the auxiliary service are relevant factors.

A large national museum has hourly guided tours of a popular major exhibition. It provides a radio microphone system for hearing aid users to accompany the tour and on one day a week has a BSL interpreter available. The museum advertises this service and encourages BSL users to book space with the interpreter on the tours on that day. These are likely to be reasonable steps for the museum to have to take.

A small, private museum with limited resources provides a daily guided tour of its exhibits. It investigates the provision of equipment for hearing aid users such as an induction loop in the main gallery or a radio microphone system to accompany the tour, but, after careful consideration, it rejects both options as too expensive and impracticable. Instead, with little effort or cost, the museum decides to provide good quality audio taped guides (with an option of plug-in neck loops) which can be used by people with hearing aids who want to follow the guided tour. This is likely to be a reasonable step for the museum to have to take.

5.18. The reasonableness of the service provider's response to disabled people's requirements will inevitably vary with the circumstances. The kinds of factors which may be relevant are described in paragraphs 4.21 to 4.27 above.

A hospital physiotherapist has a new patient who uses BSL as his main means of communication. The hospital arranges for a qualified BSL interpreter to be present at the initial assessment, which requires a good level of communication on both sides. At this initial assessment the physiotherapist and the disabled patient also discuss what other forms of communication services or aids would be suitable. They agree that for major assessments a BSL interpreter will be used but that at routine treatment appointments they will communicate with a notepad and pen. This is because these appointments do not require the same level or intensity of communication. This is likely to be a reasonable step for the hospital to have to take.

5.19. For a deaf person who uses British Sign Language as his or her main form of communication, having a qualified BSL interpreter is the most effective method of communication. This is because for people whose first language is BSL (rather than spoken or written English) exchange of written notes or lipreading can be an uncertain means of communication.

British Sign Language Interpretation may not be easily available and should be arranged in advance wherever possible. If an interpreter is not available, the service provider should consider an alternative method of communication, in consultation with the deaf person.

5.20. A service provider will have to consider what steps it can reasonably take to meet the individual requirements of disabled people. How effectively the service provider is able to do so will depend largely on how far it has anticipated the requirements of its disabled customers. Many things that seem impossible at the time they are confronted might have been accommodated relatively easily if prior thought had been given to the question.

5.21. The Act leaves open what particular auxiliary aids or services might be provided in specific circumstances. Disabled people may be able to help the service provider to identify difficulties in accessing the service and what kind of auxiliary aid or service will overcome them. It is good practice to include disabled customers in the process of considering what reasonable adjustments should be made. However the duty remains on the service provider to determine what steps it needs to take.

Using auxiliary aids or services to improve communication

5.22. In many cases, a service provider will need to consider providing auxiliary aids or services to improve communication with people with a sensory impairment (such as those affecting hearing or sight) or a speech impairment or learning disabilities. The type of auxiliary aid or service will vary according to the importance, length, complexity or frequency of the communication involved. In some cases, more than one type of auxiliary aid or service might be appropriate, as different people have different communication requirements. Account should also be taken of people with multiple communication disabilities, such as deaf-blindness or combined speech and hearing disabilities.

A cinema offers patrons a telephone booking service. Its booking office installs a text-phone and trains its staff to use it. This offers access to deaf patrons and is likely to be a reasonable step for the cinema to have to take.

The booking office of a small heritage railway decides to communicate with passengers who have speech or hearing impairments by exchanging written notes. This is likely to be a reasonable step for this service provider to have to take.

However, it is unlikely to be a sufficient reasonable adjustment for the booking office at a mainline rail terminus to make for such passengers. Instead, it installs an induction loop system and a textphone. These are likely to be reasonable steps for a large station to have to take.

Provision for people with a hearing disability

5.23. For people with hearing disabilities, the range of auxiliary aids or services which it might be reasonable to provide to ensure that services are accessible might include one or more of the following:

- written information (such as a leaflet or guide);
- (a facility for taking and exchanging written notes;
- (a verbatim speech-to-text transcription service;
- (induction loop systems;
- (subtitles;
- (videos with BSL interpretation;
- (information displayed on a computer screen;
- (accessible websites;
- (textphones, telephone amplifiers and inductive couplers;
- (teletext displays;
- (audio-visual telephones;
- (audio-visual fire alarms;
- (qualified BSL interpreters or lipspeakers.

A deaf defendant (or defender) in court proceedings uses BSL as his main form of communication. The court arranges for a qualified BSL interpreter to interpret and voice over his evidence in court. This is likely to be a reasonable step for the court to have to take.

A hearing impaired person who lipreads as her main form of communication wants a secured loan from a bank. In the initial stages it might be reasonable for the bank to communicate with her by providing printed literature or information displayed on a computer screen. However, before a secured loan agreement is signed, this particular bank usually provides a borrower with an oral explanation of its contents. At that stage it is likely to be reasonable, with the customer's consent, for the bank to arrange for a qualified lipspeaker to be present so that any complex aspects of the agreement can be fully explained and communicated.

A television broadcasting company provides teletext sub-titles to some of its programmes. This allows viewers with a hearing impairment to follow the programmes more easily. This is likely to be a reasonable step for the broadcasting company to have to take.

5.24. Where sign language interpretation is used as an auxiliary service the interpreter should be capable of communicating accurately and efficiently with both the disabled person and the other parties involved. Other interpretation services such as lipspeakers and Makaton communicators should similarly be capable of communicating accurately and effectively.

5.25. Service providers should bear in mind that hearing impairments take many forms and are of varying degrees. What might be a reasonable auxiliary aid or service for a person with tinnitus or reduced hearing might not be a reasonable adjustment for someone who is profoundly deaf.

A bus station fits an induction loop system at its booking office. This ensures that customers who have reduced hearing and use hearing aids are able to communicate effectively with the booking office. However, this does not help profoundly deaf customers. The bus company instructs its staff to take time to communicate by using a pen and notepad to discover what the customer wants and to give information. The staff are also trained to speak looking directly at the customer to allow those customers who can lipread to do so. These are likely to be reasonable steps for the bus station to have to take.

Provision for people with a visual impairment

5.26. For people with visual impairments, the range of auxiliary aids or services which it might be reasonable to provide to ensure that services are accessible might include one or more of the following:

- (readers;
- (documents in large or clear print, Moon or braille;
- (information on computer disk or e-mail;
- (information on audiotape;
- (telephone services to supplement other information;
- (spoken announcements or verbal communication;
- (accessible websites;
- (assistance with guiding;
- (audiodescription services;
- (large print or tactile maps/plans and three-dimensional models;
- (touch facilities (for example, interactive exhibits in a museum or gallery).

A restaurant changes its menus daily. For that reason it considers it is not practicable to provide menus in alternative formats, such as braille. However, its staff spend a little time reading out the menu for blind customers and the restaurant ensures that there is a large print copy available. These are likely to be reasonable steps for the restaurant to have to take.

A utility company supplying gas and electricity to domestic customers sends out quarterly bills. On request, the company is willing to provide the bills in alternative formats such as braille or large print for customers with visual impairments. This is likely to be a reasonable step for the utility company to have to take.

Every year a local council sends out information to local residents about new council tax rates. Because the information is important, the council provides copies in large print. On request, it is also prepared to supply the information in alternative media such as braille or audiotape or to explain the new rates to individual residents with visual impairments. These are likely to be reasonable steps for the council to have to take.

A customer with a visual impairment wishes to buy a compact disc player from a small specialist hi-fi shop. The shop arranges for a member of staff to assist the customer by reading out product details, packaging information or prices. This is likely to be a reasonable step for the shop to have to take.

5.27. As with other forms of sensory impairments, visual disabilities are of varying kinds and degrees. Service providers need to consider what is the most appropriate auxiliary aid or service to provide. More than one auxiliary aid or service may be necessary according to the circumstances.

A small estate agent is reviewing the accessibility of its sales literature for clients who are partially sighted or blind. Because of the nature of the service it provides and the size of its business, the estate agent concludes that it is not practicable to make particulars of houses for sale available in braille. However, the estate agent decides to change the print size and redesign the appearance of its written sales particulars. This makes the estate agent's sales information more accessible to its partially sighted clients, but does not assist those who are blind. It therefore also decides to put the information on audio tape on request. These are likely to be reasonable steps for the estate agent to have to take.

A housing benefit office ensures that claim forms and information literature are available in large print for partially sighted claimants. It also arranges for the forms and literature to be provided in braille or audiotape on request. These are likely to be reasonable steps for the housing benefit office to have to take.

Provision for people with other disabilities or multiple disabilities

5.28. There are many examples of how auxiliary aids or services can be used to improve communication with people who have hearing disabilities or visual impairments. Service providers should also consider how communication barriers can be overcome for people with other disabilities. For example, a customer with a learning disability may be able to access a service by the provision of documents in large, clear print and plain language or by the use of colour coding and illustrations.

A coach company issues its staff at a ticket office with a card showing destinations, types of tickets and prices. It trains the staff so that customers with learning disabilities can point to or ask for the options on the card that they want. These are likely to be reasonable steps for the coach company to have to take.

5.29. Service providers should not assume that their services are made accessible to customers with multiple disabilities simply by providing auxiliary aids or services which are suitable for people with individual disabilities.

5.30. For example, deafblind people (individuals who have a severe combined sight and hearing impairment) are not necessarily assisted in accessing services by the simple provision of communication aids designed for use by people with hearing disabilities or visual impairments. Such aids could assist deafblind people if appropriately used (for example, information leaflets produced in braille or Moon, good lighting and acoustics, induction loop systems, etc). However, what is appropriate will depend on the nature and extent of the individual's dual sensory impairment and the methods he or she uses to communicate and access information. Adjustments which may be of assistance to a deafblind person might include engaging a deafblind manual interpreter for important meetings or having a member of staff trained in specific ways to help a deafblind person. Where service providers give their staff disability awareness training, they should consider including ways of helping deafblind people, such as guiding them safely and tracing capital letters and numbers on the palm of the hand.

A branch of a bank with a regular customer who is deafblind has a particular staff member trained in communicating with deafblind people. At the customer's request, the bank arranges for statements and letters to be sent in braille. These are likely to be reasonable steps for the bank to have to take.

Overcoming barriers created by physical features

What is the duty to make reasonable adjustments in relation to physical features?

s 21(2)

5.31. Where a 'physical feature' makes it impossible or unreasonably difficult for disabled people to make use of any service which is offered to the public, a service provider must take reasonable steps to:

- remove the feature; or
- alter it so that it no longer has that effect; or
- provide a reasonable means of avoiding the feature; or
- provide a reasonable alternative method of making the service available to disabled people.

The meaning of a 'physical feature' is explained in paragraph 5.44 below and includes, for example, a feature arising from the design or construction of a building or the approach or access to premises.

5.32. The duty to make reasonable adjustments in relation to a physical feature sets out four possible ways in which the barriers created by such features might be overcome. The fourth duty (to provide a reasonable alternative method of making the service available (has been in force since 1 October 1999. The other duties come into force on 1 October 2004.

5.33. Whilst service providers are not obliged to comply with these latter duties—to remove, alter or provide a reasonable means of avoiding a physical feature—prior to 1 October 2004, the Code of Practice has been issued in advance of this date to give service providers an opportunity to consider the adjustments that they need to make under these provisions. The period between the issue of this Code and 1 October 2004 is intended to be a 'transitional' period during which service providers can prepare for their new obligations. It will be good practice and may make business sense to take action to remove or alter a physical feature or to provide a reasonable means of avoiding it before October 2004 and there is nothing to prevent a service provider from doing so.

5.34. In considering whether or not a service provider has taken reasonable steps to comply with its duties after 1 October 2004, a court might take into account the time that the service provider has had prior to that date to make preparations.

A public inquiry point is located on the second floor of a government office building and is accessed by a flight of stairs. This makes it impossible or unreasonably difficult for some disabled people to get to it. People with a mobility disability or a mental health disability (like anxiety related depression) may find using the stairs difficult.

Since 1 October 1999 the government department has had to consider what it could do to provide a reasonable alternative method of making its inquiry service accessible to disabled members of the public. For example, it might provide the service in the form of a telephone inquiry line. This may be a reasonable alternative method of providing the service if it effectively delivers the service in another way.

However, if it does not do so (for instance, if staff at the inquiry point also help people to complete forms and that cannot be done by telephone), the provision of a telephone service may not be a reasonable alternative. The department will then have to consider whether there are other reasonable steps it can take to provide the same service. For example, it might provide a courtesy telephone on the ground floor to enable disabled people to call staff down to help them.

Despite this, if the service is still not accessible to all disabled people, from 1 October 2004 further reasonable steps may involve a physical alteration of some kind. For example, it might be reasonable to install a lift or to move the inquiry point to the ground floor. Although there is no requirement to make physical alterations before 1 October 2004, it may be sensible to consider and give effect to such possibilities before then, especially if refurbishment of the building is being planned.

5.35. It would be sensible for service providers to plan ahead and to apply for any necessary consents before 1 October 2004 so they are able to make any physical alterations. Whenever a service provider is planning and executing building or refurbishment works, such as extending existing premises or making structural alterations to an existing building, it is sensible to provide for the removal or alteration of physical features which create a barrier to access for disabled people or to consider providing a reasonable means of avoiding the physical feature. Even though the Act does not require this until 1 October 2004, it might be more cost effective to make these alterations as part of planned refurbishment before 2004.

A public launderette is planning to install new washing machines and tumble dryers in 2002. In doing so, it chooses the machines and their positioning so as to facilitate their use by disabled customers. This has the effect of improving the accessibility of the launderette to disabled people.

A firm of accountants is refurbishing its offices in 2001. In replacing the carpets, the firm ensures that low pile, high density carpeting is fitted. This helps many of its clients with mobility impairments (for example, those who use a wheelchair, artificial limb or walking aid) to move with greater ease within the office. The firm also decides to make improvements to the office lighting and signage. This aids its clients with visual, hearing or learning disabilities. As part of the refurbishment, the firm also fits braille markings to lift buttons and installs an induction loop system in one of its meeting rooms. By these means, the firm has placed itself in a good position to provide accessible services to its disabled clients.

What are a service provider's obligations in respect of physical features?

s 19(1)(b), s 21(2)

5.36. The Act does not require a service provider to adopt one way of meeting its obligations rather than another. The focus of the Act is on results. Where there is a physical barrier, the service provider's aim should be to make its services accessible to disabled people. What is important is that this aim is achieved, rather than how it is achieved. If a service remains inaccessible, a service provider may have to defend its decisions.

5.37. For example, a service provider may decide to provide a service by the option of an alternative method. If the result is that disabled people are then able to access the service without unreasonable difficulty, that will satisfy the service provider's obligations under the Act. If, on the other hand, it is still unreasonably difficult for a disabled person to make use of the service, the service provider would then have to show that it could not have reasonably removed or altered the physical feature, or provided a reasonable means of avoiding it. The cost of taking such action may be a relevant consideration. Similarly, if the service provider takes no action, it will have to show that there were no steps which it could reasonably have taken. The kinds of factors which may be relevant in deciding what are reasonable steps for a service provider to have to take are described in paragraphs 4.21 to 4.27 above.

An estate agent is marketing a new residential property development. It decides to hold detailed presentations for prospective buyers at the company's premises, at which there will be a talk illustrated with slides. However, the only meeting room available in the building is inaccessible to many disabled people. The estate agent obtains a quotation to make its premises more accessible, but the cost is more than it anticipated, and it delays making the alterations.

When disabled people who are unable to attend a presentation because the room is inaccessible to them make enquiries, they are merely sent copies of comparatively brief promotional literature. This is unlikely to be a reasonable alternative method of making the service available.

If an issue arose under the Act as to whether the estate agent had failed to comply with its obligations to disabled people who are unable to make use of its service, regard might be had to the reasonableness of making the service available by any of the four different ways set out in the Act for complying with the duty to make reasonable adjustments in relation to barriers created by physical features. In this case, this would involve consideration of whether it would have been reasonable to avoid the feature, such as by holding the meeting at another venue, whether there was a more effective alternative method of providing the service that could reasonably have been adopted, or whether the cost the company would have incurred in altering its premises was such that this would have been a reasonable step for it to have to take.

Adopting an 'inclusive' approach

5.38. It is in the interests of both service providers and disabled people to overcome physical features that prevent or limit disabled people from using the services that are offered. Although the Act does not place the different options for overcoming a physical feature in any form of hierarchy, it is recognised good practice for a service provider to consider first whether a physical feature which creates a barrier for disabled people can be removed or altered.

5.39. This is because removing or altering the barriers created by a physical feature is an 'inclusive' approach to adjustments. It makes the services available to everyone in the same way. In contrast, an alternative method of service offers disabled people a different form of service than is provided for non-disabled people.

5.40. Removing or altering the barriers created by a physical feature will also be preferable to any alternative arrangements from the standpoint of the dignity of disabled people. In addition, it is likely to be in the long-term interests of the service provider, since it will avoid the ongoing costs of providing services by alternative means and may expand the customer base.

5.41. Therefore, it is recommended that service providers should first consider whether any physical features which create a barrier for disabled people can be removed or altered. If that is not reasonable, a service provider should then consider providing a reasonable means of avoiding the physical feature. If that is also not reasonable, the service provider should then consider providing a reasonable alternative method of making the service available to disabled people.

How can service providers identify possible adjustments?

5.42. Service providers are more likely to be able to comply with their duty to make adjustments in relation to physical features if they arrange for an access audit of their premises to be conducted and draw up an access plan or strategy. Acting on the results of such an evaluation may reduce the likelihood of legal claims against the service provider.

5.43. In carrying out an audit, it is recommended that service providers seek the views of people with different disabilities, or those representing them, to assist in identifying barriers and developing effective solutions. Service providers can also draw on the extensive experience of local and national disability groups or organisations of disabled people.

550

What is a 'physical feature'?

s 21(2)
SI 1999/1191
regs 2–3

5.44. *The Disability Discrimination (Services and Premises) Regulations 1999* make provision for various things to be treated as physical features. A 'physical feature' includes:

- any feature arising from the design or construction of a building on the premises occupied by the service provider;

- any feature on those premises or any approach to, exit from or access to such a building;

- any fixtures, fittings, furnishings, furniture, equipment or materials in or on such premises;

- any fixtures, fittings, furnishings, furniture, equipment or materials brought onto premises (other than those occupied by the service provider) by or on behalf of the service provider in the course of (and for the purpose of) providing services to the public;

- any other physical element or quality of land comprised in the premises occupied by the service provider.

All these features are covered whether temporary or permanent. A building means an erection or structure of any kind.

5.45. Physical features will include steps, stairways, kerbs, exterior surfaces and paving, parking areas, building entrances and exits (including emergency escape routes), internal and external doors, gates, toilet and washing facilities, public facilities (such as telephones, counters or service desks), lighting and ventilation, lifts and escalators, floor coverings, signs, furniture, and temporary or movable items (such as equipment and display racks). This is not an exhaustive list.

5.46. Where physical features are within the boundaries of a service provider's premises and are making it impossible or unreasonably difficult for disabled people to use the service, then the duty to make reasonable adjustments will apply. This will be the case even if the physical features are outdoors; for example, the paths and seating in a pub garden.

5.47. Where the physical features are within the remit of a highway authority and the highway authority is a service provider, it will have a duty to make reasonable adjustments.

A highway authority has placed some benches on the pavement of a busy main road which is also a shopping street. These benches are very low and have no arms. Some disabled people are finding them very difficult to use. The highway authority decides to make simple alterations to the benches so that they have arms and are slightly higher. This is likely to be a reasonable step for the authority to have to take.

Removing the physical feature

5.48. Removing the physical feature may be a reasonable step—and the most effective one—for a service provider to take. Physical features often create physical barriers which impede disabled people accessing services.

Display units at the entrance of a small shop restrict the ability of wheelchair users to enter the shop. The owner decides that, without any significant loss of selling space, the display units can be removed and repositioned elsewhere in the shop. This is likely to be a reasonable step for the shop to have to take.

A countryside visitor centre includes, as an attraction, a lakeside walk. However, a stile prevents access to the lakeside walk for those with mobility difficulties. The park authority which runs the centre removes the stile and replaces it with an accessible gate. This is likely to be a reasonable step for the service provider to have to take.

Altering the physical feature

5.49. Altering the physical feature so that it no longer has the effect of making it impossible or unreasonably difficult for disabled people to use the services may also be a reasonable step for a service provider to take.

A local religious group holds prayer meetings in a building entered by steps. The room in which the prayer meetings are held has a narrow entrance door. To ensure that its prayer meetings are accessible to disabled people, the religious group installs a permanent ramp at the entrance to the building. It also widens the door to the room. These are likely to be reasonable steps for the religious group to have to take.

Providing a reasonable means of avoiding the physical feature

5.50. Providing a reasonable means of avoiding the physical feature may also be a reasonable step for a service provider to take.

A public art gallery is accessible by a flight of stairs at its front entrance. It is housed in a listed building, and has not been able to obtain consent to install a ramped entrance to the gallery. A side entrance for staff use is fully accessible and always open. The gallery arranges for people with a mobility impairment to use this entrance. This is likely to be a reasonable step for the gallery to have to take. It could of course go further and adopt an inclusive approach by also making the side entrance available to everyone.

5.51. The Act requires that any means of avoiding the physical feature must be a 'reasonable' one. Relevant considerations in this respect may include whether the provision of the service in this way significantly offends the dignity of disabled people and the extent to which it causes disabled people inconvenience.

A firm of solicitors is located in a building whose front entrance is only accessible by climbing a flight of stairs. At ground level there is a bell and a sign saying 'Please ring for disabled access.' However, the bell is not answered promptly, even in bad weather, so that a disabled person often has to wait for an unreasonable time before gaining access to the building. This is unlikely to be a reasonable means of avoiding the feature.

Providing a reasonable alternative method of making services available

5.52. Providing a reasonable alternative method of making services available to disabled people may also be a reasonable step for a service provider to take. The Act requires that any alternative method of making services available must be a 'reasonable' one. Relevant considerations in this respect may include whether the provision of the service in this way significantly offends the dignity of disabled people and the extent to which it causes disabled people inconvenience.

A small self-service pharmacist's shop has goods displayed on high shelving separated by narrow aisles. It is not practicable to alter this arrangement. The goods are not easily accessible to many disabled people. The shop decides to provide a customer assistance service. On request, a member of staff locates goods and brings them to the cash till for a disabled customer. This is the provision of a service by an alternative method, which makes the service accessible for disabled people. This is likely to be a reasonable step for the shop to have to take.

The changing facilities in a women-only gym are located in a room which is only accessible by stairs. The service provider suggests to disabled users of the gym with mobility impairments that they can change in a corner of the gym itself. This is unlikely to be a reasonable alternative method of making the service available, since it may significantly infringe their dignity.

Index